# THE
# DRAMATIC WORKS OF
# THOMAS DEKKER

# THE
# DRAMATIC WORKS OF
# THOMAS DEKKER

EDITED BY
## FREDSON BOWERS
*Professor of English Literature*
*University of Virginia*

### *VOLUME III*

## CAMBRIDGE
## AT THE UNIVERSITY PRESS
1966

CAMBRIDGE UNIVERSITY PRESS
Cambridge, New York, Melbourne, Madrid, Cape Town, Singapore, São Paulo, Delhi

Cambridge University Press
The Edinburgh Building, Cambridge CB2 8RU, UK

Published in the United States of America by Cambridge University Press, New York

www.cambridge.org
Information on this title: www.cambridge.org/9780521102964

First published 1958
Reprinted 1966
This digitally printed version 2009

A catalogue record for this publication is available from the British Library

ISBN 978-0-521-10294-0 paperback (Volume 1)
ISBN 978-0-521-04808-8 hardback (Volume 1)
ISBN 978-0-521-10295-7 paperback (Volume 2)
ISBN 978-0-521-04809-5 hardback (Volume 2)
ISBN 978-0-521-10296-4 paperback (Volume 3)
ISBN 978-0-521-04810-1 hardback (Volume 3)
ISBN 978-0-521-10297-1 paperback (Volume 4)
ISBN 978-0-521-04811-8 hardback (Volume 4)

# CONTENTS

# The Roaring Girle.

## OR
### Moll Cut-Purse.

As it hath lately beene Acted on the Fortune-ſtage by
the Prince his Players.

Written by *T. Middleton* and *T. Dekkar*.

My caſe is alter'd, I muſt worke for my liuing.

Printed at *London* for *Thomas Archer*, and are to be ſold at his
ſhop in Popes head-pallace, neere the Royall
Exchange. 1611.

# TEXTUAL INTRODUCTION

*The Roaring Girl* (Greg, *Bibliography*, no. 298), a collaboration by Dekker and Thomas Middleton, was not entered in the Stationers' Register by its publisher Thomas Archer; nevertheless, the transfer of the copy to Hugh Perrey in February of 1631 indicates that he held a good copyright.

The ornaments show that Nicholas Okes was the printer. Since a single skeleton-forme was used throughout to impose the type-pages of the inner and outer formes of every sheet, it is clear that printing was done on a single press. Evidence that is not wholly clear cut suggests the presence of more than one compositor, perhaps as many as three workmen who, in general, set the start, the middle, and the latter part of the quarto.[1]

The limited number of copies preserved does not encourage very far-reaching speculation about the extent of the proof-reading. None of the known variant formes offers evidence to suggest that any other but the printing-house proof-reader was concerned with correcting the text, and none of the various alterations suggests reference to the manuscript for authority. On the evidence available, we find moderately extensive correction in the inner forme of sheet B, followed by somewhat similar alteration in only one page of inner C. Thereafter, until sheet H no further press-correction has been preserved. However, the rise in the number of literals in these non-variant sheets suggests a possibility that at least the later ones in the sequence were not formally proof-read in the same manner as sheets B and C. Beginning with sheet D (II.i.129) we find three and perhaps four literals that ought to have been caught by a proof-

---

[1] The evidence is surveyed in a recent study by G. R. Price, 'The Manuscript and the Quarto of *The Roaring Girl*', *The Library*, 5th ser., XI (1956), 182–183. Dr Price finds signs of five different compositors, a quite impossible number for a one-press shop. (Price states that Okes had other presses, but all external and internal evidence indicates the contrary.) The evidence for his Compositor *C* as distinguished from *B* is very thin, and I rather think that his *D* and *E* (like *B* and *C*) are only one compositor. A close study of Okes's work of this period would be necessary for certainty in the compositorial division.

reader (II.i.177, 289, 369, 374), two in sheet E (II.ii.92; III.i.108), three in sheet F (III.i.139, 146; III.ii.17), a rise to ten in sheet G (III.ii.207, 209, 223, 232; III.iii.3, 54, 117, 150, 164, 168), and four in the inner forme of sheet H (IV.i.1, 34, 35, 168). Sheet G, incidentally, marks the major start of the third compositor.

The variation in the inner forme of sheet I, with some resetting of the type, is—except accidentally—confined to the half of the forme containing sigs. I1ᵛ and I4. Obviously, the type loosened and pied; and it is perhaps a trifle easier to suppose that this accident happened somewhere during the process of proof-correction than in the machining of the sheets. If so, the forme had been unlocked, perhaps to correct such readings as *duckmee* (IV.ii.69), *Sommer* (IV.ii.219 S.D.), *headsir* (IV.ii.225), and *Crastina* (IV.ii.230).

Two pages, sigs. I1ᵛ and I4, irregularly pied and had to be reset in part. The resetting seems to have been done in haste and without subsequent proof-reading, on the evidence of the number of literals that were produced. At least one positive substantive error was made in the resetting, the omission of *the* at IV.ii.49; and there is no reason to suppose that the transposition of *deale they* at IV.ii.53 is anything but a mistake. The variants in sigs. I2 and I3ᵛ seem to have resulted exclusively from displaced or dropped-out loose type. Hence no alteration in the second state of inner forme I can be considered to be authoritative; and the text in this edition (save for the few necessary corrections) follows that of the earlier state as being closer to the manuscript.

If one were to depend upon the evidence of the readings alone, the question of which was the earlier and which the later state of the type in inner I might well seem to be a stand-off. Fortunately, a neat example of pure bibliography settles the case (see J. G. McManaway in *The Library*, 4th ser., XIX [1938], 176–179). The typesetting of the variant running-title on sig. I1ᵛ (and also the typesetting of the running-title on sig. I4) is found as part of the originally constructed skeleton-forme that imposed the type-pages for sheet B and also sheets C–H and this state of inner I. The typesetting for the two running-titles in the other state of inner I is not found earlier, but subsequently replaces the typesetting found in sheets B–H. Therefore, the reset running-titles must enclose the pages of

4

the later state of the text. Since these reset running-titles, first appearing in the later state of inner forme I, are also found in the outer forme, we know that the inner forme of this sheet was first through the press. This information has no textual significance, however, since with one-skeleton printing the order of the formes through the press does not bear on the method of proof-reading.

That the manuscript given to the printer was a good one is attested to not only by the fact of Middleton's preface but also by the comparatively correct substantive reproduction of the print, in so far as this can be estimated.[1] The nature of the manuscript is difficult to conjecture. If the preface to *The Family of Love* is Middleton's, and if it is candid, its statement shows that a dramatist could still write an introduction even though he had not provided the manuscript: 'Too soone and too late, this work is published: Too soone, in that it was in the Presse, before I had notice of it, by which meanes some faults may escape in the Printing. Too late, for that it was not published when the general voice of the people had seald it for good, and the newnesse of it made it much more to be desired.' On the other hand, the tone of the preface to *The Roaring Girl* appears to be that of an author introducing an approved publication to the public. But even if one of the authors thus approves publication, no guarantee is thereby made that he furnished the manuscript or that the manuscript was necessarily autograph.

When one examines the accidentals of this play with some care, one finds by and large a general consistency in forms between scenes that may reasonably be attributed to Middleton and scenes that are unquestionably by Dekker. In such cases one might argue that the compositors have so overlaid the originals with their own characteristics as to obscure what would be variable accidentals in autograph copy by the two dramatists. This condition might obtain in fact; nevertheless, common experience indicates that compositors

---

[1] Dr Price believes that on sig. K1ᵛ two different lines are omitted (following IV.ii.303 and 310), but the breaking of the rhyme is insufficient evidence when unaccompanied by any break in the sense. The three literals on the same page that he cites as evidence of the compositor's carelessness have no relation to substantive omission. The case is better for his assumption that a short speech has been omitted at the foot of sig. I1 (following IV.ii.48), but the compositor may not be to blame here.

are frequently influenced by the accidentals of their copy and that scenes in different autograph might be expected to reveal themselves by detectable differences in the form of the accidentals. In this particular case positive statements cannot be made in the absence of the identification and rigorous study against controls of the compositors in Okes's shop who typeset this quarto. However, a few considerations may be mentioned.

(1) If a transcript intervenes between autograph and printer's copy, the smoothing-out result of this transcript added to the tendency of a compositor to impose certain of his own characteristics would normally result in an approximately uniform texture in the accidentals despite the collaborated nature of the original. Distinctive characteristics do not appear to be present in the accidentals of scenes of different authorship in *The Roaring Girl*, and this fact is the more noteworthy if, as seems possible, three different compositors set the play.

(2) Experience shows that as a general rule a compositor may often impose a roughly similar form on the abbreviation of speech-prefixes, but he is less likely to interfere with variant prefixes for the same character. Also, when two dramatists collaborate, the odds are (as seen in *Westward Ho*, cf. II, 314–315) that variant speech-prefixes will appear in autograph. In *The Roaring Girl*, except for minor compositorial variants, the speech-prefixes are remarkably uniform save for one exception: In I.i Sir Davy Dapper's prefix takes forms like *S. Dap.*, Sir *Dap.*, and *Dap*; but in III.iii, the only other scene in which he appears, his prefixes are *Sir Da.* or *S. Davy*. However, since each scene is almost certainly Dekker's, nothing is proved by this divergence, and we may return to the otherwise rather remarkable uniformity as some indication that a fair-copy transcript may have smoothed out possible variance.

If the printer's copy be provisionally accepted as a transcript, the inevitable query follows whether the manuscript was a prompt copy or a transcript of a prompt copy. To estimate the nature of a manuscript from the form and position of stage-directions is an art subject to varying interpretations and, except in the most obvious cases of stage origin, to considerable uncertainty. In this matter I can only express my own conviction that whereas the directions are not inconsistent with those an author would write, I see no clear indication that any direction necessarily originated in the theatre. My opinion is that if the printer's copy was a transcript, as I believe, it had no connexion with the prompt-book.[1]

A non-theatrical transcript might be made by a professional scribe, or as a fair copy by either author. Although a scribal transcript made for the theatre from the authors' foul papers is not an impossibility—a working transcript from which in turn the prompt-book would be made up—in this case simplicity of argument suggests that either Middleton or Dekker wrote out a fair copy of his own and of the other dramatist's papers for the formal sale of the play to the actors.[2] What evidence there is points away from Middleton as the transcriber of the fair copy.

Since Middleton's signed preface was manifestly written for publication, we may conjecture that it was set directly from autograph copy. The text is too brief to offer much opportunity for analysis. Nevertheless, it is worth pointing out that the digraph œ found in *obscœne* (line 20) is very likely an authorial characteristic and is present nowhere else in the text in similar words. Less certain is the double appearance of *scœne* in the prologue (lines 2, 7) since this spelling is more conventional, and it may be that the prologue is Dekker's. The two appearances of the short suffix form *-nes* in the preface (line 6) may be authorial, though matched by two in *-nesse* (lines 27, 28); but the full form is that found throughout the text.[3]

If Middleton provided the printer with the preface, perhaps the list of persons would be his also. Certainly, the list and its particular

---

[1] In this I find myself in disagreement with Dr Price, who feels that the inconsistencies between the imperative and indicative in the stage-directions are more probably due to the transcriber's incomplete adaptation of the stage-manager's directions in a prompt-book used as the source than to the dramatists' having partially adopted a book-holder's idiom. I do not myself attach any significance to this normal authorial inconsistency, nor do I think it ascertained that a transcriber would alter imperative to indicative directions.

[2] For such authorial fair copies, see Bowers, *On Editing Shakespeare and the Elizabethan Dramatists* (1955), pp. 13–22.

[3] Dr Price finds the preface short form *sprucenes* and *nicenes* a Middleton spelling, but I do not understand his assignment of the commonplace spelling *onely* as Middletonian. I am happy to find him in agreement that the text itself is printed from a transcript by Dekker, even though we may differ about the circumstances and the source of the transcription.

7

form does not seem to be one that would come from the printer, although here one may only speculate. In this connexion the curious error by which Sir Alexander's name is spelled *Wentgrave* (for *Wengrave*) and Neat-foot is *Neats-foot* does not indicate such familiarity with the characters as would come from a transcriber of the whole; and the casual identification of Sir Alexander's son as *Yong Wentgrave* (thus confirming the spelling) instead of *Sebastian* is odd.

To sum up, what evidence there is suggests a non-theatrical manuscript that was a fair copy, not foul papers. Under the circumstances it is reasonable to expect that one or other of the authors made the fair copy from his own and his fellow's foul papers. Evidence of some weight suggests that the transcriber was not Middleton, even though Middleton was concerned in the publication. The conclusion is that Dekker made the fair copy. If so, as I believe, he wrote out the copy not for printing but, instead, for the actors, and from this manuscript they transcribed their prompt book. The printer's copy, by this hypothesis, would have come from the manuscript preserved by the company and would represent Dekker's fair copy made for the original sale of the play. Although every link in this chain of reasoning is not of equal strength, the hypothesis is consistent with the available evidence and our present ability to interpret it, and I know of no evidence against it. Although this is not the place for an analysis of the authorship, I may say that I lean more to Fleay's views which assign a very considerable portion of the play to Dekker than to Bullen's which allow him only a few scenes. Moreover, this hypothesis helps to explain a scene or two in which the authorship seems somewhat mixed. In transcribing Middleton's papers it would be quite possible for Dekker to make minor alterations for dramatic interest and to tidy up any loose ends.

*The Roaring Girl* was edited first in Dodsley's *A Select Collection of Old Plays* (1780), vol. 6; and subsequently by Sir Walter Scott in vol. 2 of *The Ancient British Drama* (1810); by J. P. Collier in vol. 6 of Dodsley (1825); then by the Rev. Alexander Dyce, *The Works of Thomas Middleton* (1840), vol. 2; the Pearson reprint of 1873; and A. H. Bullen, *The Works of Thomas Middleton* (1885), vol. 4. A photographic facsimile of the British Museum copy

(162.d.35) was issued in 1914 by J. S. Farmer for Tudor Facsimile Texts.

The present text is based on a collation of the ten copies that are known to be preserved: British Museum copy 1 (162.d.35), copy 2 (Ashley 1159); Bodleian (Mal. 246[1]); Dyce Collection in the Victoria and Albert Museum; Bute Collection in the National Library of Scotland; Henry E. Huntington Library; Folger Shakespeare Library; Boston Public Library; Carl H. Pforzheimer Collection; and a copy privately owned by Robert H. Taylor of Yonkers, New York, this last purchased in 1956 at the Harlech sale by the Seven Gables Bookshop and not previously recorded.

## *To the Comicke Play-readers,*
## *Venery, and Laughter.*

The fashion of play-making, I can properly compare to nothing, so naturally, as the alteration in apparell: For in the time of the Great-crop-doublet, your huge bombasted plaies, quilted with mighty words to leane purpose was onely then in fashion. And as the doublet fell, neater inuentions beganne to set vp. Now in the time of sprucenes, our plaies followe the nicenes of our Garments, single plots, quaint conceits, letcherous iests, drest vp in hanging sleeues, and those are fit for the Times, and the Tearmers: Such a kind of light-colour Summer stuffe, mingled with diuerse colours, you shall finde this published Comedy, good to keepe you in an afternoone from dice, at home in your chambers; and for venery you shall finde enough, for sixepence, but well coucht and you marke it. For *Venus* being a woman passes through the play in doublet and breeches, a braue disguise and a safe one, if the Statute vnty not her cod-peice point. The booke I make no question, but is fit for many of your companies, as well as the person it selfe, and may bee allowed both Gallery roome at the play-house, and chamber-roome at your lodging: worse things I must needs confesse the world ha's taxt her for, then has beene written of her; but 'tis the excellency of a Writer, to leaue things better then he finds 'em; though some obscœne fellow (that cares not what he writes against others, yet keepes a mysticall baudy-house himselfe, and entertaines drunkards, to make vse of their pockets, and vent his priuate bottle-ale at mid-night) though such a one would haue ript vp the most nasty vice, that euer hell
belcht forth, and presented it to a modest Assembly; yet we
rather wish in such discoueries, where reputation
lies bleeding, a slackenesse of truth,
then fulnesse of slander.

THOMAS MIDDLETON

# Prologus.

*A Play (expected long) makes the Audience looke*
*For wonders: — that each Scœne should be a booke,*
*Compos'd to all perfection; each one comes*
*And brings a play in's head with him: vp he summes,*
*What he would of a Roaring Girle haue writ;*
*If that he findes not here, he mewes at it.*
*Onely we intreate you thinke our Scœne,*
*Cannot speake high (the subiect being but meane)*
*A Roaring Girle (whose notes till now neuer were)*
*Shall fill with laughter our vast Theater,*     10
*That's all which I dare promise: Tragick passion,*
*And such graue stuffe, is this day out of fashion.*
*I see attention sets wide ope her gates*
*Of hearing, and with couetous listning waites,*
*To know what Girle, this Roaring Girle should be.*
*(For of that Tribe are many.)  One is shee*
*That roares at midnight in deepe Tauerne bowles,*
*That beates the watch, and Constables controuls;*
*Another roares i'th day time, sweares, stabbes, giues braues,*
*Yet sells her soule to the lust of fooles and slaues.*     20
*Both these are Suburbe-roarers. Then there's (besides)*
*A ciuill Citty-Roaring Girle, whose pride,*
*Feasting, and riding, shakes her husbands state,*
*And leaues him Roaring through an yron grate.*
*None of these Roaring Girles is ours: shee flies*
*With wings more lofty. Thus her character lyes,*
*Yet what neede characters? when to giue a gesse,*
*Is better then the person to expresse;*
*But would you know who 'tis? would you heare her name?*
*Shee is cal'd madde* Moll; *her life, our acts proclaime.*     30

# DRAMMATIS PERSONÆ

SIR ALEXANDER WENGRAUE, and NEAT-FOOT his man

SIR ADAM APPLETON

SIR DAUY DAPPER

SIR BEWTEOUS GANYMED

[SIR THOMAS LONG]

LORD NOLAND

YONG [SEBASTIAN] WENGRAUE

IACKE DAPPER, and GULL his page

GOSHAWKE

GREENEWIT                                                    10

LAXTON

TILT-YARD ⎫
OPENWORKE ⎬ Ciues et Vxores
GALLIPOT ⎭

MOL the Roaring Girle

TRAPDOORE

[TEAR-CAT]

SIR GUY FITZ-ALLARD

MARY FITZ-ALLARD his daughter

CURTILAX a Sergiant, and HANGER his Yeoman      20

[A Fellow with a Rapier. Several Cutpurses]

Ministri.

1, 7 Wengraue] Dodsley; Wentgraue Q
1 Neat-foot] Dodsley; Neats-foot Q

12

## *The Roaring Girle.*

### ACT I, Scene i

*Enter* Mary Fitz-Allard *disguised like a sempster with a case for bands, and* Neatfoot *a seruingman with her, with a napkin on his shoulder, and a trencher in his hand as from table.*

*Neat.*  The yong gentleman (our young maister) Sir *Alexanders* sonne, is it into his eares (sweet Damsell) (embleme of fragility) you desire to haue a message transported, or to be transcendent.

*Mary.*  A priuate word or two Sir, nothing else.

*Neat.*  You shall fructifie in that which you come for: your pleasure shall be satisfied to your full contentation: I will (fairest tree of generation) watch when our young maister is erected, (that is to say vp) and deliuer him to this your most white hand.

*Mary.*  Thankes sir.

*Neat.*  [*Aside*]  And withall certifie him, that I haue culled out for 10 him (now his belly is replenished) a daintier bit or modicome then any lay vpon his trencher at dinner — hath he notion of your name, I beseech your chastitie.

*Mary.*  One Sir, of whom he bespake falling bands.

*Neat.*  Falling bands, it shall so be giuen him, — if you please to venture your modesty in the hall, amongst a curle-pated company of rude seruingmen, and take such as they can set before you, you shall be most seriously, and ingeniously welcome.

*Mary.*  I haue dyned indeed already sir.

*Neat.*  — Or will you vouchsafe to kisse the lip of a cup of rich 20 *Orleans* in the buttry amongst our waiting women.

*Mary.*  Not now in truth sir.

*Neat.*  Our yong Maister shall then haue a feeling of your being here presently, it shall so be giuen him.          *Exit* Neatfoote.

*Mary.*  I humbly thanke you sir, but that my bosome
Is full of bitter sorrowes, I could smile,

19 dyned] Dodsley; dyed Q          *24 presently,] ~ ‸ Q

13

To see this formall Ape play Antick tricks:
But in my breast a poysoned arrow stickes,
And smiles cannot become me, Loue wouen sleightly
(Such as thy false heart makes) weares out as lightly,                    30
But loue being truely bred ith the soule (like mine)
Bleeds euen to death, at the least wound it takes,
The more we quench this fire, the lesse it slakes:
Oh me!

*Enter* Sebastian Wengraue *with* Neatfoote.

*Seb.*       A Sempster speake with me, saist thou.

*Neat.*   Yes sir, she's there, *viua voce*, to deliuer her auricular
confession.

*Seb.*   With me sweet heart. What ist?

*Mary.*   I haue brought home your bands sir.

*Seb.*   Bands: *Neatfoote.*

*Neat.*   Sir.                    40

*Seb.*   Prithee look in, for all the Gentlemen are vpon rising.

*Neat.*   Yes sir, a most methodicall attendance shall be giuen.

*Seb.*   And dost heare, if my father call for me, say I am busy with a
Sempster.

*Neat.*   Yes sir, hee shall know it that you are busied with a needle
woman.

*Seb.*   In's eare good *Neat-foote.*

*Neat.*   It shall be so giuen him.                    *Exit* Neat-foote.

*Seb.*   Bands, y'are mistaken sweete heart, I bespake none,
When, where, I prithee, what bands, let me see them.                    50

*Mary.*   Yes sir, a bond fast sealed, with solemne oathes,
Subscribed vnto (as I thought) with your soule:
Deliuered as your deed in sight of heauen,
Is this bond canceld, haue you forgot me.

*Seb.*                    Ha:
Life of my life: Sir *Guy Fitz-Allards* daughter,
What has transform'd my loue to this strange shape:
Stay: make all sure, — so: now speake and be briefe,
Because the wolfe's at dore that lyes in waite

---

33 fire] Dyce; *om.* Q (*cf.* I.ii.178)        34 saist] Q(c); saith Q(u)

To prey vpon vs both, albeit mine eyes
Are blest by thine, yet this so strange disguise                    60
Holds me with feare and wonder.
*Mary.*                         Mines a loathed sight,
Why from it are you banisht else so long.
*Seb.*  I must cut short my speech, in broken language,
Thus much sweete *Moll*, I must thy company shun,
I court another *Moll*, my thoughts must run,
As a horse runs, thats blind, round in a Mill,
Out euery step, yet keeping one path still.
*Mary.*  Vmh: must you shun my company, in one knot
Haue both our hands byt'h hands of heauen bene tyed,
Now to be broke? I thought me once your Bride:                    70
Our fathers did agree on the time when,
And must another bed-fellow fill my roome.
*Seb.*  Sweete maid, lets loose no time, tis in heauens booke
Set downe, that I must haue thee: an oath we tooke,
To keep our vowes, but when the knight your father
Was from mine parted, stormes began to sit
Vpon my couetous fathers brow, which fell
From them on me: he reckond vp what gold
This marriage would draw from him, at which he swore,
To loose so much bloud, could not grieue him more.                80
He then diswades me from thee, cal'd thee not faire,
And askt what is shee, but a beggars heire?
He scorn'd thy dowry of (fiue thousand) Markes.
If such a summe of mony could be found,
And I would match with that, hee'd not vndoe it,
Prouided his bags might adde nothing to it,
But vow'd, if I tooke thee, nay more, did sweare it,
Saue birth from him I nothing should inherit.
*Mary.*  What followes then, my ship-wracke?
*Seb.*                         Dearest no:
Tho wildly in a laborinth I go,                                    90
My end is to meete thee: with a side winde
Must I now saile, else I no hauen can finde

*77 brow,] Dyce [brows]; ~ : Q

But both must sinke for euer. There's a wench
Cal'd *Mol*, mad *Mol*, or merry *Moll*, a creatur
So strange in quality, a whole citty takes
Note of her name and person, all that affection
I owe to thee, on her in counterfet passion,
I spend to mad my father: he beleeues
I doate vpon this *Roaring Girle*, and grieues
As it becomes a father for a sonne,                                          100
That could be so bewitcht: yet ile go on
This croked way, sigh still for her, faine dreames,
In which ile talke onely of her, these streames
Shall, I hope, force my father to consent
That heere I anchor rather then be rent
Vpon a rocke so dangerous. Art thou pleas'd,
Because thou seest we are way-laid, that I take
A path thats safe, tho it be farre about?
*Mary.*   My prayers with heauen guide thee.
*Seb.*                                 Then I will on,
My father is at hand, kisse and begon;                                        110
Howres shall be watcht for meetings; I must now
As men for feare, to a strange Idoll bow.
*Mary.*   Farewell.
*Seb.*              Ile guide thee forth, when next we meete,
A story of *Moll* shall make our mirth more sweet.
                                                              *Exeunt.*


## [ACT I, Scene ii]

*Enter Sir* Alexander Wengraue, *Sir* Dauy Dapper, *Sir* Adam
Appleton, Goshawke, Laxton, *and Gentlemen.*

*Omn.*   Thanks good Sir *Alexander* for our bounteous cheere.
*Alex.*   Fy, fy, in giuing thankes you pay to deare.
*Dauy.*   When bounty spreads the table, faith t'were sinne,
   (At going of) if thankes should not step in.
*Alex.*   No more of thankes, no more, I mary Sir,

Th'inner roome was too close, how do you like
This Parlour Gentlmen?
*Omn.*                    Oh passing well.
*Adam.*   What a sweet breath the aire casts heere, so coole.
*Gosh.*   I like the prospect best.
*Lax.*                    See how tis furnisht.
*Dauy.*   A very faire sweete roome.
*Alex.*                         Sir *Dauy Dapper*,                    10
The furniture that doth adorne this roome,
Cost many a faire gray groat ere it came here,
But good things are most cheape, when th'are most deere,
Nay when you looke into my galleries,
How brauely they are trim'd vp, you all shall sweare
Y'are highly pleasd to see whats set downe there:
Stories of men and women (mixt together
Faire ones with foule, like sun-shine in wet wether)
Within one square a thousand heads are laid
So close, that all of heads, the roome seemes made,                    20
As many faces there (fill'd with blith lookes)
Shew like the promising titles of new bookes,
(Writ merily) the Readers being their owne eyes,
Which seeme to moue and to giue plaudities,
And here and there (whilst with obsequious eares,
Throng'd heapes do listen) a cut purse thrusts and leeres
With haukes eyes for his prey: I need not shew him,
By a hanging villanous looke, your selues may know him,
The face is drawne so rarely. Then sir below,
The very flowre (as twere) waues to and fro,                    30
And like a floating Iland, seemes to moue,
Vpon a sea bound in with shores aboue.

          *Enter* Sebastian *and Maister* Greene-wit.

*Omn.*   These sights are excellent.
*Alex.*                         I'le shew you all,
Since we are met, make our parting Comicall.

    10 *Dauy.*] *throughout this scene the* Q *speech-prefixes are forms of* S. Dapper

*Seb.*   This gentleman (my friend) will take his leaue Sir.
*Alex.*   Ha, take his leaue (*Sebastian*) who?
*Seb.*                              This gentleman.
*Alex.*   Your loue sir, has already giuen me some time,
   And if you please to trust my age with more,
   It shall pay double interest: Good sir stay.
*Green.*   I haue beene too bold.
*Alex.*                        Not so sir. A merry day          40
   Mongst friends being spent, is better then gold sau'd.
   Some wine, some wine. Where be these knaues I keepe.

         *Enter three or foure Seruingmen, and* Neatfoote.

*Neat.*   At your worshipfull elbow, sir.
*Alex.*   You are kissing my maids, drinking, or fast asleep.
*Neat.*   Your worship has giuen it vs right.
*Alex.*   You varlets stirre,
   Chaires, stooles and cushions: pre'thee sir *Dauy Dapper*,
   Make that chaire thine.
*Dauy.*                     Tis but an easie gift,
   And yet I thanke you for it sir, I'le take it.
*Alex.*   A chaire for old sir *Adam Appleton*.          50
*Neat.*   A backe friend to your worship.
*Adam.*   Mary good *Neatfoot*,
   I thanke thee for it: backe friends sometimes are good.
*Alex.*   Pray make that stoole your pearch, good Maister *Goshawke*.
*Gosh.*   I stoope to your lure sir.
*Alex.*                              Sonne *Sebastian*,
   Take Maister *Greenewit* to you.
*Seb.*                              Sit deere friend.
*Alex.*   Nay maister *Laxton* — furnish maister *Laxton*
   With what he wants (a stone) a stoole I would say,
   A stoole.
*Lax.*   I had rather stand sir.          *Exeunt seruants.* 60
*Alex.*   I know you had (good Maister *Laxton*.) So, so —
   Now heres a messe of friends, and (gentlemen)
   Because times glasse shall not be running long,
   I'le quicken it with a pretty tale.

*Dauy.*                    Good tales do well,
In these bad dayes, where vice does so excell.
*Adam.*  Begin sir *Alexander.*
*Alex.*                    Last day I met
An aged man vpon whose head was scor'd,
A debt of iust so many yeares as these,
Which I owe to my graue, the man you all know.
*Omn.*  His name I pray you sir.
*Alex.*                    Nay you shall pardon me,          70
But when he saw me (with a sigh that brake,
Or seem'd to breake his heart-strings) thus he spake:
Oh my good knight, saies he, (and then his eies
Were richer euen by that which made them poore,
They had spent so many teares they had no more.)
Oh sir (saies he) you know it, for you ha seene
Blessings to raine vpon mine house and me:
Fortune (who slaues men) was my slaue: her wheele
Hath spun me golden threads, for I thanke heauen,
I nere had but one cause to curse my starres,          80
I ask't him then, what that one cause might be.
*Omn.*  So Sir.
*Alex.*          He paus'd, and as we often see,
A sea so much becalm'd, there can be found
No wrinckle on his brow, his waues being drownd
In their owne rage: but when th'imperious winds
Vse strange inuisible tyranny to shake
Both heauens and earths foundation: at their noyse
The seas swelling with wrath to part that fray,
Rise vp, and are more wild, more mad then they.
Euen so this good old man was by my question,          90
Stir'd vp to roughnesse, you might see his gall
Flow euen in's eies: then grew he fantasticall.
*Dauy.*  Fantasticall, ha, ha.
*Alex.*                    Yes, and talkt odly.
*Adam.*  Pray sir proceed, how did this old man end?
*Alex.*  Mary sir thus.

85 winds‸] Scott; wind, Q          93 talkt] Dyce; talke Q

He left his wild fit to read ore his cares,
Yet then (though age cast snow on all his haires)
He ioy'd because (saies he) the God of gold
Has beene to me no niggard: that disease
(Of which all old men sicken) Auarice                           100
Neuer infected me.
*Lax.*   He meanes not himselfe i'me sure.
*Alex.*   For like a lamp,
Fed with continuall oyle, I spend and throw
My light to all that need it, yet haue still
Enough to serue my selfe, oh but (quoth he)
Tho heauens dew fall, thus on this aged tree,
I haue a sonne that like a wedge doth cleaue,
My very heart roote—
*Dauy.*                Had he such a sonne?
*Seb.*   Now I do smell a fox strongly.                        110
*Alex.*   Lets see: no Maister *Greene-wit* is not yet
So mellow in yeares as he; but as like *Sebastian*,
Iust like my sonne *Sebastian*, — such another.
*Seb.*   How finely like a fencer my father fetches his by-blowes to
hit me, but if I beate you not at your owne weapon of subtilty—
*Alex.*   This sonne (saith he) that should be
The columne and maine arch vnto my house,
The crutch vnto my age, becomes a whirlewind
Shaking the firme foundation—
*Adam.*                Tis some prodigall.
*Seb.*   Well shot old *Adam Bell.*                            120
*Alex.*   No citty monster neither, no prodigall,
But sparing, wary, ciuill, and (tho wiuelesse)
An excellent husband, and such a traueller,
He has more tongues in his head then some haue teeth—
*Dauy.*   I haue but two in myne.
*Gosh.*                So sparing and so wary,
What then could vex his father so.
*Alex.*                Oh a woman.
*Seb.*   A flesh fly, that can vex any man.

96 cares] cards Q     108 that] Dyce; thats Q

20

*Alex.*   A scuruy woman,
On whom the passionate old man swore he doated:
A creature (saith he) nature hath brought forth                    130
To mocke the sex of woman. — It is a thing
One knowes not how to name, her birth began
Ere she was all made. Tis woman more then man,
Man more then woman, and (which to none can hap)
The Sunne giues her two shadowes to one shape,
Nay more, let this strange thing, walke, stand or sit,
No blazing starre drawes more eyes after it.
*Dauy.*   A Monster, tis some Monster.
*Alex.*                          Shee's a varlet.
*Seb.*   Now is my cue to bristle.
*Alex.*   A naughty packe.
*Seb.*                  Tis false.
*Alex.*                        Ha boy.
*Seb.*                              Tis false.                      140
*Alex.*   Whats false, I say shee's nought.
*Seb.*                              I say that tongue
That dares speake so (but yours) stickes in the throate
Of a ranke villaine, set your selfe aside—
*Alex.*   So sir what then.
*Seb.*                    Any here else had lyed.
I thinke I shall fit you —                            *Aside.*
*Alex.*   Lye.
*Seb.*       Yes.
*Dauy.*         Doth this concerne him.
*Alex.*                              Ah sirra boy.
Is your bloud heated: boyles it: are you stung,
Ile pierce you deeper yet: oh my deere friends,
I am that wretched father, this that sonne,
That sees his ruine, yet headlong on doth run.             150
*Adam.*   Will you loue such a poyson.
*Dauy.*                        Fye, fye.
*Seb.*                              Y'are all mad.
*Alex.*   Th'art sicke at heart, yet feelst it not: of all these,
What Gentleman (but thou) knowing his disease

Mortall, would shun the cure: oh Maister *Greenewit*,
Would you to such an Idoll bow.
*Green.*                              Not I sir.
*Alex.*   Heer's Maister *Laxton*, has he mind to a woman
As thou hast.
*Lax.*            No not I sir.
*Alex.*                  Sir I know it.
*Lax.*   There good parts are so rare, there bad so common,
I will haue nought to do with any woman.
*Dauy.*   Tis well done Maister *Laxton*.
*Alex.*                          Oh thou cruell boy,          160
Thou wouldst with lust an old mans life destroy,
Because thou seest I'm halfe way in my graue,
Thou shouelst dust vpon me: wod thou mightest haue
Thy wish, most wicked, most vnnaturall.
*Dauy.*   Why sir, tis thought, sir *Guy Fitz-Allards* daughter
Shall wed your sonne *Sebastian*.
*Alex.*                          Sir *Dauy Dapper.*
I haue vpon my knees, wood this fond boy,
To take that vertuous maiden.
*Seb.*                        Harke you a word sir.
You on your knees haue curst that vertuous maiden,
And me for louing her, yet do you now                        170
Thus baffle me to my face: wear not your knees
In such intreates, giue me *Fitz-Allards* daughter.
*Alex.*   Ile giue thee rats-bane rather.
*Seb.*                            Well then you know
What dish I meane to feed vpon.
*Alex.*                        Harke Gentlemen,
He sweares to haue this cut-purse drab, to spite my gall.
*Omn.*   Maister *Sebastian*.
*Seb.*                I am deafe to you all.
Ime so bewitcht, so bound to my desires,
Teares, prayers, threats, nothing can quench out those fires
That burne within me.                    *Exit* Sebastian.

158 There...there] *i.e. their*
171 wear] Dodsley; were Q

*Alex.*                    Her bloud shall quench it then,
Loose him not, oh diswade him Gentlemen.                    180
*Sir Dap.*   He shall be weand I warrant you.
*Alex.*                    Before his eyes
Lay downe his shame, my griefe, his miseries.
*Omn.*   No more, no more, away.

> *Exeunt all but sir* Alexander.

*Alex.*                    I wash a *Negro*,
Loosing both paines and cost: but take thy flight,
Ile be most neere thee, when Ime least in sight.
Wilde Bucke ile hunt thee breathlesse, thou shalt run on,
But I will turne thee when Ime not thought vpon.

> *Enter* Ralph Trapdore.

Now sirra what are you, leaue your Apes trickes and speake.
*Trap.*   A letter from my Captaine to your Worship.
*Alex.*   Oh, oh, now I remember tis to preferre thee into my seruice.   190
*Trap.*   To be a shifter vnder your Worships nose of a clean trencher,
when ther's a good bit vpon't.                    [*Aside.*]
*Alex.*   Troth honest fellow — humh — ha — let me see,
This knaue shall be the axe to hew that downe
At which I stumble, h'as a face that promiseth
Much of a villaine, I will grind his wit,
And if the edge proue fine make vse of it.
Come hither sirra, canst thou be secret, ha.
*Trap.*   As two crafty Atturneys plotting the vndoing of their
clyents.                    200
*Alex.*   Didst neuer, as thou hast walkt about this towne
Heare of a wench cal'd *Moll*, mad merry *Moll*.
*Trap.*   *Moll* cutpurse sir.
*Alex.*   The same, dost thou know her then?
*Trap.*   Aswell as I know twill raine vpon *Simon* and *Iudes* day next,
I will sift all the tauerns ith citty, and drinke halfe pots with all the
Watermen ath bankside, but if you will sir ile find her out.
*Alex.*   That task is easy, doot then, hold thy hand vp.
Whats this, ist burnt.
*Trap.*   No sir no, a little sindgd with making fire workes.                    210

195 h'as] Dodsley [he has]; has Q

*Alex.* Ther's mony, spend it, that being spent fetch more.

*Trap.* Oh sir that all the poore souldiers in *England* had such a leader. For fetching no water Spaniell is like me.

*Alex.* This wench we speake of, straies so from her kind
Nature repents she made her. Tis a Mermaid
Has told my sonne to shipwracke.

*Trap.* Ile cut her combe for you.

*Alex.* Ile tell out gold for thee then: hunt her forth,
Cast out a line hung full of siluer hookes
To catch her to thy company: deepe spendings          220
May draw her thats most chast to a mans bosome.

*Trap.* The gingling of Golden bels, and a good foole with a hobby-
horse, wil draw all the whoores ith towne to dance in a morris.

*Alex.* Or rather, for thats best, (they say sometimes
Shee goes in breeches) follow her as her man.

*Trap.* And when her breeches are off, shee shall follow me.

*Alex.* Beate all thy braines to serue her.

*Trap.* Zounds sir, as country wenches beate creame, till butter
comes.

*Alex.* Play thou the suttle spider, weaue fine nets          230
To insnare her very life.

*Trap.* Her life.

*Alex.* Yes sucke
Her heart-bloud if thou canst, twist thou but cords
To catch her, Ile finde law to hang her vp.

*Trap.* Spoke like a Worshipfull bencher.

*Alex.* Trace all her steps: at this shee-foxes den
Watch what lambs enter: let me play the sheepeheard
To saue their throats from bleeding, and cut hers.

*Trap.* This is the goll shall doot.          240

*Alex.* Be firme and gaine me
Euer thine owne. This done I entertaine thee:
How is thy name.

*Trap.* My name sir is *Raph Trapdore*, honest *Raph.*

*Alex.* *Trapdore*, be like thy name, a dangerous step
For her to venture on, but vnto me —

216 told] *i.e. toll'd*

24

*Trap.*　As fast as your sole to your boote or shooe sir.
*Alex.*　Hence then, be little seene here as thou canst.
Ile still be at thine elbow.
*Trap.*　　　　　　　The trapdores set.
*Moll* if you budge y'are gon: this me shall crowne,　　　　250
A Roaring Boy, the Roaring Girle puts downe.
*Alex.*　God a mercy, loose no time.

　　　　　　　　　　　　　　　　　　　　　*Exeunt.*

## [ACT II, SCENE i]

*The three shops open in a ranke: the first a Poticaries shop, the next
a Fether shop: the third a Sempsters shop: Mistresse* Gallipot *in
the first, Mistresse* Tiltyard *in the next, Maister* Openworke *and his wife in the third, to them enters*
Laxton, Goshawke *and* Greenewit.

*Mist. Open.*　Gentlemen what ist you lacke. What ist you buy, see
fine bands and ruffes, fine lawnes, fine cambrickes, what ist you lacke
Gentlemen, what ist you buy?
*Lax.*　Yonders the shop.
*Gosh.*　Is that shee.
*Lax.*　Peace.
*Green.*　Shee that minces Tobacco.
*Lax.*　I: shees a Gentlewoman borne I can tell you, tho it be her
hard fortune now to shread Indian pot-hearbes.
*Gosh.*　Oh sir tis many a good womans fortune, when her husband　10
turns bankrout, to begin with pipes and set vp againe.
*Lax.*　And indeed the raysing of the woman is the lifting vp of the
mans head at all times, if one florish, tother will bud as fast I
warrant ye.
*Gosh.*　Come th'art familiarly acquainted there, I grope that.
*Lax.*　And you grope no better ith dark you may chance lye ith
ditch when y'are drunke.
*Gosh.*　Go th'art a misticall letcher.
*Lax.*　I will not deny but my credit may take vp an ounce of pure
smoake.　　　　　　　　　　　　　　　　　　　　　　20

*Gosh.* May take vp an ell of pure smock; away go, tis the closest striker. Life I think he commits venery forty foote deepe, no mans aware on't. I like a palpable smockster go to worke so openly, with the tricks of art, that I'me as aparantly seen as a naked boy in a viall, and were it not for a guift of trechery that I haue in me to betray my friend when he puts most trust in me (masse yonder hee is too —) and by his iniurie to make good my accesse to her, I should appeare as defectiue in courting, as a Farmers sonne the first day of his feather, that doth nothing at Court, but woe the hangings and glasse windowes for a month together, and some broken 30 wayting woman for euer after. I find those imperfections in my venerie, that were't not for flatterie and falshood, I should want discourse and impudence, and hee that wants impudence among women, is worthy to bee kickt out at beds feet. — He shall not see me yet.

*Green.* Troth this is finely shred.

*Lax.* Oh women are the best mincers.

*Mist. Gal.* 'Thad bin a good phrase for a Cookes wife sir.

*Lax.* But'twill serue generally, like the front of a newe Almanacke; as thus: Calculated for the meridian of Cookes wiues, but generally 40 for all Englishwomen.

*Mist. Gal.* Nay you shall ha'te sir, I haue fild it for you.

*Shee puts it to the fire.*

*Lax.* The pipe's in a good hand, and I wish mine alwaies so.

*Green.* But not to be vs'd a that fashion.

*Lax.* O pardon me sir, I vnderstand no french.
I pray be couerd. *Iacke* a pipe of rich smoake.

*Gosh.* Rich smoake; that's six pence a pipe ist?

*Green.* To me sweet Lady.

*Mist. Gal.* Be not forgetful; respect my credit; seem strange; Art and Wit makes a foole of suspition: — pray be warie. 50

*Lax.* Push, I warrant you: — come, how ist gallants?

*Green.* Pure and excellent.

*Lax.* I thought 'twas good, you were growne so silent; you are

29 woe] *i.e. woo*

like those that loue not to talke at victuals, tho they make a worse
noyse i'the nose then a common fidlers prentice, and discourse a
whole Supper with snuffling; — I must speake a word with you
anone.

*Mist. Gal.*  Make your way wisely then.

*Gosh.*  Oh what else sir, hee's perfection it selfe, full of manners,
but not an acre of ground belonging to 'em.                          60

*Green.*  I and full of forme, h'as ne're a good stoole in's chamber.

*Gosh.*  But aboue all religious: hee prayeth daily vpon elder
brothers.

*Green.*  And valiant aboue measure; h'as runne three streets from
a Serieant.

*Lax.*  Puh, Puh.               *He blowes tobacco in their faces.*

*Green. Gosh.*  Oh, puh, ho, ho.

*Lax.*  So, so.

*Mist. Gal.*  Whats the matter now sir?

*Lax.*  I protest I'me in extreame want of money, if you can supply  70
mee now with any meanes, you doe mee the greatest pleasure, next
to the bountie of your loue, as euer poore gentleman tasted.

*Mist. Gal.*  What's the summe would pleasure ye sir?
Tho you deserue nothing lesse at my hands.

*Lax.*  Why 'tis but for want of opportunitie thou know'st; I put
her off with opportunitie still: by this light I hate her, but for
meanes to keepe me in fashion with gallants; for what I take from
her, I spend vpon other wenches, beare her in hand still; shee has
wit enough to rob her husband, and I waies enough to consume
the money: why how now? what the chin-cough?                         80

*Gosh.*  Thou hast the cowardliest tricke to come before a mans face
and strangle him ere hee be aware, I could find in my heart to make
a quarrell in earnest.

*Lax.*  Poxe and thou do'st, thou know'st I neuer vse to fight with
my friends, thou'l but loose thy labour in't.
*Iacke Dapper!*

*Enter* Iacke Dapper, *and his man* Gull.

*Green.*  Mounsier *Dapper*, I diue downe to your anckles.

*Iac. Dap.*  Saue ye gentlemen all three in a peculiar salute.

*Gosh.* He were ill to make a lawyer, hee dispatches three at once.

*Lax.* So wel said: but is this of the same Tobacco mistresse 90
Gallipot?

[*Shee giues him money secretly.*]

*Mist. Gal.* The same you had at first sir.

*Lax.* I wish it no better: this will serue to drinke at my chamber.

*Gosh.* Shall we taste a pipe on't?

*Lax.* Not of this by my troth Gentlemen, I haue sworne before
you.

*Gosh.* What, not *Iacke dapper.*

*Lax.* Pardon me sweet *Iacke*, I'me sorry I made such a rash oath,
but foolish oathes must stand: where art going *Iacke.*

*Iac. Dap.* Faith to buy one fether.                                    100

*Lax.* One fether, the foole's peculiar still.

*Iac. Dap.*  *Gul.*

*Gull.* Maister.

*Iac. Dap.* Heer's three halfepence for your ordinary, boy, meete
me an howre hence in *Powles.*

*Gull.* How three single halfepence; life, this will scarce serue a man
in sauce, a halporth of mustard, a halporth of oyle, and a halporth of
viniger, whats left then for the pickle herring: this showes like
small beere ith morning after a great surfet of wine ore night, hee
could spend his three pound last night in a supper amongst girles 110
and braue baudy-house boyes, I thought his pockets cackeld not
for nothing, these are the egs of three pound, Ile go sup 'em vp
presently.                                                    *Exit* Gul.

*Lax.* Eight, nine, ten Angels, good wench ifaith, and one that
loues darkenesse well, she puts out a candle with the best tricks of
any drugsters wife in *England*: but that which mads her I raile vpon
oportunity still, and take no notice on't. The other night she would
needs lead me into a roome with a candle in her hand to show me
a naked picture, where no sooner entred but the candle was sent
of an arrant: now I not intending to vnderstand her, but like a 120
puny at the Innes of venery, cal'd for another light innocently, thus
reward I all her cunning with simple mistaking. I know she cosens
her husband to keepe me, and Ile keepe her honest, as long as I can,
to make the poore man some part of amends, an honest minde of

a whooremaister, how thinke you amongst you, what a fresh pipe,
draw in a third man.
*Gosh.*   No you'r a horder, you ingrose bith ounces.

*At the Fether shop now.*

*Iac. Dap.*   Puh I like it not.
*Mist. Tilt.*                    What fether ist you'ld haue sir.
These are most worne and most in fashion.
Amongst the Beuer gallants, the stone Riders,                    130
The priuate stages audience, the twelu peny stool Gentlemen,
I can enforme you tis the generall fether.
*Iac. Dap.*   And therefore I mislike it, tell me of generall.
Now a continuall *Simon* and *Iudes* raine
Beate all your fethers as flat downe as pancakes.
Shew me — a — spangled fether.
*Mist. Tilt.*                    Oh to go a feasting with,
You'd haue it for a hinch boy, you shall.

*At the Sempsters shop now.*

*Maist. Open.*   Masse I had quite forgot,
His Honours footeman was here last night wife,
Ha you done with my Lords shirt.
*Mist. Open.*                    Whats that to you sir,          140
I was this morning at his Honours lodging,
Ere such a snake as you crept out of your shell.
*Maist. Open.*   Oh 'twas well done good wife.
*Mist. Open.*                    I hold it better sir,
Then if you had don't your selfe.
*Maist. Open.*                Nay so say I:
But is the Countesses smocke almost donne mouse.
*Mist. Open.*   Here lyes the cambricke sir, but wants I feare mee.
*Maist. Open.*   Ile resolue you of that presently.
*Mist. Open.*   Haida, oh audacious groome,
Dare you presume to noble womens linnen,
Keepe you your yard to measure sheepeheards holland,          150
I must confine you I see that.

29

*At the Tobacco shop now.*

*Gosh.*  What say you to this geere.
*Lax.*  I dare the arrants critticke in Tobacco
To lay one falt vpon't.

*Enter* Mol *in a freese Ierkin and a blacke sauegard.*

*Gosh.*  Life yonders *Mol.*
*Lax.*  *Mol* which *Mol.*
*Gosh.*  Honest *Mol.*
*Lax.*  Prithee lets call her — *Mol.*
*All.*  *Mol, Mol,* pist *Mol.*
*Moll.*  How now, whats the matter.                                   160
*Gosh.*  A pipe of good tobacco *Mol.*
*Moll.*  I cannot stay.
*Gosh.*  Nay *Moll* puh, prethee harke, but one word ifaith.
*Moll.*  Well what ist.
*Green.*  Prithee come hither sirra.
*Lax.*  Hart I would giue but too much money to be nibling with
that wench, life, sh'as the Spirit of foure great parishes, and a voyce
that will drowne all the Citty, me thinkes a braue Captaine might
get all his souldiers vpon her, and nere bee beholding to a company
of mile-end milke sops, if hee could come on, and come off quicke  170
enough: Such a *Moll* were a maribone before an Italian, hee would
cry *bona roba* till his ribs were nothing but bone. Ile lay hard siege
to her, mony is that *Aqua fortis,* that eates into many a maidenhead,
where the wals are flesh and bloud Ile euer pierce through with a
golden auguer.
*Gosh.*  Now thy iudgement *Moll,* ist not good?
*Moll.*  Yes faith tis very good tobacco, how do you sell an ounce,
farewell. God b'y you Mistresse *Gallipot.*
*Gosh.*  Why *Mol, Mol.*
*Moll.*  I cannot stay now ifaith, I am going to buy a shag ruffe, the  180
shop will be shut in presently.
*Gosh.*  Tis the maddest fantasticalst girle: — I neuer knew so much
flesh and so much nimblenesse put together.

30

*Lax.* Shee slips from one company to another, like a fat Eele
between a Dutchmans fingers: — Ile watch my time for her.
*Mist. Gal.* Some will not sticke to say shees a man and some both
man and woman.
*Lax.* That were excellent, she might first cuckold the husband and
then make him do as much for the wife.

*The Fether shop againe.*

*Moll.* Saue you; how does Mistresse *Tiltyard?*                    190
*Iac. Dap.* *Mol.*
*Moll.* *Iacke Dapper.*
*Iac. Dap.* How dost *Mol.*
*Moll.* Ile tell the by and by, I go but toth' next shop.
*Iac. Dap.* Thou shalt find me here this howre about a fether.
*Moll.* Nay and a fether hold you in play a whole houre, a goose
will last you all the daies of your life. Let me see a good shag
ruffe.

*The Sempster shop.*

*Maist. Open.* Mistresse *Mary* that shalt thou ifaith, and the best
in the shop.                                                          200
*Mist. Open.* How now, greetings, loue tearmes with a pox
betweene you, haue I found out one of your haunts, I send you for
hollands, and you're ith the low countries with a mischiefe, I'me
seru'd with good ware byth shift, that makes it lye dead so long
vpon my hands, I were as good shut vp shop, for when I open it
I take nothing.
*Maist. Open.* Nay and you fall a ringing once the diuell cannot
stop you, Ile out of the Belfry as fast as I can — *Moll.*
*Mist. Open.* Get you from my shop.
*Moll.* I come to buy.                                                210
*Mist. Open.* Ile sell ye nothing, I warne yee my house and shop.
*Moll.* You goody *Openworke*, you that prick out a poore liuing
And sowes many a bawdy skin-coate together,
Thou priuate pandresse betweene shirt and smock,

194 the] *i.e. thee*

31

I wish thee for a minute but a man:
Thou shouldst neuer vse more shapes, but as th'art
I pitty my reuenge, now my spleenes vp,

*Enter a fellow with a long rapier by his side.*

I would not mocke it willingly — ha be thankfull.
Now I forgiue thee.
*Mist. Open.*   Mary hang thee, I neuer askt forgiuenesse in my life. 220
*Moll.*   You goodman swinesface.
*Fell.*   What wil you murder me.
*Moll.*   You remember slaue, how you abusd me t'other night in a
Tauerne.
*Fell.*   Not I by this light.
*Moll.*   No, but by candlelight you did, you haue trickes to saue
your oathes, reseruations haue you, and I haue reserued somewhat
for you, — as you like that call for more, you know the signe
againe.
*Fell.*   Pox ant, had I brought any company along with mee to haue 230
borne witnesse on't, 'twold ne're haue grieu'd me, but to be strucke
and nobody by, tis my ill fortune still, why tread vpon a worme
they say twill turne taile, but indeed a Gentle-man should haue
more manners.                                         *Exit fellow.*
*Lax.*   Gallantly performed ifath *Mol*, and manfully, I loue thee for
euer fort, base rogue, had he offerd but the least counter-buffe, by
this hand I was prepared for him.
*Moll.*   You prepared for him, why should you be prepared for him,
was he any more then a man.
*Lax.*   No nor so much by a yard and a handfull *London* measure. 240
*Moll.*   Why do you speake this then, doe you thinke I cannot ride
a stone horse, vnlesse one lead him bith snaffle.
*Lax.*   Yes and sit him brauely, I know thou canst *Mol*, twas but an
honest mistake through loue, and Ile make amends fort any way,
prethee sweete plumpe *Mol*, when shall thou and I go out a towne
together.
*Moll.*   Whether, to Tyburne prethee.
*Lax.*   Masse thats out a towne indeed, thou hangst so many iests

vpon thy friends stil. I meane honestly to *Brainford*, *Staines* or
*Ware*.                                                                      250
*Moll.*   What to do there.
*Lax.*   Nothing but bee merry and lye together, I'le hire a coach
with foure horses.
*Moll.*   I thought 'twould bee a beastly iourney, you may leaue out
one wel, three horses will serue, if I play the iade my selfe.
*Lax.*   Nay push th'art such another kicking wench, prethee be kind
and lets meete.
*Moll.*   Tis hard but we shall meete sir.
*Lax.*   Nay but appoint the place then, there's ten Angels in faire
gold *Mol*, you see I do not trifle with you, do but say thou wilt   260
meete me, and Ile haue a coach ready for thee.
*Moll.*   Why here's my hand Ile meete you sir.
*Lax.*   Oh good gold, — the place sweete *Mol*.
*Moll.*   It shal be your appointment.
*Lax.*   Somewhat neere Holborne *Mol*.
*Moll.*   In Graies-Inne fields then.
*Lax.*   A match.
*Moll.*   Ile meete you there.
*Lax.*   The houre.
*Moll.*   Three.                                                             270
*Lax.*   That will be time enough to sup at *Braineford*.

*Fall from them to the other.*

*Maist. Open.*   I am of such a nature sir, I cannot endure the house
when shee scolds, sh'has a tongue will be hard further in a still
morning then Saint *Antlings*-bell, she railes vpon me for forraine
wenching, that I being a freeman must needs keep a whore ith
subburbs, and seeke to impouerish the liberties, when we fall out,
I trouble you still to make all whole with my wife.
*Gosh.*   No trouble at all, tis a pleasure to mee to ioyne things
together.
*Maist. Open.*   Go thy waies, I doe this but to try thy honesty   280
*Goshawke*.

*The Fether shop.*

*Iac. Dap.* How lik'st thou this *Mol.*

*Moll.* Oh singularly, you'r fitted now for a bunch, he lookes for all the world with those spangled fethers like a noblemans bedpost: The purity of your wench would I faine try, shee seemes like *Kent* vnconquered, and I beleeue as many wiles are in her — oh the gallants of these times are shallow letchers, they put not their courtship home enough to a wench, tis impossible to know what woman is throughly honest, because shee's nere thoroughly try'd, I am of that certaine beleefe there are more queanes in this towne 290 of their owne making, then of any mans prouoking, where lyes the slacknesse then? many a poore soule would downe, and ther's nobody will push em:

Women are courted but nere soundly tri'd,
As many walke in spurs that neuer ride.

*The Sempsters shop.*

*Mist. Open.* Oh abominable.

*Gosh.* Nay more I tell you in priuate, he keeps a whore ith subburbs.

*Mist. Open.* O spittle dealing, I came to him a Gentlewoman borne. Ile shew you mine armes when you please sir.    300

*Gosh.* I had rather see your legs, and begin that way.    [*Aside.*]

*Mist. Open.* Tis well knowne he tooke me from a Ladies seruice, where I was well beloued of the steward, I had my Lattine tongue, and a spice of the French before I came to him, and now doth he keepe a subberbian whoore vnder my nostrils.

*Gosh.* There's waies enough to cry quite with him, harke in thine eare.

*Mist. Open.* Theres a friend worth a Million.

*Moll.* I'le try one speare against your chastity Mistresse *Tiltyard* though it proue too short by the burgh.    310

*Enter* Ralph Trapdore.

*Trap.*  Masse here she is.

I'me bound already to serue her, tho it be but a sluttish tricke.
Blesse my hopefull yong Mistresse with long life and great limbs,
send her the vpper hand of all balifes, and their hungry adherents.

*Moll.*  How now, what art thou?

*Trap.*  A poore ebbing Gentleman, that would gladly wait for the
yong floud of your seruice.

*Moll.*  My seruice! what should moue you to offer your seruice to
me sir?

*Trap.*  The loue I beare to your heroicke spirit and masculine  320
womanhood.

*Moll.*  So sir, put case we should retaine you to vs, what parts are
there in you for a Gentlewomans seruice.

*Trap.*  Of two kinds right Worshipfull: moueable, and immoueable:
moueable to run of arrants, and immoueable to stand when you
haue occasion to vse me.

*Moll.*  What strength haue you.

*Trap.*  Strength Mistresse *Mol*, I haue gon vp into a steeple, and
staid the great bell as 'thas beene ringing; stopt a windmill going.

*Moll.*  And neuer strucke downe your selfe.  330

*Trap.*  Stood as vpright as I do at this present.

> Mol *trips vp his heeles, he fals.*

*Moll.*  Come I pardon you for this, it shall bee no disgrace to you:
I haue strucke vp the heeles of the high Germaines size ere now, —
what not stand.

*Trap.*  I am of that nature where I loue, I'le bee at my mistresse
foot to do her seruice.

*Moll.*  Why well said, but say your Mistresse should receiue iniury,
haue you the spirit of fighting in you, durst you second her.

*Trap.*  Life I haue kept a bridge my selfe, and droue seuen at a time
before me.  340

*Moll.*  I.

*Trap.*  But they were all *Lincolneshire* bullockes by my troth.

> *Aside.*

*331 S.D.  Q *places on line with* 329

*Moll.* Well, meete me in Graies-Inne fields, between three and foure this afternoone, and vpon better consideration weele retaine you.

*Trap.* I humbly thanke your good Mistreship, Ile crack your necke for this kindnesse.          *Exit* Trapdore.

*Lax.* Remember three.          Mol *meets* Laxton

*Moll.* Nay if I faile you hange me.

*Lax.* Good wench Ifaith.          *then* Openworke. 350

*Moll.* Whose this.

*Maist. Open.* Tis I *Mol.*

*Moll.* Prithee tend thy shop and preuent bastards.

*Maist. Open.* Wele haue a pint of the same wine ifaith *Mol.*
          *[Exit with* Mol.] *The bel rings.*

*Gosh.* Harke the bell rings, come Gentlemen.

*Iacke Dapper* where shals all munch.

*Iac. Dap.* I am for *Parkers* ordinary.

*Lax.* Hee's a good guest to'm, hee deserues his boord, he drawes all the Gentlemen in a terme time thither,
Weele be your followers *Iacke*, lead the way,          360
Looke you by my faith the foole has fetherd his nest well.
          *Exeunt Gallants.*

*Enter Maister* Gallipot, *Maister* Tiltyard, *and seruants with water Spaniels and a ducke.*

*Maist. Tilt.* Come shut vp your shops, where's *Maister* Open-worke.

*Mist. Gal.* Nay aske not me *Maister Tiltyard.*

*Maist. Tilt.* Wher's his water dog, puh — pist — hur — hur — pist.

*Maist. Gal.* Come wenches come, we're going all to *Hogsden.*

*Mist. Gal.* To *Hogsden* husband.

*Maist. Gal.* I to *Hogsden* pigsny.

*Mist. Gal.* I'me not ready husband.          370

*Maist. Gal.* Faith thats well — hum — pist — pist.
          *Spits in the dogs mouth.*

Come Mistresse *Openworke* you are so long.

371 S.D. Q *places on same line as* 370

*Mist. Open.*   I haue no ioy of my life Maister *Gallipot.*
*Maist. Gal.*   Push, let your boy lead his water Spaniel along, and
weele show you the brauest sport at parlous pond, he trug, he trug,
he trug, heres the best ducke in *England,* except my wife, he, he,
he, fetch, fetch, fetch,
Come lets away,
Of all the yeare this is the sportfulst day.

[*Exeunt.*]

## [ACT II, Scene ii]

*Enter* Sebastian *solus.*

*Seb.*   If a man haue a free will, where should the vse
More perfect shine then in his will to loue.
All creatures haue their liberty in that,

        *Enter Sir* Alexander *and listens to him.*

Tho else kept vnder seruile yoke and feare,
The very bondslaue has his freedome there,
Amongst a world of creatures voyc'd and silent.
Must my desires weare fetters — yea are you

                [Sebastian *sees him.*]
So neere, then I must breake with my hearts truth;
Meete griefe at a backe way — well: why suppose
The two leaud tongues of slander or of truth                    10
Pronounce *Mol* loathsome: if before my loue
Shee appeare faire, what iniury haue I,
I haue the thing I like? in all things else
Mine owne eye guides me, and I find 'em prosper,
Life what should aile it now? I know that man
Nere truely loues, if he gainesayt he lyes,
That winkes and marries with his fathers eyes.
Ile keepe myne owne wide open.

                *Enter* Mol *and a porter with a viall on his backe.*
*Alex.*                Here's braue wilfulnesse,
A made match, here she comes, they met a purpose.

        *10 leaud] stet Q

**37**

*Port.*  Must I carry this great fiddle to your chamber Mistresse 20
*Mary.*

*Moll.*  Fiddle goodman hog-rubber, some of these porters beare
so much for others, they haue no time to carry wit for themselues.

*Port.*  To your owne chamber Mistresse *Mary.*

*Moll.*  Who'le heare an Asse speake: whither else goodman
pagent-bearer: the're people of the worst memories.

*Exit Porter.*

*Seb.*  Why 'twere too great a burthen loue, to haue them carry
things in their minds, and a'ther backes together.

*Moll.*  Pardon me sir, I thought not you so neere.

*Alex.*  So, so, so.                                               30

*Seb.*  I would be neerer to thee, and in that fashion,
That makes the best part of all creatures honest.
No otherwise I wish it.

*Moll.*  Sir I am so poore to requite you, you must looke for nothing
but thankes of me, I haue no humor to marry, I loue to lye aboth
sides ath bed my selfe; and againe ath'other side; a wife you know
ought to be obedient, but I feare me I am too headstrong to obey,
therefore Ile nere go about it, I loue you so well sir for your good
will I'de be loath you should repent your bargaine after, and therefore weele nere come together at first, I haue the head now of my 40
selfe, and am man enough for a woman, marriage is but a chopping
and changing, where a maiden looses one head, and has a worse ith
place.

*Alex.*  The most comfortablest answer from a Roaring Girle,
That euer mine eares drunke in.

*Seb.*                               This were enough
Now to affright a foole for euer from thee,
When tis the musicke that I loue thee for.

*Alex.*  There's a boy spoyles all againe.

*Moll.*  Beleeue it sir I am not of that disdainefull temper, but I
could loue you faithfully.                                         50

*Alex.*  A pox on you for that word. I like you not now,
Y'are a cunning roarer I see that already.

*Moll.*  But sleepe vpon this once more sir, you may chance shift
a minde to morrow, be not too hasty to wrong your selfe, neuer

while you liue sir take a wife running, many haue run out at heeles
that haue don't: you see sir I speake against my selfe, and if euery
woman would deale with their suter so honestly, poore yonger
brothers would not bee so often gul'd with old cosoning widdowes,
that turne ore all their wealth in trust to some kinsman, and make
the poore Gentleman worke hard for a pension, fare you well sir. 60
*Seb.*  Nay prethee one word more.
*Alex.*  How do I wrong this girle, she puts him of still.
*Moll.*  Thinke vpon this in cold bloud sir, you make as much hast
as if you were a going vpon a sturgion voyage, take deliberation
sir, neuer chuse a wife as if you were going to *Virginia.*
*Seb.*  And so we parted, my too cursed fate.    [*Stands aloofe.*]
*Alex.*  She is but cunning, giues him longer time in't.

*Enter a Tailor.*

*Taylor.*  Mistresse *Mol*, Mistresse *Mol*: so ho ho so ho.
*Moll.*  There boy, there boy, what dost thou go a hawking after
me with a red clout on thy finger.                                      70
*Taylor.*  I forgot to take measure on you for your new breeches.
*Alex.*  Hoyda breeches, what will he marry a monster with two
trinckets, what age is this? if the wife go in breeches, the man must
weare long coates like a foole.
*Moll.*  What fidlings heere, would not the old patterne haue seru'd
your turne.
*Taylor.*  You change the fashion, you say you'le haue the great
Dutch slop Mistresse *Mary.*
*Moll.*  Why sir I say so still.
*Taylor.*  Your breeches then will take vp a yard more.            80
*Moll.*  Well pray looke it be put in then.
*Taylor.*  It shall stand round and full I warrant you.
*Moll.*  Pray make em easy enough.
*Taylor.*  I know my fault now, t'other was somewhat stiffe be-
tweene the legges, Ile make these open enough I warrant you.
*Alex.*  Heer's good geere towards, I haue brought vp my sonne to
marry a Dutch slop, and a French dublet, a codpice daughter.
*Taylor.*  So, I haue gone as farre as I can go.

39

*Moll.* Why then farewell.

*Taylor.* If you go presently to your chamber Mistresse *Mary*, pray 90
send me the measure of your thigh, by some honest body.

*Moll.* Well sir, Ile send it by a Porter presently.      *Exit* Mol.

*Taylor.* So you had neede, it is a lusty one, both of them would
make any porters backe ake in *England*.      *Exit Taylor.*

*Seb.* I haue examined the best part of man,
Reason and iudgement, and in loue they tell me,
They leaue me vncontrould, he that is swayd
By an vnfeeling bloud, past heat of loue,
His spring time must needes erre, his watch nere goes right
That sets his dyall by a rusty clocke.      100

*Alex.* So, and which is that rusty clocke sir, you?

*Seb.* The clocke at Ludgate sir, it nere goes true.

*Alex.* But thou goest falser: not thy fathers cares
Can keepe thee right, when that insensible worke,
Obayes the workemans art, lets off the houre
And stops againe when time is satisfied,
But thou runst on, and iudgement, thy maine wheele,
Beats by all stoppes, as if the worke would breake,
Begunne with long paines for a minutes ruine,
Much like a suffering man brought vp with care,      110
At last bequeath'd to shame and a short prayer.

*Seb.* I tast you bitterer then I can deserue sir.

*Alex.* Who has bewitcht thee sonne, what diuell or drug,
Hath wrought vpon the weakenesse of thy bloud,
And betrayd all her hopes to ruinous folly?
Oh wake from drowsy and enchanted shame,
Wherein thy soule sits with a golden dreame
Flatred and poysoned.
I am old my sonne, oh let me preuaile quickly,
For I haue waightier businesse of mine owne      120
Then to chide thee: I must not to my graue,
As a drunkard to his bed, whereon he lyes
Onely to sleepe, and neuer cares to rise,
Let me dispatch in time, come no more neere her.

*Seb.* Not honestly, not in the way of marriage?

40

*Alex.*   What sayst thou marriage, in what place, the Sessions house,
  And who shall giue the bride, prethe, an inditement.
*Seb.*   Sir now yee take part with the world to wrong her.
*Alex.*   Why, wouldst thou faine marry to be pointed at,
  Alas the numbers great, do not o're burden't,                    130
  Why as good marry a beacon on a hill,
  Which all the country fixe their eyes vpon
  As her thy folly doates on.  If thou longst
  To haue the story of thy infamous fortunes,
  Serue for discourse in ordinaries and tauernes
  Th'art in the way: or to confound thy name,
  Keepe on, thou canst not misse it: or to strike
  Thy wretched father to vntimely coldnesse,
  Keepe the left hand still, it will bring thee to't.
  Yet if no teares wrung from thy fathers eyes,                    140
  Nor sighes that flye in sparkles, from his sorrowes,
  Had power to alter what is wilfull in thee,
  Me thinkes her very name should fright thee from her,
  And neuer trouble me.
*Seb.*   Why, is the name of *Mol* so fatall sir.
*Alex.*   Mary, one sir, where suspect is entred,
  For seeke all *London* from one end to t'other,
  More whoores of that name, then of any ten other.
*Seb.*   Whats that to her? let those blush for themselues.
  Can any guilt in others condemne her?                           150
  I'ue vowd to loue her: let all stormes oppose me,
  That euer beate against the brest of man,
  Nothing but deaths blacke tempest shall diuide vs.
*Alex.*   Oh folly that can dote on nought but shame.
*Seb.*   Put case a wanton itch runs through one name
  More then another, is that name the worse,
  Where honesty sits possest in't? it should rather
  Appeare more excellent, and deserue more praise,
  When through foule mists a brightnesse it can raise.
  Why there are of the diuels, honest Gentlemen,                  160
  And well descended, keepe an open house,

146 Mary,] Many ₐ Q

And some (ath good mans) that are arrant knaues.
He hates vnworthily, that by rote contemnes,
For the name neither saues, nor yet condemnes,
And for her honesty, I haue made such proofe an't,
In seuerall formes, so neerely watcht her waies,
I will maintaine that strict, against an army,
Excepting you my father: here's her worst,
Sh'has a bold spirit that mingles with mankind,
But nothing else comes neere it: and oftentimes          170
Through her apparell somewhat shames her birth,
But she is loose in nothing but in mirth,
Would all *Mols* were no worse.
*Alex.*   This way I toyle in vaine and giue but ayme
To infamy and ruine: he will fall,
My blessing cannot stay him: all my ioyes
Stand at the brinke of a deuouring floud
And will be wilfully swallowed: wilfully.
But why so vaine, let all these teares be lost,
Ile pursue her to shame, and so al's crost.   *Exit Sir* Alexander 180
*Seb.*   Hee is gon with some strange purpose, whose effect
Will hurt me little if he shoot so wide,
To thinke I loue so blindly: I but feed
His heart to this match, to draw on th'other,
Wherein my ioy sits with a full wish crownd,
Onely his moode excepted which must change,
By opposite pollicies, courses indirect.
Plaine dealing in this world takes no effect.
This madde girle I'le acquaint with my intent,
Get her assistance, make my fortunes knowne,          190
Twixt louers hearts, shee's a fit instrument,
And has the art to help them to their owne,
By her aduise, for in that craft shee's wise,
My loue and I may meete, spite of all spies.
                                      *Exit* Sebastian.

## [ACT III, Scene i]

*Enter* Laxton *in Graies-Inne fields with the Coachman.*

*Lax.*   Coachman.

*Coach.*   Heere sir.

*Lax.*   There's a tester more, prethee driue thy coach to the hither
end of Marybone parke, a fit place for *Mol* to get in.

*Coach.*   Marybone parke sir.

*Lax.*   I, its in our way thou knowst.

*Coach.*   It shall be done sir.

*Lax.*   Coachman.

*Coach.*   A non sir.

*Lax.*   Are we fitted with good phrampell iades.          10

*Coach.*   The best in Smithfield I warrant you sir.

*Lax.*   May we safely take the vpper hand of any coacht veluet
cappe or tuftaffety iacket, for they keepe a vilde swaggering in
coaches now a daies, the hye waies are stopt with them.

*Coach.*   My life for yours and baffle em to sir, — why they are the
same iades beleeue it sir, that haue drawne all your famous whores
to *Ware.*

*Lax.*   Nay then they know their businesse, they neede no more
instructions.

*Coach.*   The're so vsd to such iourneis sir, I neuer vse whip to em;   20
for if they catch but the sent of a wench once, they runne like
diuels.                              *Exit Coachman with his whip.*

*Lax.*   Fine *Cerberus,* that rogue will haue the start of a thousand
ones, for whilst others trot a foot, heele ride prauncing to hell vpon
a coach-horse.

Stay, tis now about the houre of her appointment, but yet I see
her not, harke whats this, one, two three, three by the clock at   The clocke
Sauoy, this is the houre, and Graies-Inne fields the place, shee   striks three.
swore shee'd meete mee: ha yonders two Innes a Court-men with
one wench, but thats not shee, they walke toward Islington out of   30

11 you] Dodsley; your Q

43

my way, I see none yet drest like her, I must looke for a shag ruffe,
a freeze ierken, a short sword, and a safeguard, or I get none: why
*Mol* prethee make hast, or the Coachman will cursse vs anon.

*Enter* Mol *like a man.*

*Moll.* Oh heeres my Gentleman: if they would keepe their daies
as well with their Mercers as their houres with their harlots, no
bankrout would giue seuen score pound for a seriants place, for
would you know a catchpoole rightly deriu'd, the corruption of
a Cittizen, is the generation of a seriant, how his eye hawkes for
venery. Come are you ready sir.

*Lax.* Ready, for what sir.                                    40

*Moll.* Do you aske that now sir, why was this meeting pointed.

*Lax.* I thought you mistooke me sir, you seeme to be some yong
barrister, I haue no suite in law — all my land's sold I praise
heauen for't; t'has rid me of much trouble.

*Moll.* Then I must wake you sir, where stands the coach?

*Lax.* Whose this, *Mol*: honest *Mol.*

*Moll.* So young, and purblind, you'r an old wanton in your eyes
I see that.

*Lax.* Th'art admirably suited for the three pigions at *Brainford*,
Ile sweare I knew thee not.                                    50

*Moll.* Ile sweare you did not: but you shall know me now.

*Lax.* No not here, we shall be spyde efaith, the coach is better,
come.

*Moll.* Stay.                    *Shee puts of her cloake and drawes.*

*Lax.* What wilt thou vntrusse a point *Mol.*

*Moll.* Yes, heere's the point that I vntrusse, 'thas but one tag,
'twill serue tho to tye vp a rogues tongue.

*Lax.* How.

*Moll.* There's the gold
With which you hir'd your hackney, here's her pace,           60
Shee rackes hard, and perhaps your bones will feele it,
Ten angels of mine own, I'ue put to thine,
Win em, and weare em.

54 S.D. Q *places below line* 55

44

*Lax.*  Hold *Moll*, Mistresse *Mary*.
*Moll.*  Draw or Ile serue an execution on thee
Shall lay thee vp till doomes day.
*Lax.*  Draw vpon a woman, why what dost meane *Mol?*
*Moll.*  To teach thy base thoughts manners: th'art one of those
That thinkes each woman thy fond flexable whore,
If she but cast a liberall eye vpon thee,                          70
Turne backe her head, shees thine, or amongst company,
By chance drinke first to thee: then shee's quite gon,
There's no meanes to help her: nay for a need,
Wilt sweare vnto thy credulous fellow letchers
That th'art more in fauour with a Lady
At first sight then her monky all her life time,
How many of our sex, by such as thou
Haue their good thoughts paid with a blasted name
That neuer deserued loosly or did trip
In path of whooredome, beyond cup and lip.                        80
But for the staine of conscience and of soule,
Better had women fall into the hands
Of an act silent, then a bragging nothing,
There's no mercy in't — what durst moue you sir,
To thinke me whoorish? a name which Ide teare out
From the hye Germaines throat, if it lay ledger there
To dispatch priuy slanders against mee.
In thee I defye all men, their worst hates,
And their best flatteries, all their golden witchcrafts,
With which they intangle the poore spirits of fooles,             90
Distressed needlewomen and trade-fallne wiues.
Fish that must needs bite, or themselues be bitten,
Such hungry things as these may soone be tooke
With a worme fastned on a golden hooke.
Those are the letchers food, his prey, he watches
For quarrelling wedlockes, and poore shifting sisters,
Tis the best fish he takes: but why good fisherman,
Am I thought meate for you, that neuer yet
Had angling rod cast towards me? cause youl'e say
I'me giuen to sport, I'me often mery, iest,                       100

45

Had mirth no kindred in the world but lust?
O shame take all her friends then: but how ere
Thou and the baser world censure my life,
Ile send 'em word by thee, and write so much
Vpon thy breast, cause thou shalt bear't in mind,
Tell them 'twere base to yeeld, where I haue conquer'd.
I scorne to prostitute my selfe to a man,
I that can prostitute a man to mee,
And so I greete thee.

*Lax.* Heare me.                                                              110

*Moll.* Would the spirits of al my slanderers, were claspt in thine,
That I might vexe an army at one time.

*Lax.* I do repent me, hold.                                    *They fight.*

*Moll.* You'l die the better Christian then.

*Lax.* I do confesse I haue wrong'd thee *Mol.*

*Moll.* Confession is but poore amends for wrong,
Vnlesse a rope would follow.

*Lax.* I aske thee pardon.

*Moll.* I'me your hir'd whoore sir.

*Lax.* I yeeld both purse and body.                            120

*Moll.* Both are mine, and now at my disposing.

*Lax.* Spare my life.

*Moll.* I scorne to strike thee basely.

*Lax.* Spoke like a noble girle i'faith.
Heart I thinke I fight with a familiar, or the Ghost of a fencer,
sh'has wounded me gallantly, call you this a letcherous viage?
Here's bloud would haue seru'd me this seuen yeare in broken
heads and cut fingers, and it now runs all out together, pox athe
three pigions, I would the coach were here now to carry mee to
the Chirurgions.                                    *Exit* Laxton. 130

*Moll.* If I could meete my enemies one by one thus,
I might make pretty shift with 'em in time,
And make 'em know, shee that has wit, and spirit,
May scorne to liue beholding to her body for meate,
Or for apparell like your common dame,
That makes shame get her cloathes, to couer shame.

111 slanderers] Collier; slanders Q

46

Base is that minde, that kneels vnto her body,
As if a husband stood in awe on's wife,
My spirit shall be Mistresse of this house,
As long as I haue time in't. — oh            *Enter* Trapdore. 140
Heere comes my man that would be: 'tis his houre.
Faith a good well set fellow, if his spirit
Be answerable to his vmbles; he walkes stiffe,
But whether he will stand to't stifly, there's the point;
H'as a good calfe for't, and ye shall haue many a woman
Choose him shee meanes to make her head, by his calfe,
I do not know their trickes in't; faith he seemes
A man without; I'le try what he is within.
*Trap.*    Shee told me Graies-Inne fields twixt three and foure,
Ile fit her Mistreship with a peece of seruice,            150
I'me hir'd to rid the towne of one mad girle.    *Shee iustles him.*
What a pox ailes you sir?
*Moll.*    He beginnes like a Gentleman.
*Trap.*    Heart, is the field so narrow, or your eye-sight:
Life he comes backe againe.            *She comes towards him.*
*Moll.*    Was this spoke to me sir.
*Trap.*    I cannot tell sir.
*Moll.*    Go y'are a coxcombe.
*Trap.*    Coxcombe.
*Moll.*    Y'are a slaue.            160
*Trap.*    I hope there's law for you sir.
*Moll.*    Ye, do you see sir.            *Turne his hat.*
*Trap.*    Heart this is no good dealing, pray let me know what house
you'r off.
*Moll.*    One of the Temple sir.            *Philips him.*
*Trap.*    Masse so me thinkes.
*Moll.*    And yet sometime I lye about chicke lane.
*Trap.*    I like you the worse because you shift your lodging so often,
Ile not meddle with you for that tricke sir.
*Moll.*    A good shift, but it shall not serue your turne.            170
*Trap.*    You'le giue me leaue to passe about my businesse sir.
*Moll.*    Your businesse, Ile make you waite on mee
Before I ha done, and glad to serue me too.

*Trap.*  How sir, serue you, not if there were no more men in
*England.*

*Moll.*  But if there were no more women in *England*
I hope you'd waite vpon your Mistresse then.

*Trap.*  Mistresse.

*Moll.*  Oh you'r a tri'd spirit at a push sir.

*Trap.*  What would your Worship haue me do.                    180

*Moll.*  You a fighter.

*Trap.*  No, I praise heauen, I had better grace and more maners.

*Moll.*  As how I pray sir.

*Trap.*  Life, 'thad bene a beastly part of me to haue drawne my
weapons vpon my Mistresse, all the world would a cry'd shame of
me for that.

*Moll.*  Why but you knew me not.

*Trap.*  Do not say so Mistresse, I knew you by your wide straddle
as well as if I had bene in your belly.

*Moll.*  Well, we shall try you further, ith meane time          190
Wee giue you intertainement.

*Trap.*  Thanke your good Mistreship.

*Moll.*  How many suites haue you.

*Trap.*  No more suites then backes Mistresse.

*Moll.*  Well if you deserue, I cast of this, next weeke,
And you may creepe into't.

*Trap.*  Thanke your good Worship.

*Moll.*  Come follow me to Saint *Thomas Apostles,*
Ile put a liuery cloake vpon your backe,
The first thing I do.                                            200

*Trap.*  I follow my deere Mistresse.

*Exeunt omnes.*


## [ACT III, Scene ii]

*Enter Mistresse* Gallipot *as from supper, her husband after her.*

*Maist. Gal.*  What *Pru,* Nay sweete *Prudence.*

*Mist. Gal.*  What a pruing keepe you, I thinke the baby would
haue a teate it kyes so, pray be not so fond of me, leaue your Citty

48

humours, I'me vext at you to see how like a calfe you come
bleating after me.

*Maist. Gal.*　　Nay hony *Pru*: how does your rising vp before all
. the table shew? and flinging from my friends so vnciuily, fye *Pru*,
fye, come.

*Mist. Gal.*　　Then vp and ride ifaith.

*Maist. Gal.*　　Vp and ride, nay my pretty *Pru*, thats farre from my　10
thought, ducke: why mouse, thy minde is nibbling at something,
whats ist, what lyes vpon thy Stomach?

*Mist. Gal.*　　Such an asse as you: hoyda, y'are best turne mid-wife,
or Physition: y'are a Poticary already, but I'me none of your drugs.

*Maist. Gal.*　　Thou art a sweete drug, sweetest *Pru*, and the more
thou art pounded, the more pretious.

*Mist. Gal.*　　Must you be prying into a womans secrets: say ye?

*Maist. Gal.*　　Womans secrets.

*Mist. Gal.*　　What? I cannot haue a qualme come vpon mee but
your teeth waters, till your nose hang ouer it.　　　　　　　　20

*Maist. Gal.*　　It is my loue deere wife.

*Mist. Gal.*　　Your loue? your loue is all words; giue mee deeds,
I cannot abide a man thats too fond ouer me, so cookish; thou dost
not know how to handle a woman in her kind.

*Maist. Gal.*　　No *Pru*? why I hope I haue handled —

*Mist. Gal.*　　Handle a fooles head of your owne, — fih — fih.

*Maist. Gal.*　　Ha, ha, tis such a waspe; it does mee good now to
haue her sting me, little rogue.

*Mist. Gal.*　　Now fye how you vex me, I cannot abide these aperne
husbands: such cotqueanes, you ouerdoe your things, they become　30
you scuruily.

*Maist. Gal.*　　Vpon my life she breeds, heauen knowes how I haue
straind my selfe to please her, night and day: I wonder why wee
Cittizens should get children so fretfull and vntoward in the
breeding, their fathers being for the most part as gentle as milch
kine: shall I leaue thee my *Pru*.

*Mist. Gal.*　　Fye, fye, fye.

*Maist. Gal.*　　Thou shalt not bee vext no more, pretty kind rogue,
take no cold sweete *Pru*.　　　　　　　*Exit Maister* Gallipot.

28 sting] Dodsley; sing Q

*Mist. Gal.* As your wit has done: now Maister *Laxton* shew your 40
head, what newes from you? would any husband suspect that a
woman crying, Buy any scurui-grasse, should bring loue letters
amongst her herbes to his wife, pretty tricke, fine conueyance? had
iealousy a thousand eyes, a silly woman with scuruy-grasse blinds
them all;
*Laxton* with bayes
Crown I thy wit for this, it deserues praise.
This makes me affect thee more, this prooues thee wise,
Lacke what poore shift is loue forc't to deuise? (toth' point)

*She reads the letter.*

*O Sweete Creature* — (a sweete beginning) *pardon my long absence,* 50
*for thou shalt shortly be possessed with my presence; though* Demophon
*was false to* Phillis, *I will be to thee as* Pan-da-rus *was to* Cres-si-da:
*tho* Eneus *made an asse of* Dido, *I will dye to thee ere I do so;*
*o sweetest creature make much of me, for no man beneath the siluer*
*moone shall make more of a woman then I do of thee, furnish me*
*therefore with thirty pounds, you must doe it of necessity for me; I*
*languish till I see some comfort come from thee, protesting not to dye*
*in thy debt, but rather to iiue so, as hitherto I haue and will.*

Thy true *Laxton* euer.

Alas poore Gentleman, troth I pitty him, 60
How shall I raise this money? thirty pound?
Tis thirty sure, a 3 before an o,
I know his threes too well; my childbed linnen?
Shall I pawne that for him? then if my marke
Be knowne I am vndone; it may be thought
My husband's bankrout: which way shall I turne?
*Laxton*, what with my owne feares, and thy wants,
I'me like a needle twixt two adamants.

*Enter Maister* Gallipot *hastily.*

*Maist. Gal.* Nay, nay, wife, the women are all vp, ha, how,
reading a letters? I smel a goose, a couple of capons, and a gammon 70
of bacon from her mother out of the country, I hold my life, —
Steale, — steale.

*Mist. Gal.*　　O beshrow your heart.

*Maist. Gal.*　　　　　　　　What letter's that?
I'le see't.

　　　　　　　　　　　　　　　*She teares the letter.*
*Mist. Gal.*　Oh would thou had'st no eyes to see
The downefall of me and thy selfe: I'me for euer,
For euer I'me vndone.

*Maist. Gal.*　　　　　What ailes my *Pru?*
What paper's that thou tear'st?

*Mist. Gal.*　　　　　　Would I could teare
My very heart in peeces: for my soule
Lies on the racke of shame, that tortures me
Beyond a womans suffering.

*Maist. Gal.*　　　　　What meanes this?

*Mist. Gal.*　Had you no other vengeance to throw downe,　　80
But euen in heigth of all my ioyes?

*Maist. Gal.*　　　　　　Deere woman.

*Mist. Gal.*　When the full sea of pleasure and content
Seem'd to flow ouer me.

*Maist. Gal.*　　　　As thou desirest
To keepe mee out of bedlam, tell what troubles thee,
Is not thy child at nurse falne sicke, or dead?

*Mist. Gal.*　Oh no.

*Maist. Gal.*　　　　Heauens blesse me, are my barnes and houses
Yonder at *Hockly hole* consum'd with fire,
I can build more, sweete *Pru.*

*Mist. Gal.*　　　　　Tis worse, tis worse.

*Maist. Gal.*　My factor broke, or is the *Ionas* suncke.

*Mist. Gal.*　Would all we had were swallowed in the waues,　　90
Rather then both should be the scorne of slaues.

*Maist. Gal.*　I'me at my wits end.

*Mist. Gal.*　　　　　Oh my deere husband,
Where once I thought my selfe a fixed starre,
Plac't onely in the heauen of thine armes,
I feare now I shall proue a wanderer,
Oh *Laxton, Laxton,* is it then my fate
To be by thee orethrowne?

*Maist. Gal.*            Defend me wisedome,
From falling into frenzie. On my knees,
Sweete *Pru*, speake, whats that *Laxton* who so heauy
Lyes on thy bosome.
*Mist. Gal.*        I shall sure run mad.          100
*Maist. Gal.*   I shall run mad for company then: speak to me,
I'me *Gallipot* thy husband, — *Pru*, — why *Pru*.
Art sicke in conscience for some villanous deed
Thou wert about to act, didst meane to rob me,
Tush I forgiue thee, hast thou on my bed
Thrust my soft pillow vnder anothers head?
Ile winke at all faults *Pru*, las thats no more,
Then what some neighbours neere thee, haue done before,
Sweete hony *Pru*, whats that *Laxton?*
*Mist. Gall.*          Oh.
*Maist. Gal.*   Out with him.
*Mist. Gall.*        Oh hee's borne to be my vndoer,    110
This hand which thou calst thine, to him was giuen,
To him was I made sure ith sight of heauen.
*Maist. Gal.*   I neuer heard this thunder.
*Mist. Gal.*          Yes, yes, before
I was to thee contracted, to him I swore,
Since last I saw him twelue moneths three times told,
The Moone hath drawne through her light siluer bow,
For ore the seas hee went, and it was said,
(But Rumor lyes) that he in *France* was dead.
But hee's aliue, oh hee's aliue, he sent,
That letter to me, which in rage I rent,      120
Swearing with oathes most damnably to haue me,
Or teare me from this bosome, oh heauens saue me.
*Maist. Gal.*   My heart will breake — sham'd and vndone for euer.
*Mist. Gal.*   So black a day (poore wretch) went ore thee neuer.
*Maist. Gal.*   If thou shouldst wrastle with him at the law,
Th'art sure to fall, no odde slight, no preuention.
Ile tell him th'art with child.
*Mist. Gal.*          Vmh.

98 frenzie. On my knees,] Dodsley; frenzie, on my knees. Q

*Maist. Gal.*                    Or giue out
One of my men was tane a bed with thee.
*Mist. Gal.* Vmh, vmh.
*Maist. Gal.*          Before I loose thee my deere *Pru,*
Ile driue it to that push.
*Mist. Gal.*          Worse, and worse still,          130
You embrace a mischiefe, to preuent an ill.
*Maist. Gal.* Ile buy thee of him, stop his mouth with Gold,
Think'st thou twill do.
*Mist. Gal.*          Oh me, heauens grant it would,
Yet now my sences are set more in tune,
He writ, as I remember in his letter,
That he in riding vp and downe had spent,
(Ere hee could finde me) thirty pounds, send that,
Stand not on thirty with him.
*Maist. Gal.*                    Forty *Pru,*
Say thou the word tis done, wee venture liues
For wealth, but must do more to keepe our wiues,          140
Thirty or forty *Pru.*
*Mist. Gal.*          Thirty good sweete,
Of an ill bargaine lets saue what we can,
Ile pay it him with my teares, he was a man
When first I knew him of a meeke spirit,
All goodnesse is not yet dryd vp I hope.
*Maist. Gal.* He shall haue thirty pound, let that stop all:
Loues sweets tast best, when we haue drunke downe Gall.

          *Enter Maister* Tiltyard, *and his wife, Maister* Goshawke,
                    *and Mistresse* Openworke.

Gods so, our friends; come, come, smoth your cheeke;
After a storme the face of heauen looks sleeke.
*Maist. Tilt.* Did I not tell you these turtles were together?          150
*Mist. Tilt.* How dost thou sirra? why sister *Gallipot?*
*Mist. Open.* Lord how shee's chang'd?
*Gosh.* Is your wife ill sir?
*Maist. Gal.* Yes indeed la sir, very ill, very ill, neuer worse.
*Mist. Tilt.* How her head burnes, feele how her pulses work.

*Mist. Open.*   Sister lie downe a little, that alwaies does mee good.

*Mist. Tilt.*   In good sadnesse I finde best ease in that too,
Has shee laid some hot thing to her Stomach?

*Mist. Gal.*   No, but I will lay something anon.

*Maist. Tilt.*   Come, come fooles, you trouble her, shal's goe 160
Maister *Goshawke?*

*Gosh.*   Yes sweete Maister *Tiltyard*, sirra *Rosamond* I hold my life
*Gallipot* hath vext his wife.

*Mist. Open.*   Shee has a horrible high colour indeed.

*Gosh.*   Wee shall haue your face painted with the same red soone
at night, when your husband comes from his rubbers in a false
alley; thou wilt not beleeue me that his bowles run with a wrong
byas.

*Mist. Open.*   It cannot sinke into mee, that hee feedes vpon stale
mutten abroad, hauing better and fresher at home.                    170

*Gosh.*   What if I bring thee, where thou shalt see him stand at
racke and manger?

*Mist. Open.*   Ile saddle him in's kind, and spurre him till hee kicke
againe.

*Gosh.*   Shall thou and I ride our iourney then.

*Mist. Open.*   Heere's my hand.

*Gosh.*   No more; come Maister *Tiltyard*, shall we leape into the
stirrops with our women, and amble home?

*Maist. Tilt.*   Yes, yes, come wife.

*Mist. Tilt.*   Introth sister, I hope you will do well for all this.      180

*Mist. Gal.*   I hope I shall: farewell good sister: sweet Maister
*Goshawke.*

*Maist. Gal.*   Welcome brother, most kindlie welcome sir.

*Omn.*   Thankes sir for our good cheere.

> *Exeunt all but* Gallipot *and his wife.*

*Maist. Gal.*   It shall be so, because a crafty knaue
Shall not out reach me, nor walke by my dore
With my wife arme in arme, as 'twere his whoore,
I'le giue him a golden coxcombe, thirty pound:
Tush *Pru* what's thirty pound? sweete ducke looke cheerely.

*Mist. Gal.*   Thou art worthy of my heart thou bui'st it deerely.    190

*Enter* Laxton *muffled.*

*Lax.*  Vds light the tide's against me, a pox of your Potticariship:
oh for some glister to set him going; 'tis one of *Hercules* labours, to
tread one of these Cittie hennes, because their cockes are stil
crowing ouer them; there's no turning tale here, I must on.

*Mist. Gal.*  Oh, husband see he comes.

*Maist. Gal.*                    Let me deale with him.

*Lax.*  Blesse you sir.

*Maist Gal.*  Be you blest too sir if you come in peace.

*Lax.*  Haue you any good pudding Tobacco sir?

*Mist. Gal.*  Oh picke no quarrels gentle sir, my husband
Is not a man of weapon, as you are,                         200
He knowes all, I haue opned all before him,
Concerning you.

*Lax.*                Zounes has she showne my letters.     [*Aside*]

*Mist. Gal.*  Suppose my case were yours, what would you do.
At such a pinch, such batteries, such assaultes,
Of father, mother, kinred, to dissolue
The knot you tyed, and to be bound to him?
How could you shift this storme off?

*Lax.*                       If I know hang me.

*Mist. Gal.*  Besides a story of your death was read
Each minute to me.

*Lax.*              What a pox meanes this ridling?

*Maist. Gal.*  Be wise sir, let not you and I be tost               210
On Lawiers pens; they haue sharpe nibs and draw
Mens very heart bloud from them; what need you sir
To beate the drumme of my wifes infamy,
And call your friends together sir to prooue
Your precontract, when sh'has confest it?

*Lax.*                       Vmh sir, —
Has she confest it?

*Maist. Gal.*        Sh'has 'faith to me sir,
Vpon your letter sending.

*Mist. Gal.*              I haue, I haue.

215 precontract] Dodsley; precontact Q

55

*Lax.* If I let this yron coole call me slaue,
  Do you heare, you dame *Prudence?* think'st thou vile woman
  I'le take these blowes and winke?
*Mist. Gal.*            Vpon my knees.          220
*Lax.* Out impudence.
*Maist. Gal.*       Good sir.
*Lax.*                You goatish slaues,
  No wilde foule to cut vp but mine?
*Maist. Gal.*            Alas sir,
  You make her flesh to tremble, fright her not,
  Shee shall do reason, and what's fit.
*Lax.*              I'le haue thee,
  Wert thou more common then an hospitall,
  And more diseased. —
*Maist. Gal.*      But one word good sir.
*Lax.*                 So sir.
*Maist. Gal.* I married her, haue line with her, and got
  Two children on her body, thinke but on that;
  Haue you so beggarly an appetite
  When I vpon a dainty dish haue fed         230
  To dine vpon my scraps, my leauings? ha sir?
  Do I come neere you now sir?
*Lax.*           Be Lady you touch me.
*Maist. Gal.* Would not you scorne to weare my cloathes sir?
*Lax.*                   Right sir
*Maist. Gal.* Then pray sir weare not her, for shee's a garment
  So fitting for my body, I'me loath
  Another should put it on, you will vndoe both.
  Your letter (as shee said) complained you had spent
  In quest of her, some thirty pound, I'le pay it;
  Shall that sir stop this gap vp twixt you two?
*Lax.* Well if I swallow this wrong, let her thanke you:    240
  The mony being paid sir, I am gon:
  Farewell, oh women happy's hee trusts none.
*Mist. Gal.* Dispatch him hence sweete husband.
*Maist. Gal.*               Yes deere wife:
  Pray sir come in, ere Maister *Laxton* part

Thou shalt in wine drinke to him.

*Mist. Gal.*                    With all my heart; —
How dost thou like my wit?

                                        *Exit Maister* Gallipot *and his wife.*
*Lax.*                    Rarely, that wile
By which the Serpent did the first woman beguile,
Did euer since, all womens bosomes fill;
Y'are apple eaters all, deceiuers still.

                                                            *Exit* Laxton.


# [ACT III, Scene iii]


*Enter Sir* Alexander Wengraue: *Sir* Dauy Dapper, *Sir* Adam
Appleton, *at one dore, and* Trapdore *at another doore.*

*Alex.*    Out with your tale Sir *Dauy*, to Sir *Adam*.
A knaue is in mine eie deepe in my debt.
*Dauy.*    Nay: if hee be a knaue sir, hold him fast.
                                        [*Walk aloofe with Sir* Adam.]
*Alex.*    Speake softly, what egge is there hatching now.
*Trap.*    A Ducks egge sir, a ducke that has eaten a frog, I haue
crackt the shell, and some villany or other will peep out presently;
the ducke that sits is the bouncing Rampe (that Roaring Girle my
Mistresse) the drake that must tread is your sonne *Sebastian*.
*Alex.*    Be quicke.
*Trap.*    As the tongue of an oister wench.                    10
*Alex.*    And see thy newes be true.
*Trap.*    As a barbars euery satterday night — mad *Mol* —
*Alex.*    Ah.
*Trap.*    Must be let in without knocking at your backe gate.
*Alex.*    So.
*Trap.*    Your chamber will be made baudy.
*Alex.*    Good.
*Trap.*    Shee comes in a shirt of male.

---

246 S.D. Q *places below line* 245 [drinke to him.]
3 *Dauy.*] *throughout this scene the* Q *speech-prefixes are forms of* Sir Da. *or* S. Dauy.

*Alex.* How shirt of male?

*Trap.* Yes sir or a male shirt, that's to say in mans apparell. 20

*Alex.* To my sonne.

*Trap.* Close to your sonne: your sonne and her Moone will be in
coniunction, if all Alminacks lie not, her blacke saueguard is turned
into a deepe sloppe, the holes of her vpper body to button holes,
her wastcoate to a dublet, her placket to the ancient seate of a
codpice, and you shall take 'em both with standing collers.

*Alex.* Art sure of this?

*Trap.* As euery throng is sure of a pick-pocket, as sure as a whoore
is of the clyents all *Michaelmas* Tearme, and of the pox after the
Tearme. 30

*Alex.* The time of their tilting?

*Trap.* Three.

*Alex.* The day?

*Trap.* This.

*Alex.* Away: ply it, watch her.

*Trap.* As the diuell doth for the death of a baud, I'le watch her,
do you catch her.

*Alex.* Shee's fast: heere weaue thou the nets; harke —

*Trap.* They are made.

*Alex.* I told them thou didst owe mee money; hold it vp: main- 40
tain't.

*Trap.* Stifly; as a Puritan does contention,
Foxe I owe thee not the value of a halfepenny halter.

                                         [*As in quarrel.*]

*Alex.* Thou shalt be hang'd in't ere thou scape so.
Varlet I'le make thee looke through a grate.

*Trap.* I'le do't presently, through a Tauerne grate, drawer: pish.

                                        *Exit* Trapdore.

*Adam.* Has the knaue vext you sir?

*Alex.*                             Askt him my mony,
He sweares my sonne receiu'd it: oh that boy
Will nere leaue heaping sorrowes on my heart,
Till he has broke it quite.

*Adam.*                     Is he still wild? 50

*Alex.* As is a russian Beare.

*Adam.*                    But he has left
His old haunt with that baggage.
*Alex.*                    Worse still and worse,
He laies on me his shame, I on him my curse.
*Dauy.*   My sonne *Iacke Dapper* then shall run with him,
All in one pasture.
*Adam.*               Proues your sonne bad too sir?
*Dauy.*   As villany can make him: your *Sebastian*
Doates but on one drabb, mine on a thousand,
A noyse of fiddlers, Tobacco, wine and a whoore,
A Mercer that will let him take vp more,
Dyce, and a water spaniell with a Ducke: oh,                    60
Bring him a bed with these: when his purse gingles,
Roaring boyes follow at's tale, fencers and ningles,
(Beasts *Adam* nere gaue name to) these horse-leeches sucke
My sonne, he being drawne dry, they all liue on smoake.
*Alex.*   Tobacco?
*Dauy.*               Right, but I haue in my braine
A windmill going that shall grind to dust
The follies of my sonne, and make him wise,
Or a starke foole; pray lend me your aduise.
*Both.*   That shall you good sir *Dauy.*
*Dauy.*                    Heere's the sprindge
I ha set to catch this woodcocke in: an action                    70
In a false name (vnknowne to him) is entred
I'th Counter to arrest *Iacke Dapper.*
*Both.*                    Ha, ha, he.
*Dauy.*   Thinke you the Counter cannot breake him?
*Adam.*                    Breake him?
Yes and breake's heart too if he lie there long.
*Dauy.*   I'le make him sing a Counter tenor sure.
*Adam.*   No way to tame him like it, there hee shall learne
What mony is indeed, and how to spend it.
*Dauy.*   Hee's bridled there.
*Alex.*                    I, yet knowes not how to mend it,
Bedlam cures not more madmen in a yeare,
Then one of the Counters does, men pay more deere                    80

There for there wit then anywhere; a Counter
Why 'tis an vniuersity, who not sees?
As schollers there, so heere men take degrees,
And follow the same studies (all alike.)
Schollers learne first Logicke and Rhetoricke.
So does a prisoner; with fine honied speech
At's first comming in he doth perswade, beseech,
He may be lodg'd with one that is not itchy;
To lie in a cleane chamber, in sheets not lowsy,
But when he has no money, then does he try,                    90
By subtile Logicke, and quaint sophistry,
To make the keepers trust him.
*Adam.*                              Say they do.
*Alex.*    Then hee's a graduate.
*Dauy.*                              Say they trust him not.
*Alex.*    Then is he held a freshman and a sot,
    And neuer shall commence, but being still bar'd
    Be expulst from the Maisters side, toth' twopenny ward,
    Or else i'th hole, be plac't.
*Adam.*                              When then I pray
    Proceeds a prisoner.
*Alex.*                    When mony being the theame,
    He can dispute with his hard creditors hearts,
    And get out cleere, hee's then a Maister of Arts;          100
    Sir *Dauy* send your sonne to Woodstreet Colledge,
    A Gentleman can no where get more knowledge.
*Dauy.*    There Gallants study hard.
*Alex.*                              True: to get mony.
*Dauy.*    'Lies bith' heeles i'faith, thankes, thankes, I ha sent
    For a couple of beares shall paw him.

                *Enter Seriant* Curtilax *and Yeoman* Hanger.

*Adam.*                              Who comes yonder?
*Dauy.*    They looke like puttocks, these should be they.
*Alex.*                                  I know 'em,
    They are officers, sir wee'l leaue you.

                    97 be] Dyce; beg Q

*Dauy.*                    My good knights,
Leaue me, you see I'me haunted now with spirits.
*Both.*   Fare you well sir.        *Exeunt* Alexander *and* Adam.
*Curt.*   This old muzzle chops should be he by the fellowes discrip-  110
tion: Saue you sir.
*Dauy.*   Come hither you mad varlets, did not my man tell you I
watcht here for you.
*Curt.*   One in a blew coate sir told vs, that in this place an old
Gentleman would watch for vs, a thing contrary to our oath, for
we are to watch for euery wicked member in a Citty.
*Dauy.*   You'l watch then for ten thousand, what's thy name, honesty?
*Curt.*   Seriant *Curtilax* I sir.
*Dauy.*   An excellent name for a Seriant, *Curtilax.*
Seriants indeed are weapons of the law,                              120
   When prodigall ruffians farre in debt are growne,
   Should not you cut them, Cittizens were orethrowne;
   Thou dwel'st hereby in Holborne *Curtilax.*
*Curt.*   That's my circuit sir, I coniure most in that circle.
*Dauy.*   And what yong toward welp is this?
*Hang.*   Of the same litter, his yeoman sir, my name's *Hanger.*
*Dauy.*   Yeoman *Hanger.*
One paire of sheeres sure cut out both your coates,
   You haue two names most dangerous to mens throates,
   You two are villanous loades on Gentlemens backs,                 130
   Deere ware, this *Hanger* and this *Curtilax.*
*Curt.*   We are as other men are sir, I cannot see but hee who makes
a show of honesty and religion, if his clawes can fasten to his liking,
he drawes bloud; all that liue in the world, are but great fish and
little fish, and feede vpon one another, some eate vp whole men,
a Seriant cares but for the shoulder of a man, they call vs knaues
and curres, but many times hee that sets vs on, worries more lambes
one yeare, then we do in seuen.
*Dauy.*   Spoke like a noble *Cerberus,* is the action entred?
*Hang.*   His name is entred in the booke of vnbeleeuers.            140
*Dauy.*   What booke's that?

108 spirits] *i.e. sprites*

*Curt.*  The booke where all prisoners names stand, and not one amongst forty, when he comes in, beleeues to come out in hast.

*Dauy.*  Be as dogged to him as your office allowes you to be.

*Both.*  Oh sir.

*Dauy.*  You know the vnthrift *Iacke Dapper.*

*Curt.*  I, I, sir, that Gull? aswell as I know my yeoman.

*Dauy.*  And you know his father too, Sir *Dauy Dapper?*

*Curt.*  As damn'd a vsurer as euer was among Iewes; if hee were sure his fathers skinne would yeeld him any money, hee would 150 when he dyes flea it off, and sell it to couer drummes for children at Bartholmew faire.

*Dauy.*  What toades are these to spit poyson on a man to his face? doe you see (my honest rascals?) yonder gray-hound is the dog he hunts with, out of that Tauerne *Iacke Dapper* will sally: sa, sa; giue the counter, on, set vpon him.

*Both.*  Wee'l charge him vppo'th backe sir.

*Dauy.*  Take no baile, put mace enough into his caudle, double your files, trauerse your ground.

*Both.*  Braue sir.                                                160

*Dauy.*  Cry arme, arme, arme.

*Both.*  Thus sir.

*Dauy.*  There boy, there boy, away: looke to your prey my trew English wolues, and so I vanish.              *Exit Sir* Dauy.

*Curt.*  Some warden of the Seriants begat this old fellow vpon my life, stand close.

*Hang.*  Shall the ambuscado lie in one place?

*Curt.*  No, nooke thou yonder.

*Enter* Mol *and* Trapdore.

*Moll.*  *Ralph.*

*Trap.*  What sayes my braue Captaine male and female?       170

*Moll.*  This Holborne is such a wrangling streete.

*Trap.*  That's because Lawiers walkes to and fro in't.

*Moll.*  Heere's such iustling, as if euery one wee met were drunke and reel'd.

*Trap.*  Stand Mistresse do you not smell carrion?

*Moll.*  Carryon? no, yet I spy rauens.

*Trap.*  Some poore winde-shaken gallant will anon fall into sore
labour, and these men-midwiues must bring him to bed i'the
counter, there all those that are great with child with debts, lie in.

*Moll.*  Stand vp.                                                    180

*Trap.*  Like your new maypoll.

*Hang.*  Whist, whew.

*Curt.*  Hump, no.

*Moll.*  Peeping? it shall go hard huntsmen, but I'le spoyle your
game, they looke for all the world like two infected malt-men
comming muffled vp in their cloakes in a frosty morning to
*London.*

*Trap.*  A course, Captaine; a beare comes to the stake.

*Enter* Iacke Dapper *and* Gul.

*Moll.*  It should bee so, for the dogges struggle to bee let loose.

*Hang.*  Whew.                                                        190

*Curt.*  Hemp.

*Moll.*  Harke *Trapdore*, follow your leader.

*Iac. Dap.  Gul.*

*Gull.*  Maister.

*Iac. Dap.*  Did'st euer see such an asse as I am boy?

*Gull.*  No by my troth sir, to loose all your mony, yet haue false
dice of your owne, why 'tis as I saw a great fellow vsed t'other day,
he had a faire sword and buckler, and yet a butcher dry beate him
with a cudgell.

*Both.*  Honest Sir fly, flie Maister *Dapper* you'l be arrested else.   200

*Iac. Dap.*  Run *Gul* and draw.

*Gull.*  Run Maister, *Gull* followes you.    *Exit* Dapper *and* Gull.

*Curt.*  I know you well enough, you'r but a whore to hang vpon
any man.

*Moll.*  Whores then are like Seriants, so now hang you, draw
rogue, but strike not: for a broken pate they'l keepe their beds, and
recouer twenty markes damages.

*Curt.*  You shall pay for this rescue, runne downe shoe-lane and
meete him.

*Trap.*  Shu, is this a rescue Gentlemen or no?                      210

*200 Sir] Serieant Q

*Moll.*   Rescue? a pox on 'em, *Trapdore* let's away,
I'me glad I haue done perfect one good worke to day,
If any Gentleman be in Scriueners bands,
Send but for *Mol*, she'll baile him by these hands.

*Exeunt.*


## [ACT IV, SCENE i]

*Enter Sir* Alexander Wengraue *solus.*

*Alex.*   Vnhappy in the follies of a sonne,
Led against iudgement, sence, obedience,
And all the powers of noblenesse and wit;          *Enter* Trapdore.
Oh wretched father, now *Trapdore* will she come?
*Trap.*   In mans apparell sir, I am in her heart now,
And share in all her secrets.
*Alex.*                         Peace, peace, peace.
Here take my Germane watch, hang't vp in sight,
That I may see her hang in English for't.
*Trap.*   I warrant you for that now, next Sessions rids her sir, this
watch will bring her in better then a hundred constables.          10
*Alex.*   Good *Trapdore* saist thou so, thou cheer'st my heart
After a storme of sorrow, — my gold chaine too,
Here take a hundred markes in yellow linkes.
*Trap.*   That will do well to bring the watch to light sir.
And worth a thousand of your Headborowes lanthornes.
*Alex.*   Place that a'the Court cubbart, let it lie
Full in the veiw of her theefe-whoorish eie.
*Trap.*   Shee cannot misse it sir, I see't so plaine,
That I could steal't my selfe.
*Alex.*                         Perhaps thou shalt too,
That or something as weighty; what shee leaues,          20
Thou shalt come closely in, and filch away,
And all the weight vpon her backe I'le lay.
*Trap.*   You cannot assure that sir.
*Alex.*                         No, what lets it?

*Trap.*   Being a stout girle, perhaps shee'l desire pressing,
   Then all the weight must ly vpon her belly.
*Alex.*   Belly or backe I care not so I'ue one.
*Trap.*   You'r of my minde for that sir.
*Alex.*   Hang vp my ruffe band with the diamond at it,
   It may be shee'l like that best.
*Trap.*   It's well for her, that shee must haue her choice, hee thinkes   30
   nothing too good for her, if you hold on this minde a little longer,
   it shall bee the first worke I doe to turne theefe my selfe; would do
   a man good to be hang'd when he is so wel prouided for.
*Alex.*   So, well sayd; all hangs well, would shee hung so too,
   The sight would please me more, then all their glisterings:
   Oh that my mysteries to such streights should runne,
   That I must rob my selfe to blesse my sonne.            *Exeunt.*

         *Enter* Sebastian, *with* Mary Fitz-Allard *like a page, and*
                  Mol [*in mans clothes*].

*Seb.*   Thou hast done me a kind office, without touch
   Either of sinne or shame, our loues are honest.
*Moll.*   I'de scorne to make such shift to bring you together else.   40
*Seb.*   Now haue I time and opportunity
   Without all feare to bid thee welcome loue.                *Kisse.*
*Mary.*   Neuer with more desire and harder venture.
*Moll.*   How strange this shewes one man to kisse another.
*Seb.*   I'de kisse such men to chuse *Moll,*
   Me thinkes a womans lip tasts well in a dublet.
*Moll.*   Many an old madam has the better fortune then,
   Whose breathes grew stale before the fashion came,
   If that will help 'em, as you thinke 'twill do,
   They'l learne in time to plucke on the hose too.            50
*Seb.*   The older they waxe *Moll,* troth I speake seriously,
   As some haue a conceit their drinke tasts better
   In an outlandish cup then in our owne,
   So me thinkes euery kisse she giues me now
   In this strange forme, is worth a paire or two,
   Here we are safe, and furthest from the eie

                  55 or] of Q

5                         65                         BCD III

Of all suspicion, this is my fathers chamber,
Vpon which floore he neuer steps till night.
Here he mistrusts me not, nor I his comming,
At mine owne chamber he still pries vnto me,                    60
My freedome is not there at mine owne finding,
Still checkt and curb'd, here he shall misse his purpose.

*Moll.* And what's your businesse, now you haue your mind sir;
At your great suite I promisd you to come,
I pittied her for names sake, that a *Moll*
Should be so crost in loue, when there's so many,
That owes nine layes a peece, and not so little:
My taylor fitted her, how like you his worke?

*Seb.* So well, no Art can mend it, for this purpose,
But to thy wit and helpe we're chiefe in debt,                    70
And must liue still beholding.

*Moll.*                              Any honest pitty,
I'me willing to bestow vpon poore Ring-doues.

*Seb.* I'le offer no worse play.

*Moll.*                              Nay and you should sir,
I should draw first and prooue the quicker man.

*Seb.* Hold, there shall neede no weapon at this meeting,
But cause thou shalt not loose thy fury idle,
Heere take this viall, runne vpon the guts,
And end thy quarrell singing.

*Moll.*                              Like a swan aboue bridge,
For looke you heer's the bridge, and heere am I.

*Seb.* Hold on sweete *Mol.*

*Mary.*                              I'ue heard her much commended sir,    80
For one that was nere taught.

*Moll.* I'me much beholding to 'em, well since you'l needes put vs
together sir, I'le play my part as well as I can: it shall nere be said
I came into a Gentlemans chamber, and let his instrument hang by
the walls.

*Seb.* Why well said *Mol* i'faith, it had bene a shame for that
Gentleman then, that would haue let it hung still, and nere offred
thee it.

63 businesse, now ̧] Dyce; ~ ̧ ~ , Q

*Moll.*    There it should haue bene stil then for *Mol*, for though the
world iudge impudently of mee, I nere came into that chamber yet,    90
where I tooke downe the instrument my selfe.

*Seb.*    Pish let 'em prate abroad, th'art heere where thou art knowne
and lou'd, there be a thousand close dames that wil cal the viall an
vnmannerly instrument for a woman, and therefore talke broadly
of thee, when you shall haue them sit wider to a worse quality.

*Moll.*    Push, I euer fall a sleepe and thinke not of 'em sir, and thus
I dreame.

*Seb.*    Prithee let's heare thy dreame *Mol.*

*Moll.*        *I dreame there is a Mistresse,*
                *And she layes out the money,*        The song.    100
            *Shee goes vnto her Sisters,*
                *Shee neuer comes at any.*

Enter Sir *Alexander* behind them.

        *Shee sayes shee went to'th Bursse for patternes,*
            *You shall finde her at* Saint Katherns,
        *And comes home with neuer a penny.*

*Seb.*    That's a free Mistresse 'faith.

*Alex.*    I, I, I, like her that sings it, one of thine own choosing.

*Moll.*    But shall I dreame againe?

        *Here comes a wench will braue ye,*
            *Her courage was so great,*                        110
        *Shee lay with one o'the Nauy,*
            *Her husband lying i'the Fleet.*
        *Yet oft with him she cauel'd,*
            *I wonder what shee ailes,*
        *Her husbands ship lay grauel'd,*
            *When her's could hoyse vp sailes,*
        *Yet shee beganne like all my foes,*
            *To call whoore first: for so do those,*
        *A pox of all false tayles.*

*Seb.*    Marry amen say I.                                    120

*Alex.*    So say I too.

*Moll.*    Hang vp the viall now sir: all this while I was in a dreame;

one shall lie rudely then, but being awake, I keepe my legges
together; a watch, what's a clocke here.

*Alex.*   Now, now, shee's trapt.

*Moll.*   Betweene one and two; nay then I care not: a watch and a
musitian are cossen Germanes in one thing, they must both keepe
time well, or there's no goodnesse in 'em, the one else deserues to
be dasht against a wall, and tother to haue his braines knockt out
with a fiddle case, what? a loose chaine and a dangling Diamond. 130
Here were a braue booty for an euening-theefe now, there's many
a younger brother would be glad to looke twice in at a window
for't, and wriggle in and out, like an eele in a sandbag. Oh if mens
secret youthfull faults should iudge 'em, 'twould be the general'st
execution, that ere was seene in *England*; there would bee but few
left to sing the ballets: there would be so much worke, most of our
brokers would be chosen for hangmen, a good day for them: they
might renew their wardrops of free cost then.

*Seb.*   This is the roaring wench must do vs good.

*Mary.*   No poyson sir but serues vs for some vse,                    140
Which is confirm'd in her.

*Seb.*   Peace, peace,
Foot I did here him sure, where ere he be.

*Moll.*   Who did you heare?

*Seb.*   My father,
'Twas like a sight of his, I must be wary.

*Alex.*   No wilt not be, am I alone so wretched
That nothing takes? I'le put him to his plundge for't.

*Seb.*   Life, heere he comes, — sir I beseech you take it,
Your way of teaching does so much content me,                    150
I'le make it foure pound, here's forty shillings sir.
I thinke I name it right: helpe me good *Mol.*
Forty in hand.

*Moll.*          Sir you shall pardon me,
I haue more of the meanest scholler I can teach,
This paies me more, then you haue offred yet.

*Seb.*   At the next quarter
When I receiue the meanes my father 'lowes me,

136 ballets: ... worke,] ~ , ... ~ : Q          146 sight] *i.e. sigh*

68

You shall haue tother forty.

*Alex.*                          This were well now,
Wer't to a man, whose sorrowes had blind eies,
But mine behold his follies and vntruthes,                    160
With two cleere glasses — how now?

*Seb.*  Sir.

*Alex.*  What's he there?

*Seb.*  You'r come in good time sir, I'ue a suite to you, I'de craue
your present kindnesse.

*Alex.*  What is he there?

*Seb.*  A Gentleman, a musitian sir, one of excellent fingring.

*Alex.*  I, I thinke so, I wonder how they scapt her.    [*Aside.*]

*Seb.*  Has the most delicate stroake sir.

*Alex.*  A stroake indeed, I feele it at my heart.    [*Aside.*] 170

*Seb.*  Puts downe all your famous musitians.

*Alex.*  I, a whoore may put downe a hundred of 'em.    [*Aside.*]

*Seb.*  Forty shillings is the agrement sir betweene vs,
Now sir, my present meanes, mounts but to halfe on't.

*Alex.*  And he stands vpon the whole.

*Seb.*  I indeed does he sir.

*Alex.*  And will doe still, hee'l nere be in other taile.

*Seb.*  Therefore I'de stop his mouth sir, and I could.

*Alex.*  Hum true, there is no other way indeed,
His folly hardens, shame must needs succeed.                  180
Now sir I vnderstand you professe musique.

*Moll.*  I am a poore seruant to that liberall science sir.

*Alex.*  Where is it you teach?

*Moll.*  Right against Cliffords Inne.

*Alex.*  Hum that's a fit place for it: you haue many schollers.

*Moll.*  And some of worth, whom I may call my maisters.

*Alex.*  I true, a company of whooremaisters; you teach to sing too?

*Moll.*  Marry do I sir.

*Alex.*  I thinke you'l finde an apt scholler of my sonne, especially
for pricke-song.                                             190

*Moll.*  I haue much hope of him.

*Alex.*  I am sory for't, I haue the lesse for that: you can play any
lesson.

*Moll.*   At first sight sir.

*Alex.*   There's a thing called the witch, can you play that?

*Moll.*   I would be sory any one should mend me in't.

*Alex.*   I, I beleeue thee, thou hast so bewitcht my sonne,

No care will mend the worke that thou hast done,

I haue bethought my selfe, since my art failes,

I'le make her pollicy the Art to trap her.                          200

Here are foure Angels markt with holes in them,

Fit for his crackt companions, gold he will giue her,

These will I make induction to her ruine,

And rid shame from my house, griefe from my heart.

Here sonne, in what you take content and pleasure,

Want shall not curbe you, pay the Gentleman

His latter halfe in gold.

*Seb.*                          I thanke you sir.

*Alex.*   Oh may the operation an't, end three,

In her, life: shame, in him; and griefe, in mee.

*Exit* Alexander.

*Seb.*   Faith thou shalt haue 'em 'tis my fathers guift,        210

Neuer was man beguild with better shift.

*Moll.*   Hee that can take mee for a male musitian, I cannot choose

but make him my instrument, and play vpon him.

*Exeunt omnes.*


# [ACT IV, Scene ii]

*Enter Mistresse* Gallipot, *and Mistresse* Openworke.

*Mist. Gal.*   Is then that bird of yours (Maister *Goshawke*) so wild?

*Mist. Open.*   A Goshawke, a Puttocke; all for prey: he angles for
fish, but he loues flesh better.

*Mist. Gal.*   Is't possible his smoth face should haue wrinckles in't,
and we not see them?

*Mist. Open.*   Possible? why haue not many handsome legges in
silke stockins villanous splay feete for all their great roses?

208 three] Q(c); there Q(u)

*Mist. Gal.*    Troth sirra thou saist true.

*Mist. Open.*    Didst neuer see an archer (as tho'ast walkt by Bun-
hill) looke a squint when he drew his bow?                            10

*Mist. Gal.*    Yes, when his arrowes haue flin'e toward Islington, his
eyes haue shot cleane contrary towards Pimlico.

*Mist. Open.*    For all the world so does Maister *Goshawke* double
with me.

*Mist. Gal.*    Oh fie vpon him, if he double once he's not for me.

*Mist. Open.*    Because *Goshawke* goes in a shag-ruffe band, with a
face sticking vp in't, which showes like an agget set in a crampe
ring, he thinkes I'me in loue with him.

*Mist. Gal.*    'Las I thinke he takes his marke amisse in thee.

*Mist. Open.*    He has by often beating into me made mee beleeue  20
that my husband kept a whore.

*Mist. Gal.*    Very good.

*Mist. Open.*    Swore to me that my husband this very morning
went in a boate with a tilt ouer it, to the three pidgions at *Brainford*,
and his puncke with him vnder his tilt.

*Mist. Gal.*    That were wholesome.

*Mist. Open.*    I beleeu'd it, fell a swearing at him, curssing of harlots,
made me ready to hoyse vp saile, and be there as soone as hee.

*Mist. Gal.*    So, so.

*Mist. Open.*    And for that voyage *Goshawke* comes hither incon-  30
tinently, but sirra this water-spaniell diues after no ducke but me,
his hope is hauing mee at *Braineford* to make mee cry quack.

*Mist. Gal.*    Art sure of it?

*Mist. Open.*    Sure of it? my poore innocent *Openworke* came in as
I was poking my ruffe, presently hit I him i'the teeth with the three
pidgions: he forswore all, I vp and opened all, and now stands he
(in a shop hard by) like a musket on a rest, to hit *Goshawke* i'the
eie, when he comes to fetch me to the boate.

*Mist. Gal.*    Such another lame Gelding offered to carry mee
through thicke and thinne, (*Laxton* sirra) but I am ridd of him now.  40

*Mist. Open.*    Happy is the woman can bee ridde of 'em all; 'las
what are your whisking gallants to our husbands, weigh 'em
rightly man for man.

*Mist. Gall.*    Troth meere shallow things.

71

*Mist. Open.* Idle simple things, running heads, and yet let 'em run ouer vs neuer so fast, we shop-keepers (when all's done) are sure to haue 'em in our pursnets at length, and when they are in, Lord what simple animalls they are.

Then they hang the head.

*Mist. Gal.* Then they droupe. 50

*Mist. Open.* Then they write letters.

*Mist. Gal.* Then they cogge.

*Mist. Open.* Then deale they vnder hand with vs, and wee must ingle with our husbands a bed, and wee must sweare they are our cosens, and able to do vs a pleasure at Court.

*Mist. Gal.* And yet when wee haue done our best, al's but put into a riuen dish, wee are but frumpt at and libell'd vpon.

*Mist. Open.* Oh if it were the good Lords wil, there were a law made, no Cittizen should trust any of 'em all.

*Enter* Goshawke.

*Mist. Gal.* Hush sirra, *Goshawke* flutters. 60

*Gosh.* How now, are you ready?

*Mist. Open.* Nay are you ready? a little thing you see makes vs ready.

*Gosh.* Vs? why, must shee make one i'the voiage?

*Mist. Open.* Oh by any meanes, doe I know how my husband will handle mee?

*Gosh.* 'Foot, how shall I find water, to keepe these two mils going? Well since you'l needs bee clapt vnder hatches, if I sayle not with you both till all split, hang mee vp at the maine yard, and duck mee; it's but lickering them both soundly, and then you shall see their 70 corke heeles flie vp high, like two swannes when their tayles are aboue water, and their long neckes vnder water, diuing to catch gudgions: come, come, oares stand ready, the tyde's with vs, on with those false faces, blow winds and thou shalt take thy husband, casting out his net to catch fresh *Salmon* at *Brainford.*

*49 Then] Dodsley; *Mist. Open.* Then Q
49 the] Q *original setting;* om. Q *reset*
53 deale they] Q *original setting;* they deale Q *reset*

*Mist. Gal.*  I beleeue you'l eate of a coddes head of your owne
dressing, before you reach halfe way thither.

*Gosh.*  So, so, follow close, pin as you go.

*Enter* Laxton *muffled.* [*They speak aloofe.*]

*Lax.*  Do you heare?

*Mist. Gal.*  Yes, I thanke my eares.                                    80

*Lax.*  I must haue a bout with your Potticariship.

*Mist. Gal.*  At what weapon?

*Lax.*  I must speake with you.

*Mist. Gal.*  No.

*Lax.*  No? you shall.

*Mist. Gal.*  Shall? away soust Sturgion, halfe fish, halfe flesh.

*Lax.*  'Faith gib, are you spitting, I'le cut your tayle pus-cat for
this.

*Mist. Gal.*  'Las poore *Laxton*, I thinke thy tayle's cut already:
you'r worst.                                                              90

*Lax.*  If I do not, —                                    *Exit* Laxton.

*Enter Maister* Openworke.

*Gosh.*  Come, ha'you done?
Sfoote *Rosamond*, your husband.

*Maist. Open.*  How now? sweete Maister *Goshawke*, none more
welcome,
I haue wanted your embracements: when friends meete,
The musique of the spheares sounds not more sweete,
Then does their conference: who is this? *Rosamond:*
Wife: how now sister?

*Gosh.*                   Silence if you loue mee.

*Maist. Open.*  Why maskt?

*Mist. Open.*                   Does a maske grieue you sir?

*Maist. Open.*                   It does.

*Mist. Open.*  Then y'are best get you a mumming.

*Gosh.*                   S'foote you'l spoyle all. 100

*Mist. Gal.*  May not wee couer our bare faces with maskes
As well as you couer your bald heads with hats?

*Maist. Open.* No maskes, why, th'are theeues to beauty, that rob eies

Of admiration in which true loue lies,
Why are maskes worne? why good? or why desired?
Vnlesse by their gay couers wits are fiered
To read the vildest lookes; many bad faces,
(Because rich gemmes are treasured vp in cases)
Passe by their priuiledge currant, but as caues
Dambe misers Gold, so maskes are beauties graues,          110
Men nere meete women with such muffled eies,
But they curse her, that first did maskes deuise,
And sweare it was some beldame. Come off with't.

*Mist. Open.*                                    I will not.

*Maist. Open.* Good faces maskt are Iewels kept by spirits.
Hide none but bad ones, for they poyson mens sights,
Shew them as shop-keepers do their broidred stuffe,
(By owle light) fine wares cannot be open enough,
Prithee (sweete *Rose*) come strike this sayle.

*Mist. Open.*                                    Saile?

*Maist. Open.* Ha? yes wife strike saile, for stormes are in thine eyes.

*Mist. Open.* Th'are here sir in my browes if any rise.          120

*Maist. Open.* Ha browes? (what sayes she friend) pray tel me why
Your two flagges were aduaunst; the Comedy,
Come what's the Comedy?

*Mist. Gal.*                    Westward hoe.

*Maist. Open.*                                    How?

*Mist. Open.* 'Tis Westward hoe shee saies.

*Gosh.*                                    Are you both madde?

*Mist. Open.* Is't Market day at *Braineford*, and your ware
Not sent vp yet?

*Maist. Open.* What market day? what ware?

*Mist. Open.* A py with three pidgions in't, 'tis drawne and staies
Your cutting vp.

*Gosh.*              As you regard my credit —

*Maist. Open.* Art madde?

*Mist. Open.*              Yes letcherous goate; Baboone.

116 them] then Q     123 *Mist. Gal.*] Scott; *Mist. Open.* Q

*Maist. Open.*                                          Baboone?
Then tosse mee in a blancket.                                    130
*Mist. Open.* Do I it well?
*Mist. Gal.* Rarely.
*Gosh.* Belike sir shee's not well; best leaue her.
*Maist. Open.*                                          No,
I'le stand the storme now how fierce so ere it blow.
*Mist. Open.* Did I for this loose all my friends? refuse
Rich hopes, and golden fortunes, to be made
A stale to a common whore?
*Maist. Open.*                   This does amaze mee.
*Mist. Open.* Oh God, oh God, feede at reuersion now?
A Strumpets leauing?
*Maist. Open.* Rosamond —                                       140
*Gosh.* I sweate, wo'ld I lay in cold harbour.
*Mist. Open.* Thou hast struck ten thousand daggers through my
                heart.
*Maist. Open.* Not I by heauen sweete wife.
*Mist. Open.* Go diuel go; that which thou swear'st by, damnes
                thee.
*Gosh.* S'heart will you vndo mee?
*Mist. Open.* Why stay you heere? the starre, by which you saile,
Shines yonder aboue *Chelsy*; you loose your shore:
If this moone light you, seeke out your light whore.
*Maist. Open.* Ha?
*Mist. Gal.*           Push; your Westerne pug.
*Gosh.*                                    Zounds now hell roares.
*Mist. Open.* With whom you tilted in a paire of oares,           150
This very morning.
*Maist. Open.*         Oares?
*Mist. Open.*              At *Brainford* sir.
*Maist. Open.* Racke not my patience: Maister *Goshawke*,
Some slaue has buzzed this into her, has he not?
I run a tilt in *Brainford* with a woman?
'Tis a lie:
What old baud tels thee this? S'death 'tis a lie.

147-148 shore: ... you,] Dyce; ~ ᴀ ... ~ : Q

*Mist. Open.* 'Tis one to thy face shall iustify
All that I speake.

*Maist. Open.*      Vd'soule do but name that rascall.

*Mist. Open.* No sir I will not.

*Gosh.*                    Keepe thee there girle: — then!

*Maist. Open.* Sister know you this varlet?

*Mist. Gal.*                    Yes.

*Maist. Open.*                    Sweare true,      160
Is there a rogue so low damn'd? a second *Iudas*?
A common hangman? cutting a mans throate?
Does it to his face? bite mee behind my backe?
A cur dog? sweare if you know this hell-hound.

*Mist. Gal.* In truth I do.

*Maist. Open.*                    His name?

*Mist. Gal.*                    Not for the world;
To haue you to stab him.

*Gosh.*                    Oh braue girles: worth Gold.

*Maist. Open.* A word honest maister *Goshawke*.

                              *Draw out his sword.*

*Gosh.*                    What do you meane sir?

*Maist. Open.* Keepe off, and if the diuell can giue a name
To this new fury, holla it through my eare,
Or wrap it vp in some hid character:                    170
I'le ride to *Oxford*, and watch out mine eies,
But I'le heare the brazen head speak: or else
Shew me but one haire of his head or beard,
That I may sample it; if the fiend I meet
(In myne owne house) I'le kill him: — the streete,
Or at the Church dore: — there — (cause he seekes to vnty
The knot God fastens) he deserues most to dy.

*Mist. Open.* My husband titles him.

*Maist. Open.*                    Maister *Goshawke*, pray sir
Sweare to me, that you know him or know him not,
Who makes me at *Brainford* to take vp a peticote                    180
Besides my wiues.

160 *Maist. Open.* Sister] Dyce; *Mist. Open.* Sister Q
181 besides] Q *original setting*; beside Q *reset*

*Gosh.*                   By heauen that man I know not.

*Mist. Open.*   Come, come, you lie.

*Gosh.*                              Will you not haue all out?
By heauen I know no man beneath the moone
Should do you wrong, but if I had his name,
I'de print it in text letters.

*Mist. Open.*               Print thine owne then,
Did'st not thou sweare to me he kept his whoore?

*Mist. Gal.*   And that in sinfull *Brainford* they would commit
That which our lips did water at sir, — ha?

*Mist. Open.* Thou spider, that hast wouen thy cunning web
In mine owne house t'insnare me: hast not thou        190
Suck't nourishment euen vnderneath this roofe,
And turned it all to poyson? spitting it,
On thy friends face (my husband?) he as t'were sleeping:
Onely to leaue him vgly to mine eies,
That they might glance on thee.

*Mist. Gal.*                   Speake, are these lies?

*Gosh.*   Mine owne shame me confounds.

*Maist. Open.*                   No more, hee's stung;
Who'd thinke that in one body there could dwell
Deformitie and beauty, (heauen and hell).
Goodnesse I see is but outside, wee all set,
In rings of Gold, stones that be counterfet:        200
I thought you none.

*Gosh.*            Pardon mee.

*Maist. Open.*                   Truth I doe.
This blemish growes in nature not in you,
For mans creation sticke euen moles in scorne
On fairest cheeks, wife nothing is perfect borne.

*Mist. Open.*   I thought you had bene borne perfect.

*Maist. Open.*   What's this whole world but a gilt rotten pill?
For at the heart lies the old chore still.
I'le tell you Maister *Goshawke*, in your eie
I haue seene wanton fire, and then to try,

196 *Maist. Open.*] Dyce; *Mist. Open.* Q
208 in] I in Q

The soundnesse of my iudgement, I told you,                    210
I kept a whoore, made you beleeue t'was true,
Onely to feele how your pulse beat, but find,
The world can hardly yeeld a perfect friend.
Come, come, a tricke of youth, and 'tis forgiuen,
This rub put by, our loue shall runne more euen.
*Mist. Open.*   You'l deale vpon mens wiues no more?
*Gosh.*                                      No: — you teach me
A tricke for that.
*Mist. Open.*      Troth do not, they'l o're-reach thee.
*Maist. Open.*   Make my house yours sir still.
*Gosh.*                                            No.
*Maist. Open.*                           I say you shall:
Seeing (thus besieg'd) it holds out, 'twill neuer fall.

   *Enter Maister* Gallipot, *and* Greenewit *like a Somner,*
    Laxton *muffled a loofe off.*

*Omn.*   How now?                                          220
*Maist. Gal.*   With mee sir?
*Green.*   You sir? I haue gone snafling vp and downe by your dore
this houre to watch for you.
*Mist. Gal.*   What's the matter husband?
*Green.*   — I haue caught a cold in my head sir, by sitting vp late
in the rose tauerne, but I hope you vnderstand my speech.
*Maist. Gal.*   So sir.
*Green.*   I cite you by the name of *Hippocrates Gallipot,* and you by
the name of *Prudence Gallipot,* to appeare vpon *Crastino,* do you
see, *Crastino sancti Dunstani* (this *Easter* Tearme) in Bow Church. 230
*Maist. Gal.*   Where sir? what saies he?
*Green.*   Bow: Bow Church, to answere to a libel of precontract on
the part and behalfe of the said *Prudence* and another; y'are best sir
take a coppy of the citation, 'tis but tweluepence.
*Omn.*   A Citation?
*Maist. Gal.*   You pocky-nosed rascall, what slaue fees you to this?
*Lax.*   Slaue? I ha nothing to do with you, doe you heare sir?
*Gosh.*   *Laxton* ist not? — what fagary is this?

    *222 snafling] stet Q

78

*Maist. Gal.*  Trust me I thought sir this storme long ago
Had bene full laid, when (if you be remembred)       240
I paid you the last fifteene pound, besides
The thirty you had first, — for then you swore —
*Lax.*  Tush, tush sir, oathes,
Truth yet I'me loth to vexe you, — tell you what;
Make vp the mony I had an hundred pound,
And take your belly full of her.
*Maist. Gal.*                    An hundred pound?
*Mist. Gal.*  What a hundred pound? he gets none: what a hundred
    pound?
*Maist. Gal.*  Sweet *Pru* be calme, the Gentleman offers thus,
If I will make the monyes that are past
A hundred pound, he will discharge all courts,       250
And giue his bond neuer to vexe vs more.
*Mist. Gal.*  A hundred pound? 'Las; take sir but threescore,
Do you seeke my vndoing?
*Lax.*                    I'le not bate one sixpence, —
I'le mall you pusse for spitting.
*Mist. Gal.*                    Do thy worst,
Will fourescore stop thy mouth?
*Lax.*                    No.
*Mist. Gal.*                    Y'are a slaue,
Thou Cheate, I'le now teare mony from thy throat,
Husband lay hold on yonder tauny-coate.
*Green.*  Nay Gentlemen, seeing your woemen are so hote, I must
loose my haire in their company I see.
*Mist. Open.*  His haire sheds off, and yet he speaks not so much in   260
the nose as he did before.
*Gosh.*  He has had the better Chirurgion, Maister *Greenewit*, is your
wit so raw as to play no better a part then a Somners?
*Maist. Gal.*  I pray who playes a knacke to know an honest man
in this company?
*Mist. Gal.*  Deere husband, pardon me, I did dissemble,
Told thee I was his precontracted wife,
When letters came from him for thirty pound,
I had no shift but that.

*Maist. Gal.*          A very cleane shift:
But able to make mee lowsy, On.

*Mist. Gal.*          Husband, I pluck'd          270
(When he had tempted mee to thinke well of him)
Gilt fethers from thy wings, to make him flie
More lofty.

*Maist. Gal.*   A'the top of you wife: on.

*Mist. Gal.*   He hauing wasted them, comes now for more,
Vsing me as a ruffian doth his whore,
Whose sinne keepes him in breath: by heauen I vow,
Thy bed he neuer wrong'd, more then he does now.

*Maist. Gal.*   My bed? ha, ha, like enough, a shop-boord will serue
To haue a cuckolds coate cut out vpon:
Of that wee'l talke hereafter: y'are a villaine.          280

*Lax.*   Heare mee but speake sir, you shall finde mee none.

*Omn.*   Pray sir, be patient and heare him.

*Maist. Gal.*   I am muzzled for biting sir, vse me how you will.

*Lax.*   The first howre that your wife was in my eye,
My selfe with other Gentlemen sitting by,
(In your shop) tasting smoake, and speech being vsed,
That men who haue fairest wiues are most abused,
And hardly scapt the horne, your wife maintain'd
That onely such spots in Citty dames were stain'd,
Iustly, but by mens slanders: for her owne part,          290
Shee vow'd that you had so much of her heart;
No man by all his wit, by any wile,
Neuer so fine spunne, should your selfe beguile,
Of what in her was yours.

*Maist. Gal.*          Yet *Pru* 'tis well:
Play out your game at Irish sir: Who winnes?

*Mist. Open.*   The triall is when shee comes to bearing.

*Lax.*   I scorn'd one woman, thus, should braue all men,
And (which more vext me) a shee-citizen.
Therefore I laid siege to her, out she held,
Gaue many a braue repulse, and me compel'd          300
With shame to sound retrait to my hot lust,

*272 Gilt] Dyce (Gelt); Get Q

Then seeing all base desires rak'd vp in dust,
And that to tempt her modest eares, I swore
Nere to presumne againe: she said, her eie
Would euer giue me welcome honestly,
And (since I was a Gentleman) if it runne low,
Shee would my state relieue, not to o'rethrow
Your owne and hers: did so; then seeing I wrought
Vpon her meekenesse, mee she set at nought,
And yet to try if I could turne that tide,                              310
You see what streame I stroue with, but sir I sweare
By heauen, and by those hopes men lay vp there,
I neither haue, nor had a base intent
To wrong your bed, what's done, is meriment:
Your Gold I pay backe with this interest,
When I had most power to do't I wrong'd you least.
*Maist. Gal.*   If this no gullery be sir —
*Omn.*                              No, no, on my life.
*Maist. Gal.*   Then sir I am beholden (not to you wife)
But Maister *Laxton* to your want of doing ill,
Which it seemes you haue not.  Gentlemen,                              320
Tarry and dine here all.
*Maist. Open.*          Brother, we haue a iest,
As good as yours to furnish out a feast.
*Maist. Gal.*   Wee'l crowne our table with it: wife brag no more,
Of holding out: who most brags is most whore.

                                        *Exeunt omnes.*


## [ACT V, Scene i]

*Enter* Iacke Dapper, Moll, *Sir* Beautious Ganymed,
           *and Sir* Thomas Long.

*Iac. Dap.*   But prethee Maister Captaine *Iacke* be plaine and
perspicuous with mee; was it your *Megge* of Westminsters courage,
that rescued mee from the Poultry puttockes indeed.

320 not.] Dodsley; ~ ∧ Q

*Moll.*  The valour of my wit I ensure you sir fetcht you off brauely, when you werre i'the forlorne hope among those desperates. Sir *Bewtious Ganymed* here, and sir *Thomas Long* heard that cuckoe (my man *Trapdore*) sing the note of your ransome from captiuty.

*Sir Bewt.*  Vds so *Mol*, where's that *Trapdore?*

*Moll.*  Hang'd I thinke by this time, a Iustice in this towne, (that speakes nothing but make a *Mittimus* a way with him to Newgate) 10 vsed that rogue like a fire-worke to run vpon a line betwixt him and me.

*Omn.*  How, how?

*Moll.*  Marry to lay traines of villany to blow vp my life; I smelt the powder, spy'd what linstocke gaue fire to shoote against the poore Captaine of the Gallifoyst, and away slid I my man, like a shouell-board shilling: hee stroutes vp and downe the suburbes I thinke: and eates vp whores: feedes vpon a bauds garbadg.

*T. Long.*  Sirra *Iacke Dapper*.

*Iac. Dap.*  What sai'st *Tom Long?*            20

*T. Long.*  Thou hadst a sweet fac't boy haile fellow with thee to your little *Gull*: how is he spent?

*Iac. Dap.*  Troth I whistled the poore little buzzard of a my fist, because when hee wayted vpon mee at the ordinaries, the gallants hit me i'the teeth still, and said I lookt like a painted Aldermans tomb, and the boy at my elbow like a deaths head. Sirra *Iacke*, *Mol*.

*Moll.*  What saies my little *Dapper?*

*Sir Bewt.*  Come, come, walke and talke, walke and talke.

*Iac. Dap.*  *Mol* and I'le be i'the midst.

*Moll.*  These Knights shall haue squiers places belike then: well 30 *Dapper* what say you?

*Iac. Dap.*  Sirra Captaine mad *Mary*, the gull my owne father (Sir *Dauy Dapper*) laid these *London* boote-halers the catch poles in ambush to set vpon mee.

*Omn.*  Your father? away *Iacke*.

*Iac. Dap.*  By the tassels of this handkercher 'tis true, and what was his warlicke stratageme thinke you? hee thought because a wicker cage tames a nightingale, a lowsy prison could make an asse of mee.

17 shilling:] Dodsley; ~ , Q
32-33 (Sir *Dauy Dapper*)] (*Dapper*) Sir *Dauy* Q

*Omn.*  A nasty plot.

*Iac. Dap.*  I: as though a Counter, which is a parke, in which all  40
the wilde beasts of the Citty run head by head could tame mee.

*Enter the Lord* Noland.

*Moll.*  Yonder comes my Lord *Noland.*

*Omn.*  Saue you my Lord.

*L. Nol.*  Well met Gentlemen all, good Sir *Bewtious Ganymed*, Sir
*Thomas Long?*, and how does Maister *Dapper?*

*Iac. Dap.*  Thankes my Lord.

*Moll.*  No Tobacco my Lord?

*L. Nol.*  No faith *Iacke.*

*Iac. Dap.*  My Lord *Noland* will you goe to Pimlico with vs? wee
are making a boone voyage to that nappy land of spice-cakes.     50

*L. Nol.*  Heeres such a merry ging, I could find in my heart to saile
to the worlds end with such company, come Gentlemen let's on.

*Iac. Dap.*  Here's most amorous weather my Lord.

*Omn.*  Amorous weather.                              *They walke.*

*Iac. Dap.*  Is not amorous a good word?

*Enter* Trapdore *like a poore Souldier with a patch o're one eie,
and* Teare-cat *with him, all tatters.*

*Trap.*  Shall we set vpon the infantry, these troopes of foot?
Zounds yonder comes *Mol* my whoorish Maister and Mistresse,
wo'ld I had her kidneys betweene my teeth.

*T. Cat.*  I had rather haue a cow heele.

*Trap.*  Zounds I am so patcht vp, she cannot discouer mee:  60
wee'l on.

*T. Cat.*  *Alla corago* then.

*Trap.*  Good your Honours, and Worships, enlarge the eares of
commiseration, and let the sound of a hoarse military organ-pipe,
penetrate your pittiful bowels to extract out of them so many
small drops of siluer, as may giue a hard strawbed lodging to a
couple of maim'd souldiers.

*Iac. Dap.*  Where are you maim'd?

*T. Cat.*  In both our neather limbs.

*Moll.* Come, come, *Dapper*, lets giue 'em something, las poore 70
men, what mony haue you? by my troth I loue a souldier with my
soule.

*Sir Bewt.* Stay, stay, where haue you seru'd?

*T. Long.* In any part of the Low countries?

*Trap.* Not in the Low countries, if it please your manhood, but in
*Hungarie* against the Turke at the siedge of *Belgrad.*

*L. Nol.* Who seru'd there with you sirra?

*Trap.* Many Hungarians, Moldauians, Valachians, and Transil-
uanians, with some Sclauonians, and retyring home sir, the
Venetian Gallies tooke vs prisoners, yet free'd vs, and suffered vs 80
to beg vp and downe the country.

*Iac. Dap.* You haue ambled all ouer *Italy* then.

*Trap.* Oh sir, from *Venice* to *Roma, Vecchio, Bononia, Romania,
Bolonia, Modena, Piacenza,* and *Tuscana,* with all her Cities, as
*Pistoia, Valteria, Mountepulchena, Arrezzo,* with the Siennois, and
diuerse others.

*Moll.* Meere rogues, put spurres to 'em once more.

*Iac. Dap.* Thou look'st like a strange creature, a fat butter-box,
yet speak'st English,
What art thou?                                             90

*T. Cat.* Ick mine Here. Ick bin den ruffling Teare-Cat,
Den braue Soldado, Ick bin dorick all Dutchlant
Gueresen: Der Shellum das meere Ine Beasa
Ine woert gaeb.
Ick slaag vm stroakes on tom Cop:
Dastick Den hundred touzun Diuell halle,
Frollick mine Here.

*Sir Bewt.* Here, here, let's be rid of their iobbering.

*Moll.* Not a crosse Sir *Bewtious,* you base rogues, I haue taken
measure of you, better then a taylor can, and I'le fit you, as you 100
(monster with one eie) haue fitted mee.

*Trap.* Your Worship will not abuse a souldier.

*Moll.* Souldier? thou deseru'st to bee hang'd vp by that tongue
which dishonours so noble a profession, souldier you skeldering
varlet? hold, stand, there should be a trapdore here abouts.

                              *Pull off his patch.*

84

*Trap.*   The balles of these glasiers of mine (mine eyes) shall be shot
vp and downe in any hot peece of seruice for my inuincible
Mistresse.

*Iac. Dap.*   I did not thinke there had bene such knauery in blacke
patches as now I see.                                                     110

*Moll.*   Oh sir he hath bene brought vp in the Ile of dogges, and
can both fawne like a Spaniell, and bite like a Mastiue, as hee finds
occasion.

*L. Nol.*   What are you sirra? a bird of this feather too.

*T. Cat.*   A man beaten from the wars sir.

*T. Long.*   I thinke so, for you neuer stood to fight.

*Iac. Dap.*   What's thy name fellow souldier?

*T. Cat.*   I am cal'd by those that haue seen my valour, *Tear-Cat.*

*Omn.*   *Teare-Cat?*

*Moll.*   A meere whip-Iacke, and that is in the Commonwealth of 120
rogues, a slaue, that can talke of sea-fight, name all your chiefe
Pirats, discouer more countries to you, then either the Dutch,
Spanish, French, or English euer found out, yet indeed all his
seruice is by land, and that is to rob a Faire, or some such venturous
exploit; *Teare-Cat,* foot sirra I haue your name now I remember
me in my booke of horners, hornes for the thumbe, you know how.

*T. Cat.*   No indeed Captaine *Moll* (for I know you by sight) I am
no such nipping Christian, but a maunderer vpon the pad I confesse,
and meeting with honest *Trapdore* here, whom you had cashierd
from bearing armes, out at elbowes vnder your colours, I instructed 130
him in the rudements of roguery, and by my map made him saile
ouer any Country you can name, so that now he can maunder
better then my selfe.

*Iac. Dap.*   So then *Trapdore* thou art turn'd souldier now.

*Trap.*   Alas sir, now there's no warres, 'tis the safest course of life
I could take.

*Moll.*   I hope then you can cant, for by your cudgels, you sirra are
an vpright man.

*Trap.*   As any walkes the hygh way I assure you.

*Moll.*   And *Teare-Cat* what are you? a wilde rogue, an angler, or 140
a ruffler?

*T. Cat.*   Brother to this vpright man, flesh and bloud, ruffling

*Teare-Cat* is my name, and a ruffler is my stile, my title, my
profession.

*Moll.* Sirra where's your Doxy, halt not with mee.

*Omn.* Doxy *Mol*, what's that?

*Moll.* His wench.

*Trap.* My doxy, I haue by the *Salomon* a doxy, that carries a kinchin
mort in her slat at her backe, besides my dell and my dainty wilde
del, with all whom I'le tumble this next darkmans in the strommel, 150
and drinke ben bouse, and eate a fat gruntling cheate, a cackling
cheate, and a quacking cheate.

*Iac. Dap.* Here's old cheating.

*Trap.* My doxy stayes for me in a bousing ken, braue Captaine.

*Moll.* Hee sayes his wench staies for him in an alehouse: you are
no pure rogues.

*T. Cat.* Pure rogues? no, wee scorne to be pure rogues, but if you
come to our lib ken, or our stalling ken, you shall finde neither him
nor mee, a quire cuffin.

*Moll.* So sir, no churle of you.                                    160

*T. Cat.* No, but a ben coue, a braue coue, a gentry cuffin.

*L. Nol.* Call you this canting?

*Iac. Dap.* Zounds, I'le giue a schoolemaister halfe a crowne a
week, and teach mee this pedlers French.

*Trap.* Do but strowle sir, halfe a haruest with vs sir, and you shall
gabble your belly-full.

*Moll.* Come you rogue cant with me.

*T. Long.* Well sayd *Mol*, cant with her sirra, and you shall haue
mony, else not a penny.

*Trap.* I'le haue a bout if she please.                              170

*Moll.* Come on sirra.

*Trap.* Ben mort, shall you and I heaue a booth, mill a ken or nip
a bung, and then wee'l couch a hogshead vnder the Ruffemans, and
there you shall wap with me, and Ile niggle with you.

*Moll.* Out you damn'd impudent rascall.

*Trap.* Cut benar whiddes, and hold your fambles and your
stampes.

148 kinchin] Dodsley; kitchin Q      151 bouse] Bullen; baufe Q
161 coue...coue] Dyce; caue...caue Q

*L. Nol.*   Nay, nay, *Mol*, why art thou angry? what was his gibberish?

*Moll.*   Marry this my Lord sayes hee; Ben mort (good wench) shal 180 you and I heaue a booth, mill a ken, or nip a bung? shall you and I rob a house, or cut a purse?

*Omn.*   Very Good.

*Moll.*   And then wee'l couch a hogshead vnder the Ruffemans: And then wee'l lie vnder a hedge.

*Trap.*   That was my desire Captaine, as 'tis fit a souldier should lie.

*Moll.*   And there you shall wap with mee, and I'le niggle with you, and that's all.

*Sir Bewt.*   Nay, nay *Mol* what's that wap?

*Iac. Dap.*   Nay teach mee what niggling is, I'de faine bee niggling. 190

*Moll.*   Wapping and niggling is all one, the rogue my man can tell you.

*Trap.*   'Tis fadoodling: if it please you.

*Sir Bewt.*   This is excellent, one fit more good *Moll.*

*Moll.*   Come you rogue sing with me.

> A gage of ben Rom-bouse
> In a bousing ken of Rom-vile.
>    *T. Cat.*   Is Benar then a Caster,
> Pecke, pannam, lap or popler,
> Which we mill in deuse a vile.                     200
>    *Both.*   Oh I wud lib all the lightmans.     *The song.*
> Oh I woud lib all the darkemans,
> By the sollamon vnder the Ruffemans.
> By the sollamon in the Hartmans.
>    *T. Cat.*   And scoure the Quire cramp ring,
> And couch till a pallyard docked my dell,
> So my bousy nab might skew rome bouse well.
>    *Both.*   Auast to the pad, let vs bing,
> Auast to the pad, let vs bing.

*Omn.*   Fine knaues i' faith.                     210

*Iac. Dap.*   The grating of ten new cart-wheeles, and the gruntling of fiue hundred hogs comming from *Rumford* market, cannot make

199 pannam] pennam Q    199 lap] lay Q    201, 208 *Both.*] *om.* Q

a worse noyse then this canting language does in my eares; pray
my Lord *Noland*, let's giue these souldiers their pay.

*Sir Bewt.*   Agreed, and let them march.

*L. Nol.*   Heere *Mol.*

*Moll.*   Now I see that you are stal'd to the rogue, and are not
ashamed of your professions, looke you: my Lord *Noland* heere
and these Gentlemen, bestowes vpon you two, two boordes and
a halfe, that's two shillings sixe pence.                          220

*Trap.*   Thankes to your Lordship.

*T. Cat.*   Thankes heroicall Captaine.

*Moll.*   Away.

*Trap.*   Wee shall cut ben whiddes of your Maisters and Mistreship,
wheresoeuer we come.

*Moll.*   You'l maintaine sirra the old Iustices plot to his face.

*Trap.*   Else trine me on the cheats: hang me.

*Moll.*   Be sure you meete mee there.

*Trap.*   Without any more maundring I'lde doo't, follow braue
Tear-Cat.                                                          230

*T. Cat.*   *I præ, sequor*, let vs go, mouse.

*Exeunt they two: manet the rest.*

*L. Nol.*   *Mol* what was in that canting song?

*Moll.*   Troth my Lord, onely a praise of good drinke, the onely
milke which these wilde beasts loue to sucke, and thus it was:
A rich cup of wine, oh it is iuyce Diuine,
More wholesome for the head, then meate, drinke, or bread,
To fill my drunken pate, with that, I'de sit vp late,
By the heeles wou'd I lie, vnder a lowsy hedge die,
Let a slaue haue a pull at my whore, so I be full
Of that precious liquor;                                          240
And a parcell of such stuffe my Lord not worth the opening.

*Enter a Cutpurse very gallant, with foure or fiue
men after him, one with a wand.*

*L. Nol.*   What gallant comes yonder?

*T. Long.*   Masse I thinke I know him, 'tis one of *Cumberland.*

*1. Cut.*   Shall we venture to shuffle in amongst yon heap of Gallants,
and strike?

2. *Cut.*   'Tis a question whether there bee any siluer shels amongst
them, for all their sattin outsides.

*All Cut.*   Let's try?

*Moll.*   Pox on him, a gallant? shaddow mee, I know him: 'tis one
that cumbers the land indeed; if hee swimme neere to the shore of   250
any of your pockets, looke to your purses.

*Omn.*   Is't possible?

*Moll.*   This braue fellow is no better then a foyst.

*Omn.*   Foyst, what's that?

*Moll.*   A diuer with two fingers, a picke-pocket; all his traine study
the figging law, that's to say, cutting of purses and foysting; one
of them is a nip, I tooke him once i'the twopenny gallery at the
*Fortune*; then there's a cloyer, or snap, that dogges any new
brother in that trade, and snappes will haue halfe in any booty;
Hee with the wand is both a stale, whose office is, to face a man   260
i'the streetes, whil'st shels are drawne by an other, and then with his
blacke coniuring rod in his hand, he by the nimblenesse of his eye
and iugling sticke, will in cheaping a peece of plate at a goldsmithes
stall, make foure or fiue ringes mount from the top of his *caduceus*,
and as if it were at leape-frog, they skip into his hand presently

2. *Cut.*   Zounds wee are smoakt.

*All Cut.*   Ha?

2. *Cut.*   Wee are boyl'd, pox on her; see *Moll* the roaring drabbe.

1. *Cut.*   All the diseases of sixteene hospitals boyle her: away.

*Moll.*   Blesse you sir.                                              270

1. *Cut.*   And you good sir.

*Moll.*   Do'st not ken mee man?

1. *Cut.*   No trust mee sir.

*Moll.*   Heart, there's a Knight to whom I'me bound for many
fauours, lost his purse at the last new play i'the *Swanne*, seuen
Angels in't, make it good you'r best; do you see? no more.

1. *Cut.*   A Sinagogue shall be cal'd Mistresse *Mary*, disgrace mee
not; *pacus palabros*, I will coniure for you, farewell.

*Moll.*   Did not I tell you my Lord?          [*Exeunt.*]

*L. Nol.*   I wonder how thou cam'st to the knowledge of these   280
nasty villaines.

248, 267 *All Cut.*] *Omnes* Q

*T. Long.* And why doe the foule mouthes of the world call thee
*Mol* cutpursse? a name, me thinkes, damn'd and odious.
*Moll.* Dare any step forth to my face and say,
I haue tane thee doing so *Mol?* I must confesse,
In younger dayes, when I was apt to stray,
I haue sat amongst such adders; seene their stings,
As any here might, and in full play-houses
Watcht their quicke-diuing hands, to bring to shame
Such rogues, and in that streame met an ill name: 290
When next my Lord you spie any one of those,
So hee bee in his Art a scholler, question him,
Tempt him with gold to open the large booke
Of his close villanies: and you your selfe shall cant
Better then poore *Mol* can, and know more lawes
Of cheaters, lifters, nips, foysts, puggards, curbers,
With all the diuels blacke guard, then it is fit
Should be discouered to a noble wit.
I know they haue their orders, offices,
Circuits and circles, vnto which they are bound, 300
To raise their owne damnation in.
*Iac. Dap.* How do'st thou know it?
*Moll.* As you do, I shew it you, they to me show it.
Suppose my Lord you were in *Venice.*
*L. Nol.* Well.
*Moll.* If some Italian pander there would tell
All the close trickes of curtizans; would not you
Hearken to such a fellow?
*L. Nol.* Yes.
*Moll.* And here,
Being come from *Venice,* to a friend most deare
That were to trauell thither, you would proclaime
Your knowledge in those villanies, to saue 310
Your friend from their quicke danger: must you haue
A blacke ill name, because ill things you know,
Good troth my Lord, I am made *Mol* cutpurse so.
How many are whores, in small ruffes and still lookes?
How many chast, whose names fill slanders bookes?

Were all men cuckolds, whom gallants in their scornes
Cal so, we should not walke for goring hornes,
Perhaps for my madde going some reproue mee,
I please my selfe, and care not else who loue mee.
*Omn.*    A braue minde *Mol* i'faith.                                    320
*T. Long.*    Come my Lord, shal's to the Ordinary?
*L. Nol.*    I, 'tis noone sure.
*Moll.*    Good my Lord, let not my name condemne me to you or to
the world: A fencer I hope may be cal'd a coward, is he so for that?
If all that haue ill names in *London*, were to be whipt, and to pay
but twelue pence a peece to the beadle, I would rather haue his
office, then a Constables.
*Iac. Dap.*    So would I Captaine *Moll*: 'twere sweete tickling
office i'faith.

>                                             *Exeunt.*


## [ACT V, Scene ii]

*Enter Sir* Alexander Wengraue, Goshawke *and* Greenewit, *and others.*

*Alex.*    My sonne marry a theefe, that impudent girle,
Whom all the world sticke their worst eyes vpon?
*Green.*    How will your care preuent it?
*Gosh.*                                    'Tis impossible.
They marry close, thei'r gone, but none knowes whether.
*Alex.*    Oh Gentlemen, when ha's a fathers heart-strings
>                                    *Enter a seruant*
Held out so long from breaking: now what newes sir?
*Seru.*    They were met vppo'th water an houre since, sir,
Putting in towards the Sluce.
*Alex.*                        The Sluce? come Gentlemen,
'Tis *Lambith* workes against vs.
*Green.*                        And that *Lambith*,
Ioynes more mad matches, then your sixe wet townes,       10
Twixt that and *Windsor-bridge*, where fares lye soaking.

319 loue] Collier; loues Q

*Alex.*   Delay no time sweete Gentlemen: to Blacke Fryars,
Wee'l take a paire of Oares and make after 'em.

*Enter* Trapdore.

*Trap.*   Your sonne, and that bold masculine rampe my mistresse,
Are landed now at Tower.
*Alex.*                    Hoyda, at Tower?
*Trap.*   I heard it now reported.
*Alex.*   Which way Gentlemen shall I bestow my care?
I'me drawne in peeces betwixt deceipt and shame.

*Enter sir* Fitz-Allard.

*Fitz-All.*   Sir *Alexander.*
You'r well met, and most rightly serued,                    20
My daughter was a scorne to you.
*Alex.*                    Say not so sir.
*Fitz-All.*   A very abiect shee, poore Gentlewoman,
Your house had bene dishonoured.  Giue you ioy sir,
Of your sons Gaskoyne-Bride, you'l be a Grandfather shortly
To a fine crew of roaring sonnes and daughters,
'Twill helpe to stocke the suburbes passing well sir.
*Alex.*   O play not with the miseries of my heart,
Wounds should be drest and heal'd, not vext, or left
Wide open, to the anguish of the patient,
And scornefull aire let in: rather let pitty                    30
And aduise charitably helpe to refresh 'em.
*Fitz-All.*   Who'd place his charity so vnworthily,
Like one that giues almes to a cursing beggar.
Had I but found one sparke of goodnesse in you
Toward my deseruing child, which then grew fond
Of your sonnes vertues, I had eased you now.
But I perceiue both fire of youth and goodnesse,
Are rak'd vp in the ashes of your age,
Else no such shame should haue come neere your house,
Nor such ignoble sorrowe touch your heart.                    40
*Alex.*   If not for worth, for pitties sake assist mee.
*Green.*   You vrge a thing past sense, how can he helpe you?

22 abiect ˄ shee,] Dyce; ~ , ~ ˄

All his assistance is as fraile as ours,
Full as vncertaine, where's the place that holds 'em?
One brings vs water-newes; then comes an other
With a full charg'd mouth, like a culuerins voyce,
And he reports the Tower; whose sounds are truest?
*Gosh.*   In vaine you flatter him. Sir *Alexander* —
*Fitʒ-All.*   I flatter him, Gentlemen you wrong mee grosly.
*Green.*   Hee doe's it well i'faith.
*Fitʒ-All.*                       Both newes are false,          50
Of Tower or water: they tooke no such way yet.
*Alex.*   Oh strange: heare you this Gentlemen, yet more plundges?
*Fitʒ-All.*   Th'are neerer then you thinke for, yet more close
Then if they were further off.
*Alex.*                       How am I lost
In these distractions?
*Fitʒ-All.*                       For your speeches Gentlemen,
In taxing me for rashnesse; fore you all,
I will engage my state to halfe his wealth,
Nay to his sonnes reuenewes, which are lesse,
And yet nothing at all, till they come from him;
That I could (if my will stucke to my power)          60
Preuent this marriage yet, nay banish her
For euer from his thoughts, much more his armes.
*Alex.*   Slacke not this goodnesse, though you heap vpon me
Mountaines of malice and reuenge hereafter:
I'de willingly resigne vp halfe my state to him,
So he would marry the meanest drudge I hire.
*Green.*   Hee talkes impossibilities, and you beleeue 'em.
*Fitʒ-All.*   I talke no more, then I know how to finish,
My fortunes else are his that dares stake with me,
The poore young Gentleman I loue and pitty:          70
And to keepe shame from him, (because the spring
Of his affection was my daughters first,
Till his frowne blasted all,) do but estate him
In those possessions, which your loue and care
Once pointed out for him, that he may haue roome,

48 him. Sir] Dodsley; him sir Q

To entertaine fortunes of noble birth,
Where now his desperate wants casts him vpon her:
And if I do not for his owne sake chiefly,
Rid him of this disease, that now growes on him,
I'le forfeit my whole state, before these Gentlemen.           80
*Green.*   Troth but you shall not vndertake such matches,
Wee'l perswade so much with you.
*Alex.*                    Heere's my ring,
He will beleeue this token: fore these Gentlemen,
I will confirme it fully: all those lands,
My first loue lotted him, he shall straight possesse
In that refusall.
*Fitʒ-All.*       If I change it not,
Change mee into a beggar.
*Green.*                    Are you mad sir?
*Fitʒ-All.* 'Tis done.
*Gosh.*             Will you vndoe your selfe by doing,
And shewe a prodigall tricke in your old daies?
*Alex.* 'Tis a match Gentlemen.
*Fitʒ-All.*                    I, I, sir I.           90
I aske no fauour; trust to you for none,
My hope rests in the goodnesse of your son.     *Exit* Fitz-Allard.
*Green.*   Hee holds it vp well yet.
*Gosh.*                    Of an old knight i'faith.
*Alex.*   Curst be the time, I laid his first loue barren,
Wilfully barren, that before this houre
Had sprung forth fruites, of comfort and of honour;
He lou'd a vertuous Gentlewoman.

*Enter* Moll [*in mans clothes*].

*Gosh.*                    Life, heere's *Mol.*
*Green.* *Iack.*
*Gosh.*       How dost thou *Iacke?*
*Moll.*                    How dost thou Gallant?
*Alex.*   Impudence, where's my sonne?
*Moll.*                    Weaknesse, go looke him.
*Alex.*   Is this your wedding gowne?

94

*Moll.*                    The man talkes monthly:    100
Hot broth and a darke chamber for the knight,
I see hee'l be starke mad at our next meeting.        *Exit* Moll.
*Gosh.*  Why sir, take comfort now, there's no such matter,
No Priest will marry her, sir, for a woman,
Whiles that shape's on, and it was neuer knowne,
Two men were married and conioyn'd in one:
Your sonne hath made some shift to loue another.
*Alex.*  What ere' she be, she has my blessing with her,
May they be rich, and fruitfull, and receiue
Like comfort to their issue, as I take              110
In them, ha's pleas'd me now, marrying not this,
Through a whole world he could not chuse amisse.
*Green.*  Glad y'are so penitent, for your former sinne sir.
*Gosh.*  Say he should take a wench with her smocke-dowry,
No portion with her, but her lips and armes?
*Alex.*  Why? who thriue better sir? they haue most blessing,
Though other haue more wealth, and least repent,
Many that want most, know the most content.
*Green.*  Say he should marry a kind youthfull sinner.
*Alex.*  Age will quench that, any offence but theft      120
And drunkennesse, nothing but death can wipe away.
There sinnes are greene, euen when there heads are gray,
Nay I dispaire not now, my heart's cheer'd Gentlemen,
No face can come vnfortunately to me,
Now sir, your newes?                    *Enter a seruant.*
*Seru.*                Your sonne with his faire Bride
Is neere at hand.
*Alex.*              Faire may their fortunes be.
*Green.*  Now you'r resolu'd sir, it was neuer she.
*Alex.*  I finde it in the musicke of my heart,

      *Enter* Mol *maskt, in* Sebastians *hand, and* Fitz-Allard.

See where they come.
*Gosh.*              A proper lusty presence sir.
*Alex.*  Now has he pleas'd me right, I alwaies counseld him    130

    122 There...there] i.e., *their*

95

To choose a goodly personable creature,
Iust of her pitch was my first wife his mother.
*Seb.*    Before I dare discouer my offence,
I kneele for pardon.
*Alex.*                My heart gaue it thee,
Before thy tongue could aske it,
Rise, thou hast rais'd my ioy to greater height,
Then to that seat where griefe deiected it.
Both welcome to my loue, and care for euer,
Hide not my happinesse too long, al's pardoned,
Here are our friends, salute her, Gentlemen.    *They vnmaske her.* 140
*Omn.*    Heart, who is this *Mol?*
*Alex.*    O my reuiuing shame, is't I must liue,
To be strucke blind, be it the worke of sorrow,
Before age take't in hand.
*Fitʒ-All.*                Darkenesse and death.
Haue you deceau'd mee thus? did I engage
My whole estate for this.
*Alex.*                You askt no fauour,
And you shall finde as little, since my comforts,
Play false with me, I'le be as cruell to thee
As griefe to fathers hearts.
*Moll.*                Why what's the matter with you,
Lesse too much ioy, should make your age forgetfull?                150
Are you too well, too happy?
*Alex.*                With a vengeance.
*Moll.*    Me thinkes you should be proud of such a daughter,
As good a man, as your sonne.
*Alex.*                O monstrous impudence.
*Moll.*    You had no note before, an vnmarkt Knight,
Now all the towne will take regard on you,
And all your enemies feare you for my sake,
You may passe where you list, through crowdes most thicke,
And come of brauely with your pursse vnpickt,
You do not know the benefits I bring with mee,

141  is] Dyce [who's]; *om.* Q
149–150 you, ...forgetfull?] Dyce; ~ ? ... ~ , Q

No cheate dares worke vpon you, with thumbe or knife,          160
While y'aue a roaring girle to your sonnes wife.
*Alex.*   A diuell rampant.
*Fitꝁ-All.*          Haue you so much charity,
Yet to release mee of my last rash bargaine?
And I'le giue in your pledge.
*Alex.*          No sir, I stand to't,
I'le worke vpon aduantage, as all mischiefes
Do vpon mee.
*Fitꝁ-All.*     Content, beare witnesse all then,
His are the lands, and so contention ends.
Here comes your sonnes Bride, twixt two noble friends.

*Enter the Lord* Noland, *and Sir* Bewtious Ganymed, *with* Mary
Fitz-Allard *betweene them, the Cittiꝁens and their wiues with them.*

*Moll.*   Now are you gull'd as you would be, thanke me for't,
I'de a fore-finger in't.
*Seb.*          Forgiue mee father,          170
Though there before your eyes my sorrow fain'd,
This still was shee, for whom true loue complain'd.
*Alex.*   Blessings eternall, and the ioyes of Angels,
Beginne your peace heere, to be sign'd in heauen,
How short my sleepe of sorrow seemes now to me,
To this eternity of boundlesse comforts,
That finds no want but vtterance, and expression.
My Lord your office heere appeares so honourably:
So full of ancient goodnesse, grace, and worthinesse,
I neuer tooke more ioy in sight of man,          180
Then in your comfortable presence now.
*L. Nol.*   Nor I more delight in doing grace to vertue,
Then in this worthy Gentlewoman, your sonnes Bride,
Noble *Fitꝁ-Allards* daughter, to whose honour
And modest fame, I am a seruant vow'd,
So is this Knight.
*Alex.*          Your loues make my ioyes proud,
Bring foorth those deeds of land, my care layd ready,
And which, old knight, thy noblenesse may challenge,

7                          97                          **B C D III**

Ioyn'd with thy daughters vertues, whom I prise now,
As deerely as that flesh, I call myne owne.                       190
Forgiue me worthy Gentlewoman, 'twas my blindnesse
When I reiected thee, I saw thee not,
Sorrow and wilfull rashnesse grew like filmes
Ouer the eyes of iudgement, now so cleere
I see the brightnesse of thy worth appeare.
*Mary.*   Duty and loue may I deserue in those,
And all my wishes haue a perfect close.
*Alex.*   That tongue can neuer erre, the sound's so sweete,
Here honest sonne, receiue into thy hands,
The keyes of wealth, possession of those lands,             200
Which my first care prouided, thei'r thine owne,
Heauen giue thee a blessing with 'em, the best ioyes,
That can in worldly shapes to man betide,
Are fertill lands, and a faire fruitfull Bride,
Of which I hope thou'rt sped.
*Seb.*                          I hope so too sir.
*Moll.*   Father and sonne, I ha' done you simple seruice here.
*Seb.*   For which thou shalt not part *Moll* vnrequited.
*Alex.*   Thou art a madd girle, and yet I cannot now
Condemne thee.
*Moll.*                     Condemne mee? troth and you should sir,
I'de make you seeke out one to hang in my roome,          210
I'de giue you the slip at Gallowes, and cozen the people.
Heard you this iest my Lord?
*L. Nol.*                        What is it *Iacke?*
*Moll.*   He was in feare his sonne would marry mee,
But neuer dreamt that I would nere agree.
*L. Nol.*   Why? thou had'st a suiter once *Iacke*, when wilt marry?
*Moll.*   Who I my Lord, I'le tell you when ifaith,
                    When you shall heare,
                    Gallants voyd from Serieants feare,
                    Honesty and truth vnslandred,
                    Woman man'd, but neuer pandred,            220
                    Cheaters booted, but not coacht,

221 Cheaters] Dyce *query*; Cheates Q

98

Vessels older e're they'r broacht.
If my minde be then not varied,
Next day following, I'le be married.

*L. Nol.*    This sounds like domes-day.
*Moll.*                              Then were marriage best,
For if I should repent, I were soone at rest.
*Alex.*    Introth tho'art a good wench, I'me sorry now,
The opinion was so hard, I conceiu'd of thee.
Some wrongs I'ue done thee.

                    *Enter* Trapdore.

*Trap.*                          Is the winde there now?
'Tis time for mee to kneele and confesse first,                    230
For feare it come too late, and my braines feele it,
Vpon my pawes, I aske you pardon mistresse.
*Moll.*    Pardon? for what sir? what ha's your rogueship done now?
*Trap.*    I haue bene from time to time hir'd to confound you,
By this old Gentleman.
*Moll.*                    How?
*Trap.*                          Pray forgiue him,
But may I counsell you, you should neuer doo't.
Many a snare to entrapp your Worships life,
Haue I laid priuily, chaines, watches, Iewels,
And when hee saw nothing could mount you vp,
Foure hollow-hearted Angels he then gaue you,                    240
By which he meant to trap you, I to saue you.
*Alex.*    To all which, shame and griefe in me cry guilty,
Forgiue mee, now I cast the worlds eyes from mee,
And looke vpon thee freely with mine owne:
I see the most of many wrongs before mee,
Cast from the iawes of enuy and her people,
And nothing foule but that, Il'e neuer more
Condemne by common voyce, for that's the whore,
That deceiues mans opinion; mockes his trust,
Cozens his loue, and makes his heart vniust.                    250

243 mee, now‸] Dyce; ~ ‸ ~ , Q        245 mee] Dyce; hee Q

*Moll.* Here be the Angels Gentlemen, they were giuen me
As a Musitian, I pursue no pitty,
Follow the law, and you can cucke mee, spare not,
Hang vp my vyall by me, and I care not.
*Alex.* So farre I'me sorry, I'le thrice double 'em
To make thy wrongs amends,
Come worthy friends, my honourable Lord,
Sir *Bewteous Ganymed*, and Noble *Fitz-Allard*,
And you kind Gentlewomen, whose sparkling presence,
Are glories set in mariage, beames of society,                    260
For all your loues giue luster to my ioyes,
The happinesse of this day shall be remembred,
At the returne of euery smiling spring:
In May time now 'tis borne, and may no sadnesse
Sit on the browes of men vpon that day,
But as I am, so all goe pleas'd away.


## Epilogus.

A Painter hauing drawne with curious Art
The picture of a woman (euery part,
Limb'd to the life) hung out the peece to sell:
People (who pass'd along) veiwing it well,
Gaue seuerall verdicts on it. Some dispraised
The haire, some sayd the browes too high were raised,
Some hit her o're the lippes, mislik'd their colour,
Some wisht her nose were shorter; some, the eyes fuller,
Others sayd roses on her cheekes should grow,
Swearing they lookt too pale, other cry'd no,                    10
The workeman still as fault was found, did mend it,
In hope to please all; (but this worke being ended)
And hung open at stall, it was so vile,
So monstrous and so vgly all men did smile
At the poore Painters folly. Such wee doubt

259 Gentlewomen] Dyce: Gentlewoman Q          264 May] my Q

Is this our Comedy. Some perhaps do floute
The plot, saying; 'tis too thinne, too weake, too meane,
Some for the person will reuile the Scœne.
And wonder, that a creature of her being
Should bee the subiect of a Poet, seeing                          20
In the worlds eie, none weighes so light: others looke
For all those base trickes publish'd in a booke,
(Foule as his braines they flow'd from) of Cut-purses,
Of Nips and Foysts, nastie, obscœne discourses,
As full of lies, as emptie of worth or wit,
For any honest eare, or eye vnfit.
And thus,
If we to euery braine (that's humerous)
Should fashion Sceanes, we (with the Painter) shall
In striuing to please all, please none at all.                    30
Yet for such faults, as either the writers wit,
Or negligence of the Actors do commit,
Both craue your pardons: if what both haue done,
Cannot full pay your expectation,
The *Roring Girle* her selfe some few dayes hence,
Shall on this Stage, giue larger recompence.
Which Mirth that you may share in, her selfe does woe you,
And craues this signe, your hands to becken her to you.

23 Cut-purses] Dodsley; Cut-purse Q

*FINIS*

# TEXTUAL NOTES

## I.i

24 here presently, it shall] All editors have placed a stop like a semi-colon after *here*, thus beginning a new clause with *presently*. The sense is indifferent whatever the modification, but if repetition of a cant phrase for comic effect is considered, then line 48 suggests the punctuation adopted here.

77 brow,] Dyce and Bullen, of course, modernize to *brows* in consideration of the pronoun *them* in the next line. Nothing would be easier than for a compositor to fail to see a terminal *s*; on the other hand, Elizabethan grammar does not forbid reference of this sort.

## II.ii

10 two leaud] Collier confidently altered to *lewd*; Dyce printed *leav'd* but queried *loud*; Bullen retained *leav'd* and remarked only that the sense was intelligible. I take it that the primary sense intended is the comparison of the tongue to the two hinged parts of a door or gate, each of which can move independently and thus pronounce either slander or truth. The common phrase is 'double-tongued', or 'two-tongued', or 'fork-tongued'. The lines in Crashaw's *Hymn of the Nativity* doubtless do not apply here: 'Shee spreads the red leaves of thy Lips, | That in their Buds yet blushing lye' (*Poems*, ed. L. C. Martin [1927], p. 108).

## III.iii

200 Honest Sir] Q *Serieant* (*Seriant* [u]) is manifestly wrong. Dyce, followed by Bullen, emends to *Servant*. This is not much better, since there is small point in sounding the alarm to Gull before Jack Dapper. The odds are that the compositor mistook an abbreviation like S$^r$ and expanded it wrongly.

## IV.ii

49 Then they hang the head.] Q prefixes the speech-heading *Mist. Open.*, which duplicates the same prefix at line 45. Line 49 begins a new page (sig. I1$^v$). There is about a third of a line of white space after the end of the last line on sig. I1$^r$, '. . .animalls they are', and the catchword is '*Mist. Open.*', repeated at the first line of the next page, as '*Mist. Open.* Then they hang the head.' This line does not join very smoothly to 'Lord what simple animalls they are.' and it would seem that some brief intervening remark by Mistress Gallipot has been dropped in error, but whether by the compositor or in the manuscript is not to be determined. However, if we may trust the evidence of the catchword, the manuscript could have been at fault.

222 snafling] Dyce and Bullen emend to *snuffling*, presumably on the
assumption of u:a misreading. Curiously, O.E.D. quotes this passage as
v.¹ ? Obs. *intr.* to saunter. However, since the only other illustration is a
doubtful one of 1743, and line 225 *I haue caught a cold in my head sir* is
ignored, this definition need not be taken seriously. The u:a confusion
should not be posited, since *snaffle* and *snaffling* associated with catarrh and
speaking through the nose with a snuffling noise are well represented in
O.E.D.

272 Gilt] Q reads *Get*, a crux that Collier solved simply by omitting the
word, whereas Dyce doubtfully read *Gelt* (for *Gold*) doubtfully followed
by Bullen. O.E.D. sanctions the spelling *gelt* meaning gold, or money,
as a substantive but not as an adjective, seemingly. It is safer, therefore,
to emend to *Gilt*, where we know where we stand. The original reading
can be defended only with excessive straining. *Get* is a common spelling
of *jet*, and here three possibilities might exist. O.E.D. lists *jet* (get) under
v¹ II, 6 *intrans.* as 'to move the tail up and down jerkily', as in a bird. One
might stretch the sense and propose that jet-feathers were feathers that
assisted the bird in this movement, or in the other movements described
by *jet*. The word *jet* is also associated with a protrusion. Then, of course,
*jet* means *black*; and if one were sufficiently ingenious one might remark
on the opposition of worldly gain with the white feathers of angels' wings.
But *Gilt*, whether as *gilt* or the form *gelt*, is apparently right, on the
analogy of the following lines from *Lust's Dominion*, I. iv. 36–40 (see
vol. IV):

> *Alvero.* *Mendoça* woo's the King to banish thee;
>     Startle thy wonted spirits, awake thy soul,
>     And on thy resolution fasten wings,
>         Whose golden feathers may out-strip their hate.
> *Eleaçar.* I'le tye no golden fethers to my wings.

If, as I take it, this is a reference to bribery, then the parallel with Mistress
Gallipot is exact, for she has given her husband's money to Laxton.

# PRESS-VARIANTS IN Q (1611)

[Copies collated: BM¹ (British Museum 162.d.35), BM² (Ashley 1159); Bodl (Bodleian Mal. 246[1]); Dyce (Victoria and Albert Museum); NLS (National Library of Scotland); CSmH (Henry E. Huntington Library); DFo (Folger Shakespeare Library); MB (Boston Public Library); Pforz (Carl H. Pforzheimer Collection); Taylor (Robert H. Taylor).]

## SHEET A (*outer forme*)

*Corrected:* BM², Bodl, Dyce, NLS, CSmH, DFo, Pforz, Taylor.
*Uncorrected:* BM¹, MB.

Sig. A 3.
  *Preface.*
  15  cod-peece] cod-peice
  15  book] booke
Sig. A 4ᵛ.
  *Persons.*
  Dramatis] Drammatis

## SHEET B (*inner forme*)

*Corrected:* BM¹⁻², Bodl, Dyce, NLS, CSmH, MB, Pforz, Taylor.
*Uncorrected:* DFo.

Sig. B 1ᵛ.
  I.i.22  in truth ſir] intruthſir
      33  ſlakes] ſlackes
      34  ſaiſt] ſaith
      35  *viua*] *viue*
      37  What] Wthat
      39  *Neatfoote*] *Neatfootte*
Sig. B 2.
  I.i.54  Ha!] Ha:
      56  ſhape?] ſhape:
      59  prey] pray
      59  eyes] eyes,
      61  a loathed] aloathed
      78  gold] gold,
      82  heire?] heire,

Sig. B4.
    I.ii.66  met] met,
        88  fray] fray,
        89  mad,] mad
        90  question] question,

## SHEET C (*inner forme*)

*Corrected:*    BM², Bodl, Dyce, NLS, CSmH, DFo, Pforz, Taylor.
*Uncorrected:* BM¹, MB.

Sig. C2.
    I.ii.185  I'me] Ime
       187  I'me] Ime
       205  *Simon*] *Simon*
       207  Ile] ile
       209  burnt?] burnt.

## SHEET H (*outer forme*)

*Corrected:*    BM¹⁻², Bodl, Dyce, CSmH, DFo, MB, Pforz, Taylor.
*Uncorrected:* NLS.

Sig. H1.
    III.iii.179  child] child,
         179  debts,] debts
         200  Serieant] Seriant
         205  Serieants] Seriants

Sig. H2ᵛ.
    IV.i.65  *Moll*] *Moll,*
      67  nine] mine
      71  pitty] pitty,
      77  viall,] viall
      83  wel] well

Sig. H3.
    IV.i.108  againe?] againe.

Sig. H4ᵛ.
    IV.i.201  them] them.
       204  houſe,] houſe
       204  heart   .] heart.
       208  three] there

## SHEET I (*inner forme*)

(*Note.* An asterisk indicates a variant occurring in reset type.)

Reset (*first state*): BM¹, CSmH
Original:            BM², Dyce, NLS, DFo, MB, Pforz, Taylor.

Sig. I1ᵛ.
  *running-title*
    Girle] Girle

  *IV.ii.49 *om.*] the
      *53 they deale] deale they
      *56 donc] done
      *58 will] wil
      64 whᴧ] why
      65 do] doe
      69 duck mee] duckmee
      *81 Poticariſhip] Potticariſhip

Sig. I2.
  IV.ii.83 *Lax..*] *Lax.*
      85 *Lax*] *Lax.*

Sig. I3ᵛ.
  IV.ii.180 m akes] makes
      180 peticot e] peticote
      181 beſide] besides
      183 moon] moone

Sig. I4.
  IV.ii.*209 try] try,
      *210 you] you,
      *211 'twas] t'was
      *212 beate] beat
      *216 *Miſt,*] *Miſt.*
      *216 No:----] No:—
      *218 *Mai.*] *Maiſt.*
      *219 S.D. aud] *and*
      *219 S.D. *Somner*] *Sommer*
      *221 *Gall.*] *Gal.*
      *222 *Greene.*] *Green.*
      *222 ſnaffling] ſnafling
      *224 *Gall.*] *Gal.*
      *225 ---- I] —— I
      *225 head ſir] headſir
      *227 ſir.] ſir,
      *228 *Greene.*] *Green.*

\*228 and | you] and you |
\*229 doe] do
\*230 *Craftino*] *Craftina*
\*231 *Gall.*] *Gal.*
\*232 *Greene.*] *Green.*

*Reset (second state):* Bodl

Sig. I 1ᵛ.
   IV.ii.64 why] whⱯ

## SHEET K (*outer forme*)

*Corrected:* BM¹⁻², Bodl, NLS, DFo, MB, Pforz, Taylor.
*Uncorrected:* Dyce, CSmH.

Sig. K 1.
   IV.ii.286 being] beng

## SHEET M (*outer forme*)

*Corrected:* Bodl, Dyce, DFo
*Uncorrected:* BM¹⁻², NLS, CSmH, MB, Pforz, Taylor

Sig. M 1.
   V.ii.162 charity,] charity?
     163 bargaine?] bargaine,
     166 *Fitz-All.*] *Aitz-All.*

# EMENDATIONS OF ACCIDENTALS

## Preface

14 Statute] Sta-|ute
hd. *Comicke*ᴧ] ~ ,
   15 cod-peice] Q(u); cod-peece Q(c)

15 booke] Q(u); book Q(c)
18 ha's] *text*; has *cw*

## Prologue

7 *Scœne,*] ~ .

## Persons

DRAMMATIS] Q(u); DRAMATIS Q(c)

## I.i

16 curle-pated] curle-|pated
33–34 The more...me!] *one line in*
   Q
50 When] | when
54 Ha:] Q(u); ~ ! Q(c)
54–55 Ha! | Life...] *one line* [life] *in*
   Q
56 shape:] Q(u); ~ ? Q(c)

58–59 waiteᴧ ... both,] ~ , ...
   ~ ᴧ
70 broke?] ~ ,
78 me:] ~ ,
89 ship-wracke?] ~ .
106 dangerous.] dangerours,
108 about?] ~ ,

## I.ii

S.D. Goshawke] Goshake
4 (At] | (at
16 Y'are] Y are
20 seemes] seeemes
21 fill'd] fiil'd
29 rarely.] ~ ,
59 A stoole.] *run-on with line* 58
87 foundation: ... noyseᴧ] ~ ᴧ
   ... ~ :
88 fray,] Q(u); ~ ᴧ Q(c)
89 madᴧ] Q(u); ~ , Q(c)
90 question,] Q(u); ~ ᴧ Q(c)
94 Pray...end?] Q *lines:* proceed, |
   How

109 roote —] ~ ,
109 sonne?] ~ ,
115 subtilty —] ~ .
119 foundation —] ~ ,
124 teeth —] ~ ,
143 aside —] ~ . —
185, 187 Ime] Q(u); I'me Q(c)
204 then?] ~ ,
207 ile] Q(u); Ile Q(c)
209 burnt.] Q(u); ~ ? Q(c)
222–223 hobby-|horse] hobbyhorse
223 towne to] to wneto
245 dangerous] dangerons
246 me —] ~ .

## II.i

23 on't.] ~ ,
26 hee] *text*; he *cw*
60 but] | But
97 What,] ~ .
127 you'r] your
129 fashion.] ~ ,
130 gallants, ... Riders,] ~ ᴀ ...
   ~ .
143–145 *prose in* Q
157 Honest] honest
171 Italian] *Italian*
177 an] an an
186–187 Q *lines*: man | And
199 *Maist. Open.*] *text*; *Mist. Open*
   cw
233 Gentle-man] Gentle-|man

240 measure.] ~ ..
247 Whether,] ~ ᴀ
283 you'r] your
289 thoroughly] thorougly
310 though] | Though
328 Strength] Strengh
331 S.D. Mol] Mols
331 S.D. *heels,*] ~ ᴀ
358–359 Q *lines*: boord, | He
362–363 *Open-|worke*] *Openworke*
369 pigsny] pigs ny
372 Come] *cw*; *Maist. Gal.* Come
   *text*
374 and] aud
378 Q *runs-on with line above*
378 away,] ~ ᴀ

## II.ii

9 suppose ᴀ] ~ .
25 goodman] good-|man
36 side;] ~ ,
45 That] that
45–48 *prose in* Q
92 presently] persently
98 loue,] ~ ᴀ
101 sir, you?] ~ ᴀ ~ .
108 breake,] ~ ᴀ
110 care,] ~ .
113 bewitcht] bewitch

118–120 Q *lines*: Flatred...sonne, |
   Oh...owne
118 poysoned.] ~ ,
125 marriage?] ~ ,
126–127 *prose in* Q
145 Why,] ~ ᴀ
162 (ath good] ᴀ ~ (~
184 th'other,] ~ .
186–187 change, ... indirect.] ~ .
   ...~ ,

## III.i

29 shee'd] she'ed
29 Court-men] Court-|men
37 deriu'd] *text* deri-|riu'd; *cw* -ued
42–44 Q *lines*: I...sir, | You...
   barrister, | I...sold | I...
   trouble,
45 coach?] ~ ,
47 you'r] your
59–63 Q *lines*: There's...pace, |
   Shee...it, | Ten...em,

74 letchers ᴀ] ~ .
75–76 Q *lines*: That...sight
   Then...time,
88 their] there
108 prostitute] prostitue
111 thine,] ~ .
126 sh'has] | Sh'has
139 Mistresse] Mistrsse
145 H'as] Has
146 make] meke

146–147 calfe,... in't;] ~ ; ... ~ ,
164 you'r] your
168 often,] ~ ʌ |
172–173 prose in Q

179 you'r] your
190–191 prose in Q
199–200 one line in Q

## III.ii

7 fye] fiye
13 mid-wife] mid-|wife
17 Must] Mnst
23 ouer me] ouerme
25 handled ʌ —] ~ . —
46–47 Q runs-on with above as prose
72 Steale, — steale.] Q runs-on with above as prose
73–74 What...see't.] one line in Q
74–76 Oh would...tear'st?] prose in Q
82–85 When...dead?] prose in Q
99–100 Sweete...bosome.] one line in Q
112 To him] Tohim
127–128 Or...thee.] prose in Q
138–141 Forty...Pru.] prose in Q

141 sweete,] ~ ʌ
191 Potticariship] Potticarishp
202 Concerning you] Q runs-on with line above
207 know] kuow
209 minute] minnte
216–218 Vmh...sending:] prose in Q
217 Mist.] M.ist.
223 fright] frighr
224–226 Q lines: I'le...common | Then...diseased. —
232 now] uow
236 Another] Anothcr
243–244 Yes...part] one line in Q
245–246 With...wit?] one line in Q

## III.iii

12 Mol —] ~ .
35 Away:] ~ ʌ
38 harke —] ~ ,
54 sonne] sonnne
61 these:] ~ ,
97–98 When...prisoner.] one line in Q
104 'Lies] 'lies
105 S.D. Yeoman] Yeomau
106–107 I...you.] one line in Q
107 knights,] ~ .
110–111 Q lines: he | By

117 for] fot
117 name,] ~ ʌ
122 them, ... orethrowne;] ~ ; ... ~ ,
150 money] mouey
155 sally:] ~ ʌ
164 and] and and
168 No,] ~ ʌ [doubtful]
168 nooke] uooke
185 malt-men] malt-|men
205 Seriants] Q(u); Serieants Q(c)

## IV.i

1 Vnhappy] Vnahppy
6 peace.] peacc.
9 this] | This
18–19 Shee...selfe.] prose in Q

34 hangs] haugs
35 glisterings] gilsterings
49 'twill] 't will
57 fathers] fathets

71 pitty,] Q(u); ~ ∧ Q(c)
80–81 I'ue...taught.] *prose in* Q
83 well] Q(u); wel Q(c)
108 But] Bnt
122–123 dreame; ... then,] ~ , ...
  ~ ;
131–135 Q *lines*: Here...now, |
  There's...glad | To...for't, |
  And...sandbag, | Oh...'em, |
  'Twould...execution, |
  That....

133 sandbag.] ~ ,
140–146 *prose in* Q
152 *Mol.*] ~ ,
164–165 Q *lines*: you, | I'de
168 thinke] thiuke
199 selfe,] ~ ∧
201 them,] ~ . Q(u); ~ ∧ Q(c)
212–213 Q *lines*: Hee...musitian,
  I...instrument, | And....

## IV.ii

2 prey:] [*point clear in few copies*]
9–10 Bun-|hill] Bun-|hill
17 a crampe] acrampe
69 duck mee] *reset*; duckmee [*original*]
87 pus-cat] pus-|cat
90 you'r] your
97 conference] conferenc
107 vildest] vild'st
116 Shew] *cw*; Show [*text*]
125–130 *prose in* Q
128 credit—] ~ .
140 *Rosamond*—] ~ ,
146–158 *prose in* Q
149 pug] png
150 in] ln
152 patience] patieuce
161–164 *prose in* Q
161 rogue so] rogueso
162 hangman] hang-|man
168–175 *prose in* Q
169 through] throngh
172 I'le heare] I'leheare

174 meet] mect
175 streete,] ~ .
179 him not] hiw not
180–181 *one line in* Q
192 spitting] spittiug
198 hell).] ~ )∧
203 euen] cuen
216–217 *one line in* Q
219 S.D. *Somner*] *reset*; *Sommer* [*original*]
225 head sir] *reset*; headsir [*original*]
230 *Crastino*] *reset*; *Crastina* [*original*]
239–242 *prose in* Q
242 swore —] ~ .
244 you] vou
253–254 *one line in* Q
269–273 *prose in* Q
280 hereafter] hercafter
294–295 *prose in* Q
304 presumne] prsumne
306 Gentleman] Gentlman
316 wrong'd] wroug'd
317 sir —] ~ ,

## V.i

5 desperates.] ~ ,
13 How] ho w
31 you] y ou
32, 44 Sir] *Sir*
76 Turke] *Turke*

78–79 Hungarians...Venetian]
  *names italic*
88 butter-box] butter-|box
91–97 *black-letter in* Q
92 Dutchlant∧] ~ .

95 on] ou
97 mine] miue
120 Commonwealth] Common-|
   wealth
148 My doxy,] ~ ~ ‸
150 darkmans] dark-|mans
173, 184 Ruffemans] Ruffe-|mans
207 well.] ~ ‸
231 *I*] I
231 go,] ~ ‸
232 S.D. *two:*] ~ ‸

234 milke which] milke | Which
236 then] :hen
240-241 Q *lines:* Of...Lord |
   Not....
253 better] bettet
273 trust] rrust
297 With all] Withall
323-327 Q *lines:* Good...world: |
   A...that? | If...whipt, | And
   ...rather | Haue...Constables.

## V.ii

3 impossible] im possible
9-11 *prose in* Q
14-15 Q *lines:* Your...rampe |
   My...Tower.
32-33 vnworthily, ... beggar.]
   ~ .... ~ ,
48 *Alexander* —] ~ .
53 for, ... close‸] ~ ‸ ... ~ ,
54 Then] then
54-55 How...distractions?] *one
   line in* Q
67 impossibilities] impossibilites
86-87 If...beggar.] *one line in* Q
91 aske] akse
96 fruites] friutes
99 Weaknesse] Weakensse
110-111 Q *lines:* Like...them, |
   H'as...this,
120-121 Q *lines:* Age...drunken-
   nesse, | Nothing...away.

125-126 *one line in* Q
133-134 *one line in* Q
134-135 *one line in* Q
136 height,] ~ .
137 it.] ~ ,
154 Knight] Knight
162 charity,] Q(c); ~ ? Q(u)
163 bargaine?] Q(c); ~ , Q(u)
164-166 Q *lines:* No...aduantage, |
   As...mee.
166 then,] ~ ‸
184 *Fitz-Allards*] *first* 'l' *scarcely
   inks*
208-209 *one line in* Q
235 By] by
236 counsell] connsell
242 which,] ~ ‸
248 that's the] that' sthe
253 not,] ~ ‸
257 friends,] ~ ‸

## Epilogue

5 Some] some

16 Comedy.] ~ ,
26-27 *one line in* Q

# IF

# IT BE NOT GOOD

## The Diuel is in it.

## A

## Nevv Play,

# AS IT HATH BIN

lately Acted, vvith great
applause, by the Queenes Maiesties
Seruants : At the Red Bull.

Written by THOMAS DEKKER.

*Flectere si nequeo Superos, Acheronta mouebo.*

**LONDON,**
Printed for I. T. And are to be sold by *Edward Marchant,*
at his shop against the Crosse in *Pauls*
Church-yarde. 1612.

# TEXTUAL INTRODUCTION

*If This Be Not a Good Play, the Devil Is In It* (Greg, *Bibliography,* no. 305) appeared in 1612 printed by Thomas Creede, probably for John Trundle. The play was not entered in the Stationers' Register. The title given here is that found as the head-title and hence followed by the running-titles. The variant title-page form 'If It Be Not Good, the Diuel Is In It' is less likely to be authorial, and its brevity doubtless reflects the demands of title-page advertisement.

Printing was performed using four sets of skeleton-formes, a pair for the inner and outer formes of alternate sheets. Although this is one of the patterns that can be associated with typesetting by formes, or with two-press work, occasional evidence from type substitutions, as of italic *k* and *I* for roman in sheet K, and of *k* in sheet H, suggest *seriatim* composition.[1] Precise determination would require a study made under magnification of the distribution and composition pattern of identifiable type sorts, which has not been attempted. On the other hand, ordinary tests suggest inconclusively that one compositor set the whole. This evidence is difficult to equate with the two-press pattern for the running-titles; but in the absence of highly exacting and elaborate typographic tests for the presence of more than one typesetter it has seemed somewhat more probable to assume the existence of only one regular compositor.

The compositor appears to have had some trouble with his manuscript, and as a consequence he seemingly attempted to reproduce what he read, whether it made sense or not. The proof-reading, certainly non-authorial, by no means made up for the compositorial lapses and in some cases added fresh error.

That the manuscript given to the printer was authorized is shown beyond any doubt by the author's dedication. Although such evidence is to be offered (and accepted) with caution, certain characteristics of Dekker's spelling come through strongly enough to lead me to feel that the manuscript was autograph. On the other hand, theatrical intervention has apparently taken place. The strongest

[1] For a discussion of 'setting by formes' see pp. 255–258 below.

indication comes with the addition to the stage-direction heading
V.i of 'Iouinelli here', apparently a prompter's note to have the actor
ready and waiting for his entrance after line 12. The several cases in
which directions are printed as part of the text, such as 'Flourish' at
I.ii.6, 'One ringes' at II.ii.157, and 'Musick' at IV.iv.6, may indicate
theatrical additions. Possibly the precise direction at II.ii.174 is an
addition to the author's more general notation at line 170. However,
errors such as the original direction at I.ii.151 or at I.iii.18 are
difficult to explain unless there was a tentative misunderstanding on
the part of an annotator. Even more difficult to account for is the
extraordinarily high proportion of error involving speech-prefixes.

No precision of assignment is possible, but it might appear that
the printer's manuscript was either a worked-over set of autograph
papers preceding the preparation of the prompt-book, or else a
rather rough autograph manuscript serving itself as the prompt-
book. Dekker's prefatory remark that the play was at first a failure
but was later revived successfully with an expansion of what I take
to be the first scene, in Hell, is not overly helpful, since the same
errors in speech-prefixes and stage-directions are found in I.i as in
later scenes. Editorially, the general signs of difficulty in the manuscript and of non-authorial intervention encourage some boldness
in emendation.

Except for its appearance in the Pearson reprint this text has not
previously been edited. The present text is based on a collation of
the following thirteen copies: British Museum, copy 1 (C.34.c.25)
and copy 2 (C.12.f.4[2]), Bodleian Library Mal. 235(9), Dyce copy
in the Victoria and Albert Museum, Eton College, the Bute Collection in the National Library of Scotland, the Henry E. Huntington
Library, Yale University, Folger Shakespeare Library, Houghton
Library of Harvard University, and the New York Public Library.
Owing to the rareness of this play and the interest therefore of its
press-variants, I welcomed the opportunity to collate two copies in
private hands, the first the property of the Seven Gables Bookshop
of New York City and the second the Roxburgh-Heber copy in the
collection of Robert H. Taylor of Yonkers, New York, to whom my
thanks for the courtesy are due.

# [PERSONS

ALPHONSO, King of Naples

DUKE OF CALABRIA

OCTAVIO  
ASTOLFO } Uncles to Alphonso

NARCISSO  
JOVINELLI  
BRISCO  
SPENDOLA } Counts of Naples

BARTERVILE, a Merchant

PRIOR  
SUB-PRIOR  
ALPHEGE  
HILLARY } Friars

SCUMBROTH, a cook

RUFMAN (disguised as BOHOR)  
SHACKLESOULE (disguised as FRIAR RUSH)  
LURCHALL  
LUCIFER } Devils

GLITTERBACK, a spirit

Two Gentlemen

FARNEZE, a Gentleman

ERMINHILD, Princess of Calabria

PLUTO         RAVILLAC  
CHARON        GUY FAWKES  
MINOS         A PRODIGAL  
ÆACUS         A PURITAN  
RHADAMANTH } tormented in Hell

A Soldier, Scholar, Mariner, Bravo, Italian Zany, Courtesans, Friars, Pilgrims, Servants, Devils, Furies.]

118

## To my *Loving, and Loved Friends and Fellowes,* the *Queenes Maiesties Seruants.*

*Knowledge* and *Reward* dwell far a-sunder. *Greatnes* lay once betweene them. But (in his stead) *Couetousnes* now. An ill neighbour, a bad *Benefactor,* no paymaister to *Poets.* By *This Hard-Houskeeping,* (or rather, *Shutting* vp of *Liberalities Doores,*) *Merit* goes a *Begging,* and *Learning* starues. *Bookes,* had wont to haue *Patrons,* and (now,) *Patrons* haue *Bookes.* The *Snuff* that is *Lighted,* consumes *That* which *Feeds* it. A *Signe,* the *World* hath an ill *Eare,* when no *Musick* is good, vnles it *Strikes-vp* for *Nothing.* *I* haue *Sung* so, but wil no more. A *Hue-and-Cry* follow, his *Wit,* that sleeps, when sweete *Tunes* are sounding. But tis now the *Fashion.* Lords, look wel: *Knights, Thank* well; *Gentlemen,* promise well; *Citizens, Take* well; *Gulles, Sweare* well: but *None, Giue* well. I leaue therefore *All,* for *You:* And *All* (that *This* can be) to *You.* Not in hope to *Haue;* but in *Recognition* of *What I Haue* (as I think) *Already* (your *Loues.*)

*Acknowledgement* is part of payment sometimes, but it neither is, nor shall be (betweene you and me) a *Cancelling.* I haue cast mine eye vpon many, but find none more fit, none more worthy, to *Patronize this,* than *you,* who haue *Protected it.* Your *Cost, Counsell,* and *Labour,* had bin ill spent, if a *Second* should by my hand snatch from you *This Glory.* No: When *Fortune* (in her blinde pride) set her foote vpon *This imperfect Building,* (as scorning the *Foundation* and *Workmanship:*) you, gently raizd it vp (on the same *Columnes,*) the *Frontispice* onely a little more *Garnished:* To you therefore deseruedly is the *Whole Frame* consecrated. For I durst sweare, if *Wishes* and *Curses* could haue become *Witches,* the necke of this *Harmles Diuell* had long a goe bin broken.

But I am glad that *Ignorance* (so insolent for being flattered) is now stript naked, and her deformities discouered: And more glad, that *Enuie* sits maddingly gnawing her owne *Snakes,* whose *Stinges* she had armed to strike *Others.* *Feede* let her so still. So, still let the

6 *Snuff* that] *Snufft hat* Q

*Other* be laughed at. Whilst I (*pittying* the *One*, and not *Dreading* the *Other*,) send these *my Wishes* flying into your *Bosomes*; That the *God* of *Poets*, may neuer pester your *Stage* with a *Cherilus*, nor a *Suffenus*, (*Males*, *Eminent* in nothing but in Long *Eares*, in *Kicking* and in *Braging* out *Calumnies*) vpon whose *Cruppers* may be aptly pind, *That Morrall* of poore *Ocnus* making *Ropes* in *Hell*, whil'st an Asse stands by, and (as he twists) bites them in sunder. But if *His Versifying Deity*, sends you *Any*, *I wish* they may be such, as are worthy to sit, *At the Table of the Sun*. None els.                   40

I wish a *Faire* and *Fortunate Day*, to your *Next New-Play* (for the *Makers-sake* and your *Owne*,) because such *Braue Triumphes* of *Poesie*, and *Elaborate Industry*, which my *Worthy Friends Muse* hath there set forth, deserue a *Theater* full of very *Muses* themselues to be *Spectators*. To that *Faire Day* I wish a *Full*, *Free*, and *Knowing Auditor*. And to that *Full Audience*, *One Honest Doore-keeper*. *So*, *Fare-well*.

Yours. Tho: Dekker.

## *Prologue.*

Would t'were a Custome that at all New-playes
*The Makers* sat o'th *Stage*, either with *Bayes*
To haue their *Workes Crownd*, or beaten in with *Hissing*,
*Pied* and bold *Ideotes*, durst not then sit *Kissing*
A *Muses* cheeke: *Shame* would base *Changelings* weane,
From *Sucking* the mellifluous *Hypocrene*:
Who write as blinde-men shoote, (by *Hap*, not *Ayme*,)
So, Fooles by lucky *Throwing*, oft win the Game.
*Phœbus* has many Bastards, *True Sonnes* fewe,
I meane of those, whose quicke cleare-eyes can viewe          10
*Poesies* pure *Essence*, It being so diuine,
That the *Suns Fires*, (euen when they brightest shine)
Or *Lightning*, when most subtillie *Ioue* does spend it,
May as soone be approchd, weyed, touchd, or comprehended.
  But tis with *Poets* now, as tis with Nations,
  Th'il-fauouredst *Vices*, are the brauest *Fashions.*
A Play whose *Rudenes*, *Indians* would abhorre,
Ift fill a house with Fishwiues, *Rare, They All Roare.*
It is not Praise is sought for (Now) but *Pence*,
Tho dropd, from Greasie-apron *Audience.*          20
Clapd may he bee with *Thunder*, that plucks *Bayes*,
With such *Foule Hands*, and with *Squint-Eyes* does gaze
On *Pallas Shield*; not caring (so hee *Gaines*,
A Cramd *Third-Day*,) what *Filth* drops from his *Braines.*
Let *Those* that loue *Pans pipe*, daunce still to *Pan*,
They shall but get *long Eares* by it: Giue me *That Man*,
Who when the *Plague* of an Impostumd *Braynes*
(*Breaking*-out) infects a *Theater*, and hotly raignes,
Killing the *Hearers* hearts, that the vast roomes
Stand empty, like so many Dead-mens toombes,          30
Can call the *Banishd* Auditor home, And tye
His Eare (with golden chaines) to his Melody:
Can draw with *Adamantine Pen*, (euen creatures

Forg'de out of th'*Hammer*,) on tiptoe, to *Reach*-vp,
And (from *Rare silence*) clap their *Brawny hands*,
T'*Applaud*, what their *charmd* soule scarce vnderstands.
That Man giue mee; whose Brest fill'd by the *Muses*,
With Raptures, Into a second, them infuses:
Can giue an Actor, Sorrow, Rage, Ioy, Passion,
Whilst hee againe (by selfe-same Agitation)                           40
    Commands the *Hearers*, sometimes drawing out *Teares*,
    Then smiles, and fills them both with *Hopes* and *Feares*.
That Man giue mee: And to bee such-a-*One*,
Our *Poet* (this day) striues, or to bee *None*:
Lend not (*Him*) hands for *Pittie*, but for *Merit*,
If he *Please*, hee's *Crownd*, if *Not*, his *Fate* must beare it.

## *If This be not a Good Play, the Diuell is in It.*

### [ACT I, SCENE i]

*Enter (at the sound of hellish musick,) Pluto, and Charon.*

*Pluto.*   Ha!
*Char.*         So.
*Pluto.*             What so.
*Char.*                   Ile be thy slaue no longer.
*Pluto.*   What slaue?
*Char.*                   Hels drudge, her Gally-slaue. I ha' wore,
My flesh toth' bones, bones marrowles, at the *Oaer*
Tugging to waft to'thy Stygian empire, Soules,
Which (but for *Charon*) neuer had come in Sholes,
Yet (swarmde they nere so,) them on shore I set,
Hell gets by *Charon*, what does *Charon* get?
*Pluto.*   His Fare.
*Char.*                   Scuruy fare, ile first cry garlick.
*Pluto.*                                   Doe:
And make hel stinck, as that does hither.
*Char.*                             If I doe!
Some like that smell! my boate to shore ile pull;                    10
Not worke a stroake more.
*Pluto.*                   How?
*Char.*                             Not touch a Scull.
*Pluto.*   Why?
*Char.*         I ha' no doings: Graues-end-barge has more,
And caries as good as any are in hell;
I feare th'infernall riuers are frozen or'e
So few by water come: els the whores that dwell
Next dore to hell, goe about: besides, tis thought,
That men to find hell, now, new waies haue sought,
As Spaniards did to the *Indies*. *Pluto*, mend
My wages, or row thy selfe.

*Pluto.*                    Vgly, grumbling slaue,                     20
Haue I not raisde thy price? yet still do'st craue?
Such bold braue beggers (heard off ner'e before)
Are thy fares now, they teach thee to beg more.
Thy fare was (first) a halfe-peny, then the soules gaue thee
A peny, then three-halfe-pence, we shall haue thee
(As market-folkes in dearth,) so damned-deere,
Men will not come to hell, crying out th'are heere
Worse rackt then th'are in tauernes: why doest howle?
*Char.*   For mony: Ile haue two pence for each soule
I ferry ouer; Im'e old, craz'd, Stiffe, and lam'de,
That soule thats not worth two pence wou'ld twere damb'd.      30
*Pluto.*   Thou shalt not.
*Char.*                    I will haue it, or lye still,
If *Charon* fill hell, hell shall *Charon* fill:
For Ghosts now come not thronging to my boate,
But drop by one and one in; none of note
Are fares now: I had wont braue fellowes to ply,
Who, (hack't and mangled) did in battailes dye.
But now these gallants which doe walke hells Rowndes,
Are fuller of diseases, than of woundes.
If wounded any take my boate, they roare,
Being stabd, either drunke, or slaine about some whore.      40
Thats all the fight now.
*Prod.*                *Charon.*              *Within* [*Prodigal*].
*Pluto.*                    Get thee gon:
Th'at call'd for.
*Prod.*          *Charon.*
*Char.*                    Ball not. Ile come anon.
Hagges of hell gnaw thee with their fowle furd-gummes.
*Pluto,* no wonder if so few hither comes?
*Pluto.*   Why?
*Char.*   Gingerly: See See,

25 in dearth] on darth Q                    27 rackt] racke Q
27 howle?] howle for mony? Q [*see* N & Q IX (1962), 334]
42 Th'at] That Q(u); Thart Q(c)
44 *Pluto*] *Plu:* Pluto Q [*indented with speech-prefix*]
45 *Pluto.*] *Cha.* Q                    46 *Char.*] *om.* Q

One of thine owne promooters, (with hawkes eyes,
That should for prey be watching) here snoring lyes.
*Pluto.*   With a mischife! cabind! a fury.
*Char.*                                    Ile Ferret out more.

Ruffman *comes vp, Furie Enters.*

Another: looke: dancing a bawde on's knee.                                    50

*Enter* Shackle-soule *comes vp.*

*Shac.*   I doe enquire if rich bawdes Carted bee
On earth as well as poore ones: I sleepe not *Pluto.*
*Pluto.*   Twist stronger-knotted whips, Ile wake you (slaues!)

Lurchall *and another Spirit comes vp.*

*Char.*   Two of thy Sumners dead-drunke here too.
*Lurch.*                                    Thou lyest.
*Prod.*   *Charon.*                           [*Within.*]
*Char.*        I come: If I must worke, let these
Thy Prentices, plye their occupation,
T'vphold hells Kingdome, more must worke then one.        *Exit.*
*Pluto.*   Ha; Are there whipping-posts for such as dwell
In Idlenes on Earth, and yet shall Hell
(As if wee tooke bribes here too,) let such passe!                          60
Ile haue you tawde: Is not the world as t'was?
Once mother of Rapes, Incests, and Sodomies,
Atheisme, and Blasphemies, plump Boyes indeed,
That suck'd (our Dams brest) is shee now barren? Ha!
Is there a dearth of villaines?
*Omn.*                          More now then euer?
*Pluto.*   Is there such penurie of man-kinde, Hell-houndes?
You can lye snoring.
*Ruf.*                    Each Land is full of Rake-hells.
*Shac.*   But sholes of Sharkes eate vp the Fish at Sea.
*Lurch.*   Braue pitchy villaines there.

50 Another] *Cha.* Another Q
53 S.D. Lurchall *and*...] Q *places below* '*Charon.*' *in line* 55
55 *Prod.*] *om.* Q

125

*Pluto.*                                   Yet you playing here.
*Omn.*   No, No; most awefull *Pluto.*                        70
*Pluto.*   Were you good Hell-hounds, euery day should bee
A *Symon*-and-*Iude*, to crowne our bord with Feasts
Of blacke-eyde-soules each minute: were you honest diuels
Each officer in hell should haue at least,
A brace of whores to his break-fast: aboue vs dwell,
Diuells brauer and more subtill then in Hell.
*Omn.*   Weele fill thy pallace with them.
*Pluto.*                              Ile trye that: goe:
*Rufman,* take instantly a Courtiers shape
Of any country: choose thine owne disguize
And returne swiftly.
*Ruf.*            Yes.                          *Exit.*
*Pluto.*                   *Shackle-soule* weare thou        80
A Friers graue habit.
*Shac.*           Well.                          *Exit.*
*Pluto.*                   *Grumball* walke thou
In trebble-ruffes like a Merchant.
*Lur.*                      So: tis don.         *Exit.*
*Pluto.*   The barres of our latigious Courts had wont
To crack with thronging pleaders, whose lowde din
Shooke the infernall hell, as if't had bin
An earth-quake bursting from the deepe Abisse,
Or els *Ioues* thunder, throwne at the head of *Dis*
(The God of gold,) for hiding it below,
Thereby to tempt churles hither. Nor did we know
What a Vacation ment: continuall terme            90
Fattend hels Lawyers, and shall so againe.

*Enter* Rufman, Shackle-soule *and* Lurchall [*in different shapes*].

*Ruf.*  Here.
*Shac.*        Here.
*Lurch.*            Command vs.
*Pluto.*                   Fly into the world:
As y'are in shapes transformde be so in name,

*73 Of] A Q                81 *Grumball*] *Grumshall* Q

126

For men are out-sides onely: be you the same;
Hye thee to *Naples*, (*Rufman*), thou shalt finde
A Prince there (newly crownde,) aptly inclinde
To any bendings; least his youthfull browes
Reach at Stars only, wey down his loftiest boughes
With leaden plomets, poison his best thoughts with tast
Of things most sensuall; if the heart once wast                100
The body feeles consumption; good or bad kings
Breede Subiects like them: cleere streames flow from cleere springs.
Turne therefore *Naples* to a puddle: with a ciuill
Much promising face, and well oylde, play the court diuell.
*Ruf.*  Ile doo't in brauery: if as deepe as hell,
Thy large eares heare a Land curse me, my part's playd well.
*Pluto.*  Fly *Shackle-soule.*
*Shac.*                    Whither?
*Pluto.*                         To the Friery,
Best-famde in *Naples* for strict orders: throw
What nets thou seest can catch them: Amongst 'em sow
Seedes of contention, or what euer sin                         110
They most abhor, sweate thou to bring that in.
*Shac.*  A wolfe in lambe-skin leapes into the rout,
Bell, booke, or candle cannot curse me out:
Ile curse faster than they.
*Pluto.*                  Doe: *Grumball.*
*Lurch.*                              Here.
*Pluto.*  Be thou a cittie-diuell, make thy hands
Of Harpyes clawes, which being on courtiers lands
Once fastend, ne're let loose, the Merchant play,
And on the Burse, see thou thy flag display
Of politicke banck-ruptisme: traine vp as many
To fight vnder it, as thou canst, for now's not any            120
That breake, (theile breake their necks first). If, beside
Thou canst not through the whole citie meete with pride,
Riot, lechery, enuy, Auarice, and such stuffe,
Bring 'em all-in coach'd, the gates are wide enough.
The spirit of gold instruct thee: hence all.
*Omn.*                              Fly.

*Pluto.*   Stay, least you should want helper, at your calling
Any diuels shall come, (*Starch-hound, Tobacco-spawling,*
*Vpshotten, Suckland, Glitterbacke,*) or any
Whom you shall neede to imploy, but call not many,
The'rs but few good in hell. And stay, remember          130
We all meete to heare how you prosper.
*Omn.*                              Where?
*Pluto.*                                   The Tree
Blasted with Goblins, that about whose roote
Fiue Mandrakes growe, i'th Groue by *Naples* there,
Meete there.
*Omn.*       Wee shall.
*Pluto.*                Our blessings with you beare.
*Ruf.*   Dread king of Ghosts, weele plye our thrift so well,
Thou shalt be forc'd to enlarge thy Iayle of Hell.
*Pluto.*   Be quicke th'at best, let sawcy mortals know,
How ere they sleepe, there's one wakes here below.

                                        *Exeunt.*


# [ACT I, SCENE ii]

¶ *Enter* Alphonso (*King of* Naples) *Crownde, wearing Robes*
*Imperiall, Swordes of State, Maces, &c. being borne before him, by*
Octauio, Astolfo (*two vnckles*), Narcisso, Iouinelli, Brisco (*Counts*),
*with others, Counte* Spendola *meeting them.*

*Spend.*   One of those gallant Troupes went forth to meete
Your admirde Mistris (*Erminhild* the faire)
Hath left your Conuoy with her on the way.
*King.*   And brings glad newes of her being here (this day)
Let Canons tell in Thunder her Arriuall,
When shee's at hand our selfe will meete her.
*Omn.*                              On.        *Flourish.*

126 helper,] Q(u); helpers ∧ Q(c)
6 *Flourish.*] Q *places as start of line* 6 *before* 'When'

128

*Hee takes his Seate; All kneele.*

*King.*    Pray rise; vntill about our browes were throwne,
These sparkling beames, such adoration
Was not bestowde on vs: whom does the knee
Thus lowely worship? this Idoll, (Gold) or mee?                    10
Indeed t'is the worlds *Saynt*, if that you adore,
Goe, pray to your coffers. None to vs shall bow,
Giue God your knees.
*Oct.*                    Whose owne voice does allow
That Subiects should to those who are *Supreme*,
Bend, as to God, (all Kings being like to him.)
*Ast.*    Thou wonder of thy time, Ile pay no more
To thee of dutie than has bene before
And euer shall be payd to those sit Hye.
*King.*    Pray mocke not mee with such Idolatry,
Kings, Gods are, (I confesse) but Gods of clay,                    20
Brittle as you are, you as good as they,
Onely in weight they differ, (this poore dram)
Yet all but flesh and bloud; And such I am.
If such, pray let mee eate, drinke, speake, and walke,
Not look'd cleane through, with superstitious eyes,
(Not star'de at like a Comete.) As you goe
Or speake, or feede, (vn-wondered at) let mee so.
*Oct.*    Not Kings of Ceremonie.
*King.*                    Vncle what then?
Still are they Kings.
*Oct.*                    But shew like common men.
*King.*    Good vncle know, no Sunne in this our Spheare,            30
Shall rule but Wee, let others shine as cleare,
In goodnes, None in greatnes shall.
*Ast.*                    Blest raigne!
The Golden worlde is molding new againe.
*King.*    All that I craue is this, and tis not newe,
Pay vnto *Cæsar* onely *Cæsars* due.

10 lowely] louely Q [*see* II.i.158, V.iv.69]
27 mee so] Q(u); mee be so Q(c)

*Oct.* We owe thee loyall hearts, and those weele pay,
Each minute (Mirrour of Kings.)
*Iouin.* Marke, the olde Lords promise their hearts, but no money.
*Oct.* Here are the Names of bold conspirators,
(Yong *Catilines*, and farre more desperate)  40
Who in your Fathers dayes kindled the fires
Of hote Rebellion.
*King.*                    Which are now burnt out.
*Oct.* Who knowes that? embers in dead Ashes lye.
King, Set thy hand to this, let Traytors dye.
*Ast.* Tis fit you should doe so.
*Oct.*                              Sound Pollicie.
*King.* Men many things hold fit, that are not good,
A yong Beginner and set vp in blood!
(Butchers can doe no more.) Shall Recordes say
Being Crownde, he playd the Tyran the first day,
How should that Chronicler be curs'd? your paper.  50
When such a fatall booke comes in my sight,
Ile with *Vespasian* wish I could not write,
Their bond is canceld. I forgiue the debt,
See that at liberty, they all be set.
*Omn.* A Princely Act.
*Oct.*                  If wisely tis well done.
*Spend.* That raigne must bost, which mercy has begun.
*King.* Beare witnes all, what pace the Chariot wheeles
Of our new gilded Soueraigntie shall run.
*Bris.* A mayne gallop I hope.
*King.* And here I vow to end as tis begun.  60
*Ast.* Heauen fill thee full of dayes, but (being all told)
Ending no worse, their summe weele write in gold.
*Oct.* The course youle take deere Lord.
*King.*                              This: pray obserue it.
*Iouin.* Call you this Coronation day? woud I were ith streetes
where the conduites run claret wine, there's some good fellowship
*Oct.* Peace.
*King.* Each weeke within the yeere shall be a booke

59 *Bris.*] *Rus.* Q

130

Which each day ile reade or'e: I well may doe't,
The booke being but six leaues (six dayes,) the seuenth
Be his that owes it; sacred is that and hye;                    70
And who prophanes one houre in that, shall dye.
*Spend.* How manie wilbe left aliue then this day fortnight?
*Oct.* First, beate all Tauernes downe then, Soules are lost
(Being drownde in Surfets) on that seuenth day most.
Stay (best of Kings) mine owne hand shall set downe
What lawes thou mad'st first day thou wor'st a Crowne.
Begin, begin thy weeke.
*King.* Write Monday.
*Oct.* So so,—Monday.
*Iouin.* They say Monday's Shooemakers holliday, Ile fall to that 80
trade.
*Oct.* I haue writ it downe my liege.
*Iouin.* Peace, harken to your lesson.
*King.* That day, from morne till night, Ile execute
The office of a Iudge, and wey out lawes
With euen scales.
*Iouin.* Thats more than grocers doe.
*King.* The poore and rich mans cause
Ile poize alike: It shall be my chiefe care
That bribes and wrangling be pitch'd o're the barre.                90
*Iouin.* We shall haue old breaking of neckes then.
*King.* Downe with that first.
*Oct.*                              O for a pen of gold!
Youle haue no bribes.
*King.*                    None.
*Oct.*                              Yet terme-time all the yeere!
A good strong law-suite cannot now cost deere.
*King.* Haue you done?
*Oct.* I'me at bribes and wrangling, done presently.
*Narc.* We must all turne pettifoggers, and in stead of gilt rapiers,
hang buckram bags at our girdles.
*Iouin.* All my clients, shalbe women.
*Spend.* Why?                                                      100

*Iouin.* Because they are easiest fetched ouer: there's something to
be gotten out of them.

*Oct.* Thy monday's taske is done: whats next?

*Iouin.* Sunday if the weeke goes backward.

*King.* Tuesdayes weel'e sit to heare the poore-mans cryes,
Orphans and widowes: our owne princely eyes
Shall their petitions reade: our progresse then
Shalbe to hospitalls which good minded men
Haue built to pious vse, for lame, sicke, and poore
Weele see whats giuen, what spent, and what flowes or'e:          110
Churles (with Gods mony) shall not feast, swill wine,
And fat their rancke gutts whilest poore wretches pine.

*Iouin.* This is a braue world for beggers, if it hold.

*Oct.* Poore wretches pine, So are they left: tot'h next.

*King.* Wednesdaies weele spend—

*Iouin.* In fish dinners.

*King.*          In th'affaires
Of forren states, treate with embassadors,
Heare them and giue them answeres. Thursday, for warres.

*Iouin.* That's well: better be together byth' eares, then to goe     120
halting to hospitalls.

*King.* Our Neapolitane youths (that day) shall try
Their skill in armes, poore scorned Soldiers
Shall not be suffer'd beg here (as in some landes)
Nor stoope slaue-like to Captaines proud commands,
Starue, and lie nastie, when the selfe-same pay,
The Souldier fights for, keepes the Leaders gay.
Nor shall he through ice and fire make gray his head,
Weare out new Moones, onely to earne his bread,
Wade vp to'th beard in torrents; and be drownd          130
All saue the head; march hard to meete a wound,
I'th very face, and euen his heart-strings cracke,
To win a towne, yet not to cloath his backe:
And the blacke storme of troubles being gon,
Shund like a creditor, not looked vpon,
But as court-pallats (when bright day drawes nye)
Rold vp in some darke corner is throwne by.

Vncle write that.
*Oct.*                    Fast as my pen can trot.
*Spend.*    What a number of tottred roagues wilbe turn'd into braue
fellowes a this new change of the moone.                            140
*Iouin.*    The brauer they are, the sooner are mercers vndon.
*Oct.*    Souldiers are downe too.
*King.*                        Downe with Learning next.
For friday shalbe spent it'h reuerend Schooles,
Where weele sift branne from floure, (hisse babling fooles,
But crowne the deepe-braind disputant) none shall hold
Three or foure Church-liuings (got by *Symonious* gold)
In them, to fat himselfe as in a stye,
When greater Schollers languish in beggery:
And in thin thred-bare cassacks weare out their age,
And bury their worth in some by vicorage:                          150
This weele see mended.
*Iouin.*    Tyth pigges youl'e smoake for this.
*King.*    So set it downe.
*Oct.*    Schollers languish in beggery—So:
Thy fridaies law is writ; for Satterday, what?
*King.*    I mary sir, All our cares now for that.
Well to begin, and not end so were base,
The winning of the gole crownes each mans race.

Narcisso *stepping in before in the Scene, Enters here.*

*Narc.*    Sir, theres a stranger newly ariu'de your court,
And much importunes to behold your Highnes.                        160
*King.*    What is he?
*Narc.*                    Of goodly presence.
*King.*                                Let him see vs.

Rufman [*as Bohor*] *brought in by all.*

*Ruf.*    The powers that guide me, guard thee, I haue heard thy name
In regions far hence, where it does resound
Lowder than here at home; to touch this ground
I ha pass'd through countries, into which none here

    151 mended.] *below this line Q prints the direction, 'Enter Iouenella.'*

Would willingly saile I thinke, and with me bring,
My loue and seruice, which to your grace I tender.
*King.*    What are you, and whence come you?
*Ruf.*                              From *Heluetia.*
*Spend.*    What hell sayes hee?
*Iouin.*    Peace you shall know hot hell time enough.                170
*Ruf.*    I am an Heluetian borne, the house from which
I am descended, ancient and well knowne
To many princes: *Bohor* is my name.
*Iouin.*    Zounds! *Bohor!* h'as struck two of my teeth out with his
name.
*Ruf.*    A Shalcan Tartar being my grandfather
Men call me *Shalkan Bohor.* About the world
My trauailes make a girdle (perfect round:)
So that, what wonders Kings on earth euer found
I know, and what I know, Is yours.
*King.*                              Braue Heluetian,                180
We giue you thankes and welcome: your arriuall
Is faire and to our wish, of all those dayes
Which Time sets downe, to number vp a weeke,
Euery day haue we tasked, saue only one;
How in these courts of Kings (through which you haue gon,)
Doe Princes wast their howres?
*Ruf.*                              How but in that,
For which they are borne Kings? (Pleasure:) euery mans ayme,
Is to hit pleasure: onely tis changde in name,
Thats all the difference; Are Kings Tirants? Blood
Is then their pleasure: thirst they after warres!                190
Ambition tickles them: that for which man most cares,
Good or bad, tis his pleasure, and to gaine it,
His soule must compasse it, tho hell restraine it:
To this marke all mens thoughts, Creation drew,
That all might striue for a thing, thats got by fewe:
Who are those few but Kings? and tis fit they
Should haue it, because true pleasure does soone decay.
*King.*    How like you his counsell?
*Omn.*                              Rarely.

*Oct.*                                    What ruffians this?

*King.*   *Bohor* tha'st warm'd our yong blood; Al cares of state,
Shall that day sleepe, to our selfe weele Saturday haue,        200
Pleasure (the slaue of Kings) shall then be our slaue,
Lords let there be a proclamation drawne,
What man soeuer (strange or natiue borne,)
Can feast our spleene, and heigthen our delight,
He shall haue gold and be our fauorite.
Tilts, turneys, masques, playes, dauncing, drinking deepe
Tho ere noone all *Naples* lye dead-drunke a sleepe.

*Oct.*   How King?

*King.*   Weele haue it so vncle.

*Omn.*   Downe with that too.        210

*Iouin.*   Print Satterday in great text letters.

*Oct.*   Well, well, it shall.
Our swan turnes crow, poisond with one drop of gall.

*King.*   Ile haue this proclamation forthwith drawne.

*Narc.*   And publish al the daies.

*Bris.*   And Satterday.

*Iouin.*   Especially that at large if you can in red, like a Dominicall
letter.

*King.*   Goe see it don.

*Iouin.*   My taske.                                    *Exit.* 220

*King.*   Why sigh you? Of six dayes wo'd you not spare me one?

*Oct.*   Thine owne lawes from thine owne mouth, weele proclaime,
If thine owne words thou eat'st, bee't thine owne shame.

*Enter* Iouinelli *hastily.*

*Iouin.*   Your long expected happines is arriu'd,
The princesse of *Calabria.*

*King.*                      Thou crown'st me agen:
Deere vncle, honored Lords, with our whole court
Honor her hither; I am rapd with Ioy,
And lost till I behold her: fetch me my loue.

*Oct.*   I feare deepe whirlepooles tho it run smooth aboue.

*King.*   To our worthy friend your welcomes.        230

*Exeunt* Octauio *and* Astolpho.

135

*Iouin.* But pray Sir tell vs, meane you that we indeed
Shall haue but one playing day through the whole weeke?
*King.* All *Iouinelli,* weele be Iouiall all.
*Bris.* Till Satterday came, we liu'de in terrible feare.
Thanke *Bohor,* who your dead spirits vp did reare.
*King.* Had I (as first I did begin) gon on,
I like a Schoole-boy should haue worne my crowne,
As if I had borrowed it.
*Ruf.*                           Had bin most vile.
*King.* Ile be a Sea, (boundles.)
*Spend.*                           Thou art a sunne,
And let no base cloudes muffle thee.
*King.*                           Braue Kings all!          240
Crowne, Scepter, Court, Cittie, Country, are at your call.
*Iouin.* There spake young *Ioue* indeede.
*Bris.*                           The tyde now turnes.
*Narc.* And now weele swim.
*King.*                   And laugh, tho the whole world mournes.
*Omn.* Tantara, hey.

> *Florish. Trumpets.* Erminghild *brought in.*

> *Enter* Octauio *and* Astolpho, *vshering* Erminhild,
> *attended by Ladies and others.*

*Narc.* Call vp your lustiest spirits: the Lady's come.
*King.* O my earthly blisse! embraces! kisses! how sweete
Are you to parted Louers when they meete?
That entertainement which the Duke your Father,
Lent royellie (late to mee,) I now can pay
At a Kings charge: to our Neapolitane Court,          250
None (brightest *Erminhild*) can come longd for
More then your selfe. You haue stolne vpon vs (Ladie.)
*Erm.* You haue good Law against me, (playing the thiefe)
Your Grace may keepe mee prisoner.
*King.*                           In these Armes;

244 Tantara, hey.] *Tantara, hey.* Q
244 S.D. *Florish.*] Q *prints to left of speech-prefix;* '*Tꝛupets.* Erminghild *brought in.*'
*is printed to the right on line* 244.

From whence not *Ioue* shall raunsome thee; We Twaine
Will wed, and bed, and get a Prince shall raigne
In *Naples* brauely, when wee both lye dead:
Till then, Pleasures wings, to their full bredth be spread.

*Exeunt.*

## [ACT I, Scene iii]

*Enter* Scumbroth, *ringing a Bell*; Alphege, *a Fryer, and*
Shackle-soule, *in a Friers weede* [*as Frier* Rush], *with cloth to lay.*

*Scum.*   A mangier, a mangier, a mangier, I must needs haue a
mangie voice, when I doe nothing but ball for a company of
hungry Scabs; a mangier.
*Alph.*  You must be nimble *Rush.*
*Shac.*   As a drawer in a new Tauern, first day the bush is hung vp.
*Scum.*   A mangier, a manger, a mangier.                      *Exit.*
*Alph.*  So: the Lord Priors napkin here, there the Subpriors: his
knife and case of pick-toothes thus: as for the couent, let them
licke their fingers in stead of wiping, and suck their teeth in steede
of picking.                                                          10
*Shac.*  What other dutie Sir, must I call mine?
*Alph.*  As you are nouice, you are to say grace demurely, waite on
the Priors Trencher soberly, steale away a mouthfull cunningly,
and munch it vp in a corner hungerly. Ply your office, *Rush.*

*Exit.*

*Shac.*  Thankes good Frier *Alphege*: yes, *Shackle-soule* will play
The taske hee's set to: Diuels neuer idle lye:
Frier *Rush*! ha, ha: y'haue now an excellent quire,
To sing in hell, the Diuell and the Frier.

*Enter Prior, Subprior,* Alphege, Hillary, *and other Friers.*
*All sit: dishes brought in before.*

*Prior.*   Where's *Rush,* our *Iunior Nouice?*
*Shac.*                                      Here Lord Prior.
*Prior.*   Stand foorth, and render thankes.

18 S.D. Hillary, *and*] Hillary, Rush, *and* Q      19, 20 *Shac.*] *Ru.* Q

*Shac.*                                          Hum, hum:               20
For our bread, wine, ale and beere,
For the piping hot meates heere:
For brothes of sundrie tasts and sort,
For beefe, veale, mutton, lamb, and porke.
Greene-sawce with calfes head and bacon,
Pig and goose, and cramd-vp capon.
For past raiz'd stiffe with curious art,
Pye, custard, florentine and tart.
Bak'd rumpes, fried kidneys, and lam-stones,
Fat sweete-breads, luscious maribones,               30
Artichoke, and oyster-pyes,
Butterd Crab, prawnes, lobsters thighes,
Thankes be giuen for flesh and fishes,
With this choice of tempting dishes:
To which preface: with blythe lookes sit yee,
*Rush* bids this Couent, much good do't yee.
*Prior.*  How dar'st thou mock vs thou ill nurtur'd slaue?
*Sub.*  Contemn'st thou our order and religious fare?
*Scum.*  He has spoken treason to all our stomaches.
*Omn.*  Downe with the villaine.
*Sub.*                            Mischiefe on vs waites       40
If wee feede so vile a wretch.
*Prior.*                          Thrust him out at gates.
*Shac.*  I doe coniure you by my hallowed beades
To heare me speake.
*Prior.*                        Canst thou excuse thy selfe?
*Shac.*  Alas (my Lord) I thought it had bin here
As in the neighbouring Churches, where the poor'st Vicar
Is filled vp to the chin with choice of meates,
Yet seekes new wayes to whet dull appetite,
As there with holy spels mens soules they cherish,
So with delitious fare, they themselues nourish.
Nor want they argument for sweete belly-cheere       50
To proue it lawfull.

36 *Rush* bids] *Rush.* Bids [*treated as speech-prefix*] Q
39 *Scum.*] *Shac.* Q

138

*Sub.*                Most prophane and fearefull.

*Shac.*  But since your order (pious and reuerend)
Tyed to religious fasts, spends the sad day
Wholy in meager contemplation,
I absolution beg on both my knees,
For what my tongue offended in: las! poore *Rush*
(See't by his cheekes) eates little: I can feede
On rootes, and drinke the water of the Spring
Out of mine owne cup: make an Anatomy
Of my most sinfull carcas: then pardon mee.                    60

*Prior.*  Thy ignorance is thy pardon, wee beleeue thee.

*Shac.*  *Gratias reuerende domine Prior.*

*Prior.*  But do our brethren in parts more remote,
Feede so delitious saist thou?

*Shac.*                *Rush* cannot lye.

*Sub.*  Thou falsely doest accuse those holy men.

*Prior.*  How can it stand with their profession?

*Sub.*  Thou saist (vile yongman) they haue arguments
To proue it lawfull gluttonously to feede.

*Omn.*  *Rush,* answere the Sub-prior.

*Shac.*  *Audite fratres,* they doe not onely proue it lawfull, but make 70
it palpable, that hee who eates not good meate is damde.

*Sub.*  *Benedicite.*

*Scum.*  What shall become of all vs then?

*Prior.*  Thou art distracted, whence canst thou force argument?

*Shac.*  From sillie reason, would you heare me speake?

*Prior.*  Speake freely and be bold, listen.

*Omn.*  Hum, hum, hum.

*Shac.*  He that eats not good meate is dambd: *Sic Disputo.*
If he that feedes well hath a good soule, then *è Contra*
No, he that feedes ill, hath a bad and a poore soule.            80

*Scum.*  Thats wee.

*Shac.*  And so consequently is dambd, for who regards poore
soules? and if they be not regarded they are cast foorth, and if cast
foorth, then they are dambde.

*Sub.*  I deny your minor, he that feedes well hath a good soule.

*Shac.*   *Sic probo*: the soule followes the temperature of the body,
hee that feedes well hath a good temperature of body, *Ergo*, he
that feedes well hath a good soule.

*Prior.*   A ful and edyfying argument.

*Omn.*   Hum, hum, hum.                                                        90

*Sub.*   I deny that the soule followes the temperature of the body.

*Shac.*   *Anima sequitur temperaturam Corporis*, It is a principle, *et
contra principia non est disputandum*.

*Scum.*   All wee.

*Prior.*   Its most apparent.

*Scum.*   O most learned *Rush*!

*Sub.*   A shallow Sophister, heare me farder.

*Prior.*                                       Subprior,
Weele heare the rest disputed at our leisure:
You take too much vpon you.

*Scum.*   Shall I take this vpon me my Lord?                                  100

*Prior.*   Hence with this trash, we haue too long forborne
To tast heauens blessings fully, which to our dutie
Had more enabled vs, *Rush* thart some Angel.

*Sub.*   Rather some diuell sent to bewitch our soules.

*Prior.*   Sub-prior no more.

*Sub.*                           I must speake, heare me brethren,
Shall we (bound by solemne oathes) t'abiure the world,
And all her sorceries? to whom night and day
Are as one hower of prayer? whose temperance makes vs
Endure what ful-fild bellie Gods admire;
Shall we (by zealous patrons) tyde to obserue                                 110
*Dirges* and *Requiems* for their peacefull soules,
In glottonous riot bury sacred almes!
Turne Sanctimonious zeale and Charitie
To loathsome surfet? and those well-got goods
Our benefactors sau'd, by their owne fasts
And moderate liuing, shall we feede vpon
Ful-gorging vs till we vomit? fore-fend it heauen!
By all the Saints, by him first taught our order

94 *Scum.*] *om.* Q, *which prints* 'All wee.' *after a space following* '*disputandum*', *in the
line above*

What temperance was, here shall poore *Clement* feede,
Till his ore-wearied life, takes her last leaue                        120
Of this all tempting world where all sinnes breede.
*Prior.*   Howes this? are you become our confessor?
Best thrust vs out at gates, locke vp the Cloister,
And cal in whom you like: be you the Prior.
Speake are you agreed, *Rush* be our maister-cooke?
*Scum.*   You haue my voice.
*Alph.*                          And mine.
*Prior.*                                  Doe you all consent?
*Omn.*   Yes, all.
*Sub.*              First send this fiend to banishment.
*Prior.*   We haue most voices on our side.
*Sub.*                                  You may;
Las! most men couet still the broadest way.
*Prior.*   Giue *Rush* his charge then, *Scumbroath* you must resigne. 130
*Scum.*   With a good maw, I shal haue a fatter office to be his
scullion.
*Shac.*   Worthy Lord Prior, heare me yet,
I must not my profession let,
To *Scumbroath*, what I know ile teach,
To make caudels, Iellies, leach,
Sirrup of violets, and of roses,
Cowslip sallads, and kick-choses,
Preserue the apricock, and cherry,
Damsin-peare-plom, raspis berry;                                      140
Potates eke if you shall lack,
To corroborate the back:
A hundred more shall *Rush* deuise,
And yet to early mattins rise,
Our ladies office, sing at prime,
At euen-song, and at compline time.
Chant Anthems, Aniuersaries, Dirges,
And the dolefull *de profundis.*
*Prior.*   Thou shalt not change thy order: Sirra, cooke,

*130 *Scumbroath*] *Scumb:* Q

141

From *Rush* take lessons against night, for fare                    150
Abundant and delitious.

*Scum.*   I shall be greedy to learne of him sir, since your lordship is
turnde, our very Iack and his spits shall turne too.     *Exit.*

*Enter two Pilgrimes.*

*Prior.*   What men are these?
*Sub.*   Welcome good holy fathers.
*Both.*   Thankes reuerend maister.
1. *Pilg.*   Blest sir, according to the Churches rite
We (Pilgrimes, to *Ierusalem* bound) this night
Desire repose, and pious charitie
In your most holy Couent.
*Prior.*           You are most welcome.                 160
  *Alphege,* goe lead 'em in.
*Shac.*          By no meanes.
*Prior.*             Why?
*Shac.*   Tis mortall sin.
*Sub.*          O black impietie!
*Prior.*   How? sin to feed religious votaries!
*Shac.*   Rather to nourish idle vagabonds:
The Cleargy of other lands, haue with much pietie
And thrift destroyde those drones, that lazily
Liue eating vp the labours of the bee.
A churchman there cares but to feede the soule,
He makes that charge his office. Almisdeeds! alas!
They through the Lawyers hands are fitt'st to passe.        170
*Sub.*   Can you heare this Diuell?
*Shac.*          Besides my reuerend Lord,
These manderers here are spies, and soone beare word
To Princes eares of what they heare and see.
*Prior.*   Ha *Rush!* thou speak'st right.
*Sub.*          Dambd iniquitie!
*Prior.*   Hence with those runnagates.
*Omn.*          Come, hence.

151 Abundant] Abundance Q       155 fathers] father Q
*172 are] Q (c); as Q (u)

*Prior.*                                          Spurne 'em away.
*Sub.* Oh had mine eyes drop'd out ere seene this day.
Stay comfortles poore soules, my pittying teares
Shall speake what my tongue dares not, here holy men,
You nere shall say when next we meete againe,
Frier *Clement* to the hungrie grutch'd his meate,            180
Or to the weary pilgrim lodging, this makes you eate,
And when you haue relieu'd your fainting limbes,
Commend me in your prayers, and midst your hymmes
Thus wish, that he who did your Iorney furder,
May neuer liue, to breake his holy order.
*Prior.* Old superstitious dotard; beate hence these beggers.
1. *Pilg.* Many old mens curses will on his soule be spent,
Who thus defaces, Charities monument.                    *Exeunt*
*Shac.* I told you they were curs, that cease to barke,
No longer then you feede them.
*Prior.*                              Frier, thou speak'st right:      190
Make hast with fare delitious, weele crowne the night.
                         *Exeunt. Manet* Shackle-soule.
*Shac.* Ha ha, laugh *Lucifer*, dance grim fiends of hell,
Of soules thou iudge iust, but most terrible,
I must exact a double pay from thee,
Nere hadst thou Iorneyman deserude such fee,
Let me cast vp my reckonings, what I ha won
In this first voiage: Charity! shees vndon:
Fat gluttony broke her back: next her step'd in
Contention (who shakes Churches) now the sweete sin
(Sallow lechery,) should march after: Auarice,          200
Murder, and all sinnes els, hell can deuice,
Ile broach: the head's in, draw the body after,
Begin thy feast in full cuppes, end in slaughter.
Th'at damnedst fury: oh, but Frier *Clement's* free!
True: ha'st no snare t'intrap him? let me see.
Hees old, choake him with gold; hold on thy Reuells,
*Pluto makes Shackle-soule president of Diuels.*

                                                *Exit.*

        193 iust] Q(u); must Q(c)          204 Th'at] That Q

## [ACT II, SCENE i]

*Enter King,* Octauio, Narcisso, Iouinelli, Spendola.

*King.*  What pictur's that (Vncle *Octauio?*)
*Oct.*  The picture of thy state, (drawne by thy selfe,)
This is that booke of statutes, were enacted
In the high Parliament of thy roiall thoughts
Where wisedome was the speaker.  And because
Thy subiects shall not be abusde by lawes
Wrap'd vp in caracters, crabbed and vnknowne,
These thine owne language speake.
*King.*                              Hang 'em vp vncle.
*Oct.*  What sayes the King?
*Iouin.*                              You must hang vp the lawes.
*Oct.*  Like cob-webbe in fowle roomes, through which great flies 10
Breake through, the lesse being caught bith wing, there dies.
No no, thy lawes ile fix full in thy sight,        *Hangs a table vp.*
(Like sea-markes,) that if this great ship of sway
And kingly ventures, loose her constant way,
Ith bottomles gulph of state, (beaten by the stormes
Of youthfull follie, raging in monstrous formes)
Shee may be sau'de from sinking and from wrack,
(Steerd by this compasse,) for the points of it
Shall guide her so, on rockes she cannot split.
*King.*  You are our carefull pilot. In this voiage                    20
Of Gouernment, be you our Admirall.
Wisedome and Age being props, realmes seldome fall.

*Enter* Brisco

*Oct.*  Oraculous is thy voice.
*King.*                              How now count *Brisco?*
Me thinkes I read a comedy in thy lookes.
*Narc.*  H'as met some merry painter, hees drawne so liuely.
*Omn.*  Come count your newes.

20 pilot. In] pilat ‸ In Q(u); pilot ‸ in Q(c)

144

*Bris.*                       I shall bestow them freely:
The physicke of your proclamation workes:
Your guilded pills (roll'd vp in promises
Of princely fauours to his wit, who highest
Can raise your pleasures) slip so smoothly downe          30
Your Subiects throates, that all (vpon a sudden)
Are loosely giuen.
*King.*          How? loosely giuen? why count?
*Bris.*    Name but what sport, your Highnes would haue Acted,
I'me prologue toot: your court must haue more gates
To let in rufling Saterday: without (now) waites
Musicke in some ten languages: each one sweares
(By *Orpheus* fiddle-case) they will tickle your eares
If they can doo't with scraping.
*Narc.*    Theres seuen score Noise at least of english fidlers.
*Iouin.*    Seuen score! they are able to eate vp a citie in very scraps. 40
*Bris.*    Very base-viall men most of 'em: besides whole swarmes of
welsh harpes, Irish bag-pipes, Iewes trompes, and french kitts.
All these made I together play:
But their dambd catter-wralling,
Frighted me away.
*Oct.*             These sports to please
A Princes eyes?
*Bris.*             How like you then of these?
The cittie-waterbearers (trimly dight)
With yellow oaker-tankerds (pind vpright)
Like brooches in their hatts; In their fresh loues
A may-game bring, All, wearing dog-skin gloues,          50
Made not to shrinke it'h wetting.
*King.*                      Bid these poore men
Drinke well, and so be gon.
*Bris.*                      What will you haue then?
Will you see the Turners shew, brauely preparde
With colours, drumes, and gunnes (with rust halfe mar'de)
Bearing that, of which they long haue bin depriu'de.
*King.*    What ist?

39 *Narc.*] *Bri.* Q

*Bris.*        Their daring Giant, (newly reuiu'de).

*Omn.*   For *Ioues* sake lets see that.

*Oct.*                          O fie (Prince) fie!

In thy court painted monsters, they come not here,
Ride forth, thou shalt meete Giants euery where.
Me thinkes (yong Lords) your soules being new refinde        60
With beames of honor, should not be declin'de
To sports so low and vulgar: but since the King
Of birdes (the Eagle) letts you spred a wing
So neere his owne, you should put vp such game
As fits an Eagle, and pursue the same.
And not like rauens, kites, or painted Iayes
Soare high, yet light on dunghills, for stinking preyes.

*Iouin.*   Old Lord you raue.

*Narc.*                          What sports wood you deuise?

*Oct.*   Most fit for Kings. Were I (before his eyes)        70
To present obiects, they should all be rare,
Of Romane triumps, laden w'th the spoiles of warre:
Or Lions, and wilde-Boares kill'd by actiue force:
Or sea-fights: or land-battailes on foote, or horse:
Such sights as these, kindle in Kings braue fire,
And meeting spirits that dare mount, mount 'em higher,
Where apish pastimes lay our soules downe flat,
Groueling on earth, base and effemminate.

*Bris.*   I haue bowles of this bias too, for your Lordships alley.

*King.*   Trondle 'em out before him.

*Bris.*                          The wodden-leg Souldier,

Waites to present you with his show of warre.        80

*Oct.*   I mary my liege.

*Bris.*   The Scholler has his deuice, the Mariner his.

*Oct.*   These are Kings sports indeed.

*Bris.*                          Will you see these?

*King.*   Faith be it so; because weele now rather please
Our vncle than our selfe, pray fetch in these.
The rest cashere.

*Spend.*                Send the fidlers merily home.

*Bris.*   And yet pa'em scuruily! tis impossible.

*Iouin.*    And bid the water-bearers clense the citie,
Ther's many a foule thing in it.
*King.*                              Marshall 'em in.
*Oct.*    Ile fetch these worthy spirits in my selfe.                    90
*Bris.*    No, no, weele ayde you sir.
*Iouin.*                              March: and giue vs roome.

                    *Exeunt* [Octauio, Brisco, Iouinelli].
*King.*    Sdeath? if these doting gray-beards might haue their wills,
We neuer shall haue ours: let vs crosse them
As they crosse vs.
*Omn.*              How, how!
*King.*                              Euery deuice
Their Ningles bring in, abuse with scuruie iest,
Beet nee're so good.
*Omn.*    Agreed.
*Narc.*    If *Ninies*, bring away the Nest.
*King.*    Teach *Iouinelli* and *Brisco* when to giue fire.

            *Dromes and trompets sounding,*

        *Enter* Octauio, Iouinelli, Brisco, Rufman,
            *the Souldier, Scholler, Mariner.*

*Sold.*    I am a Souldier.                                              100
*Iouin.*    We know that by your legges.
*Sold.*    Does my stump grieue you?
*Bris.*    Not if you bestir your stumps nimbly sir.
*Narc.*    What hot shot's this?
*Sold.*                              A Souldier sir: thats all:
Thats more than sir I thinke you dare be. Zounds! bafful'd
For my limbes lost in seruice! your noble father
Has clapd this buff-ierkin, when this Stump of wood
Has vp tot'h knee stucke three howres in french blood:
When such as you, with your Spangled roses, that day
Brauely bestird their heeles, and ran away:                             110
Ile stand toot, I.

89 *King.*] *Oct.* Q        90 *Oct. Bri.* Q        91 *Bris.*] om. Q
99 S.D. *Dromes...sounding,*] Q *prints in roman as second line of King's speech above*

*Spend.*     With one leg.
*Sold.*                     Yes: with one.
*Oct.*   Yong Lords, thus to scorne Souldiers, tis ill don.
*King.*   Vncle, heres no man scornes 'em; must we be brau'de
By a staring fellow, for a little fighting? goe.
*Sold.*   Fighting! I cannot halt I, but speake plaine,
No King on earth baffalls me, ide baffall againe
Th'whole race of great turkes, had I 'em ith field:
I ha brought with me a hundred Souldiers, (old Seruitors)
Poore as my selfe in clothes; picke out fiue hundred          120
Of such silke-stocken men, if they beate vs, hang vs,
S'bloud if we tosse not them, hang's agen: a fort
We ha built without, and mand it, this was the sport
A Souldier wood ha giuen thee: my one hundred
Had taught thee all the rules i'th Schoole of warre.
*King.*   All this ile read without mayme, wound or scarre.
*Sold.*   What say you to an Engine, that at once
Shall spoile some thirtie men?
*Iouin.*                     Thirtie men! nothing.
*Sold.*   If nothing! hast thou bin beate for this? farewell.
*Iouin.*   I can fetch twenty scriueners haue don more
With a bare goose-quill.
*Sold.*                     Maist thou but liue, to need          130
A Souldiers arme, that laught to see him bleed.          *Exit.*
*Bris.*   You haue lost the day sir, for your Souldiers fly.
*King.*   Fly to the diuell let 'em.
*Iouin.*                     Your leaders before.
*Spend.*   You fight all vnder one cullors? doe you not?
*Schol.*   Sir: these pleasures to the King which I prefer,
Flow from *Ioues* braine.
*Narc.*   Heyda! heres one has beaten out *Ioues* braines.
*Seaf.*   Wud I had thee hung vp at our maine kite.          [*Aside.*]
*Schol.*   No Sir, *Ioues* braine, (*Minerua* queene of wit)
If all the *Muses* and the Arts can fit          140
With their high Tunes, such choice and Princely eares,
*Apollo* (Father to them all) — appeares —
*Iouin.*   *Apollo* was an Asse; he let a wench whom he lou'de to be

turnd into a Bay-tree, and now shees glad for a peny to stick
Ale-house-windowes, and wynde dead coarses.

*Bris.*  Let *Apollo* goe and lye with his owne Daughters.

*King.*  Are you a Scholler Syr?

*Iouin.*  A school-master as I take it, and comes to present a verie
prettie show of his schollers in broken Latin.

*Oct.*  Can wee be dumb and see this?

*Schol.*                    O haples Learning!                    150
Flie and complaine, to Heauen (where thou wert borne)
That thou (whome Kings once nursde,) art now their scorne.

                                                        *Exit.*

*Narc.*  How blowes the winde Syr?

*Seaf.*                    Wynde! tis *Nore-Nore-West.*

*Narc.*  To hoyse your sayles vp too, I thinke tis best.

*Seaf.*  A blacke Gust is comming: vp a-low-there hey: A young-
man vp toth Top-mast-head, and looke-out: stand to your Sayles:
stand to your Top-sailes: let goe your Harriars, let goe, amaine
lowere amaine, quicke, quick, Goodfellowes.

*Omn.*  Hees mad.

*Seaf.*  Whoes at Helme? beare vp hard: and hard vp: and thou  160
beest a man beare vp; Star-borde, Port-agein: off with your
Drablers, and your Banners; out with your Courses: Ho, — I spie
two Shippes yonder, that yaw too and agen, they haue both sprung
a Leake, I thinke the Diuell is sucking Tabaccho, heeres such a
Mist: out with your boate, and you Bosmen, cut-downe Maste-
bith-borde; beare vp,
Ime a Blunt-fellow you see, All I say is this,
You that scorne Sea-men, shall a Sea-man misse.          *Exit.*

*Oct.*  Now by my life I haue patient stood too long,
To see rich merit and loue, payde with base wrong:          170
Learning! and Armes! and Traffique! the triple wall
That fortifies a Kingdome, race em downe All!
This Seaman, (hee that dearest earnes his bread)
Had rigd and mann'd four Gallies brauely furnisht,
With Souldiers, Rowers, and Fire-workes for a Sea-fight.

*King.*  You are full of Squibs too, pray goe fire em all.

                    153 tis] is Q

                    **149**

*Oct.*   Must I bee then cashierde too? mary and shall.
To saue thy sinking Honour, Ile send hence
These men with thankes, with praise, and recompence.     *Exit.*
*Omn.*   Pray doe.
*King.*                Braue *Shalcan-Bohor*, all this while                    180
Our eye has followed yours, and seene it smile,
(As twere in scorne) of what these men could doe,
Which made vs slight them off; to ingrosse you
(Our best and richest prize:) ith Courts of Kings
Through which you ha passd, you ha seene wonders, shew em.
*Ruf.*   I shall at opportune howers. If your Grace
Arride the toyes, they bragd of (Fire-workes,
And such light-stuffes) Sit fearelesse without danger
Of murdring shot, which villaines might discharge
(In idle counterfet Sea-fights) you shall see                              190
At opening of this hand, a thousand Balles
Of wilde-Fire, flying round about the Aire — there.

*Fire-workes on Lines.*

*Omn.*   Rare, Rare.
*King.*                Tis excellent, Sdeath from whence flew they?
*Bris.*   Hell, I thinke.
*Iouin.*   Hell! Nay, if any that are in Hell, skip vp euer so nye
Heauen, as these Diuells that spit fire did, Ile drinke nothing but
Gun-pouder.
*Ruf.*   Ha, ha, a trifle this. Your Scholler there,
Come with his Arts and Muses shallow, leaden braine,
Your swaggering Souldier, lead a tottered traine                           200
Of ruffianly Boote-hallers: I noted all
These feasts for Kings: ith garden of varietie
The vast world! you are staru'de midst your satietie,
Plucke no one Apple from the golden Tree,
But shake the fruite of euery pleasure downe.
*King.*   Thanks *Bohor*; why else weares a King his Crowne?
*Shalcan*, all *Naples* shall not buy thee from mee.
*Ruf.*   Nor you and these from me.

207 Shalcan] K. Shalcan Q [indented as speech-prefix]

*King.*                          Aske what thou wilt haue
But to stay here.
*Ruf.*              Loe, this is all I craue.        [*Hug him.*]
*King.*    Thou hast our fast embraces.
*Ruf.*                          Swift as mans thought,        210
Various delights shall bee each minute borne,
And dye as fast that fresh may rise; wee scorne
To serue vp one dish twice, bee't nere so rare;
Will you that gainst to morrow I prepare
A Feast of strange Mirth for you?
*King.*                          Deare *Bohor* doe.
*Ruf.*    I shall; Nor doe I thus your loue pursue,
With seruile hopes of Golde, I neede it not:
If out the jawes of Hell Golde may bee got
*Blacke Artes* are mine to doo't; and what delights
Those worke bee yours.
*King.*                      Thou art gratious in our sight.        220
                                        *Exeunt.*


## [ACT II, SCENE ii]

❡ *A Table is set out by young fellowes like Merchants men, Bookes
of Accounts vpon it, small Deskes to write vpon, they
sit downe to write Tickets, Lurchall with them.*

1. *Ser.*    Come fellow *Lurchall* write.
*Lurch.*                          Fuh, Stay not for mee,
I shall out-goe you all.
2. *Ser.*              I hold fiue Crownes,
Wee all leaue you behinde vs.
*Lurch.*                  Don; but I          [*Aside.*]
Must not leaue you behinde mee; what paines a poore Diuell
Takes to get into a Merchant? hees so ciuill,
One of Hell must not know him, with more ease
A Diuell may win ten Gallants, then one of these,
Yet a Merchants wife, before these ten, is wonne
To entertaine her Diuell, if Pride be one.

But *Lurchall*, now tha'rt in, and for yeares bound,            10
To play the Merchant, play him right: th'ast found
A Master, who more villenie has by hart,
Then thou by rote; See him but play his owne part,
And thou doest Hell good seruice; *Barteruile*,
Theres in thy name a Haruest makes mee smile.

*Bart.*   *Lurchall*: —                        [Barteruile] *within.*
*Omn.*            My master calls.
*Lurch.*                        I.

     *Enter* Barteruile.

  *Men too and fro bring in Bags, and haue Bills.*       *Exit.*

*Bart.*                        Oh, art there?
 This day twixt one and two a Gallants bound
To pay four hundred Crownes to free his Landes
Fast morgag'de to mee, *Lurchall*, get thee vp hye
Into my Turret, where thou mayest espie            20
All commers euery way; if by thy guesse,
Thou seest the Gull make hither—
*Lurch.*                  So Syr.
*Bart.*                     That his Hower
 Lye gasping, at the last Minutes, let him beate at dore;
Within Ile beate his heart out.
*Lurch.*                  Ile let him stand.
*Bart.*   Do, take my *Watch*, go faster. All his Land
 Is sumd with these two Figures, (two and one.)
At past one, (his,) strike but two, tis mine owne.
*Lurch.*   Ile turne the wheeles: and spin the howers vp faster.
*Bart.*   The Citie-clockes then strike, and kill thy Master.
 Would all the Citie-Sextons, at my cost            30
Were drunke this day four howres.
*Lurch.*                  Troth so wud I,
 And wee their Iackes ath Clocke-house.
*Bart.*                        Wee'de strike merily.
 Fly vp to'th top ath house.
*Lurch.*            There sir, Ile sit,
 And croake like a Rauen, to damb thee in hels pit.       *Exit.*

*Barteruile set amongst his men reading a long scroll.*

*Bart.*  How goes this moneth?
*Omn.*                              Much shorter than the last.
*Bart.*  Weddings this moneth twelue thousand: not worth the
   scoring,
But thinke ther's little marying, we ha so much whoring.
Grynding milles so much-vsde; about the citie
Such grinding, yet no more mony; suites in law,
Full brought to an end this moneth, no more but ten:              40
This law will begger vs: had I the bags againe,
I bought this combrous office with, the King
Should make his best of't: hee that did farm't before
Had it for lesse than I, yet receiude more.
How much remaines of the salt tribute due?
*1. Ser.*  Seuen thousand Crownes.
*Bart.*                              Thats well: a sauorie summe:
These our Italian tributes, were well deuisde,
Me thinkes tis fit a subiect should not eate
But that his Prince from euery dish of meate
Should receiue nourishment: for (being the head)              50
Why should he pine, when all the body is fed?
Besides, it makes vs more to awe a King,
When at each bit we are forc'd to thinke on him.

*Enter a Brauo with mony.*

*1. Ser.*  What payment's this?
*Brauo.*  The pension of the Stewes, you neede not vntye it, I
   brought it but now from the sealers office: ther's not a peece there,
   but has a hole in't, because men may knowe where twas had, and
   where it will be taken againe: blesse your worship? Stew-mony
   sir, Stew-Prune cash sir.
*Bart.*  They are sure, tho not the soundest paymaisters,              60
Read whats the summe.
*1. Ser.*                              But bare two hundred crownes.

52 makes] make Q

153

*Brauo.* They are bare crownes indeede sir, and they came from Animals and vermin that are more bare: wee that are clarkes of these flesh-markets haue a great deale of rotten mutton lying vpon our hands, and finde this to bee a sore payment.

*Bart.* Well, well, the world will mend.

*Brauo.* So our surgeons tell 'em euery day; but the pox of mendment I see.

*Bart.* Doe not your gallants come off roundly then?

*Brauo.* Yes sir, their haire comes off fast enough, we turne away 70 crack't french crownes euery day. I haue a suite to your worship in behalfe of all our dealers in small wares, our free-whores sir, you know my meaning.

*Bart.* If your whores are knowne, whats thy suite?

*Brauo.* I should haue brought a petition from 'em, but that tis put off sir, till clensing-weeke, that they may all be able to set to their hands, or else a whores marke.

*Bart.* Well, well, whats their request?

*Brauo.* Mary sir, that all the shee-tobacco-shops, that creepe vp daily in euery hole about the Citie, may bee put to scilence. 80

*Bart.* Why pray thee honest fellow?

*Brauo.* I thanke your good worship, I had not such a sweete bit giuen me this seuen yeeres, honest fellow: marry sir Ile open to you your suppliants cases: they that had wont to spend a crowne about a smocke, haue now their delight dog-cheape, but for spending one quarter of that mony in smoake: besides sir, they are not contented to robbe vs of our customes only, but when their pipes are fowle with spitting and driueling in those foresaide shops, they haue no place to burne 'em in, but our houses.

*Bart.* Draw their petition, and weele see all cur'de. 90

*Brauo.* Let a frost come first sir: I thanke your venerable worship; the pox gnaw out so many small guts as haue payde thee crownes.

*Exit.*

*Enter* Lurchall *running.*

*Lurch.* The tyd's against you sir, the crownes are come.

*Bart.* How goes my watch?

*Lurch.* As most watches vse to goe sir, sleepily, heauily.

*Bart.*   Not reach'd to one yet; wert thou to be hangd,
The hower had gallop'd.
*Lurch.*                 I spurd it all that I could.
*Bart.*   S'death keep his howre, heauen helpe poore Citizens,
If Gentlemen grow thus warie: let him in.          *Exit* Lurchall.
Barren now, that hast in craft so fruitfull bin.                    100
Your businesse sir to me.

               *Enter* [Lurchall] *with two Gentlemen.*

1. *Gent.*                 Doe you not know me sir?
*Bart.*   No in good truth sir.
1. *Gent.*                 To know you I am bold sir,
You haue lands of mine in morgage, this is my day,
And heres your crownes.
*Bart.*                 Signior *Innocentio*;
My memorie had quite lost you, pray sit both,
A bowle of wine here.
1. *Gent.*                 Sir it shall not neede:
Please you to fetch my euidence, whil'st we tell.
*Bart.*   What needes this forward spring? faith two moneths hence
Had bin to me as welcome.
1. *Gent.*                 Sir I thanke you.
2. *Gent.*   Your hower drawes on Signior *Innocentio*.          110
*Bart.*   Goe beate a drumme ith garret, that no tongues
Of clockes be heard but mine.
*Lurch.*                 Little past one.
*Bart.*   Winde, winde.
*Lurch.*                 Thus wind'st thou to damnation.
2. *Gent.*   Ile part with none sir, pardon me, till I see
Your writings: will you fetch the euidence sir.
*Bart.*   What euidence sir, haue I of yours?
1. *Gent.*                         My friend sir, —
Whose mony hee lends me to redeeme my morgage.
*Bart.*   Which you would haue for your securitie.
2. *Gent.*   Tis so sir?
*Bart.*                 No sir *Innocentio*,
To morrow on your bare word will I lend you                    120

155

Thirty crownes more: I loue you sir, and wish you
Beware whose hands you fall into: the worlds a serpent.

*2. Gent.*   This does but spend the hower sir, will you take your
mony?

*Bart.*   With all my heart.

*1. Gent.*                    Let him see my writings then.

*Bart.*   Haue you such couenant from mee? I remember none.

*1. Gent.*   Your conscience is sufficient couenant sir.

*Bart.*   Ha! whats that conscience? I know no law-termes I,
Talke to me as to a Citizen.

*2. Gent.*                    Weele dally no longer;
We knew what snake would sting vs, and therefore brought
Our medcine gainst his venome: youle keepe the writings,          130
And weele ith Court of conscience tender your crownes,
Whither this writ does summon you.

*Lurch.*                          A fox, and ore-taken?

*Bart.*   Serue writs vpon me, yet keepe my mony too?
Dull slaue hast thou no braine?          [*Aside to* Lurchall.]

*Lurch.*                    Braine! trye this.     [*Whisper.*]

*Bart.*                              Peace.

*2. Gent.*   Will you as fits a Christian giue vs in
What is our right, and take your crownes sir yet?

*Bart.*   Tis good to try mens patience, fetch me downe
Those writings on my pillow, there they ha slept

*Exit* Lurchall

These two howers for you: must not friends iest? ha!

*Both.*   Yes sir: let your men tell, iust four hundred crownes.          140

*Bart.*   Besides the vse.

*1. Gent.*          The vse is there too.

*Bart.*                              Hold:
Ile take it without telling, put it vp.

*Both.*   Not till we see the writings.

*Enter* Lurchall.

*Bart.*                    Dare you touch it?
*Both.*    Dare! yes sir, and dare stab him to the heart,
Offers to take it from vs.
*Bart.*                    Who stabs first?
                                    *Flings mony amongst it.*
Now touch it if you dare: ther's gold of mine,
And if they lay one finger on't, cry theeues,
They come to rob me, touch it if you dare.
1. *Gent.*    Dambde wretch, thou wilt goe quicke to hell I feare.
*Bart.*    No sir, the diuell shall fetch me when I goe.          150
*Lurch.*    Th'at all my errand.                    [*Aside.*]
2. *Gent.*                    We are cheated both.
*Bart.*    Proceede, in your chancery suite, I haue begun your bill.
Humbly complayning.
1. *Gent.*              Of thee villaine Ile complaine
That sels thy soule for mony, diuels on earth dwell,
And men are no where, all this world is hell.          *Exeunt.*
*Bart.*    I kisse thy forhead, my wittie *Oedipus*
That canst vnfold such riddels.    *One ringes. Exit* 1. *Seruant.*
*Lurch.*                    Sir, I am bound
To doe you all seruice, till I you all confound.          [*Aside.*]
1. *Ser.*    Maister *Siluerpen* the procter sir, sends word, if you come
not in to morrow and personally depose your payment of the two  160
hundred crownes, youle be non-suited.
*Bart.*    That is a law-draught goes downe coldly.
*Lurch.*    Why sir? Tis but your swearing the mony is payde.
*Bart.*    If oathes had back-dores to come in at, without danger of
damnation, to catch a mans soule bith back, swearing were braue.
1. *Ser.*    What answere shall I giue the Proctors man?
*Lurch.*    Tell him my maister shall come in and sweare.

145 S.D. *Flings....*] Q *prints in roman as part of the text, line* 145
151 Th'at] That Q
157 S.D. *One ringes.*] Q *prints in roman as part of the text, line* 157 [riddels: one
ringes.]

*Exit [Seruant] and Enters.*

*Bart.*  Doe, tell him: on thee Ile build: now all my feare,
Is for apparance at the Chancellors Court.
No trick to saue that?
*Lurch.*                I haue a braue one fort.          170

*Exit* 1. *[Seruant] for wine: bring't in.*

Bring in a pottle of wine: will *Carlo* here,
My fellow, depose a truth if he see it, to helpe
His maister?
*Bart.*          Wut thou not honest *Carlo?*
2. *Ser.*                                Yes sir.
1. *Ser.*   Here's the wine.              *Enter with wine.*
*Lurch.*   Set this to your head anon sir, when tis there
Away you, and to morrow thou mai'st sweare
Before the Chancelor, and sweare true, if hee
Were in that case thou leftst him, twere in vaine
To hope he could liue, till thou camst back againe.
*Bart.*   All Knights a'th Post learne this trick: the fits vpon me now. 180
*Lurch.*   Take a good draught, twill helpe you sir: It gulpes,
Hees almost breathles. *Carolo,* away.
1. *Ser.*                  I am gon.              *Exit.*
*Lurch.*   Hees gon, hees gon sir.
*Bart.*                     One gulpe more had choaked me;
This wine has washed my feares off, tha'st giuen mee power
To make me doate vpon thee. *Carolos* gon?
*Lurch.*   Yes and will sweare his heart out, to your good.
Sweare let him; bee thy selfe and hee dambde too.      *[Aside.]*
*Bart.*   So I may get by it. In my bosome sleepe
(My doue, my loue,) prosper but thou and I.
*Lurch.*   And let all els sinck.
*Bart.*                  Let 'em: so I kisse gold,          190
The yongmans whore, the saint of him thats old.

                                             *Exeunt.*

173 Wut] What Q          180 *Bart.*] *om.* Q
182 1. *Ser.*] *Car.* Q          184 has] had Q

## [ACT II, SCENE iii]

*Enter Prior,* Alphege, Hillary, *and Friers with pruning kniues, spades, &c. met by Subprior, and* Shackle-soule.

*Sub.*    Whither (mad-men) run you?
*Omn.*                                    To our Vines.
*Sub.*                                    Your Vines?
(The tree of sin and shame?) this Serpent here,
Has with that liquorish poison, so set on fire
The braines of *Nicodeme* and *Siluester,*
That they in drunken rage haue stabd each other.
*Prior.*    Stabd!
*Shac.*            Yes, they bleede a little, but haue no harme,
Their yong blood with the grapes Iuice being made warme,
They brawld and struck, but I kept off the blowes,
Yet the Subprior saies from me their quarrell rose.
*Sub.*    It did.
*Shac.*            In very deede (for I not sweare)                    10
It did not sir: to me you malice beare,
As if that all such mischife don, were mine,
But cause your selfe shall see how I repine
To see vice prosper, pardon me good Lord Prior,
If I a tell-tale be of what mine eyes
Beheld with water in them: sin will rise
In holy sircles I see sometimes.
*Prior.*                          What sin?
*Sub.*    What hast thou seene?
*Shac.*                          Wud present I had not beene,
But till I vtter it, my clogd conscience beares
A man vpon a woman.
*Omn.*                    Ha!
*Shac.*                          I speak't in teares:                    20
*Scumbroth* our cooke, and a female I beheld
Kissing in our orchard: on her lippes he dwelld
I thinke some halfe howre.

*Sub.*                     Shame to our reuerend order!
A woman in our couent! Sin black as murder.
*Prior.*   Our cooke shalbe seuerely punished: a woman,
A tempter here.
*Omn.*   Abhominable!
*Prior.*   *Rush,* thoul't rebuke sin.
*Shac.*                     Tho my Lord I'me bad,
I'me not giuen that way.
*Prior.*                     Let vs some plagues inuent
To lay on this lecherous knaue.
*Shac.*                     Some light punishment          30
(Good my Lord Prior) suppose twere your owne fault,
Whip as you woud be whipd, the best's naught.
*Sub.*   He shalbe punisht, and then loose his place.
*Prior.*   That sir shall be as we will: to our Vines: away.
*Sub.*   For shame giue or'e, dare you prophane this day
That is to holy vses consecrate?
*Prior.*   Why? what day is this?
*Omn.*                     *Lambert* the marter.
*Prior.*                     No matter,
To vex thee deeper, this whole day weele spend,
Onely about our Vines.
*Sub.*                     You vex not me,
But heauen: what warrants you to this?
*Prior.*                     Our will.          40
*Sub.*   Thou hast thy will, thy wish thou ne're shalt haue,
In sight of heauen who sees and punishes
Mens blacke impieties; And in sight of these
(Sharers in thy full sin:) And in his sight,
T'expresse whose vilenes, there's no epithite.
*Prior.*   No matter what he saies *Rush.*
*Shac.*                     I'me knowne what I am.
*Sub.*   To thee I prophecie, (vitious old man to thee,)
Who er'st with lift-vp-hands, and downe-bowed knee,
Seemest to'haue had worke in heauen: now (full of spite,)
Onely to sate a liquorish appetite;          50

Digst our religious wales vp, planting there
Luxurious fruits to pamper belly-cheere:
(For all thy paines to dresse it,) of this Vine
Thy lustfull lips shall neuer tast the wine.
*Prior.*   Distracted foole, in stead of my iust anger,
Thou onely hast my pittie: thou prophecie?
*Omn.*   Ha, ha.
*Sub.*   Laugh on, but since nor prayers preuaile nor teares,
Ile powre my griefe into my Princes eares.          *Exit.*
*Shac.*   Heele goe and complaine to the King.
*Prior.*                                    Let him complaine,   60
Kings cannot Subiects of their foode restraine.
Away.
                              *Exeunt: Manet* Shackle-soule.
*Shac.*   Ingender sin with sin; that wines rich heate
May bring forth Lust, Lust murder may beget,
But here strike saile, this barke awhile hale in,
And lanch into the deepe, a brighter sin:
Ho, *Glitterbacke*, ascend, to *Shackle-soule*,
To *Shackle-soule* ascend, ho *Glitterbacke*;
Thou richest spirit, thrust vp thy golden head
From hell thus hie: when? art imprisoned          70
In misers chests so fast thou canst not come?
Or fearst thou theeues, or cutpurses? here be some
Can saue thee from their fingers: when? Arise;
And dazle th'approching night with thy glistring eyes.
*Glitt.*   Here.
                    *A golden Head ascends.*

*Shac.*   How thou sweatst with comming? Saue me those drops
(Golds pure *Elixar*) stilling from thy lockes:
Shake from thy browes and hayre that golden showre,
So: get home: quicke: (to hell) least hell grow poore,
If Richmens pawes once fasten thee, and beware          80
It'h way thou meetst no Lawyers: theile pull thee bare,
Hence: downe.
*Glitt.*   Ime gon.                              *Descendit.*

*Shac.*　Coole night will call Frier *Clement* forth anon:
Angels, be you his strong temptation:
Wines lustfull fires him warme not: At this spring,
(Scornde by the rest) for him, spred thy gilt wing,
Full in his eye; As he drinks water downe,
In streames of *Auarice*, let his weake soule drowne.

*Exit.*

## [ACT III, Scene i]

*Enter the King*, Narcisso, Brisco, Spendola,
Iouinelli, Rufman, *followed by* Astolfo.

*Ast.*　I doe beseech your Highnes, yet turne backe
And comfort the sad Lady, whose faire eyes
Are worne away with weeping.
*Iouin.*　If her eyes be worne away, what should a man doe with a
blind wife? kill her with flyes?
*King.*　I cannot abide a woman thats fond of me.
*Spend.*　Nor I.
*Narc.*　I would loue a woman but as I loue a walnut, to cracke it,
and peele it, eate the meate, and then throw away the shell.
*Iouin.*　Or as noble-men vse their great horses, when they are past 10
seruice: sell 'em to brewers and make 'em drey-horses: So vse a
woman.
*Ast.*　So so.
*Ruf.*　The Indians are warme without clothes, and a man is best at
ease without a woman: or if your Highnes must needs haue one,
Haue factors to buy the fairest, doate not any,
But like the turke, regard none, yet keepe many.
*King.*　You heare the Iuries verdit.
*Ast.*　　　　　　　　　　　　Whose foreman's the diuell?
These counsell thee to thy destruction.
*King.*　Destruction? why? tho heauen can abide but one sun, I hope 20
we on earth may loue many mens daughters: Tell *Erminhilda* so:

20 tho] the Q

162

send her home to the duke her father: And tell him too, because
the disease of mariage brings the stone with it, I hate a woman;
I loue not to be cut: inclosde grounds are too rancke.
*Ruf.*   Best feeding on the Commons.
*Ast.*   Will you not mary this chast Lady then?
*King.*   No sir, and will you now my reason haue?
A woman is an insatiate graue
Wherein hee's dambd that lyes buried.
*Omn.*                              On, on, away.
*Ruf.*   Braue battailes! fight you, but ile win the day.       *Exeunt.* 30

    *Manet,* Astolpho. *Enter* Octauio *and* Ermynhilda.

*Erm.*   I heard the storie, tell't not or'e againe,
Twere crueltie to wound men, being halfe slaine.
*Oct.*   Tis crueltie too much, and too much shame
That one of your high birth, youth, beautie, name,
And vertues shining bright, should hence be sent
(Like some offender into banishment)
Abusde by a King, and his luxurious traine,
Of parasites, knaues, and fooles, (a kingdomes bane,)
For them, by him not carde for; you came not so,
But as his bride, his Queene, and bedfellow.                          40
*Erm.*   And yet am neither, from my fathers court
Came I (being sude by Princes too) for this?
To see him, his subiects scorne, and my selfe his?
Once thought I that his loue had bin (as fate)
Vnmoueable; and ist now turn'd to hate?
Yes, yes, hees wauering as the running streame,
And far more ydle than a mad-mans dreame.
*Ast.*   Send to the duke your father, let him inforce
Your plighted mariage.
*Erm.*                       Worse than a diuorce.
No: to his eyes since hatefull I am growne,                          50
Ile leaue his Court and him, and dye vnknowne.             *Exit.*
*Ast.*   All runnes I see to ruine.

          25 Commons.] commons then. Q       26 *Ast.*] *om.* Q
          28 woman] womans Q

*Oct.*                              If he persue,
These godles courses, best we leaue him too,
That land to it selfe must a quick downefall bring,
Whose King has lost all, but the name of King.

                                                *Exeunt.*


## [ACT III, Scene ii]

*Enter Subprior with an earthen pot, and a lanthorne;*
*Scumbroath with him with a peice.*

*Sub.*   Get thee to bed thou foolish man and sleepe.
*Scum.*   How? Sleepe? no sir no, I am turnd a tyrant and cannot
sleepe:
I stand centinell perdu, and somebody dyes if I sleepe,
I am possest with the diuell and cannot sleepe.
*Sub.*   What diuell possesses thee?
*Scum.*   The fencers diuell, a fighting diuell; *Rush* has committed
a murder vpon my body, and his carcas shall answere it; the cock
of my reuenge is vp.
*Sub.*   Murder! what murder?                                      10
*Scum.*   He has taken away my good name, which is flat man-
slaughter, and halfe hangd me, which is as much as murder, he told
the Lord Prior and you that I was kissing a wench: Its a lye, I giue
him the lye, and he shall fight with me at single pistall against my
caliuer, do I looke like a whore-monger? when haue you seene a
wencher thus hairy as I am: *Rush* thou diest for this treason against
my members concupiscentiallitie.
*Sub.*   Thou wut not kill him, wut thou?
*Scum.*   No, but Ile make him know what tis to boile a cooke in's
owne grease.                                                      20
I am scalding hot, I am chargd with furie, I carie a heart-burning
within me. I kisse a whore? I shall haue boyes cry out to me now,
who kist *Mary?* No *Rush*, *Scumbroth* shall giue thee suger pellets
to eate, I will not be danc'de vpon.

21 *indented* 2 *ems*

*Sub.*  Let me perswade thy peace of minde to night,
  Get thee to rest, if *Rush* haue thee belide,
  Reioyce, by wrongs to haue thy patience tride.
  He shall forgiuenes aske thee.
*Scum.*  Let me but haue one blow ats head with my cleauer ith
  kitchin, and I freely forgiue him, or let me bownce at him.     30
*Sub.*  These bloudie thoughts will dam thee into hell.
*Scum.*  Doe you thinke so? what becomes of our roaring boyes
  then that stab healths one to another, doe you thinke they will be
  dambd vp too?
*Sub.*  I thinke so, for I know it, deere sonne to prayer,
  Two sinnes beset thee, murder, and despaire,
  I charge thee meete me at my cell anon,
  To saue thee will I spend my orison.
  In name of heauen I charge thee to be gon.
*Scum.*  Well sir, the cold water of your counsell has laid the heate     40
  of my furie: he had met with his match, but I wil shoote off my
  anger, I will be gon, and why? Looke you, because the moone is
  vp and makes hornes at one of vs; As the noble-mans coach is
  drawne by foure horses, the knights by two, and the cuckold by
  three, euen so am I drawne away with none at all. *Vale, Bonos
  Noches*: I am possest still: It buzzes here. *Vale.*          *Exit*
*Sub.*  Blest star of light, stucke there to illuminate
  This world darkned or'e with sin: thou watchest late,
  To guide mans comming home, shewing thereby
  Heauens care of vs, seeing how we tread awry.          50
  We haue two great lights for midnight and for noon,
  Because blacke deeds at no time should be don.
  All haile to thee (now my best guide) be giuen,
  What needs I earths candle, hauing the lamp of heauen?
  Now *Benedicite?* where am I?

                    *Enter* [Shackle-soule *as*] Rush [*aloof*].

O whether am I going? which way came I?
Ah wellada, I come to fill my pot,
With water not with thee; thou art mis-begot,

           56 O] Rush. O Q [*not indented*]

**165**

Else wouldst thou not lye there; what Orphans blood
Hast thou suckt out, to make this golden flood?                    60
None drinke this well but I, how is it than
Thou thus way-lay'st me, (theefe to the soule of man?)
Would some poore wretch (by losse of law vndone)
Had thee: goe doe him good: me canst thou none.
My wholesome cup is poysond, it flowes or'e
With mans damnation (gold,) drinke there no more.
*Shac.*    Not tast what all men thirst for? old and so braue,
When mony assaults, one combat more Ile haue.

*Enter* Scumbroth.

*Scum.*    So, ho, ho, father Subprior.
*Sub.*    Whoes there? what art thou callst me?                    70
*Scum.*    One that feeds the hungry, the cooke sir, *Scumbroth.*
*Sub.*    Come hither, I haue for thee a golden prize.
*Shac.*    Ha ha: heele take it.
Villaines and fooles will ha gold, (tho got from hell,)
But they who doe so, (as thou shalt) pay for't well.        *Exit.*
*Scum.*    But stay, father Subprior, before we goe one step farder,
what doe you thinke I haue done since I went from you?
*Sub.*    No hurt I hope, say hast thou?
*Scum.*    Hurt? If I did hurt in that, how much harme doe Almanake
makers, who lye coldly quiuering at it all the yeare long? I did doe 80
nothing but stand staring at the man in the moone.
*Sub.*    And what good thoughts bred that within thee?
*Scum.*    This: I thought to my selfe, what a happy fellow that man
in the moone was, to see so many fooles and knaues here below,
and yet neuer to be troubled with 'em, nor meddle with 'em.
*Sub.*    Hees happy that meddles not with this world indeed.
*Scum.*    If that man in the moone should write a prognostication,
oh he should not neede to tell astronomicall lyes to fill his booke,
nor talke gibrish no man vnderstands, of *Quartiles, Aspects,*
*Stations, Retrogradations, Peragrations; Centricall, Eccentricall,* 90
*Cosmicall, Acronicall,* and such *Palquodicall, Solar, Lunar, Lunati-*

89 talke] Q(u); talke in Q(c)

*call* vaulting ouer the railes of heauen, that no Christian dare looke
vpon their tricks, for feare his wit breake his necke.

*Sub.*　Thou putst into a Sea, thou canst not sound,
Ignorance still is foe to Arts profound.
Come hither man, come hither.

*Scum.*　Arts profound, Arts make men as very asses as women doe,
I haue no Art, and yet I knowe this Moone that shines to night,
sees more than you or I doe, for all your spectacles.

*Sub.*　True, tis the eye of heauen.　　　　　　　　　　　　100

*Scum.*　Which of the eyes? tis but the left eye: and the Sun is the
right: and yet the left sometimes sees more than the right, and the
right as much as the left, there's paxonisme for you father, globicall
paxonisme.

*Sub.*　I vnderstand thee not.

*Scum.*　No, why heres the oyster opend, I say the Sun sees much
knauery in a yere, and the Moone more in a quarter: the Moone sees
men caryed by a quarelling watch to prison, and the Sun sees the
constable and the booke-keeper share fees the next morning.

*Sub.*　Thats not well.　　　　　　　　　　　　　　　　110

*Scum.*　Yes, but they sweare tis well: the Moone sees bastards come
bawling into the world, and the Sun sees 'em shifted and shuftled
in dossers, away to nurse, and thats the cause we haue so many
dosser-heads: the Moone sees old curmudgeons come reeling from
Tauerns with sipping of halfe pintes of Sack, and the Sun sees the
same churles the next day, soberly cutting any mans throate for a
pennie.

*Sub.*　Enough of this: come hither: looke what here lyes.

*Scum.*　What here lyes: mary, father Subprior, the diuell and some
Vsurers mony haue bin here at their lecherie, and see what goodly 120
children they haue begot: if you will ile keepe the bastards at
nurse.

*Sub.*　I am content that halfe this gold be thine,
(If it bee ask'd for neuer, for tis not mine,)
So thou wilt promise tother halfe to giue
To such as I appoint.

*Scum.*　By this gold I will lay it out brauely, as you appoint me.

127 *Scum.*] *Sub.* Q

*Sub.*   Looke not to prosper; if thou dealst amisse;
Good workes are keyes opening the gates of blisse;
That golden key, thou in that heape maist find,                    130
If with it thou relieue the lame, sick, blind,
And hungry.
*Scum.*          I will doe it I protest.
*Sub.*   One halfe bestow'd so, take thy selfe the rest.
So fare thee well.                                                    *Exit.*
*Scum.*   Farewell good father, — foole: Ile giue the blinde a dog to
lead 'em, the lame shall to the whipping-post, the sick shall dye in
a cage, and the hungry leap at a crust: I feede roagues, the pox
shall: the world is changde: a begger yesterday, and full of gold
to day: an asse to day, and a prow'd scab to morrow.

*Golden head ascends.*

*Glitt.*   Stay: stand.                                              140
*Scum.*   Stand: cannot a Gentleman grow rich, but he must keepe
knaues about him?
*Glitt.*   That gold is none of thine.
*Scum.*   But all the craft in that great head of yours cannot get it out
of my fangers. Zounds who the diuel art thou?
*Glitt.*   A spirit sent vp from hell to make thee rich.
*Scum.*   Thanke hell for it: hell makes worse fooles rich in a yeere.
*Glitt.*   That gold I laide there for thee.
*Scum.*   When doe you lay againe, that I may haue more of these
egges?                                                               150
*Glitt.*   Spend those I charge thee first.
*Scum.*   Yes, Head.
*Glitt.*   And brauely I charge thee.
*Scum.*   What neede you be at such charges, Ile doe't: but shall the
poore be a pennie the better for me, as the old fellow chargd me,
yea, or no?
*Glitt.*   No.
*Shac.*   No.                                                   *Within.*
*Scum.*   Whose that?
*Glitt.*   Tis thine owne Genius cryes vnto thee no.                 160

147 fooles] foole Q      155 chargd] charge Q      158 S.D. *Within.*] Within? Q

*Scum.* My Genius, I am a cooke, my Genius then belike is a
scullion; but when this is spent, can my Genius tell mee whither
I shall haue more.

*Shac.* More.⎫
*Glitt.* More. ⎪
1. More.   ⎬    *Within.*
2. More.   ⎪    *In a big voice.*

*Scum.* Because my Genius keepes company with a great man, Ile
take all their wordes; and his bond.

*Glitt.* When thou hast spent all that: I charge thee come          170
To the blacke tree, that stands in *Naples* groue,
Clymbe boldly to the top, and keepe fast hold,
For there ile rayne on thee a showre of gold,
If what thou seest there, thou to any tell,
Diuels shall teare thee.

*Shac.*              Away.                    [*Within.*]
*Omn.*               Away.
*Scum.*                     Farewell.                *Exit.*

*Enter* Shacklesoule *laughing.*

*Shac.* Ha, ha! downe downe bright spirit, thou wut bee mist anon,
Hell mynt stands ydle.
*Glitt.*              Loose not that foole.
*Shac.*                      Be gon.
*Glitt.* Haue care to meete at next infernall court:
The day drawes nye.                        *Goes downe.*
*Shac.*              I thanke thee for this spirit.
                                              *Exit.*


## [ACT III, Scene iii]

*Enter King,* Rufman, Narcisso, Spendola, Brisco, Iouinelli,
[Barteruile, Lurchall, *the two Gentlemen, and* Farneze.]

*King.* You that complaine gainst *Barteruile,* (receiuer
Of all our tribute-monies) speak your wrongs;

169

Nay you haue deaff'd our eares too much already,
Hee does confesse your crownes (payde and receiude)
But to giue backe your writings ther's no clause,
If them youle win, fight it out by our lawes.

*Bart.*   I humbly thanke your highnes. A gratious doome.

1. *Gent.*   One day to try this plea, to hel thowlt come.

*Exeunt two [Gentlemen].*

*King.*   Toth' next, we ha businesse of our owne, toth' next:
O *Barteruile*! for these two hundred crownes.                    10

*Bart.*   I payde 'em to that man.

*Far.*                         Now afore the King
And his Lords here, thou liest: th'ast payde me none.

*King.*   Your chollers sirra too hye.

*Far.*                         Tho my collar stand
So hye, it scarce beares vp this falling band.
Thou say'st thowlt sweare th'ast payd it: vds nailes sweare so,
And the fowle feende goe with't: two hundred crownes?
I ha lost as much at loggets: sweare but to reuel,
And spend't in hel, gallop thee and that toth' diuel.

*Lurch.*   Man wherefore doest not sweare?

*King.*                         Reach me a booke.

*Bart.*   Let me before I sweare, on my notes look,          20
Ile tell you the very day; pray hold my staffe,
Till I draw out my false eyes.

*Far.*   Draw thy heart out an't wut: thou maist wel say thy false
eyes.

*Bart.*   The day: August, 14.

*Far.*   Thats now, be dambd, and so away.

*Bart.*   On this day (August, 14.) I sweare I payde
Into these handes, two hundred crownes in gold.

*Far.*   Zounds nor in siluer: by this booke I had none.

*King.*   One of you two is periuriously forsworne.          30

*Far.*   He, he, as I am true Christian man.

*Iouin.*                         He sweares,
To your owne hands he payde them.

*Bart.*                         Else let that eye,

19 *Lurch.*] *Far.* Q

170

Which sees me play false, scourge my periury
With fearefull stripes.
*Far.*                    O iustice! falne downe dead!
                              Lurchall *and* Rufman *about him.*
Wud I had lost all, tho I had bin cozened,
Rather than thou thy soule.
*Omn.*                    He bleedes at mouth.
*Far.*   See his staffe (beating the earth, for heauen loues truth)
Is burst in shiuers, and that gold he swore
Was pay'd to me, lyes scattred on the flore.
*Ruf.*   He comes againe, the diuell will not receiue him.      40
*King.*   Take him away, weele punish him for this cryme.
*Ruf.*   Beg his office: you a Courtier?
*Spend.*   I haue a suite to your highnes.
*King.*   What ist count *Spendola?*
*Lurch.*   Maister, looke vp man.
In this black trance had thy soule flyen away,          [*Aside.*]
I had wrought hard and made a holliday.
*Ruf.*   Loose not a minute (pue-fellow) leaue him not yet,
I haue whales here too, lye playing in the net.
                              *Exit* [Lurchall *with* Barteruile].
*Far.*   Ile take this gold at venture, (sweete yong King,)      50
For all this hel-hound owes me.
*King.*                    Doe, and be gone.
*Far.*   I am pay'd: the diuels turn'd puritane I feare,
He hates (me thinkes) to heare his own child sweare.      *Exit.*
*King.*   The office of this periurde *Barteruile,*
I frankly giue away, diuiding it
To the Count *Spendola,* and our worthy friend
Braue *Bohor* here; farme it to whom you please.
*Both.*   We thanke your Highnes.
*Spend.*   Who bids most, he buyes it.
*King.*   If to his life, the diuel giues longer lease,      60
To build more worke for hel, goe see; and from him
Exact a strict account of what he owes vs.
*Ruf.*   That strict account ile take.          *Exit.*
*King.*                    Show him no fauour.

*Enter* Octauio *with petitions.*

*Oct.*  If now thou art a iust King, keepe thy word,
With thy poore subiects.

*King.*                              How now vncle, why?

*Oct.*  This is thy day to heare the poore mans crye:
And yonders crying enough, at thy Court gates;
Fiue hundred white heads, and scarce ten good hats,
Yet haberdashers too, of all trades some,
Crying out they are vndon.

*Omn.*                          Vndon, by whom?                    70

*Oct.*  Mary, looke: by such as you are, who goe gay,
Weare't out, booke downe more, set to their hands but neuer pay;
Neuer in deare yeares was there such complayning
Of poore staru'd seruants, or (when plagues are raigning)
Mourne orphans so and widdowes, as those doe
That owe these sorrowfull papers.

*King.*                          Pray how can I
To their complainings adde a remedy?

*Oct.*  Ile tell thee how: are any here in debt
To Merchants, Mercers, Taylors? let 'em iet
In their owne sattins, pay for what they ha tane,                80
And these will goe lesse braue, tother lesse complaine.

*Omn.*  Ha ha!

*Oct.*  The mightie wrongs the weake, the rich the poore,
This man should haue his owne, could he greaze more
His too-fat lawyer; that wretch for's coate does sue,
But his coat's gon, and his skin flead off too,
If his purse bee ore-match'd: these grosse impure
And ranck diseases, long vnto thy cure,
Thy word's in pawn fort, these are the poores cryes,
How wilt thou stop their throates?

*King.*                          With halters.

*Omn.*                                    Hang 'em.          90

*Oct.*  Hang 'em! any halters here! ist so set down?

76 owe] *i.e.* owne                    87 If] Ist Q

This law-booke speakes not so, yet tis thine own.
*King.* Still brauing me with this? burne it.
*Oct.*                                              Yes doe.
If you burne all the weeke, burne saterday too:
Doe one good dayes-deed first, read poore mens plaints.
*King.* Hels plagues confound 'em: in their heads and thine.
Vex me no more.
*Oct.*                    I warrant thee ile saue mine.
                                        *Meetes the Subprior.*
Holy Saint pardon me, (las good father,) my braine
So wilde is I forgot thee, but ile to him againe,
Tis but an old mans head off. King take it, ile speake      100
Whilest this stands on my shoulders.
*King.*                              But that you are —
*Oct.* An honest man, thoud'st haue this: ô I beseeke
Thy attention to this Reuerend sub-Prior,
Who plaines against disorders of this House;      [*Giues paper.*]
Where once Deuotion dwelt and Charitie,
Ther's Drunkennesse now, Gluttonie, and Lecherie,
Tell thou the Tale.
*Sub.*              Bad Storie soone is tolde;
Because tis foule, that Leafe does all in-folde.
Their sinnes grow hye, and fearefull, and strike at Heauen,
Punish them *THOV*, whose power from thence is giuen.      110
*King.* Your Friers so lustie!
*Iouin.* All the Barbers in *Naples* tell newes of that Priorie.
*Bris.* I would your Grace would let me purge this house of her
infection; bestowe the Liuings of it on mee, ile sweeten it in one
Moneth.
*Iouin.* Heele lay it in Lauender.
*King.* The Couent, the Demeasnes, Immunities,
Rents, Customes, Chartres, what to this house of *Baall*
Soeuer is belonging — *Brisco* tis thine.
*Oct.* Wut rob the Church too, (Now th'ast nothing left      120
Scarce for thy selfe?)
*Sub.*                O heauen for-fend such theft!
*King.* Bestowe it at thy pleasure.

173

*Oct.*                              Woe to those dayes,
When to raise Vpstarts, the poore *CHVRCH* decayes.
*Sub.*   Call backe thy gift (ô King) and ere these eyes
Behold vnhallowed hands to Tyrannize
Where many a good man has his Orisons said,
And many a *Requiem* bene sung out for the Dead,
(Till I am thrust out by Death) ô let mee haue
My dwelling there, there let me dig my Graue,
With mine owne Nayles, (shut vp from worldly Light,          130
Betweene two walls,) and dye an *Anchoryte*.
*King.*   I referre you to your Patron there.
*Bris.*                              Thats I:
Shew mee first where your Abbey-gold sleeps, then goe dye.
*Sub.*   I feare *RELIGIONS* Fall: Alacke I see
This world's a Cittie built by the most Hie,
But kept by man, (*GODS*) greatest enemie.          *Exit.*
*Oct.*   Let ill-Newes flye together, thou art full of teares,
But I more full of woes, of cares, of feares.          *Exit.*

*Enter* Astolpho.

*King.*   S'death shall wee haue yet faire weather?
*ouin.*   Heeres one storme more.          140
*Ast.*   *Calabrias* Duke demaunds of you a Daughter.
*King.*   Let me but lye with's wife, Ile giue him a Sonne.
*Ast.*   Hee sends for *Erminghild.*
*King.*                              Deliuer her.
*Ast.*   Shees not to be found.
*King.*                              Ya're an olde Foole,
To aske for that which is not.
*Ast.*                              Thus hee sayes,
Denie her and looke for warres.
*King.*                              So: goe your wayes.
*Ast.*   I'me quickly gone.          *Exit.*

*Enter* Ruffman *and* Barteruile.

*King.*                              With Sacke ile sweare you are,
This was short and sweete, — Seemes then we shal ha warres,

174

*Bohor*, the Drumme must scolde, the Canon thunder:
Fighting about a wench.
*Omn.*                    Tush, thats no wonder.                    150
*King.*  Who bayld him out of Hell? dambd periurde caytiff!
Out of mine eye.
*Ruf.*              I neuer begd before,
Pardon his crime (I intreate) and backe restore
Both your hye fauour to him, and his place.
*Bart.*  Let me want life, rather then want your Grace.
*Spend.*  Doe you thinke Ile loose the Kings gift?
*Bart.*                    Ile send you Golde.
*Spend.*  That stops my mouth, pray let him still Sir hold
This Office of *Receiuer*, I resigne
That part which I haue in it.
*Ruf.*                    And I all mine.
*King.*  Sirra, thanke these Lords.
*Bart.*                    I shall their loues deserue.    160
*King.*  *Barteruile*, wee haue warres, Ile haue thee lend mee
Some thirty thousand Chicquines at least.
*Bart.*                    Take all my Golde.
*King.*  Wel, get you home: with your bags sir, weele make bold.
*Bart.*  Your Maiestie shall haue what bags you will,
Bags onely, but Ile keepe my money still.              *Exit.*

            *Enter* Octauio *and* Astolpho.

*King.*  Now *Shalcan*, some newe Spirit.
*Ruf.*                    A thousand wenches
Stark-nak'd, to play at Leap-frog.
*Omn.*                    Oh rare sight!
*Iouin.*  Your vncle—
*King.*              Sdeath, still haunted with this gray sprite.
*Oct.*  You need no Taylors now, but Armorers,
Theres a deere reckoning for you all to pay,              170
About a Ladie; the *Calabrian* Duke
Is on a March: the Lightning flashes now,
Youle heare the cracke anone. Before the starre

            163 home:] ~ ‸ Q

                        175

To call whome vp, the wakefull Cocke doth sing,
Bee twice more seene abroad; at your Citie gates
The Diuells purseuant will beate (the Canon.)
Will these briske leaders (stucke with Estridge-feathers)
Goe braue your enemie now, and beate him backe?
Saue thee, thy Kingdome, and themselues from wracke?

*King.*   Dotard, I scorne to take prescription                    180
From any breath to which ours is supreame,
Stood Diuels with fire-works on your battlements,
A thousand Armed *Ioues* at your proude walls
Hurling forked Thunder, and the gates ramd vp
With piles of Citizens heads, our spring-tyde pleasures
No aduerse windes, no *Torrent* shall resist:
Midst flames weele dance, and dye a *Nerenist.*          *Exit.*

*Omn.*   Fight you, yare good for nothing else.          *Exeunt.*

*Ast.*   They mocke vs.

*Oct.*              All starke mad: let vs be wise,
And flye from buildings falling to'th surer side,          190
If wee can his safety, if not, (our owne prouide.)

                                                        *Exeunt.*


## [ACT IV, SCENE i]

*Enter* Barteruile *like a Turke;* — Lurchall.

*Bart.*   Thou hadst like t'ha sent mee swearing into Hell,
Ile weaue my Nettes my selfe, how doest thou like mee?
Is not this habite Turke-Merchant-like?

*Lurch.*   A meere Turke sir, none can take you for lesse.

*Bart.*   King borrow thirty thousand Chequines of mee! ha, ha!

*Lurch.*   But pray sir, what ist turnes you into a Turke?

*Bart.*   That, for which manie their Religion,
Most men their Faith, all chaunge their honestie,
*Profite,* (that guilded god) *Commoditie.*
Hee that would grow damnd-Rich, yet liue secure,          10
Must keepe a case of Faces, sometimes demure,
Sometimes a grum-surly sir, now play the Iewe,

Then the Precisian; Not a man weele viewe,
But varies so. My selfe, (of bashfull nature)
Am thus supplyed by Arte.

*Lurch.*                    Mine owne deere creature.
But sir, your Aymes, and endes in this.

*Bart.*                         Mary these —
A hundred thousand-Florens fill my Coffers,
Some of it is mine owne, and some the Kings,
Some taken vp at vse of sundry Merchants,
To pay at six six monthes, (on mine owne band,)          20
Sue that, Ile keepe the monies in my hand.

*Lurch.*   Youle breake sir.

*Bart.*                         Not mine owne necke, but their backes;
To get their monies, *Bartaruile* must die,
Make will, name an executur, which am I.

*Lurch.*   Rare!

*Bart.*           Giuen out his kinsman, lately imployed
By him in *Turky*.

*Lurch.*               What will hence befall?

*Bart.*   Like an executur will I cozen all.
Make creditors Orphans, and widowes spend those teares
They sau'de from their late husbands burialls;
They get not two pence it'h pound.

*Lurch.*                    Theile tell the King.          30

*Bart.*   The King? ha ha:
The King is going this way; he meanes to borrow,
(If the warres holde) my gold: yes: when? to morrow!
All debts of mine, on him shall be conferd,
I ha breifes and tickets which from time to time
Shew what large summes his minions ha fetcht from me,
His tribute mony has payd it, that's no matter,
The world bites these dead, whom aliue they flatter.
And so must I; then giue it out I left
A compleate state, but the Kings death bereft          40
Me of those summes he owde.

*Lurch.*               Say the King preuailes.

26 By] *om.* Q                    33 holde] holds Q

*Bart.*  With that wind must I likewise shift my sailes:
And where the fox gets nothing, will turne Ape,
Make legges, crouch, kisse my paw, present some stale
Deuice of vertues triumph to expresse
How much I ioy him safe, wish nothing lesse.

*Lurch.*  But how can you excuse your turning Turke?

*Bart.*  Easiest of all: Ile sweare, this saude my life,
Pursued by kennells of barking creditors,
For my much loue to him: and thus being forcde                    50
To walke obscure, my credit fell to wracke,
Want of returne made all my factors breake,
In parts remote; to recompence which losse,
And that with safetie I may giue direction
To my disturbd state, craue I the Kings protection.

*Lurch.*  Protection! whats that?

*Bart.*                               A merchant, and yet know'st not
What a protection is? Ile tell thee.

*Lurch.*  Pray sir, for I neuer broke with any man.

*Bart.*  It is a buckler of a large fayre compasse
Quilted within with Fox-skinnes: In the midst                     60
A pike sticks out, (sometimes of two yeeres long,
And sometimes longer.) And this pike keepes off
Serieants and Bailiffs, Actions, and Arrests:
Tis a strong charme gainst all the noisome smels
Of Counters, Iaylors, garnishes, and such hels;
By this, a debtor craizde, so lustie growes,
He may walke by, and play with his creditors nose.
Vnder this buckler, here ile lye and fence.

*Lurch.*  You haue out-reachd me.

*Bart.*                               Ile out-reache the diuell:
But I tempt danger: goe thou and featch some Frier                70
As if (at point of death,) I did desire,
(No, *Barteruile* did desire) to make confession:
If any creditors beate, or raile at dore,
Vp starts this Turke and answeres them.

*Lurch.*                               Why fetch I a Frier?

42 sailes] saile Q                    53 to] ore Q

*Bart.*   I haue a reaching plot in that (boy) hasten,
That we may smile in our securer port:
Seeing others sea-tost: why tis but a sport
For him thats safe, to see the proud waues swallow
Whole fleetes of wretched soules: it needes must follow,
Nature sent man into the world, (alone,)                    80
Without all company, but to care for one,
And that ile doe.
*Lurch.*            True Citie doctrine sir.
*Bart.*   Away, thy hast, our richest loue shall earne.
*Lurch.*   I came to teach, but now (me thinkes) must learne.

*Exeunt.*

## [ACT IV, Scene ii]

*Enter* Scumbroth *like a begger.*

*Scum.*   What saies the prodigall child in the painted cloth? when
all his mony was spent and gon, they turnd him out vnnecessary;
then did hee weepe and wist not what to don, for he was in's hose
and doublet: verily, the best is, there are but two batches of people
moulded in this world, thats to say Gentlemen and Beggers; or
Beggers and Gentlemen, or Gentlemanlike Beggers, or Beggerlike
Gentle-men; I ranck with one of these I am sure, tag and rag one
with another: Am I one of those whom Fortune fauours? No no,
if Fortune fauourd me, I should be full, but Fortune fauours no
body but Garlicke, nor Garlike neither now, yet she has strong   10
reason to loue it; for tho Garlicke made her smell abhominably in
the nostrills of the gallants, yet she had smelt and stuncke worse
but for garlike: One filthy sent takes away another. She once
smilde vpon me like a lambe, when shee gaue me gold, but now she
roares vpon me like a Lion. Stay: what said head? Spend this
brauely, and thou shalt haue more: can any prodigall new-come
vpstart spend it more brauely? and now to get more, I must goe
into the groue of *Naples*, thats here, and get into a blacke tree,
heares a blacke tree too, but art thou he?

*Glitt.*  He.                                                    *Within.* 20
*Scum.*  Ha ha, where art thou my sweete great head?
*Glitt.*  Head.
*Scum.*  O at the head, thats to say at the top: how shall I get vp?
for tis hard when a man is downe in this world to get vp, I shall
neuer climbe hie.
*Glitt.*  Hye.
*Scum.*  I will hie me then, but I am as heauy as a sow of lead.
*Glitt.*  Leade.
*Scum.*  Yes, I will lead (big Head) whatsoeuer followes,
Many a gallant for gold, has climbde higher on a gallowes.          30
The storme (euen as Head nodded) is comming: Cooke, licke thy
fingers, now or neuer.
*Glitt.*  Now or neuer.

*Rayne, Thunder and lightning: Enter* Lucifer *and Diuels.*

*Omn.*  Oooh.
*Luc.*  This is the tree.
*Scum.*  On which would you all were hang'd, so I were off it, and
safe at home.
*Luc.*  And this (I am sure tis this) the horrid groue
Where witches broodes ingender, (our place of meeting.)
*Scum.*  Doe witches ingender here: zounds I shall bee the diuels 40
bawde whilest he goes to his lecherie.
*Luc.*  And this the hideous black infernall howre:
Ha! no appearance yet? if their least minute
Our vassailes breake, sinck shall these trees to hell.
*Scum.*  Alas!
*Luc.*  This groue ile turne into a brimstone lake
Which shall be euer-burning.
*Scum.*  The best is, if I be a match in the diuels tinderbox, I can
stinck no worse than I doe alreadie.
*Luc.*  Not yet come? Oooh!                                         50
*Omn.*  Oooh, oooh.

*Enter* Shacklesoule, Rufman, *and* Lurchall, *at seuerall*
*dores with other diuels. Embrace.*

*Scum.*   Sure these are no Christian diuels, they so loue one another.
*Luc.*   Stand forth.
                              *Sits vnder the tree, all about him.*
*Scum.*   Frier *Rush* amongst 'em!
*Luc.*   And here vnlade you of that pretious freight
  For which you went, (mens soules;) what voyage is made?
*Omn.*   No sauing voyage, but a damning.
*Luc.*                              Good.
*Scum.*   I thought the diuell was turnde Merchant, theres so many
  Pirates at Sea.
*Ruf.*   Ith Court of *Naples* haue I prospred well,                    60
  And braue soules shall I shortly ship to hell:
  In sensuall streames, Courtier and King I ha crownde,
  From whence warre is flowing, whose tyde shall all confound.
*Scum.*   Are there gentlemen diuels too? this is one of those, who
  studies the black Art, thats to say, drinkes Tobacco.
*Luc.*   Are all then good ith Citie?
*Lurch.*                              No *Lucifer.*
*Scum.*   No nor scarce ith suburbes.
*Lurch.*   Great Prince of diuels, thy hests I haue obayde,
  I am bartring for one soule, able to lade
  An Argocy; if Citie-oathes, if periuries,                            70
  Cheatings, or gnawing mens soules by vsuries,
  If all the villanies (that a Citty can,)
  Are able to get thee a sonne, I ha found that man.
*Luc.*   Serue him vp.                              *Stands vp.*
*Scum.*   Alas, now now.
*Lurch.*   Damnation giues his soule but one turne more,
  Cause he shall be enough.
*Scum.*   Its no meruaile if markets be deere, when the Citie is bound
  to find the diuell roast-meate.
*Luc.*   Has *Rush* lyen ydle?
*Shac.*                    Ydle? no *Lucifer.*                          80

*51 S.D. Embrace] stet Q

181

*Scum.*    All the world is turnd diuell. *Rush* is one too.
*Shac.*    Ydle? I haue your nimblest diuell bin,
 In twentie shapes begetting sin.
*Scum.*    One was to get me thrust out of the priory.
*Shac.*    I am fishing for a whole schoale of Friers.
 Al are gluttoning or muttoning, stabbing or swelling:
 Ther's onely one Lambe scapes my killing,
 But I will haue him: then theres a cooke —
*Scum.*    Whose arse makes buttons.
*Shac.*    Of whom I some reuenge haue tooke.                    90
*Scum.*    The diuell choake you fort.
*Shac.*    He mickle scath has done me,
 And the knaue thinkes to out-run me.
*Scum.*    Not too fast.
*Luc.*    Kick his guilty soule hither.
*Shac.*                          Ile driue him to despaire,
 And make him hang himselfe.
*Scum.*    For hanging I stand faire.
*Luc.*    Goe, ply your workes, our Sessions are at hand.
*All 3.*    We fly to execute thy dread command. *Exeunt* [*the*] *three.*
*Scum.*    Would I could flye into a bench-hole.               100
*Luc.*    But what haue you don? nothing.
*1. Diu.*                          We haue all like bees
 Wrought in that Hyue of soules (the busie world:)
 Some ha lyen in cheesmongers shops, paring leaden waites.
*Scum.*    Wud I were there but with a paring of cheese.
*1. Diu.*    For one halfe ounce, we had a chandlers soule.
*Scum.*    If he melted tallow, hee smelt sweetly as I doe.
*1. Diu.*    Walke round hels shambles, thou shalt see there sticks
 Some foure butchers soules, puft queintly vp with pricks.
*Scum.*    Foure sweete-breads I hold my life, that diuels an asse.
*1. Diu.*    Taylors ore-reach vs, for to this tis growne,      110
 They scorne thy hell, hauing better of their owne.
*Scum.*    They feare not sattin nor all his workes.
*1. Diu.*    I haue with this fist beate vpon rich-mens hearts,

*99 *All* 3.] *Fire.* Q                    102 soules] soule Q
110 ore-reach vs] ore-reachers Q

To make 'em harder: and these two thumbes thrust,
(In open Churches) into braue dames eares,
Damning vp attention; whilst the loose eye peeres
For fashions of gowne-wings, laces, purles, ruffes,
Fals, cals, tires, wires, caps, hats, and mufs, and pufs.
For so the face be smug, and carkas gay,
Thats all their pride.

*Luc.*                    Twill be a festiuall day          120
When those sweete Duckes comes to vs: loose 'em not: goe:
More soules you pay to hell, the lesse you owe.
This Ewe-tree blast with your hot-scorching breath,
A marke, (toth' witch who next sits here) of death.

*Omn.*  Ooooh.                    *Fireworkes:* Scumbroath *falls.*

                                        *Exeunt Omnes.*

*Scum.*  Call you this, rayning downe of gold? I am wet toth'
skinne in the showre, but tis with sweating for feare: had I now
had the conscience that some Vintners and Inholders haue? here
might I haue gotten the diuell and all. But two sinnes haue vndone
me, prodigalitie, and couetousnesse: and three Pees haue pepperd  130
me, the Punck, the Pot, and Pipe of smoake, out of my pocket my
gold did soake. I cannot sweare now, zounds I am gallant: but
I can sweare as many of the ragged Regiment doe, zounds I haue
bin a gallant. But I am now downe, deiected, and debash'd, and
can better drawe out a thirdendale gallant, thats to say, a gallant
that wants of his true measure, than any tapster can draw him out
of his scores: thus he sets vp, and thus hee's pulld downe; thus is
he raised, and thus declinde:          *Singulariter,*
*Nominatiuo, Hic* Gallantus, a Gallant.
*Genetiuo, Hugious,* Braue.                                        140
*Datiuo Huic,* If he gets once a lick,
*Accusatiuo Hunc,* Of a taffaty Punck.
*Accusatiuo Hanc,* His cheekes will growe lanck,
*Hunc, Hanc, et Hoc,* With lifting vp her smock.
*Vocatiuo, ô!* Hees gon if he cryes so.
*Ablatiuo, ab hoc,* Away with him, he has the pock.
*Pluraliter, Nominatiuo, Hi gallanti,* If the pox he can defie,
*Genetiuo, Horum,* Yet hees a begger in coram.

*Datiuo, His:* His gilt rapier he does misse.
*Accusatiuo Hos,* Without his cloake he goes.                    150
*Accusatiuo Has,* To the Counter he must passe.
*Hos, has, et Hæc,* With two Catchpols at his back.
*Vocatiuo, ó!* A hole he desirde, and toth' hole he must goe.
*Ablatiuo, ab His,* Thus many a Gallant declined is.

Exit.

## [ACT IV, SCENE iii]

*Enter* Erminhild *to the Subprior.*

*Sub.*   What art thou?
*Erm.*                 Daughter to the *Calabriam* Duke.
   The haples troth-plight wife to your sad King.
*Sub.*   Alack! what notes are these I heare you sing?
   Pardon me madam:
   O Lady! want of you has bred much woe;
   Calamitie does euery where ore-flow,
   All long of your strange absence.
Drommes afar off marching.
*Erm.*                    I confesse,
   Loaden with your Kings contempt, and loath to beare
   Shame to my country, who from thence came freighted
   With many glorious honours, I preferd              10
   An obscure life before a publick shame;
   O then (good father) be it not my blame
   If my supposde death, on the King haue throwne,
   Dangers, which from himselfe are meerely growne.
*Sub.*   What (princely Mayden) would you wish me doe?
*Erm.*   I doe coniure you sir, by all the bonds
   Tye you to pious Acts, you would make way
   To my incensed father; giue him these lines,
   This Ring, pledge of that blessing he deliuerd me
   At our last parting: adde vnto these, if euer       20
   His daughters memory to him were deare,
   To wound the Prince let his rash hand forbeare:

Since through each wound he giues him, I am slaine,
If the sad king you meete, venture to tell him
That more for him, than he for me, I bide,
And am his subiect stil, tho not his bride.
*Sub.*    This shall I doe, how shall we meete againe?
*Erm.*    Feares follow me so, I know not where nor when.
*Sub.*    Hearke how the sound of horror beates the Ayre,
Your fathers vp in Armes and does prepare                    30
Sharpe vengeance, for this citie, woe is me: trust you
To me, who nere made much of woman yet,
Rest here sweete maide, till an old Frier beget
What ioyes he can to comfort thee? Is *Clement* growne
A womans man now? No, I am not mine owne,
Where your command may sway me: much more in this,
Where heauen (through vertues triall) makes you his.

> *Exeunt.*

## [ACT IV, SCENE iv]

*A table is set out with a candle burning, a deaths head, a cloke and a crosse; Subprior sits reading: Enter* Shackle-soule, *leading in an Italian Zany, fiue or six Curtizans, euery one holding a Iewell.*

*Shac.*    Thats he, and theres your golden hire to charme him
Your fees ile treble, let but lusts flame be felt;
The Alpine-snow at the sun's beames does melt,
So let your beauties thaw his frozen Age,
First t'act an old Lecher, then a diuell on hells black Stage:
Strike, strike your siluer strings: braue set of whores?

> *Musick.*

At your striking vp, diuells dance, and all hell roares.

> *Zany and Curtizans fall into a short dance.*

*Sub.*    What sound offends mine eare? Soule of temptation?
Enchanters I defie yee, get you gon;

37 S.D. *Exeunt*] *Exit* Q
6 S.D. *Musick.*] Q *prints in roman as text, line* 5 [Musick first t'act....]

Ime blind to your enticements, from this I learne,                    10
At how deere rate the careles world does earne,
That thing calld pleasure: how many soules doe fall?
(Sold for a little guilt to daube this wall?)
Hence with your witchcrafts, the sight of this driues hence,
All thoughts besieging our voluptuous sence.
*Shac.*    Another baite, at this he will not bite.

*The Zany singes: Subprior holds his head downe as fast a sleepe.*

*Zany.*    Will you haue a daintie girle? here tis:
  Currall lippes, teeth of pearle: here tis:
  Cherry cheekes, softest flesh; that's shee;
  Breath like *May*, sweete and fresh; shee shee.          20
  Be she white, blacke, or browne,
  Pleasure your bed shall crowne,
   Choose her then, vse her then,
   Women are made for men.
    Prettie, prettie wast:
    Sweete to be embracde:
   Prettie leg, ô prettie foote,
   To beauties tree the roote,
   This is she shall doo'te,
Or she shall doo't, or she shall doo't, she shall doo't, she shall doo't. 30
   Kisse, kisse, play, play, come and dally,
  Tumble, tumble, tumble, in beauties valley.
*Shac.*    His soule is chaind in pleasures, bind it fast,
If he breake your charmes, the strongest spell comes last.    *Exit.*

*All wake him.*

*Sub.*    Hence diuells incarnate, tis not the sorcerie
Of your deceitfull tunes, shuts vp mine eye,
Mine eares are likewise stop'd, hence, hence I say.
*Omn.*    Ha ha, a man of yce, a clod of clay.          *Exeunt.*

*Enter* Shackle-soule, *or some spirit in a frightfull shape.*

*Sub.*    Are all thy incantations spent now? art come againe?
Base workmanship of heauen, what other traine,          40

Were all hells frightfull horrors stucke in thy looke,
Thou canst not shake me.
*Shac.*                    I can.
*Sub.*                         Thou liest, thou shalt not.
*Shac.*   I bring thee tydings of thy death this night.
*Sub.*   How doest thou know that houre of my last sight?
False herald, Minister of despaire and lyes.
*Shac.*   I know to how many minutes thy daies must rise.
*Sub.*   Who giues thee the number.
*Shac.*                         All things to vs are knowne,
What euer haue bin, are, or shalbe don.
*Sub.*   Ile pose thee presently, whats this thou fiend
Which now I haue turnd too, doe but tell me that            50
And ile belieue thee.
*Shac*                 I scorne to be thy slaue.
*Sub.*   Downe, downe, and sincke into thy damned caue:
Looke here, doest fly thou hell-hound? I dare thee stand,
Or'e thee by these holy spells haue I strong command,
Thy battries are too weake: by goodmens prayers,
The continence of saints, (by which as stayres,
They ascend to heauen) by Virgins chastitie;
By Martirs cround deaths, which recorded lye
In siluer leaues, aboue: I charge thee downe,
Howle where tha'rt bound in slauerie, till the last dome.    60
*Shac.*   Stormes, thunder, lightning, rip vp the earths wombe.
*Sub.*   Eternall power, thankes on my humbled knee,
Thou still to constant brests giu'st victory.            *Exit.*
*Shac.*   No way to conquer thee? Ile giue thee ore:
Ne're fishd I so, (yet lost a soule) before.

                                                 *Exit.*

[ACT V, Scene i]

*Allarums. Enter King*, Rufman, Spendola, Brisco,
*with drawne weapons.*

*King.*   Blacke horrors, mischiefe, ruine and confusion
Affright vs, follow vs.
*Ruf.*                     Dare them to the face,
And you fright them.
*Spend.*               No safetie but to fly.
*King.*   Whither *Spendola*, whither? better stay, and die.

*Enter* Narcisso [*to the*] *King, Allarums a far of.*

*Omn.*   What hope? what newes?
*King.*                     Is my vncle fled?
*Narc.*                                   Hees gon: —
And fights against you.
*King.*               Follow him damnation,
That leaues his Prince so in distresse, in miserie;
O bane of Kings! (thou inchanting flatterie,)
Thy venome now I feele, eating my heart,
More mortall than an Indians poisned dart.                    10
*Ruf.*   Yar'e too deiected, gather head and fight it out.
*King.*   The head's here, where are hands to lay about?

*Enter* Iouinelli.

*Iouin.*   Where is the King?
*King.*                     The man that title mockes
Is here, (thou sad-visage man) are any hirde
To kill me, or betray me? let 'em come:
Griefes growing extreame, death is a gentle doome.
*Iouin.*   Prepare then for the worst.
*King.*                     I am armd fort: shew it.
*Iouin.*   Thy kingdome is a weake ship, bruizd, split, sinking,
Nor hast thou any pilot to waft vs o're

S.D. *weapons.*] Q adds, '*Iouinelli here.*'      5 Hees] Hees is Q

Out of this foule Sea, to some calmer shore.                              20
Thy peoples hearts are turnd to rocks of flint,
The Scholler, Souldier, and the Mariner,
Whom (as themselues say) once thou trodst vpon,
Now serue as wheeles of thy destruction.
*King.*   Flying swiftly backward, the kingly Lion quaild,
What shall the weaker heardes doe, if he fall?
*Spend.*   Lets fly.
*Omn.*          Zounds whither?
*Bris.*                    So we may be safe—
*Iouin.*                              But where?
*Spend.*   At *Barteruile*: the churle's to me beholden,
His house so stands, we may enter without feare.
*Omn.*   Beet so, to *Barteruile.*
*Spend.*                    What will your Highnes doe?       30
*King.*   Die *Spendola*, a miserable King,
None here can hinder vs of that.
*Spend.*                    How? die? —
Ha you any stomach to death sirs?
*Omn.*                    Not I.
*Spend.*                    Nor I.
Troth's, tho you grow desperate, weele grow wise.
*Omn.*   Farewell sir, weele saue one.              *Exeunt.*
*King.*                    Oh my cruelst enemies!
Stabs *Brutus* at me too?
*Ruf.*                    Now mine owne or neuer.      [*Aside.*]
*King.*   Why art not thou gon?
*Ruf.*                    I, Ile sticke to you euer:
I am no Courtier sir of fortunes making.
*King.*   Thou art no wiseman to preferre thy loue
To me, before thy life, pray thee leaue me.                              40
*Ruf.*   Not I.
*King.*      I shall not hate the world so really
As else I would, O had the ancient race
Of men (who had long leases of their liues)
Bin wretched as we are, no recompence

25 *King.*] *Iou.* Q          25 Lion] Lions Q

Could the Gods haue giuen them for their being here,
But now more pittifull wise nature growes,
Who cuts of mans yeeres to cut off his woes.
*Ruf.*  True sir, and teaches him a thousand waies
To leade him out this horrid giddy maze.
*King.*  I apprehend thee, a small daggers point,          50
Opens the vaines to cure our plurizy.
*Ruf.*  Than to be made your foes-slaue, better dye.
*King.*  A hundred thousand deaths, than like a captiue
Be chaind to grace prowd *Cæsars* Chariot wheele.
*Ruf.*  Much lesse a pettie Dukes.
*King.*                              Fetch me deare friend,
An armed Pistoll, and mouth it at my brest:
Ile make a way my selfe, and all my sorrowes
Are made away.
*Ruf.*                  The best and nobler spirits
Haue done the like.
*King.*                  Your brauest men at Armes
Haue done the like.
*Ruf.*                  Philosophers haue don it.          60
*King.*  Great peeres haue don it.
*Ruf.*                              Kings haue done the like.
*King.*  And I will doe it.
*Ruf.*                      Nay it shall nere be said,
I liu'd a minute after you: here, here.
*King.*  I embrace thee noblest friend.
*Ruf.*                              Lets saile together.
*King.*  Content braue *Bohor*: oh! but whither? whither?
*Ruf.*  From hell, (this world,) from fiends, (in shapes of men.)
*King.*  No: into hel, from men to be dambd black with fiends.
Me thinkes I see hell iawne to swallow vs.
*Ruf.*  Fuh, this is but the swimming of your braine,
By looking downe-wards with a timerous eye.          70
*King.*  My soule was sunck too low, to looke more hye,
Forgiuenes heauen.                          *Allarums.*
*Ruf.*  The whippes of furies lash mee: the foe comes on.
*King.*  And we will meete him, dare confusion,

And the worlds mixed poisons, there is a hand
That fights for Kings, and vnder that weele stand.

*Allarum, still a farre off: Enter a Frier running.*

*Ruf.*　Whither runnes this Frier?
*Frier.*　　　　　　　To saue my wretched life,
From th'insolent soldier, threatning the Cities spoile.
*King.*　Of what house art thou?
*Frier.*　　　　　　Of father *Clements* Order,
The Capachines Subprior: a quick messenger　　　　　　80
Fetched me to be rich *Barteruiles* confessor,
Who lyes a dying.
*King.*　　　A dying!
*Frier.*　　　　　　He does, but I
Haue come thus far, with so much ieopardy,
That could I safely get to the lee shore,
Him nor the priory would I see more.
For charities sake, direct me, and defend me.
*King.*　To helpe destressed men, religion bindes me,
Shouldst thou in this hot broiles, be met abroad,
It will be iudgde you leaue your Priory,
Carying gold and siluer with you.
*Frier.*　　　　　　Las I haue none.　　　　　90
*King.*　But Frier if you be thus taken, your life is gon,
Here, here, cast off thy habit, better that lye
Ith Streetes than thou poore wretch; weare mine, and away:
Strike downe that lane.
*Frier.*　　　　　Thankes maister, for your liues ile pray.
　　　　　　　　　　　　　　　　　　　　*Exit.*

*King.*　This *Bohor* shall disguise me, whither wilt thou fly?
*Ruf.*　Ile shift I warrant: hast thou toth' Priory.
*King.*　If we nere meete againe, (best friend) farewell.
*Ruf.*　Not meete, yes, I hope, you must not thus cheate hel.
　　　　　　　　　　　　　　　　　　　　*Exit.*

*King.*　I will not trust this fellow: toth' Priory, no:
*Barteruiles* Confessor: if to betray　　　　　　100

84 get to the lee] get the keys Q　　85 Him nor] Nor Q

Thou findst the churle apt, leaue him, if not, there stay.
The downefall of that Prince, is quick and steepe,
Who has no heart to leaue, nor power to keepe.

                                                              *Exit.*

### [ACT V, Scene ii]

*Enter* Barteruile [*as a Turk*] *and* Lurchall, *with the Courtiers.*

*Lurch.*   Make the doore sure, the house is round beset.
*Omn.*                                            Beset!
*Bart.*   Put vp: feare nothing: Armies should they enter,
  Cannot here find you.
*Omn.*                    How shall we escape?
*Bart.*   Send for your truncks and iewels, ile ship you this night:
  meane time, this vnknowne way, leads to a cellar, where a world
  cannot fetch you forth: In, In, if danger pursue you, in a dry-fat
  ile packe you hence.
*Omn.*   Zounds into the dungeon?
*Bart.*                    So to *Sardini*:
                                            *Exeunt* [*Courtiers*].
  Your cloakes and your gilt rapiers, downe, downe, downe.

            [*Enter King as a frier, aloofe.*]

*King.*   How soone meetes Babels-pride, confusion?          10
*Lurch.*   What nest of birds are these new-kild with feare?
*Bart.*   Fowle cannot last long sweete, therefore kept there
  In my cold cellar; stay, house beset? what fees?
*Lurch.*   Such as strike dead the heart, yet giue no blowes.
  Serieants.
*Bart.*   This — footra for 'em: proclamations *Lurchall*,
  Six thousand Crownes are his, can these betray,
  Soone earnd, weele share; fetch the *Calabriam* hither,
  They are here say: dam 'em.
*Lurch.*                    You shall be dambd together.
                                                              *Exit.*

*Enter King as a Frier [comes forward].*

*King.* Wher's that deuote sicke man desires to take        20
Leaue off this world? *Deus hic* to all now here.
*Bart.* Now Domine Frier; what I to you confesse
You are bound by oath to keepe.
*King.*                          I auer no lesse.
*Bart.* Keepe then this close, I am no Turke, not I,
But *Barteruile* disguisde in pollicy.
*King.* Are you the Sickman?
*Bart.*                          Sick of a disease,
Bad as a plague to Citizens, I must breake,
(Play a banckrowts part) I haue monie of the kings,
Of merchants, Ile keepe all, these are Citie-springs;
Here lyes Serieants Leaguer: about my doores:        30
My house to me is an hospitall, they the sores
Which run vpon me vily, (peepe I but out,)
To raize this Dunkirke seige, thus cast I about.
*King.* Lets heare, pray how?
*Bart.*                          Thus, thus sweete Domine Frier,
Ile be like you, a Capuchine: So, by your Prior,
Sub-prior, and couent, I may be fetcht hence,
Spite of all Showlder-clappers violence.
Tho the King should lay hands on me, I wud not tary.
*King.* You neede not.
*Bart.*                          You are my guard, my Sanctuary.
*King.* But what your leuel in this, when this is don?        40
*Bart.* Alas! what leuell but pure deuotion?
*King.* The Diuell you haue.        [*Aside.*]
*Bart.*                          When I dye there, take All:
Will you goe to your prior and tell this?        *A March a far.*
*King.*                          Yes I shall.
*Bart.* Ile send him an earnest peny (a hundred Crownes)
As the first stone my charitie builds vpon.
What drom's this? come, dispatch Frier, and be gon.

46 gon.] gon. *Exit.* Q

[*As King starts to leaue,* Barteruile *takes off his disguise.*]

*King.*   Out of this hell thou meanest: yes ile fly from thee
As from the Diuels hangman: thowl't else betray mee.
World! to what crest of villanie art thou growne?
When (of good men) whole kingdomes scarce breede *One.*     50

                                              *Exit.*

[*Enter* Lurchall, *bound, and Duke of* Calabria,
*with* Astolpho. *Soldiers.*]

*Lurch.*   Heres the Duke of *Calabria* sir: if you haue made mee tell
a lye, theile send me of a voiage to the yland of Hogs and Diuels,
(the *Barmudas,*) the Duke sir.
*Bart.*   His grace is welcome, las! I had more neede
To haue Phisitions and Apothecaries,
Than fighters at my gates: *Lurchall* why come they?
*Cal.*   Deliuer vp those monsters in thy house,
That haue deuourd a Kingdome and the King.
Tis death to thee, and him, if thou detainst 'em.
*Bart.*   I detaine 'em, here, here, here.                          60
*Ast.*   Reward if thou deliuerst them.
*Bart.*   Ime past rewarding in this world, I looke
Onely for good mens prayers, theres the key *Lurchall.*
*Cal.*   Vnbind him: stay why did thy house receiue them?
*Bart.*   Full sore against my will: the bed I rize from
Count I my death-bed; for (each minute) I looke
When Angells (heauens good porters) will let me in,
Yet (like my betters) I'me heauy laden with sin.
And being thus sicke, and at last gaspe, I sent
For my neerst cozen, my executor,                                   70
Who seeing braue fellowes beating at my gates,
Tooke 'em for honest men, let 'em in simply,
And vndertooke this night, to ha shipd 'em hence;
My faithfull Seruant telling me this, (In zeale,
To you and my country) I bid him, All reueale.
*Cal.*   Thast plaid a Subiects part in't.
*Bart.*                                   Heele lead you to them.

*Cal.*   My Lord, take force and seize 'em, nere stand vpon
More trialls; giue 'em speedie execution.
*Ast.*   Come fellow.

> *Exeunt* Astolpho *and* Lurchall *cum Militibus.*

*Bart.*   Your grace has don with me?
*Cal.*                              Goe, looke to thy health:    80
The crownes the proclamation promised,
Shall to thy man be payd.
*Bart.*                        Thankes to your Grace:
Las what I did in this, was for no hire.    *Exit* [Barteruile].
*Cal.*   Ha ha, the rent of a cellar neuer was so deere.
On, beate the drum.

> *As they goe off; Enter* Octauio *with* Rufman *and a guard.*

*Oct.*   Are the rest tane?
*Cal.*                    Yes.
*Oct.*                        The graund-Pyrat's here.
Heres the Diuells bellowes, kindled all those fires,
Which now are burning: This is the Snake, whose sting
(Being kept warme in the bosome of a King)
Struck him to'th-heart: This hee, who by the force    90
Of his damb'd Arguments, was the first diuorce,
Of the Kings Loue, this is *Bohor.*
*Cal.*                           This that Serpent?
Y'haue all (like Traytors) wrought a Princes fall,
And all shall taste one death.
*Oct.*                             Sirra, wheres the King?
*Ruf.*   Warrant mee life, ile bring you to the place
Where you shall take him.
*Oct.*                          Wult thou betray him Slaue?
*Ruf.*   Yes.
*Cal.*   Thou shalt haue life.
*Ruf.*                           And you the King shall haue.
*Oct.*   And the Gallows shall haue thee, else hang me. Away.

> *Exeunt.*

83 S.D. *Exit.*] Q *prints after line* 84

## [ACT V, Scene iii]

*Enter* Scumbroth [*to the Sub-Prior*].

*Scum.*   Alas, wheres the sub-Prior?

*Sub.*   Here; what ailest thou?

*Scum.*   Can you picke nothing out of my face?
Is there not a Deaths-head standing on my shoulders?

*Sub.*   Why, what's the matter?

*Scum.*   The Lord Pryor is calld away.

*Sub.*   Whither, by whome?

*Scum.*   By the Great-head, I thinke he couzened mee, Hee is gone
to the blacke-squibbe-tree, to *Iudas Oke*, set by the Diuell, I tolde
you then, I saw Frier *Rush* spit fire amongst other Hel-cats, and   10
yee woud not belieue me. Now I tell you, that the Pryor is choackt;
will his choaking goe downe your throate?

*Sub.*   How, choackt?

*Scum.*   Yes, choackt: that of which men die ore-night, and are well
the next morning, wine has kild the Lorde Pryor: he woud in a
brauerie taste the liquor of our Vines, because you threatned he
should neuer licke his lippes after. And the Kernell of a grape
stopt his winde-pipe, for want of a skowring-sticke.

*Sub.*   Art thou sure hee is dead?

*Scum.*   How, dead? because I wud be sure, I cut his throate of   20
purpose, to take out the Kernell.

*Sub.*   Most fearefull and prodigious, whither runst thou?

*Scum.*   To see more throates cut, an Execution of certaine
Gallants is this morning, and I came running to see them. Who
like a whore spoyles euery good thing that comes into his hand?
The hang-man. I leaue you to the Gallowes.                    [*Exit.*]

23 an] and Q
24 morning, and...them. Who] morning. And...them, who Q

196

*Enter* Barteruile *like a Frier, brought in by the Subprior, the King,*
Shackle-soule, *and* Lurchall, *with others [all like Friers].*

*Shac.*  Welcome deare brother: now your heede must be
Not to looke backe at this worlds vanitie,
Riches and pleasures: you haue laide aside
That Garment, and must now be mortifide.                              30
*Bart.*  I am mortifide, I warrant you.
*King.*                     So is the Diuell.        [*Aside.*]
*Sub.*  Your Gold and siluer, you must see no more.
*Bart.*  O Fye! giue it euery farthing to the poore,
When I haue sent for't hither.
*Lurch.*                  That will be neuer.        [*Aside.*]
*Shac.*  Your money shalbe spent in pious sort.
*Bart.*  I know that: Let my soule be the better for't,
Thats all I craue for, after I am dead.
*Sub.*  Many a *Requiem* for it shall be said.
*Omn.*  What Drum is this?
*Shac.*                  Fryers stand vpon your Guard.
The Priorie is beset with Armed-men,                                 40
Of which some Troupes are entred.
*King.*  I am betrayd.
*Bart.*  *Lurchall* I feele my wezand pipe cut.
*Lurch.*  I warrant you.

*Enter* Calabria, Octauio, Astolfo, Rufman *led by two
holding pistalls, Souldiers, drums, and Cullors.*

*Cal.*  Guard the Abbey gates, let not a Frier goe forth:
You haue a King amongst you, which is he?
*Omn.*  A King!
*Sub.*            I know of none here.
*Cal.*                     Villaines you lie.
*Oct.*  This caitife does delude you, tortur him.
*Cal.*  Hang him, and these vp or'e the Abbey walls,
Our wrath shall smite like thunder where it falls.                   50
*Bart.*  I shall like a dog, die without mony, *Lurchall.*

27, 35 *Shac.*] *Rush.* Q          32, 38 *Sub.*] *Pri.* Q

*Lurch.*   I warrant you.

*King.*   Tyran, that royall hart thou huntst, is here,
Stand from me all, you haue betrayd me all,
And ile trust none of you, if the Lion must fall,
Fall shall he like a Lion; thinkst thou (base Lord)
Because the glorious Sun behind blacke cloudes
Has a while hid his beames, hees darkned for euer?
Ecclipsd neuer more to shine, yes, and to throw
Fires from his sparkling eyes, thee to confound.                    60
Touch not that noble friend of mine, (It seemes,
For my sake markd for danger,) let your arrowes
(Dipd in rancke poyson) be shot all at me,
Since all is lost, die nobly, and loose life too:
O vncle! must the first dart fly from you?

*Oct.*   Into thy bosome fly I.

*King.*                           To betray me?

*Oct.*   To fight for thee till I can fight no more:
Hadst thou possest this Kingly spirit before,
We ne're had left thee: what makes Iudas here?

*Ast.*   Heres he that to the Duke thy life betraide.                 70

*King.*   *Bohor!*

*Oct.*                I, *Bohor.*

*Ruf.*                          I told him where you were.

*Oct.*   I tell thee tha'rt a traitor and ile haue
Thy head off, or thou mine.

*Ruf.*                          Head?

*Oct.*                                Thart a slaue?
Thou seest Duke what to trust too.

*Bart.*   I haue confest, and shal be hangd, the King?

*Cal.*   Our faire game come to this? our swordes I see
Must from your hearts-blood let out al my wronges,
A murdred daughter for iust vengeance cryes,
Whom to appease, your liues weele sacrafize:
Beate the drom.

*King.*                Thunder mock thunder, beate ours.              80

*Sub.*   O let these fires be quenchd out with my teares.
If waters cannot, (Duke) I bind thy rage

With this strong charme, and this: read ore that spell,
And let thy hard brest grow more flexible.                    *Exit.*
*King.*   Wheres *Iouinelli*; and that bastard crue
Of my false friendes?
*Oct.*            Beheaded.
*King.*                         They haue their due.
*Cal.*   The ring I gaue her, and her hand: old man, —
Wheres the old Frier deliuerd these?
*Omn.*                         Hees gon.
*Cal.*   Make after him, tis some delusion.

*Enter Subprior and* Erminhild.

*Erm.*   Tis no delusion (father) am I the ground          90
Of this your quarrell, which must both confound
If you goe on: your battailes thus ile part,
The first blow giuen, shall run cleane through my heart.
*King.*   Oh noble constant maid, forgiue my wrongs,
The warmth of heauen to a pyning spring
Cannot such comfort giue as thy glad presence
Does to my bosome.
*Oct.*            Will you fight or no?
*Cal.*   Twere madnes to wish stormes when faire windes blow:
Will you your faith yet keepe?
*King.*                         Inuiolate.
*Cal.*   Then here end all my warres.
*King.*                         And all my hate.          100
Hast all these Friers vp to the Abbey walles,
And with shrill voyces, this our peace proclaime,
Stay holy father: *Bohor*, See you this don.
*Ruf.*   Vengeance, I haue now lost more than I haue won.   *Exeunt.*
*Bart.*   I shall goe scot-free *Lurchall.*
*Lurch.*                       Passing well?
*Bart.*   They doe not smell me, yet my selfe I smell.      *Exeunt.*
*Oct.*   Why sends your Highnes thus, these Friers to play
Your heralds parts in publishing this peace?
*King.*   There's in't a riddle (vncle) which by none

94 *King.*] *om.* Q

But by these Friers onely, can be don.          *Enter Friers aboue* 110
So: are you mounted? Sing now.
*Omn.*                     Sing?
*King.*                          Yes sing,
  Like Swannes before your deathes: there you all shall dye,
  Giue fire to this most damned priory.
*Sub.*   Alacke for pitty!
*King.*                     Father, but for thee,
  Thunder from heauen had (long ere this) to dust
  Grinded these hellish buildings: that hand was iust,
  Which struke your vitious Prior, so is our doome,
  That Synagogue of diuells, let fire consume.
*Bart.*   But meanes the King that I shall burne here too?
*King.*   Thou? the grand villaine, giue him a villaines due.          120
*Bart.*   I am no Frier, see I'me poore *Barteruile.*
*Omn.*   How? *Barteruile?*
*King.*                     He lyes: the slaue's a Turke.
*Bart.*   A Christian by this hand, Your officer.
*King.*   The cittie canker, the courts cozener,
  A diuell in shape of man.
*Bart.*                     Halfe that I haue
  I freely giue, so you my life will saue.
  Ile lend your Hyghnes thirty thousand chequines.
*King.*   Ten Kingdomes cannot buy thee; were there ten hels
  Thart dambd in all. S'death! fire that house of diuels.
*3. Diuells.*   Doe: lets not want light to set forth our Reuels.          130
*Ruf.*   King, little doest thou know, whom (all this while)
  Thy court, this Couent, and this *Barteruile,*
  Haue entertaind: of hell, three Spirits we are.
*Omn.*   How?
*Ruf.*   Sent to catch soules for *Pluto,* our Prince and maister.
*Omn.*   Defend vs heauens.
*Ruf.*                     Thy selfe hast burst those bandes
  In which I once held thee: these are in our handes.
*Bart.*   If you be right Serieants, for mony youle let mee goe.
  Fiue thousand crownes ile giue but to goe home.

129 fire] fie Q

200

*All* 3.  No.                             140

*Bart.*  Ile put in foure brokers to be my baile: I hope theile be taken.

*Ruf.*  Yes as thou art, (to hell,) you dog leaue howling.

This pile of greene young diuels, needes no fire

Of mortals kindling to consume these frames,

You shall with vs to hell ride, all in flames.

*Shac.*  Catch.

*All* 3.      Come.

*Ruf.*          Let euery spirit his owne prize beare.

*All* 3.  They are so heauy with sin, theile soone be there.

*Ruf.*  Away then and be dambd, wud you all were here.

*Omn.*  Oooh.                 *Sinck downe, aboue flames.*

*King.*  Immortall thankes for our deliuerance:       150

Race to the ground those wals: no stone shall stand,

To tell such place was euer in our land,

What welth can there be found, giue to the poore,

Another house weele build and thee restore,

To former virginitie: weepe not for these ruines,

Thou shalt from vs haue honours. Here we begin

Our reigne anew, which golden threds shall spin,

Iustice shall henceforth sit vpon our throne,

And vertue be your Kings companion.

Warre here resignes his black and horrid stage     160

To sportfull *Hymen,* God of Mariage.

                                   *Exeunt.*

## [ACT V, SCENE iv]

*The play ending, as they goe off, from vnder the ground in seuerall places, rise vp spirits, to them enter, leaping in great ioy,* Rufman, Shacklesoule, *and* Lurchall, *discouering behind a curten,* Rauillac, Guy Faulx, Barteruile, *a Prodigall, standing in their torments.*

*Omn. Spir.*  Ha, ha, ha.

*Omn. Dam.*  Torments in-vtterable! oh! dambd for nothing?

*Rau.*  Terrors incomprehensible.

*Faulx.* Back: y'are blowne vp else.

*Bart.* Whooh: hot, hot, hot, — drinck, — I am heart-burnt.

*Prod.* One drop, a bit.

*Faulx.* Now, now, now.

*Bart.* I am perboild, I am stewd, I am sod in a kettle of brimstone pottage. — it scaldes, — it scaldes, — it scaldes, — it scaldes — whooh.                    10

*Omn. Diu.* Ha ha ha.

*Prod.* But one halfe crom, a little little drop, a bit.

*Faulx.* Towers, towers, towers, towers, pinnacles and towers, battlements and pynnacles, steeples, abbeys, churches and old chimneys.

*Bart.* Zounds drinke, shall I choake in mine Inne? drinck.

*Omn. Dam.* Drinck, drinck, oh! one drop, one drop, to coole vs.

*Ruf.* So many tapsters in hell, and none fill drinck here?

*Omn. Diu.* Ball no more, you shall be liquord.          *Exeunt.*

*Rau.* Why art thou dambd toth' horrors of one hell,        20
Yet feelst ten thousand.

*Faulx.*                    Wherefore is thy soule
Made sensible of tortures which (each minute)
Kill thee ten thousand times, yet canst not dye?

*Bart.* Some sacke.

*Prod.* Why for a few sinnes that are long hence past,
Must I feele torments that shall euer last?
Euer euer.

*Bart.* Let the sacke be mulld.

*Rau.* Why is the diuell,
(If man be borne good) suffred to make him euill?        30

*Bart.* Man is an asse, if he sit broyling thus ith glasse house without drinke: two links of my chaine for a three halfe peny bottle of mother consciences Ale: drinke.

*Omn. Dam.* One drop of puddle water to coole vs.

11, 19 *Omn.*] *om.* Q          17, 34, 52 *Dam.*] *om.* Q

*Enter* Shacklesoule *with a burning torch, and a long knife,* Lurchall *with a handfull of Snakes, A third spirit with a ladle full of molten gold, All three make a stand, laughing.*

*Omn. Diu.*    Leaue howling and be dambd.
*Shac.*    Heres drinke for thee royall villaine.        *Stabs* Rauillac.
*Rau.*    Oh!
*Shac.*    Ist not good!
    For bloud th'ast thirsted, and thy drinke is bloud.
    Strikes it so cold to thy heart? heres that shall warme thee. *Agen.* 40
*Rau.*    Damnation, furies, fire-brandes.        *Hand burn't off.*
*Omn. Diu.*    Ha, ha, ha.
*Prod.*    One drop of moisture, but one crum.
*Lurch.*    Art hungry, eate this adder: dry? Sucke this Snake.
*Prod.*    Sucke and be dambd thy selfe: Ile starue first. Away.
*Bart.*    Is not this all waters? Ruby water, some Ruby water, or
    els a bottle of posterne water to saue charges, or els a thimble-full
    of lymon water, to coole my stomach.
*3. Diu.*    The ruby is swilld vp all, heres lymon, downe with't.
                                            [*Molten gold.*]
*Bart.*    Foh, the great diuell or els some *Aquauite* woman has made 50
    water, It scalds me.
*Omn. Dam.*    Oooh.
*Omn. Diu.*    Ha ha ha.        *Curtaines are drawne ouer them.*

                    *Enter* Rufman.

*Ruf.*    Hell grinnes to heare this roaring: wheres this black child
    Of faddomles perdition? rarest diuell
    That euer hould in *Barathrum?* here, (deere pupill)
                                    [Faulx *brought in.*]
    Of a new damnations stamp, Saucer-eyde *Lucifer,*
    Has drunke to thee this deepe infernall boule off,
    Wut pledge his vglines?
*Faulx.*    Reach it mee.                                    60

35, 42 *Diu.*] *om.* Q
48–49 stomach. | 3. *Diu.* The ruby is] stomach ∧ the ru- | *Spir.* By is
53 *Omn.*] *om.* Q

203

*Ruf.*  Choake with it.
*Omn. Diu.*  Ha ha ha.
*Faulx.*  Giue fire, blow all the world vp.
*Ruf.*  Bounce: tis don. Ha ha ha. —

*Fires the barrell-tops.*

*Faulx.*  I shalbe grinded into dust; It falls: I am mad.  [*Exit.*]
*Omn. Dam.*  I am mad, I am mad.  *Within.*
*All 4.*  Ha ha ha.
*Others.*  Ho ho ho.  *Spirits from below.*

*Enter* Pluto, *attended by* Minos, Æacus, *and*
Rhadamanth, *and three Furies.*

*Pluto.*  Fetch whippes of poysoned steele, strung with glowing
    wires,
And lash these saucie hell-hounds: ducke their soules,  70
Nine times tot'h bottome of our brimstone lakes,
From whence vp pull them by their sindged hayre,
Then hang 'em in ropes of yce nine times frozen o're:
Are they scarce hot in hell, and must they roare?
What holliday's this? that heres such grinning, ha!
Is hell a dancing Schoole? y'are in extreames,
Snoring, or els horne-mad? who are set on shore,
On this vast land of horror, that it resounds,
With laughter stead of shrikes, who are come to our bounds? ha!
*Ruf.*  Dread Lord of this lower tortary, to thy Iayle  80
Haue we thy busie Catch-polls (prisoners) brought
Soules, for whose comming all hell long hath sought.
*Pluto.*  Their names: Is *Ward* and *Dantʒiker* then come?
*Omn.*  Yes: *Dantʒiker* is come.
*Pluto.*  Wheres the dutch *Schellum*? wheres hells factor! ha?
*Ruf.*  *Charon* has bound him for a thousand yeeres,
To tug ats oare: he scourd the Seas so well,
*Charon* will make him ferriman of hell.
*Pluto.*  Where's *Ward*?
*Shac.*  The Merchants are not pilld nor pulld enough,  90

They are yet but shauen, when they are fleade, hee'le come.
And bring to hell fat booties of rich theeues,
A crew of swearers and drinkers the best that liues.
*Omn.*   *Ward* is not ripe for damming yet.
*Pluto.*                                      Who is it then?
*Cutlar* the Serieant: ha! he come?
*Ruf.*                           Yes *Pluto*:
*Cutlar* has bin here long, sent in by a carman,
But his sterne lookes the feindes did so displease,
Bound hand and foote, he houles in little ease,
Hauing onely mace to comfort him: he does yell,
And raue, because he cannot rest in hell.                    100
*Shac.*   Tis not for him, that we this holliday hold.
*Pluto.*   The baude of Shorditch, Is that hellcat come?
*Ruf.*   No: but sha's bin a long time lanching forth,
In a Rosa-solis-barke.
*Pluto.*                      Diuells! who is it then?
*Mall Cutpurse* is she come?
*Omn.*                          Our cosen come? No.
*Shac.*   Tis not yet fit *Mall Cutpurse* here should houle,
Shee has bin too late a sore-tormented soule.
*Pluto.*   Where is our daughter? ha? Is shee ydle?
*Omn.*                                      No.
Shee was beating hemp in bridewell to choke theeues,
Therefore to spare this shee-ramp she beseeches,          110
Till like her selfe all women weare the breeches.
*Lurch.*   *Mall Cutpurse* plyes her taske and cannot come.
*Pluto.*   For whom then is this wilde Shroue-tuesday kept?
*Ruf.*   See King of gloomie shades what soules resort,
To this thy most iust, and least-fying court.
*Pluto.*   Stay, since our Iayle is with braue-fellowes storde,
Bid *Charon* that no more yet come aboard.
Seeing our Iudges of hell here likewise are
Sit: call a Sessions: set the soules to a barre.
*Minos* (the iust:) *Rhadamanth* (the temperate:)          120
And *Æacus* (the seuere,) each take his state.
*Minos.*   Not an officer here?

*Omn.*                 A Fury.

3. *Iud.*              Make an Oyes?

*Fury.*   Oyes! All manner of soules, if they loue their owne quietnes, keepe out of hell, vnlesse they haue horrible businesse at this infernall sessions, vpon paine of being damnably plagued for their lustines. Back there, let those shackeld rakehels shew their faces.

*Some.*   Roome here, we must come into the court.     *Within.*

*Pluto.*   What damned fiends are those dare make this noise?

*Shac.*   A Iury of Brokers impanelde, and deepely sworne,     130
To passe on all the villaines in hell.

*Rhad.*   *Euill-Conscience* be their keeper.

*Fury.*   Looke to the Iury: *Euill-Conscience* looke to the Brokers.

*Pluto.*   Now proceede.

*Æac.*   Stay, let the King of Ghosts haue first a vew
Of those who are doom'd to paines horrid, but new.
Then produce those who came to your prison vntryed.

*Fury.*   Peace there.

*Omn.*   Heres one, hels tortures does deride.

                               Rauillac [*brought in*].

*Rau.*   Arraigne me, rend me peece-meale, ile confesse nothing.    140

*Ruf.*   Peace, thou shalt ball thy throate out.

*Rau.*   Merciles hangmen! to tiranize ouer so braue a Roman spirit.

*Pluto.*   Ho, ho, what country diuell is this?

*Rau.*   Thine owne.

*Ruf.*   A french.
The eagerest bloodhound that ere came from thence;
Is there a King to be murdred, whilest he does stand
Colossus-like, supporting a whole land,
And when by his fall that Land most feares a wracke,
Send forth this diuell; his name is *Rauillac.*     150

*Rau.*   *Rauillac*: I am *Rauillac*, that laughes at tortures, spurnes at death, defies all mercy: Iybbets, racks, fires, pincers, scalding oyle, wilde-horses, I spit in the face of all.

*Fury.*   Peace.

      128 *Some.*] *Omn.* Q
      128 S.D. *Within.*] Q prints in roman as end of the sentence

*Rau.*  No: were my tongue torne out with burning flesh-hookes,
  Fames thousand tonges shall thunder out *Rauillacs* name, extoll it,
  eternise it, Cronicle it! Canonise it: oh!
*Minos.*  Downe with this diuell to'th dungeon, there let him houle.
*Rau.*  Worlds shall applaud my Act, and crowne my soule.  *Exit.*
*Pluto.*  Another.                                                   160
*Omn.*  Come, you leane dog.          *Prodigall brought in.*
*Prod.*  One drop, a bit.
*Pluto.*  Whats he? what staruelings this?
*Prod.*  One that lacks a medicine for hunger: I am falne away.
*Omn.*  From heauen.
*3. Iud.*  To'th common Iayle with him.
*Fury.*  He must feede on beggeries basket: leaue balling sirra.
*Prod.*  Shall I be vndon for a little drinke.
*Lurch.*  No, thart vndon for drinking.
*Pluto.*                          Starue him, away.
                                          *Exit Prodigall.*
  What was he when he liu'de.
*Lurch.*                    A prodigall:                              170
  Who (in one yeare,) spent on whores, fooles and slaues,
  An Armies maintenance, now begges for cromes, and raues
  To see his sumptuous buildings, pastures, woodes,
  That stood in vplands, dround in Rhenish floodes.
*Pluto.*  Is here all?
*Shac.*              All! no, the Arch-helhound's here.

                         Faulx *Enters.*

*Pluto.*  What *Peter Goner*'s this?
*Faulx.*  Speake softly, within an inch of giuing fire, within an inch.
*Shac.*  Had all thy gray diuells in their highest lust sat,
  T'haue litterd furies, they could not haue begot
  One to match this: ith' darke he groapd damnation —            180
*Faulx.*  Now, now.
*Shac.*  Digd cellars to find where hel stood and has found it;
  There was but one villainy vnborne, and he crownd it.
*Faulx.*  So: all the billets lye close; glorious bonfire? pontificall

166 3.] *om.* Q     179 T'haue] *M.* T'haue Q [*indented as speech-prefix*]

bonfire; braue heads to contriue this, gallant soules to conspire in't,
resolute hand to seale this with my blood, through fire, through
flint; ha, ha, ha, whither fly my selfe to heauen, friends to honour,
none to the halter, enemies to massacre, ha ha, dismall tragicall-
Comedy now?

*Pluto.*   What does he?

*Shac.*                    As he thinkes, giuing fire to powder;          190
  Nere in any land could diuels haue found, such walkes,
  As he was beating out.

*Pluto.*                His name.

*Omn.*                          *Guy Faulx.*

*Faulx.*   Who cals? damnation stops throate.

*3. Iud.*   Let it stop thine.

*Faulx.*   Am I betrayd? giue fire, now, now, giue fire.

*Omn.*   To burne thine owne soule, villaine.

*Pluto.*                          Pay him his hire:
                                  *Exit* [Faulx].

  He has a desperate rakehels face.

*Shac.*                    Had his plot tane fire,
  One realme before any other had doomesday seene,
  Kings who in tombes lay at rest had wakened beene,
  He was within twelue howers of hewing downe                200
  A whole land at one blow, and at once drowne
  In a flood of flames, an Ark-roiall with his whole fleete,
  Of nobilitie and clergy: in a leaden-sheete
  Law and her children had bin hotly wrap'd;
  Millions ere this had in our iayle bin clap'd,
  For damned Arts not known now, which had then
  Bin rife, but now lye dead (th'Acts with the men.)

*Pluto.*   Make much of this our ningle: for the rest
  Deliuer 'em to our head-hangman.

*Omn.*   When?

*Pluto.*        In a twinckling.

*Minos.*                    How applaudes *Pluto*          210
  Our enginous tortures, and most rigorous doome?

---

210 *Omn.* When?] Q *prints at foot of sig.* M 2 *and in error repeats at top of sig.* M 2ᵛ,
*although* M 2 *cw is* '*Plu.* In'

*Pluto.*   *Minos,* thy doome is iust; — But you ill-fac'de Caitiffs,
What fish in your infernall Nets, drew you vp
Ith *Naples* Court, Citie, and Frierie?
We charg'de you saile thither: Is mischiefs Riuer there drie?
*Ruf.*   Drie, No: Fat preyes for hell we all did meete,
In Court, Citie, Countrey, Nay, in euery streete,
In euery house, within-him, and without-him,
Hee that wore best cloathes, had some Diuell about him:
Courtiers from *Naples* hither in sholes are come,                    220
Some for Ambition, for Flattery, and Enuie some:
Some, who (each meale) eate subiects vp, and wore
Whole Families in their shoo-strings, such, and others more,
Being here, haue bene examining (euer since
They came) by Hells-clarke, (*Spotted-Conscience.*)
*Minos.*   Till the next Sessions, these wee must deferre.
*Pluto.*   None come fro'th Citie, so many bad being there!
*Lurch.*   Yes, (King of endles horror) see who's here.
                                                    Barteruile [*brought in*].
*Pluto.*   Rich-men in hel! they are welcom, whats the graybeard.
*Bart.*   One that can buy thee and ten such as thou art out of thy  230
Sea-coale-pits here. Is not this *Newcastle?*
*Lurch.*   No couetous wretch: tis Hell, thy blacke-soules prison.
*Bart.*   Soule in prison! I never had any soule to speake on.
*Lurch.*   Now thou shalt finde th'ast one.
*Bart.*   Can Angells Bayle mee?
*Minos.*   Not all the wealth which the worlds back does beare
Can Bayle thy wretched soule hence, Now tis here.
*Bart.*   A thousand Pounds. ——
*Fury.*   Where ist foole?
*Rhad.*   Thy wealths now gone,                                       240
Thy hands still catch at bags, but they gripe none.
*Bart.*   Whats this? ——
*Omn.*   Ha, ha, ha.
*Æac.*   Ayre, shadowes, things Imaginary:
That is thy Torment now, which was thy Glory.

212 you] your Q                      212 ill-] all- Q
228 S.D. Barteruile] Q *prints as text ending line* 228 *after* 'here:'

*Bart.*   If you giue me bags full of Saw-dust, in stead of money, my
Ghost shall walke.

*3. Iud.*   To thy grim Father of Hell.

*Bart.*   No, to my olde brother, Syr *Achitophell Pinch-gut* shall I:
shall I?                                                                    250

*Pluto.*   Hence with him, the Churl's mad:
In *Lethes*-flood drownd all the wealth hee had.

*Bart.*   My chaine, Let me hang in chaines, so it bee my Golde
chaine; Theeues, theeues, theeues.          *Exit [led by three deuils].*

*Minos.*   Throwe him head-long into our boyling-Lake,
Where molten Golde runnes.

*Lurch.*                              His thirst it cannot slake,
Seas could not quench his dropsie: Golde to get
Hee would hang a Citie, starue a Countrey. Euen yet
Raues hee for Bonds and incombers: to saue whose soule,
(Tho hee fed none liuing) Saw-sages were his dole.                          260

*A confused noyse to come pressing in.*

*Omn.*   What coyle is that?                              *A Noise.*

*Enter a [Puritan] Ghoast, cole-blacke.*

*Pur.*   Tis a burning zeale must consume the wicked, and therefore
I will not bee kept out, but will chastize and correct the foule
Fiend.

*3. Iud.*   Whats this blacke *Incubus?*

*Shac.*   An Arch-great Puritane once.

*Omn.*   Ha! How! a Puritane?

*Minos.*   An Arch-great Puritane! How comes thy soule so little?

*Pur.*   I did exercise too much with a liuely Spirit.

*Pluto.*   Are there any more of his Synagogue?                            270

*Ruf.*   Yes, a whole Hoy-full are Landed.

*Omn.*   Ha!

*Pluto.*   Are they all so blacke as he is?

*Omn.*   Worse.

*Minos.*   Syrra, why being a Puritane is your soule so black?

254 S.D. *Exit.*] 3—*Exit.* Q

*Pur.*   Wee were all smoakt out of our owne Countrey, and sent to *Rotterdam.*

*Minos.*   How camst thou lame and crooked, why do'st halt?

*Pur.*   All the brethren and sisters for the better part are crooked, and halt: for my owne part, I neuer went vpright.                    280

3. *Iud.*   And yet a puritane? hence with him.

*Pur.*                                     Alacke!
How can I choose but halt, goe lame, and crooked?
When I pulld a whole church downe vpon my backe.

*Minos.*   Hence with him, he will pull all hell downe too.

*A noise to come in [and then to go out].*

*Pur.*   Let in the brethren, to confound this wicked assembly.

3. *Iud.*   Thrust him out at hell gates.            *Exit [Puritane].*

*Pluto.*                             Theile confound our kingdome,
If here they get but footing: rise therefore, away;
Keepe the Iurie of brokers till our next court day.

*Minos.*   Adiourne this.

*Fury.*                   Oyes! Sessions is deferd,
Because of Puritanes, Hell cannot be cleerd.                    290

*Pluto.*   Set forward to our Hall paued all with brasse,
Iudges we thanke you: let our officers drinke,
I'th bottome of hells celler, for their good seruice.
Since to this heigth our Empyre vp you reare,
Hell shall hold triumphes, and (thats don,) prepare,
Agen to walke your circuites o're the earth,
Soules are hells Subiects, and their grones our mirth.

*FINIS.*

## *Epilogue.*

If't be not good, the Diuell is in't, (they say,)
The Diuell was in't, this then is no good play
By that conclusion, but hereby is meant,
If for so many nones, and midnights spent
To reape three howres of mirth, our haruest-seede
Lyes still and rot, the Diuels in't then indeed:
Much Labour, Art, and Wit, make vp a Play
As it does a Ship, yet both are cast away,
(When brauely they haue past the humorous Seas)
At landing, What black fates curseth both these?                10
Sayle it, or sinck it, now tis forth, and nere
The Hauen at which it longs t'ariue: if there
It suffers wrack, the spitefuller Rockes shoote forth,
Yet non may bring it home laden with much worth.
By wonted gentle gale, (sweete as the Balme,)
Or by extending your faire liberall Palme,
To fan away all stormes, if you see it lowers,
The ayre shall ring thankes, but the glory's yours.

15 By] By your Q                    16 your] *om.* Q

# TEXTUAL NOTES

## I.i

73 Of] Although *a* for *of* is perfectly good idiom in such contractions as *a'th* for *of the*, the present Q reading *A*, emended to *Of*, more probably arose through confusion with the *A* beginning the line above.

## I.iii

130 *Scumbroath*] It seems more likely that Q *Scumb:* (with its colon) is an abbreviation used in the manuscript than that the Prior is using a nickname.

172 manderers here are spies] Clearly the line must read either 'These mander here as spies' or 'These manderers here are spies'. That the proof-reader chose the latter means very little, since elsewhere he did not consult the manuscript. The compositor misread the handwriting, or gained a too hasty false impression, of one of the two operative words. Although the context might at first sight seem to support *here as spies* by giving a greater force to *here* as *this monastery* rather than merely as a redundant identification of the pilgrims, yet two arguments may support the present editorial choice. (1) It would seem easier to mistake *are* for *as* than the shorter verb *mander* for the longer form of the slightly unusual noun *manderers*; (2) the use of *here* following a noun is a perfectly acceptable idiom, as in 'Lord Christofero here would ask of thee' from *Lust's Dominion*, V.vi.27 (see vol. 4).

## IV.ii

51 S.D. *Embrace*] Q prints this whole direction as a side-direction to the right of lines 50–52. In this direction *Embrace* [Q *embrace.*] begins a line after line 51, where it seems to belong, although typographically it gives the appearance of intervening between *Rufman* and *and Lurchall*. Despite the appearance of Shacklesoul and Rufman together at one point in the King's court (III.iii.34 S.D.), there is no particular reason for them to embrace while ignoring Lurchall. Scumbroth's description of the action recounted in the direction seems to apply to all the devils embracing with the three just arriving, as indicated by the alteration made in this text.

99 *All 3.*] Q *Fire.* may represent a stage-direction to the left, but the fact that it comes where a speech-prefix is required leads more naturally to the supposition that an error is involved. Although some stage effect of fire would not be inappropriate to accompany the departure of the three devils, perhaps it would unduly detract from the effect of the direction at line 125.

# PRESS-VARIANTS

[Copies collated: BM¹ (British Museum C.34.c.25), BM² (C.12.f.4[2]); Bodl
(Bodleian Library Mal. 235[9]); Dyce (Victoria and Albert Museum); Eton
(Eton College); NLS (National Library of Scotland); CSmH (Huntington
Library); CtY (Yale University); DFo (Folger Shakespeare Library); MH
(Harvard University); NN (New York Public Library); 7Gab (Seven Gables
Bookshop, New York City); Taylor (Roxburgh-Heber copy property of
Robert H. Taylor, Yonkers, N.Y.)]

## SHEET A (*inner forme*)

*Corrected:*   BM¹⁻², Bodl, Dyce, Eton, CSmH, CtY, DFo, MH, NN,
            7Gab, Taylor.
*Uncorrected:* NLS.

Sig. A4.
   *Prologue,* l.  4 *Kiſsing*] *Kiſsing.*
          18 Fiſhwiues] Fiſhwins

## SHEET B (*outer forme*)

*Corrected:*   BM¹⁻², Bodl, Dyce, Eton, NLS, CtY, DFo, MH, NN,
            7Gab.
*Uncorrected:* CSmH, Taylor.

Sig. B3.
   I.i.109 can] coan
     116 lǎds] lǎds.
     120 To fiight] Fight
     126 helpers] helper,
     128 Glitterbacke] Gltterbacke

Sig. B4ᵛ.
   I.ii.51 fatall] fatell
     52 *Veſpaſian*] *Eſpaſian*
     53 forgiue] fnrgiue
     58 guilded] gilded
     62 weele] wheele
     70 Sacred] Saered

## SHEET B (*inner forme*)

*Corrected:* Eton, MH, NN.
*Uncorrected:* BM[1–2], Bodl, Dyce, NLS, CSmH, CtY, DFo, 7Gab, Taylor.

Sig. B 1[v].
I.i.42 Thart] That
49 miſchiefe] miſchife
Sig. B 4.
I.ii.27 mee be ſo] mee ſo

## SHEET C (*inner forme*)

*Corrected:*  BM[1], Bodl, Dyce, CSmH, CtY, MH, NN.
*Uncorrected:* BM[2], Eton, NLS, DFo, 7Gab, Taylor.

Sig. C 1[v].
I.ii.138 pen] thing

## SHEET D (*outer forme*)

*Corrected:*  BM[1–2], Bodl, Eton, NLS, CSmH, CtY, DFo, MH, NN, 7Gab, Taylor.
*Uncorrected:* Dyce.

Sig. D 1.
I.iii.71 dambde] damde
92 *Corporis*] *Corporib*
Sig. D 2[v].
I.iii.172 are] as
193 muſt] iuſt

## SHEET D (*inner forme*)

*Corrected:*  BM[1–2], Bodl, Eton, NLS, CSmH, CtY, DFo, MH, NN, 7Gab, Taylor.
*Uncorrected:* Dyce.

Sig. D 1[v].
I.iii.112 gluttonous] glottonous
112 almes!] almes ¡
117 heauen!] heauen?
Sig. D 3[v].
II.i.20 pilot in] pilat In

Sig. D 4.
    II.i.59 Ride] Rirde
        71 with] w'th
        79 Trundle] Trondle

### SHEET F (*outer forme*)

*Corrected:* BM¹.
*Uncorrected:* BM², Bodl, Dyce, Eton, NLS, CSmH, CtY, DFo, MH, NN,
        7Gab, Taylor.
Sig. F 2ᵛ.
    II.iii.23 our] or
        23 order] ourder

### SHEET G (*inner forme*)

*Corrected:* BM¹⁻², Bodl, Dyce, Eton, NLS, CtY, DFo, MH, NN
        7Gab.
*Uncorrected:* CSmH, Taylor.

Sig. G 2.
    III.ii.89 in] *omitted*

### SHEET H (*outer forme*)

*Corrected:* BM¹⁻², Bodl, Dyce, Eton, NLS, CSmH, CtY, DFo, MH,
        NN, 7Gab.
*Uncorrected:* Taylor.

Sig. H 2ᵛ.
    III.iii.158 refigne] refi g e
        164 bags] dags
Sig. H 3.
    III.iii.184 rambd] ramd
    IV.i.7 their] their
        7 Religion,] Religion·
Sig. H 4ᵛ.
    IV.ii.30 gallant] gallanr
        31 thy] hy

### SHEET H (*inner forme*)

*Corrected:* BM¹, Bodl, Dyce, Eton, NLS, CSmH, CtY, DFo, MH,
        NN, 7Gab.
*Uncorrected:* BM², Taylor.

Sig. H 1ᵛ.
    III.iii.108 infolde] in-folde

109 Their] Thəir
118 Cuſtomes] Cuſtoɯes
121 heauen] beauen

Sig. H2.
III.iii.149 the Drumme] tbe Drumme
150 wench.] wench
151 periurde caytiffe] periuade caytiff

Sig. H3ᵛ.
IV.i.24 executer] executur

Sig. H4.
IV.i.69 out-reacht] out-reachd
70 fetch] featch

## SHEET K (*inner forme*)

*Corrected:* BM¹⁻², Eton, NLS, CSmH, DFo, MH, NN, 7Gab, Taylor.
*Uncorrected:* Bodl, Dyce, CtY.

Sig. K1ᵛ.
V.i.67 to] ro

Sig. K2.
V.i.84 That [*to margin*]] That [*indented*]

Sig. K3ᵛ.
V.ii.65 riſe] rize
67 heauens] heaunes
68 betters] bettors
74 My] my
80 me?] me,

Sig. K4.
V.ii.91 damb'd] daɯb'd
V.iii.1 ſub Prior] ſub-Prior
9 *Oke*] *Okes*

## SHEET M (*outer forme*)

*Corrected:* Eton, DFo, MH, NN, 7Gab.
*Uncorrected:* BM¹ ², Bodl, Dyce, NLS, CSmH, CtY, Taylor.

Sig. M2ᵛ.
V.iv.215 charg'de] chard'de

# EMENDATIONS OF ACCIDENTALS

## Dedication

9 and-*Cry*] and *Cry*  
11 *Gentlemen*] *Gntlemen*  
12 *well.*] ~ ,  
46 *Audience*] *Andience*

## Prologue

2 o'th‸] ~ ,  
7 (by *Hap*]‸ ~ ( ~  
10 viewe‸] ~ .  
16 Th'il-] Thil-  
24 -*Day*,)] ~ , ‸  
24 *Braines.*] ~ ·  
25 loue] louc  
34 *Hammer*,)] ~ , ‸

## I.i

10 smell!] ~ ,  
12 *Pluto.*] *Pln.*  
18 Spaniards] Spanirards  
21 before)] ~ ‸  
45 Why?] ~ :  
48 snoring] suoring  
49 mischife] Q(u); mischiefe Q(c)  
50 a bawde] abaw'de  
53 S.D. *Spirit*] *Sqirit*  
54 Sumners] Summers  
57 T'vphold] T.vphold  
63 indeed,] ~ .  
66 -kinde,] ~ ‸  
91 S.D. Shackle-] Srackle-  
104 oylde,] ~ ‸  
118 display‸] ~ .  
120 fight] fiight  
121 first). If] ~ )‸ if  
128 *Glitterbacke*,)] ~ , ‸

## I.ii

S.D. Octauio,] ~ ‸  
S.D. Astolfo‸ (*two vnckles*),] ~ ,  
  (~ ~)‸  
S.D. Brisco (*Counts*),] ~ , (~)‸  
6 On] *On*  
44 this,] ~ ‸  
46–48 Q *lines*: Men...fit, | That  
  ...good, | A...blood! |  
  (Butchers...more.) | Shall...  
  say  
56 Q *lines*: bost, | Which  
58 gilded] Q(u); guilded Q(c)  
61–62 Q *lines*: Heauen...dayes, |  
  But...told) | Ending no worse, |  
  Their...gold.  
70–71 Q *lines*: Be...it; | Sacred...  
  hye; | And...that, | Shall dye.  
94 law-suite] law, suite  
96 bribes‸ ...wrangling,] ~, ...  
  ~ ‸  
110 or'e:] ~ ‸  
118 forren] farren  
158 each mans] eachmans Q (*almost*)  
171–173 *prose in* Q

174 h'as] has
184 tasked, ... one;] ~ ; ... ~ ,
201 Kings)] ~ ₐ
216 *Bris.] Pris.*
217–218 Q *lines:* Especially...red, |
    like...letter.
222–223 *prose in* Q
223 eat'st] e'atst

242 *Bris.] Pris.*
244 S.D. Trumpets] *Ttŭpets*
244 S.D. Astolpho] *Astolphe*
250 Neapolitane] *Neapolitane*
251 *Erminhild)*] ~ ₐ
252 selfe.] ~ .)
256 Prince] Ptince

### I.iii

7 Subpriors] Subpiors
35 preface] proface
61 ignorance] ignornnce
71 damde] Q(u); dambde Q(c)
79 *Contra*ₐ] ~ .
82 consequently] cōsequenly
97–103 Subprior....] *prose in* Q
106 abiure] abuire
112 glottonous] Q(u); gluttonous
    Q(c)

130 Giue] Ciue
136 caudels] candels
141 eke] ike
143 deuise] deuice
169 Almisdeeds] Alsmisdeeds
172–173 *prose in* Q
189–190 *prose in* Q
199 Churches] Ghurches
207 *Shackle-] Sackle-*

### II.i

1 pictur's] pictar's
14 way,] ~ .
18 compasse,)] ~ , ₐ
25 H'as] Has
33 Acted,] ~ ₐ
41–45 Q *lines:* ...whole | swarmes
    ...trompes, | And...play; |
    But...away.
50 gloues,] ~ .
51–52 Bid...gon.] *one line in* Q
54 mar'de)] ~ ₐ
56 reuiu'de] reui'de
67 Soare] So'are
71 w'th] Q(u); with Q(c)
79 Trondle] Q(u); Trundle Q(c)
88 citie,] ~ ₐ
94 deuice] dcuiee

98 *Ninies,*] ~ ₐ
106 Q *indents 2 ems*
116 againeₐ] ~ ,
117 I 'em] iem
117–118 Q *lines:* Th'whole...
    brought | With...Seruitors)
130–131 Q *lines:* Maist...arme,
    That...bleed.
138 *Seaf.] Seap.*
138 kite] kit
139 Sir,] ~ ₐ
155 young-|man] young-man
158 lowere] louere
165 Bosmen] Besmen
169 long,] ~ .
190 (In idle] ₐ ~ (~
213 twice, ... rare;] ~ ; ... ~

### II.ii

S.D. *fellowes] fellewes*
5 Takes] takes
8 ten,] ~ ₐ

16 I] *I*
19 thee] thce
22 hither —] ~ .

219

22 *Bart.*] *Barr.*
22 That‸] ~ ,
23 Minutes, . . . dore;] ~ ; . . . ~ ,
53 S.D. *Brauo*] *Brano*
71 crownes] erownes
87 their] rheir
98 keep] keek
99 grow] gtow
99 S.D. *Exit*] *Extit*
116–117 My. . .morgage.] *one line n?*
Q
120–122 *prose in* Q

141–142 Hold. . .vp.] *one line in* Q
150 *Bart.*] *Aar.*
157 S.D. *Exit*‸] ~ .
167 S.D. *Exit*‸] ~ .
170 S.D. *Exit*‸] ~ .
171–173 Q *lines:* Bring. . .fellow,
      Depose. . .maister?
171 here,] ~ ‸
182 Hees] hees
182 breathles.] ~ ‸
185 gon?] ~ .

## II.iii

7 ‸warme] (warme
28–29 Tho. . .way.] *one line in* Q
29–30 Let. . .knaue.] *one line in* Q
47 thee,)] ~ ,‸
49 spite,)] ~ ,‸

67, 68 *Shackle-soule*] shackle-soule
74 thy] rhy
77 *Elixar*] *Elipar*
87 rest) for him,] ~ ‸ ~ ~ ,)
88 downe,] ~ ‸

## III.i

S.D. Narcisso] Narcisco
4–5 Q *lines:* doe | With
8–9 Q *lines:* I. . .cracke | It. . .
   the | Shell
10–12 Q *lines:* Or. . .they|Are. . .
   drey-|horses. . .woman.
14–16 Q *lines as prose:* The. . .
   man | Is. . .must | needs. . .
   notany,

20–24 Q *lines:*Destruction. . .sun,|
   I. . .daughters:| Tell. . .father:|
   And. . .mariage | Brings. . .
   not | To. . .rancke.
28 graue‸] ~ .
34 That] Tbat
49 diuorce.] ~ ‸
54 downefall] downefull

## III.ii

11 man-|slaughter] man-|slaughter
15 whore-] whorme-
16 hairy] hiary
21 heart-burning] heart-|burning
22 me‸ now,] ~ , ~ ‸
27 patience] patiencee
29 ith] Ith
32–34 Q *lines:* Doe. . .roaring |
   boyes. . .thinke | they. . .too?

40 *Scum.*] *Suc.*
43 noble-mans] noble-|mans
45 am I] amI
50 awry.] *full stop may loosen and
   drop out in some copies*
58 mis-begot,] ~ .
62 man?)] ~ ? ‸
69 father‸] ~ ,
91 such] sueh

220

120 Vsurers] Vsuters
129 blisse;] ~ ,
130 find,] ~ ;
131–132 If...hungry.] *one line in* Q

146, 148, 157, 160 *Glitt.*] *Gilt.*
165 *Glitt.*] *Flit.*
176–177 *prose in* Q

## III.iii

S.D. Iouinelli,] ~ .
 1–6 *prose in* Q
31 Christian] Curstian
37 truth)] ~ ◬
43 your] yout
45 man.] ~ ,
49 S.D. *Exit*] *Ezit*
61 hel, ... see;] ~ ; ... ~ ,
65 vncle, why?] ~ ? ~ ◬
91 *Oct.*] *Ost*
96 thine.] ~ ◬
98 father,)] ~ , ◬
100–101 *prose in* Q
101 are —] ~ . —
102 this:] ~ ,
103 Thy] thy
108 in-folde.] ~ , Q(u); infolde,
   Q(c)

116 *Iouin.*] *Ion:*
119 Soeuer] soeuer
121 Scarce] scarce
122 those] thoses
126 has] hes
132 *Bris.*] *Rris.*
138 S.D. Astolpho] Astolphe
146 So:] ~ ◬
151 caytiff] Q(u); caytiffe Q(c)
157 hold◬] ~ ,
162 Some] some
165 S.D. Astolpho] Astolphe
168 vncle —] ~ .
174 sing,] ~ ◬
175 at] At   176 Canon.)] ~ ◬)
177 -feathers)] ~ .)
184 ramd] Q(u); rambd Q(c)
190 buildings] buidldings

## IV.i

3 Is] *indented* 4 *ems*
3, 4, 6 Turke] *Turke*
11 demure,] ~ .
13 viewe,] ~ .
20 (on] ◬ ~
24 executur] Q(u); executer Q(c)
26 befall?] ~ ¿
31–32 Q *lines*: The...way; | He
  ...borrow,
33 when?] ~ ◬

33 morrow!] ~ .
49 creditors,] ~ :
50 him:] ~ ,
55 craue] eraue
69 out-reachd] Q(u); outreacht
   Q(c)
70 featch] Q(u); fetch Q(c)
72 desire)] ~ (
74 Vp starts] V pstarts
81–82 *one line in* Q

## IV.ii

4 doublet:] ~ ◬
5 to say] tosay
13 another] anoher

18 *Naples,*] ~ ◬
23 O at] O'at
28 *Glitt.*] *Giltt.*

30 gallowes.] ~ ·
31 (euen)_∧ ~
41 to] ro
52 Q *lines*: Christian | Diuels
54 S.D. *tree*,] ~ _∧
68 Q *lines*: diuels, | Thy
86 swelling:] *colon clear only in*
　BM²
88 cooke —] ~ . —

93 -run] -rnn
95 guilty] guily
99 execute] sxecute
109 Foure sweete-] 4. Sweete-
115 eares,] ~ .
137 pulld] pulls
140 Braue] braue
147 *Hi*_∧] ~ .
154 Gallant] Callant

## IV.iii

36 Q *lines*: me: | Much

37 (through] ) ~

## IV.iv

S.D. *Curtiʒans*] *Gurtiʒans*
11 earne,] ~ .
19 that's] that‚s
19 shee;] ~ ,
23 Choose] Chose

30 doo't.] ~ _∧
34 S.D. *Exit*.] *Eexit*.
35 *Sub*.] *Snb*.
38 S.D. Shackle-soule] Shackle
　soule

## V.i

1 mischiefe,] ~ _∧
2 Affright] affright
4 S.D. Narcisso_∧] Narcisco:
5–6 Hees...you.] *one line in* Q
13–15 Q *lines*: The man...mockes|
　Is...me, | Or...come:
32–33 How?...sirs?] *one line in* Q
39 loue_∧] ~ .
76 S.D. *Allarum*,] *comma only a
　speck in all copies but* BM¹

80–82 *prose in* Q
81 *Barteruiles*] *Bateruiles*
83 ieopardy,] ~ .
90 *Frier*.] *Eri*.
93 away:] ~ _∧
101 stay.] ~ ,
102 steepe,] ~ .
103 keepe.] ~ ,

## V.ii

1 sure,] ~ _∧
4 night:] ~ _∧
15 Serieants.] Q *turns-up after line*
　14
18 share; fetch_∧] ~ _∧ ~ ,
22 Frier] Ftier
28 (Play]_∧ ~
51 sir:] ~ _∧

63 Onely] onely
65 rize] Q(u); rise Q(c)
69–70 *prose in* Q
85 On,] ~ _∧
89 (Being) (being
92 Serpent?] ~ ,
96 Where] where
97 *Ruf*.] *Rnff*.

## V.iii

1 sub-Prior] Q(u); sub Prior
    Q(c)
7 Whither] Whtiher
8–12 Q *lines*: By...mee, | Hee
    ...to | *Iudas*...then, | I...
    Hel-cats, | and...you, | that...
    choaking | goe...throate?
13 How,] ~ ∧
20 How, dead?] ~ ∧ ~ ,
20–22 Q *lines*: How...sure, | I...
    the | Kernell.
25 hand?] ~ .
26 -man.] ~ ,
39 *Shac.*] *Shæck.*

59 shine] shind
60 sparkling] sparklings
60 confound.] ~ ,
83 this:] ~ ∧
104 *Ruf.*] *Suf.*
107 Highnes ∧ thus,] Hignes, thus ∧
109–110 *prose in* Q
111 Sing?] ~ .
113 Giue] Ciue
122 lyes:] ~ ∧
139 crownes] Crownes
144 consume∧] ~ ,
146–147 *All*] *Au.*

## V.iv

8 perboild] perbold
8 brimstone∧] brim-|stone,
18 here?] ~ :
27 Euer euer.] Q *runs-on with line*
    *above*
31 without] | Without
32 three halfe] threehalfe
46 or] | Or
47 thimble-] | Thimble-
53 S.D. *Enter*] *Euter*
54–55 *prose in* Q
68 S.D. Æacus] Æac us
69 glowing] glouing
69 wires,] ~ .
76 y'are] yare
95 come?] ~ .
108 daughter?] ~ ¿
120 temperate:] ~ .
125 plagued] plagude
126 rakehels] rake-|hels
136 new.] ~ ·
155 flesh-hookes] flesh-|hookes
161 S.D. *Prodigall brought in.*] *Prodi-*
    *gall. Brought in.*

167 sirra] serra
169 him,] ~ ∧
175 helhound's] helhoud's
179 begot∧] ~ . [*followed by* cw:
    *Fau.* One]
180 damnation —] ~ ,
182 it;] ~ ∧
192 *Faulx*] *Eaulx*
193 *Faulx.*] *Fan.*
196 To] Te
196 soule,] ~ ∧
207 men.)] ~ . ∧
212 Caitiffs,] ~ .)
213 drew] Drew
218 without-him,] ~ .
222 wore∧] ~ ,
225 *Spotted-Conscience*] spotted-
    Conscience
251 him, the] ~ ∧ ~ ,
281 puritane] puaitane
289 Oyes] O yes
289 deferd,] ~ ∧

## *Epilogue*

6 rot, the Diuels] rot. The Diuelt

16 Palme,] ~ .

*Troia-Noua Triumphans.*

# London Triumphing,

### O R,

The Solemne, Magnificent, and Me-
*morable Receiuing of that worthy Gentle-*
man, Sir I o h n   S v v i n e r t o n  Knight, into
the Citty of L o n d o n , after his Returne from
*taking the Oath of Maioralty at Westminster,*
on the Morrow next after *Simon* and
*Iudes* day, being the 29. of
*October.* 1612.

All the Showes, Pageants, Chariots of Triumph, with
*other Deuices,(both on the water and Land)*
here fully expressed.

By *Thomas Dekker.*

*LONDON,*
Printed by *Nicholas Okes,* and are to be sold by *Iohn*
*Wright* dwelling at Christ Church-gate. 1612.

# TEXTUAL INTRODUCTION

*Troia-Nova Triumphans* (Greg, *Bibliography*, no. 302) was entered to Nicholas Okes in the Stationers' Register on 21 October 1612 (the Show itself taking place on 29 October), as follows: 'Entred for his copie vnder thand of m$^r$ Harison Warden. to be prynted When yt is further Aucthorised. A booke called. Troia Nova triũphans. London triũphinge. Or the solemne receauinge, of S$^r$ Io. Swynerton K$^t$. into the citye. [at *interlined above* after *deleted*] his Retourne from Westm̃ after taking his oathe written by Tho. Decker     vj$^{d}$' (Greg's transcription). The further authority required was perhaps the assurance that this was authorized as the official account, or that the Merchant Taylors were willing to release the description.

The accidentals of the printed text suggest that Dekker's holograph served as printer's copy, as we should expect.

A type facsimile of this account was printed in R. T. D. Sayle, *Lord Mayor Pageants of the Merchant Taylors* (1931), with transcripts of the contributions and payments for expenses.

The present text is based on a collation of the following five copies, all that are known to exist: British Museum (C.33.e.7[17]), Bodleian Library copy 1 (4°P 42[3] Art.) and copy 2 (Wood 537[7]), Henry E. Huntington Library, and the Chapin Collection in the Williams College Library (wants sig. D 1 [ll. 534–90]).

*To the Deseruer of all those Honors, which the*
*Customary Rites of this Day, And the generall*
*Loue of this City bestow vpon him; Sir Iohn*
*Swinerton, Knight, Lord Maior of the*
*renowmed City of London.*

Honor (*this day*) *takes you by the* Hand, *and giues you* welcomes *into your* New-Office *of* Pretorship. *A* Dignity *worthie the* Cities bestowing, *and most worthy your* Receiuing. *You haue it with the* Harts *of many people,* Voices *and* Held-vp *hands: they know it is a* Roabe *fit for you, and therefore haue clothed you in it. May the* Last-day *of your wearing the* same, *yeeld to your* Selfe *as much* Ioy, *as to* Others *does this* First-day *of your putting it on. I swimme (for my owne part) not onely in the* Maine Full-sea *of the* General praise *and* Hopes *of you. But powre out also (for my particular) such a* streame *as my* Prayers *can render, for a successe answerable to the* 10 On-set: *for it is no* Field, *vnlesse it be* Crowned *with victory.*

*I present* (Sir) *vnto you, these labours of my Pen, as the first and* newest Congratulatory Offrings *tendred into your hands, which albeit I should not (of my selfe) deserue to see accepted, I know notwith-standing you will giue to them a generous and gratefull entertainement, in regard of that* Noble Fellowship *and* Society, *(of which you* Yesterday *were a* Brother, *and* This Day *a* Father*) who most freely haue bestowed these their Loues vpon you. The* Colours *of this* Peece *are mine owne; the Cost theirs: to which nothing was wanting, that could be had, and euery thing had that was required. To their* Lasting 20 memory *I set downe* This; *And to your* Noble Disposition, *this I* Dedicate. *My wishes being (as euer they haue bene) to meete with any* Obiect, *whose reflexion may present to your* Eyes, *that* Loue *and* Duty, *In which*

I stand Bounden
To your Lordship.
*Thomas Dekker.*

229

# *Troia Noua Triumphans.*

# London Triumphing.

*Tryumphes*, are the most choice and daintiest fruit that spring from *Peace* and *Abundance*; *Loue* begets them; and *Much Cost* brings them forth. *Expectation* feeds vpon them, but seldome to a surfeite, for when she is most full, her longing wants something to be satisfied. So inticing a shape they carry, that *Princes* themselues take pleasure to behold them; they with delight; common people with admiration. They are now and then the *Rich* and *Glorious Fires* of *Bounty*, *State* and *Magnificence*, giuing light and beauty to the *Courts* of *Kings*: And now and then, it is but a debt payd to *Time* and *Custome*: And out of that debt come *These*. *Ryot* hauing no 10 hand in laying out the *Expences*, and yet no hand in plucking backe what is held decent to be bestowed: A *sumptuous Thriftinesse* in these *Ciuil Ceremonies* managing *All*. For it were not laudable, in a City (so rarely gouerned and tempered) superfluously to *exceed*; As contrariwise it is much honor to her (when the *Day* of *spending* comes) not to be *sparing* in any thing. For the *Chaires* of *Magistrates* ought to be adorned, and to shine like the Chariot which caries the *Sunne*; And *Beames* (if it were possible) must be thought to be shot from the *One* as from the *Other*: As well to dazle and amaze the common *Eye*, as to make it learne that there is some *Excellent*, and 20 *Extraordinary Arme* from heauen thrust downe to exalt a *Superior* man, that thereby the *Ga3er* may be drawne to more obedience and admiration.

In a happy houre therefore did your Lordship take vpon you this inseperable burden (of *Honor* and *Cares*) because your selfe being *Generous* of mind, haue met with men, and with a *Company* equall to your Selfe in *Spirit*. And vpon as fortunate a *Tree* haue they ingrafted their *Bounty*; the fruites whereof shoot forth and ripen, are gathered, and taste sweetly, in the mouthes not onely of this *Citty*, but also of our best-to-be-beloued friends, the *Noblest* 30 *strangers*. Vpon whom, though none but our *Soueraigne King* can bestow *Royall welcomes*; yet shall it be a *Memoriall* of an *Exemplary Loue* and *Duty* (in those who are at the *Cost* of these *Triumphs*) to haue *added* some *Heightning* more to them then was intended at first, of purpose to do honor to their Prince and Countrey. And I make no doubt, but *many worthy Companies* in this City could gladly be content to be partners in the *Disbursements*, so they might be sharers in the *Glory*. For to haue bene leaden-winged now, what infamy could be greater? When all the streames of *Nobility* and *Gentry*, run with the *Tide* hither. When all *Eares* lye listning for no 40 newes but of *Feasts* and *Triumphs*: All *Eyes* still open to behold them: And all harts and hands to applaud them: When the heape of our *Soueraignes Kingdomes* are drawne in *Little*: and to be seene within the Walles of this *City*. Then to haue tied *Bounty* in too straight a girdle: *Proh scelus infandum!* No; she hath worne her garments loose, her lippes haue bene free in Welcomes, her purse open, and her hands liberall. If you thinke I set a flattering glasse before you, do but so much as lanch into the *Riuer*, and there the *Thames* it selfe shall shew you *all the Honors*, which this day hath bestowed vpon her: And that done, step againe vpon the *Land*, and 50 *Fame* will with her owne *Trumpet* proclaime what I speake; And her I hope you cannot deny to beleeue, hauing at least twenty thousand eyes about her, to witnesse whether she be a *True-tong'd Fame* or a *Lying*.

By this time the Lord Maior hath taken his oath, is seated in his barge againe; a lowd thundring peale of *Chambers* giue him a *Farewell* as he passes by. And see! how quickly we are in ken of land, as suddenly therefore let vs leap on shore, and there obserue what honorable entertainement the Citty affoords to their new *Prætor*, and what ioyfull salutations to her noble *Visitants*. 60

## *The first Triumph on the Land.*

The Lord *Maior*, and *Companyes* being landed, the first *Deuice* which is presented to him on the shore, stands ready to receiue him at the end of *Pauls-Chayne*, (on the south side the Church) and this it is.

231

A *Sea-Chariot* artificially made, proper for a God of the sea to sit in; shippes dancing round about it, with *Dolphins* and other great *Fishes* playing or lying at the foot of the same, is drawne by two *Sea-horses*.

## *Neptune.*

In this Chariot sits *Neptune*, his head circled with a *Coronet* of siluer *Scollup-shels*, stucke with branches of Corrall, and hung 70 thicke with ropes of pearle; because such things as these are the treasures of the *Deepe*, and are found in the shels of fishes. In his hand he holds a siluer *Trident*, or *Three-forked-Mace*, by which some Writers will haue signified the three *Naturall qualities* proper to *Waters*; as those of fountaines to bee of a delitious taste, and Christalline colour: those of the Sea, to bee saltish and vnpleasant, and the colour sullen, and greenish: And lastly, those of standing Lakes, neither sweet nor bitter, nor cleere, nor cloudy, but altogether vnwholesome for the taste, and loathsome to the eye. His roabe and mantle with other ornaments are correspondent to the quality of 80 his person; Buskins of pearle and cockle-shels being worne vpon his legges. At the lower part of this Chariot sit *Mer-maids*, who for their excellency in beauty, aboue any other creatures belonging to the sea, are preferred to bee still in the eye of *Neptune*.

At *Neptunes* foot sits *Luna* (the *Moone*) who beeing gouernesse of the sea, and all petty Flouds, as from whose influence they receiue their ebbings and flowings, challenges to herselfe this honour, to haue rule and command of those Horses that draw the Chariot, and therefore she holds their reynes in her hands.

She is atired in light roabes fitting her state and condition, with 90 a siluer *Crescent* on her head, expressing both her power and property.

The whole Chariot figuring in it selfe that vast compasse which the sea makes about the body of the earth: whose *Globicall Rotundity* is *Hieroglifically* represented by the wheele of the Chariot.

Before this *Chariot* ride foure *Trytons*, who are feyned by Poets to bee Trumpeters to *Neptune*, and for that cause make way before him, holding strange Trumpets in their hands, which they sound as they passe along, their habits being Antike, and Sea-like, and sitting

vpon foure seuerall fishes, *viz.* two *Dolphins*, and two *Mer-maids*, 100
which are not (after the old procreation), begotten of painted cloath,
and browne paper, but are liuing beasts, so queintly disguised like
the natural fishes, of purpose to auoyd the trouble and pestering of
Porters, who with much noyse and little comlinesse are euery yeare
most vnnecessarily imployed.

The time being ripe, when the scope of this *Deuice* is to be
deliuered, *Neptunes* breath goeth forth in these following *Speeches*.

## Neptunes *Speeches*.

*Whence breaks this warlike thunder of lowd drummes,*
(Clarions *and* Trumpets) *whose shrill eccho comes*
*Vp to our* Watery Court, *and calles from thence*    110
Vs, *and our* Trytons? *As if violence*
*Weere to our Siluer-footed* Sister *done*
(*Of* Flouds *the Queene*) *bright* Thamesis, *who does runne*
*Twice euery day to our bosome, and there hides*
*Her wealth, whose* Streame *in liquid* Christall *glides*    \* Ebbe and
*Guarded with troopes of* Swannes? *what does beget*    Flow.
*These* Thronges? *this* Confluence? *why do voyces beate*
*The* Ayre *with acclamations of applause,*
Good wishes, Loue, *and* Praises? *what is't drawes*
*All* Faces *this way? This way* Rumor *flyes,*    120
*Clapping her infinite wings, whose noyse the Skyes*
*From earth receiue, with* Musicall *rebounding,*
*And strike the Seas with repercussiue sounding.*
*Oh! now I see the cause: vanish vaine feares,*
*Isis no danger feeles: for her head weares*    \* Thamesis
Crowns *of* Rich Triumphes, *which* This day *puts on,*
*And in* Thy Honor *all these* Rites *are done.*
*Whose* Name *when* Neptune *heard, t'was a strange* Spell,
*Thus farre-vp into th'*Land *to make him swell*
*Beyond his* Bownds, *and with his* Sea-troops *wait*    130
Thy wish't arriuall *to congratulate.*
*Goe therefore on, goe boldly: thou must saile*
*In rough Seas* (now) *of* Rule: *and euery* Gale

*Will not perhaps befriend thee: But (how blacke*
*So ere the Skyes looke) dread not* Thou *a* Wracke,
*For when* Integrity *and* Innocence *sit*
*Steering the* Helme, *no* Rocke *the* Ship *can split.*
*Nor care the* Whales *(neuer so great) their* Iawes
*Should stretch to swallow thee:* Euery good mans cause
Is in all stormes his Pilot: He that's sound        140
To himselfe (in Conscience) nere can run-a-ground.
*Which that thou mayst do, neuer looke on't still:*
*For (Spite of Fowle gusts) calmer* Windes *shall fill*
*Thy* Sayles *at last. And see! they home haue brought*
*A* Ship *which* Bacchus *(God of* Wines) *hath fraught*
*With richest Iuice of* Grapes, *which thy* Friends *shall*
*Drinke off in* Healths *to this* Great Festiuall.
*If any at* Thy happinesse *repine,*
*They gnaw but their* Owne hearts, *and touch not* Thine.
*Let* Bats *and* Skreech-Owles *murmure at bright* Day,        150
*Whiles* Prayers *of* Good-men *Guid* Thee *on the way.*
*Sownd old* Oceanus Trumpeters, *and lead on.*

The *Trytons* then sownding, according to his command, *Neptune*
in his *Chariot* passeth along before the *Lord Maior.* The foure
*Windes* (habilimented to their quality, and hauing both *Faces* and
*Limbes* proportionable to their blustring and boisterous condition)
driue forward that *Ship* of which *Neptune* spake. And this concludes
this first *Triumph* on the Land.

These two *Shewes* passe on vntill they come into *Pauls-Church-*
*yard*, where standes another *Chariot*; the former *Chariot* of *Neptune*,  160
with the *Ship*, beeing conueyd into *Cheape-side*, this other then takes
the place: And this is the *Deuice.*

## The second Land-Triumph.

It is the *Throne of Vertue*, gloriously adorned and beautified with
all things that are fit to express the *Seat* of so noble and diuine a
*Person.*

Vpon the height, and most eminent place (as worthiest to be

exalted) sits *Arete* (*Vertue*) herselfe; her temples shining with a *Diadem* of starres, to shew that her *Descent* is onely from heauen: her roabes are rich, her mantle white (figuring *Innocency*) and powdred with starres of gold, as an *Embleme* that she puts vpon 170 *Men*, the garments of eternity.

Beneath *Her*, in distinct places, sit the *Seauen liberall Sciences*, *viz*. *Grammer*, *Rhetoricke*, *Logicke*, *Musicke*, *Arithmetike*, *Geometry*, *Astronomy*.

Hauing those roomes alotted them, as being *Mothers* to all *Trades*, *Professions*, *Mysteries* and *Societies*, and the readiest guide to *Vertue*. Their habits are *Light Roabes*, and *Loose* (for *Knowledge* should be free.) On their heads they weare garlands of *Roses*, mixt with other flowers, whose sweet *Smels* are arguments of their cleere and vnspotted thoughts, not corrupted with vice. Euery one carrying 180 in her hand, a *Symbole*, or *Badge* of that *Learning* which she professeth.

At the backe of this *Chariot* sit foure *Cupids*, to signifie that vertue is most honored when she is followed by *Loue*.

This *Throne*, or *Chariot*, is drawne by foure *Horses*: vpon the two formost ride *Time* and *Mercury*: the first, the *Begetter* and *Bringer forth* of all things in the world, the second, the *God* of *Wisedome* and *Eloquence*. On the other two *Horses* ride *Desire* and *Industry*; it beeing intimated hereby, that *Tyme* giues wings to *Wisedome*, and sharpens it, *Wisedome* sets *Desire* a burning, to attaine to *Vertue*, 190 and that *Burning Desire* begets *Industry* (earnestly to pursue her.) And all these (together) make men in *Loue* with *Arts*, *Trades*, *Sciences*, and *Knowledge*, which are the onely staires and ascensions to the *Throne* of *Vertue*, and the onely glory and vpholdings of Cities. *Time* hath his wings, *Glasse*, and *Sythe*, which cuts downe *All*.

*Mercury* hath his *Caduceus*, or *Charming Rod*, his fethered *Hat*, his *Wings*, and other properties fitting his condition, *Desire* caries a burning heart in her hand.

*Industry* is in the shape of an old *Country-man*, bearing on his 200 shoulder a *Spade*, as the *Embleme* of *Labour*.

Before this *Chariot*, or *Throne* (as *Guardians* and *Protectors* to *Vertue*, to *Arts*, and to the rest; and as *Assistants* to *Him* who is

*Chiefe* within the *Citty* for that yeare) are mounted vpon horsebacke twelue *Persons* (two by two) representing the twelue superior *Companyes,* euery one carrying vpon his left arme a faire *Shield* with the armes in it of one of the twelue *Companies,* and in his right hand a launce with a light streamer or pendant on the top of it, and euery horse led and attended by a *Footman.*

The Lord *Maior* beeing approached to this *Throne, Vertue* thus 210 salutes him.

## *The Speech of* Arete (Vertue.)

Haile (*worthy* Pretor) *stay, and do* Me *grace,*
(*Who still haue cald thee* Patron) *In this place*
*To take from me heap'd welcomes, who combine*
*These peoples hearts in* one, *to make them* thine.
*Bright* Vertues *name thou know'st and heau'nly birth,*
*And therefore (spying thee) downe she leapd to earth*
*Whence* vicious men *had driuen her: On her* throne
*The* Liberall Arts *waite: from whose* brests *do runne*
*The* milke *of* Knowledge: *on which,* Sciences *feed,*                  220
Trades *and* Professions: *And by* Them, *the* seed
*Of* Ciuill, Popular gouernment, *is sowne;*
*Which springing vp, loe! to what* heigth *tis growne*
* The Alder-    *In* Thee *and* *These *is seene. And (to maintaine*
   men.    *This* Greatnesse) Twelue *strong* Pillars *it sustaine;*
* The twelue    *Vpon whose* Capitals, *Twelue Societies *stand,*
   Companies.    (Graue *and* well-ordred) *bearing chiefe* Command
*Within this* City, *and (with* Loue) *thus reare*
*Thy* fame, *in* free election, *for this* yeare.
*All* arm'd, *to knit their* Nerues (*in* One) *with* Thine,          230
*To guard* this new Troy: *And, (that* She *may shine*
*In* Thee, *as* Thou *in* Her) *no* Misers *kay*
*Has bard the* Gold *vp; Light flies from the* Day
*Not of more free gift, than from them their* Cost:
*For whats now* spar'd, *that only they count* Lost.
*As then their* Ioynd-hands *lift* Thee *to thy* Seate,
* Lord Maior.    (*Changing thereby thy* Name *for one* More *Great*).

236

*And as this* City, *with her* Loud, Full Voice,
(*Drowning all* spite *that murmures at the* Choice,
*If at least* such *there be*) *does* Thee *preferre,*          240
*So art thou bound to loue, both* Them *and* Her.
*For* know, *thou art not like a* Pinnacle, *plac'd*
*Onely to stand aloft, and to be grac'd*
*With wondring eyes, or to haue caps and knees*
*Heape worship on thee: for* that Man *does lee*ȝ*e*
*Himselfe and his* Renowne, *whose growth being* Hye
*In the weale-publicke* (*like the* Cypres tree)
*Is neither good to* Build-with, *nor beare* Fruit;
*Thou must be now,* Stirring, *and* Resolute,
*To be what thou art* Sworne, (*a waking Eye*)        250
*A farre off* (*like a* Beacon) *to descry*
*What stormes are comming, and* (*being come*) *must then*
*Shelter with spred armes, the poor'st* Citizen.
*Set* Plenty *at thy* Table, *at thy* Gate
Bounty, *and* Hospitality: *hee's most* Ingrate
*Into whose lap the* Publicke-weale *hauing powr'd*
*Her* Golden shewers, *from* Her *his wealth should hoord.*
*Be like those* Antient Spirits, *that* (*long agon*)
*Could thinke no* Good deed *sooner, than twas* Don;
Others *to pleasure,* hold *it* Thou *more* Glory,          260
*Than to be pleas'd* Thy Selfe. *And be not sory*
*If* Any *striue* (*in best things*) *to exceed thee,*
*But glad, to* helpe thy Wrongers, *if they need thee.*
*Nor feare the Stings of* Enuy, *nor the* Threates
*Of her inuenomd Arrowes, which at the* Seates
*Of those* Who Best Rule, *euermore are shot,*
*But the Aire blowes off their fethers, and they hit not.*
*Come therefore on; nor dread her, nor her* Sprites,
*The poyson she spits vp, on her owne* Head *lights.*
*On, on, away.*          270

This Chariot or Throne of Vertue is then set forward, and followes that of *Neptune,* this taking place iust before the Lord Maior:
And this concludes the second Triumphant shew.

## *The third Deuice.*

The third *Deuice* is a *Forlorne Castle*, built close to the little *Conduit* in *Cheap-side*, by which as the *Throne* of *Vertue* comes neerer and neerer, there appeare aboue (on the battlements) *Enuy*, as chiefe Commandresse of that infernall *Place*, and euery part of it guarded with persons representing all those that are fellowes and followers of *Enuy*: As *Ignorance, Sloth, Oppression, Disdaine,* &c. *Enuy* her selfe being attired like a *Fury*, her haire full of Snakes, her 280 countenance pallid, meagre and leane, her body naked, in her hand a knot of Snakes, crawling and writhen about her arme.

The rest of her *litter* are in as vgly shapes as the *Dam*, euery one of them being arm'd with black bowes, and arrows ready to bee shot at *Vertue*. At the gates of this *Fort* of *Furies*, stand *Ryot* and *Calumny*, in the shapes of *Gyants*, with clubs, who offer to keep back the *Chariot* of *Vertue*, and to stop her passage. All the rest likewise on the battlements offering to discharge their blacke Artillery at her: but she onely holding vp her bright shield, dazzles them, and confounds them, they all on a sudden shrinking in their 290 heads, vntill the *Chariot* be past, and then all of them appearing againe: their arrowes, which they shoote vp into the aire, breake there out in fire-workes, as hauing no power to do wrong to so sacred a Deity as *Vertue*.

This caue of *Monsters* stands fixed to the Conduit, in which *Enuie* onely breathes out her poyson to this purpose.

## *The speech of* Enuy.

ENVY.  Adders *shoote, hysse speckled Snakes;*
Sloth *craule vp, see* Oppression *wakes;*
(*Baine to learning*) Ignorance
*Shake thy* Asses *eares,* Disdaine, *aduance*        300
*Thy head* Luciferan: Ryot *split*
*Thy ribbes with curses:* Calumny *spit*
*Thy rancke-rotten gall vp. See, See, See,*
*That* Witch, *whose bottomelesse Sorcery*

238

*Makes fooles runne mad for her; that* Hag
*For whom your* Dam *pines, hangs out her flag*
*Our* Den *to ransacke :* Vertue, *that whoore;*
*See, see, how braue shee's, I am poore.*
VERTVE.  *On, on, the beames of* Vertue, *are so bright,*
*They daȝle* Enuy, *on: the* Hag's *put to flight.*                    310
ENVY.  Snakes, *from your virulent spawne ingender*
Dragons, *that may peece-meale rend her:*
Adders *shoote your stings like quils*
*Of* Porcupines (*Stiffe,*) *hot* Aetnean *hils*
*Vomit sulphure to confound her,*
*Fiendes and Furies (that dwell vnder)*
*Lift hell gates from their hindges: come*
*You clouen-footed-broode of* Barrathrum,
*Stop, stay her, fright her, with your shreekes,*
*And put fresh bloud in* Enuies *cheekes.*                    320
VERTVE.  *On, on, the beames of* Vertue, *are so bright,*
*They daȝle* Enuy: *On, the* Hag's *put to flight.*
OMNES.  *Shoote, Shoote, &c.      All that are with* Enuy.

Either during this speech, or else when it is done, certaine Rockets
flye vp into the aire; The *Throne of Vertue* passing on still, neuer
staying, but speaking still those her two last lines, albeit, shee bee
out of the hearing of *Enuy*: and the other of *Enuies* Faction, crying
still, shoote, shoote, but seeing they preuaile not, all retire in, and
are not seene till the *Throne* comes backe againe.

And this concludes this Triumphant assault of *Enuy*: her conquest 330
is to come.

## *The fourth Deuice.*

This *Throne* of *Vertue* passeth along vntill it come to the Crosse
in Cheape, where the presentation of another Triumph attends to
welcome the Lord Maior, in his passage, the *Chariot* of *Vertue* is
drawne then along, this other that followes taking her place, the
Deuice bearing this argument.

*Vertue* hauing by helpe of her followers, conducted the Lord

318 *-footed-*] *-foote-* Q

Maior safely, euen, as it were, through the iawes of *Enuy* and all her Monsters: The next and highest honour shee can bring him to, is to make him ariue at the house of *Fame*, And that is this *Pageant.* 340 In the vpper seat sits *Fame* crowned in rich attire, a Trumpet in her hand, &c. In other seuerall places sit Kings, Princes, and Noble persons, who haue bene free of the *Marchant-tailors*: A perticular roome being reserued for one that represents the person of *Henry* the now Prince of *Wales.*

The onely speaker heere is *Fame* her selfe, whose wordes sound out these glad welcomes.

### The speech of Fame.

*Welcome to* Fames high Temple: *here fix fast*
*Thy* footing; *for the* wayes *which thou hast past*
*Will be forgot and worne out, and no* Tract            350
*Of steps obseru'd, but what thou* now *shalt Act.*
*The booke is shut of thy* precedent deedes,
*And* Fame *vnclaspes another, where shee reades*
(*Aloud*) *the* Chronickle *of a* dangerous yeare,
*For* Each Eye *will looke through thee, and* Each Eare
*Way-lay thy* Words *and* Workes. *Th'hast yet but gon*
*About a* Pyramid's *foote; the* Top's *not won,*
*That's* glasse; *who slides there, fals, and once falne downe*
*Neuer more rises*: No Art cures Renowne
The wound being sent to'th Heart. *Tis kept from thence*    360
*By a strong Armor,* Vertues influence;
She *guides thee,* Follow *her. In this* Court *of* Fame
*None else but* Vertue *can enrole thy* Name.
    Erect *thou then a* Serious Eye, *And looke*
*What Worthies fill vp* Fames *Voluminous booke,*
*That now* (*thine owne name read there*) *none may blot*
*Thy leafe with foule inke, nor thy* Margent *quoate*
*With any Act of* Thine, *which may disgrace*
*This* Citties choice, *thy* selfe, *or this* thy Place:
*Or, that which may dishonour the high* Merits        370
*Of thy* Renown'd Society: Roiall Spirits

*Of* Princes *holding it a grace to weare*
*That* Crimson Badge, *which these about them beare,*
*Yea,* Kings themselues *'mongst you haue* Fellowes *bene,*
*Stil'd by the* Name *of a* Free-citizen:
*For instance, see,* seuen English Kings *there plac'd,*
*Cloth'd in your Liuery, The first* Seate *being grac'd*
*By second* Richard: *next him* \*Bullingbrooke:                    \* *Henry the 4*
*Then, that* Fift (*thundring*) Henry: *who all* France *shook:*
*By him, his* sonne (sixth Henry) *By his side*                    380
Fourth Edward: *who the* Roses *did diuide:*
Richard *the* third, *next him, and then that King,*
*Who made* both Roses *in* one Branch *to spring:*
*A* Sprig *of which* Branch, (Highest *now but* One)
*Is* Henry Prince of Wales, *followed by none:*
*Who of this* Brotherhood, *last and best steps forth,*
*Honouring your* Hall. *To* Heighthen *more your* worth,
*I can a Register show of seuenteene more,*
(Princes *and* Dukes All:) *entombed long before,*
*Yet kept aliue by* Fame; Earles *thirty one,*                    390
*And* Barons *sixty six that path haue gone:*
*Of* Visecounts *onely one, your* Order *tooke:*
*Turne ouer one leafe more in our vast booke*
*And you may reade the* Names *of Prelates there,*
*Of which one* Arch-biship *your cloth did weare.*
*And* Byshops *twenty foure: of* Abbots *seuen,*
*As many* Priors, *to make the number euen:*
*Of* forty Church-men, I, *one sub-prior adde,*
*You from all these, These from you honour had:*
*Women of high bloud likewise laid aside*                    400
*Their greater* State *so to be dignified:*
*Of which a* Queene *the first was, then a paire*
*Of* Dukes wiues: *And to leaue the* Roll *more faire*
*Fiue* Countesses *and two* Ladies *are the last,*
*Whose* Birth *and* Beauties *haue your* Order *gracd.*
*But I too long spin out this* Thrid *of* Gold;
*Here breakes it off.* Fame *hath them* All *en-rold*
*On a* Large File (*with* Others,) *And their* Story

*The world shall reade, to* Adde *vnto thy* Glory,
*Which I am loath to darken: thousand eyes*　　　　　410
*Yet aking till they enioy thee, win then that prise*
*Which* Vertue *holds vp for thee, And (that done)*
Fame *shall the end crowne, as she hath begun.*
*Set forward.*

Those Princes and Dukes (besides the Kings nominated before)
are these.

*Iohn* Duke of Lancaster. ⎫
*Edmond* Duke of Yorke. ⎬ In the time of *Richard* the second.
The Duke of Gloster. ⎪
The Duke of Surrey. ⎭　　　　　420

*Humfry* Duke of Gloster. ⎫ In the time of *Henry* the fifth.
*Richard* Duke of Yorke. ⎭

*George* Duke of Clarence.　In the time of *Edward* the fourth.

Duke of Suffolke. ⎫
*Iohn* Duke of Norfolke. ⎬ In the time of *Richard* the third.
*George* Duke of Bedford. ⎭

*Edward* Duke of Buckingham, In the time of *Henry* the seuenth with
　others, whose Rol is too long, here to be opened.
The Queene spoken of, was *Anne* wife to *Richard* the second.
　Dukes wiues these, *viz.*　　　　　430
The Dutchesse of Gloster. In the time of *Richard* the second.
*Elionor* Dutchesse of Gloster. In the time of *Henry* the fifth.
*Now for Prelates, I reckon onely these,*
*The* Prior *of Saint* Bartholmewes,
*And his* Sub-Prior.
*The* Prior *of* Elsinge-spittle.
Thomas Arundell *Arch-bishop of* Canterbury.
Henry Bewfort *Bishop of* Winton.
*The Abbot of* Barmondsey.
Philip Morgan *Bishop of* Worster　　　　　440

439 *After this line* Q *prints:* The Abbot of Towrchill [*first* b *in* Abbot *broken and*
*resembles an* h]

*The Abbot of* Tower-hill.
*The* Prior *of Saint* Mary Ouery.
*The* Prior *of Saint* Trinity *in* Cree-church.
*The* Abbot *and* Prior *of* Westminster.
Kemp *Bishop of* London.
W. Wainfleete *Bishop of* Winchester.
George Neuill *Bishop of* Winchester, *and Chauncelor of* England.
Iohn May, *Abbot of* Chertsay.
Laurence *Bishop of* Durham.
Iohn Russell *Bishop of* Rochester.                           450

If I should lengthen this number, it were but to trouble you with
a large Index of names onely, which I am loath to do, knowing your
expectation is to bee otherwise feasted.

The *Speech* of *Fame* therefore being ended, as 'tis set downe
before, this *Temple* of *Hers* takes place next before the Lord *Maior*,
those of *Neptune* and *Vertue* marching in precedent order. And as
this *Temple* is carryed along, a *Song* is heard, the *Musicke* being
queintly conueyed in a priuate roome, and not a person discouered.


## THE SONG.

*Honor, eldest Child of Fame,*
*Thou farre older then thy Name,*                              460
*Waken with my Song, and see*
*One of thine, here waiting thee.*
           *Sleepe not now*
           *But thy brow*
*Chac't with Oliues, Oke and Baies*
*And an age of happy dayes*
           *Vpward bring*
           *Whilst we sing*
*In a* Chorus *altogether,*
*Welcome, welcome, welcome hither.*                           470

*Longing round about him stay*
*Eyes, to make another day,*

*Able with their vertuous Light*
*Vtterly to banish Night.*
   *All agree*
   *This is hee*
*Full of bounty, honour, store*
*And a world of goodnesse more*
   *Yet to spring*
   *Whilst we sing*          480
*In a* Chorus *altogether,*
*Welcome, welcome, welcome hither.*

Enuy *angry with the dead,*
*Far from this place hide thy head:*
*And* Opinion, *that nere knew*
*What was either good or true*
   *Fly, I say*
   *For this day*
*Shall faire* Iustice, Truth, *and* Right,
*And such happy sonnes of* Light        490
   *To us bring*
   *Whilst we sing*
*In a* Chorus *altogether,*
*Welcome, welcome, welcome hither.*

*Goe on nobly, may thy Name,*
*Be as old, and good as Fame.*
*Euer be remembred here*
*Whilst a blessing, or a teare*
   *Is in store*
   *With the pore*         500
*So shall* SWINERTON *nere dye,*
*But his vertues vpward flye*
   *And still spring*
   *Whilst we sing*
*In a* Chorus *ceasing neuer,*
*He is liuing, liuing euer.*

And this concludes this fourth *Triumph,* till his Lordships returne
from the *Guild-hall.*

244

In returning backe from the *Guild-hall*, to performe the Cere-
moniall customes in *Pauls Church*, these shewes march in the same 510
order as before: and comming with the *Throne* of *Vertue*, *Enuy* and
her crue are as busie againe, *Enuy* vttering some three or foure lines
toward the end of her speech onely: As thus:

> ENVY.   Fiends *and* Furies *that dwell vnder,*
> *Lift* Hell-gates *from their hindges: Come*
> *You clouen-footed-brood of* Barathrum,
> *Stop, stay her, fright her with your shreekes,*
> *And put fresh bloud in* Enuyes *cheekes.*
> VERTVE.   *On, on, the beames of* Vertue *are so bright,*
> *They dazzle* Enuy: *On, the* Hag's *put to flight.*                520

This done, or as it is in doing, those twelue that ride armed
discharge their *Pistols*, at which *Enuy*, and the rest, vanish, and are
seene no more.

When the Lord *Maior* is (with all the rest of their *Triumphes*)
brought home, *Iustice* (for a fare-well) is mounted on some conuenient scaffold close to his entrance at his *Gate*, who thus salutes
him.

## The speech of IVSTICE.

> *My* This-dayes-sworne-protector, *welcome home,*
> *If* Iustice *speake not now, be she euer dumbe:*
> *The world giues out shee's blinde; but men shall see,*                530
> *Her* Sight *is cleere, by influence drawne from* Thee.
> *For* One-yeare *therefore, at these* Gates *shee'l sit,*
> *To guid thee* In *and* Out: *thou shalt commit*
> (*If* Shee *stand by thee) not* One *touch of wrong:*
> *And though I know thy* wisdome *built vp strong,*
> *Yet men (like great ships) being in storms, most neere*
> *To danger, when vp their sailes they beare.*
> *And since all* Magistrates *tread still on yce,*
> *From mine owne* Schoole *I reade thee this* aduice:
> > *Do good for no mans sake (now) but thine* owne,                540

*Take leaue of* Friends *and* foes, *both must be knowne*
*But by one* Face: *the* Rich *and* Poore *must lye*
*In* one euen Scale: *All* Suiters, *in thine Eye*
*Welcome alike; Euen* Hee *that seemes most base,*
*Looke not vpon his* Clothes, *but on his* Case.
*Let not* Oppression *wash his hands ith'* Teares
*Of* Widowes, *or of* Orphans: Widowes *prayers*
*Can pluck downe* Thunder, *and poore* Orphans *cries*
*Are* Lawrels *held in fire; the violence flyes*
*Vp to* Heauen-gates, *and there the wrong does tell,*                550
*Whilst* Innocence *leaues behind it a sweet smell.*
*Thy* Conscience *must be like that* Scarlet Dye;
*One fowle spot staines it* All: *and the quicke* Eye
*Of this prying world, will make that spot thy scorne.*
*That* Collar (*which about thy* Necke *is worne*)
*Of* Golden Esses, *bids thee so to knit*
Mens hearts *in* Loue, *and make a* Chayne *of it.*
*That* Sword *is seldome drawne, by which is meant,*
*It should strike seldome: neuer th'innocent.*
*Tis held before thee by anothers* Hand,                560
*But the* point *vpwards* (heauen *must that command*)
*Snatch it not then in* Wrath; *it must be giuen,*
*But to cut none, till* warranted *by* Heauen.
*The* Head, *the* politike Body *must aduance*
*For which thou hast this* Cap *of* Maintenance,
*And since the most iust* Magistrate *often* erres,
*Thou guarded art about with* Officers,
*Who knowing the pathes of* Others *that are gone,*
*Should teach thee* what to do, what leaue vndone.
*Nights* Candles *lighted are, and burne amaine,*                570
*Cut therefore here off,* Thy Officious Traine
*Which* Loue *and* Custome *lend thee: All* Delight
*Crowne both this* Day *and* Citty: *A good* Night
*To* Thee, *and these* Graue Senators, *to whom*
*My last* Fare-wels, *in these glad wishes come,*
*That* thou *and* they (*whose strength the City beares*)
*May be as old in* Goodnesse *as in* Yeares.

246

The *Title-page* of this *Booke* makes promise of all the *Shewes by water*, as of these *On the Land*; but *Apollo* hauing no hand in them, I suffer them to dye by that which fed them; that is to say, *Powder* 580 and *Smoake*. Their thunder (according to the old *Gally-foyst-fashion*) was too lowd for any of the *Nine Muses* to be bidden to it. I had deuiz'd *One*, altogether *Musicall*, but *Times Glasse* could spare no sand, nor lend conuenient *Howres* for the performance of it. *Night* cuts off the glory of this *Day*, and so consequently of these *Triumphes*, whose brightnesse beeing ecclipsed, my labours can yeeld no longer shadow. They are ended, but my *Loue* and *Duty* to your *Lordship* shall neuer.

— *Non displicuisse meretur,*
*Festinat (Prætor) Qui placuisse Tibi.*　　590

*FINIS.*

# PRESS-VARIANTS IN Q (1612)

[Copies collated: BM (British Museum C.33.e.7[17]), Bodl¹ (Bodleian Library 4° P 42[3] Art.), Bodl² (Wood 537[7]), CSmH (Henry E. Huntington Library), MWiW-C (Chapin Collection of Williams College).]

SHEET C (*outer forme*)

*Corrected:* Bodl¹, MWiW-C
*Uncorrected:* BM, Bodl², CSmH

Sig. C1.
322 *On,*] on
Sig. C2ᵛ.
403 *Of*] of
Sig. C3.
432 *Eleonor*] *Elionor*
447 George] Gcorge

# EMENDATIONS OF ACCIDENTALS

## Dedication

11 *vnlesse*] *unlesse*

## Text

10 debt] dept
12 bestowed:] ~ .
56 *Fare-|well*] *Fare-well*
70 siluer₍ₐ₎] ~ ,
71 thicke] *a partly inked space makes the word resemble* thickei
74 *qualities*] qualiies
75 of fountaines] offountaines
159 *-Church-|yard*] *-Church-yard*
180 vice] uice
191 earnestly] earnest-|nestly
234 *than*] *thau*
236 Seate,] ~ .
237 Great).] ~ )₍ₐ₎
249 Resolute,] ~ .
260 *pleasure,* hold] *pleasure.* Hold
283 *no paragraph indentation in* Q

314 Porcupines ₍ₐ₎ (*Stiffe,*)] ~ , (~ ₍ₐ₎)
329 *Throne*] Throne
332 *Throne. . . Vertue*] Throne. . . Vertue
334 *Chariot. . . Vertue*] Chariot. . . Vertue
343 bene free] benefree
387 Hall.] ~ :
387 worth,] ~ .
424 Suffolke.] ~ ₍ₐ₎
425 Norfolke.] ~ ₍ₐ₎
432 Elionor] Q(u); Eleonor Q(c)
436 -spittle.] ~ ,
437 Canterbury.] ~ ₍ₐ₎
448 Chertsay.] ~ ,
511 of] *of*

249

# A
# TRAGI-COMEDY:
## Called,

*Match mee in* LONDON.

---

As it hath beene often Prefented ; Firft,
at the *Bull* in St. IOHNS - ftreet ; And lately,
at the Priuate-Houfe in DRVRY-Lane,
called the PHOENIX

*Si non, Hù vtere Mecum.*

Written by THO: DEKKER.

LONDON.
Printed by B. ALSOP and T. FAVVCET, for H. SEILE,
at the *Tygers*-head in St. *Pauls* Church.
yard. 1631.

# TEXTUAL INTRODUCTION

*Match Me in London* (Greg, *Bibliography*, no. 440) was re-licensed without fee by Buc on 21 August 1623 as 'An Old Playe' (Bentley, *Jacobean Stage*, III, 256). On 8 November 1630 it was entered in the Stationers' Register to H. Seile. Despite the 1631 date on its title-page, the quarto could well have appeared in December of 1630, or even in late November.

Since Dekker signed the dedication to Lodowick Carlell, he doubtless furnished the printer with the manuscript in this case,[1] and indeed the print shows no clear sign of stage influence.[2] The text was typeset by one compositor and printed on one press using two skeleton-formes per sheet for imposition. Mechanically, the only obvious irregularity is the appearance of a set of running-titles in inner forme B in a small type that disappears thereafter. From the skeleton that had imposed outer B two running-titles reappear in inner C, apparently from a turned forme since the running-title on sig. B4$^v$ goes to C1$^v$, and that on B3 to C2. The running-title of B2$^v$ does not reappear, and since there had been no running-title on sig. B1, newly set running-titles are found on sigs. C3$^v$ and C4. The running-titles in the outer forme of C are all newly set in the larger type. In the transfer of the skeleton from outer C to outer D, the running-titles of sigs. C1 and C2$^v$ go, regularly, to D1 and D2$^v$, but the C3 running-title with a different quad arrangement that seems to reflect some accident is found on D4$^v$, and the C4$^v$ running-title may have pied, since that on D3 is a different setting. Thereafter the transfer is quite regular except for a switch in skeletons between formes in the imposition of sheet K.

The quarto was printed in ten sheets with the collation A² B–K⁴ L². Half-sheets A and L were demonstrably printed together by

---

[1] However, on the evidence of the apparent confusion that lists *Lupo* as a separate character from *Gazetto*, Dekker did not provide the Persons.

[2] Irregularities that might reflect reworking, or annotation, for the stage are only three, and none is very definite: (1) the misplacement of the direction 'florish' for I.iv; (2) the ghost character *Fuentes* in the direction for III.ii; and (3) the use of *Clown* for *Bilbo* in IV.ii.

twin half-sheet imposition on one full sheet and then sected to form one copy of each fold of two leaves. The proof comes in the running-title pattern whereby $K_1 = L_1$, $K_4^v = L_2^v$, $K_1^v = L_1^v$, and $K_4 = L_2$. Since quarters were taken from both skeleton-formes of sheet K to impose the half-sheet L, it is obvious that the two formes of L were not imposed together in one skeleton (from inner or outer K) by single half-sheet imposition. Instead, one forme of A must have been imposed in each chase with one forme of L. The transfer of the quarters from the two skeletons of K is to the appropriate similarly placed quarters of L if imposed with A for twin half-sheet printing.[1]

The evidence indicates that in *Match Me* inner A was imposed with outer L, and outer A with inner L, the imposition preferred in eighteenth-century printers' manuals and seemingly also exemplified in the printing of half-sheets A and M in *The Virgin Martyr* (1622). If the imposition were this inner with outer, as suggested, the first stage of correction of inner A and outer L was performed at the same time; and, correspondingly, the second stopping of the press for further correction resulted in the simultaneous alteration of the same two formes in the second stage. If, on the contrary, inner A and inner L were imposed together, we would have had the press while printing white paper stopped twice for corrections only to sigs. $A_1^v$, 2; and stopped twice while perfecting for corrections only to sigs. $L_1$, $2^v$. This latter process though not impossible is most improbable. In the first place if inner L were printed with inner A, setting of sigs. $L_1^v$, 2 (V.v.12–68) must have been superlatively correct from the start since no press variants would have been made in these pages although the forme was twice unlocked for minor correction to inner A (preliminaries). If so, it is difficult to understand why, on the contrary, outer L was so carelessly set by the same compositor as to require the press to be stopped twice for a total of eighteen variants in its two pages (V.iv.4–V.v.11; V.v.69–88). These two states of the text of the four L pages, distinguished by formes,

---

[1] For the principle involved and the interpretation of such running-title evidence, see 'Running-Title Evidence for Determining Half-Sheet Imposition', *Papers of the Bibliographical Society of the University of Virginia* [*Studies in Bibliography*], 1 (1948), 199–202.

are clearly most irregular, and the case could rest on this evidence alone, in conjunction with the abnormal double stopping of the press required for *both* formes.

Evidence that is suggestive though of less weight may be noticed, however. None of the extensive variation elsewhere in this quarto affects capitalization. On the other hand, the first stage of correction of inner A and of outer L contains three rather arbitrary examples of the raising of lower-case to a capital; and it is reasonable to assume that they were so ordered in the same proof-reading (and by the same agent). And if, as will be suggested below, the agent differed from the proof-reader for the rest of the book, we should have a ready explanation why in the second stage of the correction of inner A the venial change from *Dramatis* to *Drammatis* was made. If inner A and inner L were together, in one skeleton, the press would have been stopped for this change alone. However, if inner A and outer L were imposed together, the press was stopped a second time for the major correction of twelve variants on sigs. L 1, 2ᵛ, and the alteration on A 1ᵛ was quite secondary.

The process by which books composed *seriatim* and printed with two skeleton-formes were ordinarily proof-read and corrected seems to be established.[1] Usually only one forme will be press-variant since proofs for the perfecting forme would have been pulled while proof alterations were being made in the white-paper forme, and corrections in the perfecting-forme type would have been completed while the white-paper forme was finishing the edition-sheet. Two assumptions thereupon follow: (1) the type of the invariant forme when perfecting starts will have been proof-corrected; and (2) because proofs for the perfecting forme are pulled only a few minutes after the return of corrected proof for the white-paper forme, the same agent would normally have read and marked the proof for both formes.

However, recent bibliographical studies have shown that typesetting was not always performed *seriatim*, but instead that it was by no means unknown for compositors to set type-pages by formes

[1] See 'An Examination of the Method of Proof Correction in *King Lear*', *The Library*, 5th ser., II (1947), 20–44; and 'Elizabethan Proofing', *Joseph Quincy Adams Memorial Studies* (1948), pp. 571–586.

from cast-off copy that marked the precise amount of material to be set on each page.[1] Which method of compostion was employed is of some textual consequence, for the proof-reading procedures would necessarily differ between the two systems.

There is abundant evidence that *Match Me* was set by formes, at least in large part. For instance, in sheet C the speech-prefix for *King* strained the supply of the italic capital *K*; and hence it was found necessary to supplement the twenty-one italic *K* sorts by twenty-one roman K types. The pattern of substitution demonstrates that the outer forme of C was typeset before the inner forme. Whereas with a single anomalous exception on sig. C3$^v$ all settings of the letter K in the inner forme of C are in roman,[2] sig. C1 uses ten italic types, C2$^v$ six italic (and one anomalous roman), and C3 begins with four italic before continuing with five roman in the lower half of the page. It is clear, therefore, that composition started with sig. C1, jumped to C2$^v$, and thence to C3. On sig. C3 the italic *K* types were exhausted and the roman substitution began, continued through the three pages of inner C that required the speech-prefix. Distribution of a forme of sheet B would not have helped since no italic *K* types had been present there.

Further evidence is found in sheet D, in which a shortage of italic *L* developed. Sig. D1 contains four italic *L*, D2$^v$ has two, D3 has one at the top followed by the substitution of six roman L types, D4$^v$ has six italic, D1$^v$ had three italic and one roman (the roman at the foot), D2 has three roman, D3$^v$ has ten italic, and D4 has five. Here it would seem that setting also could not have been *seriatim* but was instead by formes, with distribution that restocked the cases occurring after outer D3 and inner D2 respectively.

In sheet F the supply of italic capital *I* was depleted. On F1 appear eight italic *I* and on F2$^v$ appear eleven italic. Then on F3 after five italic the italic sorts are exhausted and the lower half of the page substitutes five roman. Distribution apparently then took place, since F4$^v$ continues with three italic. In the inner forme, F1$^v$

---

[1] See Charlton Hinman, 'Cast-off Copy for the First Folio', *Shakespeare Quarterly*, VI (1955), 259–273; and George Walton Williams, 'Setting by Formes in Quarto Printing,' *Studies in Bibliography*, XI (1958), 39–53.

[2] An italic *K* on C2 (I.iii.64) is a later press variant.

has seven italic, F2 has one italic and eight roman, F3ᵛ has one italic and eleven roman, and F4 has one italic. The pattern of depletion makes it impossible for the typesetting of the pages to have been in regular order, like F1ᵛ, F2, F2ᵛ, F3, but instead composition must have been by formes.

Hence the usual standards for the proof-reading do not apply to *Match Me*. With *seriatim* setting and two-skeleton printing, the visible press-alteration to the white-paper forme and the invisible correction of the perfecting forme are managed so close together as almost to require the same agent to act as the proof-reader for both formes. But with quarto setting by formes, the proof-reading is an independent action for each forme, performed some hours apart and therefore not necessarily by the same agent. Moreover, since no other forme can be imposed to place on the press for proofing while the type of the opposite forme is being corrected, we should normally expect each forme to be independently press-variant, as in one-skeleton printing from *seriatim*-set type-pages.

The effect of this analysis on the textual problems of *Match Me* is to demonstrate that each press-variant forme must be considered on its own merits and that we can make no direct inferences about the agent who corrected any one forme from evidence present in the opposite forme of the sheet. Moreover, when one forme of a sheet is variant and the other invariant, it does not necessarily follow that the invariant forme has been proof-read, although probability dictates the assumption that it is in a corrected state and that an uncorrected state not yet discovered was printed.[1] Finally, when both formes of a sheet are variant, we must assume in the absence of some contrary evidence that the uncorrected type in each has the same status; that is, the only visible stage of alteration in either

[1] In a play showing such extensive correction to most of the formes as *Match Me*, we should expect all to have been proof-read and press-corrected. Here, at least, it is a natural inference that an invariant forme represents the corrected state, with the uncorrected state as yet not viewed. As an example, one may perhaps cite I.iv.2 in the invariant outer C forme, 'It spake! not, did it?' This wrongly placed exclamation point may be simple compositorial confusion, but analogy suggests that a proof-reader had marked the page to substitute the exclamation for the comma after *not*, and that the compositor correcting the type mistook the position. See III.i.54 for exactly the same mistake made in the known correction of outer F.

forme should represent the initial stage of press-correction unless there is some reason to believe the contrary.

The evidence from collation indicates that the sheets of *Match Me* were proof-read according to a regular system that occasionally gave a double check to the proofing. That is, we know that inner C, inner F, and the forme containing inner A and outer L had been once corrected and had resumed printing when the press was stopped for a second round of alteration consequent upon a rereading of the first corrected state. It is possible that the single alterations in outer B and outer E, and possibly the two variants in outer G and outer I, represent a second round and that an unrecovered initial state underlies them.

If as many as seven formes were reread (and perhaps even more not yet established), we should be chary of assigning the rereading to other than printing-house routine; that is, to take it that one round might represent the printer's reader but the other the author is to conjecture authorial intervention in a situation that seems to be mechanically systematic. Moreover, a significant consistency is not present. We cannot assign all of the first proof-reading to Dekker and the second to the press-reader, for too many of the first-stage variants differ no whit from the standard printing-house alterations seen in the dramatic quartos of the period. Many of the variants in the first corrected state of inner F—the small-change correction of literals, punctuation, and eccentric spelling—are quite representative and are precisely similar to the alterations made in the formes where only a single round of correction appears.[1] And the first-stage correction of inner F can be established as non-authorial by the alteration of the spelling *Farentes* to *Fuentes*, a careful change except that this is a ghost character.

On the other hand, it is equally difficult to assign the initial reading to the press-corrector and the second to Dekker. Characteristic of this quarto is the large number of exclamation points in the text, and the relatively large number added by the press-corrector. For

[1] For these single-stage corrected formes we must assume that the printer was the correcting agent: either the author did not attend the press or else the first-round author's variants have not been recovered. In view of the number of literals and obvious errors corrected in some of these once-altered formes it is difficult to believe that the author (or any other formal agent) had previously surveyed them.

example, in the formes that were corrected only once, he added eight such exclamations. When in the second round of alteration of inner A +outer L we find five added exclamations, therefore, we may be doubtful of an authorial second-round correction.

The best case for the assignment of the second reading to Dekker would come with the final alterations in inner C. Though the correction at I.iv.64 is obviously required, it was not so obvious—on the evidence—as to have been caught in the initial reading. Moreover, even admitting that the alteration at I.iv.40 is not overly difficult to make, yet that at II.i.41 required some subtlety, and the original reading of I.iv.73 made sense and did not cry out for change. The presence of the first corrected state in thirteen of the twenty-six collated copies shows that more than the usual delay (if we may be guided by the six copies showing the first state of corrected inner F and the two of inner A +outer L) obtained before rereading. Thus it is just possible that Dekker dropped in at the shop and made these changes to a forme that had earlier satisfied the proof-reader. Yet if he did so here, the gravity of the errors corrected might well have persuaded him to follow other formes and sheets with equal care, one would think; but of any such authoritative review there would appear to be no certain evidence elsewhere. In view of the arguments presented above about the place of the second reading in the printing-house routine, it is as easy to assume, hence, that this second round originated with the printer's agent like the other second rounds, that the extra number of copies printed of the first stage of correction merely indicates some extra delay before review (similar to that in a few formes before initial reading), and that the two added exclamation points suggest the hand of the regular proof-reader.[1] If the substantive alterations in the second stage of correction in inner C are authoritative—as they appear to be in a concentration not found elsewhere—it is possible to assume reference to manuscript, a procedure that may have occurred sporadically elsewhere though with no observable consistency.

This proof-reader was a curious man and one wishes that some information were available about his operation in other books. In

---

[1] This evidence may gain in weight if the arguments below about the correction of A(i)+L(o) are accepted.

certain respects he seems to have tried to carry forms of words in mind. His correction at III.i.90 of *Vm* to *Vmh* is a case in point, although the oddest is certainly his change of *Vindicadoes* to *Vindicados* on sig. K 4, V.ii.75. (The name *Vindicado's* had appeared before only at III.ii.92, sig. G 1, and was not to come again until V.v.5, on sig. L 1.) But the alteration of *Farentes* to *Fuentes* at III.ii.S.D. shows that he knew something of Spanish. Aware that he was working with a compositor who was careless about substantives as well as accidentals (and who was prone to omit both), this reader apparently took extraordinary responsibility upon himself. His metrical tinkerings at IV.iv.30 (I inner) and at V.ii.48 (K inner) are remarked in the Textual Notes, as are a few of his sophistications, especially where the usage of a word was not familiar to him (as at II.ii.55). A startling example of his assumption of responsibility is the alteration of 'ill-look'd Iade' to 'ill-fac'd Bawd' at II.ii.93; but the most egregious is the quite mistaken change at III.ii.51 of original 'Father' to 'Father in law', an alteration that shows his confidence in his own judgement and the quite cursory reading of the text that must have caused his misunderstanding of Don Valasco's position.

There remains one variant forme, however, where the details suggest the strong possibility that Dekker may actually have read proof. When an author dedicates a book to an important patron, it is possible he will wish to assure himself that the dedication (perhaps the only part of the book that will be read) is without embarrassing error, since there he is speaking in his own person. When we examine the variant forme of inner A+outer L, three peculiarities are immediately apparent. First, in contrast to the only other recovered sheets with a forme in two visible stages of alteration, the number of copies printed of the first corrected state is strikingly low before the press was stopped again for further correction: two against six for inner F and thirteen for inner C.

The second peculiarity concerns the changes made in the first stage of correction. In inner A the only two variants raise lower-case to capitals in the dedication, perhaps rather arbitrarily, and another such instance is found in outer L. This last, the raising of 'but two' to 'but, Two', at V.v.87, is interesting because it seems to conform to the usage at V.v.19, sig. L1$^v$, 'he in disguise | Has followed Both thus long to be reueng'd.' Unless we are to conjecture that this 'Both' (like *Two* a reference to Tormiella and her husband) was raised in a hypothetical correction of A(o)+L(i) to conform to the raising of *two* to *Two*, we are bound to take it that the capitalized *Both* stood in the manuscript and was faithfully reproduced by the compositor in the print. That being so, unless we are to infer such a close consultation of the manuscript by the press-corrector at V.v.87, and perhaps also in inner A, as has not been previously encountered—one that is doubtful in the extreme as likely to affect such minutiae—we may legitimately enquire into the possibility of another agent having ordered this particular group of variants.

That it is not the standard work of the printing-house reader seems clear. Nowhere else in all his correction of this quarto has this reader capitalized a single word. Yet three in this forme are so altered. The third detail now becomes pertinent. Whereas variants in the first stage of correction of A(i)+L(o) like the capitalization are unique, the rather large number of alterations in the two pages of L in the second round is entirely characteristic. For example, it is interesting in the light of his previous addition of exclamation points to notice that five exclamations and a query are ordered. It seems difficult to believe that the same agent performed both acts of correction as separate entities within an interval that ought to have been much less than an hour, and that he withheld his most frequent and characteristic changes until the second round.[1] Since the dedication forme is affected, for which the author may well have had some concern, I am willing to contemplate the hypothesis that the evidence favours assigning to Dekker the first-round alterations in this forme; and they have been adopted in the present text, accordingly.

---

[1] It is a pertinent fact that he made more alterations in the second round than in the first, a procedure differing from the second correction of inner C and inner F, to say nothing of the possibility that outer B, outer E, outer G, and outer I represent second rounds of alteration. (Acceptance of this part of the argument based on the addition of exclamation points, chiefly, will strengthen the pertinence of the evidence of the exclamations that the second stage of alteration to inner C was ordered by the printing-house reader despite what seems to be the generally authoritative nature of the substantive variants.)

The only other matter of interest about the variants is the statement that the resetting of lines at the foot of sig. K4 as part of the first stage of proof-correction seems to have resulted from accidentally pied type and was not ordered for any textual reason.

*Match Me in London* has not been edited previously save for the Pearson reprint. The present edition is based on a collation of the following twenty-six copies: British Museum, copy 1 (644.b.22), copy 2 (Ashley 618), copy 3 (C.12.f.4[4]), wanting sheets E–I; Bodleian Library, copy 1 (Mal. 195[8]), copy 2 (Mal. 235[10]), copy 3 (Mal. 914[3]), copy 4 (Douce D.205); Dyce Collection in the Victoria and Albert Museum, copy 1 and copy 2; Eton College; National Library of Scotland; Worcester College, Oxford; Henry E. Huntington Library; Yale University; Folger Shakespeare Library; Library of Congress; Newberry Library; University of Chicago; Boston Public Library; Harvard University; Chapin Collection at Williams College; The Pierpont Morgan Library; University of Pennsylvania; University of Virginia. Because of the special interest of the press-variants my thanks are due to Mr and Mrs Donald F. Hyde for permission to collate their private copy, the more especially since its evidence for inner A was unique in the copies consulted; and also to Mr Carl H. Pforzheimer for permission to collate and record the variants in the copy in the Pforzheimer Collection.

# DRAMATIS PERSONÆ

KING OF SPAINE

DON IOHN, Prince [of Spain and brother to the King]

DON VALASCO, Father to the Queene

[LUKE] GAZETTO, Louer of Tormiella

[ANDRADA] MALEVENTO, Father to her

CORDOLENTE, her Husband

ALPHONSO [DE GRANADA] ⎫
IAGO                             ⎬ Courtiers
MARTINES [DE BARAMEDA] ⎭                                    10

DOCTOR

2. CHVRCHMEN

BILBO [CAVEARE, servant to Malevento, and after journeyman to Cordolente]

PACHECO [, page to Prince Iohn]

LAZARILLO [, apprentice to Cordolente]

QVEENE [of Spain]

TORMIELLA

DILDOMAN, a Bawd

[A Coxcomb, two Friars, Gallants, Officers, Ladies and Gentlemen   20
of the Court]

---

10 MARTINES] *in a line between this and* DOCTOR, Q *inserts* LVPO

264

## To The Noble Louer,
### (and deseruedly beloued) of the Muses,
## LODOWICK CARLELL,
### Esquire, Gentleman of the Bowes, and Groome of the King, and Queenes Priuy-Chamber.

*That I am thus bold to sing a Dramatick Note in your Eare, is no wonder, in regard you are a Chorister in the Quire of the Muses. Nor is it any Over-daring in mee, to put a Play-Booke into your hands, being a Courtier;* Roman *Poets did so to their Emperours, the* Spanish, *(Now) to their Grandi'es, the* Italians *to their Illustrissimoes, and our owne Nation, to the Great-ones.*

*I haue beene a Priest in* APOLLO'S *Temple, many yeares, my voyce is decaying with my Age, yet yours being cleare and aboue mine, shall much honour mee, if you but listen to my old Tunes. Are they set Ill! Pardon them; Well! Then receiue them.*                    10

*Glad will you make mee, if by your Meanes, the King of* Spaine, *speakes our Language in the Court of* England; *yet haue you wrought as great a wonder, For the Nine sacred Sisters, by you, are (There) become Courtiers, and talke with sweet Tongues, Instructed by your Delian Eloquence. You haue a King to your Master, a Queene to your Mistresse, and the Muses your Play-fellowes. I to them a Servant: And yet, what Duty soeuer I owe them, some part will I borrow to waite vpon you, And to Rest*

Ever,
So devoted.    20
THO: DEKKER.

## Match Mee in London.

### ACTVS, I [SCENA i]

*Enter* Malevento.

*Male.*  *Tormiella* Daughter — nor in this roome — Peace:
1. 2. 3. 4. 5. 6. 7. 8. 9. 10. 11. 12.
The dawne of Midnight, and the Drunkards noone,
No honest soules vp now, but Vintners, Midwiues,
The nodding Watch, and pitious Constable,
Ha; *Bilbo*!
My street doore open! *Bilbo, Puskeena, Bilbo.*
Bawds, Panders, to a young Whore.

*Enter* Bilbo.

*Bilbo.*  Theeues, Theeues, Theeues, where are they Master?
*Male.*  Where are they *Bilbo*? What Theefe seest thou?          10
*Bilbo.*  That ilfauor'd Theefe in your Candle sir, none else not I.
*Male.*  Why didst thou cry Theeues then?
*Bilbo.*  Because you cry'd Whores; I knew a Theefe was alwayes
within a stones cast of a Whore.
*Male.*  What mak'st thou vp at Midnight?
*Bilbo.*  I make them which are made euery houre i'th day (patches.)
*Male.*  Slaue what art doing?
*Bilbo.*  That which few men can doe, mending Sir.
*Male.*  What art mending?
*Bilbo.*  That which few men care to mend, a bad sole.          20
*Male.*  Looke here, come hither, dost thou see what's this?
*Bilbo.*  I see tis our Wicket, master.
*Male.*  Stop there and tell me, is *Tormiella* forth?
*Bilbo.*  I heard *Puskeena* our Kitchin-maid say, she was going
about a murther.
*Male.*  A murther; of whom?
*Bilbo.*  Of certaine Skippers; she was fleaing her selfe.

266

*Male.* She dwels not in her Chamber, for my Ghost
(Call'd from his rest) from Roome to roome has stalk'd,
Yet met no *Tormiella.*                                                30
Was not her sweet heart here to night, *Gazetto?*
*Bilbo.* *Gazetto!* no sir, here was no *Gazetto* here.
*Male.* Walke round the Orchard, holla for her there.
*Bilbo.* So, ho, ho, ho, ho.                                    *Exit.*
*Male.* She's certaine with *Gazetto,*
Should he turne Villaine, traine my poore child forth
Though she's contracted to him, and rob her youth
Of that Gemme none can prize (because nere seene)
The Virgins riches (Chastity) and then
(When he has left her vgly to all eyes)                          40
His owne should loath her, vds death I would draw
An old mans nerues all vp into this arme,
And nayle him to the Bed —

*Enter* Bilbo.

*Bilbo.* So, ho, ho, ho, the Conyes vse to feed most i'th night Sir,
yet I cannot see my young mistris in our Warren.
*Male.* No!
*Bilbo.* No, nor you neither, tis so darke.
*Male.* Where should this foolish girle be? tis past twelue,
Who has inuited her forth to her quicke ruine!
*Bilbo.* My memory jogs me by the elbow, and tels me —        50
*Male.* What *Bilbo,* out with all.
*Bilbo.* A Barber stood with her on Saturday night very late, when
he had shau'd all his Customers, and as I thinke, came to trimme
her.
*Male.* A Barber! To trim her! Sawst thou the Muskcod?
*Bilbo.* A chequer'd aprone Gentleman I assure you: he smelt
horrible strong of Camphire, Bay leaues and Rose water: and he
stood fidling with *Tormiella.*
*Male.* Ha?
*Bilbo.* Fidling at least halfe an houre, on a Citterne with a mans 60
broken head at it, so that I thinke 'twas a Barber Surgion: and

there's one *Cynamomo* a Shopkeeper, comes hither a batfowling euery Moone-shine night too.

*Male.* What's he! *Cynamomo*!

*Bilbo.* I take him to be a Comfitmaker with rotten teeth, for he neuer comes till the Barber's gone.

*Male.* A Comfitmaker!

*Bilbo.* Yes Sir, for he gaue *Tormiella* a Candied roote once, and she swore 'twas the sweetest thing —

*Male.* Dwels he here i'th City?                70

*Bilbo.* He has a house i'th City, but I know not where he liues.

*Male.* Sheele follow her kind, turne Monster; get a light.

*Bilbo.* My sconce is ready Sir.

*Male.* Call at *Gazettoes* Lodging, aske how he dares
Make a Harlot of my child, — slaue say no more:
Begon, beat boldly.

*Bilbo.* Ile beat downe the doore; and put him in mind of a Shroue-tuesday, the fatall day for doores to be broken open.        *Exit.*

*Male.* For this night I'm her Porter; Oh haplesse Creatures!        80
There is in woman a Diuell from her birth,
Of bad ones we haue sholes, of good a dearth.

                                        *Exit.*


[ACT I, Scene ii]

*Enter* Cordolente *and* Tormiella.

*Cordo.*   No more my *Tormiella*, night hath borne
Thy vowes to heauen, where they are fyl'd by this
Eyther one day to crowne thy constant Soule
Or (if thou spot it with foule periury,)
For euer to condemne thee.

*Tormi.*                    Come it shall not:
Here am I sphear'd for euer, thy feares (deare Loue)
Strike coldly on thy jealous breast I know
From that my Fathers promise to *Gazetto*
That he should haue me: contract is there none,

For my heart loath'd it, is there left an oath                    10
Fit for a Maid to sweare by?
*Cordo.*                    Good sweet giue o're,
What need we binding oathes being fast before?
I dare the crabbed'st Fate, shee cannot spin
A thred thus fine and rotten; how now! sad!
*Tormi.*   Pray Heauen, I bee not mist at home, deare *Cordolente*
Thou shalt no farther, Ile venter now my selfe.
*Cordo.*   How, sweet! venture alone!
*Tormi.*                    Yes, yes, good rest.
*Cordo.*   By that are Louers parted, seldome blest.

*Enter* Bilbo.

*Bilbo.*   Who goes there, if you be a woman stand, for all the men
I met to night, lye in the Kennell.                              20
*Tormi.*   My Fathers man! I am betray'd.
*Cordo.*                    Feare nothing.
*Tormi.*   *Bilbo*!
Whether art thou running?
*Bilbo.*   Out of my wits and yet no Churles Executor, 'tis not
money makes me mad, but want of money.
*Tormi.*   Good tell me whether art going?
*Bilbo.*   I am going to Hell (that's to say home) for my Master
playes the Diuell, and I come from seeking out a house of euer-
lasting Thunder, (that's to say a Woman) I haue beene bouncing
at Signior *Gazetto*'s Chamber for you.                          30
*Tormi.*   Ha!
*Bilbo.*   You'l be haa'd when you come home.
*Tormi.*   I am vndone for euer.
*Cordo.*                    Thou art not, peace.
*Bilbo.*   Signior *Gazetto* is horne-mad, and leapt out of his Bed, (as
if fleas had bit him) so that I thinke he comes running starke naked
after me.
*Tormi.*   Oh me, what helpe my dearest Soule?
*Cordo.*                    To desperate wounds
Let's apply desperate cure, dar'st thou flye hence?

13 dare the] Q(c); Q(u) *omits* the          24 not] no | Q

*Tormi.* Dare! try me.

*Cordo.*              Then farewell *Cordoua*;
Horses wee'l forthwith hire, and quicke to *Siuell*        40
My birth-place, there thou shalt defie all stormes.

*Tormi.* Talke not, but doe.

*Bilbo.*   She would haue you doe much but say little.

*Tormi.* *Bilbo*, thou seest me not.

*Bilbo.*   No, no, away, mum I.

*Cordo.* To shut thy lips fast, here are lockes of Gold.

*Bilbo.*   I spy a light comming, trudge this way.

*Tormi.* You dally with fire, haste, haste, *Bilbo* farewell.

*Cordo.* O starre-crost Loue!
To find way to whose Heauen, man wades through Hell.        50

*Exeunt: manet* Bilbo.


*Enter* Gazetto.


*Gaʒ.* Wo, ho, ho, ho, — whew.

*Bilbo.*   Another Fire-drake! More Salamanders! Heere Sir.

*Gaʒ.* *Bilbo*! How now!
Is the Dy-dapper aboue water yet?

*Bilbo.*   Signior *Gaʒetto*! Mine Eyes are no bigger then litle pinnes
heads with staring, my heeles ake with trotting, my candle is come
to an vntimely end through a Consumption, yet my yong Mistris
your sweet hart, like sweet breath amongst Tobacco-drinkers, is
not to be found.

*Gaʒ.* On, take my Torch, apace: the neer'st way home.        60
Fluttering abroad by Owle-light!

*Bilbo.*   Here sir, turne downe this Lane; shall I knocke your Torch
Signior?

*Gaʒ.* Prithee doe what thou wilt, the Diuell! where is she?

*Bilbo.*   Had you knockt your Torch well before *Tormiella* (ware
the post) and held it well vp when it was lighted, she had neuer
giuen you the slip, and i'faith Signior when is the day?

*Gaʒ.* The wedding (meanst thou) on Saint *Lukes* day next,
'Tis mine owne name thou know'st: but now I feare
She's lost, and the day too.        70

*Bilbo.*  If she should driue you by foule weather into Cuckolds
Hauen before Saint *Lukes* day comes, Signior *Luco* how then?

*Gaȝ.*  If she dares let her, I haue her Fathers promise,
Nay oath that I shall haue her.

*Bilbo.*  Here is my Masters Gate.

*Gaȝ.*  Stay she's at home sure now: Ile slip aside,
Knocke thou, and if she answeres (as 'tis likely)
Weel try if still th'old fencing be in vse,
That faulty women neuer want excuse.

*Bilbo.*  They are made for the purpose to lye and cullor,          80
Ile knocke.

*Male.*  Who's there?                              [*Within.*]

*Bilbo.*  'Tis I, open the doore.

*Male.*  What! to a Common!

*Bilbo.*  What, common! You doe me wrong sir, though I goe in
breeches, I am not the roaring girle you take me for.

*Male.*  Wert thou with *Gaȝetto*?

*Bilbo.*  Yes.

*Male.*  Was she with *Gaȝetto*?

*Bilbo.*  No.                                               90

*Male.*  Was *Gaȝetto* alone?

*Bilbo.*  No sir, I was with him.

*Male.*  Foole, knew not he she was forth?

*Bilbo.*  Yes when I told him.

*Gaȝ.*  Signior *Malevento* open the doore pray.

[*Enter* Malevento.]

*Male.*  Oh *Luke Gaȝetto.*

*Gaȝ.*  Not yet come home!

*Male.*          No, no.

*Gaȝ.*                    Not yet! vds death
When I shall take the Villaine does this wrong,
H'ad better stolne away a Starre from Heauen:
No *Spaniard* sure dares doe it.                          100

*Bilbo.*  'Tis some *English* man has stolne her, I hold my life, for
most Theeues and brauest Cony-catchers are amongst them.

*Gaȝ.*  All *Cordoua* search ere morning, if not found

Ile ride to *Siuill*, Ile mount my Iennet Sir
And take the way to *Madrill*.

*Male.*            Ne're speake of *Madrill*,
The iourney is for her too dangerous,
If *Cordoua* hold her not, lets all to *Siuill*.
Haste, haste, by breake of day Signior *Gazetto*
Let vs meet agen.

*Gaz.*       Agreed.

*Male.*       We'll hunt her out.      *Exit.*

*Bilbo.*  But you know not when, will you take your Torch. *Exit.* 110

*Gaz.*  Keepe it: lustfull maiden!
Hot *Spanish* vengeance followes thee, which flyes
Like three forkt Lightning, whom it smites, he dyes.

                                     *Exit.*


[ACT I, Scene iii]

*Enter Prince* Iohn *all vnready, and* Pacheco *his Page.*

*Iohn.*  Pacheco?

*Pach.*  My Lord.

*Iohn.*  Is't so earely! What a Clocke Is't?

*Pach.*  About the houre that Souldiers goe to bed, and Catchpoles rise: Will your Lordship be truss'd vp this morning?

*Iohn.*  How dost meane, goe to hanging!

*Pach.*  Hanging! does your Lordship take me for a crack-rope?

*Iohn.*  No, but for a notable Gallowes, too many Lordships are truss'd vp euery day (boy) some wud giue a thousand Crownes to haue 'em vnty'd, but come sir tye vp my Lordship.   10

*Pach.*  As fast as I can, Oh my Lord and a man could tye friends to him as fast as I doe these points, 'twere a braue world.

*Iohn.*  So he does, for these are fast now, and loose at night.

*Pach.*  Then they are like the loue of a woman.

*Iohn.*  Why boy! Do you know what the loue of a woman is!

*Pach.*  No faith my Lord, nor you neither, nor any man else I thinke.

*Iohn.*   Y'are a noble Villaine.

*Pach.*   Would I were, then I should be rich.

*Iohn.*   Well get you gon —                    *Exit* [Pacheco]. 20
Here's a braue fyle of noble *Portugals*
Haue sworne to helpe me, its hard trusting strangers,
Nay more, to giue them footing in a Land
Is easie, hard to remoue them; say they and I
Should send my Brother King out of this world,
And inthrone me (for that's the Starre I reach at,)
I must haue *Spaine* mine, more then *Portugall*,
Say that the *Dons* and *Grandi'es* were mine owne,
And that I had the Keyes of the Court Gates
Hang at my Girdle, in my hand the Crowne;              30
There's yet no lifting it vp to my head
Without the people: I must ride that Beast,
And best sit fast: who walkes not to his Throne
Vpon their heads and hands, goes but alone;
This Dogfish must I catch then, the Queenes Father!
(*Pedro Valasco*) what if I got him!
Its but a shallow old fellow, and to build
On the great'st, wisest Statesman, in a dessigne
Of this high daring, is most dangerous;
We see the tops of tall trees, not their heart;       40
To find that sound or rotten, there's the Art.
How now *Iago*?

                    *Enter* Iago.

*Iago.*                    Good morrow to your Lordship,
The King lookes for you, you must come presently.

*Iohn.*   Well Sir: must come! So:
As I must come, so he ere long must goe.

                              *Exeunt.*

## [ACT I, SCENE iv]

*Florish. Enter King,* Valasco, Martines, Alphonso.

*Val.*   And broad awake!
*King.*              As is that eye of Heauen.
*Val.*   It spake not, did it?
*King.*            No; but with broad eyes,
  Glassie and fierie stair'd vpon me thus,
  As blacke, as is a Soule new dipt in Hell;
  The t'other was all white, a beard and haire
  Snowie like *Portugall,* and me thought his looke:
  But had no armes.
*Val.*         No armes!
*King.*            No: just my height,
  Now, and e're this it was shot vp so high,
  Me thought I heard the head knocke at a Starre,
  Cleane through the Seeling.
*Val.*         Fancy, Fancy.
*King.*            I saw it.       10
*Val.*   A meere *Deceptio visus.*
*King.*            A vice Asse;
  Y'are an incredulous Coxcombe, these saw it.
*Val.*   Well; they did, they did.
*King.*            I call'd for helpe;
  These enter'd, found mee dead with feare!
*Omn.*               'Tis right Sir.
*King.*   Did not the Spirits glide by thee?
*Mart.*   Your Grace must pardon me, I saw none.
*King.*   'Shart doe I lye! doe you braue me! you base Peasant?
*Mart.*   No my Lord, but I must guard my life against an Emperor.
*King.*   One of my wiues men, is't not! Ha!
  What a Pox fawnes the Curre for here! away.     20
  Her Spye Sir! Are you!          *Exit* Martines.

S.D. *Florish.*] Q [*florish*] places to the right of I.iii.44
21 S.D. *Exit* Martines.] Q *places after line* 20

*Val.*                     Sooth him vp, y'are fooles,
If the Lyon say the Asses eares are hornes
The Asse if he be wise will sweare it, la Sir
These tell me they all saw it.
*Omn.*                     Yes my Lord.

                    *Enter* Iago.

*King.*  And yet I lye! a whoreson buzzard — Now sir.
*Iago.*  Prince *Iohn* is comming.
*King.*                     When sir!
*Iago.*                             Instantly.
*King.*  Father Ile tell you a Tale, vpon a time
The Lyon, Foxe and silly Asse did jarre,
Grew friends and what they got, agreed to share:
A prey was tane, the bold Asse did diuide it                    30
Into three equall parts, the Lyon spy'd it,
And scorning two such sharers, moody grew,
And pawing the Asse, shooke him as I shake you.
*Val.*  Not too hard good my Lord, alas I am craz'd.
*King.*  And in rage tore him peace meale, the Asse thus dead,
The prey was by the Foxe distributed
Into three parts agen; of which the Lyon
Had two for his share, and the Foxe but one:
The Lyon (smiling) of the Foxe would know
Where he had this wit, he the dead Asse did show.                    40
*Val.*  An excellent Tale.
*King.*                     Thou art that Asse.
*Val.*                                  I!
*King.*                                      Thou:
You, and the Foxe my Brother cut my Kingdome,
Into what steakes you list, I haue no more,
Then what you list to giue.
You two broach Warre or Peace; you plot, contriue,
You flea off the Lyons skinne, you sell him aliue,
But hauing torne the Asse first limbe from limbe
His death shall tell the Foxe Ile so serue him.

         *40 Asse] Q(c²); *om.* Q(u, c¹)      *43 haue] Q(u); *share* Q(c¹)

*Val.*   I doe all this! 'tis false: in Prince *Iohns* face
Ile spit if he dares speake it, you might ride me                    50
For a right Asse indeed if I should kick
At you, vndermine you, or blow you vp?
In whom the hope of my posterity
(By marriage of my child your wife) doth grow:
None but an Asse would doe it.
*King.*                     If I know,
Your little finger was but in't; neither age,
Your place in Court, and Councell, respect of honour,
Nor of my wife (your Daughter) shall keepe this head
Vpon these shoulders —

*Enter Prince* Iohn.

*Val.*                    Take it; now here's Prince *Iohn.*
*King.*   How now Brother! Sick!
*Iohn.*                    Not very well.
*King.*                              Our Court   60
Is some Inchanted Towre, you come not neare it
Are you not troubled with some paine i'th head?
Your Night-cap shewes you are?
*Iohn.*                    Yes wonderously, —
A kind of Megrim Sir.
*King.*              I thinke to bind
Your Temples with the Crowne of *Spaine* would ease you.
*Iohn.*   The Crowne of *Spaine*! my Temples!
*King.*                              Nay I but iest,
A Kingdome would make any Sicke man well,
And *Iohn* I would thou hadst one.
*Iohn.*                    It shall goe hard else.
                                        [*Aside.*]

*Val.*   The King I thanke him sayes that you and I —
*King.*   What?                                    70
*Val.*              Cut you out sir in steakes, Ile not be silent,
And that I am an Asse, and a Foxe you,
Haue I any dealings with you?

64 *King.*] Q(c²); *Ioh.* Q(u, c¹)        69 him] Q(c¹); *om.* Q(u)

276

*Iohn.*                    When I am to deale sir
A wiser man then you shall hold the Cards.
*Val.*   Now I'm call'd foole too.
*King.*                    Sir if you remember
Before he came, you buzz'd into mine eare,
Tunes that did sound but scuruily.
*Val.*                    I buz! What buz!
*King.*   That he should sell me to the *Portugall.*
*Val.*   Wer't thou as big as all the Kings i'th world,
'Tis false and I defie thee.
*King.*                    Nay Sir, and more, —
*Val.*   Out with't; no whispering.
*King.*                    I shall blush to speake it,          80
Harke you, a Poxe vpon't, cannot you sooth
His sullen Lordship vp, you see I doe.
Flatter him, confesse any thing.
*Val.*                    A good Iest!
I should confesse to him I know not what,
And haue my throat cut, but I know not why.
*Iohn.*   W'ud your Grace
Would licence me a while to leaue the Court
To attend my health.
*King.*                    Doe.
*Iohn.*                    I take my leaue — as for you Sir —
                                                        *Exit.*
*King.*   My Lord doe you see this Change i'th Moone, sharpe hornes
Doe threaten windy weather, shall I rule you?          90
Send to him dead words, write to him your mind
And if your hearts be vnsound purge both, all humors
That are corrupt within you.
*Val.*   Ile neuer write, but to him in person.          *Exit.*

              *Enter old Lady* [Dildoman].

*King.*   Pray Madam rise.                [*She whispers him.*]
*Iago.*   Doe you know this old furie?

*73 wiser man then you shall] Q(c²) [than]; wise man then shall Q(u, c¹)
*82 doe.] ~ ₄ Q

277

*Alph.* No: what is she?

*Iago.* She's the Kings nuthooke (if report has not a blister on her tongue) that when any Filberd-tree is ripe; puls downe the brauest bowes to his hand: a Lady Pandresse, and (as this yeares Almanacke 100 sayes) has a priuate hot-house for his Grace onely to sweat in: her name the Lady *Dildoman*: the poore Knight her Husband is troubled with the City Gowt, lyes i'th Counter.

*King.* Ile hang him that stirres in't, the proudest Fawlcon that's pearcht vp nearest the Eagle, if he dare, make this his prey, how many yeares!

*Lady.* Fifteene and vpwards if it please your Grace.

*King.* Some two-footed Diuell in our Court,
Would thrust you out of all. Inclos'd! or Common!

*Lady.* 'Tis yet inclos'd if it like your Grace. 110

*King.* Entayl'd!

*Lady.* Newly Entayl'd, as there 'tis to be seene in blacke and white.

*King.* This case my selfe will handle; fee no Lawyer,
Ile stand for you, ha! Servants of mine turn'd grinders!
To oppresse the weake! What slaue is't! from my sight,
Least my heau'd hand swerue awry, and Innocence smite.

*Alph.* This Bawd belike has her house pull'd downe.

                                   *Exeunt* [Alphonso, Iago].

*King.* So: come hither, nearer, where shines this starre?

*Lady.* I'th City, brightly, sprightly, brauely, oh 'tis a Creature — 120

*King.* Young!

*Lady.* Delicate, piercing eye, inchanting voyce, lip red and moyst, skin soft and white; she's amorous, delicious, inciferous, tender, neate.

*King.* Thou madst me, newly married!

*Lady.* New married, that's all the hole you can find in her coate, but so newly, the poesie of her wedding Ring is scarce warme with the heate of her finger; therefore my Lord, fasten this wagtayle, as soone as you can lime your bush, for women are Venice-glasses, one knocke spoyles 'em. 130

*King.* Crackt things! pox on 'em.

*Lady.* And then they'l hold no more then a Lawyers Conscience.

*King.*   How shall I get a sight of this rich Diamond.

*Lady.*   I would haue you first disguis'd goe along with mee, and
buy some toy in her shop, and then if you like *Danae* fall into her
lap like *Ioue*, a net of Goldsmiths worke will plucke vp more
women at one draught, then a Fisherman does Salmons at fifteene.

*King.*   What's her Husband?

*Lady.*   A flatcap, pish; if he storme, giue him a Court-Loafe; stop
his mouth with a Monopoly.                                                    140

*King.*   Th'ast fir'd me.

*Lady.*   You know where to quench you.

*King.*   Ile steale from Court in some disguise presently.

*Lady.*   Stand on no ground good your Highnesse.

*King.*   Away, Ile follow thee, speake not of hast,
Thou tyest but wings to a swift gray Hounds heele,
And add'st to a running Charriot a fift wheele.
Thou now dost hinder me, away, away.

                                                          [*Exeunt.*]

                    *Finis Actus primi.*


## ACTVS, II [Scena i]

*A shop opened, Enter* Bilbo *and* Lazarillo.

*Bilbo.*   *Laʒarillo* art bound yet?

*Laʒ.*   No, but my Indentures are made.

*Bilbo.*   Make as much haste to seale, as younger Brothers doe at
taking vp of Commodities: for *Laʒarillo*, there's not any *Deigo*
that treads vpon *Spanish* leather, goes more vpright vpon the soles
of his Conscience, then our Master does.

*Laʒ.*   Troth so I thinke, now I like my little smirking Mistris as
well.

*Bilbo.*   Like her, did not I like her simply, to runne away from her
father (where I had both men Seruants and maid Seruants vnder   10
me) to weare a flat cap here and cry what doe you lacke.

            139–140 stop his] Q(u); stop's Q(c¹)
            3 at] Q(c¹); a | Q(u)

                            279

*Enter Gallants.*

*La*ʒ. What is't you lacke Gentlemen, rich garters, spangled roses,
silke stockins, embrodered gloues or girdles.

*Bilbo.* Don sweet *Don*, see here rich *Tuscan* hatbands, *Venetian*
ventoyes, or *Barbarian* shoo-strings — no poynt —

*Exeunt Gallants.*

*La*ʒ. Their powder is dankish and will not take fire.

*Bilbo.* Reach that paper of gloues, what marke is't?

*La*ʒ. *P.* and *Q.*

*Enter* Malevento.

*Bilbo.* *P.* and *Q.*, chafe these, chafe, chafe, here's a world to make
Shopkeepers chafe.                                                         20

*La*ʒ. What is't you buy Sir, gloues, garters, girdles.

*Bilbo.* *La*ʒ*arillo, La*ʒ*arillo*, my old master *Andrada Malevento*; do
you heare sir, the best hangers in *Spaine* for your worship.

*Male.* Vmh! I haue knowne that voyce, what! Run away! Why
how now *Bilbo*! growne a Shopkeeper!

*Bilbo.* Iogging on Sir, in the old path to be call'd vpon to beare all
offices, I hope one day.

*Male.* 'Tis well: good fortunes blesse you.

*Bilbo.* Turn'd Citizen sir, a Counter you see still before me, to put
me in mind of my end, and what I must goe to, if I trust too many    30
with my ware, it's newes to see your worship in *Siuill*.

*Male.* 'Tis true: but *Bilbo*, no newes yet of my Daughter?

*Bilbo.* None.

*Male.* Not any!

*Bilbo.* What will your worship giue me, if I melt away all that sow
of lead that lyes heauy at your heart, by telling you where shee is.

*Male.* Prithee step forth, speake softly, thou warm'st my blood,
Ile giue thee the best suite Prentize e're wore.

*Bilbo.* And I can tell you Prentizes are as gallant now, as some that
walke with my cozen *Bilbo* at their sides, you can scarce know 'em   40
for Prentizes of *Siuill*.

*Male.* Fly to the marke I prithee?

*41 for] Q(c²); from Q(u, c¹)

280

*Bilbo.*  Now I draw home, doe you see this shop, this shop is my
Masters.

*Male.*  So, so, what of all this?

*Bilbo.*  That master lies with my yong mistris, and that mistris is
your Daughter.

*Male.*  Ha!

*Bilbo.*  Mum: she's gone forth, this morning to a Wedding, he's
aboue, but (as great men haue done) he's comming downe.          50

*Enter* Cordolente.

*Male.*  Is this he?

*Bilbo.*  This is he.

*Cordo.*  Looke to the shop.

*Male.*  Pray sir a word?

*Cordo.*                 You shall.

*Male.*                           You doe not know me?

*Cordo.*  Trust me not well.

*Male.*                        Too well, thou hast vndone me,
Thou art a Ciuill Theefe with lookes demure
As is thy habit, but a Villaines heart.

*Cordo.*  Sir —

*Male.*            Heare me sir — to rob me of that fire
That fed my life with heate (my onely Child)
Turne her into —

*Cordo.*            What sir! She's my wife.          60

*Male.*  Thy Strumpet, she's a disobedient Child,
To crosse my purposes; I promis'd her
To a man whom I had chosen to be her Husband.

*Cordo.*  She lou'd him not; was she contracted to him?
Can he lay claime to her by Law?

*Male.*                            Ile sweare,
She told me I should rule her, that she was
Affy'd to no other man, and that to please me
She would onely take *Gazetto.*

*Cordo.*                       I will forbeare Sir
To vexe you; what she spake so, was for feare,
But I ha' done, no Begger has your child,          70

I craue no Dowrie with her, but your Loue,
For hers I know I haue it.
*Male.*                    Must I not see her!
*Cordo.*    You shall but now she's forth sir.
*Male.*                                She has crackt
My very heart-strings quite in sunder.
*Cordo.*                                Her loue
And duty shall I hope knit all more strongly.
Sir I beseech your patience, when my bosome
Is layd all open to you, you shall find
An honest heart there, and you will be glad
You ha met the Theefe that rob'd you, and forgiue him,
I am ingag'd to businesse craues some speed,                    80
Please you be witnesse to it.
*Male.*                    Well I shall,
Parents with milke feed Children, they them with gall.
                    *Exeunt* [Malevento *and* Cordolente].
*Bilbo.*    As kind an old man *Laȝarillo*, as euer drunk mull'd Sack.
*Laȝ.*    So it seemes, for I saw him weepe like a Cut Vine.
*Bilbo.*    Weepe; I warrant that was because hee could not find in's
heart to haue my Master by th'eares.

                    *Enter* Tormiella.

*Laȝ.*    My Mistris.
*Bilbo.*    Chafe chafe.
*Tormi.*    Where's your master.
*Bilbo.*    Newly gone forth forsooth.                    90
*Tormi.*    Whether, with whom.
*Bilbo.*    With my old Master your Father.
*Tormi.*    Ha! my Father! when came he! who was with him?
What said he, how did my Husband vse him?
*Bilbo.*    As Officers at Court vse Citizens that come without their
Wiues, scarce made him drinke, but they are gone very louingly
together.
*Tormi.*    That's well, my heart has so ak't since I went forth, I am
glad I was out of the peales of Thunder, askt hee not for mee, was
*Gaȝetto* with him, *Luke* was not hee with him ha!                    100

*Bilbo.*    No onely the old man.

*Tormi.*    That's well, reach my workebasket, is the imbrodered Muffe perfum'd for the Lady?

*Bilbo.*    Yes forsooth, she neuer put her hand into a sweeter thing.

*Tormi.*    Are you sure *Gazetto* was not with my Father?

*Bilbo.*    Vnlesse he wore the invisible cloake.

*Tormi.*    Blesse me from that disease and I care not, one fit of him would soone send me to my graue; my hart so throbs?

> *Enter* Gazetto [*disguised as* Lupo] *and Officers.*

*Laz.*    What is't you lacke.

*Bilbo.*    Fine Garters, Gloues, Glasses, Girdles, what is't you buy.  110

*Gaz.*    I haue a warrant you see from the King to search all *Siuell* for the woman that did this murther, the act of which has made me mad, misse no shop, let me haue that which I can buy in some Country for seuen groates — *Iustice.*

*Offi.*    Your searching house by house thus is so spread abroad that 'tis as bad as a scarcrow to fright away the bird you seeke to Catch, me thinks if you walke soberly alone from shop to shop, your bat fowling would catch more wagtailes.

*Gaz.*    Well shot *Sagitarius*, Ile nock as thou bidst mee.

*Offi.*    What thinke you of yonder parrot i'th Cage.        120

*Gaz.*    A rope — ha — puffe — is the wind with mee.

*Tormi.*    What stares the man at so.

*Offi.*    His wits are reeld a little out of the road way; nothing else.

*Bilbo.*    Alas mistris, this world is able to make any man mad.

*Gaz.*    Ha ha ha ha.

*Offi.*    What doe you laugh at, is this shee.

*Gaz.*    No, but I saw a doue fly by that had eaten Carrion; it shewd like a corrupted Churchman; farewell.

*Offi.*    Doe you discharge vs then.            *Exeunt Officers.*

*Gaz.*    As haile shot at a dunghill where Crowes are.        130
Th'art mine; thankes vengeance; thou at last art come,
(Tho with wolly feet) be quick now and strike home.        *Exit.*

---

*113–114 some Country] *stet* Q          *115 thus] this Q

283

*Enter King and Lady* [Dildoman].

*La*. What is't you lacke.
*Bilbo.* What is't you buy.
*Lady.* That's shee.
*King.* Peace; Madam lets try here.
*Bilbo.* What is't you lack sir!
*King.* A gloue with an excellent perfume.
*Bilbo.* For your selfe sir!                                    140
*King.* I would fit my selfe sir, but I am now for a woman: a pritty
little hand: the richest you haue.
*Lady.* About the bignesse of this gentlewomans will serue.
*King.* Yes faith Madam, at all adventures Ile make this my measure,
shall I mistrisse!
*Tormi.* As you please sir.
*King.* It pleases mee well.
*Bilbo.* Then sir go no farder, heer's the fairest in all *Spaine*, fellow
it and take mine for a dogskin.
*Lady.* Pray forsooth draw it on, if it fit you it fits the party surely.
*Bilbo.* Nay Madam, the gloue is most genuine for any young 150
Ladies hand vnder the Coape, I assure you.
*King.* I but the Leather.
*Bilbo.* Nay, the Leather is affable and apt to bee drawn to any
generous disposition.
*King.* Pray (faire Lady) does it not come on too stiffe?
*Tormi.* No sir very gently.
*Bilbo.* Stiffe; as prolixious as you please: nay sir the sent is
*Aromaticall* and most odorous, the muske vpon my word Sir is
perfect *Cathayne*, a Tumbasine odor vpon my credit, not a graine
either of your *Salmindy*, Caram or Cubit musk.                  160
*King.* Adulterated I doubt.
*Bilbo.* No adultery in the world in't, no sophistication but pure as
it comes from the cod.
*Tormi.* Open more, you shall haue what choyce you please.
*Bilbo.* You shall haue all the ware open'd i'th shop to please your
worship but you shall bee fitted.

*King.*    No no, it needs not: that which is open'd already shall serue
my turne.

*Lady.*    Will you goe farther sonne and see better.

*King.*    And perhaps speed worse: no: your price?                    170

*Bilbo.*    Foure double Pistolets.

*King.*    How!

*Bilbo.*    Good ware cannot be too deare: looke vpon the cost,
relish the sent, note the workemanship.

*King.*    Your man is too hard, Ile rather deale with you: three Ile
giue you.

*Lady.*    Come pray take it, will three fetch 'em?

*Tormi.*    Indeed we cannot, it stands my Husband in more.

*King.*    Well lay these by, a Cordouant for my selfe.

*Bilbo.*    The best in *Siuell*: Lacke you no rich *Tuskan* Garters, 180
*Venetian* ventoyes Madam, I haue maskes most methodicall, and
facetious: assay this gloue sir?

*King.*    The Leather is too rough.

*Bilbo.*    You shall haue a fine smooth skin please your feeling better,
but all our *Spanish Dons* choose that which is most rough, for it
holds out, sweat you neuer so hard.

*King.*    The price?

*Bilbo.*    The price!
Foure Crownes, I haue excellent *Hungarian* shag bands Madam
for Ladies, cut out of the same peece that the great Turkes Tolibant 190
was made of.

*King.*    The Great Turke be damn'd.

*Bilbo.*    Doe you want any *French* Codpeece points Sir?

*King.*    Poxe on 'em, they'l not last, th'are burnt i'th dying.

*Bilbo.*    If they be blacke they are rotten indeed, sir doe you want
no rich spangled *Morisco* shoo-strings.

*King.*    I like this beard-brush, but that the haire's too stiffe.

*Bilbo.*    Flexable as you can wish, the very bristles of the same
Swine that are fatten'd in *Virginia*.

*Lady.*    What comes all to before vs?                                200

*Bilbo.*    It comes to four, fiue, sixe in all, sixe double Pistolets, and a
*Spanish* Ducket ouer.

180 you] Q(c); *om.* Q(u)

*King.* Too deare, let's goe.

*Bilbo.* Madam, worshipfull *Don*, pray sir offer, if any shop shew
you the like ware —

*Lady.* Prithee peace fellow, how d'ee like her?

*King.* Rarely. What lure canst thou cast to fetch her off.

*Lady.* Leaue that to me, giue me your purse.

*Bilbo.* Doe you heare Madam!

*King.* The fatall Ball is cast, and though it fires                    210
All *Spaine*, burne let it, hot as my desires:
Haue you dispatch'd?

*Lady.* Yes.

*Bilbo.* I assure your worship, my master will be a looser by you.

*King.* It may be so, but your Mistris will not say so.

*Lady.* Sonne I tell her of the rich imbrodered stuffe at home for
the tops of gloues, and to make mee muffes, if it please the Gentlewoman to take her man along, shee shall not onely see them, but
certaine stones, which I will haue set onely in one paire. I can tell
you, you may so deale with me, you shall gaine more then you    220
thinke of.

*Bilbo.* Mistris strike in with her.

*Tormi.* My Husband is from home, and I want skill
To trade in such Commodities, but my man
Shall wait vpon your Ladiship.

*Lady.*                    Nay, nay, come you,
Your man shall goe along to note my House
To fetch your Husband, you shall dine with vs.

*King.* Faith doe forsooth, you'l not repent your match.

*Lady.* Come come you shall.

*Tormi.* Ile wait vpon you Madam, Sirrah your cloake.        230

*Bilbo.* Make vp that ware, looke to th'shop.

*Tormi.* If your Master come in, request him to stay till your fellow
come for him.

*Lady.* Come Mistris, on Sonne, nay, nay indeed you shall not,
My Gloue, one of my gloues lost in your shop.

*Tormi.* Runne backe sirrah.

*King.* Doe, wee'll softly afore.

*Tormi.* Make haste.                                        *Exeunt.*

*Laᶻ.* A Gloue! I saw none.
*Bilbo.* Nor I, it drop'd from her somewhere else then.                    240
*Laᶻ.* I am call'd vp to Dinner *Bilbo.*
*Bilbo.* Are you, then make fast the shop doore, and play out your
set at Maw, for the Mistris of my Masters alley is trundled before,
and my bowles must rub after.
*Laᶻ.* Flye then and a great one.                              *Exit.*
*Bilbo.* She's out a'th Alley, i'th Cranck belike, run, run, run.
                                                               *Exit.*


## [ACT II, Scene ii]

*Enter Lady,* Tormiella, *and King.*

*Lady.* Low stooles, pray sit, my man shall fetch the stuffes
And after Dinner you shall haue those stones:
A cup of wine; what drinke you! Loue you bastard!
Ile giue you the best in *Spaine.*
*Tormi.*                    No wines at all.
*Lady.* Haue you beene married long?
*Tormi.*                              Not long.
*Lady.*                                        I thinke
Your wedding shooes haue not beene oft vnty'd.
*Tormi.* Some three times.
*Lady.*                     Pretty Soule; No more! indeed
You are the youngest Vine I e're saw planted,
So full of hope for bearing; me thinks 'tis pitty
A Citizen should haue so faire a Tree                          10
Grow in his Garden.
*Tormi.*             I thinke him best worthy,
To plucke the fruit, that sets it.
*Lady.*                             Oh you'd h'a shon
At Court like a full Constellation,
Your Eyes are orbes of Starres.
*Tormi.*                         Muse my man stayes.
*Lady.* Your man is come, and sent to fetch your Husband,
Trust me you shall not hence, till you haue fill'd

This banqueting roome with some sweet thing or other:
Your Husband's wonderous kind to you.
*Tormi.*                              As the Sunne
To the new married Spring, the Spring to th'Earth.
*Lady.*   Some children looke most sweetly at their birth,                    20
That after proue hard fauor'd; and so doe Husbands:
Your honey Moones soonest waine and shew sharpe hornes.
*Tormi.*   Mine shall shew none.
*Lady.*                         I doe not wish it should,
Yet be not too much kept vnder, for when you would
You shall not rise.
*Tormi.*            Vmh!
*Lady.*                       I was once as you are,
Young (and perhaps as faire) it was my Fate
Whilst Summer lasted and that beauty rear'd
Her cullors in my cheekes, to serue at Court:
The King of *Spaine* that then was, ey'd me oft:
Lik't me, and lou'd me, woo'd me, at last won me.                              30
*Tormi.*   'Twas well you were no City.
*Lady.*                        Why?
*Tormi.*                              It seemes,
You yeelded e're you needed.
*Lady.*                         Nay, you must thinke,
He ply'd me with fierce batteries and assaults:
You are coy now, but (alas) how could you fight
With a Kings frownes! your womanish appetite
Wer't ne're so dead and cold would soone take fire
At honors, (all women would be lifted higher)
Would you not stoope to take it, and thrust your hand
Deepe as a King's in Treasure, to haue Lords
Feare you, t'haue life or death fly from your words.                          40
The first night that I lay in's Princely armes,
I seem'd transform'd, me thought *Ioues* owne right hand
Had snatcht mee vp and in his starry spheare
Plac'd me (with others of his Lemmans there)
Yet was he but the shaddow, I the sunne.
In a proud zodiake, I my Course did runne.

Mine eye beames was the dyals stile; and had power
To rule his thoughts, as that Commands the hower.
Oh you shall find vpon a Princes pillow
Such golden dreames.
*Tormi.*          I find 'em.
*Lady.*                    Cry you mercy.                    50
*Tormi.*  My husband comes not, I dare not stay.
*Lady.*  You must.
*King.*          You shall.
*Lady.*                    Before you lyes your way
Beaten out by mee, if you can follow doe.
*Tormi.*  What meanes this, are there bawds Ladies too?
*King.*  Why shake you, feare not, none here dreads your life.
*Tormi.*  Shall not a lambe tremble at the butchers knife.
Let goe your hold, keepe off, what violent hands
Soeuer force mee, ne're shall touch woman more,
Ile kill ten Monarches ere Ile bee ones whore.
*King.*  Heare mee.
*Tormi.*          Avoyd thou diuell.
*Lady.*                    Thou puritan foole.          60
*Tormi.*  Oh thou base Otter hound, help, help.
*King.*                              In vaine.
*Tormi.*  The best in *Spaine* shall know this.
*Lady.*                              The best now knowes it.
*Tormi.*  Good pitch let mee not touch thee, *Spaine* has a King.
If from his royall throne Iustice bee driuen
I shall find right, at the Kings hands of Heauen.
*Lady.*  This is the King.
*Tormi.*          The King, alas poore slaue.
A Rauen stucke with Swannes feathers, scarcrow drest braue.
*King.*  Doe you not know me?
*Tormi.*                    Yes, for a whore-master.
*Lady.*  No matter for her scoulding, a womans tongue
Is like the myraculous Bell in *Aragon*,                    70
Which rings out without the helpe of man.

*47 was] Q(u); *om.* Q(c)                    *50 I find 'em.] Q *stet*
*55 dreads] Q(u); threats Q(c)

*King.* Heare me, thou striu'st with Thunder, yet this hand
That can shake Kingdomes downe, thrusts into thine,
The Scepters, if proud fool, thou let'st them fall
Thou beat'st thy selfe in peeces on a rocke
That shall for euer ruine thee and thine,
Thy Husband, and all opposites that dare
With vs to cope, it shall not serue your turne
With your dim eyes to iudge our beames, the light
Of Common fires. We can before thy sight          80
Shine in full splendor, though it suites vs now
To suffer this base cloud to maske our brow.
Be wise, and when thou mayst (for lifting vp
Thine arme) plucke Starres, refuse them not; I sweare
By heauen I will not force thee 'gainst thy blood;
When I send, come: if not, withstand thy good;
Goe, get you home now, this is all, farewell.
*Tormi.* Oh me! what way to heauen can be through hell.   *Exit.*
*King.* Why diue you so?
*Lady.*                    I hope your Maiesty,
Dare sweare I ha play'd the Pylot cunningly,          90
Fetching the wind about to make this Pinnace
Strike Sayle as you desir'd.
*King.*                    Th'art a damn'd Bawd:
A soaking, sodden, splay-foot, ill-look'd Iade;
Not all the wits of Kingdomes can enact
To saue what by such Gulphes as thou art wrack'd,
Thou horie wickednesse, Diuels dam, do'st thou thinke
Thy poysonous rotten breath shall blast our fame,
Or those furr'd gummes of thine gnaw a Kings name!
If thou wouldst downe before thy time, to thy crew,
Prate of this — yes, doe; for gold, any slaue          100
May gorge himselfe on sweetes, Kings cannot haue.
By helpe of such a hag as thou, I would not
Dishonour her for an Empire, from my sight.

74 fool,] fall, Q
*93 ill-look'd Iade‸] Q(u); ill-fac'd Bawd; Q(c)
97 poysonous] poysons Q

*Lady.*    Well sir.
*King.*            Giue o're your Trade.
*Lady.*                    Ile change my Coppy.
*King.*    See you doe.
*Lady.*            I will turne ouer a new leafe.
*King.*    We search for Serpents, but being found destroy them,
Men drinke not poysons, though they oft imploy them.    *Exit.*
*Lady.*    Giue o're! how liue then! no, Ile keepe that still.
If Courtiers will not, I'me sure Citizens will.
                                        *Exit.*


## [ACT II, Scene iii]

*Enter* Tormiella, *and* Gazetto [*disguised*].

*Gaʒ.*    Speake with you.
*Tormi.*            Ha! good fellow keepe thy way.
*Gaʒ.*    Y'are a whore.
*Tormi.*            Th'art a base Knaue, not the streets free!
                                        *Exit.*
*Gaʒ.*    Though dead, from vengeance earth thee shall not saue,
*Hyæna* like, Ile eate into thy Graue.
                                        *Exit.*


## [ACT II, Scene iv]

*Enter* Cordolente, *and* Malevento.

*Cordo.*    I dare now bestow on you a free,
And hearty welcome to my poore house.
*Male.*                        Thankes Sonne:
Good Ayre, very good Ayre, and Sonne I thinke,
You stand well too for trading.
*Cordo.*                Very well sir.
*Male.*    I am glad on't.

*Enter* Lazarillo.

*Cordo.*   Sirrah where's your Mistris?

*Male.*                              I, I, good youth call her,
She playes the Tortoyes now, you shall 'twixt her and me,
See a rare Combat; tell her here's her Father,
No, an old swaggering Fencer, dares her at the weapon,
Which women put downe men at, Scoulding! (boy)                10
I will so chide her, Sonne.

*Cordo.*                        Pray doe Sir, goe call her?

*Laʒ.*   She's forth Sir with my fellow, a Lady tooke her along.

*Male.*   Taken vp already, it's well, yet I commend her,
She flyes with birds that are of better wing
Then those she spreads her selfe.

*Cordo.*                              Right Sir.

*Male.*                                          Nay she's wise,
A subtill Ape, but louing as the Moone,
Is to the Sea.

*Cordo.*      I hope she'l proue more constant.

*Male.*   Then is the needle to the Adamant,
The God of gold powre downe on both your heads
His comfortable showers.

*Cordo.*                        Thankes to your wishes.                20

*Male.*   May neuer gall be fill'd into your Cup,
Nor wormewood strew your Pillow; so liue, so loue,
That none may say, a Rauen does kisse a Doue,
I am sorry that I curst you, but the string
Sounds as 'tis play'd on, as 'tis set we sing.

*Enter* Bilbo.

*Cordo.*   Where's thy Mistresse?

*Male.*   Oh — pray Sonne, vse *Bilbo Caueare* well.
Where's thy Mistresse?

*Bilbo.*   She's departed Sir.

*Cordo.*   Departed! whether prithee!                          30

*Bilbo.*   It may be to a Lord, for a Lady had her away, I came backe

31 be] *om.* Q

292

to fetch a Gloue which dropt from the Lady, but before I could
ouertake them, they were all dropt from me; my Mistris is to me
Sir, the needle in the bottle you wot where.

*Male.*   Of hay thou mean'st, she'l not be lost I warrant.

*Enter* Tormiella, *and passes ouer the Stage.*

*Cordo.*   Here she comes now sir.—

                    *Tormiella!*—call her.

*Bilbo.*   What shall I call her?                        *Exit.*

*Male.*   Nothing by no meanes,
No let her flutter, now she's fast i'th net,
On disobedience, a gracefull shame is set.         40

*Cordo.*   A strange dead palsie, when a womans tongue
Has not the power to stirre, dumb! call her I say!

*Enter* Bilbo.

*Bilbo.*   Strange newes Sir!

*Cordo.*   What is't?

*Bilbo.*   Yonders a Coach full of good faces.

*Cordo.*   That so strange?

*Bilbo.*   Yes to alight at our Gate; They are all comming vp as
boldly, as if they were Landlords and came for Rent, see else.

*Enter Gentlemen and Gentlewomen.*

1. *Gent.*   The woman of the House sir pray?

*Cordo.*   She's in her Chamber, sirrah shew the way.     50

        *Exeunt* [Gentlewomen, *with* Bilbo *before:*]
                *manent Gentlemen and walke.*

*Male.*   Doe you know these!

*Cordo.*              Troth not I sir, I'me amaz'd
At this their strange ariuall.

*Male.*             By their starcht faces,
Small shancks, and blisterd shoo-knobs, they should be Courtiers.

*Cordo.*   Our *Spanish* Mercers say, th'are the brauest fellowes.

*Male.*   For braue men, th'are no lesse i'th Taylors bookes,
Courtiers in Citizens Houses, are Summer fires,

      50 S.D. *manent*] *manet* Q        53 blisterd] blisted Q

May well be spar'd, and being cleane out are best.
They doe the house no good, but helpe consume,
They burne the wood vp, and o're-heat the roome,
Sweetening onely th'ayre a little, that's all,                    60
Play the right Citizen then, whil'st you gaine by them,
Hug 'em, if they plucke your feathers, come not nigh them.

*Cordo.* Ile close with them.

*Male.* Doe.

*Cordo.* Welcome Gentlemen.

*Omn.* Thanks.

*Cordo.* Pray sir what Ladies may these be with my Wife?

1. *Gent.* Faith sir if they would cast themselues away vpon Knights,
they may be Knights Ladies, but they are onely Gentlewomen of
an exceeding sweet carriage and fashion, and 'tis so Sir, that your  70
wiues doings being bruited and spread abroad to be rare for her
handling the *Spanish* needle, these beauties are come onely to haue
your wife pricke out a thing, which must be done out of hand,
that's the whole businesse Sir.

*Cordo.* In good time Sir.

*Male.* Of Court I pray Sir are you?

2. *Gent.* Yes Sir, we follow the Court now and then, as others
follow vs.

*Cordo.* He meanes those they owe money too.

*Male.* Pray Sir what newes at Court?                              80

1. *Gent.* Faith Sir the old stale newes, blacke Iackes are fill'd, and
standing Cups emptyed.

*Male.* I see then Iackes are sawcie in euery corner, I haue giuen it
him vnder the list of the eare.

*Cordo.* 'Twas soundly, you see he's strucke dead.

*Male.* Dauncing Baboone!

*Enter* Tormiella, *mask'd, and in other Garments, the Gentlewomen
with her, and Gentlemen leading her away.*

*Tormi.* Farewell.

*Omn.* To Coach, away.

1. *Gent.* The *Welch* Embassador has a Message to you sir.

294

**2. *Gent.*** Hee will bee with you shortly, when the Moones Hornes 90
are i'th full.　　　　　　　　　　　　　　　　　*Exeunt.*

*Male.* What's that they talke!

*Cordo.* Nothing but this, they haue giuen it me soundly, I feele it
vnder the lists of both eares, where's my wife!

*Enter* Bilbo.

*Bilbo.* She's falne sicke sir.

*Cordo.* The Night-mare rides her.

*Male.* Ha! sicke! how sicke!

*Bilbo.* Of the falling sicknesse; you and my Master haue vs'd her
to runne away, that she has shew'd you another light paire of
heeles, she's gon Sir.　　　　　　　　　　　　　　　　100

*Cordo.* Thou lyest.

*Bilbo.* It may be she lyes by this time, but I stand to my words,
I say agen She's gon sir; cast your Cap at her, but she's gon, hurried
into a Coach drawne with foure Horses.

*Cordo.* These her oathes, vowes, protestations, damnations; a
Serpent kist the first woman, and euer since the whole sexe haue
giuen sucke to Adders.

*Male.* Run into th'Street, and if thou seest the priuiledg'd Bawdy
house she went into —

*Bilbo.* That runs on foure wheeles, the Caroach sir.　　　11c

*Cordo.* Cry to the whole City to stop her.

*Bilbo.* I will sir, 'tis euery mans case i'th City, to haue his wife
stop'd. —　　　　　　　　　　　　　　　　　　*Exit.*

*Male.* Well; what wilt thou say, if this be a plot,
Of merriment betwixt thy wife and them,
For them to come thus, and disguise her thus,
Thus whorry her away to some by-Towne,
But foure or fiue miles distance from the City,
Then must we hunt on Horsebacke, find our game,
See and not know her in this strange disguise,　　　120
But the jest smelt out, showts, and plaudities
Must ring about the Table where she sits,
Then you kissing her, I must applaud their wits.

*Cordo.* Well, I will once be gull'd in this your Comedy,

A while Ile play the Wittall, I will winck Sir,
One Bird you see is flowne out of the nest—
*Male.*  What Bird!
*Cordo.*          A wagtaile: after, flye all the rest.
*Male.*  Come then.

Exeunt.

*Finis Actus secundi.*

## ACTVS, III [Scena i]

*Enter* Iohn, *a Doctor, and* Pacheco.

*Iohn.*  Pacheco.
*Pach.*  My Lord.
*Iohn.*  It shall be so, to the King presently,
See my Caroach be ready, furnish me
To goe to Court sir.
*Pach.*  Well Sir.                                    *Exit.*
*Doct.*  Why my Lord?
*Iohn.*  What sayst thou?
*Doct.*              You will ouerthrow the state
Of that deare health which so much cost and time
Haue beene a building vp, your pores lying open          10
Colds, Agues, and all enemies to pure bloods
Wil enter and destroy life.

*Enter* Pacheco, *with Cloake and Rapier.*

*Iohn.*                I will to Court.
*Doct.*  Pray my Lord stirre not forth.
*Iohn.*                        Lay downe, begon.
                                        *Exit* Pacheco.

*Doct.*  The Ayre will pierce you.
*Iohn.*                    I ha tooke cold already.
*Doct.*  When sir?
*Iohn.*            When you councell'd me to ride my horse.

3 presently,] ~ ∧ Q

*Doct.*     Nay that was well, how slept you the next night?

*Iohn.*     Not a winck.

*Doct.*                    All the better.

*Iohn.*                                   But i'th next morning,
I could not in a Russian stoue sweat more
Then I did in my Bed.

*Doct.*                    Marry I'me glad on't.

*Iohn.*     And had no clothes vpon me.

*Doct.*                                   Still the better.                    20

*Iohn.*     My bones Sir pay'd for all this, and yet you cry, still the
better: when you ha' purg'd your pockets full of gold out of a
Patient, and then nayl'd him in's Coffin, you cry then still the better
too, a man were better to lye vnder the hands of a Hangman, than
one of your rubarbatiue faces; sirrha Doctor, I doe not thinke but
I haue beene well, all this time I haue beene Sicke?

*Doct.*     Oh my good Lord.

*Iohn.*     Oh good Master Doctor, come no more of this, I haue
another Diaphragma for you to tickle, you minister poyson in
some Medicines, doe you not?                    30

*Doct.*     Yes my good Lord, in Purgatiue and Expulsiue.

*Iohn.*     So, so, breake not my head with your hard words, you can
for a need poyson a Great man?

*Doct.*     Your Lordship's merry.

*Iohn.*     Right Sir, but I must haue it done in sadnesse, 'tis your
Trade Master Doctor to send men packing: harke you, 'tis no
lesse Bug-beare then *Don Valasco*!

*Doct.*     The Admirall of *Castile*!

*Iohn.*     Him you must sincke.

*Doct.*     'Tis my certaine death to doe it.                    40

*Iohn.*     And thy certaine death to deny it, if you will not shew him
a cast of your Office, Ile be so bold, as bestow this vpon you of
mine, I am sharpe set, will you doe it?

*Doct.*     I will by these two hands.

*Iohn.*     When?

*Doct.*     When you please.

*Iohn.*     This day?

*Doct.*     This hower.

*Iohn.* And make him fast.

*Doct.* Fast. 50

*Iohn.* For speaking.

*Doct.* For speaking.

*Iohn.* Why then good Doctor rise
To honour by it, be secret and be wise.

*Enter* Pacheco.

*Pach.* The Admirall is come my Lord.

*Iohn.* A way with these, show him the way in. Doctor —

*Doct.* Oh my Lord!

*Enter* Valasco.

*Iohn.* If you faile —

*Val.* All health to your good Lordship, I wish that,
Which most I thinke you want.

*Iohn.* Thankes my good Lord, 60
Doctor dispatch, take heed your Compositions,
Hit as I told you.

*Doct.* Oh my Lord, I am beaten to these things. *Exit.*

*Iohn.* Goe then, this visitation of your Lordship,
I take most kindly.

*Val.* Two maine wheeles my Lord,
Haue hither brought mee, one the Kings Command,
To'ther my loue, with a desire to know
Why I mong'st all the trees that spread it'h Court
Should still be smote with lightening from your eye;
Yours th'onely dangerous Arrowes shootes at me: 70
You haue the Courtiers dialect right, your tongue
Walkes ten miles from your heart, when last you saw me,
Doe you remember how you threaten'd; as for you Sir —

*Iohn.* These notes are strange.

*Val.* Oh my good Lord, be my good Lord, I read
Harsh Lectures in your face, but meet no Coment
That can dissolue the riddle, vnlesse it be
Out of that noble fashion that great men

56 in. Doctor—] ~ , ~ . Q      66 one] on Q
70 th'] *om.* Q

298

Must trip some heeles vp, tho they stand as low
As Vintners when they coniure, onely to shew                              80
Their skill in wrastling, 'tis not well to strike
A man whose hands are bound, like should chuse like.
*Iohn.*   I strike you not, nor striue to giue you falls,
'Tis your owne guilt afflicts you, if to the King
The song I set of you, did to your eare
Vnmusically sound, 'twas not in hate
To you, but in desire to giue the state
True knowledge of my innocence, be sure a bird,
Chanted that tune to mee, that onely you
Incenc'd the King that I should sell him.
*Val.*                            Vmh!                                    90
*Iohn.*   Doe you thinke I lye?
*Val.*                            I doe beleeue your Lordship.
*Iohn.*   'Twas a man most neare you.
*Val.*                            A bosome villaine!
*Iohn.*   For you must think that all that bow, stand bare
And giue Court Cakebread to you, loue you not.
*Val.*   True loue at Court my Lord, is hardly got.
*Iohn.*   If I can friend you, vse me.
*Val.*                            Humble thankes.
*Iohn.*   Oh my good Lord, times siluer foretop stands
An end before you, but you put it by.
Catch it, 'tis yours, scap'd neuer yours, your shoulders
Beare the Weale-publique vp, but they should beare,                       100
Like Pillars to be strong themselues: would I
Want fish at Sea, or golden showers at Court
I'de goe awry sometimes, wer't but for sport.
*Val.*   Say you so!
*Iohn.*   Sell Iustice and she'l buy you Lordships, cloath her
(As Citizens doe their wiues) beyond their worth,
She'll make you sell your Lordships and your plate,
No wise man will for nothing serue a state,
Remember this, your Daughter is the Queene,

95 at Court my Lord,] Q(u); my Lord at Court, Q(c¹)
98 An] Q(u, c¹); On Q(c²)               105 buy] by Q

Braue phrase to say my Sonne in Law the King,                    110
Whil'st sweet showers fall, and Sunne-shine, make your Spring.
*Val.*   You looke not out I see, nor heare the stormes
Which late haue shooke the Court.
*Iohn.*                          Not I! what stormes!
*Val.*   You in your Cabbin know nothing, there's a Pinnace
(Was mann'd out first by th'City,) is come to th'Court,
New rigg'd, a very painted Gally foist,
And yet our *Spanish* Caruils, the Armada
Of our great vessels dare not stirre for her.
*Iohn.*   What Pinnace meane you?
*Val.*                          From his lawfull pillow,
The King has tane a Citizens wife.
*Iohn.*                          For what?                    120
*Val.*   What should men doe with Citizens wiues at Court,
All will be naught, poore Queene 'tis she smarts for't.
*Iohn.*   Now 'tis your time to strike.
*Val.*                          He does her wrong,
And I shall tell him soundly.
*Iohn.*                    Tell him!
*Val.*                          Ile pay it home.
*Iohn.*   Were you some Father in Law now —
*Val.*                          What lyes heere,
Lyes here, and none shall know it.
*Iohn.*                          How easie were it,
For you to set this warping Kingdome straight?
*Val.*   The peoples hearts are full —
*Iohn.*                          And weed the State.
*Val.*   Too full of weeds already.
*Iohn.*                          And to take all,
Into your owne hands.
*Val.*                    I could soone doo't.
*Iohn.*                          Then doo't.                    130
*Val.*   Doe what! misprize me not, pray good my Lord,
Nor let these foolish words we shoot i'th Ayre,

112 out] Q(c²); on Q(u, c¹)

Fall on our heads and wound vs: to take all
Into mine owne hands, this I meane.
*Iohn.*                                    Come on.
*Val.*    Boldly and honestly to chide the King.
*Iohn.*    Vmh.
*Val.*    Take his minx vp short.
*Iohn.*    Take her vp!
*Val.*    Roundly, to rate, her Wittall husband: to stirre vp —
*Iohn.*    The people, since mens wiues are common Cases.        140
*Val.*    You heare not me say so.
*Iohn.*    To force this Tyrant to mend or end.
*Val.*    Good day to your Lordship.
*Iohn.*    Shoot off the Peece you haue charg'd.
*Val.*    No, it recoyles.
*Iohn.*    You and I shall fall to cutting throates.
*Val.*    Why!
*Iohn.*    If euer you speake of this.
*Val.*    If we cut one anothers throates, I shall neuer
Speake of this: fare your Lordship well.                        150
*Alphonso de Granada.*

                    *Enter* Alphonso.

*Alph.*    Good health to both your Lordships.
*Iohn.*    Thankes good *Alphonso*, nay pray stay.
*Val.*    Where hast thou beene *Alphonso*!
*Alph.*    In the Marquesse of *Villa Noua del Rios* Garden,
Where I gathered these Grapes.
*Val.*    And th'are the fairest Grapes I euer toucht.
*Iohn.*    Troth so they are; plump *Bacchus* cheekes were neuer
So round and red, the very God of Wine,
Swels in this bunch, *Lyæus* set this Vine.                     160
*Val.*    I haue not seene a louelier.
*Alph.*    'Tis your Lordships, if you vouchsafe to take it.
*Val.*    Oh I shall rob you, of too much sweetnesse.
*Alph.*    No my Lord.
*Val.*    I thanke you.

            149 anothers] another Q

*Alph.*   Make bold to see your honour —
*Iohn.*   Good *Alphonso.*
*Alph.*   And (loath to be too troublesome) take my leaue.
*Iohn.*   My duty to the King.
*Val.*    Farewell good *Alphonso.*          *Exit* [Alphonso]. 170
*Iohn.*   How doe you like your Grapes?
*Val.*                        Most delicate, taste 'em:
  Is it not strange, that on a branch so faire,
  Should grow so foule a fruit, as Drunkards are!
*Iohn.*   These are the bullets that make Cities reele,
  More then the Cannon can.
*Val.*                       This Iuice infus'd
  In man, makes him a beast, good things abus'd,
  Conuert to poyson thus; how now!
*Iohn.*                        I'me dizzie:
  Oh! does not all the house run round on wheeles!
  Doe not the Posts goe round! my Lord this fellow,
  Loues you I hope?
*Val.*             Ile pawne my life he does.          180
*Iohn.*   Would all we both are worth, were laid to pawne
  To a Broaker that's vndamn'd, for halfe a dram,
  For halfe a scruple, — oh we are poyson'd.
*Val.*                             Ha!
*Iohn.*   What doe you feele?
*Val.*                       A giddynesse too me thinkes.
*Iohn.*   Without there, call the Doctor (slaue).

                    *Enter* Pacheco.

*Pach.*   He's here Sir.

                    *Enter Doctor.*

*Iohn.*   Oh Doctor now or neuer — giue him his last,
  We are poyson'd both.          *Exit Doctor.*
*Val.*                    I thinke our banes are ask'd.
*Iohn.*   Hee'l bring that shall forbid it, call him (villaine).
*Pach.*   Well Sir I will call him villaine.          *Exit.* 190
*Val.*    All thriues not well within me: On my soule     [*Aside.*]

  189 bring] Q(c¹); *om.* Q(u)          191 On] Q(c¹); Oh Q(u)

T'is but Conceipt, Ime hurt with feare: *Don Iohn*
Is my Close mortall enemy, and perhaps
Vnder the Cullor I am poyson'd, sends
To pay me soundly! to preuent the worst,
Preseruatiue or poyson, he drinkes first.

*Enter Doctor.*

*Iohn.*   Giue it him.
*Val.*          No, begin.
*Iohn.*               What is't?
*Doct.*                    Cordiall.
*Iohn.*   The Doctor shall begin, quickly, so heere,
Halfe this: to both our deathes if't come too late.
*Val.*   I pledge them both, death is a common fate.          200
*Iohn.*   Shift hands, is't mortall!
*Doct.*                It strikes sure.
*Iohn.*                        Let it runne.
*Val.*   'Tis downe.
*Iohn.*          Ime glad, thy life's not a span long.   [*Aside.*]
How is't!
*Val.*     Worse.
*Iohn.*          [*Aside*] Better, — I doe feare this physick
Like pardons for men hang'd is brought too late.

[*Valasco falls.*]

*Doct.*   Hee's gone.
*Iohn.*   Who's without!
*Doct.*   Some of his men attending with his Caroach.
*Iohn.*   Take helpe; bestow the body in't, convey it,
To his owne house and there sir, see you sweare,
You saw him in your presence fall dead heere.          210
*Doct.*   This I can safely sweare.
*Iohn.*                    Helpe then, away,
Thou art next, for none must liue that can betray.

*Exeunt.*

192 Ime] I'me Q(c¹); Fue Q(u)
195 soundly!] Q(c¹); some lye! Q(u)     199 this:] ~ ‸ Q
202 Ime glad] I'me glad Q(c¹); Fine clad Q(u)

## [ACT III, Scene ii]

*Florish. Enter King, Queene,* Tormiella, *Ladies,*
Iago, Martines, *and* Alphonso.

*King.* So sweetnesse, Ile now walke no longer with you.

*Queen.* Are you weary of my Company!

*King.* Neuer shall:
Prithee keepe thy Chamber a while, the Ayre bites.

*Queen.* 'Tis because the Sunne shines not so hot as't had wont.

*King.* There's some Cloud betweene then.

*Queen.* Yes, and a horrible foule one.

*King.* I see none but faire ones.

*Queen.* No! Looke yonder, it comes from the City.

*King.* Let it come, by these Roses I am angry that you let me not go.  10

*Queen.* Nay looke you, your Grace takes all from me too; I pray
Sir giue me my roses, your Highnesse is too couetous.

*King.* I must of necessitie haue one.

*Queen.* You shall, so you take it of my choosing.

*King.* I will, so you choose that which I like.

*Queen.* Which will you haue, the bud, or that which is blown?

*King.* The bud sure, I loue no blowne ware.

*Queen.* Take your bud then.    *Offers to goe, and throwes it down.*

*King.* Doe you heare? are you angry?

*Queen.* No, you are jealous, you are so loath to haue me out of  20
your sight, you need not, for I keepe the fashion of the Kings of
*China,* who neuer walke abroad, but besides their Attendants, haue
fiue or sixe as richly attired as themselues, to cut off treason.

*King.* So.

*Queen.* Here are others in the Troupe will be taken for Queenes
sooner then I.

---

*S.D. Martines,] *after* Martines, *and before* and Q(u) *reads* Farentes, *changed in*
Q(c¹) *to* Fuentes,
    11 looke you, your] Q(c¹) [look]; looke your Q(u)      *11 I] Q(u); *om.* Q(c¹)
24–32 *the last lines on sig.* F 4, *reset in* Q(c¹) *presumably after the type had pied when
unlocked for correction*
    *25 Here are] Q(u); Here be Q(c¹)      25 others] Q(c¹); other Q(u) [*cf.* III.i.149]

*King.*  You are vext I haue prefer'd a creature to you.

*Queen.*  Who dares checke the Sunne, if he make a stinking weed
grow close to a bed of Violets, vext! not I, and yet me thinkes you
might giue me leaue to chuse mine owne women, as well as you ₃₀
doe your men, I commend no man to you, for lifting joyne-stooles,
to be one of your guard.

*King.*  Your Muffe.

*Queen.*  Take it good wife.                         [*To* Tormiella.]

*King.*  You will make me angry: good wife! so, take it.

*Queen.*  Now I hope you'l take it, you need not scorne a Queenes
leauings, for a Queene has had yours.

*King.*  What!

   [Tormiella *takes vp the muffe and giues it to the Queene.*]

*Queen.*  You see; does your Maiestie frowne because I take it from
her?                                                                40
Come hither, put your hand here? so, well met,
All friends now, yet tho ty'd neuer so fast,
Being a bow knot, it slips it selfe at last.

   *Exeunt Queene,* Tormiella, *Ladies and* Martines.

*King.*  Is't so! wer't thou a Diamond worth the world,
And ne're so hard, yet thine owne Dust shall cut thee:
Goe call that Lady backe.

*Alph.*     Which?

*King.*     Tormiella,
No doe not! 'Tis a Cocke the Lyon can fright,
The Hen does't now, the Case is alter'd quite.

    *Enter Doctor.*

*Doct.*  Your gracious pardon to call backe a life
That's halfe lost with despaire.

*King.*    What hast thou done?        50

*Doct.*  Poyson'd a man.

*King.*   Whom hast thou poyson'd?

*Doct.*    The Queenes Father.

30–31 you doe] Q (c¹); *om.* Q (u)
48 does't] *i.e.* does it; Q *reads* do'st
*51 Father] Q (u); Father in law Q (c)

*King.* Would it had beene the Daughter: thou shalt feele,
A double death, one heere, and one in Hell.
*Doct.* I must haue company with me then: *Don Iohn*
Your Highnesse Brother, set against my throat —
*King.* Back.
*Doct.* His arm'd sword; I had dy'd, had I not done't.
*King.* Our Guard;
Goe fetch *Don Iohn* our brother to the Court.
*Doct.* A word in your Highnesse eare —                    60
*King.* Search him.
*Omn.*                    He has nothing.
*Doct.*                                   I in stead of poyson,
Gaue him a sleepy Potion, he's preseru'd;
*Don Iohn* thinkes not: the noble Admirall
Feares plots against his life, forbeares the Court
But sends me to your Grace, to bid you set
Your footing stiffe and strongly, for *Don Iohn*
Trips at your life and Kingdome, to his throat
*Valasco* this will iustifie.
*King.*                    He shall:
Goe you and fetch him secretly to Court.
*Alphonso* take the Doctor and returne.                    70
Death! when!                    *Exeunt* [Alphonso *and Doctor*].
*Iago* with your smoothest face go greet
*Don Iohn* from vs, say we haue worke of State,
Both presently and closely bid him come.
*Iago.* I shall.                                   *Exit.*

            *Enter* Gazetto [*disguised as* Lupo].

*King.* How now what's he, giue vs leaue, come hither:
We haue perus'd your paper Sir, and thinke
Your promises Spring-tides, but we feare you'll ebbe
In your performance.
*Gaz.*                    My deeds and speeches Sir,
Are lines drawne from one Center, what I promise                    80
To doe, Ile doe, or loose this.

            59 to the Court] (Q(u); to Court Q(c)

                              306

*King.*                    You giue me physicke
After I'm dead, the *Portugals* and we
Haue hung our drummes vp, and you offer heere
Models of Fortification, as if a man
Should when Warre's done, set vp an Armorors shop.
*Gaʒ.*  I bid you set vp none Sir, you may chuse.
*King.*  This fellow Ile fitly cast i'th Villaines mold,
I find him crafty, enuious, poore, and bold:
Into a Saw Ile turne thee, to cut downe
All Trees which stand in my way; what's thy name?          90
*Gaʒ.*  You may reade in my paper.
*King.*  *Lupo Vindicado's*; Vmh! nay we shall imploy you,
Merrit went neuer from vs with a forehead,
Wrinckled or sullen, what place would you serue in?
*Gaʒ.*  Any, but one of your turne broaches; I would not be one of
your blacke Guard, there's too much fire in me already.
*King.*  You say, you haue the Languages.
*Gaʒ.*  Yes.
*King.*  What thinke you of an Intelligencer, we'll send you —
*Gaʒ.*  To th'Gallowes, I loue not to be hang'd in State.          100
*King.*  You hauing trauel'd as you said so farre,
And knowing so much, I muse thou art so poore.
*Gaʒ.*  Had the confusion of all tongues began,
In building me, could I sing sweet in all,
I might goe beg and hang, I ha' seene *Turkes*
And *Iewes*, and *Christians*, but of all, the *Christians*
Haue driest hands, they'l see a Brother starue,
But giue Duckes to a water-Spaniell.
*King.*                    Well obseru'd.
Come sir, faith let's crow together, in what stamp
Dost thou coyne all thy Languages.
*Gaʒ.*                    I doe speake *English*          110
When I'de moue pittie, when dissemble, *Irish*,
*Dutch* when I reele, and tho I feed on scalions,
If I should brag Gentility, I'de gabble *Welch*,
If I betray, I'me *French*, if full of braues,
They swell in loftie *Spanish*, in neat *Italian*

I Court my Wench, my messe is all seru'd vp.
*King.*   Of what Religion art thou?
*Gaʒ.*                              Of yours.
*King.*   When you were in *France?*
*Gaʒ.*                        *French.*
*King.*                              Without there.

                    *Enter* Alphonso.

*Alph.*                              Sir?
*King.*   Giue this Gentleman fiue hundred Pistolets.
Be neere vs.
*Gaʒ.*      In thy bosome, for thy Pistolets            [*Aside.*] 120
Ile giue thee Pistols, in a peece might ha beene mine
Thou shoot'st or mean'st to shoot, but Ile charge thine.
Thy heart off goes it in thunder.
*King.*                    Through the Gallerie,
Vnseene conuay him hither, giue vs leaue sir.
*Gaʒ.*   Leaue haue you —      *Exeunt* [Gazetto *and* Alphonso].

        *Enter Doctor,* Valasco, *and* Alphonso [*after them*].

*Val.*   I'm glad to see your Maiesty.
*King.*                        You haue reason.
*Val.*   I was going to cry all hid.
*King.*                    Come hither
Dead man, you'l iustifie this treason?
*Val.*                        To his teeth,
Throate, mouth to mouth, bodie to bodie.
*King.*                        So.
                    *Enter* Iago.

*Iago.*   Don *Iohn* of *Castile*'s come.
*King.*                    A Chaire, stand you          130
Full here and stirre not, front him, bring him in:
How, now, did a Hare crosse your way?

                    128 man,] ~ ‸ Q

*Enter* Don Iohn.

*Iohn.*                                    The Diuell!     [*Aside.*]
Doctor Ile giue you a purge for this, Ile make
Your Highnesse laugh.
*King.*                    You must tickle me soundly then.
*Iohn.*   In this retreat of mine from Court, my bodie
(Which was before a cleane streame) growing foule
By my minds trouble, through your high displeasure
Which went to th'bottome of my heart; I call'd
That sound Card to me, gaue him fees and bid him
(By all the fairest props that Art could reare)                     140
To keepe my health from falling, which I felt
Tottering and shaken, but my Vrinalist
(As if he sate in Barber-Surgions Hall
Reading Anatomy Lectures) left no Artery
Vnstretcht vpon the Tenters.
*King.*                    So he vext you to the guts.
*Iohn.*   My bowels were his coniuring roomes, to quit him
I tempted him to poyson a great man.
I knowing this my honourable friend —
*Val.*   Keepe backe, hee'l poyson my gloue else.
*Iohn.*   Comming to visit me,                                     150
This was the man must die.
*King.*                    Why did you this?
*Iohn.*   Onely to hatch a jest on my pill'd Doddy,
I knew he durst not doo't.
*King.*                    But say he had?
*Val.*   Then he had beene hang'd.
*Iohn.*                    That had made me more glad.
*Doct.*   I am bound to your Lordship.
*Iohn.*   Being a Doctor you may loose your selfe.
*King.*   Mens liues then are your Balls, disarme him.
*Iohn.*                                             How!
Not all thy Kingdome can.                     *Drawes.*

*148 this_∧] stet Q

309

*King.*                         Hew him in peeces,
Our Guard, s'death kill him.
*Iohn.*                         Are you in earnest?
*King.*                                        Looke.
*Iohn.*    See then, I put my selfe into your Den:          160
What does the Lyon now with me?
*King.*                         Th'art a traytor.
*Iohn.*    I am none.
*King.*              No!
*Val.*              Yes, an arrant traytor.
*Iohn.*                                        You sir;
Spit all thy poyson forth.
*Val.*                         No, I dranke none sir.
*King.*    Come to your proofes, and see you put 'em home.
*Val.*    You and I one day, being in conference,
You nam'd this noble King (my Soveraigne)
A tyrant, bid me strike, 'twas now my time,
Spake of a Peece charg'd, and of shooting off,
Of stirring vp the Rascals to rebell,
And to be short, to kill thee.
*Iohn.*                         I speake this!          170
*Val.*    Yes Traytor, thou.
*Iohn.*              Where!
*Val.*                         In your Chamber.
*Iohn.*                                        Chamber!
Was it not when you told me, that the King
Had got a strumpet.
*King.*              Ha.
*Val.*              How!
*Iohn.*                         A Citizens wife;
'Twas when you swore to pay him soundly.
*Val.*                                        See, see!
*Iohn.*    The peoples hearts were full.
*Val.*                                        Poxe, a'my heart then.
*Iohn.*    Or was't not when you threaten'd to take all,
Into your owne hands?
*Val.*                         There's my gloue, thou lyest.

*King.*   Good stuffe, I shall find traitors of you both,
If you are, be so; with my finger, thus
I fanne away the dust flying in mine eyes                    180
Rais'd by a little wind; I laugh at these now,
'Tis smoake, and yet because you shall not thinke
We'll dance in Earth quakes, or throw squibs at Thunder,
I charge both keepe your Chambers for a day
Or so. —
*Val.*        Your will.                           *Exit.*
*Iohn.*             Chambers!
*King.*                      We bid it.
*Iohn.*                          You may.        *Exit.*

           *Enter Queene, and Ladies.*

*Omn.*   The Queene.
*Queen.*   I thanke your highnesse for the bird you gaue me.
*King.*   What bird?
*Queen.*          Your Tassell gentle, shee's lur'd off
And gone.
*King.*      How, gon! what's gone!
*Queen.*                      Your woman's fled,
Whom you prefer'd to me, she's stolne from Court.          190
*King.*   You iest.
*Queen.*      Bee it so. —                    *Goes away.*
*King.*                 I haue hotter newes for you,
Your Fathers head lies here, art thou still shooting
Thy stings into my sides! Now doe you looke
I should turne wild, and send through all the winds
Horsemen in quest of her, because you weare
A kind of yellow stocking; let her flie:
If *Ioue* forsooth would fixe a starre in Heauen,
*Iuno* runnes mad; thou better mightst haue spurn'd
The gates of hell ope, then to looke into
Our bosome.
*Queen.*      Where your Trull lyes.
*King.*                  Y'are a Toad.            200
*Queen.*   Womans reuenge awake thee, thou hast stirr'd

                       311

A blood as hot and high as is thine owne.
Raise no more stormes; your treasure is not gon,
I fear'd the Sea was dangerous, and did sound it,
Mischiefe but halfe vp, is with ease confounded.     *Exit.*

*King.*   In thine owne ruine,—me canst thou hit
But with one finger which can doe no harme,
But when a King strikes, 'tis with his whole arme.

    *Exit.*


### [ACT III, SCENE iii]

*Enter Queene and* Tormiella.

*Queen.*   Make fast the Closet — so — giue me the key,
I meane to kill thee.

*Tormi.*          Kill me, for what cause?

*Queen.*   Guesse.

*Tormi.*       I know none, vnlesse the Lambe should aske
The Butcher why he comes to cut his throat.

*Queen.*   I could through loope holes hit thee, or hire slaues
And send death to thee twenty secret wayes.

*Tormi.*   Why would you doe all this?

*Queen.*          Or (as the Hart
Drawes Serpents from their Den) with subtill breath
I could allure thee to sit downe, and banquet
With me as with the King thou hast.

*Tormi.*         Oh neuer —       10

*Queen.*   Yet poyson you most sweetly.

*Tormi.*          Now you doe it.

*Queen.*   And I could make thee a Queenes bedfellow
As thou hast beene a Kings.

*Tormi.*       Neuer by —

*Queen.*          Sweare,
Yet stifle you in a pillow, but I scorne
To strike thee blindfold, onely thou shalt know
An Eagles nest, disdaines to hatch a Crow:
Why are all mouthes in *Spaine* fill'd to the brim,

Flowing o're with Court newes onely of you and him,
The King I meane, where lies the Court?
*Tormi.*                                        Sure here.
*Queen.*   It remou'd last, to th'shop of a *Millaner*,                    20
The gests are so set downe, because you ride
Like vs, and steale our fashions and our tyers,
You'l haue our Courtiers to turne shopkeepers,
And fall to trading with you, ha!
*Tormi.*                              Alas
The Court to me is an inchanted tower
Wherein I'me lockt by force, and bound by spels,
A Heauen to some, to me ten thousand Hels.
I drinke but poyson in gold, sticke on the top
Of a high Pinnacle like an idle vaine
(As the wind turnes) by euery breath being tost;                          30
And once blowne downe, not miss'd, but for euer lost.
*Queen.*   Out Crocadile, —                        *Spurne her.*
*Tormi.*                      You will not murther me!
*Queen.*   Ile cure you of the Kings euill. —      *Draw two kniues.*
*Tormi.*                        To one woman
Another should be pittifull, heare me speake?
*Queen.*   How dares so base a flower follow my Sunne
At's rising to his setting.
*Tormi.*              I follow none.
*Queen.*              How dar'st thou Serpent wind about a tree,
That's mine.
*Tormi.*       I doe not.
*Queen.*                Or to shake the leaues.
*Tormi.*   By Heauen not any.
*Queen.*                  Or once to taste the fruit
Tho throwne into thy lap; if from a Harlot                                 40
Prayers euer came, pray, for thou dy'st.
*Tormi.*                        Then kill me.
*Queen.*   How did my Husband win thee?
*Tormi.*                          By meere force;
A Bawd betray'd me to him.

27 A] To Q

313

*Queen.* Worse and worse.

*Tormi.* If euer I haue wrong'd your royall bed
In act, in thought, nayle me for euer fast,
To scape this Tyger of the Kings fierce lust
I will doe any thing, I will speake treason
Or Drinke a Cup of poyson, which may blast
My inticing face, and make it leprous foule:
Ruine you all this, so you keepe vp my Soule;                    50
That's all the wealth I care for.

*Queen.*                                         I haue now
No hart left to kill thee, rise, thou and I
Will like two quarrelling Gallants faster tye
A knot of Loue, we both i'th Field being wounded.
Since we must needs be sharers, vse me kindly
And play not the right Citizen, to vndoe
Your partner, who 'ith stocke has more than you.

*A noyse within. Enter the King.*

*King.* Must you be closetted?
*Queen.*                                         Yes.
*King.*                                         What are you doing?
*Queen.* Not getting Children.
*King.*                                         Naked kniues; for what,
Speake, s'death speake you.
*Tormi.*                                         They both fell from her side.          60
*King.* You lie, away.                                 [*To the Queen.*]
*Queen.*                                         Must you be closetted?
*King.*                                         Yes.
*Queen.* When hart break'st thou, thou dost too much swell,
This Aspish biting, is incurable.                                 *Exit.*
*King.* Be true to me I charge you, did the Queene
Offer no violence to you.
*Tormi.*                                         None at all.
*King.* Why were these drawne?
*Tormi.*                                         I know not.
*King.*                                         Know not; what's heere,

314

Why is this rose dim'd with a pearled teare,
When the sunne shines so warme, you know not that too.
The lambe has tam'd the *Lyon*, the vulture tyers
Vpon the Eagles hart, these subtill wyers                    70
Chaine *Ioue*, these balls, from whose flames *Cupid* drew,
His wild fire burnes heere, this you know not too.
I loue you, that you know not neither, y'are coy,
And proud, and faire, you know this?
*Tormi.*                    I beseech you
Let me shake off the golden fetters you tye
About my body, you inioy a body
Without a soule, for I am now not heere.
*King.*   Where then.
*Tormi.*                At home in my poore husbands armes,
This is your Court, that mine.
*King.*                Your husbands armes,
Thou art his whore, he plai'd the theefe and rob'd         80
Another of thee, and to spoyle the spoyler,
Is Kingly iustice, 'tis a lawfull prize
That's ta'ne from Pirates; their's are fellow wiues.
*Tormi.*   Which of your subiects (which abroad adore
Your state, your greatnesse, presence and your throne
Of sunne beames) thinke you now are with a wanton,
Or working a chast wife to become one.
*King.*   I worke thee not to be so, for when time
Shall iog his glasse and make those sands lye low
Which now are at the top, thy selfe shalt grow              90
In selfe same place my Queene does.
*Tormi.*                What tree euer stood
Long and deepe rooted, that was set in blood;
I will not be your whore to weare your Crowne,
Nor call any King my Husband, but mine owne.
*King.*   No!
*Tormi.*    No, 'twere shame 'mongst all our City Dames
If one could not scape free, their blasted fames.

67 dim'd] deni'd Q          69 tam'd] am'd Q
83 their's] there's Q

*King.* The sound of Bels and Timbrels make you mad
As it does a Tyger, the softer that I stroke you
The worse you bite, your father and your Husband
Are at my sending come to Court, Ile lay                        100
Honours on both their backs, here they shall stay
Because Ile keepe you here, if you doe frowne,
The engine which reares vp, shall plucke all downe.
Ile fetch 'em to you my selfe.                            *Exit.*
*Tormi.* Oh who can stifling scape in baser throngs,
When Princes Courts threaten the selfe-same wrongs.
                                                         *Exit.*

*Finis Actus tertij.*


ACTVS, IV [SCENA i].

*Flourish. Enter King,* Maleuento, Cordolente, Iago, Alphonso,
Gazetto [*disguised as* Lupo], *and* Tormiella.

*King.* Y'aue the best welcome which the Court can yeeld,
For the King giues it you.
*Male.*                        Your Grace is gracious.
*King.* Is this your Father?                    [*To* Tormiella.]
*Male.*                        My proper flesh and bloud Sir.
*King.* And that your Husband?
*Cordo.* Not I sir; I married an honest wench that went in a cap,
no whim whams; I did but shuffle the first dealing, you cut last,
and dealt last, by the same token you turn'd vp a Court Card.
*King.* Is the man iealous!
*Cordo.* No, but a little troubled with the yellow Iaundize, and you
know if it get to the Crowne of the head, a man's gon.          10
*King.* We send not for you hither to be brau'd,
Sirrah cast your darts elsewhere.
*Cordo.* Amongst the wild *Irish* Sir hereafter.
*King.* 'Tis our Queenes pleasure that your wife be call'd
Her woman, and because she will not loose her,

She hath importun'd vs to raise you both;
Your name sir?

*Male.*                Mine, *Andrada Maleuento.*

*King.* *Andrada Maleuento* we make you
Vice-Admirall of our Nauy.

*Cordo.* Oh spitefull Comedy, he's not a Courtier of halfe an houres 20
standing, and he's made a Vice already.

*King.* We make thy Husband —

*Cordo.* A Cuckold doe you not.

*Male.* Sonne you forget your selfe.

*Cordo.* Meddle with your owne office; there's one will looke that
none meddles with mine.

*Male.* Is not a change good?

*Cordo.* Yes, of a louzie shirt.

*King.* Take hence that fellow, he's mad.

*Cordo.* I am indeed horne-mad, oh me, in the holyest place of the 30
Kingdome haue I caught my vndoing, the Church gaue mee my
banes.

*Tormi.* What the Church gaue thee, thou hast still.

*Cordo.* Halfe parts, I thought one had tane thee vp.

*Tormi.* Take me home with thee, Ile not stay here.

*King.* Ha!

*Tormi.* Let me not come to Court.

*Male.* The King is vext, let me perswade thee Sonne
To wincke at small faults.

*Cordo.* What sir *Pandarus.*

*Tormi.* Sends the King you to blush in's roome.                    40

*Male.* Y'are a baggage.

*King.* Goe tell the lunatique so; *Andrada* harke —

*Iago.* The King sir bids me sing into your eare,
Sweet notes of place and office which shall fall —

*Cordo.* Into my mouth, I gape for 'em.

*Iago.* He bids me aske what will content you.

*Cordo.* Nothing, nothing, why Sir the powers aboue cannot please
vs, and can Kings thinke you? when we are brought forth to the

*32 banes] Q(u); bane Q(c)

world, we cry and bawle as if we were vnwilling to bee borne; and 50
when we are a dying we are mad at that.

*King.*   Take hence that Wolfe that barkes thus.

*Cordo.*   I am muzzel'd, but one word with your Maiestie, I am
sober sir.

*King.*   So sir.

*Cordo.*   You oft call Parliaments, and there enact
Lawes good and wholesome, such as who so breake
Are hung by th'purse or necke.   But as the weake
And smaller flyes i'th Spiders web are tane
When great ones teare the web, and free remaine,                 60
So may that morall tale of you be told,
Which once the Wolfe related: in the Fold
The Shepheards kill'd a sheepe and eate him there;
The Wolfe lookt in, and seeing them at such cheere,
Alas (quoth he) should I touch the least part
Of what you teare, you would plucke out my hart.
Great men make Lawes, that whosoe're drawes blood
Shall dye, but if they murder flockes 'tis good:
Ile goe eate my Lambe at home sir.

*King.*   Part, and thus reckon neuer to see her more.                 70

*Cordo.*   Neuer!

*Tormi.*          Neuer thus, but thus a Princes whore.

*Exeunt.* [*Manent* Cordolente *and* Gazetto.]

*Cordo.*   Thou dar'st not, if thou do'st, my heart is great,
Thus wrong'd, thou canst doe little if not threat.

*Gaȝ.*   Ha, ha, ha, ha.

*Cordo.*   At what dost laugh?

*Gaȝ.*   At a thing of nothing, at thee; why shouldst thou be afraid
to fall into the Cuckolds disease.

*Cordo.*   Because it makes a Doctor an Asse, nothing can cure it, are
you answer'd Sir?

*Gaȝ.*   Come th'art a foole, to grieue that thy wife is taken away by 80
the King to his priuate bed-chamber,
Now like a booke call'd in, shee'l sell better then euer she did.

*Cordo.*   Right sir, but could he chuse no stocke to graft vpon, but
that which was planted in my nurserie.

*Gaz.*   Ile shew thee a reason for that.

*Cordo.*   Why?

*Gaz.*   Leachers comming to women, are like Mice amongst many
Cheeses, they taste euery one, but feed vpon the best: hornes
rightly weigh'd are nothing.

*Cordo.*   How, nothing! oh sir, the smallest Letters hurt your eyes   90
most, and the least head-ach which comes by a womans knocking
hurts more then a cut to the scull by a mans knocking.

*Gaz.*   Yet I warrant thou dar'st sweare the party's honest?

*Cordo.*   Ha; sweare; not I, no man durst euer sweare for his wife
but *Adam*, nor any woman for her husband but *Eue*, fare you well
sir.

*Gaz.*   Whether art flying?

*Cordo.*   In peices, dost not see I'me shot out of a Cannon.   *Exit.*

*Gaz.*   Downewards Ile shoote thee, but as Diuels vse
Ile tickle at thy tortures, dance at thy stumbling,                      100
Play with thee, and then paw thee, 'shalt make me merry:
The Crowne of blacke deeds that are hatcht in Hell
Is to out-liue and laugh, and all's play'd well.

                                                            *Exit.*


## [ACT IV, Scene ii]

*Enter* Bilbo, *and* Coxecombe.

*Bilbo.*   I haue not pass'd by a *Don*, to touch whose hand mine
owne was neuer more troubled with a more terrible itch.

*Cox.*   I haue not met a Signior, at whom mine owne eyes (as if
roasted enough) did euer burne more in desire to flye out: so that
whether to recoyle or aduance on, I am betweene Hawke and
Buzzard.

*Bilbo.*   The honey of sweet Complement so turne vp your Tuskes
or Mochatoes, that they be not too stiffe, to brisle against my
acquaintance.

*Cox.*   Your acquaintance is a Limbeck, out of which runneth a   10

S.D. Bilbo] *Clowne* Q          1 *Bilbo.*] *Clo.* Q

perfum'd water, bathing my nosthrils in a strong scent of your
embracings: are you of Court, Signior?

*Bilbo.* No Signior, of the City: are you a Don of the Citie!

*Cox.* No Signior, of the Court; City, I smile.

*Bilbo.* Why.

*Cox.* I assure you Signior, you are to vs of the Court but *Animals.*
You are held but as shoeing hornes to wait on great Lords heeles.

*Bilbo.* Let em pay vs what they owe then, and pull on their shoes,
and wee'll wait no more.

*Cox.* You are our Apes.                                    20

*Bilbo.* But you are fuller of Apish trickes.

*Cox.* No sooner leape our Ladies into a fashion, but your Wiues
are ready to creepe into the same.

*Bilbo.* Why not; for tho some of your Ladies invent the fashion,
some of our wiues husbands are neuer pay'd for the stuffe or
making.

*Cox.* Giue way with your poore scull to our oares: for I tell thee
Signior, you of the city are the flatten milke of the kingdome, and
wee of the Court the Creame.

*Bilbo.* I tell thee Signior! wee of the City eate none of your Court 30
butter, but some of you munch vp our flatten milk cheese.

*Cox.* Be not too loud; tho you are good ringers in the City, for
most of you haue bels at your doores.

*Bilbo.* Be not you too loud: for you might be good singers at
Court but that most of you are spoyled in learning your pricksong.

*Cox.* Bee temporate: I will shew you your City Cinquipace, you
beare, sweare, teare, reare, and weare; you beare the Tanckerd,
sweare shop oathes, teare money out of debtors throates, reare rich
estates, weare good clothes, but carry your Conscience in torne
pockets.                                                   40

*Bilbo.* Bee attentiue, I will shew you your Court Coranto pace,
it consisteth of fiue bees and three cees; you borrow of any man,
are braue on any termes, brag at any hand to pay, bellow at any
that demands it, bite any Catchpole that fangs you, but carry
neither Conscience nor coyne in your whole pockets.

*Cox.* Tell mee Signior, tell mee why in the City does a harmelesse
signe hang at the doore of a subtill *Nicodemus* sitting in a shop?

*Bilbo.* And tell me Signior, tell me, why when you eate our good cheare i'th City, haue you handsome wide chops, but meeting vs at Court, none; your gumme's glew'd vp, your lips coup'd like a 50 Ferret, not so much as the corner of a Custard; if a could cup, and a dry cheate loafe 'tis well.

*Cox.* Come, come, You are Acornes, and your Sonnes the Prodigals that eate you vp.

*Bilbo.* Goe, goe, you are Prodigals, and glad of the yellow Acornes we leaue our Sonnes.

*Cox.* I will crosse my selfe when I owe money to a Citizen, and passe by his doore.

*Bilbo.* I will blesse my selfe, when a Courtier owing me no money, comes neare my doore.                                                    60

*Cox.* You are discended from the tanckerd generation.

*Bilbo.* You are ascended vp to what you are, from the blacke Iacke and bumbard distillation.

*Cox.* Deere Signior.

*Bilbo.* Delicious *Don.*

*Exeunt.*


## [ACT IV, Scene iii]

*Enter* Don Iohn [*and* Pacheco *his boy*].

*Iohn.* Boy.

*Pach.* My Lord.

*Iohn.* Art sure thou saw'st the Admirall at Court!

*Pach.* Am I sure I see your Lordship in your gowne.

*Iohn.* And talking with the King?

*Pach.* Most familiarly.

*Iohn.* And what say the people about my committing to mine owne house?

*Pach.* The beast grinnes at it, there's a Libell already of you my Lord.                                                                     10

*Iohn.* A Libell, away.

*Pach.* Yes faith my Lord, and a Song to the tune of Lament Ladies, Lament.

*Iohn.* I'me glad the stinkards are so merry, a halter on 'em, it's musick to them to haue euery man thrown off, you haue seen the Kings Mistris, boy, haue you not, what manner of peice is't?

*Pach.* Troth my Lord I know not, I neuer saw her shot off, a pretty little pocket dag.

*Iohn.* What report giues she?

*Pach.* A very good report of her Husband, but he giues an ill 20 report of her.

*Iohn.* How does the Ladies take it; now the King keepes a Wench vnder the Queenes nose?

*Pach.* They take it passing heauily, it goes to the heart of some of them, that he keepes not them too.

*Iohn.* I heard say they were all once leauing the Court?

*Pach.* True sir, but there was a deuise which stopp'd 'em.

*Iohn.* Who are you! *Knocking within.*

*Val.* My Lord, we must speake with you.

*Iohn.* What are you? fetch me a weapon. 30

*Omn.* Your friends.

*King.* 'Sdeath breake it open.

*Enter King, Valasco, and others.*

*Iohn.* The King;
I did not vnderstand your Maiesty.

*King.* You shall, for Ile speake plaine to you, know you these?
[*Shews papers.*]

*Iohn.* Not I.

*King.* You doe not, a Kings arme thou seest
Has a long reach, as farre as *Portugall*
Can We fetch treason backe hatcht here by you.

*Iohn.* Me!

*King.* Thee and the trayterous *Portugals* to depriue me
Of life and Crowne, but I shall strike their King 40
And them, and thee beneath into the earth.

*Iohn.* And lower then earth you cannot.

*King.* Halfe your body
Is in the graue, it only lackes our hand
To cast the dust vpon you, yet you stand

On slippery Ice your selfe, and trip at vs
Whose foot is fixt on Rocks, but since th'ast throwne
Thy selfe downe, neuer looke to rise.

*Iohn.*   I care not, I will be little so
In debt to you, that I will not owe you
So much as God a mercy for my life.                                    50

*King.*   You shall not then, stand not to ayme at markes,
Now roue not but make choyse of one faire white,
Th'ast but one arrow to shoote, and that's thy flight.
The Admirall knowes our pleasure.          *Exit [with train].*

*Iohn.*                              And Heauen knowes mine.
Left in mine enemies hand, are you my Iaylor?

*Val.*   No my Lord, I thinke I'me rather left
To be your Confessor.

*Iohn.*                  I need not any,
That you and I should both meet at one Ball,
I being the stronger, yet you giue the fall.

*Val.*   A kind of foot-ball slight, my Lord, men vse          60
Exceeding much at Court, your selfe has heard
Little shrimps haue thrown men higher then the Guard;
But barring this rough play, let's now consider,
For what I stay, and what you are to doe.

*Iohn.*   Doe what?

*Val.*            To die.

*Iohn.*                  And must you play the Hangman.

*Val.*   Breake in fellowes.                      *Guard.*

*Iohn.*   'Sdeath what are these?

*Val.*   Your Executioners appointed by the King.

*Iohn.*   These my Executioners,
And you my ouer-seer, wherefore kneele they?        70

*Val.*   To beg your pardon, for they feare their worke
Will neuer please you.

*Iohn.*               What booke's that they hold,
This is no time for Dedications.

*Val.*   That booke is sent in Loue to you from the King,
It containes pictures of strange sundry deaths,
He bids you choose the easiest.

*Iohn.*                        Then I chuse this.

                                                                    *Snatches a Halbert.*

*Val.*    Your choyce is ill made.

*Iohn.*                        I'me more sorry Sir,
I had rather haue my body hackt with wounds,
Then t'haue a Hangman fillip me.

*Val.*                        My Lord pray pardon me,
I'me forct to what I doe, 'tis the Kings pleasure                          80
To haue you die in priuate.

*Iohn.*                        Any where;
Since I must downe, the King might let me fall
From lofty Pinacles, to make my way
Through an arm'd Feild, yet for all that, euen then
Vnlesse I slew a kingdome full of men
I should at last be pay'd home: blackest fate
Thy worst, I heere defie thee, what the State
Appoints 'tis welcome.

*Val.*                        That's to haue your head.

*Iohn.*    'Tis ready.

*Val.*                        Hee'l be quiet when you are dead.

                                                                    *Exeunt.*


[ACT IV, Scene iv]

*Enter* Tormiella, Malevento, *and* Alphonso.

*Alph.*    Madam there's a fellow stayes without to speake with you.

*Tormi.*    With me!

*Enter* Cordolente [*disguised*].

*Alph.*    Your shoo-maker I thinke.

*Tormi.*    Hast brought my shooes?

*Cordo.*    Yes Madam.

*Tormi.*    You drew them not on last.

*Cordo.*    No Madam, my Master that seru'd you last has very good
custome, and deales with other Ladies as well as you, but I haue
fitted you before now, I should know the length of your foote.

*Tormi.*　I doe not remember thee.　　　　　　　　　　　10

*Cordo.*　I'me sorry you haue forgotten me.

*Tormi.*　What shooe was the last you drew on?

*Cordo.*　A yellow.

*Tormi.*　A yellow! I neuer wore that cullor.

*Cordo.*　Yes Madam by that token when I fitted you first, you wore not your shoes so high i'th instep, but me thinks you now go cleane awry.

*Tormi.*　A fault I cannot helpe, manie Ladies besides me goe so, I hope 'twill grow to a fashion.

*Male.*　Has not that fellow done there?　　　　　　　　20

*Cord.*　Yes sir, I haue now done, I haue a suit to you Madam, that none may be your shoo-maker but I.

*Tormi.*　Thy Master thou sayst serues me, I should wrong him then.

*Cordo.*　Yet doe you me more wrong, oh my *Tormiella*!
Is the leafe torne out where our Loue was writ,
That I am quite forgot!

*Tormi.*　　　　　　　　Softly good sweet.

*Cordo.*　Oh miserie, I make my selfe a theefe,
To steale mine owne, another at my fire
Sits whiles I shake with cold, I fatten a stranger,　　　30
And starue my selfe.

*Tormi.*　　　　　　　Danger throwes eyes vpon thee,
Thus visit me, watch time for my escape,
To any Country by thy dearest side
Ile lackey all the world or'e, Ile not change
Thee for a thousand Kings; there's gold.

*Male.*　Not yet done?

*Cor.*　Yes sir, I'me onely taking instructions to make her a lower Chopeene, she finds fault that she's lifted too high.

*Male.*　The more foole shee.

*Enter* Iago.

*Iago.*　The King comes Madam, he enquires for you.　　40

32-33 escape, ...Country<sub>Λ</sub>] ~ <sub>Λ</sub> ... ~ , Q

*Enter King,* Valasco, Gazetto [*as* Lupo], *and others.*

*King.* My brother *Iohn* is gone then?
*Val.* I ha bestow'd him as you commanded, in's graue.
*King.* Hee's best there,
Except the Gods, Kings loue none whom they feare.
How now!
*Tormi.* My Shoo-maker.
*King.* Oh hast fitted her, so, hence sir.
*Cordo.* As a worme on my belly: what, should the Ant,
On his poore Mole-hill braue the Elephant,
No, Signior no, 50
No braines to stay, but saues a head to goe. *Exit.*
*King.* Let me haue no more of this: haue not we eyes
Pointed like Sun-beames, goe to, get you in.
*Tormi.* Angell from Heauen, falne a Kings Concubine. *Exit.*

*Enter* Martines.

*Mart.* May it please your Grace —
*King.* Ha!
*Mart.* Her Highnesse drown'd in sorrow, that your brow
Has beene so long contracted into frownes,
Wishing to die vnlesse she see it smooth'd,
Commends her best loue to you in this Iewell 60
The Image of her heart.
*King.*                     My Lord Admirall,
My wife's growne kind, see!
*Vl.*                     One of the happiest houres
Mine age e're numbred; would your Highnesse now
Would fetch vp the red blood her cheekes hath lost
By sending her, some simbole of your loue.
*King.* Pray step your selfe vnto her, say I locke
My heart vp in your bosome to her vse,
And giue it her.
*Val.*               Ile lend it in your name.
*King.* Doe.
*Val.*          She shall pay her heart for it in interest. *Exit.*

326

*King.* Ile see her anon,                                            70
Leaue vs, stay you, and set that Table here.
                    *Exeunt.* [*Manent King and* Martines.]
A chaire, none trouble vs, doe you serue the Queene?
*Mart.* Yes sir.
*King.*            We know you now, y'are in our eye.
Are the doores fast?
*Mart.*            They are Sir.
*King.*                    Nearer yet,
Doe not you know of a conspiracie,
To take away my life vpon Saint — tush,
No matter for the day, you know the plot Sir?
*Mart.* By Heauen I know of none!
*King.*                    Blushing does you staine!
*Mart.* It is not guilt but anger.
*King.*                    Y'aue all fixt
Your hands and Seales to an Indenture drawne            80
By such a day to kill me.
Mart.                For my part
My Loyaltie like a rough Diamond shines
The more 'tis cut, I haue no hand in that
Or any basenesse else against your Life
Or Kingdome.
*King.*        No!
*Mart.*            None.
*King.*                    Fetch me Inke and Paper,
I soone shall try that, come Sir write your name:
Stay, your owne words shall choake you, 'twas a letter
Wrap'd vp in hidden Characters, and sent
Inclos'd in a Pomgranet, to a great *Don*
And thus subscrib'd: *At your pleasure your obsequious vassaile.*   90
Write this, and then your name, here.
*Mart.*                    *At your pleasure.*
*King.* Thy hand shakes.
*Mart.*                No sir, *Your obsequious Vassaile.*
*King.* Here sir, your name now there so low it stood.

78 does you staine!] do you staine? Q

327

*Mart.*  *Martines Caʒalla de Barameda.*

*King.*  There's in thy face no Traytor, I cannot tell,
Good mouthes haue giuen thee to mee, on your life
Be not you like a Wolfes-skin Drom to fright
The whole Heard by your sound, I will compare
Your hand with this, that's all, but sir beware
You prate to none of what 'twixt vs is past.                              100

*Mart.*  Were I i'th world aboue, I would desire
To come from thence, to giue that man the lye,
That once should dare to blot my Loyalty.

*King.*  Here take this Key, meet mee some halfe houre hence
I'th priuy Gallery with two naked Poniards.

*Mart.*  Two ponyards.                                                    *Exit.*

*Enter* Gazetto [*as* Lupo].

*King.*  Yes, goe send some body in, stay, *Lupo*
Can you write?

*Gaʒ.*  Yes.

*King.*  Indite a Letter — 'sdeath sir — heere begin.                    110

*Gaʒ.*  After my heartie Commendations, so sir.

*King.*  How! write — *My most admired Mistris.*

*Gaʒ.*  *Mired Mistris,*

*King.*  *With the fire you first kindled in me, still I am burnt.*

*Gaʒ.*  *Still I am burnt:*

*King.*  *So that Thunder shall not hinder mee from climbing the
highest step of the Ladder.*

*Gaʒ.*  *Climbing the highest step of the Ladder.*

*King.*  *Of your perfections, though I bee confounded for euer.*

*Gaʒ.*  *Be confounded for euer.*                                        120

*King.*  *Your high pleasures are mine, mine yours.*

*Gaʒ.*  *Mine yours.*

*King.*  *And I dye euerlastingly vntill I bee in your bosome.*

*Gaʒ.*  *And I dye — vntill I be in your bosome.*

*King.*  So.

*Gaʒ.*  So.

*King.*  Hold.

97 Drom] Drone Q(u); Drum Q(c)

*Gaȥ.*  Here sir.
*King.*  Where are the Gentlemen of our Chamber?
*Gaȥ.*  Without Sir.                                          130
*King.*  Bid them attend vs close.
*Gaȥ.*  I shall.

                                              *Exeunt.*

## [ACT IV, SCENE V]

*Enter* Martines *with two Poniards.*

*Mar.*  Would this dayes worke were done, I doe not like
To see a Bull to a wild Fig-tree ty'd
To make him tame, beasts licking 'gainst the hayre
Fore-shew some storme, and I fore-see some snare:
His sword is dipt in oyle, yet does it wound
Deadly: yet stand it, innocence wrong'd is crown'd.

*Enter the King,* Alphonso, *and* Gazetto [*as* Lupo, *and others*].

*Omn.*  Treason!
*King.*         Where?
*Omn.*              Kill the Villaine.           *All draw.*
*King.*                         Stay, none touch him
On your liues; on Kings shoulders stand
The heads of the Colossie of the Goddes
(Aboue the reach of Traitors) were the beds              10
Of twenty thousand Snakes layd in this bosome,
There's thunder in our lookes to breake them all,
Leaue vs.
*Omn.*  You are too venturous.
                              *Exeunt.* [*Manent King and* Martines.]
*King.*                         *Ioue* cannot fall:
Both person, place and businesse were quite lost
Out of our memorie, lay aside these poniards,
We haue alter'd now our businesse, you shall beare sir
Our salutation to the Queene — not seal'd!

                        329

'Sfoot, nor indors'd! some Inke, come let thy forehead
Haue no more wrincles in't — but this, to the Queene,
Write it.
*Mart.*     To the Queene, no more!
*King.*                    No, no, 'tis well,                    20
Hast thou no Seale about thee? if my wife
Exceptions take missing our royall signet
Say that not hauing that, I borrowed yours.
*Mart.* I shall Sir.                                *Exit.*
*King.*          Hide it, goe — without there.
*Omn.*                              Sir.    *Enter All.*
*King.*   You met him did you not, how lookt the slaue?
*Omn.*   Most strangely.
*King.*   Vnparalel'd Villaine! Diuels could not set
To hatch such spitefull mischiefe, guard me closely,
When you see him at the stake then worry him,
Are all weapon'd?
*Omn.*              All, all.
*King.*                  When Darts inuisible flye,          30
A slaue may kill a Lyon in the eye.
                                        *Exeunt.*


[ACT IV, SCENE vi]

*Enter Queene, and* Tormiella.

*Queen.*   Who gaue you this?
*Tormi.*                  A Gentleman of your Chamber.
*Queen.*   Call in the Villaine,

            *Enter* Martines.

                Thou audatious Serpent!
How dar'st thou wind in knotted curles thy lust
About our honour; where hadst thou this Letter?

                18 thy] the Q          24 *Enter All.* Q *places in line after* Exit.
                *30 inuisible flye] Q(u); inuisible doe flye Q(c)
                *2 S.D. *Enter* Martines.] Q *places below line* 1

                            330

*Mart.*    I had it from the King.
*Queen.*                        Out impudent Traytor.

*Enter King,* Iago, Gazetto [*as* Lupo], Alphonso.

*King.*    How now at Barle-brake, who are in Hell?
What's that? to the Queene, what Queene!
*Queen.*                              Me, 'tis to me!
Your mistris there the Messenger, her Secretary
Hee heere.
*King.*        Vds death.
*Queen.*                    Your Trull and hee haue laid
Traines to blow vp mine honour, I am betray'd.                    10
*King.*    *Lupo,* Fasten her.
*Queen.*                    Fasten mee!
*King.*                            *Iago* see.
Looke all, bind fast this Diuell, is there no Circle
To be damn'd in but mine.
*Queen.*                    Slaue let me goe.
*King.*    Oh thou lustfull harlot.
*Queen.*                        Guard me Heauen.
*Mart.*                                    I'me sold.
*Queen.*    Thou Villaine speake truth.
*King.*                            Keepe her off.
*Mart.*                                    Most basely
Betray'd and baffled, is that Letter the same
I sent in to the Queene.
*Tormi.*                    The very same.
*King.*    Is this thy hand?
*Mart.*    'Tis sir, but heare me.
*King.*                        And this thy name, thy hand?
*Mart.*    My name, my hand.
*Queen.*                    Saue him and let him spit                    20
His blackest poyson forth?
*King.*                    Spare him, vnhand her.
*Queen.*    Let me haue Iustice as thou art a King!
*King.*    To prison with them both.

*Queen.*                      As I am thy wife
Make not thy selfe a strompit of me.
*King.*                           Hence, guard her.
*Queen.*  I come Heauen, guarded with innocence.          *Exit.*
*King.*  Follow your Mistris, you.
*Tormi.*                    Yes, to her graue.
Oh that I now were swallowed in some Waue.          *Exit.*
*King.*  Oh that I
Should in a womans lap my Kingdome lay,
Honour and life, and she should all betray          30
To a Groome, a slaue.
*Iago.*                Let not her poyson run
Too neare your heart.
*King.*                    *Iago* I haue done,
Pray let my greife want company, this wracke
So great, shall make th'whole Kingdome mourn in black.
                              *Exeunt [Court].*
*Lupo!*
*Ga.*  Did your Highnesse call!
*King.*  Yes, harke thee *Lupo*:
It may bee th'art a Serpent dull of sight,
Be quicke of hearing, may be th'art a Hare,
And canst see side-wayes, let me locke vp here,          40
What euer's layd in there.
*Ga.*  I am strongly charm'd.
*King.*  Wilt venter for me?
*Ga.*  To the threshold of hell.
*King.*  May I trust thee?
*Ga.*  Else imploy me not.
*King.*  Didst euer kill a Scorpion?
*Ga.*  Neuer, I ha beene stung by one.
*King.*  Didst neuer bait a wild Bull?
*Ga.*  That's the pastime I most loue and follow.          50
*King.*  A strange disease
Hangs on me, and our Doctors say the bloud
Onely of these two beasts must doe me good,
Dar'st thou attempt to kill them?

*Gaʒ.*                    Were they Diuels
With heads of Iron, and Clawes ioynted with brasse,
Encounter them I shall, in what Parke run they?
*King.*   The Queene that Scorpion is, *Tormiellas* husband
The mad Oxe broken loose; in a small volume
What mischiefe may be writ! in a maze?
*Gaʒ.*                         No, in a muse,
I'me plotting how to doe't, and to come off.                    60
*King.*   This does it, by this key burst ope all doores
That can betray thee, done, be sure to rise,
Let a Kings royall breath, send the hence flying.
*Gaʒ.*   As Powder does the Bullet.
*King.*                    Heap'd vp honours
Are scedules to thine enterprise annext,
Doe it and mount —
*Gaʒ.*              [*Aside*] To th'Gallowes.
*King.*                  [*Aside*] Thy selfe goes next.   *Exit.*
*Gaʒ.*   I scorne to be thy bloud hound,
Why should I vexe a Soule did neuer greeue me?
The Queenes an honest Lady: should I kill her
It were as if I pull'd a Temple downe                    70
And from the ruines of that built vp a stewes,
She liues, but Butcher like the Oxe Ile vse.

                                        *Exit.*


## ACTVS, V [Scena i]

*Enter King.* [*At another door*] Valasco, Malevento, Alphonso.

*Male.*   Oh royall Sir, my Daughter *Tormiella*
Has lost her vse of reason and runne mad.
*King.*   When!
*Male.*              Not halfe an houre since.
*King.*                                   Mad now! now frantique!
When all my hopes are at their highest pitch
T'inioy her beauties! talke no more: thou ly'st.

*Enter* Gazetto [*as* Lupo].

*Gaz.*  May it please your Maiestie —
*King.*                              Curses consume thee — oh —
                                                    *Strikes.*
*Gaz.*  It is dispatch'd, the Queene is lost, neuer to be found.
*King.*  Waue vpon Waue,
  Hard hearted Furies, when will you dig my Graue:
  You doe not heare him, thunder shakes Heauen first          10
  Before dull Earth can feele it:
  My deere, dearest Queene is dead.
*Val.*                              Ha!
*Omn.*                              The Queene dead!
*King.*  What said she last!
*Gaz.*                        Commend me to the King
  And tell him this, mine honour is not wrack'd,
  Though his Loue bee.
*King.*                  And so her heart-strings crackt!
*Val.*  Some tricke vpon my life, State-coniuring
  To raise vp Diuels in Prisons, and i'th darke:
  If she be dead, Ile see her.
*King.*                        Villanous man,
  Thou see what we haue inioy'd, thou impudent foole
  Away, *Iago* giue this tumbling Whale                        20
  Empty barrels to play with till this troublous Seas
  (Which he more raging makes) good Heauen appease.
*Val.*  Well I say nothing, Birds in Cages mourne
  At first, but at last sing; I will take my turne.          *Exit.*
*King.*  My Queene dead, I shall now haue riming slaues
  Libell vpon vs, giuing her innocent wings
  But say we murdered her, scandall dare strike Kings:
  Then here's another Moone of *Spaine* Eclips'd,
  One whom our best lou'd Queene put in her bosome,
  For sweetnesse of pure life, integritie,                    30
  And (in Court beauties wondrous) honesty,
  Shee's mad too, *Lupo, Tormiella*'s mad!
*Gaz.*  Mad!

334

*Iago.*   As a March whore.                              [*Aside.*]
*Ga₹.*   Mad, shall I worke vpon her?
*King.*   Vse thy skill.                          *Exit* Gazetto.
*Iago.*   I would to Heauen your highnesse —
*King.*   Ha! the Queene! was she not at my elbow?
*Omn.*   Here was nothing.
*King.*   I must not liue thus, *Iago* if I lye                    40
After the kingly fashion without a woman
I shall run mad at midnight; I will marry
The Lunaticke Lady, she shall be my Queene,
Proclaime her so.
*Iago.*         Your highnesse does but jest!
*King.*   All the world's franticke, mad with mad are best.   *Exit.*
*Iago.*   Wretched state of Kings, that standing hye,
Their faults are markes shot at by euery eye.

                                              *Exeunt.*


## [ACT V, Scene ii]


*Enter* Tormiella, Malevento, Gazetto [*disguised as a Doctor*].

*Ga₹.*   Giue me the key, make all fast, leaue vs, Ile skrew her wits
to the right place.
*Male.*   *Apollo* blesse thee.                        *Exit.*
*Tormi.*   Are not you a woollen-Draper?
*Ga₹.*   Yes.
*Tormi.*   Whether is a womans life measured by the Ell or the Yard.
*Ga₹.*   All women by the Yard sure, it's no life else.
*Tormi.*   I'me now neare seuenteene yeares old, if I should dye at
these yeares, am I not a foole.
*Ga₹.*   Yes, marry are you, for the Law allowes none to be of dis- 10
cretion, till they come to twenty one.
*Tormi.*   Out vpon you, you are a Lawyer, pray get you hence, for
you'l not leaue me clothes to my backe if I keepe you company,
Ime mad enough now, and you'l make me starke mad.
*Ga₹.*   I am not what I seeme, no Doctor I

            47 S.D. *Exeunt*] *Exit* Q

                    335

But by your Husband sent in this disguise
To sound your bosome.

*Tormi.*    You bob for Eeles, doe you not?

*Gaʒ.*    Here has he lockt his mind vp, but for mee
To put a burning linstocke in a hand                              20
That may giue fire, and send my Soule in powder,
I know not, pardon me, fare you well Lady?

*Tormi.*    Hist doe you heare?

*Gaʒ.*                            The eyes of mercy guard thee,
Were't knowne for what I venter'd thus, 'twere death,
Ile to your husband.

*Tormi.*                            Stay, I am not mad
Yet I haue cause to raue, my wits like Bels
Are backward rung, onely to fright the Tyrant
That whilst his wild lust wanders, I may flye
To my sweet husbands armes, here I haue hid
The traines I meane to lay for mine escape.    [*Shews letters.*] 30

*Gaʒ.*    Excellent, he shall second you.

*Tormi.*                            Should any watch vs!

*Gaʒ.*    All's fast, run mad agen then, the King thinks
Me some rare fellow, you shall leaue the Court
Now if you'l taste my Counsell.

*Tormi.*                            Ile drinke gall
To cure mee of this sicknesse.

*Gaʒ.*                            Sit then downe here,
Ile bind you fast because it shall appeare,
That you grow worse and worse, then will I tell
The King, the onely course to leaue you well,
Is to remoue you home to mine owne Lodging,
Ile bind you.

*Tormi.*    For euer to thee.

*Gaʒ.*                            Once hence, you may flye    40
To th'*Straights*, and then crosse ouer to *Barbary*:
So, th'art a Strumpet.

*Tormi.*                            What's that you speake!

41 ouer] Q(u); o're Q(c)

*Ga*ȝ.                                    A damn'd one,
Dost thou not know me, I am *Gaȝetto*!
*Tormi.*                                         Mercy.
*Ga*ȝ. Who like a ball of wild-fire haue beene tost
To make others sport, but here I burst and kill:
A periur'd Strumpet.
*Tormi.*          I am none, my Father swore
That I should marry thee, and then a Tyger
And a Lambe had beene together, I ne're was thine,
Nor neuer will be.
*Ga*ȝ.                    Sweare thou art not mine,
That when I see thy heart drunke with hot oathes,                    50
This Feind may pitch thee reeling into Hell,
Sweare that thou art not mine.
*Tormi.*                      By heauen I am not,
To proue I sweare right to thee, change that weapon,
See at my Girdle hang my wedding kniues,
With those dispatch mee.
*Ga*ȝ.                    To th'heart?
*Tormi.*                              Ayme right
I beseech thee.
*Ga*ȝ.          Ile not kill thee now for spight
Because thou begst it.
*Tormi.*                  Then good villaine spare me!
*Ga*ȝ. Neither, heere's that shall sinke thee; to the King
Thy iugling and these Letters shall be showne.
*Tormi.* Vpon thy head be my confusion:                              60
The King, I shall both feed his rage and lust,
First doome me to any Tortures!
*Ga*ȝ.                      Thou shalt then sweare —
                                    *Vnbinds her.*
Because I know he'll force the tye a knot,
The Church must see and sigh at, if he marries thee

45 kill:] Q (c); ∼ ∧ Q (u)
46–49 Q *lines*: I...none, | My...thee, | And...beene together [*u*] *or* met [*c*] | I...
be.
*48 beene together] Q (u); met Q (c)      49 neuer] Q (u); euer Q (c)
63 the] *i.e.* thee                       64 thee∧] Q (u); ∼ , Q (c)

Sweare when he comes to touch thy naked side
To bury him in those sheets, thou art his Bride.

*Tormi.* By Heauen that night's his last, my iust hart keepes
This vow grauen there.

*Gaʒ.* Till then my vengeance sleepes,
Where is the King?

*Enter King,* Iago, Alphonso, Malevento.

*Gaʒ.* I haue refin'd 70
That Chaos which confounded her faire mind.

*King.* Moue in thy voice the Spheares, when next thou speakst
*Tormiella.*

*Tormi.* I am well, my fearefull dreame
Is vanisht, thankes to Heauen and that good man.

*King.* Thou giu'st me another Crowne, oh *Vindicado's,*
The axletree on which my Kingdome moues,
Leanes on thy shoulders, I am all thine, *Tormiella*
Bright *Cynthia* looke not pale, *Endimions* heere,
*Hymen* shall fetch a leape from Heauen t'alight
Full in thine armes, backe thou blacke ominous night. 80

*Exeunt.* [*Manet* Gazetto.]

*Enter* Cordolente.

*Cordo.* Signior *Lupo,* why *Don,* not know me, I am the poore
Shopkeeper, whose ware is taken vp by the King.

*Gaʒ.* You lye.

*Cordo.* True, as Iudges doe with their wiues, very seldome, I am
*Cordolente* a poore Gudgin diuing thus vnder water, to see how
*Neptune* and his Mermaides swim together, but dare not come neare
him, for feare he sets Dogfish to deuoure me.

*Gaʒ.* An excellent maske against the marriage, now get a private
Coat, the King meanes to haue you stab'd.

*Cordo.* He does that already, with the bodkin that sticks in my 90
wifes hayre.

*Gaʒ.* He has not the patience to stay the dressing of his meat of

thy prouiding, he will haue it taken vp, and eate the flesh raw, he
will be married incontinently.

*Cordo.* Will she set her hands to my hornes?

*Ga⁊.* Yes, and set them to your head, she followes the steps of her
old grandam, all euils take their names from her, the ills of *Eue*,
thy wife for the hoope ring thou marriedst her withall, hath sworne
to send thee a Deathes head.

*Cordo.* Sworne!                                                                    100

*Ga⁊.* Sworne, were thy case my case; I would set a Diuell at her
elbow in the very Church, I would kill her as she gaue away her
hand.

*Cordo.* Wilt helpe me to a fit Circle to play the Diuell in?

*Ga⁊.* Ile place thee, Ile put thy foot into the stirrup.

*Cordo.* And I will rid the world of one of his diseases, a loose
woman.

*Ga⁊.* Farewell, eate her very hart.                                    *Exit.*

*Cordo.* As we feed one vpon another, hungerly —

                                                                                        *Exit.*


## [ACT V, Scene iii: *Dumbshew*]

*Hoboyes: Enter two Fryers setting out an Altar, Enter* Iago,
Alphonso, Gazetto, Malevento, *two Churchmen,* Tormiella *next and
the King, Ladies attending,* Cordolente *steales in, and stands in some
by place, the King stayes or sits in a chayre,* Tormiella *is brought to
him, as she is comming the King meets her; as the ring is putting on,*
Cordolente *steps in rudely, breakes them off,* Tormiella *flyes to his
bosome, the King offers to stab him, is held: she kneeles, sues, weepes,*
Cordolente *is thrust out,* Gazetto *laughs at all, they are preparing to
it againe, it Thunders and Lightens: all affrightedly — Exeunt.*


109 S.D. *Exit*] *Exeunt* Q

## [ACT V, SCENE iv]

*Enter* Cordolente.

*Cordo.*  Dost thou tell me of thy Proclamations that I am banisht
from the Court, that Court where I came to thee, was none of
thine, it belongs to a King that keepes open Court, one that neuer
wrong'd a poore Begger, neuer tooke away any mans wife, vnlesse
he sent his Purseuant death for her: oh thou daring Sacrilegious
royall Theefe; wilt thou rob the Church too, as thou hast me,
thrust me out of that house too in the Sanctuary, turn'd Diuell in
a crowd of Angels.

*Enter* Gazetto.

*Gaʒ.*  Why didst not kill her?
*Cordo.*                          I had no power to kill her,                 10
Charmes of Diuinity pull'd backe mine Arme,
She had Armor of proofe on, (reuerence of the place)
She is not married, is she, shorten my paines.
*Gaʒ.*  Heauen came it selfe downe, and forbade the Banes.

*Enter* Iago.

*Iago.*  You must both to th'King.
*Gaʒ.*  Must! we are for him.
*Cordo.*  Now doe I looke for a fig.
*Gaʒ.*  Chew none, feare nothing.

*Exeunt.*

## [ACT V, SCENE v]

*Flourish. Enter King,* Tormiella, Valasco, Malevento, Alphonso.

*King.*  Has heauen left chiding yet, there's in thy voice
A thunder that worse frights mee, didst thou sweare
In bed to kill me, had I married thee?

6 me,] Q(c¹); *om.* Q(u)        7 the] Q(c¹); thy Q(u, c¹)

*Tormi.*   It was my vow to doe so.

*King.*                        And did that Villaine,
That *Lupo Vindicado's*, thrust this vengeance
Into thy desperate hand.

*Tormi.*                  That Villaine swore me
To speed you, I had dy'd else; me had he murdered
When in a Doctors shape he came to cure
The madnesse which in me was counterfeit,
Onely to shun your touches.

*King.*                      Strange preseruation.              10

*Enter* Iago, Gazetto, *and* Cordolente.

*Val.*   Here comes the traytor!

*King.*   Diuell, didst thou tempt this woman 'gainst my life?

*Gaʒ.*   Has she betray'd me, yes, hence Anticke vizors,
Ile now appeare my selfe.

*Male.*                  *Gaʒetto!*

*Gaʒ.*                          The same.

*Cordo.*   I ha warm'd a Snake in my bosome.

*Male.*                              This is he,
To whom by promise of my mouth, (not hers)
*Tormiella* should ha' beene married, but flying him
To runne away with this, he in disguise
Has followed Both thus long to be reueng'd.

*Gaʒ.*   And were not my hands ty'd by your preuention      20
It should goe forward yet, my plot lay there
(King) to haue her kill thee, this Cuckold her,
Then had I made him Hawkes-meat.

*Val.*                          Bloudy Varlet.

*King.*   Rare Prouidence, I thanke thee, what a heape
Of mischiefes haue I brought vpon my Kingdome,
By one base Act of lust, and my greatest horror
Is that for her I made away my Queene
By this destroyers hand, this crimson Hell-hound
That laughes at nothing but fresh Villanies.

*Gaʒ.*   The laughing dayes I wisht for, are now come sir,   30

341

I am glad that leaping into such a Gulph,
I am not drown'd, your Queene liues.

*King.* Ha!

*Gaz.* She liues,
I had no reason to kill her.

*Val.* A better Spirit
Stood at his elbow, then you planted there,
My poore Girle your sad Queene, breathes yet.

*King.* Long may she,
Fetch her, commend me to her, cheere her (Father.)

*Val.* With the best hart I haue. *Exit.*

*King.* Let that slye Bawd,
Engine of Hell, who wrought vpon thy Chastity
Be whipt through *Sivill,* foure such tempting witches
May vndoe a City: come, you wronged paire,                40
By a King that parted you, you new married are.
Inioy each other and prosper.

*Cordo.* I doe already,
Feeling more ioyes then on my Wedding day,
I nere till now was married.

*Tormi.* Nor I euer happy vntill this houre.

*Male.* Nor I, as I am true Lord.

*King.* No sir, y'are no true Lord, you haue a title,
A face of honour, as in Courts many haue,
For base and seruile prostitutions,
And you are such a one, your Daughters fall                50
Was first step to your rising, and her rising
Againe to that sweet goodnesse she neuer went from,
Must be your fall, and strip you of all honours,
Your Lordship is departed.

*Male.* Does the Bell ring out! I care not.
Your Kingdome was a departing too, I had a place in Court for
nothing, and if it be gon, I can loose nothing; I ha' beene like a
Lord in a play, and that done, my part ends.

*King.* Yes sir, I purge my Court of such Infection.

*Male.* I shall find company i'th City I warrant; I am not the first 60
hath giuen vp my Cloake of honour. *Exit.*

*Enter* Valasco, Iohn, *and Queene.*

*King.*  Oh my abused heart, thy pardon, see
I haue sent home my stolne goods.
*Queen.*                                    Honestly!
*King.*  As she was euer; now with full cleere eyes
I see thy beauty, and strange Cheekes despise.
*Queen.*  You call me from a graue of shame and sorrow,
In which I lay deepe buried.
*Iohn.*                                    From a graue likewise
Your Maiestie calls me, I haue lookt backe
On all my poore Ambitions, and am sorry,
That I fell euer from so bright a Spheare,                    70
As is the Loue of such a royall brother.
*King.*  Be as you speake, we are friends, it was our will
To let you know, we can, or saue, or kill.
*Iohn.*  Your mercy new transformes me.
*King.*                                    Sirrah your sauing
My Queene, when I confesse (lust me so blinded)
I would haue gladly lost her; giues thee life.
*Queen.*  First I thanke Heauen, then him, and at last you.
*Gaʒ.*  I had not the heart to hurt a woman, if I had, your little face
had beene mall'd ere this, but my Angers out, forgiue me.
*Tormi.*  With all my heart.                    80
*King.*  Pray noble brother loue this man, he's honest,
I ha' made of him good proofe, we should haue had
A wedding, but Heauen frown'd at it, and I
Am glad 'tis crost, yet we'll both Feast and dance,
Our Fame hath all this while laine in a Trance:
Come *Tormiella*, well were that City blest,
That with but, Two such women should excell,
But there's so few good, th'ast no Paralell.

*Exeunt.*

*FINIS.*

76 her] Q(c²); the Q(u, c¹)

343

# TEXTUAL NOTES

## I.iv

40 Asse]  This addition from the second proof-correction of inner C may be
a sophistication.  On the other hand, emphasis and balance cry out for it;
and though these could have been the factors influencing the corrector to
insert the word on his own responsibility, a survey of the other substantive
alterations in this forme made in the second correction suggests the fair
possibility that the proof-reader on this occasion consulted copy.

43 haue]  Whether *share* substituted in the first round of correction is
authoritative may perhaps be a matter of opinion.  I prefer the original *haue*
on the ground that no clear evidence exists for consultation of copy during
this first correction of inner C (especially if we are to infer the possibility of
such consultation in the second round).  For what it is worth—and it is
doubtless a quibble—a *king* does not *share* his kingdom with anyone even
though he may be the victim of withheld power and revenues. This press-
corrector was very keen on carrying such words in his mind and substi-
tuting them later. The classic case is the error he made about *Father* at
III.ii.51.

73 wiser man then you]  The alteration comes in the second round of correction for inner C, one that may refer to some authority.  Although the
press-corrector several times elsewhere tinkers with the metre, there is no
reason why Dekker should have written less than a pentametre here. If so,
the uncorrected reading would represent memorial failure by the compositor.

82 doe.]  Metrical accent requires a stress on *doe*; indeed, the line would scan
very oddly if *doe* did not end a clause.  For the sense, the king has not been
flattering John although he has been stimulating him. Hence the omission
of a stop seems to represent merely another of the compositor's almost
congenital faults of this kind.

## II.i

41 for]  The sense is almost indifferent, but on the basis of the justness of the
other substantive changes made in this forme during the second round of
correction, *for* has also been accepted instead of uncorrected *from*.

113–114 some Country]  If this turns out to be doubtful idiom, it is as
possible that a word like *other* has been dropped after *some* as that singular
*Country* appears in error for plural *Countries*.

115 thus]  As in the line above—except that here emendation is imperative—
a word may be dropped, as *by this*. Perhaps minim error and the emendation

344

*thus* is a trifle simpler, but I should not myself lean much weight on that as an argument. A compositor can skip a word as easily as misread minims. Interestingly, the Hyde copy, which has a few corrections in an early hand, contains a manuscript alteration to *thus*.

## II.ii

47 beames was]   It is guesswork whether (1) the corrector objected to the metre and thought it improved by the omission of *was*; or (2) he objected to *was* instead of *were* and the compositor, charged with the alteration, saw the deletion but not the substitution. Whatever the reason, *was* does not appear to be wrong: if we compare line 55 below on the same page (D 4ᵛ), we may take it that the proof-reader is sophisticating here without reference to copy.

50 I find 'em.]   Some temptation exists to alter the full stop to a query. It could be that Tormiella takes literally lines 49–50, 'Oh you shall find vpon a Princes pillow Such golden dreames' and exclaims in surprise, '*I* find 'em?' On the other hand, her surprise in line 54 at the Lady's suggestion 'Before you lyes your way' *etc.* does not favour the view that she has previously seen the meaning of lines 49–50; and the Lady's 'Cry you mercy' is a bit odd if in reply to any astonishment in 'I find 'em'. Very likely, therefore, Q's punctuation is right. In 'I find 'em' Tormiella states by implication that she finds golden dreams upon her husband's pillow and need not envy those who dream upon a prince's pillow. The Lady's 'Cry you mercy', then, would be an ironic commentary on the lowness of Tormiella's ambitions.

55 dreads]   The press-corrector seems not to have been acquainted with the idiomatic use of *dreads* ('to cause to fear, to affright, terrify') as illustrated in O.E.D. 5. *v. trans.*, and took the easy road of sophistication.

93 ill-look'd Iade]   It is difficult to imagine a compositor setting *ill-look'd Iade* when his copy read *ill-fac'd Bawd* (this last the press-corrected reading), especially since *Iade* carries on the equine reference of *splay-foot*. Reference to manuscript by the proof-reader seems ruled out, therefore, and we must posit either sophistication or a revising author. Since this alteration is the only variant in the outer forme of sheet E, the type had presumably already been proof-read, and hence the alteration very likely represents a second go-through. Dekker *could* have stopped by the shop after a very few copies of outer D had been machined, read the sheet, and discovered he wanted to make this change. But since he clearly did not do so for the second-round variants of all other sheets where they may be suspected, or are physically present, it is more reasonable to suppose that outer E resembles them than that it is unique. The variant does not seem to have authority, therefore.

## III.ii

S.D. Martines,] Q's addition of *Fuentes* (c¹) changed from *Farentes* (u) represents a ghost character. That Fuentes is not given in the Persons is of no significance since (on the evidence of *Lupo* listed as a separate character from *Gaʒetto*) Dekker did not furnish this list. The three named courtiers—Martines, Iago, and Alphonso—are all specified in this direction, and so Fuentes is not to be identified with one of them in any early state of the text. Very likely *Fuentes* is a fossil, a minor character whose name inadvertently escaped from a reworking. No speeches are assigned to him here or elsewhere, nor does any action require his presence.

11 I] The omission of this pronoun in Q(c¹) was undoubtedly the responsibility of the compositor who was pressed for space when directed to insert *you* earlier in the line. We may notice that he also excised the final *e* from *looke*.

25 Here are] Whether the Q(c¹) change to *Here be* was a proof-reader's marking (implying reference to copy) or a compositorial saving of space in order to add an *s* to *other* in the next word is doubtful. It is true that still farther on in the line the compositor of c¹ in his resetting expanded *be* to *bee*; but at the time of setting *Here be* he could not have contemplated this later change or that he would have the space for it, especially since in the same line of his copy he would see the abbreviation *Qu.* that called for expansion. The difficulty is caused by the fact this change takes place in the reset lines, not in standing type. I lean to the compositorial explanation, partly because there is no sign of consultation of copy elsewhere in the forme (although no evidence to bar such consultation), partly because there is a question whether the proof-reader would order this change without such consultation, and partly because the queen elsewhere does not use such pert language even under stress.

51 Father] Valasco, the queen's father, is the *king's* father-in-law. When Q(c) on sig. F4ᵛ of the outer forme alters to *Father in law* the Q(u) reading *Father*, we cannot believe that this forme was read by the author unless we take it that the change was to be part of a thorough revision of reference, and the compositor retained in error *Queenes* and did not insert the rest of the addition. Hence with some certainty we can pin this alteration on the proof-reader. Since F(o) was probably first through the press, it is not likely that he picked it up from reading proof on sig. F2 of the inner forme, *Were you some Father in Law now* (III.i.125).

148 I knowing this my honourable friend—] Presumably *was* is to be understood after *friend*: 'I knowing that this man my honourable friend was coming to visit me, this (my honourable friend) was the man who must die.' Otherwise, less likely, a comma would be required after *this*, and its reference would then be not to *friend* but instead to some previous statement as line 147.

## IV.i

32 banes]    It may be a question whether the proof-reader was right and it was the compositor who had been in error in misunderstanding the pun and adding the plural *s*, or whether the proof-reader wanted to increase its obviousness.  If the proof-reader were indeed correcting a compositorial error, he was probably right only by guesswork since there is no sign of reference to copy elsewhere in the forme.  *Banes* is a perfectly acceptable spelling for *bans*.

## IV.v

30 inuisible flye]    Whether or not these words complete a pentametre as printed in this text (and Dekker frequently does not count the second element of a repetition like *All, all* in his metre), it would seem that the proof-reader thought a tetrametre better than a trimetre as the first line of a couplet.

## IV.vi

2 S.D. *Enter* Martines.]    The exact position of this direction is a trifling matter.  But it should be remarked that line 2 is split in Q as printed in this text, though both half-lines are flush against the left margin, of course.

## V.ii

48 beene together]    Q(c) substitute *met* seems to be another example of unauthoritative metrical tinkering.  If the verse is relined as in the present text, then *met* is clearly impossible.  According to Q's lining, *beene together* made the line seem hypermetrical.

# PRESS-VARIANTS IN Q (1631)

[Copies collated: BM¹ (British Museum 644.b.22), BM² (Ashley 618), BM³ (C.12.f.4[4]; wants sheets E–I), Bodl¹ (Bodleian Mal. 195[8]), Bodl² (Mal. 235[10]), Bodl³ (Mal. 914[3]), Bodl⁴ (Douce D.205), Dyce¹ (Victoria and Albert), Dyce², Eton (Eton College), NLS (National Library of Scotland), Worc (Worcester College), CSmH (Huntington), CtY (Yale), DFo (Folger), DLC (Library of Congress), Hyde (Mr and Mrs Donald F. Hyde), ICN (Newberry), ICU (University of Chicago), MB (Boston Public), MH (Harvard), MWiW-C (Chapin, Williams Coll.), NNP (Pierpont Morgan), Pforz (Carl H. Pforzheimer Library), PU (University of Pennsylvania), ViU (University of Virginia).]

## SHEET A (*inner forme*)

1st stage corrected: CSmH.
Uncorrected:         Hyde.

Sig. A2.
*Dedication*
3 Over-daring] over-daring
5 (*Now*)] (now)

2nd stage corrected: BM¹⁻³, Bodl¹⁻⁴, Dyce¹⁻², Eton,. NLS, Worc, CtY, DFo, DLC, ICN, ICU, MB, MH, MWiW-C, NNP, Pforz, PU, ViU.

Sig. A1ᵛ.
*Persons*
1 Drammatis] Dramatis

## SHEET B (*outer forme*)

Corrected:   BM¹⁻³, Bodl¹⁻⁴, Dyce¹⁻², Eton, NLS, Worc, CSmH, DFo, DLC, Hyde, ICN, ICU, MB, MH, MWiW-C, NNP, Pforz, PU, ViU.

Uncorrected: CtY.
Sig. B2ᵛ.
I.ii.13 dare the] dare [*om.* the]

## SHEET C (*inner forme*)

*1st stage corrected:* BM², Bodl¹, Dyce¹, Eton, Worc, DFo, ICU, MB, MH,
MWiW-C, NNP, Pforz, PU.
*Uncorrected:* CtY, Hyde, ICN.

Sig. C1ᵛ.
  I.iv.35 peece] peace
      39 Foxe] FoXe
      43 ſhare] haue
      48 death] death
Sig. C2.
  I.iv.52 you vp] yo  vp
      61 Tower] Towre
      65 Temples] Templet
      66 Nay,] Nay
      69 him] *omitted*
      70 ſteakes:] ſteakes,
      71 you;] you,
Sig. C3ᵛ.
  I.iv.139 flatcap,] flatcap
     139 ſtop's] ſtop his
     144 Highneſſe] Higneſſe
  II.i.3 at] a
Sig. C4.
  II.i.18 S.D. *Malevento*] MALEVENTO

*2nd stage corrected:* BM¹⁻³, Bodl²⁻⁴, Dyce², NLS, CSmH, DLC, ViU.

Sig. C1ᵛ.
  I.iv.25 lye!] lye
     40 Aſſe] *omitted*
     49 falſe:] falſe
Sig. C2.
  I.iv.64 *King.*] *Ioh.*
     73 wiſer man than you ſhall] wiſe man then ſhall
Sig. C4.
  II.i.34 any!] any.
     41 for] from

## SHEET D (*outer forme*)

*Corrected:* BM¹⁻³, Bodl¹⁻⁴, Dyce¹⁻², Eton, NLS, Worc, CSmH, CtY, DFo, DLC, Hyde, ICN, ICU, MB, MH, MWiW-C, NNP, Pforz, ViU.

*Uncorrected:* PU.

Sig. D 1.
II.i.79 h'a] ha
  80 ſpeed,] ſpeed
  81 ſhall,] ſhall
  91 whom?] whom.
  93 Ha!] Ha
  93 Father!] Father,
  93 he!] he
  93 him?] him

Sig. D 2ᵛ.
II.i.173 coſt,] coſt
  180 you] *omitted*
  181 *Ve-* | *tian*] *Vene* | *tian*
  200 to,] to
  203 deare,] deare

Sig. D 3.
II.i.207 off?] off.
  211 deſires:] deſires
  226 Houſe,] Houſe
  229 Come,] Come

Sig. D 4ᵛ.
II.ii.47 beames] beames was
  55 threats] dreads
  63 King:] King.
  64 driuen,] driuen

## SHEET D (*inner forme*)

*Corrected:* BM¹⁻³, Bodl¹⁻⁴, Dyce¹⁻², Eton, NLS, Worc, CSmH, CtY, DFo, DLC, Hyde, ICN, ICU, MB, MH, MWiW-C, NNP, Pforz, ViU.

*Uncorrected:* PU.

Sig. D 1ᵛ.
II.i.113 that,] that
  114 Iuſtice!] Iuſtice.
  121 puffe —] puffe

II.i.123 (elfe;] (elfe) [*both tucked up at end of line*]
  124 miftris,] miftris
  129 *Exeunt Officers.*] *Exeunt* | *Officers.* [lines 128–129]
Sig. D2.
 II.i.166 worfhip,] worfhip
Sig. D3ᵛ.
 II.i.243 before,] before.
Sig. D4.
 II.ii.20 fweetly] fwcetly
  38 it,] it.

## SHEET E (*outer forme*)

*Corrected:* BM¹⁻², Bodl¹⁻⁴, Dyce¹⁻², Eton, NLS, Worc, CSmH., CtY,
     DFo, DLC, Hyde, ICU, MB, MH, MWiW-C, NNP,
     Pforz, PU, ViU.
*Uncorrected:* ICN.

Sig. E1.
 II.ii.93 ill-fac'd Bawd;] ill-look'd Iade

## SHEET F (*outer forme*)

*Corrected:* BM¹⁻², Bodl¹⁻⁴, Dyce¹⁻², NLS, CSmH, DFo, DLC, Hyde,
     ICU, MB, MH, MWiW-C, NNP, Pforz, ViU.
*Uncorrected:* Eton, Worc, CtY, ICN, PU.

Sig. F1.
 III.i.53 rife] rife,
  54 by,] by
  56 the way] the wey
Sig. F4ᵛ.
 III.ii.51 Father in law.] Father.
  56 *Kin.*] *Ki.*
  59 to Court.] to the Court.

## SHEET F (*inner forme*)

*1st stage corrected:* Bodl¹⁻², Dyce¹, DFo, ICN, MWiW-C.
*Uncorrected:*  Eton, Worc, CtY, Hyde, PU.

Sig. F1ᵛ.
 III.i.76 Comment] Coment
  90 Incens'd] Incenc'd
  90 Vmh!] Vm!
  95 my Lord at Court,] at Court my Lord,

Sig. F 2.
  III.i.115 City,)] City,
      115 Court,] Court,)
      125 Father] Farher

Sig. F 3ᵛ.
  III.i.189 Hee'l] Heel
      189 bring] *omitted*
      191 On] Oh
      192 Conceipt] Concerpt
      192 I'me] Fue
      192 feare,] feare:
      195 foundly!] fome lye!
      202 I'me glad,] Fine clad,

Sig. F 4.
  III.ii.S.D. *Fuentes*] *Farentes*
       1 fweetneffe,] fweetneffe
      11 look you, your] looke your
      11 pray] I pray
      12 Sir] r
      15 choofe] take

[*The following variants in reset type.*]
      24 K*in*. So] K*i*. So [in (u) printed continuously; but in (c) given a
          separate line]
      25 Here be] Here are
      25 others] other
      25 bee] be
      25 Queenes] Qu.
      27 vext,] vext
      29 Violets?] Violets,
      30–31 you doe] *omitted*
      31 joyne- | to] joyne-ftooles | to

  2*nd stage corrected:* BM¹⁻², Bodl³⁻⁴, Dyce², NLS, CSmH, DLC, ICU,
          MB, MH, NNP, Pforz, ViU

Sig. F 1ᵛ.
  III.i.98 On] An

Sig. F 2.
  III.i.108 ftate,] ftate
      111 Sunne-fhine,] Sunne-fhine
      112 out] on
      119 Pinnace] Pinnace!
      121 Court?] Court,

Sig. F3ᵛ.
 III.i.197 No,] No
  197 is't?] is't,
Sig. F4.
 III.ii.19 heare?] heare
  20 No,] No
  31 joyne- | ſtooles to] joyne- | to

### SHEET G (*outer forme*)

*Corrected:* Dyce¹, DFo, DLC.
*Uncorrected:* BM¹⁻², Bodl¹⁻⁴, Dyce², Eton, NLS, Worc, CSmH, CtY,
     Hyde, ICN, ICU, MB, MH, MWiW-C, NNP, Pforz,
     PU, ViU.
Sig. G1.
 III.ii.93 forehead] forehead,
Sig. G3.
 III.ii.174 See,] See.

### SHEET G (*inner forme*)

*Corrected:* BM¹⁻², Bodl²⁻⁴, Dyce¹⁻², NLS, CSmH, CtY, DFo, DLC,
    ICN, ICU, MB, MH, MWiW-C, NNP, Pforz, ViU.
*Uncorrected:* Bodl¹, Eton, Worc, Hyde, PU.

Sig. G1ᵛ.
 III.ii.103 began] began,
  111 diſſemble,] diſſemble
  114 betray,] betray
  122 thine;] thine.
Sig. G3ᵛ.
 III.iii.1 Make] Male
  2 *Tor.*] *Vor.*
  6 thee,] thee
Sig. G4.
 III.iii.18 newes,] newes
  29 Pinnacle,] Pinnacle
  32 S.D. *her*] *hər*
  33 S.D. *kniues.*] *kniues·*
  37 tree] tree,
  39 Heauen,] Heauen

## SHEET H (*inner forme*)

Corrected:   BM¹⁻², Bodl¹⁻⁴, Dyce¹⁻², Eton, NLS, Worc, CSmH, CtY,
            DFo, DLC, Hyde, ICN, ICU, MB, MH, MWiW-C,
            NNP, Pforz, ViU.
Uncorrected: PU.

Sig. H1ᵛ.
III.iii. 95  No!] No.
        106 wrongs!] wrongs.

Sig. H2.
IV.i.32 bane] banes
     40 *Pandarus*!] *Pandarus.*

Sig. H3ᵛ.
*headline* 45] 46
IV.ii.14 City,] City
      17 fhooing] fhoeing
      29 Court,] Court
      31 butter,] butter
      36 Cinqui- | pace] Cinqui- | place

Sig. H4.
IV.ii.48 Signior,] Signior
      50 coap'd] coup'd
      51 cold] could
      55 Goe,] Goe

## SHEET I (*outer forme*)

Corrected:   BM¹⁻², Bodl²⁻⁴, Dyce¹⁻², NLS, Word, CSmH, DFo, DLC,
            Hyde, ICU, MB, MH, MWiW-C, NNP, Pforz, ViU.
Uncorrected: Bodl¹, Eton, CtY, ICN, PU.

Sig. I3.
IV.iv.96 your] yhur
      97 Drum] Drone

## SHEET I (*inner forme*)

Corrected:   BM¹⁻², Bodl¹⁻⁴, Dyce¹⁻², NLS, Worc, CSmH, CtY, DFo,
            DLC, Hyde, ICN, ICU, MB, MH, MWiW-C, NNP,
            Pforz, ViU.
Uncorrected: Eton, PU.

Sig. I1ᵛ.
IV.iii.85 kingdome] kindome
       89 dead] deɇd
IV.iv.4 Ha'ft] Haft

Sig. I 2.
    IV.iv.42 him] him
        49 braue] braue
Sig. I 4.
    IV.v.30 inuifible doe flye] inuifibleflye
    IV.vi.2 S.D. Martines] Martineo

SHEET K (*outer forme*)

*Corrected:* BM¹⁻³, Bodl¹·³⁻⁴, Dyce², NLS, DFo, DLC, Hyde, ICU,
             MB, MH, MWiW-C, NNP, Pforz, PU, ViU.
*Uncorrected:* Bodl², Dyce¹, Eton, Worc, CSmH, CtY, ICN.

Sig. K 1.
    IV.vi.39 Hare] Hare,
Sig. K 2ᵛ.
    V.i.21 with,] with
        23 Well,] Well
        47 markes,] markes
Sig. K 3.
    V.ii.10 Yes] Yes,
        14 I'me] Ime
        21 powder,] powder
Sig. K 4ᵛ.
    V.ii.93 raw,] raw
        95 Cor.] Gor.

SHEET K (*inner forme*)

*Corrected:* BM¹⁻³, Bodl¹⁻⁴, Dyce¹⁻², Eton, NLS, Worc, CSmH, DFo,
             DLC, Hyde, ICU, MB, MH, MWiW-C, NNP, Pforz,
             PU, ViU.
*Uncorrected:* ICN, CtY.

Sig. K 1ᵛ.
    IV.vi.55 braffe,] braffe
        62 rife,] rife
        68 me?] me
        69 her,] her
        70 downe,] downe
Sig. K 2.
    V.i.11 it:] it
      17 darke:] darke

Sig. K3ᵛ.
  V.ii.41 o're] ouer
     41 *Barbary*:] *Barbary*
     42 one,] one
     43 me!] me,
     45 kill:] kill
     46 none,] none
     48 met,] beene together,
     49 euer] neuer
     51 Hell,] Hell
     53 weapon,] weapon

Sig. K4.
  V.ii.61 King!] King,
     64 thee,] thee
     65 fide,] fide
     72 whē] when
     72 thou] to
     72 fpeakft,] fpeakft
     75 *Vindicados*] *Vindicadoes*
     77 thine;] thine,
     77 *Tormiella*!] *Tormiella*
     78 *Endimions*] *Endemions*
     78 heere,] heere
     84 wiues,] wiues

SHEET L (*outer forme*)

   *1st stage corrected:* PU.
   *Uncorrected:*    Hyde.

Sig. L1.
  V.iv.6 me,] *omitted*
  V.v.1 voice] voice,

Sig. L2ᵛ.
  V.v.73 can,] can
     83 wedding,] wedding
     87 but, Two] but two
     88 [*rule*] | *FINIS.* | [*rule*] ] [*rule*] | *FINIS.*

  *2nd stage corrected:* BM¹⁻³, Bodl¹⁻⁴, Dyce¹⁻², Eton, NLS, Worc, CSmH,
                CtY, DFo, DLC, ICN, ICU, MB, MH, MWiW-C,
                NNP, Pforz, ViU.

Sig. L1.
  V.iv.5 her:] her,
     6 me!] me,

V.iv.7 the] thy
    8 Angels!] Angels.
    10 Arme,] Arme
    11 (reuerence...place)] reuerence...place
    15 Muſt!] Muſt,
V.v.1 yet!] yet,
    6 hand?] hand.
    7 murdered,] murdered
    10 preſeruation!] preſeruation.
Sig. L 2ᵛ.
    V.v.76 her] thee

# EMENDATIONS OF ACCIDENTALS

## Persons

DRAMATIS] Q(u, c¹); DRAMMATIS Q(c²)

## Dedication

3 *Over-daring*] Q(c¹); *over-daring*
Q(u)

5 *(Now)*] Q(c¹); *(now)* Q(u)

### I.i

5–6 *one line in* Q
22 Wicket,] ~ ∧
30 *Tormiella*] *Tormelia*
34 So, ho,] ~ , ~ ∧
42 arme,] ~ .

51 *Bilbo,*] ~ ∧
68 *Bilbo.*] *Bii.*
72 kind, ...Monster;] ~ ; ... ~ ,
77 Shroue-|tuesday] Shroue-tues-
day

### I.ii

9 me:] ~ ,
11 by?] ~ .
17 How,] ~ ∧
28 euer-|lasting] euer-|lasting
50 S.D. *Exeunt:*] ~ ∧
53–54 *Bilbo*...yet?] *one line in* Q
57 Consumption,] ~ .
73–74 *prose in* Q

85 What,] ~ ∧
93 Foole,] ~ ∧
99 H'ad] Had
99 Heauen:] ~ ∧
108–109 Q *lines:* Haste...day
Signior...agen.
111 it:] ~ ,

### I.iii

4 Catchpoles] Catch-|poles
7 -rope?] ~ ,
11 fast] ast

30 Girdle, ...Crowne;] ~ ; ...
~ ,
43 Q *lines:* The...you, | You...
presently.

### I.iv

2 spake∧] ~ !
13–14 I...feare !] *one line in* Q
21 *Exit*∧] ~ .
28 Lyon,] ~ ∧
35 peace] Q(u); peece Q(c¹)
41–42 Thou: | You...Kingdome,]
*one line in* Q

54 grow:] ~ ∧
55–56 If...age,] *one line in* Q
56 in't; ...age,] ~ , ... ~ ;
60–61 Our...it.] *one line in* Q
61 Towre,] ~ ∧ [Towre ∧ Q(u);
Tower ∧ Q(c¹)]
63–64 Yes...Sir.] *one line in* Q

66 Nay‸] Q(u); ~ , Q(c¹)
70 steakes,] Q(u); ~ : Q(c¹)
71 you,] Q(u); ~ ; Q(c¹)
73 then] Q(u); than Q(c²)
90 you?] ~ ‸
109 all.] ~ ,
114 Lawyer,] ~ ‸

123 inciferous,] ~ ‸
130 'em] em
134 mee] mec
137 fifteene] fiftecne
139 -Loafe;] ~ ‸
141 Th'ast] T'hast

## II.i

5 vpon Spanish] vponSpanish
17 gloues,] ~ ‸
19 Q.,] ~ .
70 child,] ~ ‸
73–74 She...sunder.] one line in Q
74–75 Her...strongly.] one line in Q
75 strongly.] ~ ‸
79 ha] Q(u); h'a Q(c)
91 whom.] Q(u); ~ ? Q(c)
110 Girdles,] ~ ‸
113 that‸] Q(u); ~ , Q(c)
114 groates—] ~ ‸
114 Iustice.] Q(u); ~ ! Q(c)
117 alone‸...shop,] ~ , ... ~ ‸
123 way;] ~ ‸
123 else.] ~ ‸ Q(u); ~ ; Q(c)
127 Carrion;] ~ ‸

128 Churchman;] ~ ‸
141 hand:] ~ ,
160 Salmindy,] ~ ‸
166 worship‸] Q(u); ~ , Q(c)
174 relish] | Relish
181 Venetian] Q(u); Ve-|tian Q(c)
193 Sir?] ~ ,
198 Bilbo.] Bii.
200 fo‸] Q(u); ~ , Q(c)
205 ware—] ~ .
207 What] what
207 off.] Q(u); ~ ? Q(c)
217 Gentle-|woman] Gentlewoman
219 paire.] ~ ,
226 House‸] ~ Q(u); ~ , Q(c)
229 Come‸] Q(u); ~ , Q(c)
237 Doe,] ~ ‸

## II.ii

5–6 I...vnty'd.] one line in Q
40 words.] point only a speck in most copies
42 hand‸] ~ .
43 spheare‸] ~ .
45 shaddow,] ~ ‸
47 power‸] ~ .
49 pillow‸] ~ .
54 too?] ~ ‸
63 King.] Q(u); ~ : Q(c)
64 driuen‸] Q(u); ~ , Q(c)

69–71 prose in Q, though line 70 has Is with capital
76 thine,] ~ ‸
80 fires.] ~ ,
82 brow.] ~ ‸
84 not;] ~ ,
85 blood;] ~ ,
90 cunningly,] ~ .
98 gummes] gummmes
100 yes, doe;] ~ ; ~ ,
101 haue.] ~ ‸
108 still.] ~ ‸

## II.iv

3 thinke,] ~ .
10 (boy)]ᴧ ~ ᴧ
11 her,] ~ ᴧ
13 her,] ~ ᴧ
15 wise,] ~ ᴧ
16–17 A...Sea.] *one line in* Q
36 sir.—Tormiella!—call her.] ~ ,
   ~ , ~ ~ .
38 meanes,] ~ ᴧ (*may be a speck in*
   *some copies*)
57 best.] ~ ᴧ

103 gon,] ~ ᴧ
105–106 damnations; ...woman,]
   ~ , ... ~ ;
108 *Male.*] *Mvl.*
109 into—] ~ ,
119 game,] ~ ᴧ
121 plaudities] plandities
124 your Comedy] yourComedy
126 nest—] ~ ,
127 wagtaile:] ~ ,

## III.i

19 I did] Idid
54 byᴧ it,] ~ , ~ ᴧ Q (c); ~ ᴧ ~ ᴧ
   Q(u)
58 faile—] ~ .
76 Coment] Q(u); Comment
   Q(c¹)
90 Incenc'd] Q(u); Incens'd Q(c¹)
106 worth,] ~ ᴧ
107 plate,] ~ ᴧ
109 Queene,] ~ ᴧ
114 nothing,] ~ ᴧ
121 Court,] Q(u); ~ ? Q(c²)
125 now—] ~ .
128 full—] ~ ,

134 this] ɪhis
151 *Granada*] *Gramada*
155 *Rios*ᴧ Garden,] ~ , ~ ᴧ
159 Wine,] ~ .
162 'Tis] Q *text*; Tis Q *cw*
166 honour—] ~ .
177 dizzie:] ~ ᴧ
182 vndamn'd, ...dram,] ~ ᴧ ...
   ~ ᴧ
189 Hee'l Q(c²) *text*; He'll Q *cw*;
   Heel Q(u)
192 feare :] Q(u); ~ , Q(c¹)
192 *Iohn*ᴧ] ~ .
203 Better,—] ~ ,ᴧ

## III.ii

S.D. *Florish* Q *cw*; *Flourish* Q *text*
11 looke] Q(u); look Q(c¹)
25 be] Q(u); bee Q(c²)
25 Queenes] Q(c²); Qu̲. Q(u)
27 vextᴧ] Q(u); ~ , Q(c¹)
29 Violets,] Q(u); ~ ? Q(c¹)
31 -stooles,] ~ ᴧ
40 her?] ~ ᴧ
52 Daughter: ...feele,] ~ , ...
   ~ :
58–59 *one line in* Q
60 eare—] ~ :
62 preseru'd;] ~ ᴧ

68 shall:] ~ ᴧ
69 Court.] ~ ᴧ
71–74 Q *lines*: Death! ...face | Go
   ...vs, | Say...presently | And
   ...come.
79 performance] peformance
81–82 You...we] *one line in* Q
92 you,] ~ ᴧ
93 forehead,] Q(u); ~ ᴧ Q(c)
103 began,] Q(u); ~ ᴧ Q(c)
108 obseru'd.] ~ ᴧ
119 Pistolets.] ~ ᴧ
122 thine.] Q(u); ~ ; Q(c)

131 in:] ~ ∧
132 Diuell!] ~ ∧
147 man.] ~ ,
157–158 How!...can.] *one line in* Q
162–163 You...forth.] *one line in* Q
168 off,] ~ ∧
177 owne] ow ne
177 hands?] ~ :
188–189 Your...gone.] *one line in* Q

189 How,] ~ ∧
191 Bee] bee
196 flie:] ~ ∧
198–199 mad;...ope,] ~ , ... ~ ;
202 owne.] ~ ∧
204 it,] ~ ∧
206 ruine, —] ~ , ∧
207 harme,] ~ ∧

## III.iii

1 key,] ~ ∧
6 thee∧] Q(u); ~ , Q(c)
18 newes∧] Q(u); ~ , Q(c)
18 him,] ~ ∧
20 *Millaner*,] ~ ∧
24–25 Alas...tower] *one line in* Q
26 spels,] ~ ∧
27 Hels.] ~ ∧
29 Pinnacle∧] Q(u); ~ , Q(c)
29 idle] jdle
30–31 tost;...downe,] ~ ∧ ... ~ ;
37 tree,] Q(u); ~ ∧ Q(c)
39 Heauen∧] Q(u); ~, Q(c)

40–41 lap;...came,] ~ , ... ~ ;
42–43 By...him.] *one line in* Q
51–52 I haue...and I] *one line in* Q
54 wounded.] ~ ∧
66 drawne?] ~ ,
67–68 teare, ...too.] ~ .... ~ ,
71 Chaine] Chanie
74 this?] ~ ,
93 Crowne,] Q *punctuation uncertain and may be full stop*
95 No,] ~ ∧
102 frowne,] ~ ∧
106 wrongs.] Q(u); ~ ! Q(c)

## IV.i

S.D. IV] IIII
40 *Pandarus*.] Q(u); ~ ! Q(c)
43 harke —] ~ ,
49 you?] ~ ,
58 necke. But] necke, but
60 remaine,] ~ .

63 there;] ~ ∧
66 out] our
66 hart.] ~ ,
90 How,] ~ ∧
98 peices,] ~ ∧
101 merry:] ~ ∧

## IV.ii

13, 14 Signior,] ~ ∧
14 Court;] ~ ∧
16 *Animals*.] ~ ∧
17 shoeing] Q(u); shooing Q(c)
28 Signior, ...city∧] ~ ∧ ... ~ ,
29 Court∧] Q(u); ~ , Q(c)

36 Cinquipace] Q(c); Cinqui-|place
Q(u)
46 harmelesse] Harme-| Q *cw*;
harmlesse Q *text*
50 coup'd] Q(u); coap'd Q(c)
51 could Q(u); cold Q(c)
61 *Cox*.] *Cor*.

## IV.iii

16 boy,] ~ ∧
33–34 *one line in* Q
42–43 Halfe...hand] *one line in* Q
46 th'ast∧] ~ ,
47 downe,] ~ ∧
48–50 I...life.] *prose in* Q
51 markes,] ~ ∧
52 white,] ~ ∧

53 flight.] ~ ∧
54 mine.] ~ ∧
72 hold,] ~ ∧
74 King,] ~ ∧
75 deaths,] ~ ∧
79 me,] ~ ∧
81 where;] ~ ∧

## IV.iv

4 Hast] Q(u); Ha'st Q(c)
7 *Cordo.*] *Gor.*
48 belly: what,] ~ , ~ ∧
55 Grace —] ~ ,
51–62 My...see!] *one line in* Q
63 Highnesse] Hignesse
67–68 My...her.] *one line in* Q
70 anon,] ~ ∧

73 eye.] ~ ∧
85 Paper,] ~ ∧
90 *vassaile.*] ~ ∧
95 Traytor,] ~ ∧
95 tell,] ~ ∧
105 I'th] i'th
130 Sir.] ~ ¿

## IV.v

6 Deadly:] ~ ,
13 fall:] ~ ,

14 person,] ~ ∧
15 poniards,] ~ ∧

## IV.vi

2 *Queen.*] *Qn.*
7 me!] ~ ∧
39 Hare,] Q(u); ~ ∧ Q(c)
59 writ! ...maze?] ~ , ... ~ !

62 done,] ~ ∧
67 hound,] ~ ∧
69 her∧] Q(u); ~ , Q(c)
70 downe∧] Q(u); ~ , Q(c)

## V.i

S.D. Malevento,] ~ ∧
21 with∧] Q(u); ~ , Q(c)

23 Well∧] Q(u); ~ , Q(c)
47 markes∧] Q(u); ~ , Q(c)

## V.ii

10 Yes,] Q(u); ~ ∧ Q(c)
14 Ime] Q(u); I'me Q(c)
23 thee,] ~ ∧
34–35 Ile...sicknesse.] *one line in* Q

35 here,] ~ ∧
43 me,] Q(u); ~ ! Q(c)
55–56 Ayme...thee.] *one line in* Q
60 confusion:] ~ ∧

61 King,] Q(u); ~ ! Q(c)
65 side,] Q(u); ~ , Q(c)
72 speakst,] Q(u); ~ , Q(c)
73 well,] ~ ,

75 *Vindicado's*] *Vindicadoes* Q(u); *Vindicados* Q(c)
77 thine,] Q(u); ~ ; Q(c)
77 *Tormiella*,] Q(u); ~ ! Q(c)

## V.iv

6 me,] Q(c¹); ~ ! Q(c²)
8 Angels.] Q(u); ~ ! Q(c²)

9 her,] ~ ,

## V.v

1 yet,] Q(u); ~ ! Q(c²)
6 hand.] Q(u); ~ ? Q(c²)
7 murdered,] Q(u); ~ , Q(c²)
10 preservation.] Q(u); ~ ! Q(c²)
13 vizors,] ~ ,
30 sir,] ~ ,

32–33 She...her.] *one line in* Q
37 Bawd,] ~ ,
40 paire,] ~ ,
53 honours,] ~ ,
55 not.] ~ ,
66 sorrow,] ~ .

# THE
# VIRGIN
## MARTIR,
### A
## TRAGEDIE.

AS IT HATH BIN DIVERS
times publickely Acted with great
Applause,

*By the seruants of his Maiesties Reuels.*

---

Written    { *Phillip Messenger* and }
by      { *Thomas Deker.* }

---

---

L ONDON,
Printed by *B. A.* for *Thomas*
*Iones.* **1 6 2 2.**

[Greg, 380 (a†)]

# THE
# VIRGIN
## MARTIR,
### A
## TRAGEDIE.

### AS IT HATH BIN DIVERS
times publickely Acted with great
Applause,

*By the seruants of his Maiesties Reuels.*

Written by *Phillip Messenger* and
*Thomas Decker.*

LONDON,
Printed by *Bernard Alsop* for *Thomas
Iones.* 1622.

# TEXTUAL INTRODUCTION

*The Virgin Martyr* by Dekker and Massinger (Greg, *Bibliography*, no. 380) was 'reformed' and licensed by Buc for the Red Bull on 6 October 1620; and was entered in the Stationers' Register to Thomas Jones on 7 December 1621. Jones's edition, printed by Bernard Alsop and dated 1622, would likely have appeared late in 1621 or early in 1622. G. E. Bentley, *The Jacobean Stage*, III, 265–266 usefully discusses the 1620 licensing.

The manuscript serving as printer's copy seems to have been a collection of papers written in two different hands, in large part coinciding with conventional estimates of the division by authorship. This manuscript was apparently not a theatrical one. No signs of professional intervention appear, and no one has troubled to remove the redundant character identifications from Dekker's stage-direction heading II.ii or the direction following II.iii.56.

It is evident that only one compositor set the type for this play: an examination of spelling and typographical characteristics discloses no such distinctions as can be remarked when more than one workman is present.[1] Moreover, distinctive broken types and the mixed fount that placed many roman capitals at the head of italic names demonstrates that only one set of type-cases was utilized.[2]

[1] The most marked typographical peculiarity concerns the variation in setting names in stage-directions in roman or in italic. So far as can be determined the practice is quite random and bears no relation either to authorial shares or to bibliographical units. For example, italic names appear in the directions at I.i.1 (B1), I.i.74 (B2), I.i.409 (C3$^v$); II.i.1 (C4$^v$); II.ii.1 (D3$^v$); II.iii.1 (E1); III.i.1 (G1), III.ii.22 (G1), III.ii.32 (G1$^v$); IV.i.59 (H3$^v$), IV.i.108 (H4$^v$), IV.i.169 (I1$^v$); IV.ii.1 (I1$^v$), IV.ii.61 (I2$^v$), IV.iii.131 (K2$^v$), IV.iii.187 (K3); V.i.1 (K3), V.i.38 (K3$^v$), V.i.56 (K4), V.i.84 (K4), V.i.122 (L1), V.i.156 (L1$^v$); V.ii.1 (L1$^v$), V.ii.62 (L2$^v$), V.ii.219 (M1), V.ii.238 (M1$^v$). On the other hand, the names are set in roman in the directions at I.i.23 (B1$^v$), I.i.118 (B3); II.i.86 (D1$^v$); II.iii.133 (E3$^v$); III.i.1 (F1$^v$), III.i.41 (F2); III.iii.1 (G3); IV.i.1 (H2$^v$); IV.ii.85 (I3), IV.ii.104 (I3$^v$); IV.iii.1 (I4), IV.iii.32 (I4$^v$), IV.iii.113 (K1$^v$), IV.iii.165 (K2$^v$). The difference in spelling *Hircius* as *Hercius* in the Persons and in the stage-direction at II.i.1 and II.iii.56 (with *Her.* as the speech-prefix at II.i.20 and II.iii.63) seems equally without significance.

[2] Not much can be told from the evidence of type-shortage enforcing the use of wrong-fount letters, for the italic fount of capitals was apparently in a somewhat mixed

This conclusion fits the pattern of the running-titles that suggests the use of only one press. The quarto was printed with two skeleton-formes that appear throughout in every sheet, the only unusual matter being the regularity with which, beginning with the transfer from sheet D to E, the skeletons interchange formes back and forth for each successive sheet, save for sheet L that follows the order of the formes in K. One may perhaps interpret this regular irregularity as indicating that the compositor was comfortably ahead of the press. The quarto collates A² B–L⁴ M². The press-variants indicate that half-sheets A and M were separately imposed and machined, a conclusion that the blanks A1 and M2 would also suggest and one confirmed by the running-title transfer from L2 to M1 and from L4ᵛ to M1ᵛ.

Since only one compositor was concerned with the typesetting, variable characteristics in the 'accidentals' that conform to the scene-division in the most conservative allocation of authorship by scenes may safely be regarded as due to differences in the respective portions of the underlying manuscript.

The question is, however, whether holograph papers constituted the printer's copy or whether the manuscript was a transcript of some sort of the holographs, either by one collaborator of the other's work, or by an independent scribe of the work of one or of both. Ordinarily the case would be undemonstrable and subject only to opinion. It is my own cautious conjecture that the amount of variation in *The Virgin Martyr* quarto may be too significant, and the kind of variation too minute, for us to believe that a scribal transcript formed the whole of the printer's copy. Minor variants like the double appearance of *Roome* (for *Rome*) in I.i, a Massinger scene,[1] or of *Dorothæa* (for *Dorothea*) twice at II.ii.43, 49, in a Dekker scene, may have no significance that can be assessed when further repetition is wanting. On the other hand, when in five out of six appearances in scenes that are certainly Dekker's one finds the spelling *Cesarea* versus the invariable *Cæsarea* in Massinger scenes,

condition when typesetting started, and hence some of the use of wrong-fount letters is quite arbitrary and without relation to necessity. At least, one can say that no evidence seems to exist to suggest the casting-off of copy and setting by formes.

[1] These seem to be compositorial, anyway: see below.

and, statistically, a very high proportion of hyphenated compounds in Dekker versus a very low proportion in Massinger, one is justified in assigning these differences to the varying characteristics of the printer's copy according to the authorship of the scenes. Once this hypothesis is established, such other characteristics as the appearance a few times of the apostrophus *I'am* in Dekker scenes but never in Massinger's, or possibly a high proportion in Dekker of *ile* to *Ile* in Massinger, may assume a significance that otherwise might not be felt.

The conservative assignment of scenes may be referred to Gifford, who on critical grounds allocated to Massinger I.i; III.i, ii; IV.i, iii; and V.ii; and to Dekker II.i, ii, iii; III.iii; IV.ii; V.i. With the possible exception of IV.i, iii, the characteristics of the accidentals in the 1622 quarto agree with Gifford's literary allocation. We may, therefore, temporarily set aside these two scenes and survey the evidence found in the remaining.

In Massinger's undoubted scenes (*i.e.* in I.i; III.i, ii; V.ii) we find the invariable spellings *Cæsarea*, *dietie* (for *deity*), *Emperour*, and *Gouernour* (except *Gouernor* in I.i.458). We also find some preference for *ere* (V.ii.136, 153, 198, 221) and *nere* (I.i.94; V.ii.9, 170, 234). On four occasions appears the form with the apostrophe *eu'n* (I.i.54, 237, 256; III.i.71). Although doubling of the vowel in pronouns may appear frequently in such contractions as *weele*, and so on, it is rare otherwise and is found only in *mee* (I.i.151). The contraction *ile* with lower-case appears only once (V.ii.204). Contractions involving *it* are rare: *do't* (I.i.242), *of't* (I.i.369), *on't* (I.i.401) and *wer't* (I.i.25). Hyphenation of compounds occurs only four times (III.i.153; III.ii.12; V.ii.36, 43). Only a slight use is made of the dash, and relatively few exclamation marks are employed. Punctuation seems to have been so light as to cause the compositor occasional difficulty in interpreting the desirable pointing.

In Dekker's undoubted scenes (*i.e.* in II.i, ii, iii; III.iii; IV, ii; V.i) we find five spellings *Cesarea* (II.ii.65; II.iii.26, 56 S.D.; IV.ii.69; V.i.3) to one of *Cæsarea* (II.iii.217), the single *Emperor* (II.iii.27), and two *Gouernor* (II.iii.56 S.D.; IV.ii.69). The word *deity* does not occur; no forms of *eu'n* with or without apostrophe appear; and there is only one *nere* (II.iii.106) and no *ere*. The doubled vowel in *mee* is printed twice (II.i.1, 50), in *wee* seven times (II.iii.122; III.iii.16, 71, 78, 161; IV.ii.105, 130), in *hee* four times (III.ii.161, 174, 181; V.i.72), in *shee* twice (III.iii.217; V.i.52); and in *bee* six times (II.i.24, 106, 190; II.ii.29; III.iii.62; IV.ii.51). The contraction *ile* occurs ten times (II.i.191; IV.ii.9, 50, 55; V.i.82, 134, 136, 142, 148, 150), and *i'me* once at V.i.132. Contractions of *it* are *doo't* twice (II.i.208; V.i.140), *on't* twice (III.iii.109, 202), *in't* once (V.i.130) and *ist* five times (II.iii.195 (twice); III.iii.2; V.i.1, 88). A contraction of *his* as *'s* is *in's* (III.iii.172). Other contractions are *ith'* five times (II.i.78; II.ii.39; III.iii.165; V.i.34, 138), *to'th* thrice (II.iii.5; V.i.35, 133), *ath'* twice (III.iii.195, 196), *thou't* once (IV.ii.13) and *y'are* very frequently. The word *a* is used for *of* in II.i.62. The apostrophus *I'am* appears thrice (II.iii.149, 247; IV.ii.87). In contrast to the four hyphenations in all of Massinger's scenes, nineteen are found in II.i, seven in II.ii, ten in II.iii, nine in III.iii, five in IV.ii, and ten in V.i. A marked use is made of the dash, and the exclamation point is liberally employed. Punctuation does not appear to be noticeably light.

When we survey the characteristics of IV.i, we find from Massinger's list the spelling *dieties* (line 2), which—since the word does not appear in Dekker's undoubted scenes—may or may not be compositorial; and we find the spelling *Gouernour* (line 170). On the other hand, from Dekker's list we have the somewhat doubtful value *shee* (line 33). More important, five exclamation marks are used (lines 21, 89, 137, 151, 181), and three hyphenated compounds (lines 51, 88, 117). What may be a typical Dekker spelling *bonefire* (line 114) occurs (see III.iii.146), and in *Phlegmatike* (line 112) a *k* spelling not found in the Massinger scenes but present in *Arithmatike* (II.iii.9) and *Zodiake* (III.iii.143) by Dekker. Stronger evidence comes in the contractions, however, for in this one scene we have *too't* (line 78), *i'th* (line 139), *doo't* (lines 142, 152, 156), *bi'th* (line 165), and *too'th* (line 183).

In the language employed, a Massinger-scene phrase is repeated in *powers I serue* at line 179 (see I.i.18). Both writers have joined in applying the label *witch* of line 172 (see Massinger, III.i.2, V.ii.56; Dekker, IV.ii.136) or *sorceress* of line 60 (see Massinger, III.i.2; Dekker II.iii.91) to Dorothea. Dekker had used the word *pash* (line 140) at II.ii.59; and had liberally *whored* Dorothea (line 75) as in II.iii.115 and IV.ii.96. More important, the phrase *proud Thing* applied to her (line 75 and see line 149) was repeated from Dekker's II.iii.171–172, 'let not this Christian *Thing*, in this her pageantry | Of prowd deriding...'. At V.i.74 Angelo, though with different intent, is called a *Thing*. The word *a* is used for *of* or *on* (line 96), a usage that an independent study made of Massinger's linguistic characteristics does not record as present in his unaided plays.[1]

In IV.iii we have what seems to be the characteristic Massinger-scene *eu'n* (line 75)[2] and a spelling *Karkasse* (line 184) that is found later in V.ii.22.[3] The *power* Dorothea *serves* (lines 52, 90, 127) can, as in IV.i, be compared to Massinger's I.i.18. The idiom *to me* as in lines 12, 73, and 76 may be paralleled in Massinger's I.i.422, 425, although Dekker's II.iii.38 must be noticed. Massinger had applied *Apostata* (line 63) to Dorothea in III.i.28, and to Antoninus in V.ii.52, and the word is used in *Believe As You List*. On the other hand, although little weight may be placed on the spelling *bee* (line 72), the form *ile* (line 185) might suggest Dekker, as might *ist* (line 128) and the two exclamation marks (lines 12, 113). The references to Dorothea as a witch (lines 116, 123) are not distinctive. That she is a 'prowd contemner | Of vs and of our gods' (lines 50–51) is very like Dekker's II.iii.171–172 quoted above in connexion with IV.i. And Theophilus on Harpax affected by Angelo, 'He is distracted and I must not loose him' (line 122) parallels Theophilus to Harpax, 'I will not loose thee then, her to confound' in Dekker's II.ii.85.

Since both the language and the accidental characteristics of IV.i resemble those found in scenes that are Dekker's, and the characteristics of Massinger scenes are so weak and uncertain, it may be that the scene should be assigned wholly to Dekker, to whom one

---

[1] Cyrus Hoy, 'The Shares of Fletcher and his Collaborators in the Beaumont and Fletcher Canon (I)', *Studies in Bibliography*, VIII (1956), 145.

[2] Although found in other printed texts, like *The Bondman*, this form does not appear in the manuscript *Believe As You List*, or *The Duke of Milan* printed by Alsop a year later than the *Martyr*. However, the infrequency of this word's occurrence in elided form in both plays makes for doubt about their value as evidence, except negatively.

[3] On the evidence of *Believe As You List*, this spelling seems to be compositorial and of doubtful value. See below.

24-2

would wish, surely, to give the British-slave speeches at the very least. However, it is the function of the critical editor and commentator of this edition to decide questions of authorship, and the point is raised here in the textual introduction only in connexion with the enquiry into the nature of the printer's copy. Hence if literary critics on stylistic and parallel-passage evidence decide that there are well-grounded signs of Massinger in IV.i, the characteristics of the printed text would suggest the conjecture that in this scene Dekker had rewritten a Massinger version.

It will be noticed that Dekker was responsible solely for scenes involving Hircius and Spungius, but that he was not confined to such scenes, on the evidence of II.ii and V.i; and in fact the lines devoted to Dorothea and her associates in II.i and II.iii outweigh the low-comedy sections. Thus if Massinger were responsible for all of Act I, and Dekker for all of Act II, and Act V were split between the two, we should expect something of an equal division of major responsibility in Acts III and IV. Act III, except for the Hircius-Spungius III.iii is, indeed, Massinger's for the remaining two scenes. Thus we might expect Dekker to have been responsible for two of the three scenes in Act IV, and, so supported, add to undoubted IV.ii the IV.i scene in which his hand seems to be present.

The accidental characteristics of the Dekker scenes are very slight in IV.iii and perhaps ought not to be taken seriously were it not for the parallel language that Theophilus used of Harpax and possibly the reference to Dorothea as *prowd*. If Dekker may be associated with this probable Massinger scene on literary grounds, the evidence would suggest that he merely touched it up. Whether in the process he copied it out fair would be doubtful, certainly.

If then such variation in accidental characteristics between scenes as betray the hands of two different authors may be detected throughout the 1622 quarto, the question arises whether the single compositor set from the holograph papers of these two authors, from a transcript of both, or from a transcript only of one. That such small distinguishing characteristics as the spellings *Cesarea* or *Cæsarea*, and the use of hyphens in compounds (perhaps the two strongest pieces of evidence) would survive scribal transcription and then compositorial typesetting could be questionable; but such an argument is no more than an appeal to general probability and can scarcely qualify as evidence.

In a collaboration one author may transcribe the other's foul papers to make a fair copy to deliver to the theatre, but such a process should give us more of a mixture of characteristics than we find in *The Virgin Martyr* save perhaps in the two somewhat doubtful scenes IV.i and IV.iii. That one author, or both, should hire a scribe to copy out his portion fair is possible but not wholly probable. Thus if the distinction of characteristics noticed in the various scenes of *The Virgin Martyr* is valid, the odds are it should stem from the use of the holographs of the two dramatists as printer's copy. Of Dekker's dramatic composition in manuscript we have only the *More* scene, too little to assist us greatly;[1] but of Massinger we have the holograph manuscript play *Believe As You List*, though written out about eleven years later than the manuscript for *The Virgin Martyr*.

On the positive side this manuscript contains not one hyphenated compound or dash, and its spelling of *Ile* is invariably with a capital. Some, but not any extraordinary number of exclamation marks are present. In a scattering of spellings it and the Massinger scenes of the quarto are in some agreement, although—as one would expect—the disagreement is more frequent. If the printer's copy for the *Martyr* was a Massinger holograph, then such spellings as *Roome* (I.i.124, 229), *exspect* (I.i.235), *exscusde* (I.i.394) are compositorial. If the single evidence of *deitie* in *Believe As You List* (Malone Society, line 525) is trustworthy, the invariable use of *dietie* in the *Martyr* must also be compositorial; and hence its appearance in IV.i cannot be used as evidence for Massinger. Similarly, on the evidence of *Believe's* three-times spelling *carkase(s)*, the Martyr spelling *Karkasses* at IV.iii.184 and V.ii.22 has no significance as evidence for Massinger's hand. Again, if the *Martyr* scenes by Massinger were holograph in the printer's copy, the appearance of the form *eu'n* may be compositorial, although the very few occurrences of *euen* in *Believe* are doubtless insufficient to determine the facts.

[1] However, from Dekker's printed texts it is certain that he freely hyphenated compounds as a constant characteristic.

On the whole, the decision is not easy. *The Virgin Martyr* betrays few positive characteristics of the Massinger accidentals as seen in *Believe As You List*;[1] and hence what chiefly distinguish the Massinger scenes in the *Martyr* are what may be called the non-Dekker, or negative characteristics presenting the obverse of the Dekker scenes. Yet probability lies with the view that insufficient contrary direct evidence exists in the accidentals of the Massinger scenes in the print[2] to discount these conclusions: (1) significant variations exist in some characteristics between scenes of different authorship; and (2) the overall evidence is clearly against the possibility that one dramatist copied out the other's work as a regular procedure.[3] Under these conditions we have remaining the choice of conjecturing either that the printer's copy was the combined foul papers of the two authors or else that it was a scribal transcript of such papers. Simplicity argues for the first; in favour of the second is the oddity that there are not more distinguishing characteristics in the accidentals of the two men and the oddity that the specific characteristics found in *Believe As You List* are scarcely perceptible in the *Martyr* print. Although we may perhaps feel that the foul-papers hypothesis is slightly preferable, on the whole, it must be admitted that only a provisional decision is possible so long as we want a detailed study of the compositor who set *The Virgin Martyr*.

The press-variants during the course of printing indicate only casual proof-reading. When the obvious error of *reader* for *readier* was not noticed at I.i.474, but a comma added as the proof-reader's contribution, we have sufficient evidence that copy was not con-

[1] *The Duke of Milan*, printed by Alsop in 1623, shows few more, in fact, and exhibits somewhat different variations, as in the usual forms *ne're* and *e're* for the invariable *nere* and *ere* of *Believe* and the *Martyr*. Despite a number of common spelling characteristics, it may be doubtful whether this play and the *Martyr* were set by the same compositor.

[2] On the evidence of *Believe As You List*, the increase in doubled vowels as in *mee*, *hee*, *bee*, and so on, in the *Martyr* Dekker scenes as against the Massinger scenes must be fortuitous if a manuscript resembling *Believe* served as printer's copy, for these doubled forms are invariable in the holograph. Closer examination shows that the highest incidence of these in the Dekker scenes occurs in the prose, where perhaps the doubling is a justification device, although the forms are not unknown in the verse.

[3] The final caution is intended to take care of the possibility that the mixed characteristics seen in IV.i, iii resulted from just such authorial copying.

sulted, at least with any regularity. It could be argued that the change from *Directly* to *Deiectedly* at I.i.253 could have required the suggestion of the copy; but it is by no means impossible for the correction to have been an inspired guess. The lack of parallelism between the particular forme of a sheet corrected and the forme that, according to the running-title pattern, ought to have gone first through the press suggests the possibility that formes like corrected B(o), G(o), I(i), and L(i), at the least, represent a second round of proof-reading and not the original correction.

The quartos of 1631 (Q2), 1651 (Q3), and 1661 (Q4) are mere reprints, each of its immediate predecessor, and hence without authority. An additional scene licensed on 7 July 1624 (Chambers, *Elizabethan Stage*, III, 298; Bentley, *Jacobean Stage*, I, 174–175) never found its way into print.

*The Virgin Martyr* was first edited by Thomas Coxeter in vol. I of *The Dramatic Works of Mr Philip Massinger* (1759), then by John Monck Mason in the *Works*, vol. I (1779), and then by William Gifford in vol. I of *The Plays of Philip Massinger* (1805, revised 1813). The bowdlerized edition of 1831 in Harper's Family Library is of no consequence. In 1840 the play appeared as part of *The Dramatic Works of Massinger and Ford*, edited by Hartley Coleridge; and in 1887 in vol. II of *Philip Massinger*, edited in the Mermaid Series by Arthur Symons. Earlier, in 1868 Francis Cunningham included it in his edition of Gifford's *Plays*. Emendations first made by any of these editions have been recorded when the reading was not first adopted in one of the quartos.

The present text is based on a collation of the following ten copies, all that have been recorded by Greg as preserved: British Museum copy 1 (644.f.1), copy 2 (162.d.19), copy 3 (Ashley 1110), and copy 4 (1077.k.4); Bodleian copy 1 (Douce M.671) and copy 2 (Mal. 233[4]); Dyce Collection in the Victoria and Albert Museum copy 1 (Dyce 25.A.103) and copy 2 (Dyce 25.A.104); Henry E. Huntington Library copy 1 (17644) and copy 2 (17644a). The Historical Collation was made up from the Folger Shakespeare Library copies of Q2 (1631), Q3 (1651), and Q4 (1661).

# THE ACTORS NAMES.

DIOCLESIAN
MAXIMINUS } Emperours of Rome

A King of Pontus

A King of Epire

A King of Macedon

SAPRITIUS, Gouernour of Cæsaria

THEOPHILUS, a zealous persecutor of the Christians

SEMPRONIUS, Captaine of Sapritius Guards

ANTONINUS, sonne to Sapritius

MACRINUS, friend to Antoninus

HARPAX an euill spirit, following Theophilus in the shape of a
Secretary

ARTEMIA, daughter to Dioclesian

CALISTE
CHRISTETA, } Daughters to Theophilus

DOROTHEA, The Virgin Martyr

ANGELO, a good spirit, serving Dorothea in the habite of a Page

A Brittish Slaue

HIRCIUS, a Whoremaster
SPUNGIUS, a Drunkard, } Seruants to Dorothea

A Priest to Iupiter

Officers and Executioners

[Doctors
Geta and Iulianus, servants to Theophilus]

## The Virgin Martir.

### ACTUS PRIMUS, Scena i

*Enter* Theophilus, Harpax.

*Theoph.*  Come to *Cæsarea* to night?
*Harpax.*                         Most true Sir.
*Theoph.*  The Emperour in person?
*Harpax.*                         Do I liue?
*Theoph.*  Tis wondrous strange, the marches of great Princes
Like to the motions of prodigious Meteors,
Are step, by step obseru'd, and lowd tong'd Fame
The harbinger to prepare their entertainment:
And were it possible, so great an armie,
Though couer'd with the night, could be so neere:
The Gouernour cannot be so vnfriended
Among the many that attend his person,                    10
But by some secret meanes he should haue notice
Of *Cæsars* purpose, in this then excuse me
If I appeare incredulous.
*Harpax.*                At your pleasure.
*Theoph.*  Yet when I call to mind you neuer faild me
In things more difficult, but haue discouered
Deeds that were done thousand leagues distant from me,
When neither woods, nor caues, nor secret vaults,
No nor the power they serue, could keep these Christians,
Or from my reach or punishment, but thy magicke
Still layd them open: I begin againe                       20
To be as confident as heretofore.
It is not possible thy powerfull art
Should meete a checke, or fayle.

12 purpose, in this$_\wedge$] Mason; $\sim$ $_\wedge$ $\sim$ $\sim$ , Q 1-4

*Enter a Priest with the image of Iupiter,* Caliste, Christeta.

*Harpax.* Looke on these vestals,
The holy pledges that the gods haue giu'n you,
Your chast faire daughters. Wer't not to vpbraid
A seruice to a maister not vnthankfull,
I could say these in spite of your preuention,
Seduc'd by an imagin'd faith, not reason,
(Which is the strength of Nature) quite forsaking
The Gentile gods, had yeelded vp themselues               30
To this new found religion. This I crosd,
Discouerd their intentions, taught you to vse
With gentle words and milde perswasions,
The power, and the authority of a father
Set of with cruell threats, and so reclaimd em,
And whereas they with torments should haue dy'd,
(Hels furies to me had they vndergone it)                 *Aside.*
They are now votaries in great *Iupiters* temple,
And by his Priest instructed, growne familiar
With all the Mysteries, nay the most abstruse ones        40
Belonging to his Dietie.
*Theoph.* Twas a benefit
For which I euer owe you, Haile *Ioues Flamen,*
Haue these my daughters reconcilde themselues
(Abandoning for euer the Christian way)
To your opinion.
*Priest.* And are constant in it,
They teach their teachers with their depth of iudgement,
And are with arguments able to conuert
The enemies to our gods, and answer all
They can obiect against vs.
*Theoph.* My deere daughters.
*Caliste.* We dare dispute against this new sprung sect   50
In priuate or in publicke.
*Harpax.* My best Lady.
Perseuer in it.

*27 these ₐ] Mason; this ₐ Q 1-4 [~ , Q 3-4]      51 in] Q 3; *om.* Q 1-2

*Christeta.*        And what we maintaine
We will seale with our bloods.
*Harpax.*                        Braue resolution.
I eu'n grow fat to see my labors prosper.
*Theoph.* I yong againe: to your deuotions.
*Harpax.*                        Doe —
My prayers be present with you.
                                *Exeunt Priest and daughters.*
*Theoph.*                Oh my *Harpax.*
  Thou engine of my wishes, thou that steeldst
  My bloody resolutions, thou that armst
  My eyes gainst womanish teares and soft compassion,
  Instructing me without a sigh to looke on            60
  Babes torne by violence from their mothers brests
  To feed the fire, and with them make one flame:
  Old men as beasts, in beasts skins torne by dogs:
  Virgins and matrons tire the executioners,
  Yet I vnsatisfied thinke their torments easie.
*Harpax.* And in that iust, not cruell.
*Theoph.*                Weare all scepters
  That grace the hands of kings made into one,
  And offerd me, all crownes layd at my feete,
  I would contemne them all, thus spit at them,
  So I to all posterities might be cald                70
  The strongest champion of the Pagan gods
  And rooter out of Christians.
*Harpax.*                Oh mine owne,
  Mine owne deere Lord, to further this great worke
  I euer liue thy slaue.

                *Enter* Sapritius *and* Sempronius.

*Theoph.*            No more, the Gouernour.
*Sapr.*  Keepe the ports close, and let the guards be doubl'd,
  Disarme the Christians, call it death in any
  To weare a sword, or in his house to haue one.

      55 againe:] Q3; ~ ₐ Q1-2        66 Weare] *i.e.* were

                        379

*Semp.*  I shall be carefull Sir.

*Sapr.*                    It will well become you.
  Such as refuse to offer sacrifice
  To any of our gods, put to the torture.                          80
  Grub vp this growing mischiefe by the roots,
  And know when we are mercifull to them,
  We to our selues are cruell.

*Semp.*                    You poure oyle
  On fire that burnes already at the height,
  I know the Emperours Edict and my charge,
  And they shall find no fauour.

*Theoph.*                    My good Lord,
  This care is timely, for the entertainment
  Of our great maister, who this night in person
  Comes here to thanke you.

*Sapr.*                    Who the Emperour?

*Harpax.*  To cleere your doubts, he does return in triumph,          90
  Kings lackying by his triumphant Chariot,
  And in this glorious victory my Lord,
  You haue an ample share: for know your sonne,
  The nere enough commended *Antoninus*,
  So well hath fleshd his maiden sword, and died
  His snowy plumes so deepe in enemies blood,
  That besides publicke grace, beyond his hopes,
  There are rewards propounded.

*Sapr.*                    I would know
  No meane in thine could this be true.

*Harpax.*  My head answer the forfeit.

*Sapr.*                    Of his victory          100
  There was some rumor, but it was assurd
  The army passd a full dayes iourney higher
  Into the countrey.

*Harpax.*          It was so determin'd,
  But for the further honor of your sonne,
  And to obserue the gouerment of the citty,
  And with what rigor, or remisse indulgence

*97 hopes,] Q3; ~ ∧ Q1-2

The Christians are pursude he makes his stay here.
For proofe his trumpets speake his neere arriuall.

> *Trumpets a farre of.*

*Sapr.*   Haste good *Sempronius*, draw vp our guards,
And with all ceremonious pompe receiue                              110
The conquering army. Let our garrison speake
Their welcome in lowd shouts, the citie shew
Her state and wealth.
*Semp.*              I am gone              *Exit* Sempronius.
*Sapr.*              O I am rauish'd
With this great honour, cherish good *Theophilus*
This knowing scholler, send for your faire daughters,
I will present them to the Emperour,
And in their sweet conuersion, as a mirror
Expresse your zeale and duty.              *A lessen of Cornets.*
*Theoph.*              Fetch them good *Harpax.*

*A guard brought in by* Sempronius, *souldiers leading in three kings
bound,* Antoninus *and* Macrinus *carrying the Emperors Egles,*
Dioclesian *with a guilt laurell on his head, leading in* Artemia,
Sapritius *kisses the Emperors hand, then embraces his sonne,*
Harpax *brings in* Caliste *and* Christeta, *lowd showts.*

*Diocle.*   So at all parts I finde *Cæsarea*
Compleatly gouernd, the licentious souldier                              120
Confin'd in modest limits, and the people
Taught to obey, and not compeld with rigor;
The ancient Roman discipline reuiu'd,
(Which raysde *Roome* to her greatnes, and proclaimd her
The glorious mistresse of the conquerd world)
But aboue all the seruice of the gods
So zealously obseru'd, that (good *Sapritius*)
In words to thanke you for your care and duty
Were much vnworthy *Dioclesians* honor
Or his magnificence to his loyall seruants.
But I shall find a time with noble titles                              130
To recompence your merits.

115 for] Gifford; *om.* Q 1–4

*Sapr.*                    Mightiest *Cæsar*
Whose power vpon this globe of earth, is equall
To *Ioues* in heauen, whose victorious triumphs
On prowd rebellious Kings that stir against it
Are perfit figures of his immortall trophees
Wonne in the gyants war, whose conquering sword
Guided by his strong arme, as deadly kils
As did his thunder, all that I haue done,
Or if my strength were centupld could do,                    140
Comes short of what my loyalty must challenge.
But if in any thing I haue deseru'd
Great *Cæsars* smile, tis in my humble care
Still to preserue the honour of those gods,
That make him what he is: my zeale to them
I euer haue expressd in my fell hate
Against the Christian sect, that with one blow,
Ascribing all things to an vnknowne power,
Would strike downe all their temples, and allowes them
Nor sacrifice nor altars.
*Diocle.*                    Thou in this                    150
Walkest hand in hand with mee, my will and power
Shall not alone confirme, but honor all
That are in this most forward.
*Sapr.*                    Sacred *Cæsar*;
If your imperiall Maiestie stand pleasd
To showre your fauours vpon such as are
The boldest champions of our religion,
Looke on this reuerend man, to whom the power
Of serching out, and punishing such delinquents,
Was by your choyce committed, and for proofe
He hath deseru'd the grace imposd vpon him,                    160
And with a fayre and euen hand proceeded
Partiall to none, not to himselfe, or those
Of equall neerenesse to himselfe, behold
This paire of Virgins.
*Diocle.*                    What are these?

147 blow,] Q3; ~ ˌ Q1-2

*Sapr.*                    His daughters.

*Artemia.*   Now by your sacred fortune they are faire ones,
Exceeding faire ones, would 'twere in my power
To make them mine.

*Theoph.*              They are the gods, great Lady,
They were most happy in your seruice else,
On these when they fell from their fathers faith
I vsde a iudges power, entreaties failing                    170
(They being seduc'd) to win them to adore
The holy powers we worship, I put on
The scarlet robe of bold authority,
And as they had bin strangers to my blood,
Presented them in the most horrid forme
All kind of tortures, part of which they sufferd
With Roman constancy.

*Artemia.*               And could you endure,
Being a father, to behold their limbs
Extended on the racke?

*Theoph.*             I did, but must
Confesse there was a strange contention in me,           180
Betweene the impartiall office of a Iudge,
And pitty of a father; to helpe Iustice
Religion stept in, vnder which ods
Compassion fell: yet still I was a father,
For euen then, when the flinty hangmans whips
Were worne with stripes spent on their tender limbs,
I kneeld, and wept, and begd them though they would
Be cruell to themselues, they would take pittie
On my gray haires. Now note a sodaine change,
Which I with joy remember, those whom torture             190
Nor feare of death could terrifie, were orecome
By seeing of my suffrings, and so wonne,
Returning to the faith that they were borne in,
I gaue them to the gods, and be assurde
I that vsde iustice with a rigorous hand
Vpon such beauteous virgins, and mine owne,
Will vse no fauour where the cause commands me

To any other, but as rocks be deafe
To all intreaties.
*Diocle.*                    Thou deseru'st thy place,
Still hold it and with honor, things thus orderd                    200
Touching the gods tis lawfull to descend
To human cares, and exercise that power
Heauen has conferd vpon me, which that you
Rebels and traytors to the power of *Rome*
Should not with all extremities vndergoe,
What can you vrge to qualifie your crimes
Or mitigate my anger?
*Epire.*                    We are now
Slaues to thy power, that yesterday were kings,
And had command ore others, we confesse
Our grandsires payd yours tribute, yet left vs,                    210
As their forefathers had, desire of freedome.
And if you Romans hold it glorious honor
Not onely to defend what is your owne.
But to enlarge your Empire, (though our fortune
Denies that happinesse) who can accuse
The famishd mouth if it attempt to feed,
Or such whose fetters eate into their freedomes,
If they desire to shake them off.
*Pontus.*                    We stand
The last examples to proue how vncertaine
All humane happinesse is, and are prepard                    220
To endure the worst.
*Macedon.*                    That spoake which now is highest
In *Fortunes* wheele, must when she turns it next
Decline as low as we are. This consider'd
Taught the Egyptian *Hercules*, *Sesostris*
(That had his chariot drawne by captiue kings)
To free them from that slauery, but to hope
Such mercy from a Roman, were meere madnesse.
We are familiar with what cruelty
*Roome* since her infant greatnesse, euer vsde
Such as she triumphd ouer, age nor sexe                    230

384

Exempted from her tyranny: scepterd Princes
Kept in your common dungeons, and their children
In scorne traind vp in base Mechanicke arts
For publicke bondmen; in the catologue
Of those vnfortunate men, we exspect to haue
Our names remembred.

*Diocle.*        In all growing Empires
Eu'n cruelty is vsefull, some must suffer
And be set vp examples to strike terror
In others though far of, but when a State
Is raysde to her perfection, and her Bases                240
Too firme, to shrinke, or yeeld, we may vse mercy
And do't with safety, but to whom? not cowards?
Or such whose basenesse shames the conqueror,
And robs him of his victorie, as weake *Perseus*
Did great *Æmilius.* Know therefore kings
Of *Epire, Pontus,* and of *Macedon,*
That I with courtesie can vse my prisoners
As well as make them mine by force, prouided
That they are noble enemies: such I found you
Before I made you mine, and since you were so,      250
You haue not lost the courages of Princes,
Although the Fortune: had you borne your selues
Deiectedly, and base, no slauery
Had beene too easie for you, but such is
The power of noble valour, that we loue it
Eu'n in our enemies, and taken with it,
Desire to make them friends, as I will you.
*Epire.*   Mocke vs not *Cæsar.*
*Diocle.*                    By the Gods I do not.
Vnloosse their bonds, I now as friends embrace you,
Giue them their Crownes againe.
*Pontus.*                    We are twice ouercome,      260
By courage and by courtesie.
*Macedon.*                    But this latter
Shall teach vs to liue euer faithfull Vassals
To *Dioclesian* and the power of *Rome.*

*Epire.* All Kingdomes fall before her.
*Pontus.* And all Kings
Contend to honour *Cesar*.
*Diocle.* I beleeue
Your tongues are the true Trumpets of your hearts,
And in it I most happy. Queene of fate,
Imperious *Fortune* mixe some light disaster
With my so many ioyes to season em,
And giue them sweeter rellish, I am girt round                    270
With true felicity, faithfull subiects heare,
Heare bold Commanders, heere with new made friends,
But what's the crowne of all in thee *Artemia*,
My only child whose loue to me and duty
Striue to exceede each other.
*Artemia.* I make payment
But of a debt which I stand bound to tender
As a daughter, and a subiect.
*Diocle.* Which requires yet
A retribution from me *Artemia*
Tyde by a fathers care how to bestow
A iewell of all things to me most pretious.                     280
Nor will I therefore longer keepe thee from
The chiefe ioyes of creation, mariage rites,
Which that thou mayst with greater pleasure tast of,
Thou shalt not like with mine eyes but thine owne.
Amongst these kings forgetting they were captiues,
Or these remembring not they are my subiects,
Make choyce of any, by *Ioues* dreadfull thunder
My will shall ranke with thine.
*Artemia.* It is a bounty
The daughters of great Princes seldome meete with.
For they, to make vp breaches in the state,                     290
Or for some other politicke ends are forc'd
To match where they affect not, may my life
Deserue this fauour.

271–272 heare, | Heare] Q 1 (u); here, | Here Q 1 (c)

*Diocle.*                    Speake, I long to know
The man thou wilt make happy.
*Artemia.*                    If that titles
Or the adored name of Queene could take me,
Here would I fixe mine eyes and looke no farther.
But these are baites to take a meane borne Lady,
Not her that boldly may call *Cæsar* father.
In that I can bring honor vnto any
But from no king that liues receiue addition,                    300
To raise desert and vertue by my fortune,
Though in a low estate, were greater glory,
Then to mixe greatnesse with a Prince that owes
No worth but that name onely.
*Diocle.*                    I commend thee,
Tis like thy selfe.
*Artemia.*                    If then of men beneath me
My choyce is to be made, where shall I seeke
But among those that best deserue from you,
That haue seru'd you most faithfully, that in dangers
Haue stood next to you, that haue interposd
Their brests as shields of proofe to dull the swords                    310
Aimd at your bosome, that haue spent their blood
To crowne your browes with Lawrell.
*Macr.*                    *Citherea*
Great Queene of loue be now propitious to me.
*Harpax.*   Now marke what I foretold.        [*To* Sapritius.]
*Anton.*                    Her eyes on me,
Faire *Venus* sonne draw forth a leaden dart,
And that she may hate me, transfixe her with it,
Or if thou needs wilt vse a golden one,
Shoote in the behalfe of any other,
Thou knowst I am thy votary else where.
*Artemia.*   Sir.
*Theoph.*   How he blushes!
*Sapr.*                    Welcome, foole, thy fortune,                    320
Stand like a blocke when such an Angell courts thee.

300 receiue] Coxeter; receiues Q 1–4

*Artemia.* I am no obiect to diuert your eye
From the beholding.
*Anton.*            Rather a bright Sun
Too glorious for him to gaze vpon
That tooke not first flight from the Egles aeiry.
As I looke on the temples, or the gods,
And with that reuerence Lady I behold you,
And shall do euer.
*Artemia.*            And it will become you,
While thus we stand at distance, but if loue
(Loue borne out of th'assurance of your vertues)                330
Teach me to stoope so low —
*Anton.*            O rather take
A higher flight.
*Artemia.*        Why, feare you to be raisd?
Say I put off the dreadfull awe that waits
On Maiestie, or with you share my beames,
Nay make you to outshine me, change the name
Of subiect into Lord, rob you of seruice
Thats due from you to me, and in me make it
Duty to honor you, would you refuse me?
*Anton.* Refuse you Madam, such a worme as I am,
Refuse, what kings vpon their knees would sue for?                340
Call it, great Lady, by another name,
An humble modesty that would not match
A Molehill with *Olimpus.*
*Artemia.*            He that's famous
For honourable actions in the warre,
As you are *Antoninus,* a prou'd soldier
Is fellow to a king.
*Anton.*            If you loue valour,
As 'tis a kingly vertue, seeke it out,
And cherish it in a king, there it shines brightest,
And yeelds the brauest lustre. Looke on *Epire,*
A Prince, in whom it is incorporate,                350
And let it not disgrace him, that he was

332 Why,] Gifford; ~ ₐ Q 1-4

388

Orecome by *Cæsar*, (it was a victory
To stand so long against him,) had you seene him,
How in one bloody scene he did discharge
The parts of a Commander, and a souldier,
Wise in direction, bold in execution;
You would haue sayd, great *Cæsars* selfe excepted,
The world yeelds not his equall.
*Artemia.*                              Yet I haue heard,
Encountring him alone in the head of his troope,
You tooke him prisoner.
*Epire.*                    Tis a truth great Princesse.                360
Ile not detract from valour.
*Anton.*                        Twas meere fortune,
Courage had no hand in it.
*Theoph.*                      Did euer man
Striue so against his owne good.
*Sapr.*                          Spiritlesse villaine,
How I am tortur'd, by the immortall gods
I now could kill him.
*Diocle.*              Hold *Sapritius* hold,
On our displeasure hold.
*Harpax.*                  Why, this would make
A father mad, tis not to be endur'd,
Your honours tainted in it.
*Sapr.*                    By heauen it is,
I shall thinke of't.
*Harpax.*              Tis not to be forgotten.
*Artemia.*   Nay kneele not Sir, I am no rauisher,          370
Nor so farre gone in fond affection to you,
But that I can retire, my honour safe.
Yet say hereafter that thou hast neglected
What but seene in possession of another
Will runne thee mad with enuy.
*Anton.*                        In her lookes
Reuenge is written.
*Macr.*                As you loue your life
Study t'appease her.

*Anton.*                    Gratious madame heare me.
*Artemia.*    And be againe refusd?
*Anton.*                    The tender of
My life, my seruice, or since you vouchsafe it,
My loue, my heart, my all, and pardon me:                    380
Pardon dread Princesse that I made some scruple
To leaue a valley of securitie
To mount vp to the hill of Maiestie,
On which the neerer *Ioue* the neerer lightning.
What knew I but your grace made triall of me?
Durst I presume to embrace, where but to touch
With an vnmannerd hand was death? the Foxe
When he saw first the forrests king, the Lyon,
Was almost dead with feare, the second view
Onely a little danted him, the third                    390
He durst salute him boldly: pray you apply this,
And you shall find a little time will teach me
To looke with more familiar eyes vpon you
Then duty yet allowes me.
*Sapr.*                    Well exscusde.
*Artemia.*    You may redeeme all yet.
*Diocle.*                    And that he may
Haue meanes and opportunity to do so,
*Artemia* I leaue you my substitute
In faire *Cæsarea.*
*Sapr.*          And here as your selfe
We will obey and serue her.
*Diocle.*                    *Antoninus*
So you proue hers I wish no other heire,                    400
Thinke on't, be carefull of your charge *Theophilus,*
*Sapritius* be you my daughters guardian.
Your company I wish confederate Princes
In our Dalmatian wars, which finished
With victorie I hope, and *Maximinus*
Our brother and copartner in the Empire

379 or] Q1 (u); not Q1 (c)          *389 dead] Q2; drad Q1

At my request wonne to confirme as much,
The kingdomes I tooke from you weele restore,
And make you greater than you were before.

   *Exeunt omnes, manent* Antoninus *and* Macrinus.

*Anton.* Oh I am lost, for euer lost *Macrinus*,    410
The anchor of the wretched, hope forsakes me,
And with one blast of fortune all my light
Of happinesse is put out.
*Macr.*     You are like to those
That are ill onely, cause they are too well,
That surfetting in the excesse of blessings
Call their abundance want: what could you wish,
That is not falne vpon you? honour, greatnesse,
Respect, wealth, fauour, the whole world for a dowre,
And with a Princesse, whose excelling forme
Exceedes her fortune.
*Anton.*    Yet poyson still is poyson   420
Though drunke in gold, and all these flattring glories
To me, ready to starue, a painted banquet
And no essentiall foode: when I am scorchd
With fire, can flames in any other quench me?
What is her loue to me, greatnes, or Empire,
That am slaue to another, who alone
Can giue me ease or freedome?
*Macr.*     Sir you point at
Your dotage on the scornfull *Dorothea*,
Is she though faire the same day to be nam'd
With best *Artemia*? in all their courses    430
Wisemen propose their ends: with sweete *Artemia*
There comes along pleasure, security,
Vsher'd by all that in this life is precious:
With *Dorothea*, though her birth be noble,
The Daughter to a Senator of *Rome*,
By him left rich (yet with a priuate wealth

   410 lost, for euer~A~] ~ ~A~ ~ ~ , Q 1-4

And farre inferiour to yours) arriues
The Emperours frowne (which like a mortall plague
Speakes death is neere) the Princesse heauy scorne,
Vnder which you will shrinke, your fathers fury, 440
Which to resist euen piety forbids,
And but remember that she stands suspected
A fauourer of the Christian Sect, she brings
Not danger but assured destruction with her:
This truely wai'd, one smile of great *Artemia*
Is to be cherish't and prefer'd before
All ioyes in *Dorothea*, therefore leaue her.
*Anton.* In what thou think'st thou art most wise, thou art
Grosely abus'd *Macrinus*, and most foolish.
For any man to match aboue his ranke, 450
Is but to sell his liberty; with *Artemia*
I still must liue a seruant, but enioying
Diuinest *Dorothea*, I shall rule,
Rule as becomes a husband; for the danger,
Or call it if you will assur'd destruction,
I sleight it thus. If then thou art my friend,
As I dare sweare thou art, and wilt not take
A Gouernors place vpon thee, be my helper.
*Macr.* You know I dare and will doe any thing.
Put me vnto the test.
*Anton.* Goe then *Macrinus* 460
To *Dorothea*, tell her I haue worne,
In all the battailes I haue fought her figure,
Her figure in my heart, which like a diety
Hath still protected me, thou canst speake well,
And of thy choysest language, spare a little
To make her vnderstand how much I loue her,
And how I languish for her, beare her these iewels
Sent in the way of sacrifice, not seruice,
As to my goddesse. All lets throwne behind me,
Or feares that may deter me: say this morning 470
I meane to visite her by the name of friendship,
No words to contradict this.

*Macr.*                    I am yours,
And if my trauell this way be ill spent,
Iudge not, my readier will, by the euent.

                                        *Exeunt.*

*Finis actus primus.*


ACTUS II, SCENA i

*Enter* Spungius *and* Hircius.

*Spung.*  Turne Christian, wud he that first tempted mee to haue my
shooes walke vpon Christian soles, had turn'd me into a Capon,
for I am sure now the stones of all my pleasure in this fleshly life
are cut off.
*Hirc.*  So then, if any Coxecombe has a galloping desire to ride,
heres a Gelding, if he can but sit him.
*Spung.*  I kicke for all that like a horse, looke else.
*Hirc.*  But thats a kickish Iade, fellow *Spungius*, haue not I as much
cause to complaine as thou hast? When I was a Pagan, there was
an Infidell Punke of mine, would haue let me come vpon trust for  10
my coruetting, a pox of your christian Coxatrices, they cry like
Poulterers wiues, no money, no Cony.
*Spung.*  *Bacchus*, the God of brew'd Wine and Sugar, grand Patron
of rob-pots, vpsie-freesie-tiplers, and super-naculam takers; this
*Bacchus*, who is head warden of Vintners Hall, Ale-cunner, Maior
of all Victualing houses, the sole liquid Benefactor to bawdy-houses,
*Lanꝫe preꝫado* to red Noses, and inuincible *Adelantado* ouer the
Armado of pimpled, deepe scarletted, rubified, and carbuncled
faces.
*Hirc.*  What of all this?                                      20
*Spung.*  This boone Bacchanalion skinker, did I make legges to.
*Hirc.*  Scuruy ones, when thou wert drunke.
*Spung.*  There is no danger of loosing a mans eares by making

474 readier] Q3; reader Q1 (u, c)-2     21 skinker] Mason; stinker Q1-4
23 mans] Q2; man Q1                      23 eares] Coxeter; yeares Q1-4

these Indentures, he that will not now and then bee *Calabingo*, is worse then a *Calamoothe*: when I was a Pagan and kneeld to this *Bachhus*, I durst out-drinke a Lord, but your Christian Lords out-boule me: I was in hope to leade a sober life, when I was conuerted, but now amongst the Christians, I can no sooner stagger out of one Alehouse but I reele into another: they haue whole streets of nothing but drinking roomes, and drabbing chambers, iumbled 30 together.

*Hirc.* Bawdy *Priapus*, the first schoolemaister that taught Butchers how to sticke pricks in flesh, and make it swell, thou knowest was the onely Ningle that I cared for vnder the Moone, but since I left him, to follow a scuruy Lady, what with her praying and our fasting, if now I come to a wench and offer to vse her any thing hardly (telling her being a Christian she must endure) she presently handles me as if I were a cloue, and cleaues me with disdaine as if I were a Calues head.

*Spung.* I see no remedy fellow *Hircius*, but that thou and I must 40 be halfe Pagans and halfe Christians, for we know very fooles that are Christians.

*Hirc.* Right, the quarters of Christians are good for nothing but to feed Crowes.

*Spung.* True, Christian Brokers, thou knowest, are made vp of the quarters of Christians, parboyle one of these rogues and he is not meate for a dog: no, no, I am resolued to haue an Infidels heart, though in shew I carry a Christians face.

*Hirc.* Thy Last shall serue my foote, so will I.

*Spung.* Our whimpring Lady and Mistresse sent mee with two 50 great baskets full of Beefe, Mutton, Veale and Goose fellow *Hircius*.

*Hirc.* And Woodcocke fellow *Spungius*.

*Spung.* Vpon the poore leane Asse fellow, on which I ride, to all the Almswomen: what thinkst thou I haue done with all this good cheere.

*Hirc.* Eate it, and be choakt else.

*Spung.* Wud my Asse, basket and all were in thy maw if I did: no,

24 Indentures] Mason; Indures Q 1-4
43 nothing] Q 2; not | thing Q 1

394

as I am a demy Pagan, I sold the victuals, and coynd the money
into pottle pots of wine.                                                    60

*Hirc.*  Therein thou shewdst thy selfe a perfect demy-Christian
too, to let the poore beg, starue and hang, or dye a the pip: our
puling snotty-nose Lady sent me out likewise with a purse of
mony, to releeue and release prisoners: did I so thinke you?

*Spung.*  Wud thy ribs were turnd into grates of iron then.

*Hirc.*  As I am a totall Pagan, I swore they should be hangd first:
for sirra *Spungius*, I lay at my old ward of lechery, and cryed a poxe
on your two-penny wards, and so I tooke scuruy common flesh for
the mony.

*Spung.*  And wisely done, for our Lady sending it to prisoners, had  70
bestowed it out vpon lowsie knaues, and thou to saue that labour
casts it away vpon rotten whores.

*Hirc.*  All my feare is of that pinke-an-eye Iack-an-Apes boy, her
page.

*Spung.*  As I am a Pagan, from my cod-peece downward, that
white-fac'd Monkie, frights me to, I stole but a durty pudding last
day out of an almesbasket, to giue my dogge when he was hungry,
and the peaking chitface page hit me ith'teeth with it.

*Hirc.*  With the durty pudding; so he did me once with a cowturd,
which in knauery I would haue crumd into ones porridge, who was  80
halfe a Pagan to: the smug dandiprat smels vs out whatsoeuer we
are doing.

*Spung.*  Does he! let him take heede I proue not his backe friend;
Ile make him curse his smelling what I doe.

*Hirc.*  Tis my Lady spoyles the boy, for he is euer at her tayle:
and she's neuer well but in his company.

*Enter* Angelo *with a Booke and Taper lighted,*
*they seeing him, counterfeit deuotion.*

*Ange.*  O! now your hearts make ladders of your eyes
In shew to climbe to heauen, when your deuotion
Walkes vpon crutches: where did you waste your time
When the religious man was on his knees,                          90
Speaking the heauenly language.

68 on] Q3; in Q1-2

395

*Spung.* Why fellow *Angelo*, we were speaking in pedlars French
I hope.

*Hirc.* We ha not bene idle, take it vpon my word.

*Ange.* Haue you the baskets emptied which your Lady
Sent from the charitable hands, to women
That dwell vpon her pitty?

*Spung.* Emptied em! yes, Ide be loth to haue my belly so emptie,
yet I'm sure, I munched not one bit of them neither.

*Ange.* And went your money to the prisoners. 100

*Hirc.* Went! no, I carryed it; and with these fingers paid it away.

*Ange.* What way? the diuels way, the way of sinne,
The way of hot damnation, way of lust:
And you, to wash away the poore mans bread
In bowles of drunkennesse.

*Spung.* Drunkennesse! yes, yes, I vse to bee drunke: our next
neighbours man called *Christopher* has often seene me drunke, has
he not?

*Hirc.* Or me giuen so to the flesh, my cheekes speake my doings.

*Ange.* Auant you theeues, and hollow hypocrites. 110
Your hearts to me lie open like blacke bookes,
And there I reade your doings.

*Spung.* And what do you read in my heart?

*Hirc.* Or in mine? come amiable *Angelo*, beate the flint of your
braines.

*Spung.* And lets see what sparkes of wit fly out, to kindle your
*Carebruns.*

*Ange.* Your names euen brand you, you are *Spungius* cald
And like a Spunge you sucke vp liquorous wines
Till your soule reeles to hell. 120

*Spung.* To hell! can any drunkards legs carry him so far.

*Ange.* For blood of grapes you sold the widowes food.
And staruing them, tis murder, whats this but hell.
*Hircius* your name, and Goatish is your nature:
You snatch the meate out of the prisoners mouth,
To fatten harlots, is not this hell to,
No Angell, but the diuell waites on you.

104 you, to∧] Q3; ~ ∧ ~ , Q1-2    117 *Carebruns*] *i.e.* cerebrum

*Spung.*　Shall I cut his throate.

*Hirc.*　No, better burne him, for I thinke he is a witch, but sooth,
sooth him.　　　　　　　　　　　　　　　　　　　　　　　　130

*Spung.*　Fellow *Angelo*, true it is, that falling into the company of
wicked he-Christians for my part —

*Hirc.*　And she-ones for mine, we haue 'em swim in sholes hard by.

*Spung.*　We must confesse, I tooke too much of the pot, and he of
tother hollow commodity.

*Hirc.*　Yes indeed, we layd lill on both of vs, we cousen'd the
poore, but 'tis a common thing, many a one that counts himselfe
a better Christian then we two, has done it, by this light.

*Spung.*　But pray sweet *Angelo*, play not the tell-tale to my Lady,
and if you take vs creeping into any of these mouse-holes of sin 140
any more, let Cats flea off our skins.

*Hirc.*　And put nothing but the poysond tailes of Rats into those
skins.

*Ange.*　Will you dishonor her sweet charity,
Who sau'd you from the tree of death and shame.

*Hirc.*　Wud I were hangd rather then thus be told of my faults.

*Spung.*　She tooke vs, tis true, from the gallowes, yet I hope she
will not barre yeomen sprats to haue their swinge.

*Ange.*　She comes, beware and mend.

*Enter* Dorothea.

*Hirc.*　Lets breake his necke, and bid him mend.　　　　　　150

*Dor.*　Haue you my messages (sent to the poore)
Deliuer'd with good hands, not robbing them
Of any iot was theirs.

*Spung.*　Rob 'em Lady, I hope, neither my fellow nor I am theeues.

*Hirc.*　Deliuerd with good hands madam, else let me neuer licke
my fingers more when I eate butterd fish.

*Dor.*　Who cheate the poore, and from them plucke their almes,
Pilfer from Heauen, and there are thunderbolts
From thence to beate them euer, do not lye,
Were you both faithfull true distributers?　　　　　　　160

*Spung.*　Lye Madame, what griefe is it to see you turne Swaggerer,
and giue your poore minded rascally seruants the lye.

*Dor.*   I'm glad you doe not, if those wretched people
Tell you they pine for want of any thing,
Whisper but to mine eare, and you shall furnish them.
*Hirc.*   Whisper, nay Lady, for my part Ile cry whoope.
*Ange.*   Play no more Villaines with so good a Lady,
For if you doe —— —— ——
*Spung.*   Are we Christians?
*Hirc.*   The fowle Feind snap all Pagans for me.                    170
*Ange.*   Away, and once more mend.
*Spung.*   Takes vs for Botchers.
*Hirc.*   A patch, a patch.                              [*Exeunt.*]
*Dor.*   My booke and Taper.
*Ange.*                        Heere most holy Mistresse.
*Dor.*   Thy voyce sends forth such musicke, that I neuer
Was rauisht with a more celestiall sound,
Were euery seruant in the world like thee,
So full of goodnesse, Angels would come downe
To dwell with vs, thy name is *Angelo*,
And like that name thou art, get thee to rest,                    180
Thy youth with too much watching is opprest.
*Ange.*   No my deare Lady, I could weary starres,
And force the wakefull Moone to lose her eyes
By my late watching, but to waite on you,
When at your prayers you kneele before the Altar,
Me thinkes I'm singing with some Quire in Heauen,
So blest I hold me in your company:
Therefore my most-lou'd mistresse do not bid
Your boy so seruiceable to get hence,
For then you breake his heart.
*Dor.*                        Bee nye me still then,                    190
In golden letters downe ile set that day
Which gaue thee to me, little did I hope
To meete such worlds of comfort in thy selfe,
This little pretty body, when I comming
Forth of the temple, heard my begger-boy,
My sweete fac'd godly begger-boy, craue an almes,
Which with glad hand I gaue, with lucky hand,

And when I tooke thee home, my most chast bosome
Me thought was fil'd with no hot wanton fire,
But with a holy flame, mounting since higher                    200
On wings of Cherubines then did before.
*Ange.*   Proud am I that my Ladies modest eye,
So likes so poore a seruant.
*Dor.*                       I haue offerd
Handfuls of gold but to behold thy Parents,
I would leaue Kingdomes, were I Queene of some,
To dwell with thy good father, for the sonne
Bewitching me so deepely with his presence,
He that begot him must doo't ten times more,
I pray thee, my sweete boy, shew me thy parents,
Be not asham'd.
*Ange.*               I am not, I did neuer                    210
Know who my mother was, but by yon Pallace
Fill'd with bright heauenly Courtiers, I dare assure you,
And pawne these eyes vpon it, and this hand,
My father is in Heauen, and pretty Mistresse,
If your illustrious houre Glasse spend his sand
No worse then yet it does, vpon my life
You and I both shall meete my father there,
And he shall bid you welcome.
*Dor.*                         A blessed day,
We all long to be there, but lose the way.

*Exeunt.*

[ACT II, SCENE ii]

Macrinus *friend to* Antoninus *enters, being met
by* Theophilus *and* Harpax.

*Theoph.*   Sunne-god of the day guide thee *Macrinus.*
*Macr.*   And thee *Theophilus.*
*Theoph.*                      Gladst thou in such scorne,
I call my wish backe.

211 my] Q3; any Q 1-2

*Macr.*                I'm in hast.

*Theoph.*                One word,
Take the least hand of time vp: stay.

*Macr.*                Be briefe.

*Theoph.*    As thought: I prithee tell me good *Macrinus*
How health and our faire Princesse lay together
This night, for you can tell, Courtiers haue flyes
That buzze all newes vnto them.

*Macr.*                She slept but ill.

*Theoph.*  Double thy courtesie, how does *Antoninus*?

*Macr.*  Ill, well, straight, crooked, I know not how.

*Theoph.*                Once more,    10
Thy head is full of Winde-mils: when does the Princesse
Fill a bed full of beauty, and bestow it
On *Antoninus* on the wedding night.

*Macr.*  I know not.

*Theoph.*                No, thou art the Manuscript
Where *Antoninus* writes downe all his secrets,
Honest *Macrinus* tell me.

*Macr.*                Fare you well Sir.        *Exit.*

*Harpax.*    Honesty is some Fiend, and frights him hence,
A many Courtiers loue it not.

*Theoph.*                What peece
Of this State-wheele (which winds vp *Antoninus*)
Is broke, it runnes so iarringly? the man        20
Is from himselfe deuided: Oh thou the eye
By which I wonders see, tell me my *Harpax*,
What gad flye tickles so this *Macrinus*,
That vp-flinging the tayle, he breakes thus from me.

*Harpax.*    Oh Sir, his braine-panne is a bed of Snakes,
Whose stings shoote through his eye-balls, whose poysonous
    spawne
Ingenders such a fry of speckled villanies,
That vnlesse charmes more strong then Adamant
Bee vs'd, the Romane Egles wings shall melt,
And *Cæsars* Diadem be from his head        30

24 the] Q 3; thy Q 1-2            *29 Egles] Angels Q 1-4

Spurn'd by base feete, the Lawrell which he weares
(Returning victor) be inforc't to kisse
That which it hates (the fire.) And can this Ram,
This *Antoninus-Engine*, being made ready
To so much mischiefe, keepe a steady motion,
His eyes and feete you see giue strange assaults.

*Theoph.* I'm turnd a marble Statue at thy language,
Which printed is in such crab'd Charracters,
It puzzles all my reading, what (ith name
Of *Pluto*) now is hatching.

*Harpax.*                 This *Macrinus*          40
The line is, vpon which loue errands runne
Twixt *Antoninus* and that ghost of women,
The bloudlesse *Dorothæa*, who in prayer
And meditation (mocking all your gods)
Drinkes vp her ruby colour, yet *Antoninus*
Playes the Endymion to this pale fac'd Moone,
Courts her, seekes to catch her eyes.

*Theoph.* And what of this?

*Harpax.*                 These are but creeping Billowes
Not got to shore yet, but if *Dorothæa*
Fall on his bosome, and be fir'd with loue,          50
(Your coldest women do so) had you ynck
Brew'd from the infernall *Stix*, not all that blacknesse
Can make a thing so foule, as the Dishonours,
Disgraces, Buffettings, and most base affronts
Vpon the bright *Artemia*, Starre of Court,
Great *Cæsars* Daughter.

*Theoph.*                 I now conster thee.

*Harpax.* Nay more, a Firmament of Clouds being fild
With *Ioues* Artillery, shot downe at once
To pash your Gods in peeces, cannot giue
With all those Thunderbolts so deepe a blow          60
To the Religion there, and Pagan lore
As this; for *Dorothea* hates your gods,

41 line] Mason; time Q 1-4
52 not] Q 3; and not Q 1-2

And if she once blast *Antoninus* soule,
Making it foule like hers: Oh the example —
*Theoph.*   Eates through *Cesareas* heart, like liquid poison.
Haue I inuented tortures to teare Christians,
To see but which, could all that feeles Hels torments
Haue leaue to stand aloofe heere on earths stage,
They would be mad till they againe descended,
Holding the paines most horrid, of such soules,                    70
May-games to those of mine, has this my hand
Set downe a Christians execution
In such dire postures, that the very hangman
Fell at my foote dead hearing but their figures,
And shall *Macrinus* and his fellow *Masquer*
Strangle me in a dance.
*Harpax.*                No, on, I do hug thee,
For drilling thy quick braines in this rich plot
Of tortures gainst these Christians: on, I hug thee.
*Theoph.*   Both hug and holy me, to this *Dorothea*
Flye thou and I in thunder.
*Harpax.*                Not for Kingdomes                    80
Pil'd vpon Kingdomes, theres a villaine Page
Waites on her, whom I would not for the world
Hold trafficke with. I do so hate his sight,
That should I looke on him I must sinke downe.
*Theoph.*   I will not loose thee then, her to confound,
None but this head with glories shall be crown'd.
*Harpax.*   Oh, mine owne as I would wish thee.

                                                    *Exeunt.*


## [ACT II, Scene iii]

*Enter* Dorothea, Macrinus, Angelo.

*Dor.*   My trusty *Angelo*, with that curious eye
Of thine, which euer waites vpon my businesse,
I prithee watch those my still-negligent seruants
That they performe my will in whats enioyn'd them

To'th good of others, else will you find them flyes
Not lying still, yet in them no good lyes:
Be carefull deare Boy.

*Ange.*        Yes, my sweetest Mistresse.      *Exit.*

*Dor.* Now Sir, you may goe on.

*Macr.*           I then must study,
A new Arithmatike, to summe vp the vertues
Which *Antoninus* gracefully become,        10
There is in him so much man, so much goodnesse,
So much of honour, and of all things else
Which makes our being excellent, that from his store
He can enough lend others, yet much taken from him,
The want shall be as little as when Seas
Lend from their bounty to fill vp the poorenesse
Of needy Riuers.

*Dor.*        Sir, he is more indebted,
To you for praise, then you to him that owes it.

*Macr.* If Queens viewing his presents, paid to the whitenes
Of your chast hand alone, should be ambitious,    20
But to be parted in their numerous shares,
This he counts nothing: could you see maine Armies
Make battailes in the quarrell of his vallour,
That tis the best, the truest, this were nothing:
The greatnesse of his State, his fathers voyce
And arme, awing *Cesarea*, he neuer boasts of:
The Sun-beames, which the Emperor throwes vpon him,
Shine there but as in water, and guild him
Not with one spot of pride: no dearest beauty,
All these heap'd vp together in one scale,    30
Cannot weigh downe the loue he beares to you
Being put into the other.

*Dor.*        Could gold buy you
To speake thus for your friend, you Sir are worthy
Of more then I will number, and this your language
Hath power to win vpon another woman,

24 the best] Coxeter; *om.* the Q 1–4
*26 awing] Gifford; owing Q 1–3

Top of whose heart, the feathers of this World
Are gaily stuck, but all which first you named,
And now this last, his loue to me are nothing.
*Macr.*   You make me a sad Messenger.

*Enter* Antoninus.

But himselfe
Being come in person, shall I hope heare from you          40
Musicke more pleasing.
*Anton.*                         Has your eare *Macrinus*
Heard none then?
*Macr.*                   None I like.
*Anton.*                               But can there be
In such a noble Casket, wherein lies
Beauty and chastity in their full perfections,
A rocky heart killing with cruelty
A life thats prostrated beneath your feete?
*Dor.*   I am guilty of a shame I yet neuer knew,
Thus to hold parley with you, pray Sir pardon.
*Anton.*   Good sweetenesse, you now haue it, and shall goe,
Be but so mercifull, before your wounding me          50
With such a mortall weapon, as Farewell,
To let me murmure to your Virgin eare,
What I was loath to lay on any tongue
But this mine owne.
*Dor.*                     If one immodest accent
Flye out, I hate you euerlastingly.
*Anton.*   My true loue dares not doe it.
*Macr.*                               *Hermes* inspire thee.

*They whispering below, enter aboue* Sapritius, *father to* Antoninus,
*and Gouernor of* Cesaria, *with him* Artemia *the Princesse,*
Theophilus, Spungius *and* Hircius.

*Spung.*   See you, doe you see, our worke is done, the fish you angle
for is nibling at the hooke, and therefore vntrusse the Codpeece
point of our reward, no matter if the breeches of conscience fall
about our heeles.                                             60

*Theoph.*   The gold you earne is heere, dam vp your mouthes,
And no words of it.

*Hirc.*   No, nor no words from you of too much damming neither;
I know women sell themselues dayly, and are hacknied out for
siluer, why may not we then betray a scuruy mistresse for gold.

*Spung.*   She sau'd vs from the Gallowes, and only to keepe one
Prouerbe from breaking his necke, weele hang her.

*Theoph.*   Tis well done, go, go, y'are my fine white boyes.

*Spung.*   If your red boyes, tis well knowne, more ilfauour'd faces
then ours are painted.                                               70

*Sapr.*   Those fellowes trouble vs.

*Theoph.*                         Away, away.

*Hirc.*   I to my sweete placket.

*Spung.*   And I to my full pot.                          *Exeunt.*

*Anton.*   Come, let me tune you, glaze not thus your eyes
With selfe-loue of a vowed Virginity,
Make euery man your glasse, you see our Sex
Doe neuer murder propagation,
We all desire your sweete society,
And if you barre me from it, you doe kill me,
And of my bloud are guilty.

*Artemia.*                    O base Villaine.                    80

*Sapr.*   Bridle your rage sweete Princesse.

*Anton.*                               Could not my fortunes
(Rear'd higher farre then yours) be worthy of you,
Me thinkes my deare affection makes you mine.

*Dor.*   Sir, for your fortunes were they mines of gold,
He that I loue is richer; and for worth,
You are to him lower then any slaue
Is to a Monarch.

*Sapr.*            So insolent, base Christian.

*Dor.*   Can I, with wearing out my knees before him
Get you but be his seruant, you shall boast
Y'are equall to a King.

*Sapr.*                  Confusion on thee,                       90
For playing thus the lying Sorceresse.

68 y'are] Q2; yeare Q1

405

*Anton.* Your mockes are great ones, none beneath the Sun
Will I be seruant too: on my knees I beg it,
Pitty me wondrous maid.
*Sapr.* I curse thy basenesse.
*Theoph.* Listen to more.
*Dor.* Oh kneele not Sir to me.
*Anton.* This Knee is Embleme of an humbled heart,
That heart which tortur'd is with your disdaine,
Iustly for scorning others; euen this heart,
To which for pitty such a Princesse sues,
As in her hand offers me all the World,                                    100
Great *Cæsars* daughter.
*Artemia.* Slaue thou lyest.
*Anton.* Yet this
Is adamant to her, that melts to you
In drops of blood.
*Theoph.* A Very dogge.
*Anton.* Perhaps
Tis my religion makes you knit the brow,
Yet be you mine, and euer be your owne,
I nere will screw your conscience from that power
On which you Christians leane.
*Sapr.* I can no longer,
Fret out my life with weeping at thee villaine; sirra,
Would when I got thee, the high thunderers hand
Had strucke thee in the wombe.
*Macr.* We are betrayde.                                    110
*Artemia.* Is that your Idoll, traitor, which thou kneelst to,
Trampling vpon my beauty?
*Theoph.* Sirra, bandog,
Wilt thou in peeces teare, our *Iupiter*,
For her? our *Mars*, for her? our *Sol*, for her?
A whore, a hel-hound, in this globe of braines
Where a whole world of tortures for such furies
Haue fought (as in a Chaos) which should exceed,
These nailes shall grubbing lye, from scull to scull,

109 thunderers] Coxeter; thunder Q 1-4

406

To finde one horrider, then all, for you,
You three.

*Artemia.*        Threaten not, but strike, quicke vengeance flies      120
Into thy bosome, caitife: here all loues dies.        *Exeunt [aboue].*

*Anton.*   O I am thunder-strucke!
                              Wee are both ore whelm'd.

*Macr.*   With one high raging billow.

*Dor.*                        You a souldier,
And sinke beneath the violence of a woman?

*Anton.*   A woman! a wrongd Princesse: from such a starre
Blazing with fires of hate, what can be look'd for
But tragicall euents? my life is now
The subiect of her tyranny.

*Dor.*                    That feare, is base,
Of death, when that death doth but life displace
Out of her house of earth; you onely dread                    130
The stroke, and not what followes when you are dead,
There's the great feare indeed: come, let your eyes
Dwell where mine doe, youle scorne their tyrannies.

        *Enter below,* Artemia, Sapritius, Theophilus, *a guard.*
        Angelo *comes and is close by* Dorothea.

*Artemia.*   My fathers nerues put vigour in mine arme,
And I his strength must vse; because I once
Shed beames of fauour on thee, and with the Lyon
Playd with thee gently when thou strokst my heart,
Ile not insult on a base humbled prey,
By lingring out thy terrors, but with one frowne
Kill thee: hence with 'hem to execution.                    140
Seize him, but let euen death it selfe be weary
In torturing her: Ile change those smiles to shreekes,
Giue the foole what she is proud of (martyrdome)
In peeces racke that Bawd to.

*Sapr.*                    Albeit the reuerence
I owe our gods and you, are in my bosome
Torrents so strong, that pitty quite lies drownd

From sauing this yong man, yet when I see
What face death giues him, and that a thing within me,
Sayes 'tis my sonne, I'am forc'd to be a man,
And grow fond of his life, which thus I beg.                    150
*Artemia.*    And I deny.
*Anton.*                        Sir you dishonour me,
To sue for that which I disclayme to haue,
I shall more glory in my sufferings gaine,
Then you in giuing iudgement, since I offer
My blood vp to your anger: nor do I kneele
To keepe a wretched life of mine from ruine:
Preserue this temple (builded faire as yours is)
And *Cæsar* neuer went in greater triumph
Than I shall to the scaffold.
*Artemia.*                    Are you so braue Sir,
Set forward to his triumph, and let those two            160
Go cursing along with him.
*Dor.*                        No, but pittying,
(For my part, I) that you loose ten times more
By torturing me, than I that dare your tortures,
Through all the army of my sinnes, I haue euen
Labord to breake, and cope with death to th'face;
The visage of a hangman frights not me;
The sight of whips, rackes, gibbets, axes, fires
Are scaffoldings, by which my soule climbes vp
To an Eternall habitation.
*Theoph.*    *Cæsars* imperiall daughter, heare me speake,    170
Let not this Christian *Thing*, in this her pageantry
Of prowd deriding, both our gods and *Cæsar*,
Build to her selfe a kingdome in her death
Going laughing from vs.  No, her bitterest torment
Shall be to feele her constancy beaten downe,
The brauery of her resolution lie
Battered by the argument, into such peeces,
That she agen shall (on her belly) creepe
To kisse the pauements of our Panim gods.

157 yours] Q2; your Q1

*Artemia.*     How to be done.

*Theoph.*                    Ile send my daughters to her,          180
And they shall turne her rocky faith to waxe,
Else spit at me, let me be made your slaue,
And meete no *Romans* but a villains graue.

*Artemia.*  Thy prisoner let her be then: and *Sapritius*
Your sonne, and that be yours: death shall be sent
To him that suffers them by voyce or letters
To greet each other. Rifle her estate,
Christians to beggery brought grow desperate.

*Dor.*  Still on the bread of pouerty let me feed.

                              *Exeunt.* [*Manet* Angelo.]

*Ange.*  O my admired mistresse; quench not out          190
The holy fires within you, though temptations
Showre downe vpon you: claspe thine armour on,
Fight well, and thou shalt see, after these warres
Thy head weare Sun-beames, and thy feet touch starres.

                    *Enter* Hircius *and* Spungius

*Hirc.*  How now *Angelo* how ist? how ist? what thred spins that
whore *Fortune* vpon her wheele now.

*Spung.*  *Comesta, comesta* poore knaue.

*Hirc.*  *Com a porte vou, com a porte vou,* my petite garsoone.

*Spung.*  *Me partha whee* Comrade, my halfe inch of mans flesh,
how run the dice of this cheating world, ha?          200

*Ange.*  Too well on your sides, you are hid in gold
Ore head and eares.

*Hirc.*  We thanke our fates, the signe of the gingle-boyes hangs at
the doores of our pockets.

*Spung.*  Who wud thinke that we comming forth of the arse, as it
were, or fag end of the world, should yet see the golden age, when
so little siluer is stirring.

*Hirc.*  Nay who can say any citizen is an Asse, for lading his owne
backe, with money, till his soule crackes agen, onely to leaue his

sonne like a gilded coxecombe behinde him? will not any foole take 210
me for a wiseman now, seeing me draw out of the pit of my treasury,
this little god with his belly full of gold.

*Spung.* And this full of the same meate out of my ambrey.

*Ange.* That gold will melt to poyson.

*Spung.* Poyson, wud it wud, whole pintes for healths shall downe
my throate.

*Hirc.* Gold poyson! there's neuer a she-thrasher in *Cæsarea* that
liues on the flaile of money will call it so.

*Ange.* Like slaues you sold your soules for golden drosse,
Bewitching her to death, who stept betweene                    220
You, and the gallowes.

*Spung.* Twas an easie matter to saue vs, she being so well backt.

*Hirc.* The gallowes and we fell out, so she did but part vs.

*Ange.* The misery of that mistresse is mine owne,
She beggerd, I left wretched.

*Hirc.* I can but let my Nose drop in sorrow with wet eyes for her.

*Spung.* The petticote of her estate is vnlac'd I confesse.

*Hirc.* Yes, and the smocke of her charity is now all to peeces.

*Ange.* For loue you beare to her, for some good turnes
Done you by me, giue me one peece of siluer.                    230

*Hirc.* How! a peece of siluer! if thou wert an Angell of gold I
would not put thee into white money, vnlesse I weigh'd thee, and
I weigh thee not a rush.

*Spung.* A peece of siluer! I neuer had but two calues in my life,
and those my mother left me; Ile rather part from the fat of them,
then from a mustard-tokens worth of Argent.

*Hirc.* And so sweet Nit we crawle from thee.

*Spung.* *Adieu,* demi-dandiprat, *adieu.*

*Ange.* Stay one word yet, you now are full of gold?

*Hirc.* Ide be sorry my dog were so full of the poxe.                    240

*Spung.* Or any Sow of mine of the meazles either.

*Ange.* Go, go, y'are beggers both, you are not worth
That leather on your feete.

*Hirc.* Away, away boy.

*Spung.* Page you do nothing but set patches on the soles of your
iests.

*Ange.* I'am glad I tryde your loue, which see I want not,
So long as this is full.

*Both.* And so long as this. — so long as this.

*Hirc.* Spungius y'are a picke-pocket.                                    250

*Spung.* Hircius thou hast nimb'd — so long as, — not so much
money is left as will buy a louse.

*Hirc.* Th'art a thiefe, and thou lyest in that gut through which thy
wine runs, if thou denyest it.

*Spung.* Thou lyest deeper then the bottome of mine enraged
pocket, if thou affrontst it.

*Ange.* No blowes, no bitter language, all your gold gone?

*Spung.* Can the diuell creepe into ones breeches?

*Hirc.* Yes, if his hornes once get into the codpeece.

*Ange.* Come, sigh not, I so little am in loue                            260
With that whose losse kils you, that see tis yours,
All yours, deuide the heape in equall share,
So you will goe along with me to prison,
And in our mistresse sorrowes beare a part:
Say, will you?

*Both.* Will we?

*Spung.* If she were going to hanging, no gallowes should part vs.

*Hirc.* Lets both be turnd into a rope of Onyons if we do not.

*Ange.* Follow me then, repaire your bad deeds past,
Happy are men when their best dayes are last.                             270

*Spung.* True master *Angelo*, pray sir leade the way.

                                        *Exit* Angelo.

*Hirc.* Let him leade that way, but follow thou me this way.

*Spung.* I liue in a Iayle?

*Hirc.* A way and shift for our selues, sheele do wel enough there,
for prisoners are more hungry after mutton, then Catchpoles
after prisoners.

*Spung.* Let her starue then if a whole Iayle will not fill her belly.

                                        *Exeunt.*

           *Finis Actus secundi*

251 as, —] Gifford; ~ , ‸ Q 1–4 ±        268 not.] Gifford; *om.* Q 1–4
273 Iayle?] Q 3; ~ . Q 1–2

                        411

## ACTUS III, Scena i

*Enter* Sapritius, Theophilus, *Priest*, Caliste, Christeta.

*Sapr.* Sicke to the death I feare.

*Theoph.*                    I meete your sorrow,
With my true feeling of it.

*Sapr.*                    She's a Witch,
A sorceresse *Theophilus*, my sonne
Is charm'd by her enticing eyes, and like
An image made of waxe, her beames of beauty
Melt him to nothing; all my hopes in him,
And all his gotten honours finde their graue
In his strange dotage on her. Would when first
He saw and lou'd her, that the earth had opend
And swallowd both aliue.

*Theoph.*                    There's hope left yet.          10

*Sapr.* Not any, though the Princesse were appeasd,
All title in her loue surrenderd vp,
Yet this coy Christian, is so transported
With her religion, that vnlesse my sonne
(But let him perish first) drinke the same potion
And be of her beleefe, sheele not vouchsafe
To be his lawfull wife.

*Priest.*                    But once remou'd
From her opinion, as I rest assur'd,
The reason of these holy maydes will win her,
Youle finde her tractable, to any thing          20
For your content or his.

*Theoph.*                    If she refuse it,
The Stygian dampes breeding infectious ayres,
The Mandrakes shreekes, or Basilisks killing eye,
The dreadfull lightning that does crush the bones
And neuer singe the skin, shall not appeare
Lesse fatall to her, then my zeale made hot
With loue vnto my gods: I haue deferd it

In hope to draw backe this Apostata,
Which will be greater honour then her death,
Vnto her fathers faith, and to that end 　　　　　30
Haue brought my daughters hither.

*Caliste.*　　　　　And we doubt not
To do what you desire.

*Sapr.*　　　　　Let her be sent for,
Prosper in your good worke, and were I not
To attend the Princesse, I would see and heare
How you succeede.

*Theoph.*　　　　　I am commanded to,
Ile beare you company.

*Sapr.*　　　　　Giue them your Ring
To leade her as in triumph if they win her
Before her highnesse.　　　　　*Exit* Sapritius.

*Theoph.*　　　　　Spare no promises,
Perswasions, or threats I do coniure you,
If you preuayle, 'tis the most glorious worke 　　　　　40
You euer vndertooke.

　　　　　*Enter* Dorothea *and* Angelo.

*Priest.*　　　　　She comes.

*Theoph.*　　　　　We leaue you,
Be constant and be carefull.　　　　　*Exeunt* Theophilus, *Priest.*

*Caliste.*　　　　　We are sorry
To meete you vnder guard.

*Dor.*　　　　　But I more greeu'd
You are at libertie, so well I loue you,
That I could wish, for such a cause as mine
You were my fellow prisoners: prethee *Angelo*
Reach vs some chaires, please you sit?

*Caliste.*　　　　　We thanke you,
Our visite is for loue, loue to your safetie.

*Christeta.*　　Our conference must be priuate, pray you therfore
Command your boy to leaue vs.

*Dor.*　　　　　You may trust him 　　　　　50
With any secret that concernes my life,

Falshood and he are strangers, had you Ladies
Bene blest with such a seruant, you had neuer
Forsooke that way (your iourney euen halfe ended)
That leades to ioyes eternall. In the place
Of loose lasciuious mirth, he would haue stird you
To holy meditations, and so farre
He is from flattery, that he would haue told you,
Your pride being at the height, how miserable
And wretched things you were, that for an howre          60
Of pleasure here, haue made a desperate sale
Of all your right in happinesse hereafter.
He must not leaue me, without him I fall,
In this life he is my seruant, in the other
A wished companion.
*Ange.*                    Tis not in the diuell,          [*Aside.*]
Nor all his wicked arts to shake such goodnesse.
*Dor.* But you were speaking Lady.
*Caliste.*                    As a friend
And louer of your safety, and I pray you
So to receiue it; and if you remember
How neere in loue our parents were, that we          70
Eu'n from the cradle were brought vp together,
Our amitie encreasing with our yeeres,
We cannot stand suspected.
*Dor.*                    To the purpose.
*Caliste.* We come then as good Angels *Dorothea*,
To make you happy, and the meanes so easie,
That be not you an enemy to your selfe,
Already you enioy it.
*Christeta.*          Looke on vs
Ruin'd as you are once, and brought vnto it
By your perswasion.
*Caliste.*          But what follow'd Lady,
Leauing those blessings which our gods giues freely,          80
And showr'd vpon vs with a prodigall hand,

As to be noble borne, youth, beauty, wealth,
And the free vse of these without controule,
Checke, curbe, or stop, (such is our Lawes indulgence)
All happinesse forsooke vs, bonds and fetters
For amorous twines, the Racke and Hangmans whips
In place of choise delights, our Parents curses
Instead of blessings, scorne, neglect, contempt
Fell thick vpon vs.
*Christeta.*          This consider'd wisely,
We made a faire retreate, and reconcil'd                    90
To our forsaken gods, we liue againe
In all prosperity.
*Caliste.*          By our example
Bequeathing misery to such as loue it,
Learne to be happy, the Christian yokes too heauy
For such a dainty necke, it was fram'd rather
To be the shrine of *Venus*, or a Pillar
More precious then Christall to support
Our *Cupids* Image, our Religion Lady
Is but a varied pleasure, yours a toyle
Slaues would shrinke vnder.                                 100
*Dor.*     Haue you not clouen feete? are you not diuels?
Dare any say so much, or dare I heare it
Without a vertuous and religious anger?
Now to put on a Virgin modesty,
Or maiden silence, when his power is question'd
That is omnipotent, were a greater crime,
Then in a bad cause to be impudent.
Your Gods, your temples, brothell houses rather,
Or wicked actions of the worst of men
Pursu'd and practis'd, your religious rites,             110
O call them rather iugling mysteries,
The baytes and nets of hell, your soules the prey
For which the Diuell angles, your false pleasures
A steepe descent by which you headlong fall
Into eternall torments.

86 twines] Coxeter; Twins Q 1-4

*Caliste.*            Doe not tempt
Our powerfull gods.
*Dor.*            Which of your powerfull gods,
Your gold, your siluer, brasse, or woodden ones?
That can, nor do me hurt, nor protect you.
Most pittied women, will you sacrifice
To such, or call them gods or goddesses,            120
Your Parents would disdaine to be the same,
Or you your selues? O blinded ignorance,
Tell me *Caliste* by the truth I charge you,
Or any thing you hold more deere, would you
To haue him deifide to posterity,
Desire your father an Adulterer,
A Rauisher, almost a Paracide,
A vile incestuous wretch?
*Caliste.*            That piety
And duty answere for me.
*Dor.*            Or you *Christeta*,
To be heereafter registred a goddesse,            130
Giue your chast body vp to the embraces
Of Goatish lust, haue it writ on your forehead,
This is the common Whoore, the prostitute,
The Mistresse in the art of wantonnesse,
Knowes euery tricke and labyrinth of desires
That are immodest.
*Cristeta.*            You iudge better of me,
Or my affection is ill plac'd on you,
Shall I turne Strumpet?
*Dor.*            No, I thinke you would not,
Yet *Venus* whom you worship was a whore,
*Flora* the Foundresse of the publike Stewes,            140
And has for that her sacrifice: your great god,
Your *Iupiter*, a loose adulterer,
Incestuous with his sister, reade but those
That haue canoniz'd them, youle find them worse

118 you.] ~ , Q 1–2; ~ ? Q 3–4      128 piety] Q 3; pitty Q 1–2

Then in chast language I can speake them to you,
Are they immortall then that did partake
Of humane weakenesse, and had ample share
In mens most base affections? subiect to
Vnchast loues, anger, bondage, wounds, as men are.
Heere *Iupiter* to serue his lust turn'd Bull.                    150
The shape indeede in which he stole *Europa*.
*Neptune* for gaine builds vp the walls of *Troy*
As a day-labourer; *Apollo* keepes
*Admetus* sheepe for bread; the *Lemnian* Smith
Sweats at the Forge, for hire; *Prometheus* heere
With his still growing Liuer feedes the Vulture;
*Saturne* bound fast in hell with adamant chaines;
And thousands more, on whom abused error
Bestowes a diety, will you then deere Sisters,
For I would haue you such, pay your Deuotions       160
To things of lesse power then your selues?
*Caliste*.                         We worship
Their good deedes in their Images.
*Dor*.                         By whom fashion'd,
By sinfull men? Ile tell you a short tale,
Nor can you but confesse it was a true one.
A King of *Ægypt* being to errect
The Image of *Osiris*, whom they honour,
Tooke from the Matrons necks the richest Iewels
And purest gold, as the materialls
To finish vp his worke; which perfected,
With all solemnity he set it vp                    170
To be ador'd, and seru'd himselfe his Idoll;
Desiring it to giue him victory
Against his enemies: but being ouerthrowne,
Enrag'd against his god (these are fine gods
Subiect to humane fury) he tooke downe
The sencelesse thing, and melting it againe,
He made a Basing, in which Eunuches wash'd

150 Heere] Q3; Her Q1-2          151 shape] Coxeter; ship Q1-4
155 *Prometheus*] Coxeter; *Lyometheus* Q1; *Lymotheus* Q2-4

His Concubines feete, and for this sordid vse
Some moneths it seru'd: his mistresse proouing false,
As most indeede do so, and grace concluded,               180
Betweene him and the Priests, of the same Basing
He made his god againe, thinke, thinke of this,
And then consider, if all worldly honors
Or pleasures that do leaue sharpe stings behind them,
Haue power to win such as haue reasonable soules,
To put their trust in drosse.

*Caliste.*                    Oh that I had beene borne
Without a father.

*Christeta.*           Piety to him
Hath ruin'd vs for euer.

*Dor.*                  Thinke not so,
You may repaire all yet, the Attribute
That speakes his Godhead most, is mercifull,               190
Reuenge is proper to the Fiends you worship,
Yet cannot strike without his leaue; you weepe,
Oh tis a heauenly showre, celestiall balme
To cure your wounded conscience, let it fall,
Fall thick vpon it, and when that is spent,
Ile helpe it with another of my teares.
And may your true repentance proue the child
Of my true sorrow, neuer mother had
A birth so happy.

*Caliste.*           We are caught our selues
That came to take you, and assur'd of conquest            200
We are your Captiues.

*Dor.*                  And in that you triumph,
Your victory had beene eternall losse,
And this your losse immortall gaine, fixe heere,
And you shall feele your selues inwardly arm'd
Gainst tortures, death, and hell, but take heede sisters,
That or through weakenesse, threats, or mild perswasions
Though of a father, you fall not into
A second and a worse Apostacie.

178 Concubines] *i.e.* Concubine's

*Caliste.*   Neuer, oh neuer, steel'd by your example,
We dare the worst of tyrranny.
*Christeta.*                    Heer's our warrant,                    210
You shall along and witnesse it.
*Dor.*                    Be confirm'd then
And rest assur'd, the more you suffer heere,
The more your glory, you to heauen more deere.

                                        *Exeunt.*

## [ACT III, Scene ii]

*Enter* Artemia, Sapritius, Theophilus, Harpax.

*Artemia.*   *Sapritius* though your sonne deserue no pitty,
We grieue his sicknesse, his contempt of vs
We cast behinde vs, and looke backe vpon
His seruice done to *Cæsar*, that weighs downe
Our iust displeasure, if his malady
Haue growth from his restraint, or that you thinke
His liberty can cure him, let him haue it,
Say we forgiue him freely.
*Sapr.*                    Your grace binds vs
Euer your humblest Vassals.
*Artemia.*                    Vse all meanes
For his recouery, though yet I loue him,                    10
I will not force affection, if the Christian
Whose beauty hath out-riuald mine, be wonne
To be of our beliefe, let him enioy her,
That all may know when the cause wills, I can
Command my owne desires.
*Theoph.*                    Be happy then,
My Lord *Sapritius*, I am confident
Such eloquence and sweete perswasion dwels
Vpon my Daughters tongues, that they will worke her
To any thing they please.
*Sapr.*                    I wish they may,

Yet tis no easie taske to vndertake,                                    20
To alter a peruerse and obstinate woman.

*A shout within, loud Musicke.*

*Artemia.*    What meanes this shout.

*Enter* Sempronius.

*Sapr.*                        Tis seconded with Musicke,
Triumphant musicke, ha.
*Semp.*                    My Lord your Daughters
The pillars of our faith hauing conuerted,
For so report giues out, the Christian Lady,
The Image of great *Iupiter* borne before them
Sue for accesse.
*Theoph.*              My soule diuin'd as much,
Blest be the time when first they saw this light,
Their Mother when she bore them to support
My feeble age, fild not my longing heart                                30
With so much ioy, as they in this good worke
Haue throwne vpon me.

*Enter Priest with the Image of Iupiter, Incense and Censors,*
*followed by* Caliste, *and* Christeta, *leading* Dorothea.

Welcome, oh thrice welcome
Daughters, both of my body and my mind,
Let me embrace in you my blisse, my comfort,
And *Dorothea* now more welcome too,
Then if you neuer had falne off, I am rauish't
With the excesse of ioy, speake happy daughters
The blest euent.
*Caliste.*          We neuer gain'd so much
By any vndertaking.
*Theoph.*              Oh my deare Girle,
Our gods reward thee.
*Dor.*                      Nor was euer time                              40
On my part better spent.
*Christeta.*              We are all now
Of one opinion.

420

*Theoph.*        My best *Christeta,*
Madame if euer you did grace to worth,
Vouchsafe your Princely hands.
*Artemia.*                        Most willingly:
Doe you refuse it?
*Caliste.*                Let vs first deserue it.
*Theoph.*   My owne child still, heere set our god, prepare
The Incense quickly, come faire *Dorothea,*
I will my selfe support you, now kneele downe
And pay your vowes to *Iupiter.*
*Dor.*                        I shall doe it
Better by their example.
*Theoph.*                They shall guide you,                    50
They are familiar with the sacrifice,
Forward my Twinnes of comfort, and to teach her
Make a ioynt offring.
*Christeta.*                Thus.
*Caliste.*                        And thus.

*They both spit at the Image, throw it downe, and spurne it.*

*Harpax.*                        Profane
And impious, stand you now like a Statue?
Are you the Champion of the Gods? where is
Your holy zeale, your anger?
*Theoph.*                I am blasted,
And as my feete were rooted heere, I finde
I haue no motion, I would I had no sight too,
Or if my eyes can serue to any vse,
Giue me thou iniur'd power a sea of teares,                    60
To expiate this madnesse in my Daughters:
For being themselues, they would haue trembled at
So blasphemous a deede in any other,
For my sake hold awhile thy dreadfull thunder,
And giue me patience to demand a reason
For this accursed act.
*Dor.*                Twas brauely done.
*Theoph.*   Peace damn'd Enchantres peace, I should looke on you

45 *Caliste.*] Q2; *om.* Q1

With eyes made red with fury, and my hand
That shakes with rage should much outstrip my tongue,
And seale my vengeance on your hearts, but nature          70
To you that haue falne once, bids me againe
To be a father, O how durst you tempt
The anger of great *Ioue?*
*Dor.*                              Alacke poore *Ioue,*
He is no Swaggerer, how smug he stands,
Heele take a kick, or any thing.
*Sapr.*                              Stop her mouth.
*Dor.*   It is the pacientst godling, do not feare him,
He would not hurt the thiefe that stole away
Two of his golden locks, indeede he could not,
And still tis the same quiet thing.
*Theoph.*                              Blasphemer,
Ingenious cruelty shall punish this,                       80
Thou art past hope, but for you yet deare daughters,
Againe bewitcht, the dew of mild forgiuenesse
May gently fall, prouided you deserue it
With true contrition, be your selues againe,
Sue to the offended diety.
*Christeta.*                              Not to be
The Mistresse of the earth.
*Caliste.*                              I will not offer
A graine of Incense to it, much lesse kneele,
Not looke on it but with contempt and scorne,
To haue a thousand yeeres confer'd vpon me
Of worldly blessings, we profess our selues            90
To be like *Dorothea,* Christians,
And owe her for that happinesse.
*Theoph.*                              My eares
Receiue in hearing this, all deadly charmes
Powerfull to make man wretched.
*Artemia.*                              Are these they
You brag'd could conuert others?

---

76 pacientst] Mason (suggested); ancientst Q 1–4

*Sapr.*　　　　　　　　　That want strength
To stand themselves?
*Harpax.*　　　　　Your Honour is ingag'd,
The credit of our cause depends vpon it,
Something you must doe suddenly.
*Theoph.*　　　　　　　And I will.
*Harpax.*　They merit death, but falling by your hand,
It will be recorded for a iust reuenge　　　　　　　100
And holy fury in you.
*Theoph.*　　　　　Doe not blow,
The Furnace of a wrath thrice hot already,
*Ætna* is in my brest, wildfire burnes heere,
Which onely bloud must quench: incensed power,
Which from my infancy I haue ador'd,
Looke downe with fauourable beames vpon
The Sacrifice (though not allow'd thy Priest)
Which I will offer to thee, and be pleasde
(My fierie zeale inciting me to act it)
To call that iustice, others may stile murther.　　　110
Come you accursd, thus by the haire I drag you
Before this holy altar; thus looke on you
Lesse pittifull then Tigres to their prey.
And thus with mine owne hand I take that life
Which I gaue to you.　　　　　　*Kils them.*
*Dor.*　　　　　O most cruell Butcher.
*Theoph.*　My anger ends not here, hels dreadfull porter
Receiue into thy euer open gates
Their damned soules, and let the furies whips
On them alone be wasted: and when death
Closes these eyes, twill be *Elizium* to me,　　　　120
To heare their shreekes and howlings, make me *Pluto*
Thy instrument to furnish thee with soules
Of this accursed sect, nor let me fall
Till my fell vengeance hath consum'd them all.

　　　　　　*Exit with* Harpax *hugging him, laughing.*

*124 S.D. *him, laughing.* | *Enter* Angelo.] *him.* | *Enter* Artemia *laughing.* Q 1-4

*Enter* Angelo.

*Artemia.*   Tis a braue zeale.
*Dor.*                     O call him backe againe,
Call backe your hangman, here's one prisoner left
To be the subiect of his knife.
*Artemia.*                 Not so.
We are not so neere reconcilde vnto thee,
Thou shalt not perish such an easie way.
Be she your charge *Sapritius* now, and suffer          13c
None to come neere her till we haue found out
Some torments worthy of her.
*Ange.*                   Courage Mistresse,
These Martyrs but prepare your glorious fate,
You shall exceed them and not imitate.

                                        *Exeunt.*


## [ACT III, SCENE iii]

*Enter* Spungius *and* Hircius *ragged at seuerall doores.*

*Hirc.*   *Spungius.*
*Spung.*   My fine rogue, how ist? how goes this totterd world.
*Hirc.*   Hast any money?
*Spung.*   Money! no, the Tauerne-Iuy clings about my mony and
kils it. Hast thou any mony?
*Hirc.*   No, my mony is a mad Bull, and finding any gap opend,
away it runs.
*Spung.*   I see then a Tauerne and a Bawdy-house haue faces much
alike, the one has red grates next dore, the tother has peeping holes
within doores; the Tauerne hath euermore a bush, the bawdy close   10
sometimes neither hedge nor bush. From a Tauerne a man comes
reeling, from a bawdy house not able to stand. In the Tauerne you
are cousend with paltry Wine, in a bawdy-house by a painted Whore,
Money may haue Wine, and a Whore will haue Mony, but neither

can you cry, Drawer you Rogue, or keepe doore rotten Bawde, without a siluer Whistle, wee are iustly plagued therefore for running from our Mistresse.

*Hirc.*  Thou didst, I did not; yet I had run to, but that one gaue me turpentine pilles, and that stayde my running.

*Spung.*  Well: the thred of my life is drawne through the needle of  20 necessity, whose eye looking vpon my lowsie breeches, cryes out it cannot mend 'em: which so prickes the linings of my body, and those are Heart, Lights, Lungs, Guts, and Midriffe, that I beg on my knees to haue *Atropos* (the Tailer to the destinies) to take her sheares and cut my thred in two, or to heate the Iron goose of Mortalitie, and so presse me to death.

*Hirc.*  Sure thy father was some botcher, and thy hungry tongue bit off these shreds of complaints, to patch vp the elbowes of thy nittie eloquence.

*Spung.*  And what was thy father?  30

*Hirc.*  A low minded Cobler, a Cobler whose zeale set many a woman vpright, the remembrance of whose Awle, I now hauing nothing, thrusts such scuruy stitches into my soule, that the heele of my happines has gone awry.

*Spung.*  Pitty that ere thou trodst thy shooe awry.

*Hirc.*  Long I cannot last, for all sowterly waxe of comfort melting away, and misery taking the length of my foote, it bootes not me to sue for life when all my hopes are seame-rent, and go wetshod.

*Spung.*  This shews th'art a Coblers son by going through stitch: O *Hircius* wud thou and I were so happy to be coblers.  40

*Hirc.*  So would I, for both of vs being now wearie of our liues, should then be sure of shoomakers ends.

*Spung.*  I see the beginning of my ende for I am almost staru'd.

*Hirc.*  So am not I, but I am more then famishd.

*Spung.*  All the members of my bodie are in rebellion one against another.

*Hirc.*  So are mine, and nothing but a cooke being a constable can appease them, presenting to my nose, in stead of his painted staffe, a spit full of rost-meate.

*Spung.*  But in this rebellion, what vprores do they make, my belly  50 cries to my mouth, why dost not gape and feed me.

*Hirc.* And my mouth sets out a throate to my hand, why dost not thou lift vp meate and cramme my choppes with it.

*Spung.* Then my hand hath a fling at mine eyes, because they looke not out and sharke for victuals.

*Hirc.* Which mine eyes seeing, full of teares, crie alowd, and curse my feet for not ambling vp and downe to feede Colon, sithence if good meate be in any place, tis knowne my feet can smell.

*Spung.* But then my feet like lazie rogues lie still, and had rather do nothing, then run to and fro, to purchase any thing.  60

*Hirc.* Why mong so many millions of people, should thou and I onely bee miserable totterdemalions, rag-a-muffins, and lowsie desperates.

*Spung.* Thou art a meere *I am-an-o, I am-an-as,* consider the whole world, and tis as we are.

*Hirc.* Lowsie, beggerly, thou whorson *Assa Fætida.*

*Spung.* Worse, al tottering, al out of frame, thou *Fooliamini.*

*Hirc.* As how *arsnicke*: come make the world smart.

*Spung.* Old Honor goes on crutches, beggry rides caroched, honest men make feastes, knaues sit at tables, cowards are lapt in 70 veluet, souldiers (as wee) in ragges: Beautie turnes Whore; Whore Bawd; and both dye of the poxe: why then when all the world stumbles, should thou and I walke vpright?

*Enter* Angelo.

*Hirc.* Stop, looke who's yonder.

*Spung.* Fellow *Angelo!* how does my little man? well?

*Ange.* Yes, and would you did so, where are your clothes?

*Hirc.* Clothes! you see euery woman almost goe in her loose gowne, and why should not wee haue our clothes loose?

*Spung.* Wud they were loose.

*Ange.* Why where are they?  80

*Spung.* Where many a veluet cloke I warrant at this houre keepes them company, they are pawnd to a Broker.

*Ange.* Why pawnd, where's all the gold I left with you?

*Hirc.* The gold! we put that into a Scriueners hands, and he has cousend vs.

67 tottering] Coxeter; totterings Q 1–4

*Spung.* And therefore I prethee *Angelo,* if thou hast another purse,
let it be confiscate, and brought to deuastation.
*Ange.* Are you made all of lyes? I know which way
Your gilt-wing'd peeces flew; I will no more
Be mock'd by you: be sorry for your ryots,                    90
Tame your wilde flesh by labor, eate the bread
Got with hard hands: let sorrow be your whip
To draw drops of repentance from your heart,
When I reade this amendment in your eyes,
You shall not want, till then my pitty dies.         *Exit.*
*Spung.* Ist not a shame that this scuruy *Puerilis* should giue vs
lessons?
*Hirc.* I haue dwelt thou knowst a long time in the Suburbs of the
conscience, and they are euer bawdy, but now my heart shall take
a house within the walls of honesty.                         100

                *Enter* Harpax *aloofe.*

*Spung.* O you drawers of wine, draw me no more to the bar of
Beggery; the sound of Score a pottle of sack, is worse then the
noyse of a scolding oyster wench, or two Cats incorporating.
*Harpax.* This must not be, I doe not like when conscience
Thawes, keepe her frozen still: how now my masters?
Deiected, drooping, drownd in teares, clothes torne,
Leane, and ill colour'd, sighing! whats the whirlewinde
Which raiseth all these mischiefes? I haue seene you
Drawne better on't. O! but a spirit told me
You both would come to this, when in you thrust            110
Your selues into the seruice of that Lady,
Who shortly now must die; where's now her praying,
What good get you by wearing out your feete,
To run on scuruy errands to the poore,
And to beare money to a sort of rogues,
And lowsie prisoners.
*Hirc.* A pox on 'em, I neuer prosperd since I did it.
*Spung.* Had I bin a Pagan stil, I could not haue spit white for want
of drinke, but come to any Vintner now and bid him trust me,
because I turnd Christian, and he cries puh.               120

                              427

*Harpax.* Y'are rightly seru'd; before that peeuish Lady
Had to doe with you, weomen, wine, and money
Flow'd in aboundance with you, did it not?
*Hirc.* Oh! those dayes, those dayes.
*Harpax.* Beat not your breasts, teare not your haire in madnes,
Those dayes shall come agen, be rulde by me,
And better (marke me) better.
*Spung.* I haue seen you sir as I take it, an attendant on the Lord
Theophilus.
*Harpax.* Yes, yes, in shew his seruant, but harke hither.          130
Take heed no body listens.
*Spung.* Not a Mouse stirres.
*Harpax.* I am a Prince disguisde.
*Hirc.* Disguisde! how! drunke?
*Harpax.* Yes my fine boye, Ile drinke to, and be drunke,
I am a Prince, and any a man by me
(Let him but keepe my rules) shall soone grow rich,
Exceeding rich, most infinitely rich,
He that shall serue me, is not staru'd from pleasures
As other poore knaues are; no, take their fill.          140
*Spung.* But that sir, we are so ragged —
*Harpax.* Youle say, you'd serue me.
*Hirc.* Before any master vnder the Zodiake.
*Harpax.* For clothes no matter; I haue a mind to both.
And one thing I like in you, now that you see
The bonefire of your Ladyes state burnt out,
You giue it ouer, do you not?
*Hirc.* Let her be hangd.
*Spung.* And poxd.
*Harpax.* Why now y'are mine.
                    Come let my bosome touch you. 150
*Spung.* We haue bugges Sir.
*Harpax.* Ther's mony, fetch your cloths home, theres for you.
*Hirc.* Auoid Vermine: giue ouer our mistresse! a man cannot
prosper worse if he serue the diuell.
*Harpax.* How? the diuell! Ile tell you what now of the diuell,
He's no such horrid creature, clouen footed,

Blacke, saucer-eyde, his nostrils breathing fire,
As these lying Christians make him.
*Both.*    No!
*Harpax.*    He's more louing, to man, then man to man is.          160
*Hirc.*    Is hee so! wud wee two might come acquainted with him.
*Harpax.*    You shall: he's a wondrous good fellow, loues a cup of
wine, a whore, any thing, you haue mony, its ten to one but Ile
bring him to some Tauerne to you or other.
*Spung.*    Ile bespeake the best roome ith' house for him.
*Harpax.*    Some people he cannot endure.
*Hirc.*    Weele giue him no such cause.
*Harpax.*    He hates a ciuill Lawyer, as a souldier does peace.
*Spung.*    How a commoner?
*Harpax.*    Loues him from the teeth outward.          170
*Spung.*    Pray my Lord and Prince, let me encounter you with one
foolish question: does the diuell eate any Mace in's broth?
*Harpax.*    Exceeding much, when his burning feauer takes him, and
then hee has the knuckles of a Bailiffe boyld to his breakefast.
*Hirc.*    Then my Lord, he loues a Catchpole does he not?
*Harpax.*    As a Bearward does a dog, a Catchpole! he has sworn
if euer he dies, to make a Serieant his heire, and a Yoeman his
ouerseer.
*Spung.*    How if he come to any great mans gate, will the Porter let
him come in sir?          180
*Harpax.*    Oh, hee loues Porters of great mens gates, because they
are euer so neere the wicket.
*Hirc.*    Doe not they whom he makes much on, for all his stroking
their cheekes, leade hellish liues vnder him.
*Harpax.*    No, no, no, no, he will be damn'd before he hurts any
man. Doe but you (when y'are throughly acquainted with him)
aske for any thing, see if it does not come.
*Spung.*    Any thing!
*Harpax.*    Call for a delicate rare whore; she's brought you.
*Hirc.*    Oh my elbow itches: will the diuel keepe the dore?          190
*Harpax.*    Be drunke as a begger, he helps you home.
*Spung.*    O my fine diuell! some watchman I warrant, I wonder
who's his constable.

*Harpax.* Will you sweare, roare, swagger? he claps you.
*Hirc.* How! ath' chops.
*Harpax.* No, ath' shoulder, and cries O my braue boy.
Will any of you kill a man?
*Spung.* Yes, yes, I, I.
*Harpax.* Whats his word, hang, hang, tis nothing.
Or stab a woman?                                                    200
*Hirc.* Yes, yes, I, I.
*Harpax.* Here's the worst word he giues you, a pox on't goe on
*Hirc.* O inueagling rascall, I am rauishd.
*Harpax.* Go, get your clothes, turn vp your glasse of youth,
  And let the sands run merily; nor do I care
  From what a lauish hand your money flies,
  So you giue none away, feed beggers.
*Hirc.* Hang 'em.
*Harpax.* And to the scrubbing poore.
*Hirc.* Ile see 'em hangd first.                                    210
*Harpax.* One seruice you must do me.
*Both.* Any thing.
*Harpax.* Your Mistresse *Dorothea*, ere she suffers,
  Is to be put to tortures, haue you hearts
  To tear her into shreekes, to fetch her soule
  Vp in the Pangs of death, yet not to die.
*Hirc.* Suppose this shee, and that I had no hands, heere's my teeth.
*Spung.* Suppose this she, and that I had no teeth, heere's my nailes.
*Hirc.* But will not you be there sir.
*Harpax.* No, not for hils of diamonds, the grand Master     220
  Who schooles her in the Christian discipline,
  Abhorres my company; should I be there,
  You'd thinke all hell broke loose, we shall so quarrell.
  Plie you this businesse; he, her flesh who spares
  Is lost, and in my loue neuer more shares.              *Exit.*
*Spung.* Here's a Master you rogue.
*Hirc.* Sure he cannot chuse but haue a horrible number of seruants.

                                                        *Exeunt.*

                    *Finis Actus tertii.*

## ACTUS IV, SCENA i

*A bed thrust out,* Antoninus *vpon it sicke, with Physitions about him,* Sapritius *and* Macrinus [*, guards*].

*Sapr.*  O You that are halfe gods, lengthen that life
Their dieties lend vs, turne ore all the volumes
Of your mysterious *Æsculapian* science
T'encrease the number of this yong mans dayes,
And for each minute of his time prolong'd,
Your fee shall be a peece of Romane gold
With *Cæsars* stampe, such as he sends his Captaines
When in the warres they earne well: do but saue him,
And as he is halfe my selfe, be you all mine.
*Doct.*  What art can do, we promise: phisickes hand          10
As apt is to destroy, as to preserue,
If heauen make not the medicine; all this while
Our skill hath combat held with his disease,
But tis so armd, and a deepe melancholy
To be such in part with death, we are in feare
The graue must mocke our labours.
*Macr.*                              I haue beene
His keeper in this sicknesse, with such eyes
As I haue seene my mother watch ore me,
And from that obseruation sure I finde,
It is a Midwife must deliuer him.                            20
*Sapr.*  Is he with child, a Midwife!
*Macr.*                              Yes, With child,
And will I feare lose life if by a woman
He is not brought to bed: stand by his Pillow
Some little while, and in his broken slumbers
Him shall you heare cry out on *Dorothea*,
And when his armes flye open to catch her,
Closing together, he falls fast asleepe,
Pleas'd with embracings of her airy forme;
Physicians but torment him, his disease

Laughs at their gibrish language, let him heare                    30
The voyce of *Dorothea*, nay but the name,
He starts vp with high colour in his face,
Shee or none cures him, and how that can be,
(The Princess strick't command, barring that happines)
To me impossible seemes.
*Sapr.*                    To me it shall not.
Ile be no subiect to the greatest *Cæsar*
Was euer crown'd with Lawrell, rather then cease
To be a father.                                        *Exit.*
*Macr.*          Silence sir, he wakes.
*Anton.*   Thou kilst me *Dorothea*, oh *Dorothea.*
*Macr.*   Shees heere; enioy her.
*Anton.*                    Where, Why doe you mocke me, 40
Age on my head hath stuck no white haires yet,
Yet I'me an old man, a fond doting foole
Vpon a woman, I to buy her beauty,
(Truth I am bewitched) offer my life,
And she for my acquaintance hazards hers,
Yet for our equall suffrings, none holds out
A hand of pitty.
*Doct.*          Let him haue some Musicke.
*Anton.*   Hell on your fidling.
*Doct.*                    Take againe your bed Sir,
Sleepe is a soueraigne Physicke.
*Anton.*                    Take an Asses head Sir,
Confusion on your fooleries, your charmes,                    50
Thou stinking Glister-pipe, where's the god of rest,
Thy Pills, and base Apothecary drugges
Threatned to bring vnto me, out you Impostors,
Quacksaluing, cheating Mountebankes, your skill
Is to make sound men sicke, and sicke men kill.
*Macr.*   O be your selfe deare friend.
*Anton.*                    My selfe *Macrinus,*
How can I be my selfe, when I am mangled

40 enioy] Mason; I enioy Q 1-4

Into a thousand peeces, heere moues my head,
But wheres my heart? where euer, that lies dead.

*Enter* Sapritius *dragging in* Dorothea *by the Haire*,
Angelo *attending*.

*Sapr.*   Follow me thou damn'd Sorceres, call vp thy spirits,         60
And if they can, now let 'em from my hand
Vntwine these witching haires.
*Anton.*                     I am that spirit,
Or if I be not (were you not my father)
One made of Iron should hew that hand in peeces
That so defaces this sweete Monument
Of my loues beauty?
*Sapr.*                  Art thou sicke?
*Anton.*                              To death.
*Sapr.*   Wouldst thou recouer?
*Anton.*                        Would I liue in blisse?
*Sapr.*   And doe thine eyes shoote daggers at that man
That brings thee health?
*Anton.*                    It is not in the world?
*Sapr.*   Ist heere?
*Anton.*          Oh Treasure, by enchantment lock'd         70
In Caues as deepe as hell, am I as neere?
*Sapr.*   Breake that enchanted Caue, enter, and rifle
The spoyles thy lust hunts after; I descend
To a base office, and become thy Pandar
In bringing thee this proud Thing, make her thy Whore,
Thy health lies heere, if she deny to giue it,
Force it, imagine thou assaultst a towne,
Weake wall, too't, tis thine owne, beat but this downe.
Come, and vnseene, be witnesse to this battry,
                              [*To the others aside.*]
How the coy strumpet yeelds.
*Doct.*                    Shall the boy stay sir.         80
*Sapr.*   No matter for the boy, Pages are vs'd

71 neere?] Q3; ~ . Q1–2

To these odde bawdy shufflings, and indeede
Are those little yong snakes in a Furies head
Will sting worse then the great ones, let the Pimpe stay.

*Exeunt aside.*

*Dor.*   Oh guard me Angels,
What Tragedy must begin now?
*Anton.*                    When a Tyger
Leapes into a tymerous heard, with rauenous Iawes
Being hunger-staru'd, what Tragedy then begins?
*Dor.*   Death! I am happy so, you hitherto
Haue still had goodnes spher'd within your eyes,              90
Let not that Orbe be broken.
*Ange.*                    Feare not Mistresse,
If he dare offer violence, we two
Are strong enough for such a sickly man.
*Dor.*   What is your horrid purpose sir, your eye
Beares danger in it?
*Anton.*                    I must.
*Dor.*                    What.
*Sapr.*                    Speake it out.
*Anton.*   Climbe that sweete Virgin tree.
*Sapr.*                    Plague a your trees.
*Anton.*   And pluck that fruit which none I think euer tasted.
*Sapr.*   A souldier, and stand fumbling so.
*Dor.*                    O Kill me,      *Kneeles.*
And heauen will take it as a sacrifice,
But if you play the Rauisher, there is              100
A Hell to swallow you.
*Sapr.*                    Let her swallow thee.
*Anton.*   Rise, for the Romane Empire (*Dorothea*)
I would not wound thine honour, pleasure forc'd
Are vnripe Apples, sowre, not worth the plucking,
Yet let me tell you, tis my fathers will,
That I should seize vpon you as my prey.
Which I abhorre as much as the blackest sinne
The villany of man did euer act.

*90 spher'd] Mason; spard Q1; spar'd Q2-4

　　　　Sapritius *breakes in and* Macrinus.

*Ange.*　Dye happy for this language.
*Sapr.*　　　　　　　　Dye a slaue,
A blockish Ideot.
*Macr.*　　　　Deare sir, vexe him not.　　　　　　　110
*Sapr.*　Yes, and vexe thee too, both I thinke are geldings,
Cold, Phlegmatike Bastard, th'art no brat of mine,
One sparke of me, when I had heate like thine
By this had made a Bonefire: a tempting whore
(For whom th'art mad) thrust euen into thine armes,
And standst thou puling? had a Taylor seene her
At this aduantage, he with his crosse-capers
Had rufled her by this, but thou shalt curse
Thy dalliance, and heere before her eyes
Teare thy flesh in peeces, when a slaue　　　　　120
In hot lust bathes himselfe, and gluts those pleasures
Thy nicenesse durst not touch, call out a slaue,
You Captaine of our guard, fetch a slaue hither.
　　　　　　　　　　　　*Exit* [*attendant*].
*Anton.*　What will you do deere Sir.
*Sapr.*　　　　　　　Teach her a trade,
Which many would learne in lesse then halfe an houre,
To play the Whore.
　　　　　　　*Enter a Slaue.*

*Macr.*　　　A Slaue is come, what now.
*Sapr.*　Thou hast bones and flesh
Enough to ply thy labour, from what country
Wert thou tane Prisoner, heere to be our slaue.
*Slaue.*　From *Brittaine.*
*Sapr.*　　　　In the west Ocean.
*Slaue.*　　　　　　Yes.　　　　　　130
*Sapr.*　An Iland.
*Slaue.*　　　Yes.

116–117 her | At Q3; her | Her at Q1–2
126 come] Mason; to me Q1–2

435　　　　　　　　　　　　28-2

*Sapr.*                    I am fitted, of all Nations
Our Romane swords euer conquer'd, none comes neere
The Brittaine for true whooring: sirrah fellow,
What wouldst thou doe to gaine thy liberty?
*Slaue.*   Doe! liberty! fight naked with a Lyon,
Venture to plucke a Standard from the heart
Of an arm'd Legion: liberty! Ide thus
Bestride a Rampire, and defiance spit
I'th face of death; then, when the battring Ram
Were fetching his careere backward to pash                    140
Me with his hornes in peeces, to shake my chaines off:
And that I could not doo't but by thy death,
Stoodst thou on this dry shore, I on a rock
Ten Piramids high, downe would I leape to kill thee,
Or dye my selfe: what is for man to doe
Ile venture on, to be no more a slaue.
*Sapr.*   Thou shalt then be no slaue, for I will set thee
Vpon a peece of worke is fit for man,
Braue for a Brittaine, drag that Thing aside
And rauish her.                    150
*Slaue.*   And rauish her! is this your manly seruice,
A Diuell scornes to doo't, tis for a beast,
A villaine, not a man, I am as yet
But halfe a slaue, but when that worke is past,
A damned whole one, a blacke vgly slaue,
The slaue of all base slaues, doo't thy selfe Roman,
Tis drudgery fit for thee.
*Sapr.*                    Hees bewitch'd too,
Binde him, and with a Bastinado giue him
Vpon his naked belly two hundred blowes.
*Slaue.*   Thou art more slaue then I.          *Exit carried in.* 160
*Dor.*   That power supernall on whom waites my soule,
Is Captaine ore my chastity.
*Anton.*                    Good sir giue ore,
The more you wrong her, your selfes vex'd the more.
*Sapr.*   Plagues light on her and thee: thus downe I throw
Thy Harlot thus bi'th haire, naile her to earth,

Call in ten slaues, let euery one discouer
What lust desires, and surfet heere his fill,
Call in ten slaues.
*Ange.*          They are come sir at your call.
*Sapr.*  Ooh.                    *Falls downe.*
                    *Enter* Theophilus.

*Theoph.*  Where is the Gouernour?
*Anton.*                    There's my wretched father.    170
*Theoph.*  My Lord, *Sapritius*, hee's not dead, my Lord,
That Witch there —
*Anton.*              Tis no Romane gods can strike
These fearefull terrors, O thou happy maid,
Forgiue this wicked purpose of my father.
*Dor.*  I doe.
*Theoph.*      Gone, gone, he's peppered: tis thou
Hast done this act infernall.
*Dor.*                    Heauen pardon you,
And if my wrongs from thence pull vengeance downe
(I can no myracles worke) yet from my soule
Pray to those powers I serue, he may recouer.
*Theoph.*  He stirres, helpe, raise him vp, my Lord.
*Sapr.*                    Where am I?    180
*Theoph.*  One cheeke is blasted.
*Sapr.*                    Blasted! Wheres the *Lamia*
That teares my entrailes? I'me bewitch'd, seize on her?
*Dor.*  I'me heere, do what you please.
*Theoph.*                    Spurne her too'th barre.
*Dor.*  Come boy, being there, more neere to heauen we are.
*Sapr.*  Kicke harder, goe out witch.            *Exeunt.*
*Anton.*  O bloudy hangmen, thine own gods giue thee breth,
Each of thy tortors is my seuerall death.
                                        *Exit.*

*169 Ooh] Q 1 (u); O oh Q 1 (c)-4

437

## [ACT IV, SCENE ii]

*Enter* Harpax, Hircius, *and* Spungius.

*Harpax.* Doe you like my seruice now, say am not I
A Master worth attendance.

*Spung.* Attendance, I had rather licke cleane the soles of your
durty bootes, then weare the richest sute of any infected Lord,
whose rotten life hangs betweene the two Poles.

*Hirc.* A Lords sute! I wud not giue vp the cloake of your seruice
to meet the splay-foot estate of any leftey'd knight aboue the
Antipodes, because they are vnlucky to meete.

*Harpax.* This day ile try your loues to me, tis onely
But well to vse the agility of your armes.                          10

*Spung.* Or legs, I am lusty at them.

*Hirc.* Or any other member that has no legges.

*Spung.* Thou't runne into some hole.

*Hirc.* If I meet one that's more then my match, and that I cannot
stand in their hands, I must and will creep on my knees.

*Harpax.* Heere me my little teeme of villaines, heare me,
I cannot teach you Fencing with these Cudgels,
Yet you must vse them, lay them on but soundly,
That's all.

*Hirc.* Nay if we come to malling once, puh.                       20

*Spung.* But what Wall-nut tree is it we must beate.

*Harpax.* Your Mistresse.

*Hirc.* How! my Mistresse! I begin to haue a Christians heart,
made of sweet butter, I melt, I cannot strike a woman.

*Spung.* Nor I, vnlesse she scratch, bum my mistresse!

*Harpax.* Y'are Coxecombes, silly Animals —

*Hirc.* Whats that?

*Harpax.* Drones, Asses, blinded Moles, that dare not thrust
Your armes out to catch Fortune, say you fall off,
It must be done, you are conuerted Rascalls,                        30
And that once spred abroad, why euery slaue

16 Heere] *i.e.* Hear (cf. V.ii.104 and note)

Will kicke you, call you motley Christians,
And halfe fac'd Christians.

*Spung.* The guts of my conscience beginne to be of whit-leather,

*Hirc.* I doubt me I shall haue no sweet butter in me.

*Harpax.* Deny this, and each Pagan whom you meete
Shall forked fingers thrust into your eyes.

*Hirc.* If we be Cuckolds.

*Harpax.* Doe this, and euery god the Gentiles bow to,
Shall adde a fadome to your line of yeeres.                         40

*Spung.* A hundred fadome, I desire no more.

*Hirc.* I desire but one inch longer.

*Harpax.* The Senators will as you passe along
Clap you vpon your shoulders with this hand,
And with this hand giue you gold. When you are dead,
Happy that man shall be can get a nayle,
The paring —, nay the durt vnder the nayle
Of any of you both, to say this durt
Belong'd to *Spungius* or *Hircius.*

*Spung.* They shall not want durt vnder my nayles, ile keepe 'em 50
long of purpose, for now my fingers itch to bee at her.

*Hirc.* The first thing I doe Ile take her ore the lips.

*Spung.* And I the hips, we may strike any where?

*Harpax.* Yes, any where.

*Hirc.* Then I know where ile hit her.

*Harpax.* Prosper and be mine owne; stand by, I must not,
To see this done, great businesse calls me hence,
Hee's made can make her curse his violence.            *Exit.*

*Spung.* Feare it not sir, her ribs shall be basted.

*Hirc.* Ile come vpon her with rounce, robble-hobble, and thwicke 60
thwacke thirlery bouncing.

*Enter* Dorothea *lead Prisoner, a Guard attending, a Hangman with
Cords in some vgly shape, sets vp a Pillar in the middle of the
stage,* Sapritius *and* Theophilus *sit,* Angelo *by her.*

*Sapr.* According to our Romane customes, binde
That Christian to a Pillar.

*Theoph.*                    Infernall Furies,

Could they into my hand thrust all their whips
To teare thy flesh, thy soule, tis not a torture
Fit to the Vengeance, I should heape on thee,
For wrongs done me: me! for flagitious facts
By thee done to our gods, yet (so it stand
To great *Cesareas* Gouernors high pleasure)
Bow but thy Knee to *Iupiter* and offer                    70
Any slight sacrifice, or doe but sweare
By *Cæsars* fortune, and be free.
*Sapr.*                    Thou shalt.
*Dor.*   Not for all *Cæsars* fortune, were it chaind
To more worlds, then are kingdomes in the world,
And all those worlds drawne after him: I defie
Your hangmen; you now shew me whither to flie.
*Sapr.*   Are her tormentors ready?
*Ange.*                    Shrinke not deere mistresse.
*Both.*   My Lord, we are ready for the businesse.
*Dor.*   You two! whom I like fosterd children fed,
And lengthen'd out your starued life with bread:                    80
You be my hangmen! whom when vp the ladder
Death hald you to be strangled, I fetcht downe,
Clothd you, and warmed you, you two my tormentors.
*Both.*   Yes, we.
*Dor.*   Diuine powers pardon you.
*Sapr.*                    Strike.

        *Strike at her:* Angelo *kneeling holds her fast.*

*Theoph.*                    Beate out her braines —
*Dor.*   Receiue me you bright Angels.
*Sapr.*                    Faster slaues.
*Spung.*   Faster: I am out of breath I'am sure: if I were to beate a
bucke, I can strike no harder.
*Hirc.*   O mine armes, I cannot lift 'em to my head.
*Dor.*   Ioy aboue ioys, are my tormentors wearie                    90
In torturing me, and in my sufferings

        81 hangmen] Coxeter; hangman Q 1-4

I fainting in no limbe: tyrants strike home
And feast your fury full.
*Theoph.*　　　These dogs are curs,
*Come from his seate.*
Which snarle, yet bite not: see my Lord, her face
Has more bewitching beauty then before,
Prowd whore: it smiles, cannot an eye start out
With these.
*Hirc.*　No sir, nor the bridge of her nose fall, tis full of Iron worke.
*Sapr.*　Lets view the cudgels, are they not counterfeit.
*Ange.*　There fixe thine eye still, thy glorious crown must come　100
Not from soft pleasure, but by martyrdome,
There fixe thine eye still, when we next do meet,
Not thornes, but roses shall beare vp thy feet:
There fixe thine eye still.　　　　　　　　　　*Exit.*

*Enter* Harpax *sneaking.*

*Dor.*　　　　　Euer, euer, euer.
*Theoph.*　Wee are mock'd, these bats haue power downe to fell
　　　　gyants,
Yet her skin is not scar'd.
*Sapr.*　　　　What rogues are these.
*Theoph.*　Cannot these force a shreeke.　　　*Beats them.*
*Spung.*　Oh! a woman has one of my ribs, and now fiue more are
broken.
*Theoph.*　Cannot this make her roare.　　*Beates tother, he roares.*　110
*Sapr.*　Who hir'd these slaues? what are they?
*Spung.*　We serue that noble Gentleman there, he entisde vs to this
dry-beating, oh for one halfe pot.
*Harpax.*　My seruants! two base rogues, and sometimes seruants
To her, and for that cause forbeare to hurt her.
*Sapr.*　Vnbinde her, hang vp these.
*Theoph.*　Hang the two hounds on the next tree.
*Hirc.*　Hang vs! master *Harpax*, what a diuell shall we be thus vsde.
*Harpax.*　What bandogs but you two wud worry a woman!
Your mistresse! I but clapt you, you flew on:　　　　　120
Say I should get your liues, each rascall begger

Would when he met you, cry, out helhounds, traitors,
Spit at you, fling durt at you, and no woman
Euer endure your sight: tis your best course
(Now had you secret kniues) to stab your selues,
But since you haue not, goe and be hang'd.
*Hirc.*   I thanke you.
*Harpax.*   Tis your best course.
*Theoph.*                    Why stay they trifling here?
To gallowes drag 'em by the heeles: away.
*Spung.*   By the heeles! no sir, wee haue legges to doe vs that   130
seruice.
*Hirc.*   I, I, if no woman can endure my sight, away with me.
                                        *Exit [guarded].*
*Harpax.*   Dispatch 'em.
*Spung.*   The diuell dispatch thee.                    *Exit.*
*Sapr.*   Death this day rides in triumph, *Theophilus.*
See this witch made away to.
*Theoph.*                    My soule thirsts for it.
Come, I my selfe, thy hangmans part could play.
*Dor.*   Oh hasten me to my coronation day.
                                        *Exeunt.*


[ACT IV, Scene iii]

*Enter* Antoninus [*sick*], Macrinus, *seruants.*

*Anton.*   Is this the place where vertue is to suffer,
And heauenly beauty leauing this base earth,
To make a glad returne from whence it came,
Is it *Macrinus?*                    *A scaffold thrust forth.*
*Macr.*            By this preparation
You well may rest assurd that *Dorothea*
This houre is to die here.
*Anton.*                    Then with her dies
The abstract of all sweetnesse that's in woman.

132 S.D. *Exit*] *exeunt* Q 1-2; *om.* Q 3-4
135 rides] Q 3; ride Q 1-2        136 thirsts Q 2; thirst Q 1

Set me downe friend, that ere the iron hand
Of death close vp mine eyes, they may at once
Take my last leaue both of this light, and her:  10
For she being gone, the glorious Sun himselfe
To me's *Cymerian* darkenesse.
*Macr.*                    Strange affection!
*Cupid* once more hath chang'd his shafts with death,
And kills in stead of giuing life.
*Anton.*                    Nay weepe not,
Though teares of friendship be a soueraigne balme,
On me they are cast away: it is decreed
That I must die with her, our clew of life
Was spun together.
*Macr.*               Yet sir tis my wonder
That you who hearing onely what she suffers,
Pertake of all her tortures, yet will be  20
To adde to your calamitie, an eye witnesse
Of her last Tragicke scene, which must pierce deeper
And make the wound more desperate.
*Anton.*                    O *Macrinus,*
Twould linger out my torments else, not kill me,
Which is the end I aime at: being to die to,
What instrument more glorious can I wish for,
Then what is made sharpe by my constant loue
And true affection. It may be the duty
And loyall seruice with which I pursude her,
And seald it with my death, will be remembred  30
Among her blessed actions, and what honor
Can I desire beyond it?

*Enter a guard bringing in* Dorothea, *a headsman before her,
followed by* Theophilus, Sapritius, Harpax.

See she comes,
How sweet her innocence appeares, more like
To heauen it selfe then any sacrifice
That can be offerd to it. By my hopes
Of ioyes hereafter, the sight makes me doubtfull

In my beleefe, nor can I thinke our gods
Are good, or to be seru'd, that take delight
In offrings of this kinde, that to maintaine
Their power, deface the masterpeece of nature,                    40
Which they themselues come short of: she ascends,
And euery step raises her neerer heauen.
What god so ere thou art that must enioy her,
Receiue in her a boundlesse happinesse.

*Sapr.*    You are too blame
To let him come abrode.

*Macr.*                    It was his will,
And we were left to serue him, not command him.

*Anton.*  Good sir be not offended, nor deny
My last of pleasures in this happy obiect
That I shall ere be blest with.

*Theoph.*                    Now prowd contemner                    50
Of vs and of our gods, tremble to thinke
It is not in the power thou seru'st, to saue thee.
Not all the riches of the sea increasd
By violent shipwrackes, nor the vnsearched mines
*Mammons* vnknowne exchequer shall redeeme thee.
And therefore hauing first with horror weigh'd
What tis to die, and to die yong, to part with
All pleasures, and delights: lastly, to goe
Where all *Antipathies* to comfort dwell,
Furies behind, about thee, and before thee,                    60
And to adde to affliction the remembrance
Of the *Eliȝian* ioyes thou might'st haue tasted,
Hadst thou not turnd Apostata to those gods
That so reward their seruants, let despayre
Preuent the hangmans sword, and on this scaffold
Make thy first entrance into hell.

*Anton.*                    She smiles,
Vnmou'd by *Mars*, as if she were assur'd
Death looking on her constancy would forget
The vse of his ineuitable hand.

*Theoph.*    Derided to? dispatch I say.

*Dor.*                              Thou foole                70
That gloriest in hauing power to rauish
A trifle from me I am weary of:
What is this life? to me not worth a thought
Or if to bee esteemd, 'tis that I loose it
To win a better, eu'n thy malice serues
To me but as a ladder to mount vp
To such a height of happinesse where I shall
Looke downe with scorne on thee, and on the world,
Where circl'd with true pleasures, plac'd aboue
The reach of death or time, twill be my glory          80
To thinke at what an easie price I bought it.
There's a perpetuall spring, perpetuall youth,
No ioynt benumming cold, nor scorching heate,
Famine nor age haue any being there:
Forget for shame your *Tempe*, burie in
Obliuion, your fainde *Hesperian* Orchards:
The Golden fruite kept by the watchfull Dragon
Which did require your *Hercules* to get it
Compar'd with what growes in all plenty there,
Deserues not to be nam'd. The power I serue          90
Laughs at your happy *Arabie*, or the
*Eliȝian* shades, for he hath made his bowers
Better indeed then you can fancy yours.

*Anton.*    O take me thither with you.

*Dor.*                              Trace my steps
And be assurd you shall.

*Sapr.*                              With mine owne hands
Ile rather stop that little breath is left thee,
And rob thy killing feauer.

*Theoph.*                              By no means,
Let him go with her, do seduc'd yong man,
And waite vpon thy saint in death, do, do,
And when you come to that imagind place,              100

86 your fainde] Q3; your fainde your Q1–2
88 your] Coxeter; *om.* Q1–4

445

That place of all delights, pray you obserue me,
And meete those cursed things I once call'd daughters,
Whom I haue sent as harbingers before you,
If there be any truth in your religion,
In thankfulnesse to me that with care hasten
Your iourney thither, pray send me some
Small pittance of that curious fruit you bost of.

*Anton.* Grant that I may goe with her, and I will.

*Sapr.* Wilt thou in thy last minute dam thy selfe?

*Theoph.* The gates to hell are open.

*Dor.*                         Know thou tyrant                    110
Thou agent for the diuell thy great master
Though thou art most vnworthy to tast of it,
I can and will.

> *Enter* Angelo *in the Angels habit.*

*Harpax.*         Oh! mountaines fall vpon me,
Or hide me in the bottom of the deepe,
Where light may neuer find me.

*Theoph.*                     Whats the matter?

*Sapr.* This is prodigious, and confirms her witchcraft.

*Theoph.* *Harpax* my *Harpax* speake.

*Harpax.*                     I dare not stay,
Should I but heare her once more I were lost,
Some whirlewinde snatch me from this cursed place,
To which compar'd (and with what now I suffer)          120
Hels torments are sweet slumbers.          *Exit* Harpax.

*Sapr.*                     Follow him.

*Theoph.* He is distracted, and I must not loose him,
Thy charms vpon my seruant cursed witch,
Giues thee a short reprieue, let her not die
Till my returne.          *Exeunt* Sapritius *and* Theophilus.

*Anton.*         She minds him not, what obiect
Is her eye fixd on?

*Macr.*         I see nothing.

*Anton.*                     Marke her.

*Dor.* Thou glorious minister of the power I serue,

For thou art more then mortall, ist for me
Poore sinner, thou art pleasd awhile to leaue
Thy heauenly habitation? and vouchsafest                    130
Though glorified, to take my seruants habit,
For put off thy diuinitie, so lookd
My louely *Angelo*.
*Ange.*          Know I am the same,
And still the seruant to your pietie,
Your zealous prayers and pious deeds first wonne me
(But 'twas by his command to whom you sent 'em)
To guide your steps. I tride your charitie,
When in a beggers shape you tooke me vp
And clothd my naked limbes, and after fed
(As you beleeu'd) my famishd mouth. Learne all         140
By your example to looke on the poore
With gentle eyes, for in such habits often
Angels desire an Almes. I neuer left you,
Nor will I now, for I am sent to carry
Your pure and innocent soule to ioyes eternall,
Your martyrdome once sufferd, and before it
Aske any thing from me, and rest assur'd
You shall obtaine it.
*Dor.*          I am largely payd
For all my torments, since I find such grace
Grant that the loue of this yong man to me,                 150
In which he languisheth to death, may be
Chang'd to the loue of heauen.
*Ange.*                    I will performe it.
And in that instant when the sword sets free
Your happy soule his shall haue libertie.
Is there ought else?
*Dor.*          For proofe that I forgiue
My persecutor, who in scorne desir'd
To tast of that most sacred fruite I go to,
After my death as sent from me, be pleasd
To giue him of it.
*Ange.*          Willingly deere Mistresse.

447

*Macr.*    I am amaz'd.

*Anton.*                    I feele a holy fire                    160
That yeelds a comfortable heate within me.
I am quite alterd from the thing I was.
See I can stand, and goe alone, thus kneele
To heauenly *Dorothea*, touch her hand
With a religious kisse.

*Enter* Sapritius *and* Theophilus.

*Sapr.*                    He is well now,
But will not be drawne backe.

*Theoph.*                    It matters not,
We can discharge this worke without his helpe:
But see your sonne.

*Sapr.*            Villaine.

*Anton.*                    Sir I beseech you,
Being so neere our ends diuorce vs not.

*Theoph.*    Ile quickly make a separation of 'em.        170
Hast thou ought else to say?

*Dor.*                    Nothing but blame
Thy tardinesse in sending me to rest,
My peace is made with heauen, to which my soule
Begins to take her flight, strike, O strike quickly,
And though you are vnmou'd to see my death,
Hereafter when my story shall be read,
As they were present now, the hearers shall
Say this of *Dorothea* with wet eyes,
She liu'd a virgin, and a virgin dies.        *Her head strucke off.*

*Anton.*    O take my soule along to waite on thine.        180

*Macr.*    Your sonne sinks to.                    Antoninus *sinkes.*

*Sapr.*                    Already dead.

*Theoph.*                        Die all,
That are or fauour this accursed Sect,
I triumph in their ends, and will raise vp
A hill of their dead Karkasses, to orelooke

180 thine] Q2; mine Q1

The *Pyrenean* Hils, but ile roote out
These superstitious fooles, and leaue the World
No name of Christian.

*Loud Musicke, exit* Angelo *hauing first laid his hand vpon their mouthes.*

*Sapr.*                     Ha, heauenly Musicke.
*Macr.*   Tis in the ayre.
*Theoph.*               Illusions of the Diuell
Wrought by some one of her Religion,
That faine would make her death a miracle,                    190
It frights not me: because he is your sonne
Let him haue buriall, but let her body
Be cast forth with contempt in some high way,
And be to Vultures and to Dogs a prey.
                                              *Exeunt.*

*The end of the fourth Act.*


## ACTUS V, Scena i

*Enter* Theophilus *in his study, Bookes about him.*

*Theoph.*   Is't Holliday (Oh *Cæsar*) that thy seruant,
(Thy Prouost, to see execution done
On these base Christians in *Cesarea*)
Should now want worke: sleepe these Idolaters
That none are stirring? As a curious Painter          *Rises.*
When he has made some admirable peece,
Stands off, and with a searching eye examines
Each colour, how tis sweetned, and then hugs
Himselfe for his rare workemanship — So heere          *Sits.*
Will I my Drolleries and bloudy Lantskips               10
Long past wrap'd vp vnfold to make me merry
With shadowes, now I want the substances.              *Booke.*
My Muster-booke of Hel-hounds, were the Christians

187 S.D. *their*] *i.e.* of Dorothea and Antoninus
8 colour,] Q3; colours ᴧ Q1-2

Whose names stand heere (aliue) and arm'd; not *Rome*
Could mooue vpon her Hindges. What I haue done,
Or shall heereafter, is not out of hate
To poore tormented wretches, no I am carried
With violence of zeale, and streames of seruice
I owe our Romane gods. *Great Britaine,* what.
A thousand wiues with brats sucking their brests,                    20
Had hot Irons pinch 'em off, and throwne to swine;
And then their fleshy backparts hewed with hatchets,
Were minc'd and bak'd in Pies to feede staru'd Christians.
  Ha, ha.
Agen, agen, — *East Anglas* —, oh, East-Angles,
Bandogs (kept three dayes hungry) worried
A thousand Brittish Rascals, styed vp, fat
Of purpose, strip'd naked, and disarm'd.
I could outstare a yeere of Sunnes and Moones,
To sit at these sweete Bul-baitings, so I could                    30
Thereby but one Christian win to fall
In adoration to my *Iupiter.* Twelue hundred
Eyes boar'd with Augurs out: oh! eleuen thousand
Torne by wild beasts: two hundred ram'd i'th earth
To'th armepits, and full Platters round about 'em,
But farre enough for reaching, eate dogs, ha, ha, ha.                    *Rise.*
Tush, all these tortures are but phillipings,
Flea-bitings; I before the destinies                    *Consort, enter* Angelo
My bottome did winde vp, would flesh my selfe                    *with a Basket*
Once more, vpon some one remarkeable                    *fild with fruit and* 40
Aboue all these, this Christian Slut was well,                    *flowers.*
A pretty one, but let such horror follow
The next I feede with torments, that when *Rome*
Shall heare it, her foundation at the sound
May feele an Earth-quake. How now?                    *Musicke.*
*Ange.*                    Are you amaz'd Sir. —
So great a Roman spirit and does it tremble.
*Theoph.*   How cam'st thou in? to whom thy businesse?
*Ange.*                    To you:
I had a mistresse late sent hence by you

Vpon a bloudy errand, you intreated
That when she came into that blessed Garden          50
Whither she knew she went, and where (now happy)
Shee feedes vpon all ioy, she would send to you
Some of that Garden fruit and flowers, which heere
To haue her promise sau'd, are brought by me.
*Theoph.*   Cannot I see this Garden?
*Ange.*                    Yes, if the Master
Will giue you entrance.
                              Angelo *vanisheth.*
*Theoph.*             Tis a tempting fruit,
And the most bright cheek'd child I euer view'd,
Sweete smelling goodly fruit, what flowers are these?
In *Dioclesians* Gardens, the most beautious
Compard with these are weedes: is it not February?          60
The second day she dyed: Frost, Ice and snowe
Hang on the beard of Winter, wheres the sunne
That guilds this summer, pretty sweete boy, say
In what Country shall a man find this Garden —,
My delicate boy, gone! Vanished!
Within there, *Iulianus* and *Geta.* —

                    *Enter two seruants.*

*Both.*   My Lord.
*Theoph.*   Are my gates shut?
*1.*   And guarded.
*Theoph.*   Saw you not — a boy.          70
*2.*   Where?
*Theoph.*   Heere hee entred, a young Lad;
A thousand blessings danc'd vpon his eyes,
A smooth fac'd glorious Thing, that brought this Basket.
*1.*   No sir?
*Theoph.*   Away, but be in reach if my voyce calls you,   *Exeunt.*
No! vanish'd! and not seene, be thou a spirit
Sent from that Witch to mock me, I am sure
This is essentiall, and how ere it growes,
Will taste it.                                        *Eates.* 80

| *Harpax.* | Ha, ha, ha, ha. | *Harpax within.* |

*Theoph.* So good, ile haue some more sure.

*Harpax.* Ha, ha, ha, ha, great lickorish foole.

*Theoph.* What art thou?

*Harpax.*           A Fisherman.

*Theoph.*                     What doest thou catch.

*Harpax.* Soules, soules, a fish cal'd soules.

*Theoph.*                          *Geta.*

*Enter a seruant.*

*1.*                          My Lord.

*Harpax.* Ha, ha, ha, ha.                  *Within.*

*Theoph.* What insolent slaue is this dares laugh at me?
Or what ist the dog grinnes at so?

*1.* I neither know my Lord at what, nor whom, for there is none
without but my fellow *Iulianus*, and hee's making a Garland for 90
*Iupiter.*

*Theoph.* *Iupiter!* all within me is not well,
And yet not sicke.

*Harpax.* Ha, ha, ha, ha.                  *Lowder.*

*Theoph.* What's thy name slaue?

*Harpax.*           Goe looke.           *At one end.*

*1.*                     Tis *Harpax* voyce.

*Theoph.* *Harpax*, goe drag the Caitiffe to my foote,
That I may stampe vpon him.

*Harpax.*           Foole, thou lyest.      *At tother end.*

*1.* Hee's yonder now my Lord.

*Theoph.*                Watch thou that end
Whilst I make good this.

*Harpax.* Ha, ha, ha, ha, ha.              *At the middle.* 100

*Theoph.* Hee's at Barli-breake, and the last couple are now in hell,
Search for him, all this ground me thinkes is bloudy,

                          *Exit seruant.*

And pau'd with thousands of those Christians eyes

82 more] Q3; now Q1–2
85 *Enter a seruant.*] Gifford; Q1–4 *place after* Harpax's *line, ending* cal'd soules.
*But the catchword after this is* Theo.
102 thinkes] Q3; thinke Q1–2      102 S.D. Q1–4 *place in line* 101

452

Whom I haue tortur'd, and they stare vpon me;
What was this apparition? sure it had
A shape Angelicall; mine eyes (though dazled
And danted at first sight) tell me, it wore
A paire of glorious wings, yes they were wings,
And hence he flew; tis vanished, *Iupiter*
For all my sacrifices done to him　　　　　　　　　110
Neuer once gaue me smile: how can stone smile,　　*Musicke.*
Or woodden Image laugh? ha! I remember
Such Musicke gaue a welcome to my eare,
When the faire youth came to me: tis in the Ayre,
Or from some better place, a power diuine,
Through my darke ignorance on my soule does shine,
And makes me see a conscience all stai'nd ore,
Nay drown'd and damn'd for euer in Christian gore.
*Harpax.* Ha, ha, ha.　　　　　　　　　　　　　*Within.*
*Theoph.* Agen, what dainty rellish on my tongue　　120
This fruit hath left, some Angell hath me fed,
If so toothfull, I will be banqueted.　　　　*Eates another.*

*Enter* Harpax *in a fearefull shape, fire flashing out of the study.*

*Harpax.* Hold.
*Theoph.*　　　　Not for *Cæsar.*
*Harpax.*　　　　　　　　But for me thou shalt.
*Theoph.* Thou art no Twin to him that last was heere.
You powers whom my soule bids me reuerence,
Guard me: What art thou?
*Harpax.*　　　　　　　I'me thy Master.
*Theoph.*　　　　　　　　　　　　Mine.
*Harpax.* And thou my euerlasting slaue; that *Harpax,*
Who hand in hand hath led thee to thy Hell
Am I.
*Theoph.* Auant.
*Harpax.*　　　I will not, cast thou downe
That Basket with the things in't, and fetch vp　　130
What thou hast swallowed, and then take a drinke
Which I shall giue thee, and i'me gon.

*Theoph.* My Fruit!
Does this offend thee? see.
*Harpax.* Spet it to'th earth,
And tread vpon it, or ile peece-meale teare thee.
*Theoph.* Art thou with this affrighted? see, heares more.
*Flowers.*
*Harpax.* Fling them away, ile take thee else and hang thee
In a contorted Chaine of Isicles
I'th frigid Zone: downe with them.
*Theoph.* At the botome,
One thing I found not yet, see. *A crosse of Flowers.*
*Harpax.* Oh, I'me tortur'd.
*Theoph.* Can this doo't? hence thou Fiend infernall hence. 140
*Harpax.* Claspe *Iupiters* Image, and away with that.
*Theoph.* At thee ile fling that *Iupiter*, for me thinkes
I serue a better Master, he now checkes me
For murthering my two daughters, put on by thee;
By thy damn'd Rhetoricke did I hunt the life
Of *Dorothea*, the holy Virgin Martyr,
She is not angry with the Axe nor me,
But sends these presents to me, and ile trauell
Ore worlds to finde her, and from her white hand
To beg a forgiuenesse.
*Harpax.* No, ile bind thee heere. 150
*Theoph.* I serue a strength above thine: this small weapon
Me thinkes is Armour hard enough.
*Harpax.* Keepe from me.
*Sinkes alittle.*
*Theoph.* Art poasting to thy center? down hel-hound, down,
Me hast thou lost; that arme which hurles thee hence
Saue me, and set me vp the strong defence
In the faire Christians quarrel.

*Enter* Angelo. [Harpax *vanishes.*]

*Ange.* Fixe thy foote there,
Nor be thou shaken with a *Cæsars* voyce,
Though thousand deaths were in it: and I then

454

Will bring thee to a Riuer that shall wash
Thy bloudy hands cleane, and more white then Snow,                    160
And to that Garden where these blest things grow,
And to that martyr'd Virgin, who hath sent
That heauenly token to thee; Spred this braue wing
And serue then *Cæsar*, a farre greater King.                        *Exit.*
*Theoph.*   It is, it is some Angell, vanish'd againe!
Oh come back rauishing Boy, bright Messenger,
Thou hast (by these mine eyes fixt on thy beauty)
Illumined all my soule, now looke I backe
On my blacke Tyranies, which as they did
Out-dare the bloudiest, thou blest spirit that leades me,            170
Teach me what I must do, and to doe well,
That my last act, the best may Paralell.

                                                                     *Exit.*


[ACT V, SCENE ii]

*Enter* Dioclesian, Maximinus, Epire, Pontus, Macedon,
             *meeting* Artemia, *attendants.*

*Artemia.*   Glory and Conquest still attend vpon
Triumphant *Cæsar.*
*Diocle.*              Let thy wish faire Daughter
Be equally deuided, and hereafter
Learne thou to know and reuerence *Maximinus,*
Whose power with mine vnited makes one *Cæsar.*
*Maxim.*   But that I feare 'twould be held flattery,
The bonds consider'd in which we stand tide
As loue, and Empire, I should say till now
I nere had seen a Lady I thought worthy
To be my Mistresse.
*Artemia.*              Sir, you shew your selfe                      10
Both Courtier and Souldier, but take heede,
Take heede my Lord, though my dull pointed beauty
Stain'd by a harsh refusall in my seruant

                    164 then] *i.e.* than

                         455

Cannot dart forth such beames as may inflame you,
You may encounter such a powerfull one,
That with a pleasing heate will thaw your heart
Though bound in ribs of Ice, loue still is loue,
His Bow and Arrowes are the same, great *Iulius*
That to his successors left the name of *Cæsar*,
Whom warre could neuer tame, that with dry eyes          20
Beheld the large plaines of *Pharsalia*, couer'd
With the dead Karkasses of Senators
And Citizens of *Rome*, when the world knew
No other Lord but him, strucke deepe in yeeres to,
And men gray haird forget the lusts of youth:
After all this, meeting faire *Cleopatra*,
A suppliant to, the magicke of her eye,
Euen in his pride of conquest tooke him captiue,
Nor are you more secure.

*Maxim.*                    Were you deform'd
(But by the gods you are most excellent)                 30
Your grauity and discretion would o'recome me,
And I should be more proud in being a Prisoner
To your faire vertues, then of all the Honours,
Wealth, Title, Empire, that my sword hath purchac'd.

*Diocle.*   This meetes my wishes, welcome it *Artemia*
With out-stretch'd armes, and study to forget
That *Antoninus* euer was: thy fate
Reseru'd thee for this better choise, embrace it.

*Epire.*   This happy match brings new nerues to giue strength
To our continued league.

*Macedon.*                    *Hymen* himselfe          40
Will blesse this marriage which we will solemnize
In the presence of these Kings.

*Pontus.*                    Who rest most happy
To be eye-witnesses of a Match that brings
Peace to the Empire.

*Diocle.*                    We much thanke your loues,
But wher's *Sapritius* our Gouernour,

27 to] *i.e.* too          37 was:] Q3 [~ ;]; ~ ₐ Q1-2

And our most zealous prouost good *Theophilus?*
If euer Prince were blest in a true seruant,
Or could the gods be debtors to a man,
Both they and we stand far ingag'd to cherish
His pietie and seruice.
*Artemia.*                Sir the Gouernour          50
Brookes sadly his sonnes losse although he turnd
Apostata in death, but bold *Theophilus*
Who for the same cause in my presence seald
His holy anger on his daughters hearts,
Hauing with tortures first tride to conuert her,
Drag'd the bewitching Christian to the scaffold,
And saw her loose her head.
*Diocle.*                He is all worthy,
And from his owne mouth I would gladly heare
The manner how she sufferd.
*Artemia.*                'Twill be deliuerd
With such contempt and scorne, I know his nature,    60
That rather twill beget your highnesse laughter
Then the least pittie.

               *Enter* Theophilus, Sapritius, Macrinus.

*Diocle.*                To that end I would heare it.
*Artemia.*     He comes, with him the Gouernour.
*Diocle.*                         O *Sapritius,*
I am to chide you for your tendernesse,
But yet remembring that you are a father,
I will forget it, good *Theophilus*
Ile speake with you anone: neerer your eare —     *To* Sapritius.
*Theoph.*     By *Antoninus* soule I do coniure you,
And though not for religion, for his friendship,
Without demanding whats the cause that moues me,    70
Receiue my signet, by the power of this
Go to my prisons, and release all Christians
That are in fetters there by my command.
*Macr.*     But what shall follow?
*Theoph.*                Haste then to the port,

457

You there shall finde two tall ships ready rig'd,
In which embarke the poore distressed soules
And beare them from the reach of tyranny,
Enquire not whither you are bound, the dietie
That they adore will giue you prosperous winds,
And make your voyage such, and largely pay for             80
Your hazard, and your trauaile: leaue me here,
There is a scene that I must act alone.
Haste good *Macrinus*, and the great God guide you.
*Macr.*   Ile vndertake't, theres some thing prompts me to it,
Tis to saue innocent blood, a Saintlike act,
And to be mercifull has neuer beene
By morrall men themselues esteemd a sin.        *Exit* Macrinus.
*Diocle.*   You know your charge.
*Sapr.*                            And will with care obserue it.
*Diocle.*   For I professe he is not *Cæsars* friend
That sheds a teare for any torture that                    90
A Christian suffers. Welcome my best seruant,
My carefull, zealous Prouost, thou hast toyld
To satisfie my will though in extreames,
I loue thee for't, thou art firme rocke, no changeling:
Prethee deliuer, and for my sake do it
Without excesse of bitternesse or scoffes
Before my brother and these kings, how tooke
The Christian her death.
*Theoph.*                    And such a presence
Though euery priuate head in this large roome
Were circl'd round with an imperiall crowne,               100
Her story will deserue, it is so full
Of excellency and wonder.
*Diocle.*                     Ha! how's this?
*Theoph.*   O marke it therefore, and with that attention,
As you would here an Embassie from heauen
By a wing'd Legate, for the truth deliuerd,
Both how and what this blessed virgin sufferd:

91 Christian] Q2; Christians Q1
104 here] *i.e.* hear (cf. V.ii.136, 166–168)

And *Dorothea* but hereafter nam'd,
You will rise vp with reuerence, and no more
As things vnworthy of your thoughts, remember
What the canoniz'd *Spartan* Ladies were　　　　　　　110
Which lying *Greece* so bosts of: your owne matrons,
Your Romane dames whose figures you yet keepe
As holy relickes in her historie
Will find a second vrne. *Gracchus Cornelia,*
*Paulina* that in death desirde to follow
Her husband *Seneca,* nor *Brutus Portia*
That swallowd burning coles to ouertake him,
Though all their seuerall worths were giuen to one
With this is to be mention'd.
*Maxim.*　　　　　　　　Is he mad?
*Diocle.* Why they did die *Theophilus,* and boldly.　　　120
This did no more.
*Theoph.*　　　　　They out of desperation
Or for vaine glory of an aftername
Parted with life. This had not mutinous sonnes
As the rash *Gracchi* were, nor was this Saint
A doting mother as *Cornelia* was:
This lost no husband in whose ouerthrow
Her wealth and honour suncke, no feare of want
Did make her being tedious, but aiming
At an immortall crowne, and in his cause
Who onely can bestow it; who sent downe　　　　　130
Legions of ministring Angels to beare vp
Her spotlesse soule to heauen; who entertaind it
With choyce celestiall musicke, equall to
The motion of the spheres; she vncompeld
Chang'd this life for a better. My Lord *Sapritius*
You were present at her death, did you ere here
Such rauishing sounds?
*Sapr.*　　　　　　　Yet you sayd then it was witchcraft,
And diuellish illusions.
*Theoph.*　　　　　　I then hard it
With sinfull eares, and belch'd out blasphemous words

Against his dietie, which then I knew not,                     140
Nor did beleeue in him.
*Diocle.*            Why, dost thou now?
Or dar'st thou in our hearing?
*Theoph.*                Were my voyce
As lowd as is his thunder, to be heard
Through al the world, all potentates on earth
Ready to burst with rage should they but heare it,
Though hell to ayde their mallice lent her furies
Yet I would speake, and speake againe, and boldly,
I am a Christian, and the powers you worship
But dreames of fooles and madmen.
*Maxim.*              Lay hands on him.
*Diocle.*  Thou twice a child (for doting age so makes thee)   150
Thou couldst not else thy pilgrimage of life,
Being almost past through, in the last moment
Destroy what ere thou hast done good or great,
Thy youth did promise much, and growne a man
Thou madest it good, and with encrease of yeares
Thy actions still betterd: as the Sunne
Thou did rise gloriously, kepst a constant course
In all thy iourney, and now in the euening
When thou shouldst passe with honour to thy rest,
Wilt thou fall like a Meteor?
*Sapr.*                  Yet confesse             160
That thou art mad, and that thy tong and heart
Had no agreement.
*Maxim.*        Doe, no way is left else
To saue thy life *Theophilus.*
*Diocle.*                But refuse it,
Destruction as horrid and as sodaine
Shall fall vpon thee, as if hell stood open
And thou wert sinking thither.
*Theoph.*                Here me yet,
Here for my seruice past.
*Artemia.*              What will he say?

152 through, ...moment $_\wedge$] Gifford; $\sim$ $_\wedge$ ... $\sim$ , Q1-4±

*Theoph.*  As euer I deseru'd your fauour here me,
And grant one boone, tis not for life I sue for,
Nor is it fit that I that nere knew pitty                                    170
To any Christian, being one my selfe
Should looke for any: no, I rather beg
The vtmost of your cruelty; I stand
Accomptable for thousand Christians deaths,
And were it possible that I could die
A day for euery one, then liue againe
To be againe tormented, twere to me
An easie pennance, and I should passe through
A gentle clensing fire, but that denyde me,
It being beyond the strength of feeble nature,                               180
My sute is you would haue no pitty on me.
In mine owne house there are a thousand engines
Of studied crueltie, which I did prepare
For miserable Christians, let me feele
As the Sicilian did his brazen bull,
The horridst you can find, and I will say
In death that you are mercifull.
*Diocle.*                        Despaire not,
In this thou shalt preuaile, go fetch 'em hither,
                                   *Some go for the racke.*
Death shall put on a thousand shapes at once
And so appeare before thee, racks, and whips,                                190
Thy flesh with burning pinsors torne, shall feed
The fire that heates them, and whats wanting to
The torture of thy body, Ile supply
In punishing thy mind: fetch all the Christians
That are in hold, and here before his face
Cut 'em in peeces.
*Theoph.*                Tis not in thy power,
It was the first good deed I euer did,
They are remou'd out of thy reach: how ere
I was determin'd for my sinnes to die,
I first tooke order for their liberty,                                       200
And still I dare thy worst.

461

*Diocle.*                       Bind him I say,
Make euery artery and sinew crack,
The slaue that makes him giue the lowdest shrike
Shall haue ten thousand Drachmes, wretch ile force thee
To curse the power thou worship'st.
*Theoph.*                       Neuer, neuer,
No breath of mine shall euer be spent on him, *They torment him.*
But what shall speake his Maiesty or mercy:
I am honour'd in my suffrings, weake tormentors
More tortures, more: alas you are vnskilfull,
For Heauens sake more; my brest is yet vntorne:                    210
Heere purchase the reward that was propounded,
The Irons coole, heere are armes yet and thighes,
Spare no part of me.
*Maxim.*                       He endures beyond
The suffrance of a man.
*Sapr.*                       No sigh nor grone
To witnesse he has feeling.
*Diocle.*                       Harder Villaines.

*Enter* Harpax.

*Harpax.*   Vnlesse that he blaspheme hee's lost for euer,
If torments euer could bring forth despaire,
Let these compell him to it: oh me
My ancient enemies againe.                       *Falls downe.*

*Enter* Dorothea *in a white robe, crownes vpon her robe, a Crowne
vpon her head, lead in by* [Angelo] *the Angell,* Antoninus, Caliste
*and* Christeta *following all in white, but lesse glorious, the Angell
with a Crowne for him.*

*Theoph.*   Most glorious vision,                       220
Did ere so hard a bed yeeld man a dreame
So heauenly as this? I am confirm'd,
Confirm'd you blessed spirits, and make hast
To take that crowne of immortality
You offer to me; death till this blest minute
I neuer thought thee slow pac'd, nor could I

462

Hasten thee now for any paine I suffer,
But that thou keepst me from a glorious wreath
Which through this stormy way I would creepe to,
And humbly kneeling with humility weare it.                    230
Oh now I feele thee, blessed spirits I come,
And witnesse for me, all these wounds and scarres,
I die a souldier in the Christian warres.              *Dies.*
*Sapr.*   I haue seene thousands tortur'd, but nere yet
A constancy like this.
*Harpax.*              I am twise damn'd.
*Ange.*   Haste to thy place appointed cursed fiend,
In spite of hell this souldier's not thy prey,
Tis I haue wonne, thou that hast lost the day.

> *Exit* Angelo, *the diuell sinkes with lightning.*

*Diocle.*   I thinke the centre of the earth be crackt,
Yet I still stand vnmou'd, and will go on,                    240
The persecution that is here begun,
Through all the world with violence shall run.

> *Flourish, exeunt.*

### FINIS.

228 keepst] Q2; kepst Q1

# TEXTUAL NOTES

## I.i

27 these] The verb *had yeelded* in line 30 requires a subject, which is provided by Mason's emendation of *these* for Qq *this*. Were *this* the object of *say*, the elision of some word like *they* before *had yeelded* would be too violent and uncharacteristic. Of course, *this* in line 27 may be right, and the word *they* may have dropped out in error in line 30. The absence of a comma after *this* need not be significant, of course, given Massinger's light punctuation. In line 43 Theophilus refers to *these my daughters*, which may go back to the supposed *these* of line 27, but the argument is tenuous. Of more pertinence is the echo in the line 27 *these* of *these vestals* in line 23, so strong that the emendation is really only a repetition. Hence the confusion of *these* as *this* may seem simpler than the omission of *they*, despite the long inversion that must follow.

97 hopes,] Whether the *publicke grace* would be beyond Antoninus' hopes, or the *rewards*, is in question. Q 1–2 say the latter; Q 3–4 the first. According to the Q 1–2 text Antoninus would expect both public grace and rewards, *i.e.* both intangible honours and tangible rewards in money. It may be quibbling to point out that, as the son of a very rich father (I.i.436–437), Antoninus had no need to follow the wars for profit, and *publick grace* would be his sole concern. However, the context makes quite clear that *beyond his hopes* should properly modify *grace*, as in Q 3. Harpax knows that Artemia's choice will be the reward (see line 314). Hence, the forecast is here made that besides the *publick grace* beyond his normal expectations, there are rewards (Artemia) in store.

389 dead] Q 1 *drad* as an adjective meaning *afraid, frightened, terrified* is last noticed by O.E.D. in 1450, and at best is somewhat redundant. The emendation to the common idiom seems required.

## II.ii

29 Egles] All editors have retained Q 1–4 *Angels*, not uninfluenced, apparently, by Gifford's note alleging that *angel* is a common synonym for *bird*. The examples he gives are all of figurative uses quite unrelated to the present text, and he thus obscures the fact that the Qq reading is nonsense.

## II.iii

26 awing] Gifford's emendation of Q 1-4 *owing* seems required. *Owing* in
the sense of 'owning' fits ill with his father's *voice and arm*, whereas both
are representative of influence and authority and thus are, in a way, in
apposition to *greatnesse of his State* not dependent alone on Antoninus'
military conduct.

199 *whee*] Qq *wee*, which has driven editors to a number of ingenious emenda-
tions far from the simple truth, is actually a confusion of Dekker's comic
Welsh. For various uses of *whee* see *Patient Grissil*, II.ii.167; III.ii.182, 234;
IV.iii.111, 169.

## III.ii

124 S.D. *him, laughing. Enter* Angelo.] Gifford (1805) first saw the need to
remove the entrance of Artemia; but not until 1813 did he bring on Angelo
(after Artemia's half of line 125), and then transferred Qq *laughing* to
Angelo, as *smiling*. I take it that the confusion of the manuscript extended
to this word too, and that Harpax's exit *laughing* is meaningful, whereas
Angelo's entrance *laughing* (smiling is Gifford's silent paraphrase) is
meaningless.

## IV.i

90 spher'd] O.E.D. gives a meaning to Qq *spard* that always implies barred,
imprisoned, locked-up, all of which are inappropriate here. The next line
establishes *spher'd* as the inevitable emendation since it is the *sphere of
goodness* (and not the eyeball!) that should not be broken.
169 Ooh] If IV.i is Massinger's, untouched by Dekker, then the uncorrected
Q 1 reading *Ooh* is in error and the proof-reader's 'correction' to *O oh* no
sophistication. But if IV.i is Dekker's, whether as originator or reviser,
Q 1 (c) must be unauthoritative. The press-reader cannot be shown to have
referred to copy elsewhere, and Dekker's *Ooh* was intended to express a
particularly horrible and unearthly sound, as in *If This Be Not a Good Play*,
IV.ii.50-51, V.iii.149.

# PRESS-VARIANTS IN Q1 (1622)

[Copies collated: BM¹ (British Museum 644.f.1), BM² (162.d.19), BM³ (Ashley 1110), BM⁴ (1077.k.4); Bodl¹ (Bodleian Library Douce M.671), Bodl² (Mal. 233[4]); Dyce¹ (Dyce Collection in Victoria and Albert Museum 25.A.103), Dyce² (24.A.104); CSmH¹ (Huntington Library 17644), CSmH² (17644a).]

## HALF-SHEET A (*outer forme*)

*Corrected:* BM¹⁻³, Bodl¹, Dyce¹⁻², CSmH¹⁻².
*Uncorrected:* Bodl².

*Persons*   names] nomes

## HALF-SHEET A (*inner forme*)

*Corrected:* BM¹⁻³, Dyce¹⁻², CSmH¹.
*Uncorrected:* Bodl¹⁻², CSmH².

*Title-page*   Written   { *Phillip Meffenger* and }
            by   { *Thomas Deker.* }
|| [lace ornament] || LONDON, | Printed by *B. A.* for *Thomas* | *Iones.* 1622.] Written by *Phillip Meffenger* and | *Thomas Decker.* | [device: McK. 299, initials voided] | LONDON, | Printed by *Bernard Alfop* for *Thomas* | *Iones.* 1622.

## SHEET B (*outer forme*)

*Corrected:* BM¹⁻³, Bodl¹⁻², Dyce¹⁻², CSmH¹⁻².
*Uncorrected:* BM⁴.

Sig. B3.
I.i.124 greatnes] greatues.

## SHEET C (*outer forme*)

*Corrected:* BM¹⁻⁴, Dyce¹⁻², CSmH¹.
*Uncorrected:* Bodl¹⁻², CSmH².

Sig. C1.
I.i.252 Fortune:] Fortune,
    253 Deiectedly] Directly
    260 them] theɯ
    260 ouercome,] ouercome

I.i.261 latter,] latter
 262 Vaſſals,] Vaſſals
 271 here] heare
 272 Here] Heare

Sig. C3.
 I.i.379 not] or
 387 vnmannerd] vnmanurd
 390 danted] dant

Sig. C4ᵛ.
 I.i.474 reader will,] reader, will
 II.i.2 walke] walkes

## SHEET E (*inner forme*)

*Corrected:* BM¹⁻⁴, Dyce¹⁻², CSmH¹.
*Uncorrected:* Bodl¹⁻², CSmH².

Sig. E1ᵛ.
 II.iii.20 alone,] alone

Sig. E2.
 II.iii.47 I yet] yet I
 69 ilfa-] il-

Sig. E4.
 II.iii.183 but] bnt

## SHEET F (*outer forme*)

*Corrected:* BM¹⁻³, Dyce¹⁻², CSmH¹.
*Uncorrected:* BM⁴, Bod¹⁻², CSmH².

Sig. F1.
 II.iii.228 peeces] pe ce

Sig. F3.
 III.i.92 proſperity] poſterity

## SHEET G (*outer forme*)

*Corrected:* BM²⁻³, Bodl¹⁻², Dyce¹⁻², CSmH².
*Uncorrected:* BM¹⁻⁴, CSmH¹.

Sig. G3.
 III.ii.122 inſtrument] inſtruments

SHEET I (*inner forme*)

*Corrected:* BM¹⁻⁴, Dyce¹⁻², CSmH¹.
*Uncorrected:* Bodl¹⁻², CSmH².

Sig. I1ᵛ.
    IV.i.169  O oh] Ooh

SHEET L (*inner forme*)

*Correct:* BM¹⁻⁴, Bodl¹⁻², Dyce¹, CSmH¹⁻².
*Error:* Dyce².

Sig. L4.
    running-title   The *Virgin Martir*.] *The Virgin Martir.*

HALF-SHEET M (*outer forme*)

*Corrected:*   BM¹⁻³, Bodl¹⁻², Dyce¹⁻², CSmH¹⁻².
*Uncorrected:* BM.⁴.

Sig. M1.
    V.ii.210  vntorne:] vntorne,
        219 S.D.  *head, lead*] *head lead,*

# EMENDATIONS OF ACCIDENTALS
## Q 1 (1622)

### Persons

HIRCIUS] HERCIUS

### I.i

S.D. SCENA] Scene
2 liue?] ~ .
4 Meteors,] ~ .
23 S.D. Christeta] Christata
35 threats,] ~ ∧
74 more,] ~ ∧
75 doubl'd,] ~ ∧
115 daughters,] ~ ∧
177 endure,] ~ ∧
195 rigorous] rigorons
211 had,] ~ ∧
224 *Hercules*,] ~ ∧
261 latter∧] Q 1 (u); ~ , Q 1 (c)
262 Vassals∧] Q 1 (u); ~ , Q 1 (c)
267 happy.] ~ ∧
267 of fate] offate

277 daughter] daugher
284 owne.] ~ ∧
300 addition,] ~ ∧
302 estate,] ~ ∧
311 Aimd∧] Q 1 *text*; ~ , Q 1 *cw*
331 low —] ~ .
335 me,] ~ .
341 Call] Q 1 *text*; Cal Q 1 *cw*
372 retire,] ~ ∧
376–377 As. . . her.] *one line in* Q 1–4
388 Lyon,] ~ ∧
410 *Anton.* Oh] Q 1–4 *head speech by centered* Antoninus, Macrinus.
411 of the] ofthe
451 liberty] libetty
454 husband;] ~ ¿

### II.i

S.D. SCENA] SCENVS
S.D. Hircius] Hercius
20 What] what
26–27 out-|boule] out-boule
29 Alehouse] Alhouse
38 as if | ] asif
40 no] uo
48 face] fsce
54 ride,] Q 1 *text*; ~ ∧ Q 1 *cw*
55 haue] hue

65 of iron] ofiɹon
73 an-Apes] ~ ∧ ~
75 downward,] ~ ∧
77 almesbasket] almsebasket
132 part-] ~ .
140 mouse-holes] mouse-|holes
144 charity,] ~ .
146 be told] betold
207 Bewitching] Betwitching

469

## II.ii

14 Manuscript] Manunscript
20 Q *lines*: the | Man
60 Thunderbolts] Thunderbots

65 poison.] ~ ,
83 with.] ~ ,

## II.iii

17-18 Sir...it.] *prose in* Q 1-4
24 nothing:] ~ ,
26 of:] ~ ₳
29 pride:] ~ ,
56 S.D. Hircius] Hercius
62 And] and
90 Y'are] y'are
133 S.D. Theophilus,] ~ ₳

165 Labord] Lobord
180 daughters] daughers
195 that] | That
199 flesh] | Flesh
239 gold?] ~ .
257 gone?] ~ .
269 Follow] follow

## III.i

S.D. III,] 3.
S.D. Scena] Scenvs
 1 sorrow,] ~ .
 6 him,] ~ .
 7 honours] hononours
17 But] but
23 Basilisks] Basiliks

29 her death,] he rdeath ₳
71 together,] ~ .
88 scorne,] ~ ₳
145 speake] speakes
153 -labourer;] ~ ,
173 enemies:] ~ ,

## III.ii

3 and] aud
21 alter] altar

73 Alacke] A lacke

## III.iii

29 eloquence] eloquence
32 Awle,] ~ ₳
38 seame-rent] seame-|rent
48 of his] ofhis
52 hand,] ~ ₳
71 Whore;] Q 1 *text*; whore, Q 1 *cw*
75 well?] ~ .
98 a long] along
98 Suburbs] Sub-|vrbs
112 praying,] ~ ₳
113 out your] yout our

114 scuruy] scurny
121 rightly] righly
125 madnes,] ~ ₳
126 agen,] ~ ₳
134 drunke?] ~ ,
136 any a man] anyaman
141 ragged —₳] ~ — .
160 Q *lines*: louing, | To
185 damn'd] damn'
200 woman?] ~ .

## IV.i

S.D. IV] 4
  15 are in] arein
  44 life] llfe
  54 Mountebankes] Mountbanks
  78 downe.] ~ ,
  81–84 Q *lines*: No...boy, | Pages
    ...bawdy| Shufflings...those|

Little...head | Will...ones, |
Let...stay.
89 Death!] ~ ∧
102 Rise,] ~ ∧
124–126 Q *lines*: Teach...learne |
  In...Whore.
141 peeces, ...off:] ~ : ... ~ ,
172 there —] ~ .

## IV.ii

3 your] Q1 *text*; Your Q1 *cw*
26 Animals —] ~ ,
34 whit-leather] whit-|leather
45 When] when
49 *Hircius*] *Hercius*
53 where?] ~ .
56 not,] ~ ∧
69 *Cesareas*] *Cesaraes*

82 downe,] ~ ∧
91 sufferings] suffrings
93 curs,] *comma doubtful*
98 bridge] brigde
105–106 *prose in* Q
110 S.D. *tother*,] ~ ∧
122 traitors,] ~ ∧

## IV.iii

25 at: ...to,] ~ , ... ~ .
59 dwell,] ~ ∧
86 Orchards:] ~ ∧
156 scorne] scornd

157 to,] ~ ∧
175 death,] ~ ∧
178 eyes,] ~ ∧
181 all,] ~ .

## V.i

S.D. V] 5
  5 stirring?] ~ ,
  9 workemanship —∧] ~ —.
27 A thousand] 1000.
45–46 Are...tremble.] *prose in* Q
56–57 Tis...view'd,] *one line in* Q
63–65 Q *lines*: That...Country |
  Shall...Vanished!

72–74 *prose in* Q
73 A thousand] 1000.
101 couple] coulple
124 Q *lines*: that | Last
125 reuerence,] ~ ∧
151–152 *prose in* Q

## V.ii

19 *Cæsar*,] ~ ∧
27 to,] ~ ∧
54 hearts,] ~ .

55 tortures] tortutes
59 deliuerd] deliusrd
60 nature,] ~ ∧

471

67 eare —] ~ .
72 Christians] Dyce²; *others loosened
to* Christian
81 here,] ~ ∧
84 it,] ~ ∧
91 seruant,] ~ ∧
111 of: . . . matrons,] ~ , . . . ~ ∧
112 Romane] *Romane*
114 *Gracchus*∧] ~ ,
127 honour] hononr
133–134 equall to | The] equall to |
To the

134 spheres;] ~ ,
141–142 Why. . .hearing?] *one line
in* Q
141 Why,] ~ ∧
163 it,] ~ ∧
198 reach:] raceh, (Dyce² *may be*
raech,)
231 come,] ~ ∧
238 S.D. Angelo,] ~ ∧
242 S.D. *Flourish*,] ~ ∧

472

# HISTORICAL COLLATION OF
# EARLY EDITIONS

[The four quartos to 1661 are here collated against the present text, only substantive and semi-substantive variants being given. The lemmata are those of the present text; variants with their sigla appear after the square bracket. Omission of a siglum indicates that the quarto concerned agrees with the text.]

## I.i

2 liue.] ~ ? Q3–4
3 wondrous] wonderous Q3–4
12 purpose, in this_Λ] ~ _Λ ~ ~,
   Q1–4
19 thy] my Q4
23 these] the Q2–4
27 these] this Q1–4
29 forsaking] forsake Q4
30 Gentile] gentle Q2–4
35 em] them Q3–4
40 Mysteries] Mystries Q4
45 opinion.] ~ ? Q3–4
45 in] om. Q3; to Q4
51 in] om. Q1–2
55 againe:] ~ , Q1; ~ _Λ Q2
61 brests] brest Q3–4
70 might] may Q2–4
77 or] and Q2–4
90 does] doth Q3–4
92 this] his Q4
96 plumes] plums Q4
97 hopes,] ~ _Λ Q1–2
101 assurd] assured Q3–4
104 honor] om. Q3–4
114 honour,] ~ ! Q3–4
115 for] om. Q1–4
121 Confin'd] Cofin'd Q2
144 those] these Q2–4
146 expressd] expressed Q3–4
147 blow,] ~ _Λ Q1–2
150 Nor] No Q4

151 walkest] walk'st Q3–4
166 would 'twere] would'twere Q2;
    would't were Q3–4
176 sufferd] suffered Q3–4
200 orderd] ordered Q2–4
203 has] hath Q3–4
232 your] their Q3–4
242 cowards?] ~ , Q3–4
263 power] dower Q2
269 em] them Q3–4
283 pleasure] pleasures Q4
286 Or these...subiects,] om. Q2–4
291 politicke] publike Q2–4
296 farther] further Q3–4
298 boldly may] can boldly Q3–4
300 receiue] receiues Q1–4
303 owes] owns Q3–4
305 thy] my Q3–4
307 you,] ~ ? Q3–4
315 sonne] soone Q2
321 thee.] ~ ? Q2–4
330 th'] the Q2–4
334 or] and Q2–4
335 to] too Q4
345 prou'd] proued Q4
352 a] om. Q3–4
364 tortur'd,] ~ ? Q3–4
369 of't] of it Q3–4
375 runne] make Q3–4
377 t'] to Q3–4
378 refusd?] ~ . Q3–4

379 or] not Q1(c)–4
384 lightning] lightening Q3–4
387 vnmannerd] vnmannered Q3–4
387 was] were Q3–4
389 dead] drad Q1
410 lost, for euer‿] ~ ‿ ~ ~ , Q1–4
411 wretched,] ~ ‿ Q2–4

421 flattring] attering Q2; flattering Q3–4
432 along] a long Q4
444 assured] assur'd Q2–3
446 prefer'd] prefert'd Q3
455 assur'd] assured Q3–4
474 readier] reader Q1–2

## II.i

2 walke] to walke Q2
6 heres] here is Q3–4
8 thats] that is Q3–4
11 of] on Q3–4
21 skinker] stinker Q1–4
23 mans] man Q1
23 eares] yeares Q1–4
24 Indentures] Indures Q1–4
24 and] om. Q2–4
28 now] om. Q2–4
30 but] out Q2
43 nothing] not | thing Q1
54 ride,] ~ ‿ Q3–4 (rid Q4)
55 haue] 'aue Q2
57 and] or Q2–4
62 a] of Q3–4
63 -nose] nosed Q3–4
64 you?] ~ . Q2
68 on] in Q1–2
78 ith'] in the Q3–4
85 tayle] heeles Q2–4
86 she's] she is Q3–4
86 S.D. and] and a Q3–4
91 language.] ~ ? Q3–4
92 pedlars] om. Q3–4

96 the] her Q3–4
100 prisoners.] ~ ? Q2–4
104 you, to] ~ ‿ ~ , Q1–2
107 has...has] hath...hath Q3–4
109 flesh,] ~ ? Q3–4
110 you] ye Q3–4
115 braines] braine Q2–4
117 Carebruns] Carebrunt Q3–4
121 far.] ~ ? Q3–4
123 hell.] ~ ? Q3–4
126 to,] ~ ? Q3–4
128 throate.] ~ ? Q2–4
133 mine] my part Q3–4
136 vs, we] vs, was Q2–3; vs ‿ was Q4
138 has] hath Q3–4
145 shame.] ~ ? Q3–4
154 'em] 'm Q4
172 Takes] 'Takes Q2
174 and] end Q3–4
176 rauisht] rauished Q3–4
211 my] any Q1–2
212 you] your Q4
216 does] doth Q3–4

## II.ii

2 thee] three Q4
2 scorne,] ~ ? Q3–4
11 does] doth Q3–4
13 night.] ~ ? Q3–4
14 No,] ~ ? Q3–4
17 Fiend] Friend Q4
24 the] thy Q1–2

27 villanies] villains Q3–4
29 Egles] Angels Q1–4
35 motion,] ~ ? Q3–4
38 crab'd] crabbed Q3–4
39 ith] in 'th Q3–4
40 hatching.] ~ ? Q3–4
41 line] time Q1–4

52 not] and not Q 1–2
56 I now] Now I Q 2–4
65 like] *om.* Q 3–4
67 feeles] feel Q 3–4
69 mad] made Q 4

71 has] Hath Q 3–4
74 figures,] ~ ? Q 3–4
76 dance.] ~ ? Q 3–4
76 do] *om.* Q 3–4
77 rich] quick Q 3–4

## II.iii

12 much of] much Q 4
24 the best] *om.* the Q 1–4
26 awing] owing Q 1–4
33 your] a Q 2–4
36 World] Wold Q 2
41 Has] Hath Q 3–4
45 cruelty‸] ~ ; Q 3–4
57 See you] So now Q 3–4
57 see,] ~ ? Q 3–4
61 mouthes] moths Q 3–4
65 gold.] ~ ? Q 3–4
67 her.] ~ ? Q 3–4
68 y'are] yeare Q 1
76 glasse, ...Sex‸] ~ , ... ~ .
    Q 2; ~ ‸ ... ~ . Q 3–4
84 mines] mindes Q 2
87 Christian.] ~ ? Q 3–4
88 out] *om.* Q 2–4
109 thunderers] thunder Q 1–4
110 betrayde] betraied Q 3–4
115 whore,] ~ ? Q 3–4
115 braines‸] ~ ? Q 3–4
132 great] *om.* Q 3–4
134 put] puts Q 2–4
140 'hem] 'em Q 2–4
141 euen] ev'n Q 2
143 what] that Q 3–4
143 she is] she's Q 2–4

149 Sayes] Saith Q 3–4
157 builded] build it Q 4
180 done.] ~ ? Q 2–4
188 grow] grown Q 4
190 mistresse;] ~ ! Q 3–4
195 ist...ist] is it...is it Q 3–4
196 now.] ~ ? Q 2–4
198 *porte...porte*] *perte...perte*
    Q 3–4
198 my] me Q 3–4
199 *whee*] wee Q 1–4
212 gold.] ~ ? Q 3–4
215 Poyson,] ~ ! Q 3–4
217 there's] there is Q 3–4
222 Twas] It was Q 3–4
235 Ile] I will Q 3–4
239 gold?] ~ . Q 1–4
240 Ide] I would Q 3–4
247 I'am] I am Q 2; I'm Q 3–4
250 y'are] you are Q 3–4
253 Th'art] Thou art Q 3–4
257 gone?] ~ . Q 1–2
259 the] his Q 3–4
266 we?] ~ ! Q 3–4
268 not] *om.* Q 1–4
270 dayes] deeds Q 2–4
273 Iayle?] ~ . Q 1; ~ , Q 2

## III.i

4 enticing] enchanting Q 3–4
9 that] *om.* Q 3–4
19 reason] reasons Q 3–4
42 S.D. *Priest*] *and Priest* Q 3–4
55 leades] leade Q 1–2
61 here] here here Q 3

71 Eu'n] Euen Q 3–4
79 follow'd] followed Q 3–4
79 Lady,] ~ ? Q 3–4
82 noble] noblie Q 3
86 twines] Twins Q 1–4
90 made] made made Q 3–4

92 prosperity] Q1(c)-4; posterity
    Q1(u)
113 Diuell angles] devil-angels Q4
117 ones?] ~ , Q3-4
118 nor do] not do Q3-4
128 piety] pitty Q1-2
139 whore,] ~ ? Q4
141 has] hath Q3-4
145 speake] speakes Q1
148 most] om. Q2-4
149 are.] ~ ? Q3-4

150 Heere] Her Q1-2
151 shape] ship Q1-4
155 *Prometheus*] *Lyometheus* Q1;
    *Lymotheus* Q2-4
162 fashion'd,] ~ ? Q3-4
163 men?] ~ . Q3-4
181 him] them Q2-4
183 if] of Q2
183 worldly] wordlie Q3
193 showre] shower Q2-3
200 That] hat Q3

## III.ii

6 growth] grown Q3-4
12 mine] me Q3-4
23 ha.] ~ ! Q2-4
30 My] y Q3
45 *Caliste.*] om. Q1
53 offring] offering Q2-4
56 zeale,] ~ ? Q3-4
59 any] any other Q2-4
74 He is] He's Q3-4
76 pacientst] ancientst Q1; an-
    cientest Q3-4 (ancientst! Q2)
79 tis] it is Q3-4
81 yet] om. Q2-4
82 dew] due Q2-4

84 againe,] ~ ᴀ Q2
86 The] om. Q2-4
88 Not] Nor Q2-4
97 of] om. Q4
100 It will] 'Twill Q3-4
111 accursd] accursed Q3-4
122 instrument] Q1(c)-4; instru-
    ments Q1(u)
124 S.D. *him, laughing.* | *Enter
    Angelo.] him.* | *Enter* Artemia
    *laughing.* Q1-4
126 one] on Q1
133 but] om. Q3-4

## III.iii

2 ist] is it Q3-4
2 world.] ~ ? Q2-4
6 a mad] mad a Q2
9 has...has] hath...hath Q3-4
9 tother] other Q2-4
10 close] house Q3-4
26 presse] to presse Q2
34 has] is Q3-4
45 of] in Q3-4
50 make,] ~ ! Q3-4
51 me.] ~ ? Q3-4
53 it.] ~ ? Q3-4
61 mong] among Q3-4
63 desperates.] ~ ? Q3-4

65 and] om. Q3-4
67 tottering] totterings Q1-4
68 *arsnicke*] arsrick Q3-4
75 well?] ~ . Q1-2
76 clothes?] ~ ᴀ Q4
78 loose?] ~ ᴀ Q4
83 pawnd,] ~ ? Q3-4
84 gold!] ~ ? Q3-4
84 has] hath Q3-4
88 lyes?] ~ , Q4
96 Ist] Is it Q3-4
99 take] rake Q3-4
107 whats] Wher's Q4
109 Drawne] Drawd Q4

10) on't] on'ts Q4
113 get] got Q3-4 (Q2 *has broken* e)
113 out your] yout our Q1
116 prisoners.] ~ ? Q3-4
117 A] *om.* Q3-4
134 how!] ~ ? Q3-4
134 drunke?] ~ , Q1-2
136 any a man] anyaman Q1; any
    man Q2-4
160 He's...is.] Q1-2 *line:* louing |
    To
163 you] if you Q2-4
165 ith'] in the Q3-4
165 for] from Q3
168 does] loues Q2-4
172 does] doth Q3-4
172 in's] in his Q3-4
174 has] hath Q3-4
175 does] doth Q3-4
175 not?] ~ . Q2
176 has] hath Q3-4
184 him.] ~ ? Q3-4
185 damn'd] damn' Q1

186 y'are] you are Q3-4
187 does] doth Q3-4
189 she's] she is Q3-4
190 dore?] ~ . Q4
193 who's] who is Q3-4
193 constable.] ~ ? Q3-4
195 How!] ~ ? Q3-4
195 ath'] a'rth Q2; on the Q3-4
195 chops.] ~ ? Q3
196 ath'] on the Q3-4
196 boy.] ~ ? Q2
196 boy] boys Q3-4
199 Whats] What is Q3-4
199 word,] ~ ? Q3-4 (~ ‸ Q2)
200 woman?] ~ . Q1-2
202 Here's] Here is Q3-4
203 rascall,] ~ ! Q3-4
216 in] into Q2-4
219 sir.] ~ ? Q2-4
223 shall] should Q2-4
224 he, her flesh who] he, who her
    flesh Q3-4

## IV.i

21 Is he with child, a Midwife!] A
   midwife! is he with child? Q3-4
21 Midwife!] ~ , Q2
30 gibrish] giberish Q4
40 Where,] ~ ? Q3-4
53 me,] ~ ? Q3-4
54 Mountebankes] Mountbankes
   Q1
56 *Macrinus,*] ~ ? Q3-4
58 peeces,] ~ ? Q3-4
59 S.D. in] *om.* Q3-4
61 'em] them Q3-4
66 beauty?] ~ . Q3-4
69 world?] ~ . Q3-4
71 neere?] ~ . Q1-2
77 towne,] townes Q3-4
79 battry] battery Q2-4
80 sir.] ~ ? Q3-4
81-84 Q1-4 *line:* No...boy, |

   Pages...bawdy | Shufflngs...
   those | Little...head | Will...
   ones, | Let...stay.
89 Death!] ~ . Q1-4
90 spher'd] spard Q1; spar'd Q2-4
95 What.] ~ ? Q2-4
115 th'art] thou'rt Q3-4
115 mad)] ~ ‸ Q2
116-117 her | At] her | Her at Q1-2
122 out] our Q4
124 Sir.] ~ ? Q3-4
124-126 Q1-4 *line:* Teach...
    learne | In...Whore.
125 many] many a one Q3-4
126 come] to me Q1-4
126 now.] ~ ? Q2-4
129 slaue.] ~ ? Q2-4
130 Ocean.] ~ ? Q3-4
131 Iland.] ~ ? Q3-4

131 fitted, ...Nations‸] ~ ‸ ...
    ~ . Q2
139 I'th] In th' Q3–4
139 battring] battering Q3–4
141 peeces, ...off:] ~ : ... ~ ,
    Q1–4
151 seruice,] ~ ? Q3–4
152 doo't] doe it Q2–4
165 thus] om. Q3–4
165 bi'th] by th' Q2; by the Q3–4

167 lust] lusts Q4
167 his] her Q4
169 Ooh] O oh Q1(c)–3; Oh, oh!
    Q4
181 cheeke is] cheek's Q3–4
182 her?] ~ . Q3–4
183 Dor. I'me] Theoph. I'me Q2–4
183 Theoph. Spurne...barre.] om.
    Q2–4
186 hangmen,] ~ ! Q3–4

## IV.ii

3 Attendance,] ~ ! Q3–4
12 has] hath Q3–4
13 Thou't] Thou'lt Q3–4
19 on ‸ but soundly.] ~ ; ... ~ ‸
    Q3–4
21 beate.] ~ ? Q3–4
23 Mistresse!] ~ ? Q4
29 out] om. Q2–4
36 each] every Q3–4
45 you are] your are Q2
50 ile] I will Q3–4
50 'em] them Q3–4
52 ore] ouer Q2–4
53 where?] ~ . Q2–4
58 made] mad Q2
67 me!] om. Q2–4
68 to] vnto Q2–4
74 are] any Q4
76 hangmen] hangman Q2–4
77 tormentors] torments Q4
77 ready?] ~ . Q2–4
80 lengthen'd] lengthened Q3–4
81 hangmen] hangman Q1–4
83 tormentors.] ~ ? Q3–4

90 ioys,] ~ ! Q3–4
90 tormentors] torments Q4
91 sufferings] suffrings Q1
92 limbe:] ~ ! Q3–4
95 Has] Hath Q3–4
97 these.] ~ ? Q3–4
105 power] powred Q2
105 downe to fell] to fel down Q3–4
105–106 prose in Q1–4
107 shreeke.] ~ ? Q3–4
108 has] hath Q3–4
112 serue] seru'd Q2–4
118 vsde.] ~ ? Q3–4
119 woman!] ~ ? Q3–4
120 flew] flee Q4
122 cry,] ~ ‸ Q3–4
129 'em] them Q3–4
132 S.D. Exit.] exeunt Q1–2; om.
    Q3–4
133 'em] them Q3–4
135 rides] ride Q1–2
135 Theophilus.] ~ ‸ Q2–3; ~ , Q4
136 thirsts] thirst Q1

## IV.iii

1 suffer,] ~ ? Q3–4
3 came,] ~ ? Q3–4
12 affection!] ~ ; Q3–4
21 your] om. Q2–4

22 pierce deeper] th' deeper pierce
    Q4
24 me] om. Q4
32 it?] ~ . Q3–4

33 appeares,] ~ ? Q3; ~ ! Q4
39 offrings] offerings Q2-4
42 And] An Q1
42 neerer] nigher Q2-4
62 *Eliʒian*] *Eliʒium* Q3-4
67 *Mars*] *Mors* Q3-4
73 life? ...me_ʌ] ~ ʌ ... ~ ? Q2-4
75 eu'n] even Q3-4
78 on thee] with thee Q4
82 There's] There is Q3-4
84 haue] having Q4

86 fainde] fainde your Q1-2
88 your] *om.* Q1-4
95 mine] my Q4
101 That place...me,] *om.* Q2-4
102 call'd] called Q3-4
109 in thy] in the Q4
130 habitation?] ~ , Q3-4
136 'em] them Q3-4
156 scorne] scornd Q1
180 thine] mine Q1
181 dead.] ~ ! Q3-4
189 one] witch Q3-4

## V.i

4 worke:] ~ ? Q3-4
5 stirring?] ~ , Q1; ~ . Q2
6 admirable] honourable Q2-4
8 colour] colours Q1-2
14 names] name Q4
21 pinch] pinch'd Q2-4
21 'em] 'm Q4
22 hewed] hewen Q3-4
27 fat_ʌ] ~ , Q3-4
28 purpose,] ~ ʌ Q3-4
35 To'th] To th' Q2-4
45 S.D. *Musicke.*] *om.* Q4
45-46 Are...tremble.] *prose in* Q1-4
46 does] doth Q3-4
46 tremble.] ~ ! Q3-4
53 Garden_ʌ] ~ ? Q4
56-57 Tis...view'd,] *one line in* Q1-2
61 dyed:] ~ ? Q3-4
63-65 Q1-4 *line*: That...Country | Shall...Vanished!
63 summer,] ~ ? Q3-4
68 shut?] shut and? Q4
71 Where?] ~ . Q3-4
72-74 *prose in* Q1-4

73 eyes] eie Q3-4
75 sir?] ~ . Q3-4
77 vanish'd!] ~ , Q3; ~ ʌ Q4
77 seene,] ~ ! Q3-4
82 more] now Q1-2
84 catch.] ~ ? Q3-4
88 ist] is it Q3-4
90 hee's] he is Q3-4
94 S.D. *Lowder.*] *om.* Q3-4
96 *Harpax,*] ~ ? Q3-4
101 Hee's] He is Q3-4
102 thinkes] thinke Q1-2
102 S.D. *Exit seruant.*] *om.* Q3-4 (*seruants* Q2)
113 my] mine Q4
120 Agen,] ~ ? Q3-4
121 left,] ~ ! Q3-4
124 Q1-4 *line*: that | Last
130 in't] in it Q3-4
133 to'th] to th' Q2
139 see] *om.* Q3-4
139 I'me] I am Q3-4
150 To] *om.* Q3-4
151-152 *prose in* Q1-2
154 hast thou] thou hast Q3-4

## V.ii

5 makes] make Q3–4
16 your] you Q3
37 was:] ~ ˄ Q1–2
39 giue] bring Q4
59 sufferd] suffered Q2
67 S.D. *To*] *om.* Q2–4
75 there shall finde] shall there finde
   Q2; shall find there Q3–4
84 vndertake't,] vndertake ˄ Q2
86 has] hath Q3; had Q4
87 morrall] mortall Q2–4
91 Christian] Christians Q1
99 this] his Q2
105 deliuerd] deliuered Q2–4
106 sufferd] suffered Q2–4
108 more˄] ~ ! Q4
114 *Gracchus*˄] ~ , Q1
122 aftername] after name Q2–4
133–134 equall to | The] equall to |
   To the Q1

141–142 Why...hearing?] *one line
   in* Q1–4
152 through,...moment˄] ~ ˄ ...
   ~ , Q1–4
152 the] this Q2–4
157 did] didst Q2–4
160 Meteor?] ~ . Q2
167 Here] Heare me Q2–4
205 worship'st] worshippest Q3–4
206 *torment*] *torture* Q2–4
208 suffrings] sufferings Q2–4
212 are] *om.* Q2–4
214 suffrance] sufferance Q2–4
215 has] hath Q3–4
222 this?] ~ . Q2
225 blest] blessed Q4
228 keepst] kepst Q1; keeps Q4
228 wreath] wretch Q4
237 souldier's] prisoner's Q2–4
237 thy] they Q4
240 still stand] stand still Q2–4

480

# The Witch of Edmonton

A known true S T O R Y.

Compoſed into

## A TRAGI-COMEDY

By diverſ well-eſteemed Poets ;

*William Rowley, Thomas Dekker, John Ford,* &c

Acted by the Princes Servants, often at the Cock-Pit in *Drury-Lane,*
once at Court, with ſingular Applauſe.

*Never printed till now.*

London, *Printed by* J. Cottrel, *for* Edward Blackmore, *at the Angel in*
Paul's *Church-yard.* 1658.

# TEXTUAL INTRODUCTION

*The Witch of Edmonton* (Greg, *Bibliography*, no. 785), a collaboration by Dekker, John Ford, and William Rowley, was written in 1621 on the evidence of its drawing upon a pamphlet *The Wonderful Discovery of E. Sawyer, a Witch*, entered in the Stationers' Register on 27 April 1621, and the record of its court performance by the Prince's men on 29 December in the same year. On 21 May 1658 the quarto was entered in the Register by Edward Blackmore: 'Entred for his Copie (vnder y^e hand of M^r Thomason Warden) a booke called The Witch of Edmonton a TragiComedy by Will: Rowley &c', the usual sixpence being paid.

That the manuscript given to the printer had had some connexion with the theatre is shown by the appearance of the names of the actors Theophilus Bird and Ezekiel Fenn after the Prologue and Epilogue respectively, in Bentley's opinion (*Jacobean Stage*, I, 251–252; II, 378; III, 271–272) these representing the speakers and not the writers of the lines. Lines 5–8 of the Prologue suggest to Bentley a revival by Queen Henrietta's men (to which company Bird and Fenn belonged), and he places this event about 1635 or 1636, the manuscript deriving from this occasion.

At first sight the Actors Names list appears to have been made up by someone reading through the play and jotting down the names: at least, that is the simplest explanation for the appearance in the list of 'Poldavis, a Barbers boy', who is referred to by name and occupation in the text at III.i.57 but is not mentioned in any stage-direction and does not seem to be present in the morris. If so, we should also have explained the listing in the Actors Names of W. Hamluc, from his appearance (as W. Hamlac) in a stage-direction (and assignment of two speech-prefixes) at IV.i.14 ff. But it would seem that the listing in the Actors Names of W. Mago, for whose part in the play the quarto offers no evidence whatever, could have come only from someone familiar with a production.

Bentley has no identification for Hamluc (*Jacobean Stage*, II, 459–460); but William Mago (*J.S.*, II, 506) is known as a member of the

King's company in 1624 and in 1631. In Bentley's opinion Hamluc and Mago were actors in the original production by the Prince's men. This would be a reasonable guess did it not (1) conflict with the evidence for the inscription of the names of Bird and Fenn in the quarto, and (2) require the Actors Names to have been made up not for printing but for some other purpose years before; and it is difficult to imagine the composition of such a list as here except for the reader. Hence I should suggest the possibility that the agent who provided the manuscript added not only the names of Bird and Fenn to Prologue and Epilogue but also of Hamluc in IV.i.14 S.D. and IV.i.15, 17. It would follow that the appearance of Hamluc in the Actors Names is not solely like that of Poldavis but represents the addition of the name of an actor who—like Bird and Fenn—had taken part in the play as revived by Queen Henrietta's men. If this is so, we cannot separate the addition of the name of Mago from that of Hamluc. Thus we should be forced to conjecture not that Mago had been a member of the Prince's men, earlier; but instead that at some time after 1631 he left the King's men and joined Queen Henrietta's company. It is surely simpler to take it that the different actors' names were added at the same time, and from the same source, rather than at intervals of some years. Rowland and Jack, sometimes cited as the names of actors in the text, are more probably fictitious names for characters otherwise known only as numbers.

If the above line of argument has any validity, we can further conjecture that the agent who sold the manuscript for publication was very likely an actor (Hamluc or Mago?), and that he had originally procured the copy from the stock of the theatre at which he worked. However, it need not follow that the manuscript must thereby have been the prompt copy itself. Even if it were argued that the appearance of the name 'Hamlac' in the text of IV.i were due to another agent than the late owner of the manuscript,[1] we are long past the stage of criticism in which actors' names in texts may be taken as proof positive of prompt copy. Otherwise there is no certain evidence in favour of prompt and some evidence against, as in the different forms of speech-prefixes and stage-direction names for

---

[1] It would seem to be equally odd either for an author to write in an actor's name for two brief speeches or for an annotator to single him out for these few lines.

some characters which possibly might have been made uniform in a prompt copy. It is uncertain even whether the printer's copy was a transcript. Some small differences in spelling characteristics, some variation in the typography and in the forms of names in stage-directions and text, and major differences occasionally in speech-prefixes[1]—all these varying between scenes as units—suggest rather the possibility of authors' papers, though one can never, of course, rule out the possible presence of a scribe who followed copy in such matters with some faithfulness, as in the omission of scene number-ing only in Acts III and V for scenes other than the first. All in all, despite the evidence that the manuscript had perhaps been in the possession of an actor, and had thus come from the theatre, the odds are that it was not prompt copy but instead autograph papers or a rather literal scribal copy preliminary to the prompt book.

Previous editions consulted in the preparation of this text include that in *The Dramatic Works of John Ford*, edited by Henry Weber, vol. 2 (1811); *The Works of John Ford*, edited by William Gifford, vol. 2 (1827); *The Dramatic Works of Massinger and Ford*, edited by Hartley Coleridge (1840); *The Works of John Ford*, edited by William Gifford and revised by Alexander Dyce, vol. 3 (1869); the Mermaid edition of *Thomas Dekker*, edited by Ernest Rhys (1887); and the collection, *Elizabethan and Stuart Plays*, edited by C. R. Baskervill, V. B. Heltzel, and A. H. Nethercot (1934).

---

[1] For example, Frank Thorney has the speech-prefix *Frank.* in I.i, I.ii, IV.ii, and V.iii, but *Y. Thor.* in II.ii, and III.iii. In III.ii in the first line his prefix is *Frank* (though the stage-direction names him as *Young Thorney*), but beginning with the second prefix, at line 13, he is *Y. Thor.* consistently for the rest of the scene. In stage-directions, in I.i he is *Frank Thorney*; in I.ii and IV.ii *Frank*; in II.ii, III.ii, and III.iii *Young Thorney*; in V.iii on his first entrance he is *Young Thorney* but on his second, *Frank*.

Old Carter has the speech-prefix *O. Cart.* in I.ii, but thereafter, in II.ii, III.iii, IV.ii, V.ii, and V.iii it is *Cart.* In stage-directions he is *Old Carter* in I.ii, IV.ii, and V.iii, but *Carter* elsewhere.

Although the Witch has the invariable speech-prefix *Sawy.* in the four scenes in which she appears, in the stage-directions of II.i she is *Elizabeth Sawyer*, in IV.i *The Witch*, V.i *Mother Sawyer*, and V.iii *Sawyer*.

Cuddy Banks has the speech-prefix *Y. Bank* in II.i, but *Clow.* in III.i, III.iv, IV.i, and *Clown.* in V.i. In the stage-directions he is *Young Banks* in II.i and V.i; *Cuddy Banks* in III.i; *Banks* in III.iv; and *The Clown* in IV.i. In the text he is addressed as *Cuddy* in II.i, but as *Banks* in III.i and III.iv.

No press-variants were observed in the collation of the following eleven copies of the 1658 quarto on which the present edition is based: British Museum, copy 1 (644.c.17), copy 2 (C.12.f.1[5]); Bodleian Library, copy 1 (Mal. 238[9]), copy 2 (Gough Middlesex 14[13]); Dyce Collection in the Victoria and Albert Museum, copy 1 and copy 2; Eton College; Bute Collection in the National Library of Scotland; Henry E. Huntington Library; Harvard University; and Yale University.

# ACTORS NAMES

SIR ARTHUR CLARINGTON
OLD THORNEY, a Gentleman
OLD CARTER, a rich Yeoman
OLD BANKS, a Country-man
W. MAGO }
W. HAMLUC } two Country-men
Three other Country-men
WARBECK }
SOMERTON } Suitors to Carter's Daughters
FRANK, Thorney's Son
YOUNG CUDDY BANKS, the Clown
Four Morice-Dancers
OLD RATCLIFFE
SAWGUT, an old Fidler
POLDAVIS, a Barbers boy
Justice
Constable
Officers
Servingmen
DOG, a Familiar
A Spirit
[Country-men, Officers.]

## WOMEN

MOTHER SAWYER, the Witch
ANNE, Ratcliffs Wife
SUSAN }
KATHARINE } Carters Daughters
WINNIFRIDE, Sir Arthur's Maid

## The whole *Argument is this Dystich.*

Forc'd Marriage, Murder; Murder, Blood requires:
Reproach, Revenge; Revenge, Hells help desires.

## *Prologue.*

*The Town of* Edmonton *hath lent the Stage*
*A Devil and a Witch, both in an age.*
*To make comparisons it were uncivil,*
*Between so even a pair, a Witch and Devil.*
*But as the year doth with his plenty bring*
*As well a latter as a former Spring;*
*So has this Witch enjoy'd the first, and reason*
*Presumes she may partake the other season:*
*In Acts deserving name, the Proverb says,*
Once good, and ever; *Why not so in Plays?*                    10
*Why not in this? since (Gentlemen) we flatter*
*No Expectation: here is Mirth and Matter.*

*Mr.* Bird.

## *The Witch of Edmonton.*

### ACT. I, Scæna i

*Enter* Frank Thorney, Winnifride *with-child.*

*Frank.*   Come, Wench; why here's a business soon dispatch'd.
Thy heart I know is now at ease: thou needst not
Fear what the tattling Gossips in their cups
Can speak against thy fame: thy childe shall know
Who to call *Dad* now.
*Win.*                    You have discharg'd
The true part of an honest man; I cannot
Request a fuller satisfaction
Then you have freely granted: yet methinks
'Tis an hard case, being lawful man and wife,
We should not live together.
*Frank.*                    Had I fail'd                                10
In promise of my truth to thee, we must
Have then been ever sundred; now the longest
Of our forbearing eithers company,
Is onely but to gain a little time
For our continuing thrift, that so hereafter
The Heir that shall be born may not have cause
To curse his hour of birth, which made him feel
The misery of beggery and want;
Two Devils that are occasions to enforce
A shameful end. My plots aim but to keep                              20
My father's love.
*Win.*              And that will be as difficult
To be preserv'd, when he shall understand
How you are married, as it will be now,
Should you confess it to him.
*Frank.*                      Fathers are
Wonne by degrees, not bluntly, as our masters.

490

Or wronged friends are; and besides, I'll use
Such dutiful and ready means, that ere
He can have notice of what's past, th'inheritance
To which I am born Heir, shall be assur'd:
That done, why let him know it; if he like it not,                30
Yet he shall have no power in him left
To cross the thriving of it.
*Win.*                        You who had
The conquest of my Maiden-love, may easily
Conquer the fears of my distrust. And whither
Must I be hurried?
*Frank.*                      Prithee do not use
A word so much unsuitable to the constant
Affections of thy Husband: thou shalt live
Neer *Waltham Abbey*, with thy Unkle *Selman*:
I have acquainted him with all at large:
He'll use thee kindly: thou shalt want no pleasures,            40
Nor any other fit supplies whatever
Thou canst in heart desire.
*Win.*                        All these are nothing
Without your company.
*Frank.*                      Which thou shalt have
Once every month at least.
*Win.*                              Once every month!
Is this to have an Husband?
*Frank.*                            Perhaps oftner:
That's as occasion serves.
*Win.*                            I, I, in case
No other Beauty tempt your eye, whom you
Like better, I may chance to be remembred,
And see you now and then. Faith, I did hope
You'ld not have us'd me so: 'tis but my fortune.               50
And yet, if not for my sake, have some pity
Upon the childe I go with, that's your own.
And, 'less you'll be a cruel hearted Father,
You cannot but remember that.
Heaven knows how—

*Frank.*　　　　　　To quit which fear at once,
As by the ceremony late perform'd,
I plighted thee a faith, as free from challenge,
As any double thought; Once more in hearing
Of Heaven and thee, I vow, that never henceforth
Disgrace, reproof, lawless affections, threats,　　　　60
Or what can be suggested 'gainst our Marriage,
Shall cause me falsifie that Bridal-Oath
That bindes me thine. And, *Winnifride*, when ever
The wanton heat of youth by subtle baits
Of beauty, or what womans Art can practice,
Draw me from onely loving thee; let Heaven
Inflict upon my life some fearful ruine.
I hope thou dost believe me.
*Win.*　　　　　　　　Swear no more;
I am confirm'd, and will resolve to do
What you think most behoofeful for us.
*Frank.*　　　　　　　　Thus then;　　　　70
Make thy self ready: at the furthest house
Upon the Green, without the Town, your Unckle
Expects you. For a little time farewel.
*Win.*　　　　　　　　　　Sweet,
We shall meet again as soon as thou canst possibly?
*Frank.* We shall. One kiss. Away.　　　[*Exit* Winnifride.]

　　　　　*Enter Sir* Arthur Clarington.

*Sir Art.*　　　　　　　*Frank Thorney.*
*Frank.*　　　　　　　　　　Here Sir.
*Sir Art.* Alone? then must I tell thee in plain terms,
Thou hast wrong'd thy Master's house basely and lewdly.
*Frank.* Your house, Sir?
*Sir Art.*　　　　　Yes, Sir, if the nimble devil
That wanton'd in your blood, rebell'd against
All rules of honest duty, you might, Sir,　　　　80
Have found out some more fitting place then here,
To have built a Stewes in. All the Country whispers
How shamefully thou hast undone a Maid,

492

Approv'd for modest life, for civil carriage,
Till thy prevailing perjuries entic'd her
To forfeit shame. Will you be honest yet?
Make her amends and marry her?
*Frank.*                    So, Sir,
I might bring both my self and her to beggery;
And that would be a shame worse then the other.
*Sir Art.*   You should have thought on this before, and then          90
Your reason would have oversway'd the passion
Of your unruly lust. But that you may
Be left without excuse, to salve the infamy
Of my disgraced house, and 'cause you are
A Gentleman, and both of you my servants,
I'll make the Maid a portion.
*Frank.*                    So you promis'd me
Before, in case I married her. I know
Sir *Arthur Clarington* deserves the credit
Report hath lent him; and presume you are
A Debtor to your promise: but upon          100
What certainty shall I resolve? Excuse me
For being somewhat rude.
*Sir Art.*                    'Tis but reason.
Well *Frank*, what thinkst thou of two hundred pound
And a continual friend?
*Frank.*                    Though my poor fortunes
Might happily prefer me to a choice
Of a far greater portion; yet to right
A wronged Maid, and to preserve your favour,
I am content to accept your proffer.
*Sir Art.*                    Art thou?
*Frank.*   Sir, we shall every day have need to employ
The use of what you please to give.
*Sir Art.*                    Thou shalt have't.          110
*Frank.*   Then I claim your promise. We are man and wife.
*Sir. Art.*   Already?
*Frank.*                    And more then so, I have promis'd her
Free entertainment in her Unkle's house,

Neer *Waltham Abbey*, where she may securely
Sojourne, till time and my endeavours work
My fathers love and liking.
*Sir Art.* Honest *Frank.*
*Frank.* I hope, Sir, you will think I cannot keep her
Without a daily charge.
*Sir Art.* As for the money,
'Tis all thine own; and though I cannot make thee
A present payment, yet thou shalt be sure 120
I will not fail thee.
*Frank.* But our occasions.
*Sir Art.* Nay, nay,
Talk not of your occasions, trust my bounty:
It shall not sleep. Hast married her, yfaith *Frank?*
'Tis well, 'tis passing well: then *Winnifride,*
Once more thou art an honest woman. *Frank,*
Thou hast a Jewel. Love her; she'll deserve it.
And when to *Waltham?*
*Frank.* She is making ready.
Her Unkle stays for her.
*Sir Art.* Most provident speed.
*Frank,* I will be thy friend, and such a friend.
Thou'lt bring her thither?
*Frank.* Sir, I cannot: newly 130
My father sent me word I should come to him.
*Sir Art.* Marry, and do: I know thou hast a wit
To handle him.
*Frank.* I have a suit t'ye.
*Sir Art.* What is't?
Any thing, *Frank,* command it.
*Frank.* That you'll please,
By Letters to assure my Father, that
I am not married.
*Sir Art.* How?
*Frank.* Some one or other
Hath certainly inform'd him that I purpos'd

129 thy] Weber [your]; *om.* Q

To marry *Winnifride*; on which he threatned
To dis-inherit me; to prevent it,
Lowly I crave your Letters, which he seeing　　　140
Will credit; and I hope ere I return,
On such conditions as I'll frame, his Lands
Shall be assur'd.
*Sir Art.*　　　　　But what is that to quit
My knowledge of the marriage?
*Frank.*　　　　　　　Why you were not
A witness to it.
*Sir Art.*　　　I conceive: and then,
His Land confirmed, thou wilt acquaint him throughly
With all that's past.
*Frank.*　　　　　I mean no less.
*Sir Art.*　　　　　　　Provided,
I never was made privy to it.
*Frank.*　　　　　　　Alas, Sir,
Am I a talker?
*Sir Art.*　　　Draw thy self the Letter,
I'll put my hand to it. I commend thy policy:　　　150
Th'art witty, witty *Frank*; nay, nay, 'tis fit,
Dispatch it.
*Frank.*　　　I shall write effectually.　　　　　*Exit.*
*Sir Art.*　　Go thy way Cuckow; have I caught the young man?
One trouble then is freed. He that will feast
At others cost, must be a bold fac'd guest.

*Enter* Winnifride *in a riding-suit.*

*Win,* I have heard the news, all now is safe.
The worst is past. Thy lip, wench: I must bid
Farewel, for fashions sake; but I will visit thee
Suddenly, Girl. This was cleanly carried:
Ha? was't not *Win*!
*Win.*　　　　　Then were my happiness,

---

＊ 143 that] *stet* Q　　　　157 Thy lip] *Sir Art.* Thy lip Q
　156 *Win*, I] *Win* I Q　　　＊ 160 Then were my happiness] *stet* Q

That I in heart repent I did not bring him
The Dower of a Virginity. Sir, forgive me;
I have been much to blame. Had not my Lewdness
Given way to your immoderate waste of Vertue,
You had not with such eagerness pursu'd
The error of your goodness.

*Sir Art.*                              Dear, dear *Win.*
I hug this Art of thine, it shews how cleanly
Thou canst beguile in case occasion serve,
To practice. It becomes thee. Now we share
Free scope enough, without controle or fear,                    170
To interchange our pleasures; we will surfeit
In our embraces, Wench. Come, tell me, when
Wilt thou appoint a meeting?

*Win.*                              What to do?

*Sir Art.*   Good, good, to con the lesson of our loves,
Our secret game.

*Win.*                 O blush to speak it further!
As y'are a noble Gentleman, forget
A sin so monstrous: 'tis not gently done,
To open a cur'd wound. I know you speak
For trial; troth you need not.

*Sir Art.*                      I for trial?
Not I, by this good Sun-shine.

*Win.*                        Can you name                       180
That syllable of good, and yet not tremble,
To think to what a foul and black intent,
You use it for an Oath? Let me resolve you,
If you appear in any Visitation
That brings not with it pity for the wrongs
Done to abused *Thorney*, my kinde husband;
If you infect mine ear with any breath
That is not thoroughly perfum'd with sighs
For former deeds of lust: May I be curs'd
Even in my prayers, when I vouchsafe                            190

163 Lewdness] Dyce *query*; Laundress Q
169 thee. Now] Weber; thee, now Q

496

To see or hear you. I will change my life,
From a loose whore, to a repentant wife.
*Sir Art.* Wilt thou turn monster now? art not asham'd
After so many months to be honest at last?
Away, away, fie on't.
*Win.*                My resolution
Is built upon a Rock. This very day
Young *Thorney* vow'd with Oaths not to be doubted,
That never any change of love should cancel
The bonds in which we are to either bound,
Of lasting truth. And shall I then for my part            200
Unfile the sacred Oath set on Record
In Heaven's Book? Sir *Arthur*, do not study
To add to your lascivious lust, the sin
Of Sacriledge: for if you but endeavour
By any unchaste word to tempt my constancy,
You strive as much as in you lies to ruine
A Temple hallowed to the purity
Of holy Marriage. I have said enough:
You may believe me.
*Sir Art.*                Get you to your Nunnery,
There freeze in your old Cloyster. This is fine.          210
*Win.* Good Angels guide me. Sir, you'l give me leave
To weep and pray for your conversion.
*Sir. Art.*                Yes,
Away to *Waltham.* Pox on your honesty.
Had you no other trick to fool me? Well,
You may want mony yet.
*Win.*                None that I'll send for
To you, for hire of a damnation.
    When I am gone, think on my just complaint:
    I was your Devil, O be you my Saint!    *Exit* Winnifride.
*Sir Art.* Go, go thy ways, as changeable a baggage
As ever cozen'd Knight. I'm glad I'm rid of her.          220
Honest? marry hang her. *Thorney* is my Debtor,
I thought to have paid him too: but fools have fortune.
                              *Exit* Sir Arthur.

## [ACT I,] Scæna ii

*Enter Old* Thorney, *and Old* Carter.

*O. Thor.*    You offer Mr. *Carter*, like a Gentleman,
I cannot finde fault with it, 'tis so fair.

*O. Cart.*    No Gentleman, I, Mr. *Thorney*; spare the Mastership,
call me by my name, *John Carter*; Master is a title my Father, nor
his before him, were acquainted with. Honest *Hertfordshire*
Yeomen, such an one am I; my word and my deed shall be proved
one at all times. I mean to give you no security for the Marriage-
money.

*O. Thor.*    How? no security?
Although it need not, so long as you live;                           10
Yet who is he has surety of his life one hour?
*Men,* the Proverb says, *are mortal*: else, for my part,
I distrust you not, were the sum double.

*O. Cart.*    Double, trebble, more or less; I tell you, Mr. *Thorney*,
I'll give no security. Bonds and Bills are but the Tarriers to catch
Fools, and keep lazy Knaves busie; my security shall be present
payment. And we here, about *Edmonton*, hold present payment as
sure as an Alderman's Bond in *London*, Mr. *Thorney*.

*O. Thor.*    I cry you mercy, Sir, I understood you not.

*O. Cart.*    I like young *Frank* well, so does my *Susan* too. The Girl  20
has a fancy to him, which makes me ready in my Purse. There be
other Suitors within, that make much noise to little purpose.
If *Frank* love *Sue*, *Sue* shall have none but *Frank*. 'Tis a mannerly
Girl, Mr. *Thorney*, though but an homely man's Daughter. There
have worse Faces look'd out of black Bags, Man.

*O. Thor.*    You speak your minde freely and honestly.
I marvel my Son comes not:
I am sure he will be here sometime to day.

*O. Cart.*    To day or to morrow, when he comes he shall be
welcome to Bread, Beer and Beef, Yeoman's fare; we have no  30
Kickshaws: full Dishes, whole belly-fulls. Should I diet three days
at one of the slender City-Suppers, you might send me to Barber-

Surgeons Hall the fourth day, to hang up for an Anatomy. — Here
come they that —
How now Girls? every day play-day with you?

*Enter* Warbeck *with* Susan, Somerton *with* Katherine.

*Valentine*'s day too, all by couples? Thus will young folks do when
we are laid in our Graves, Mr. *Thorney*. Here's all the care they
take. And how do you finde the Wenches, Gentlemen? have they
any minde to a loose Gown and a strait Shooe? Win 'em, and wear
'em. They shall chuse for themselves by my consent.                    40
*Warb.*   You speak like a kinde Father. *Sue*, thou hearest
The liberty that's granted thee. What sayest thou?
Wilt thou be mine?
*Sus.*               Your what, Sir? I dare swear,
Never your wife.
*Warb.*               Canst thou be so unkinde?
Considering how dearly I affect thee;
Nay, dote on thy perfections.
*Sus.*               You are studied
Too Scholar-like in words I understand not.
I am too course for such a Gallants love
As you are.
*Warb.*       By the honour of Gentility —
*Sus.*   Good Sir, no swearing: yea and nay with us             50
Prevails above all oathes you can invent.
*Warb.*   By this white hand of thine—
*Sus.*               Take a false oath?
Fie, fie, flatter the wise: fools not regard it;
And one of these am I.
*Warb.*               Dost thou despise me?
*O. Cart.*   Let 'em talk on, Mr. *Thorney*. I know *Sue*'s minde. The
Flye may buz about the Candle, he shall but singe his Wings when
all's done. *Frank, Frank* is he has her heart
*Som.*   But shall I live in hope, *Kate*?
*Kat.*   Better so, then be a desperate man.
*Som.*   Perhaps thou thinkst it is thy Portion             60

47 words_∧] Gifford; ~ : Q

499                                         32-2

I level at: wert thou as poor in Fortunes,
As thou art rich in Goodness; I would rather
Be Suitor for the Dower of thy Vertues,
Then twice thy Father's whole Estate; and prithee
Be thou resolved so.

*Kat.*                    Mr. *Somerton*,
It is an easie labour to deceive
A Maid that will believe Mens subtil promises:
Yet I conceive of you as worthily
As I presume you do deserve.

*Som.*                    Which is
As worthily in loving thee sincerely,                    70
As thou art worthy to be so belov'd.

*Kat.*    I shall finde time to try you.

*Som.*                    Do, *Kate*, do:
And when I fail, may all my joys forsake me.

*O. Cart.*    *Warbeck* and *Sue* are at it still. I laugh to my self, Mr.
*Thorney*, to see how earnestly he beats the Bush, while the Bird is
flown into anothers bosom. A very unthrift, Mr. *Thorney*; one of
the Country roaring Lads: we have such as well as the City, and as
arrant Rake-hells as they are, though not so nimble at their prizes
of wit. *Sue* knows the Raskal to an hairs breadth, and will fit him
accordingly.                    80

*O. Thor.*    What is the other Gentleman?

*O. Cart.*    One *Somerton*, the honester man of the two, by five pound
in every stone-weight. A civil Fellow. He has a fine convenient
Estate of land in *West-ham* by *Essex*. Mr. *Ranges* that dwells by
*Enfield*, sent him hither. He likes *Kate* well. I may tell you, I think
she likes him as well. If they agree, I'll not hinder the match for
my part. But that *Warbeck* is such another —. I use him kindly
for Mr. *Somerton's* sake: for he came hither first as a Companion
of his. Honest men, Mr. *Thorney*, may fall into Knaves company,
now and then.                    90

*Warb.*    Three hundred a yeer Joynture, *Sue*.

*Sus.*    Where lies it, by Sea or by Land? I think by Sea.

*Warb.*    Do I look like a Captain?

*Sus.*                    Not a whit, Sir.

Should all that use the Seas be reckon'd Captains,
There's not a Ship should have a Scullion in her
To keep her clean.
*Warb.*          Do you scorn me, Mrs. *Susan?*
Am I a subject to be jeer'd at?
*Sus.*          Neither
Am I a property for you to use
As stale to your fond wanton loose discourse.
Pray Sir be civil.
*Warb.*          Wilt be angry, Wasp?                    100
*O. Cart.*  God-a-mercy, *Sue.* She'll firk him on my life, if he fumble
with her.

*Enter* Frank.

Mr. *Francis Thorney*, you are welcome indeed. Your Father ex-
pected your coming. How does the right worshipful Knight, Sir
*Arthur Clarington*, your Master?
*Frank.*  In health this morning. Sir, my duty.
*O. Thor.*                    Now
You come as I could wish.
*Warb.*                    *Frank Thorney*, ha!
*Sus.*  You must excuse me.
*Frank.*              Vertuous Mrs. *Susan.*
Kinde Mrs. *Katherine.*                    *Salutes them.*
              Gentlemen, to both
Good time o'th' day.
*Som.*              The like to you.
*Warb.*                    'Tis he.                    110
A word, Friend. On my life, this is the Man
Stands fair in crossing *Susan*'s love to me.
*Som.*  I think no less. Be wise, and take no notice on't.
He that can win her, best deserves her.
*Warb.*                    Marry
A Servingman? mew.
*Som.*              Prethee Friend no more.
*O. Cart.*  Gentlemen all, there's within a slight Dinner ready, if
you please to taste of it: Mr. *Thorney*, Mr. *Francis*, Mr. *Somerton.*

Why Girls? what, Huswives, will you spend all your fore-noon in
tittle-tattles? away: It's well yfaith. Will you go in, Gentlemen?
*O. Thor.*   We'll follow presently: my Son and I                    120
Have a few words of business.
*O. Cart.*   At your pleasure.                    *Exeunt the rest.*
*O. Thor.*   I think you guess the reason, *Frank*, for which
I sent for you.
*Frank.*            Yes, Sir.
*O. Thor.*                    I need not tell you
With what a labyrinth of dangers dayly
The best part of my whole Estate's encumbred:
Nor have I any Clew to winde it out,
But what occasion proffers me. Wherein
If you should faulter, I shall have the shame,
And you the loss. On these two points relie                    130
Our happiness or ruine. If you marry
With wealthy *Carter*'s Daughter, there's a Portion
Will free my Land: all which I will instate
Upon the marriage to you. Otherwise,
I must be of necessity enforc'd
To make a present sale of all: and yet,
For ought I know, live in as poor distress,
Or worse, then now I do. You hear the sum:
I told you thus before. Have you considered on't?
*Frank.*   I have, Sir. And however I could wish                    140
To enjoy the benefit of single Freedom,
For that I finde no disposition in me
To undergo the burthen of that care
That Marriage brings with it; Yet to secure
And settle the continuance of your Credit,
I humbly yield to be directed by you
In all commands.
*O. Thor.*            You have already us'd
Such thriving protestations to the Maid,
That she is wholly yours. And speak the truth,
You love her, do you not?
*Frank.*                    'Twere pity, Sir,                    150

I should deceive her.

*O. Thor.*               Better y'had been unborn.
But is your love so steady that you mean,
Nay, more, desire to make her your Wife?
*Frank.*                                    Else, Sir,
It were a wrong not to be righted.
*O. Thor.*                              True,
It were: and you will marry her?
*Frank.*                            Heaven prosper it:
I do intend it.
*O. Thor.*     O thou art a Villain!
A Devil like a Man. Wherein have I
Offended all the Powers so much, to be
Father to such a graceless godless Son?
*Frank.* To me, Sir, this? O my cleft heart!
*O. Thor.*                              To thee,                160
Son of my curse. Speak truth, and blush, thou monster,
Hast thou not married *Winnifride?* a Maid
Was fellow-servant with thee.
*Frank.*                    Some swift spirit
Has blown this news abroad. I must out-face it.     [*Aside.*]
*O. Thor.* D'you study for excuse? why all the country
Is full on't.
*Frank.*     With your license, 'tis not charitable,
I am sure it is not fatherly, so much
To be o'resway'd with credulous conceit
Of meer impossibilities. But Fathers
Are priviledg'd to think and talk at pleasure.                170
*O. Thor.* Why canst thou yet deny thou hast no wife?
*Frank.* What do you take me for? an Atheist?
One that nor hopes the blessedness of life
Hereafter, neither fears the vengeance due
To such as make the Marriage-bed an Inne,
Which Travellers day and night,
After a toylsome lodging leave at pleasure?
Am I become so insensible of losing
The glory of Creations work? My soul!

O I have liv'd too long.

*O. Thor.* Thou hast, dissembler;    180
Darest thou persevere yet? and pull down wrath
As hot as flames of hell, to strike thee quick
Into the Grave of horror? I believe thee not.
Get from my sight.

*Frank.* Sir, though mine innocence
Needs not a stronger witness then the cleerness
Of an unperish'd conscience; yet for that
I was enform'd, how mainly you had been
Possess'd of this untruth, to quit all scruple
Please you peruse this Letter: 'tis to you.

*O. Thor.* From whom?

*Frank.* Sir *Arthur Clarington* my Master.    190

*O. Thor.* Well, Sir.

*Frank.* On every side I am distracted:    [*Aside.*]
Am waded deeper into mischief,
Then virtue can avoid. But on I must:
Fate leads me: I will follow.
                    There you read
What may confirm you.

*O. Thor.* Yes, and wonder at it.
Forgive me, *Frank.* Credulity abus'd me.
My tears express my joy: and I am sorry
I injur'd innocence.

*Frank.* Alas! I knew
Your rage and grief proceeded from your love
To me: so I conceiv'd it.

*O. Thor.* My good Son,    200
I'll bear with many faults in thee hereafter.
Bear thou with mine.

*Frank.* The peace is soon concluded.

*Enter Old* Carter [*and* Susan *after*].

*O. Cart.* Why Mr. *Thorney*, d'ye mean to talk out your dinner?
the Company attends your coming. What must it be, Mr. *Frank*,
or Son *Frank*? I am plain Dunstable.

*O. Thor.*    Son, Brother, if your Daughter like to have it so.

*Frank.*    I dare be confident, she's not alter'd
From what I left her at our parting last:
Are you, fair Maid?

*Sus.*                    You took too sure possession
Of an engaged heart.

*Frank.*                Which now I challenge.                    210

*O. Cart.*    Marry and much good may it do thee, Son. Take her to
thee. Get me a brace of Boys at a burthen, *Frank*. The nursing shall
not stand thee in a pennyworth of Milk. Reach her home and spare
not. When's the day?

*O. Thor.*    To morrow, if you please. To use ceremony
Of charge and custome, were to little purpose:
Their loves are married fast enough already.

*O. Cart.*    A good motion. We'll e'en have an houshold Dinner;
and let the Fiddlers go scrape. Let the Bride and Bridegroom
dance at night together: no matter for the Guests. To morrow,    220
*Sue*, to morrow. Shall's to Dinner now?

*O. Thor.*    We are on all sides pleas'd, I hope.

*Sus.*    Pray Heaven I may deserve the blessing sent me.
Now my heart is settled.

*Frank.*                So is mine.

*O. Cart.*    Your Marriage-money shall be receiv'd before your
Wedding-shooes can be pull'd on. Blessing on you both.

*Frank.*    No Man can hide his shame from Heaven that views him.
In vain he flees, whose destiny pursues him.                    [*Aside.*]

*Exeunt Omnes.*


## ACT. II, SCÆNA i

*Enter* Elizabeth Sawyer, *gathering sticks.*

*Sawy.*    And why on me? why should the envious world
Throw all their scandalous malice upon me?
'Cause I am poor, deform'd and ignorant,
And like a Bow buckl'd and bent together,

By some more strong in mischiefs then my self?
Must I for that be made a common sink,
For all the filth and rubbish of Men's tongues
To fall and run into? Some call me Witch;
And being ignorant of my self, they go
About to teach me how to be one: urging,                    10
That my bad tongue (by their bad usage made so)
Forespeaks their Cattle, doth bewitch their Corn,
Themselves, their Servants, and their Babes at nurse.

*Enter Old* Banks.

This they enforce upon me: and in part
Make me to credit it. And here comes one
Of my chief Adversaries.
*O. Bank.*   Out, out upon thee, Witch.
*Sawy.*   Dost call me Witch?
*O. Bank.*   I do, Witch, I do: and worse I would, knew I a name
more hateful. What makest thou upon my ground?                    20
*Sawy.*   Gather a few rotten sticks to warm me.
*O. Bank.*   Down with them when I bid thee, quickly;
I'll make thy bones rattle in thy skin else.
*Sawy.*   You won't, Churl, Cut-throat, Miser: there they be.
Would they stuck cross thy throat, thy bowels, thy maw, thy
midriff.
*O. Bank.*   Sayst thou me so? Hag, out of my ground.
*Sawy.*   Dost strike me, slave? curmudgeon, now thy bones aches,
thy joynts cramps, and convulsions stretch and crack thy sinews.
*O. Bank.*   Cursing, thou Hag! take that, and that.          *Exit.* 30
*Sawy.*   Strike, do, and wither'd may that hand and arm
Whose blows have lam'd me, drop from the rotten Trunk.
Abuse me! beat me! call me Hag and Witch!
What is the name? where and by what Art learn'd?
What spells, what charms, or invocations,
May the thing call'd Familiar be purchas'd?

*Enter Young* [Cuddy] *Banks* [*the Clown*],
*and three or four more.*

*Clow.*  A new head for the Tabor, and silver tipping for the Pipe.
Remember that, and forget not five lesh of new Bells.

*1.*  Double Bells: *Crooked Lane,* ye shall have 'em straight in
*Crooked Lane:* double Bells all, if it be possible.                    40

*Clow.*  Double Bells? double Coxcombs; Trebles: buy me Trebles,
all Trebles: for our purpose is to be in the Altitudes.

*2.*  All Trebles? not a Mean?

*Clow.*  Not one: The Morrice is so cast, we'll have neither Mean nor
Base in our company, Fellow *Rowland.*

*3.*  What? nor a Counter?

*Clow.*  By no means, no hunting Counter; leave that to *Envile
Chase*-Men: all Trebles, all in the Altitudes. Now for the disposing
of Parts in the Morrice, little or no labour will serve.

*2.*  If you that be minded to follow your Leader, know me, an     50
ancient Honor belonging to our house, for a Fore-horse in a team,
and fore-gallant in a Morrice: my Father's Stable is not unfurnish'd.

*3.*  So much for the Fore-horse: but how for a good Hobby-horse?

*Clow.*  For a Hobby-horse? Let me see an Almanack. *Midsummer-*
Moon, let me see ye. When the Moon's in the full, then's wit in the
wane. No more. Use your best skill. Your Morrice will suffer an
Eclipse.

*1.*  An Eclipse?

*Clow.*  A strange one.

*2.*  Strange?                                                        60

*Clow.*  Yes, and most sudden. Remember the Fore-gallant, and
forget the Hobby-horse. The whole body of your Morrice will be
darkned. There be of us—. But 'tis no matter. Forget the Hobby-
horse.

*1.*  *Cuddy Banks,* have you forgot since he pac'd it from *Envile
Chase* to *Edmonton? Cuddy,* honest *Cuddy,* cast thy stuff.

37 *Clow.*] *throughout this scene* Q *speech-prefix is:* Y. *Bank.*
39 Lane, . . .in‸] Weber; ∼ ‸ . . . ∼ . Q
51 Fore-horse in a] Gifford [i' the]; Fore-horse, [*om.* in a] Q
52 fore-gallant] Weber; for gallant Q

*Clow.* Suffer may ye all. It shall be known, I can take mine ease as well as another Man. Seek your Hobby-horse where you can get him.

*1.* *Cuddy,* honest *Cuddy,* we confess, and are sorry for our neglect. 70

*2.* The old Horse shall have a new Bridle.

*3.* The Caparisons new painted.

*4.* The Tail repair'd.

*1.* The Snaffle and the Bosses new saffron'd o're.

                                                    Kinde:

*2.* Honest:

*3.* Loving, ingenious:

*4.* Affable *Cuddy.*

*Clow.* To shew I am not flint; but affable, as you say, very well stuft, a kinde of warm Dowe or Puff-paste, I relent, I connive, most affable *Jack:* let the Hobby-horse provide a strong back, he 80 shall not want a belly when I am in 'em. But Uds me, Mother *Sawyer.*

*1.* The old Witch of *Edmonton.* If our mirth be not cross'd—

*2.* Bless us, *Cuddy,* and let her curse her tother eye out. What dost now?

*Clow.* *Ungirt, unbless'd,* says the Proverb. But my Girdle shall serve a riding knot: and a fig for all the Witches in Christendom. What wouldst thou?

*1.* The Divel cannot abide to be cross'd.

*2.* And scorns to come at any man's whistle.                          90

*3.* Away

*4.* With the Witch.

*Omn.* Away with the Witch of *Edmonton.*

                              *Exeunt in strange postur[es].*

*Sawy.* Still vex'd? still tortur'd? That Curmudgeon *Banks,*
Is ground of all my scandal. I am shunn'd
And hated like a sickness: made a scorn
To all degrees and sexes. I have heard old Beldames
Talk of Familiars in the shape of Mice,
Rats, Ferrets, Weasels, and I wot not what,
That have appear'd, and suck'd, some say, their blood.          100

    74 Kinde:] Gifford; *1.* Kinde Q          87 knot] Gifford; knit Q

But by what means they came acquainted with them,
I'm now ignorant: would some power good or bad
Instruct me which way I might be reveng'd
Upon this Churl, I'd go out of my self,
And give this Fury leave to dwell within
This ruin'd Cottage, ready to fall with age:
Abjure all goodness: be at hate with prayer;
And study Curses, Imprecations,
Blasphemous speeches, Oaths, detested Oaths,
Or any thing that's ill; so I might work                           110
Revenge upon this Miser, this black Cur,
That barks, and bites, and sucks the very blood
Of me, and of my credit. 'Tis all one,
To be a Witch, as to be counted one.
Vengeance, shame, ruine, light upon that Canker.

*Enter* Dog.

*Dog.*  Ho! have I found thee cursing? now thou art mine own.
*Sawy.*  Thine? what art thou?
*Dog.*                      He thou hast so often importun'd
To appear to thee, the Devil.
*Sawy.*                      Bless me! the Devil?
*Dog.*  Come, do not fear, I love thee much too well
To hurt or fright thee. If I seem terrible,                        120
It is to such as hate me. I have found
Thy love unfeign'd; have seen and pitied
Thy open wrongs, and come out of my love
To give thee just revenge against thy foes.
*Sawy.*  May I believe thee?
*Dog.*                      To confirm't, command me
Do any mischief unto Man or Beast,
And I'll effect it, on condition,
That uncompell'd thou make a deed of Gift
Of Soul and Body to me.
*Sawy.*                      Out, alas!
My Soul and Body?
*Dog.*                      And that instantly,                    130

509

And seal it with thy blood: if thou deniest,
I'll tear thy body in a thousand pieces.
*Sawy.*   I know not where to seek relief: But shall I
After such Covenants seal'd, see full revenge
On all that wrong me?
*Dog.*          Ha, ha, silly woman!
The Devil is no lyer to such as he loves.
Didst ever know or hear the Devil a lyer
To such as he affects?
*Sawy.*   Then I am thine, at least so much of me,
As I can call mine own.
*Dog.*          Equivocations?          140
Art mine or no? speak, or I'll tear—
*Sawy.*          All thine.
*Dog.*   Seal't with thy blood.
                    *Sucks her arm, thunder and lightning.*
                    See, now I dare call thee mine;
For proof, command me, instantly I'll run,
To any mischief, goodness can I none.
*Sawy.*   And I desire as little. There's an old Churl,
One *Banks* —
*Dog.*          That wrong'd thee: he lam'd thee, call'd thee Witch.
*Sawy.*   The same: first upon him I'ld be reveng'd.
*Dog.*   Thou shalt: Do but name how.
*Sawy.*                    Go, touch his life.
*Dog.*   I cannot.
*Sawy.*          Hast thou not vow'd? Go, kill the slave.
*Dog.*   I wonnot.
*Sawy.*          I'll cancel then my gift.
*Dog.*                    Ha, ha!
*Sawy.*                    Dost laugh?          150
Why wilt not kill him?
*Dog.*                    Fool, because I cannot.
Though we have power, know, it is circumscrib'd,
And ti'd in limits: though he be curs'd to thee,

Yet of himself he is loving to the world,
And charitable to the poor. Now Men
That, as he, love goodness, though in smallest measure,
Live without compass of our reach. His Cattle
And Corn, I'll kill and mildew: but his life
(Until I take him, as I late found thee,
Cursing and swearing) I have no power to touch.          160
*Sawy.* Work on his corn and cattle then.
*Dog.*                                    I shall.
The Witch of *Edmonton* shall see his fall.
If she at least put credit in my power,
And in mine onely; make Orisons to me,
And none but me.
*Sawy.*              Say how, and in what manner?
*Dog.* I'll tell thee; when thou wishest ill,
Corn, Man or Beast, would spoyl or kill,
Turn thy back against the Sun,
And mumble this short Orison:
*If thou to death or shame pursue 'em,*          170
*Sanctibicetur nomen tuum.*
*Sawy.* *If thou to death or shame pursue 'em,*
*Sanctibecetur nomen tuum.*
*Dog.* Perfect. Farewel. Our first-made promises
We'll put in execution against *Banks.*          *Exit.*
*Sawy.* *Contaminetur nomen tuum.* I'm an expert Scholar;
Speak Latine, or I know not well what Language,
As well as the best of 'em. But who comes here?
                    *Enter Young* Banks [*the Clown*].
The Son of my worst Foe. *To death pursue 'em,*
*Et sanctabecetur nomen tuum.*          180
*Clow.* What's that she mumbles? the Devils *Pater noster?* Would
it were else. Mother *Sawyer*, Good morrow.
*Sawy.* Ill morrow to thee, and all the world, that flout a poor old
woman. *To death pursue 'em, and sanctabacetur nomen tuum.*
*Clow.* Nay, good Gammer *Sawyer*, what e're it pleases my Father
to call you, I know you are —
*Sawy.* A Witch.

*Clow.*  A Witch? would you were else yfaith.

*Sawy.*  Your Father knows I am by this.

*Clow.*  I would he did.                                                    190

*Sawy.*  And so in time may you.

*Clow.*  I would I might else. But Witch or no Witch, you are a
motherly woman: and though my Father be a kinde of God bless
us, as they say, I have an earnest suit to you; and if you'll be so
kinde to ka me one good turn, I'll be so courteous as to kob you
another.

*Sawy.*  What's that? to spurn, beat me, and call me Witch, as your
kinde Father doth?

*Clow.*  My Father? I am asham'd to own him. If he has hurt the
head of thy credit, there's money to buy thee a Playster: and a small  200
courtesie I would require at thy hands.

*Sawy.*  You seem a good young Man, and I must dissemble, the
better to accomplish my revenge. But for this silver, what wouldst
have me do? bewitch thee?

*Clow.*  No, by no means; I am bewitch'd already. I would have
thee so good as to unwitch me, or witch another with me for
company.

*Sawy.*  I understand thee not. Be plain, my Son.

*Clow.*  As a Pike-staff, Mother: you know *Kate Carter.*

*Sawy.*  The wealthy Yeomans Daughter. What of her?            210

*Clow.*  That same Party has bewitch'd me.

*Sawy.*  Bewitch'd thee?

*Clow.*  Bewitch'd me, *Hisce auribus.* I saw a little Devil flie out of
her eye like a Burbolt, which sticks at this hour up to the Feathers
in my heart. Now my request is, to send one of thy what d'ye call
'ems, either to pluck that out, or stick another as fast in hers.
Do, and here's my hand, I am thine for three lives.

*Sawy.*  We shall have sport. Thou art in love with her.

*Clow.*  Up to the very hilts, Mother.

*Sawy.*  And thou'ldst have me make her love thee too.           220

*Clow.*  I think she'll prove a Witch in earnest. Yes, I could finde in
my heart to strike her three quarters deep in love with me too.

*Sawy.*  But dost thou think that I can do't, and I alone?

*Clow.*  Truely, Mother Witch, I do verily believe so: and when I see it done, I shall be half perswaded so too.

*Sawy.* It's enough. What Art can do, be sure of: turn to the West, and whatsoe'er thou hearest or seest, stand silent, and be not afraid.

*She stamps.*

*Enter the* Dog; *he fawns and leaps upon her.*

*Clow.* Afraid, Mother Witch? turn my face to the West? I said I should always have a back-friend of her; and now it's out. And her little Devil should be hungry, come sneaking behinde me, like 230 a cowardly Catchpole, and clap his Talents on my Haunches. 'Tis woundy cold sure. I dudder and shake like an Aspen-leaf every joynt of me.

*Sawy.* *To scandal and disgrace pursue 'em,*
*Et sanctabicetur nomen tuum.*

How now, my Son, how is't?  *Exit* Dog.

*Clow.* Scarce in a clean life, Mother Witch. But did your Gobblin and you spout Latine together?

*Sawy.* A kinde of Charm I work by. Didst thou hear me?

*Clow.* I heard I know not the Devil what mumble in a scurvy base 240 tone, like a Drum that had taken cold in the head the last Muster. Very comfortable words: what were they? and who taught them you?

*Sawy.* A great learned Man.

*Clow.* Learned Man? learned Devil it was as soon? But what? what comfortable news about the Party?

*Sawy.* Who? *Kate Carter?* I'll tell thee, thou knowst the Style at the West-end of thy Father's Pease-Field, be there to morrow-night after Sun-set; and the first live thing thou seest, be sure to follow, and that shall bring thee to thy Love.  250

*Clow.* In the Pease-field? Has she a minde to Codlings already? The first living thing I meet, you say, shall bring me to her.

*Sawy.* To a sight of her, I mean. She will seem wantonly coy, and flee thee: but follow her close, and boldly: do but embrace her in thy arms once, and she is thine own.

*Clow.* At the Style, at the West-end of my Father's Pease-land, the first live thing I see, follow and embrace her, and she shall be

thine. Nay, and I come to embracing once, she shall be mine; I'll
go neer to make at Eaglet else. *Exit.*

*Sawy.* A ball well bandied: now the set's half won:                    260
The Father's wrong I'll wreak upon the Son.

*Exit.*

## [ACT II,] Scæna ii

*Enter [Old]* Carter, Warbeck, Somerton.

*O. Cart.* How now Gentlemen, cloudy? I know Mr. *Warbeck*,
you are in a fog about my Daughters marriage.

*Warb.* And can you blame me, Sir?

*O. Cart.* Nor you me justly. Wedding and hanging are tied up
both in a Proverb; and Destiny is the Juggler that unties the knot.
My hope is, you are reserved to a richer fortune then my poor
Daughter.

*Warb.* However, your promise —

*O. Cart.* Is a kinde of debt, I confess it.

*Warb.* Which honest men should pay.                                     10

*O. Cart.* Yet some Gentlemen break in that point, now and then,
by your leave, Sir.

*Som.* I confess thou hast had a little wrong in the Wench: but
patience is the onely salve to cure it. Since *Thorney* has won the
Wench, he has most reason to wear her.

*Warb.* Love in this kinde admits no reason to wear her.

*O. Cart.* Then love's a fool, and what wise man will take exception?

*Som.* Come, frolick, *Ned,* were every man master of his own
fortune, Fate might pick straws, and Destiny go a wool-gathering.

*Warb.* You hold yours in a string though. 'Tis well: but if there  20
be any equity, look thou to meet the like usage e're long.

*Som.* In my love to her Sister *Katherine*? Indeed, they are a pair
of Arrows drawn out of one Quiver, and should flie at an even
length: if she do run after her Sister —

* 259 make at Eaglet] *stet* Q
  1 *O. Cart.*] *throughout this scene* Q *speech-prefix is: Cart.*
  18 frolick,] Weber; ∼ ∧ Q    24 length: . . . Sister —] Weber; ∼ , . . . ∼ . Q

*Warb.*   Look for the same mercy at my hands, as I have received
at thine.

*Som.*   She'll keep a surer compass. I have too strong a confidence
to mistrust her.

*Warb.*   And that confidence is a winde, that has blown many a
married Man ashore at Cuckolds Haven, I can tell you: I wish 30
yours more prosperous though.

*O. Cart.*   Whate're you wish, I'll master my promise to him.

*Warb.*   Yes, as you did to me.

*O. Cart.*   No more of that, if you love me. But for the more
assurance, the next offer'd occasion shall consummate the Marriage:
and that once seal'd —

*Enter Young* [Frank] *Thorney and* Susan.

*Som.*   Leave the mannage of the rest to my care. But see, the
Bridegroom and Bride comes; the new pair of *Sheffeild*-Knives
fitted both to one sheath.

*Warb.*   The Sheath might have been better fitted, if some body had 40
their due. But —

*Som.*   No harsh language, if thou lovest me. *Frank Thorney* has
done —

*Warb.*   No more then I, or thou, or any man, things so standing,
would have attempted.

*Som.*   Good morrow Mr. Bridegroom.

*Warb.*                               Come, give thee joy.
Mayst thou live long and happy in thy fair choice.

*Frank.*   I thank yee Gentlemen.
Kinde Mr. *Warbeck*, I find you loving.

*Warb.*   *Thorney*, that creature, (much good do thee with her)   50
Vertue and beauty hold fair mixture in her.
She's rich no doubt in both. Yet were she fairer,
Thou art right worthy of her. Love her, *Thorney*,
'Tis nobleness in thee, in her but duty.
The match is fair and equal: the success

---

* 42 *Som.*] Gifford; *Cart.* Q
  48 *Frank.*] *throughout this scene* Q *speech-prefix is:* Y. *Thor.*

I leave to censure. Farewel, Mrs. Bride:
Till now elected, thy old scorne deride.                    *Exit.*
*Som.*   Good Mr. *Thorney.*                                [*Exit.*]
*O. Cart.*   Nay, you shall not part till you see the Barrels run a-tilt,
Gentlemen.                                                  *Exit.* 60
*Sus.*   Why change you your face, sweet-Heart?
*Frank.*                                     Who? I?
For nothing.
*Sus.*          Dear, say not so: a Spirit of your
Constancy cannot endure this change for nothing.
I have observ'd strange variations in you.
*Frank.*   In me?
*Sus.*             In you, Sir. Awake: you seem to dream,
And in your sleep you utter sudden and
Distracted accents, like one at enmity
With peace. Dear loving Husband, if I may dare
To challenge any interest in you,
Give me the reason fully: you may trust                     70
My brest as safely as your own.
*Frank.*                        With what?
You half amaze me, prithee.
*Sus.*                       Come, you shall not;
Indeed, you shall not shut me from partaking
The least dislike that grieves you. I am all yours.
*Frank.*   And I all thine.
*Sus.*                      You are not, if you keep
The least grief from me: but I find the cause;
It grew from me.
*Frank.*         From you?
*Sus.*                     From some distaste
In me or my behaviour: you are not kinde
In the concealment. 'Las, Sir, I am young,
Silly, and plain; more, strange to those contents           80
A wife should offer. Say but in what I fail,
I'll study satisfaction.
*Frank.*                 Come, in nothing.

80 more,] Gifford; ~ ‸ Q

*Sus.* I know I do. Knew I as well in what,
You should not long be sullen. Prithee Love,
If I have been immodest or too bold,
Speak't in a frown: if peevishly too nice,
Shew't in a smile. Thy liking is the glass
By which I'll habit my behaviour.
*Frank.* Wherefore dost weep now?
*Sus.*                     You, Sweet, have the power
To make me passionate as an *April*-day:                    90
Now smile, then weep; now pale, then crimson red.
You are the powerful Moon of my bloods Sea,
To make it ebb or flow into my face,
As your looks change.
*Frank.*               Change thy conceit, I prithee:
Thou art all perfection: *Diana* her self
Swells in thy thoughts, and moderates thy beauty.
Within thy left eye amorous *Cupid* sits
Feathering Love-shafts, whose golden heads he dip'd
In thy chaste brest. In the other lies
Blushing *Adonis* scarft in modesties.                     100
And still as wanton *Cupid* blows Love-fires,
*Adonis* quenches out unchaste desires.
And from these two I briefly do imply
A perfect Embleme of thy modesty.
Then, prithee Dear, maintain no more dispute,
For where thou speakst, it's fit all tongues be mute.
*Sus.* Come, come, those golden strings of flattery
Shall not tie up my speech, Sir; I must know
The ground of your disturbance.
*Frank.*                     Then look here;
For here, here is the fen in which this Hydra            110
Of discontent grows rank.
*Sus.*               Heaven sheild it: where?
*Frank.* In mine own bosom: here the cause has root;
The poysoned Leeches twist about my heart,
And will, I hope, confound me.
*Sus.*                     You speak Riddles.

*Frank.*  Take't plainly then: 'twas told me by a woman
Known and approv'd in Palmestry,
I should have two wives.
*Sus.*                    Two wives? Sir, I take it
Exceeding likely. But let not conceit hurt you:
You are afraid to bury me?
*Frank.*                    No, no, my *Winnifride.*
*Sus.*  How say you? *Winnifride?* you forget me.                    120
*Frank.*  No, I forget my self, *Susan.*
*Sus.*                    In what?
*Frank.*  Talking of wives, I pretend *Winnifride,*
A Maid that at my Mothers waited on me
Before thy self.
*Sus.*            I hope, Sir, she may live
To take my place. But why should all this move you?
*Frank.*  The poor Girl, she has't before thee,
And that's the Fiend torments me.
*Sus.*                    Yet why should this
Raise mutiny within you? such presages
Prove often false: or say it should be true?
*Frank.*  That I should have another wife?
*Sus.*                    Yes, many;                    130
If they be good, the better.
*Frank.*            Never any equal
To thee in goodness.
*Sus.*            Sir, I could wish I were
Much better for you; yet if I knew your fate
Ordain'd you for another, I could wish
(So well I love you, and your hopeful pleasure)
Me in my grave, and my poor vertues added
To my successor.
*Frank.*            Prithee, prithee, talk not
Of death or graves; thou art so rare a goodness,
As Death would rather put it self to death,
Then murther thee. But we, as all things else,                    140
Are mutable and changing.

* 126 The poor Girl] *stet* Q

*Sus.*                    Yet you still move
In your first sphere of discontent. Sweet, chase
Those clouds of sorrow, and shine cleerly on me.
*Frank.*    At my return I will.
*Sus.*                    Return? ah me!
Will you then leave me?
*Frank.*                    For a time I must:
But how? as Birds their young, or loving Bees
Their Hives, to fetch home richer dainties.
*Sus.*                    Leave me?
Now has my fear met its effect. You shall not,
Cost it my life, you shall not.
*Frank.*                    Why? your reason?
*Sus.*    Like to the Lap-wing have you all this while          150
With your false love deluded me? pretending
Counterfeit senses for your discontent,
And now at last it is by chance stole from you.
*Frank.*    What? what by chance?
*Sus.*                    Your pre-appointed meeting
Of single combate with young *Warbeck.*
*Frank.*                    Hah!
*Sus.*    Even so: dissemble not; 'tis too apparent.
Then in his look I read it: deny it not;
I see't apparent: cost it my undoing,
And unto that my life, I will not leave you.
*Frank.*    Not until when?
*Sus.*                    Till he and you be Friends.          160
Was this your cunning? and then flam me off
With an old Witch, two Wives, and *Winnifride?*
Y'are not so kinde indeed as I imagin'd.
*Frank.*    And you more fond by far then I expected.
It is a vertue that attends thy kinde.
But of our business within: and by this kiss,
I'll anger thee no more; troth Chuck I will not.
*Sus.*    You shall have no just cause.
*Frank.*                    Dear *Sue*, I shall not.

                                        *Exeunt.*

## ACT. III, Scæna i

*Enter* Cuddy Banks [*the Clown*], *and Morice-dancers.*

*1.*   Nay, *Cuddy*, prithee do not leave us now: if we part all this night,
we shall not meet before day.

*2.*   I prithee, *Banks*, let's keep together now.

*Clow.*   If you were wise, a word would serve: but as you are,
I must be forc'd to tell you again, I have a little private business,
an hours work; it may prove but an half hours, as luck may serve;
and then I take horse and along with you. Have we e're a Witch
in the Morice?

*1.*   No, no; no womans part, but Maid-marian, and the Hobby-
horse.                                                                                                          10

*Clow.*   I'll have a Witch; I love a Witch.

*1.*   Faith, Witches themselves are so common now adays, that the
counterfeit will not be regarded. They say we have three or four
in *Edmonton*, besides Mother *Sawyer*.

*2.*   I would she would dance her part with us.

*3.*   So would not I; for if she comes, the Devil and all comes along
with her.

*Clow.*   Well, I'll have a Witch: I have lov'd a Witch ever since I
play'd at Cherry-pit. Leave me, and get my horse dress'd: give
him Oats; but water him not till I come. Whither do we foot it 20
first?

*2.*   To Sir *Arthur Clarington*'s first, then whither thou wilt.

*Clow.*   Well, I'am content: but we must up to *Carter*'s, the rich
Yeoman. I must be seen on Hobby-horse there.

*1.*   O, I smell him now: I'll lay my ears *Banks* is in love, and that's
the reason he would walk melancholy by himself.

*Clow.*   Hah! who was that said I was in love?

*1.*   Not I.

*2.*   Nor I.

*Clow.*   Go to: no more of that. When I understand what you speak, 30
I know what you say: believe that.

3 2.] Weber; *1.* Q

520

*1.* Well, 'twas I, I'll not deny it: I meant no hurt in't. I have seen
you walk up to *Carter*'s of *Chessum*. *Banks*, were not you there
last Shrovetide?

*Clow.* Yes, I was ten days together there the last Shrovetide.

*2.* How could that be, when there are but seven dayes in the week?

*Clow.* Prithee peace, I reckon *stila nova*, as a *Traveller*: thou
understandest as a fresh-water Farmer, that never sawest a week
beyond Sea. Ask any Souldier that ever received his pay but in the
Low Countries, and he'll tell thee there are eight days in the week 40
there, hard by. How dost thou think they rise in high *Germany,
Italy,* and those remoter places?

*3.* I, but simply there are but seven days in the week yet.

*Clow.* No, simply as thou understandest. Prithee, look but in the
Lover's Almanack, when he has been but three days absent; Oh,
says he, I have not seen my Love these seven yeers: there's a long
cut. When he comes to her again, and embraces her, O, says he,
now methinks I am in Heaven; and that's a pretty step: he that can
get up to Heaven in ten days, need not repent his journey. You may
ride a hundred days in a Caroch, and be further off then when you 50
set forth. But I pray you, good Morrice-mates, now leave me.
I will be with you by midnight.

*1.* Well, since he will be alone, we'll back again, and trouble him
no more.

*Omn.* But remember, *Banks.*

*Clow.* The Hobby-horse shall be remembred. But hark you: get
*Poldavis*, the Barber's Boy for the Witch; because he can shew his
Art better then another.                                        *Exeunt.*

Well, now to my walk. I am neer the place where I should meet
I know not what: say I meet a Thief, I must follow him, if to the 60
Gallows: say I meet a Horse, or Hare, or Hound, still I must follow;
some slow-pac'd Beast, I hope: yet Love is full of lightness in the
heaviest Lovers. [*Enter* Dog.] Ha! my Guide is come. A Water-
Dog. I am thy first man, Sculler: I go with thee: ply no other but
my self: away with the Boat: land me but at *Katherine*'s Dock, my
sweet *Katherine*'s Dock, and I'll be a Fare to thee. That way? nay,
which way thou wilt, thou know'st the way better then I. Fine
gentle Cur it is, and well brought up, I warrant him. We go a

ducking, Spaniel; thou shalt fetch me the Ducks, pretty kinde
Rascal. 70

*Enter Spirit in shape of Katherine, vizarded, and takes it off.*

*Spir.* Thus throw I off mine own essential horror,
And take the shape of a sweet lovely Maid
Whom this Fool doats on. We can meet his folly,
But from his Vertues must be Run-aways.
We'll sport with him: but when we reckoning call,
We know where to receive: th'Witch pays for all.

Dog barks.

*Clow.* I? is that the watch-word? She's come. Well, if ever we be
married, it shall be at *Barking*-Church, in memory of thee. Now
come behinde, kinde Cur.

And have I met thee, sweet *Kate?* 80
I will teach thee to walk so late.

O see, we meet in Metre. What? dost thou trip from me? Oh that
I were upon my Hobby-horse, I would mount after thee so nimble.
Stay, Nymph, stay, Nymph, sing'd *Apollo*:

Tarry and kiss me; sweet Nymph stay:
Tarry and kiss me, Sweet.
We will to *Chessum-street,*
And then to the house stands in the high-way.

Nay, by your leave, I must embrace you. [*Exeunt Spirit and
Banks.*] Oh help, help, I am drown'd, I am drown'd. [*Within.*] 90
*Dog.* Ha, ha, ha, ha.

Enter [Banks] wet.

*Clow.* This was an ill night to go a wooing in; I finde it now in
*Pond*'s Almanack: thinking to land at *Katherine*'s Dock, I was
almost at *Gravesend*. I'll never go to a Wench in the Dog-days
again; yet 'tis cool enough. Had you never a paw in this Dog-
trick? a mangie take that black hide of yours: I'll throw you in at
*Limehouse* in some Tanner's Pit or other.
*Dog.* Ha, ha, ha, ha.
*Clow.* How now? who's that laughs at me? Hist to him. (Dog

* 90 Oh help...] stet Q

*barks*.) Peace, peace; thou didst but thy kinde neither. 'Twas my  100
own fault.

*Dog.*   Take heed how thou trustest the Devil another time.

*Clow.*   How now? who's that speaks? I hope you have not your
reading Tongue about you.

*Dog.*   Yes, I can speak.

*Clow.*   The Devil you can. You have read *Esop*'s Fables then:
I have play'd one of your parts there; the Dog that catch'd at the
shadow in the water. Pray you, let me catechize you a little: What
might one call your name, *Dog?*

*Dog.*   My Dame calls me *Tom*.                                        110

*Clow.*   'Tis well; and she may call me *Ass*: so there's an whole one
betwixt us, *Tom-Ass*. She said, I should follow you, indeed. Well,
*Tom*, give me thy fist; we are Friends: you shall be mine Ingle:
I love you; but I pray you let's have no more of these ducking
devices.

*Dog.*   Not, if you love me. Dogs love where they are beloved.
Cherish me, and I'll do any thing for thee.

*Clow.*   Well, you shall have Jowls and Livers: I have Butchers to
my Friends that shall bestow 'em: and I will keep Crusts and Bones
for you, if you'll be a kinde Dog, *Tom*.                              120

*Dog.*   Any thing: I'll help thee to thy Love.

*Clow.*   Wilt thou? That promise shall cost me a brown Loaf, though
I steal it out of my Father's Cupboard. You'll eat stollen Goods,
*Tom*, will you not?

*Dog.*   Oh best of all. The sweetest bits, those.

*Clow.*   You shall not starve, *Ningle Tom*, believe that; if you love
Fish, I'll help you to Maids and Soles. I'm acquainted with a
Fishmonger.

*Dog.*   Maids and Soles? Oh, sweet bits! Banquetting stuff, those.

*Clow.*   One thing I would request you, *Ningle*, as you have play'd  130
the Knavish Cur with me a little, that you would mingle amongst
our Morrice-Dancers in the morning. You can dance?

*Dog.*   Yes, yes, any thing: I'll be there, but unseen to any but thy
self. Get thee gone before: feare not my presence. I have work
to night. I serve more Masters, more Dames then one.

107 there] Gifford; then Q

*Clow.*   He can serve *Mammon* and the Devil too.

*Dog.*   It shall concern thee, and thy Loves purchase:
There's a gallant Rival loves the Maid;
And likely is to have her.  Mark what a mischief
Before the Morrice ends, shall light on him.          140

*Clow.*   Oh sweet *Ningle*, thy neufe once again.  Friends must part
for a time: farewel, with this remembrance; shalt have bread too
when we meet again.  If ever there were an honest Devil, 'twill be
the Devil of *Edmonton*, I see.  Farewel *Tom.*  I prithee dog me as
soon as thou canst.                            *Exit* Banks.

*Dog.*   I'll not miss thee, and be merry with thee.
Those that are joys denied, must take delight
In sins and mischiefs, 'tis the Devil's right.

                                         *Exit* Dog.

## [ACT III, Scene ii]

*Enter Young* [Frank] *Thorney, Winnifride as a Boy.*

*Frank.*   Prithee no more: those tears give nourishment
To weeds and briers in me, which shortly will
O'regrow and top my head: my shame will sit
And cover all that can be seen of me.

*Win.*   I have not shewn this cheek in company,
Pardon me now, thus singled with your self:
It calls a thousand sorrows round about,
Some going before, and some on either side;
But infinite behinde: all chain'd together.
Your second adulterous Marriage leads;          10
That's the sad Eclipse, the effects must follow.
As, plagues of shame, spight, scorn, and obloquy.

*Frank.*   Why? hast thou not left one hours patience
To add to all the rest?  One hour bears us
Beyond the reach of all these Enemies.
Are we not now set forward in the flight,

     6 now, . . .self:] ~ : . . . ~ , Q
    13 *Frank.*] *here and for the rest of this scene* Q *speech-prefix is:* Y. *Thor.*

Provided with the Dowry of my sin,
To keep us in some other Nation?
While we together are, we are at home
In any place.
*Win.*    'Tis fowl ill gotten coyn,                              20
Far worse then Usury or Extortion.
*Frank.*   Let my Father then make the restitution,
Who forc'd me take the bribe: it is his gift
And patrimony to me; so I receive it.
He would not bless, nor look a Father on me,
Until I satisfied his angry will.
When I was sold, I sold my self again
(Some Knaves have done't in Lands, and I in Body)
For money, and I have the hire. But, sweet, no more,
'Tis hazard of discovery, our discourse;                        30
And then prevention takes off all our hopes.
For only but to take her leave of me,
My Wife is coming.
*Win.*                Who coming? your Wife?
*Frank.*   No, no, thou art her: the woman; I knew
Not how to call her now: but after this day
She shall be quite forgot, and have no name
In my remembrance. See, see, she's come.

*Enter* Susan.

                                Go lead
The horses to the hills top, there I'll meet thee.
*Sus.*   Nay, with your favour, let him stay a little
I would part with him too, because he is                        40
Your sole Companion; and I'll begin with him,
Reserving you the last.
*Frank.*                I, with all my heart.
*Sus.*   You may hear, if it please you, Sir.
*Frank.*                No, 'tis not fit.
Some rudiments, I conceive, they must be,
To overlook my slippery footings. And so.

34 her] Dyce *query*; here Q

*Sus.*  No, indeed, Sir.

*Frank.*                    Tush, I know it must be so,
And 'tis necessary. On, but be brief.          [*Walks aloof.*]

*Win.*  What charge so'ere you lay upon me, Mistress,
I shall support it faithfully (being honest)
To my best strength.                                              50

*Sus.*  Believe't shall be no other. I know you were
Commended to my husband by a noble Knight.

*Win.*  Oh Gods! Oh, mine eyes!

*Sus.*                    How now? what ailst thou, Lad?

*Win.*  Something hit mine eye, it makes it water still,
Even as you said, *Commended to my Husband.*
Some door I think it was. I was, forsooth,
Commended to him by Sir *Arthur Clarington.*

*Sus.*  Whose Servant once my *Thorney* was himself.
That title methinks should make you almost Fellows,
Or at the least much more then a Servant;                        60
And I am sure he will respect you so.
Your love to him then needs no spur from me;
And what for my sake you will ever do,
'Tis fit it should be bought with something more
Then fair entreats. Look here's a Jewel for thee,
A pretty wanton Label for thine ear;
And I would have it hang there, still to whisper
These words to thee, *Thou hast my Jewel with thee.*
It is but earnest of a larger bounty,
When thou returnst, with praises of thy service,                 70
Which I am confident thou wilt deserve.
Why, thou art many now, besides thy self:
Thou maist be Servant, Friend, and Wife to him.
A good Wife is them all. A Friend can play
The Wife and Servants part, and shift enough.
No less the Servant can the Friend and Wife.
'Tis all but sweet society, good counsel,
Enterchang'd loves; yes, and counsel-keeping.

56 door] *i.e.* dor, or beetle          62 from] Rhys; for Q
74 them] Weber; then Q

*Frank.*  Not done yet?

*Sus.*  Even now, Sir.                                                              80

*Win.*  Mistress, believe my vow, your severe eye
Were it present to command; your bounteous hand,
Were it then by to buy or bribe my service,
Shall not make me more dear or neer unto him,
Then I shall voluntary. I'll be all your charge,
Servant, Friend, Wife to him.

*Sus.*                              Wilt thou?
Now blessings go with thee for't: courtesies
Shall meet thee coming home.

*Win.*                           Pray you say plainly, Mistress,
Are you jealous of him? if you be,
I'll look to him that way too.

*Sus.*                        Sayst thou so?                                         90
I would thou hadst a womans bosom now.
We have weak thoughts within us. Alas,
There's nothing so strong in us as suspicion:
But I dare not, nay, I will not think
So hardly of my *Thorney.*

*Win.*                       Believe it, Mistress,
I'll be no Pander to him; and if I finde
Any loose lubrick scapes in him, I'll watch him,
And at my return, protest I'll shew you all.
He shall hardly offend without my knowledge.

*Sus.*  Thine own diligence is that I press,                                        100
And not the curious eye over his faults.
Farewel: if I should never see thee more,
Take it for ever.

*Frank.*  Prithee take that along with thee, and haste thee
                                            *Gives his sword.*
To the hills top; I'll be there instantly.
                                            *Exit* Winnifride.

*Sus.*  No haste I prithee, slowly as thou canst.
Pray let him obey me now: 'tis happily
His last service to me. My power is e'en
A going out of sight.

*Frank.* Why would you delay?
We have no other business now but to part. 110
*Sus.* And will not that, sweet heart, ask a long time?
Methinks it is the hardest piece of work
That e're I took in hand.
*Frank.* Fie, fie, why look,
I'll make it plain and easie to you: Farewel. *Kisses.*
*Sus.* Ah, 'las! I am not half perfect in it yet.
I must have it read over an hundred times.
Pray you take some pains, I confess my dulness.
*Frank.* What a Thorne this Rose grows on? parting were sweet,
[*Aside.*]
But what a trouble 'twill be to obtain it?
Come, again and again, farewel. Yet wilt return? *Kisses.* 120
All questions of my journey, my stay, imployment,
And revisitation, fully I have answered all.
There's nothing now behinde, but nothing.
*Sus.* And that nothing is more hard then any thing,
Then all the every things. This Request —
*Frank.* What is it?
*Sus.* That I may bring you through one pasture more
Up to yon knot of trees: amongst those shadows
I'll vanish from you, they shall teach me how.
*Frank.* Why, 'tis granted: come, walk then.
*Sus.* Nay, not too fast.
They say slow things have best perfection: 130
The gentle showre wets to fertility.
The churlish storm may mischief with his bounty.
The baser beasts take strength, even from the womb:
But the Lord Lion's whelp is feeble long.

*Exeunt.*

## [ACT III, Scene iii]

*Enter* Dog.

*Dog.*  Now for an early mischief and a sudden:
The minde's about it now.  One touch from me
Soon sets the body forward.

*Enter Young* [Frank] Thorney, Susan.

*Frank.*  Your request is out: yet will you leave me?
*Sus.*                                               What?
So churlishly? you'll make me stay for ever,
Rather then part with such a sound from you.
*Frank.*  Why you almost anger me. Pray you be gone.
You have no company, and 'tis very early;
Some hurt may betide you homewards.
*Sus.*                                      Tush, I fear none.
To leave you, is the greatest hurt I can suffer:                 10
Besides, I expect your Father and mine own,
To meet me back, or overtake me with you.
They began to stir when I came after you:
I know they'll not be long.
*Frank.*                   So, I shall have more trouble.

                                                *Dog rubs him.*
Thank you for that. Then I'll ease all at once.
'Tis done now: what I ne'er thought on. You shall not go back.
*Sus.*  Why? shall I go along with thee? sweet musick!
*Frank.*  No, to a better place.
*Sus.*                         Any place, I:
I'm there at home, where thou pleasest to have me.
*Frank.*  At home? I'll leave you in your last lodging.          20
I must kill you.
*Sus.*              Oh fine! you'ld fright me from you.
*Frank.*  You see I had no purpose: I'm unarm'd.

4 *Frank.] throughout this scene* Q *speech-prefix is:* Y. Thor.

'Tis this minutes decree, and it must be.
Look, this will serve your turn.                    [*Knife.*]
*Sus.*                    I'll not turn from it,
If you be earnest, Sir. Yet you may tell me
Wherefore you'll kill me.
*Frank.*                    Because you are a whore.
*Sus.* There's one deep wound already: a whore?
'Twas ever further from me then the thought
Of this black hour: a whore?
*Frank.*                    Yes, I'll prove it,
And you shall confess it. You are my whore,                    30
No wife of mine. The word admits no second.
I was before wedded to another, have her still.
I do not lay the sin unto your charge,
'Tis all mine own. Your marriage was my theft.
For I espous'd your dowry, and I have it:
I did not purpose to have added murther;
The Devil did not prompt me: till this minute
You might have safe returned; now you cannot:
You have dogg'd your own death.                    *Stabs her.*
*Sus.*                    And I deserve it.
I'm glad my fate was so intelligent.                    40
'Twas some good Spirits motion. Die? Oh, 'twas time!
How many yeers might I have slept in sin?
Sin of my most hatred too, Adultery?
*Frank.* Nay, sure 'twas likely that the most was past;
For I meant never to return to you
After this parting.
*Sus.*                    Why then I thank you more,
You have done lovingly, leaving your self,
That you would thus bestow me on another.
Thou art my Husband, Death, and I embrace thee
With all the love I have. Forget the stain                    50
Of my unwitting sin: and then I come
A Chrystal Virgin to thee. My Soul's purity
Shall with bold Wings ascend the Doors of Mercy;

For Innocence is ever her Companion.
*Frank.*   Not yet mortal? I would not linger you,
Or leave you a tongue to blab.                    [*Stab again.*]
*Sus.*   Now heaven reward you ne'er the worse for me.
I did not think that death had been so sweet;
Nor I so apt to love him. I could ne'er die better,
Had I staid forty yeers for preparation:                    60
For I'm in charity with all the World.
Let me for once be thine example, Heaven;
Do to this man as I him free forgive.
And may he better die, and better live.          *Moritur.*
*Frank.*   'Tis done; and I am in: once past our height,
We scorn the deepst Abyss. This follows now,
To heal her Wounds by dressing of the Weapon:
Arms, thighs, hands, any place; we must not fail
                                        *Wounds himself.*
Light scratches, giving such deep ones. The best I can
To binde my self to this Tree. Now's the storm,          70
Which if blown o're, many fair days may follow.
                            Dog *ties him* [*and exit*].
So, so, I'm fast; I did not think I could
Have done so well behinde me. How prosperous
And effectual mischief sometimes is? Help, help;
Murther, murther, murther.

                *Enter* [*Old*] Carter, *and Old* Thorney.

*O. Cart.*   Ha! Whom tolls the Bell for?
*Frank.*                    Oh, oh!
*O. Thor.*                            Ah me!
The cause appears too soon: my Child, my Son.
*O. Cart.*   Susan, Girl, Child. Not speak to thy Father? Hah!
*Frank.*   O lend me some assistance to o'retake
This hapless woman.
*O. Thor.*            Let's o'retake the murtherers.          80
Speak whilst thou canst; anon may be too late.

        67 heal] *i.e.* hele, or conceal the source of
        76 *O. Cart.*] *throughout this scene* Q *speech-prefix is:* Cart.

I fear thou hast deaths mark upon thee too.

*Frank.*   I know them both; yet such an Oath is pass'd,
As pulls damnation up if it be broke;
I dare not name 'em: think what forc'd men do.

*O. Thor.*   Keep oath with murtherers? that were a conscience
To hold the Devil in.

*Frank.*                          Nay, Sir, I can describe 'em;
Shall shew them as familiar as their names.
The Taller of the two at this time wears
His Satten-doublet white, but Crimson lin'd;                    90
Hose of black Satten, Cloak of Scarlet.

*O. Thor.*   *Warbeck, Warbeck, Warbeck*: Do you list to this, Sir?

*O. Cart.*   Yes, yes, I listen you: here's nothing to be heard.

*Frank.*   Th'others Cloak branch'd Velvet black, Velvet lin'd
His Suit.

*O. Thor.*          I have 'em already: *Somerton, Somerton.*
Binal revenge, all this. Come, Sir, the first work
Is to pursue the Murtherers, when we have remov'd
These mangled bodies hence.

*O. Cart.*   Sir, take that Carcase there, and give me this.
I'll not own her now; she's none of mine.                    100
Bob me off with a dumb shew? No, I'll have life.
This is my Son too, and while there's life in him,
'Tis half mine; take you halfe that silence for't.
When I speak, I look to be spoken to:
Forgetful Slut?

*O. Thor.*          Alas! what grief may do now?
Look, Sir, I'll take this load of sorrow with me.

*O. Cart.*   I, do, and I'll have this. How do you, Sir?

*Frank.*   O, very ill, Sir.

*O. Cart.*   Yes, I think so; but 'tis well you can speak yet.
There's no musick but in sound, sound it must be.            110
I have not wept these twenty yeers before,
And that I guess was e're that Girl was born:
Yet now methinks, if I but knew the way,
My heart's so full, I could weep night and day.

                                                *Exeunt.*

## [ACT III, Scene iv]

*Enter Sir* Arthur Clarington, Warbeck, Somerton.

*Sir Art.*   Come, Gentlemen, we must all help to grace
The nimble-footed youth of *Edmonton,*
That are so kinde to call us up to day
With an high Morrice.
*Warb.*   I could wish it for the best, it were the worst now.
Absurditie's in my opinion ever the best Dancer in a Morrice.
*Som.*   I could rather sleep then see 'em.
*Sir Art.*   Not well, Sir?
*Som.*   Faith not ever thus leaden; yet I know no cause for't.
*Warb.*   Now am I beyond mine own condition highly dispos'd to   10
mirth.
*Sir Art.*   Well, you may have yet a Morrice to help both;
To strike you in a dump, and make him merry.

*Enter Fidler and Morrice; all but* Banks.

*Fidl.*   Come, will you set your selves in Morrice-ray? the fore-Bell,
second Bell, Tenor and great Bell; Maid-marion for the same Bell.
But where's the Weather-cock now? the Hobby-horse?
*1.*   Is not *Banks* come yet? What a spight 'tis?
*Sir Art.*   When set you forward, Gentlemen?
*1.*   We stay but for the Hobby-horse, Sir: all our Footmen are
ready.                                                                   20
*Som.*   'Tis marvel your Horse should be behinde your Foot.
*2.*   Yes, Sir: he goes further about: we can come in at the Wicket,
but the broad Gate must be opened for him.

*Enter* Banks [*the Clown*], *Hobby-horse and* Dog.

*Sir Art.*   Oh, we staid for you, Sir.
*Clow.*   Onely my Horse wanted a Shooe, Sir: but we shall make
you amends e're we part.
*Sir Art.*   I? well said, make 'em drink e're they begin.

*Enter servants with beer.*

*Clow.*  A bowl, I prithee, and a little for my Horse, he'll mount the
better. Nay, give me, I must drink to him, he'll not pledge else.
Here Hobby. (*Holds him the bowl.*) I pray you: No? not drink? 30
You see, Gentlemen, we can but bring our horse to the Water; he
may chuse whether he'll drink or no.

*Som.*  A good Moral made plain by History.

*1.*  Strike up, Father *Sawgut*, strike up.

*Fidl.*  E'en when you will, Children. Now in the name of the best
foot forward. How now? not a word in thy Guts? I think,
Children, my Instrument has caught cold on the sudden.

*Clow.*  My *Ningle*'s knavery: black *Tom*'s doing.          [*Aside.*]

*Omn.*  Why what mean you, Father *Sawgut*?

*Clow.*  Why what would you have him do? You hear his Fiddle is 40
speechless.

*Fidl.*  I'll lay mine Ear to my Instrument, that my poor Fiddle is
bewitch'd. I play'd *The Flowers in May*, e'en now, as sweet as
a Violet; now 'twill not go against the hair: you see I can make no
more Musick then a Beetle of a Cow-turd.

*Clow.*  Let me see, Father *Sawgut*, say, once you had a brave
Hobby-horse, that you were beholding to. I'll play and dance too.
*Ningle*, away with it.

*Omn.*  I marry, Sir!

Dog *plays the Morrice; which ended, enter a Constable and Officers.*

*Const.*  Away with jollity, 'tis too sad an hour.                         50
Sir *Arthur Clarington*, your own assistance,
In the Kings Name, I charge, for apprehension
Of these two Murderers, *Warbeck* and *Somerton*.

*Sir Art.*  Ha! flat Murtherers?

*Som.*  Ha, ha, ha, this has awakened my melancholy.

*Warb.*  And struck my mirth down flat. Murtherers?

*Const.*  The accusation is flat against you, Gentlemen.
Sir, you may be satisfied with this. I hope                    [*Warrant.*]
You'll quietly obey my power; 'twill make
Your cause the fairer.

*Ambo.*                    Oh! with all our hearts, Sir.                    60

49 S.D. Q *prints S.D. following line* 48

534

*Clow.*   There's my Rival taken up for Hang-man's meat. *Tom* told
me he was about a piece of Villany. Mates and Morrice-men, you
see here's no longer piping, no longer dancing. This news of
Murder has slain the Morrice. You that go the foot-way, fare ye
well: I am for a Gallop. Come, *Ningle.*                    *Exeunt.*
*Fidl.*   (*Strikes his Fiddle.*) I? Nay and my Fiddle be come to
himself again, I care not. I think the Devil has been abroad amongst
us to day. I'll keep thee out of thy fit now if I can.

                                                   *Exeunt* [*the rest*].
*Sir Art.*   These things are full of horror, full of pity.
But if this time be constant to the proof,                    70
The guilt of both these Gentlemen I dare take
Upon mine own danger; yet howsoever, Sir,
Your power must be obey'd.
*Warb.*                     Oh most willingly, Sir.
'Tis a most sweet affliction. I could not meet
A joy in the best shape with better will.
Come, fear not, Sir; nor Judge, nor Evidence,
Can binde him o're, who's freed by conscience.
*Som.*   Mine stands so upright to the middle Zone,
It takes no shadow to't, it goes alone.

                                                   *Exeunt.*


## ACT. IV, Scæna i

*Enter Old* Banks, *and two or three Country-men.*

*O. Bank.*   My Horse this morning runs most pitiously of the
Glaunders, whose nose yesternight was as clean as any Man's here
now coming from the Barbers; and this I'll take my death upon't is
long of this Jadish Witch, Mother *Sawyer.*
*1.*   I took my Wife and a Servingman in our Town of *Edmonton,*
thrashing in my Barn together, such Corn as Country-Wenches
carry to Market; and examining my Polecat why she did so, she
swore in her conscience she was bewitch'd: and what Witch have
we about us, but Mother *Sawyer?*

2. Rid the Town of her, else all our Wives will do nothing else 10
but dance about other Country May-poles.

3. Our Cattel fall, our Wives fall, our Daughters fall, and Maid-
servants fall; and we our selves shall not be able to stand, if this
Beast be suffered to graze amongst us.

*Enter W. Hamlac, with Thatch and a Link.*

*Haml.*   Burn the Witch, the Witch, the Witch, the Witch.
*Omn.*   What hast got there?
*Haml.*   A handful of Thatch pluck'd off a Hovel of hers: and they
say, when 'tis burning, if she be a Witch, she'll come running in.
*O. Bank.*   Fire it, fire it: I'll stand between thee and home for any
danger.                                                                 20

*As that burns, enter the Witch [Mother Sawyer].*

*Sawy.*   Diseases, Plagues; the curse of an old Woman follow and
fall upon you.
*Omn.*   Are you come, you old Trot?
*O. Bank.*   You hot Whore, must we fetch you with fire in your
tail?
*1.*   This Thatch is as good as a Jury to prove she is a Witch.
*Omn.*   Out Witch; beat her, kick her, set fire on her.
*Sawy.*   Shall I be murthered by a bed of Serpents? help, help!

*Enter Sir Arthur Clarington, and a Justice.*

*Omn.*   Hang her, beat her, kill her.
*Just.*   How now? Forbear this violence.                              30
*Sawy.*   A crew of Villains, a knot of bloody Hang-men set to
torment me I know not why.
*Just.*   Alas, neighbour *Banks*, are you a Ring-leader in mischief?
Fie, to abuse an aged woman!
*O. Bank.*   Woman? a She-hell-cat, a Witch: to prove her one, we
no sooner set fire on the Thatch of her House, but in she came
running, as if the Divel had sent her in a Barrel of Gun-powder;
which trick as surely proves her a Witch, as the Pox in a snuffling
nose, is a sign a Man is a Whore-master.

*Just.* Come, come; firing her Thatch? ridiculous: take heed Sirs 40
what you do: unless your proofs come better arm'd, instead of
turning her into a Witch, you'll prove your selves starke Fools.

*Omn.* Fools?

*Just.* Arrant Fools.

*O. Bank.* Pray, Mr. Justice what do you call 'em, hear me but in
one thing: This grumbling Devil owes me I know no good will
ever since I fell out with her.

*Sawy.* And brakedst my back with beating me.

*O. Bank.* I'll break it worse.

*Sawy.* Wilt thou? 50

*Just.* You must not threaten her: 'tis against Law. Go on.

*O. Bank.* So, Sir, ever since, having a Dun-Cow tied up in my
Back-side, let me go thither, or but cast mine eye at her, and if
I should be hang'd, I cannot chuse, though it be ten times in an
hour, but run to the Cow, and taking up her tail, kiss (saving your
Worship's Reverence) my Cow behinde; That the whole Town of
*Edmonton* has been ready to be-piss themselves with laughing me
to scorn.

*Just.* And this is long of her?

*O. Bank.* Who the Devil else? for is any man such an Ass, to be 60
such a Baby, if he were not bewitch'd?

*Sir Art.* Nay, if she be a Witch, and the harms she does end in
such sports, she may scape burning.

*Just.* Go, go; pray vex her not: she is a Subject, and you must not
be Judges of the Law to strike her as you please.

*Omn.* No, no, we'll finde cudgel enough to strike her.

*O. Bank.* I, no lips to kiss but my Cows —— ?        *Exeunt.*

*Sawy.* Rots and foul maladies eat up thee and thine.

*Just.* Here's none now, Mother *Sawyer*, but this Gentleman, my
self and you; let us to some milde Questions, have you milde 70
Answers? Tell us honestly, and with a free confession, (we'll do
our best to wean you from it) are you a Witch, or no?

*Sawy.* I am none.

*Just.* Be not so furious.

*Sawy.* I am none. None but base Curs so bark at me. I am none.
Or would I were: if every poor old Woman be trod on thus by

slaves, revil'd, kick'd, beaten, as I am daily, she to be reveng'd had
need turn Witch.

*Sir Art.*   And you to be reveng'd have sold your Soul to th'Devil.

*Sawy.*   Keep thine own from him.                                        80

*Just.*   You are too sawcie, and too bitter.

*Sawy.*   Sawcie? by what commission can he send my Soul on the
Divel's Errand, more then I can his? is he a Landlord of my Soul,
to thrust it when he list out of door?

*Just.*   Know whom you speak to.

*Sawy.*   A Man: perhaps, no Man. Men in gay clothes, whose
Backs are laden with Titles and Honours, are within far more
crooked then I am; and if I be a Witch, more Witch-like.

*Sir Art.*   Y'are a base Hell-hound. And now, Sir, let me tell you,
Far and neer she's bruited for a woman that maintains a Spirit that  90
sucks her.

*Sawy.*   I defie thee.

*Sir Art.*   Go, go, I can, if need be, bring an hundred voyces e'en
here in *Edmonton*, that shall lowd proclaim thee for a secret and
pernicious Witch.

*Sawy.*   Ha, ha!

*Just.*   Do you laugh? why laugh you?

*Sawy.*   At my name: the brave name this Knight gives me, Witch.

*Just.*   Is the Name of Witch so pleasing to thine Ear?

*Sir Art.*   Pray, Sir, give way, and let her Tongue gallop on.        100

*Sawy.*   A Witch? who is not?
Hold not that universal Name in scorne then.
What are your painted things in Princes Courts?
Upon whose Eye-lids Lust sits blowing fires
To burn Mens Souls in sensual hot desires:
Upon whose naked Paps, a Leachers thought
Acts Sin in fouler shapes then can be wrought.

*Just.*   But those work not as you do.

*Sawy.*                                   No, but far worse:
These, by Inchantments, can whole Lordships change
To Trunks of rich Attire: turn Ploughs and Teams              110
To *Flanders* Mares and Coaches; and huge trains
Of servitors, to a *French* Butter-Flie.

Have you not City-witches who can turn
Their husbands wares, whole standing shops of wares,
To sumptuous Tables, Gardens of stoln sin?
In one yeer wasting, what scarce twenty win.
Are not these Witches?
*Just.*                   Yes, yes, but the Law
Casts not an eye on these.
*Sawy.*                   Why then on me,
Or any lean old Beldame? Reverence once
Had wont to wait on age. Now an old woman          120
Ill favour'd grown with yeers, if she be poor,
Must be call'd Bawd or Witch. Such so abus'd
Are the course Witches: t'other are the fine,
Spun for the Devil's own wearing.
*Sir Art.*                   And so is thine.
*Sawy.* She on whose tongue a whirlwind sits to blow
A man out of himself, from his soft pillow,
To lean his head on Rocks and fighting waves,
Is not that Scold a Witch? The Man of Law
Whose honeyed hopes the credulous Client draws,
(As Bees by tinkling Basons) to swarm to him,          130
From his own Hive, to work the Wax in his;
He is no Witch, not he.
*Sir Art.*                   But these Men-Witches
Are not in trading with Hells Merchandize,
Like such as you are, that for a word, a look,
Denial of a Coal of fire, kill Men,
Children and Cattel.
*Sawy.*                   Tell them, Sir, that do so:
Am I accus'd for such an one?
*Sir Art.*                   Yes, 'twill be sworn.
*Sawy.* Dare any swear I ever tempted Maiden
With golden hooks flung at her chastity,
To come and lose her honour? and being lost,          140
To pay not a Denier for't? Some slaves have done it.
Men-witches can without the Fangs of Law,
Drawing once one drop of blood, put counterfeit pieces

Away for true Gold.

*Sir. Art.*                    By one thing she speaks,
I know now she's a Witch, and dare no longer
Hold conference with the Fury.

*Just.*                      Let's then away:
Old woman, mend thy life, get home and pray.

                              *Exeunt* [*Sir* Arthur *and* Justice].

*Sawy.*   For his confusion. (*Enter* Dog.) My dear *Tom*-boy
welcome.
I am torn in pieces by a pack of Curs
Clap'd all upon me, and for want of thee:                         150
Comfort me: thou shalt have the Teat anon.

*Dog.*   Bough wough: I'll have it now.

*Sawy.*                       I am dri'd up
With cursing and with madness; and have yet
No blood to moysten these sweet lips of thine.
Stand on thy hind-legs up. Kiss me, my *Tommy*,
And rub away some wrinkles on my brow,
By making my old ribs to shrug for joy
Of thy fine tricks. What hast thou done? Let's tickle.
Hast thou struck the horse lame as I bid thee?

*Dog.*   Yes, and nip'd the sucking-childe.

*Sawy.*                        Ho, ho, my dainty,        160
My little Pearl. No Lady loves her Hound,
Monkey, or Parakeet, as I do thee.

*Dog.*   The Maid has been churning Butter nine hours; but it shall
not come.

*Sawy.*   Let 'em eat Cheese and choak.

*Dog.*                       I had rare sport
Among the Clowns i'th' Morrice.

*Sawy.*                      I could dance
Out of my skin to hear thee. But my Curl-pate,
That Jade, that foul-tongu'd whore, *Nan Ratcliff*,
Who for a little Soap lick'd by my Sow,
Struck, and almost had lam'd it; Did not I charge thee,         170
To pinch that Quean to th' heart?

*Dog.*   Bough, wough, wough: Look here else.

*Enter* Anne Ratcliff *mad.*

*Ratc.*    See, see, see; the Man i'th' Moon has built a new Wind-mill,
and what running there's from all quarters of the City to learn the
Art of Grinding!
*Sawy.*    Ho, ho, ho! I thank thee, my sweet Mungrel.
*Ratc.*    Hoyda! a-pox of the Devil's false Hopper! all the golden
Meal runs into the rich Knaves purses, and the poor have nothing
but Bran. Hey derry down! Are not you Mother *Sawyer?*
*Sawy.*    No, I am a Lawyer.                                                    180
*Ratc.*    Art thou? I prithee let me scratch thy Face; for thy Pen has
flea'd off a great many mens skins. You'll have brave doings in the
Vacation; for Knaves and Fools are at variance in every Village.
I'll sue Mother *Sawyer,* and her own Sow shall give in evidence
against her.
*Sawy.*    Touch her.                                    [Dog *rubs her.*]
*Ratc.*    Oh my Ribs are made of a paynd Hose, and they break.
There's a *Lancashire* Horn-pipe in my throat: hark how it tickles
it, with Doodle, Doodle, Doodle, Doodle. Welcome Serjeants:
welcome Devil. Hands, hands; hold hands, and dance a-round, 190
a-round, a-round.

*Enter Old* Banks, *his Son the Clown, Old*
Ratcliff, *Country-fellows.*

*O. Ratc.*    She's here; alas, my poor wife is here.
*O. Bank.*    Catch her fast, and have her into some close Chamber:
do, for she's as many Wives are, stark mad.
*Clow.*    The witch, Mother *Sawyer,* the witch, the devil.
*O. Ratc.*    O my dear Wife! help, Sirs!
                                        Carry her off. [Dog *goes after.*]
*O. Bank.*    You see your work, Mother *Bumby.*
*Saw.*    My work? should she and all you here run mad,
Is the work mine?
*Clow.*    No, on my conscience, she would not hurt a Devil of two 200
yeers old.
                                        *Enter Old* Ratcliff, *and the rest.*
How now? what's become of her?

*O. Ratc.* Nothing: she's become nothing, but the miserable trunk of a wretched woman. We were in her hands as Reeds in a mighty Tempest: spight of our strengths, away she brake; and nothing in her mouth being heard, but the Devil, the Witch, the Witch, the Devil; she beat out her own brains, and so died.

*Clow.* It's any Man's case, be he never so wise, to die when his brains go a wool-gathering.

*O. Bank.* Masters, be rul'd by me; let's all to a Justice. Hag, thou 210 hast done this, and thou shalt answer it.

*Sawy.* Banks, I defie thee.

*O. Bank.* Get a Warrant first to examine her, then ship her to *Newgate*: here's enough, if all her other villanies were pardon'd, to burn her for a Witch. You have a Spirit, they say, comes to you in the likeness of a Dog; we shall see your Cur at one time or other: if we do, unless it be the Devil himself, he shall go howling to the Goal in one chain, and thou in another.

*Sawy.* Be hang'd thou in a third, and do thy worst.

*Clow.* How, Father? you send the poor dumb thing howling to 220 th'Goal? He that makes him howl, makes me roar.

*O. Bank.* Why, foolish Boy, dost thou know him?

*Clow.* No matter, if I do or not. He's baylable I am sure by Law. But if the Dog's word will not be taken, mine shall.

*O. Bank.* Thou Bayl for a Dog?

*Clow.* Yes, or a Bitch either, being my Friend. I'll lie by the heels my self, before Puppison shall: his Dog-days are not come yet, I hope.

*O. Bank.* What manner of Dog is it? didst ever see him?

*Clow.* See him? yes, and given him a bone to gnaw twenty times. 230 The Dog is no Court foysting Hound, that fills his belly full by base wagging his tayl; neither is it a Citizens Water-Spaniel, enticing his Master to go a-ducking twice or thrice a week, whilst his Wife makes Ducks and Drakes at home: this is no *Paris*-Garden Bandog neither, that keeps a Bough, wough, woughing, to have Butchers bring their Curs thither; and when all comes to all, they run away like Sheep: neither is this the black Dog of *New-gate*.

*O. Bank.* No, Good-man Son-fool, but the Dog of Hell-gate.

*Clow.* I say, Good-man Father-fool, it's a lye.

*Omn.*   He's bewitch'd.                                                 240
*Clow.*   A gross lye as big as my self. The Devil in St. *Dunstan's*
will as soon drink with this poor Cur, as with any Temple-Bar-
Laundress, that washes and wrings Lawyers.        [*Enter* Dog.]
*Dog.*   Bough, wough, wough, wough.
*Omn.*   O the Dog's here, the Dog's here.
*O. Bank.*   It was the voice of a Dog.
*Clow.*   The voice of a Dog? if that voice were a Dog's, what voice
had my Mother? so am I a Dog: bough, wough, wough: it was I
that bark'd so, Father, to make Cocks-combs of these Clowns.
*O. Bank.*   However, we'll be Cocks-comb'd no longer: away 250
therefore to th' Justice for a Warrant; and then, Gammer *Gurton,*
have at your Needle of Witch-craft.
*Sawy.*   And prick thine own eyes out. Go, peevish Fools.
                                                        *Exeunt.*
*Clow.*   *Ningle,* you had like to have spoyl'd all with your Boughings.
I was glad to put 'em off with one of my Dog-tricks, on a sudden;
I am bewitch'd, little Cost-me-nought, to love thee — a Pox, that
Morrice makes me spit in thy mouth. I dare not stay. Farewel,
*Ningle;* you whoreson Dogs-nose. Farewel Witch.        *Exit.*
*Dog.*   Bough, wough, wough, wough.
*Sawy.*   Minde him not, he's not worth thy worrying: run at a 260
fairer Game: that fowl-mouth'd Knight, scurvy Sir *Arthur,* flie at
him, my *Tommy;* and pluck out's throat.
*Dog.*   No, there's a Dog already biting's conscience.
*Sawy.*   That's a sure Blood-hound. Come, let's home and play.
Our black work ended, we'll make holiday.
                                                        *Exeunt.*


[ACT IV,] Scæna ii


*Enter* Katherine: *a Bed thrust forth, on it* Frank *in a slumber.*

*Kat.*   Brother, Brother! So sound asleep? that's well.
*Frank.*   No, not I, Sister: he that's wounded here,
As I am; (all my other hurts are bitings

263 there's] Weber; there Q

543

Of a poor flea) but he that here once bleeds,
Is maim'd incurably.

*Kat.*                    My good sweet Brother,
(For now my Sister must grow up in you)
Though her loss strikes you through, and that I feel
The blow as deep, I pray thee be not cruel
To kill me too, by seeing you cast away
In your own helpless sorrow. Good Love, sit up:          10
And if you can give Physick to your self,
I shall be well.

*Frank.*          I'll do my best.

*Kat.*                              I thank you.
What do you look about for?

*Frank.*                    Nothing, nothing;
But I was thinking, Sister.

*Kat.*                    Dear heart, what?

*Frank.*    Who but a fool would thus be bound to a bed,
Having this Room to walk in?

*Kat.*                    Why do you talk so?
Would you were fast asleep.

*Frank.*                    No, no, I'm not idle:
But here's my meaning: being rob'd as I am,
Why should my Soul, which married was to hers,
Live in divorce, and not flie after her?                  20
Why should not I walk hand in hand with death
To finde my Love out?

*Kat.*                    That were well, indeed.
Your time being come, when death is sent to call you,
No doubt you shall meet her.

*Frank.*                    Why should not I go
Without calling?

*Kat.*          Yes, Brother, so you might,
Were there no place to go to when y'are gone,
But onely this.

*Frank.*          Troth, Sister, thou sayst true:
For when a man has been an hundred yeers,
Hard travelling o're the tottering bridge of age,

He's not the thousand part upon his way.                    30
All life is but a wandring to finde home:
When we are gone, we are there. Happy were man,
Could here his Voyage end; he should not then
Answer how well or ill he steer'd his Soul,
By Heaven's or by Hell's Compass; how he put in
(Loosing bless'd Goodness shore) at such a sin;
Nor how life's dear provision he has spent:
Nor how far he in's Navigation went
Beyond Commission. This were a fine Raign,
To do ill, and not hear of it again.                         40
Yet then were Man more wretched then a Beast:
For, Sister, our dead pay is sure the best.
*Kat.* 'Tis so, the best or worst. And I wish Heaven
To pay (and so I know it will) that Traytor,
That Devil *Somerton* (who stood in mine eye
Once as an Angel) home to his deservings.
What Villain but himself, once loving me,
With *Warbeck's* Soul would pawn his own to Hell,
To be reveng'd on my poor Sister?
*Frank.*                                    Slaves!
A pair of merciless Slaves! Speak no more of them.            50
*Kate.* I think this talking hurts you.
*Frank.*                         Does me no good, I'm sure,
I pay for't everywhere.
*Kat.*                   I have done then.
Eat, if you cannot sleep: you have these two days
Not tasted any food. *Jane*, is it ready?
*Frank.* What's ready? what's ready?

[*Enter one with chicken and exit.*]

*Kat.* I have made ready a rosted Chicken for you.
Sweet, wilt thou eat?
*Frank.*            A pretty stomach on a sudden — yes —
There's one in the house can play upon a Lute:
Good Girl, let's hear him too.
*Kat.*                      You shall, dear Brother.

Would I were a Musician, you should hear       *Lute plays.* 60
How I would feast your ear. Stay, mend your Pillow,
And raise you higher.
*Frank.*              I am up too high:
Am I not, Sister, now?
*Kat.*              No, no; 'tis well:
Fall to, fall to. A Knife: here's never a Knife,
Brother, I'll look out yours.

*Enter* Dog, *shrugging as it were for joy, and dances.*

*Frank.*              Sister, O Sister,
I am ill upon a sudden; and can eat nothing.
*Kat.* In very deed you shall. The want of Food
Makes you so faint. Ha! here's none in your pocket.
I'll go fetch a Knife.                           *Exit.*
*Frank.*              Will you? 'Tis well, all's well.

*She gone, he searches first one, then the other Pocket. Knife found.*
*Dog runs off. He lies on one side: the Spirit of* Susan *his second*
*Wife comes to the Beds-side. He stares at it; and turning to the*
*other side, it's there too. In the mean time,* Winnifride *as a Page*
*comes in, stands at his Beds-feet sadly: he frighted, sits upright. The*
*Spirit vanishes.*

*Frank.* What art thou?
*Win.*              A lost Creature.
*Frank.*              So am I too.       70
*Win?* Ah, my She-Page!
*Win.*              For your sake I put on
A shape that's false; yet do I wear a heart
True to you as your own.
*Frank.*              Would mine and thine
Were Fellows in one house. Kneel by me here:
On this side now? How dar'st thou come to mock me
On both sides of my bed?
*Win.*              When?
*Frank.*              But just now:

Out-face me, stare upon me with strange postures:
Turn my Soul wilde by a face in which were drawn
A thousand Ghosts leap'd newly from their Graves,
To pluck me into a winding-Sheet.
*Win.*                              Believe it,                              80
I came no neerer to you then yon place,
At your beds-feet; and of the house had leave,
Calling my self your Horse-boy, in to come,
And visit my sick Master.
*Frank.*                    Then 'twas my Fancy.
Some Wind-mill in my brains for want of sleep.
*Win.*    Would I might never sleep, so you could rest.
But you have pluck'd a Thunder on your head,
Whose noise cannot cease suddainly: why should you
Dance at the wedding of a second wife?
When scarce the Musick which you heard at mine              90
Had tane a farewel of you. O this was ill!
And they who thus can give both hands away,
In th'end shall want their best Limbs.
*Frank.*                              *Winnifride,*
The Chamber door fast?
*Win.*                    Yes.
*Frank.*                              Sit thee then down;
And when th'ast heard me speak, melt into tears:
Yet I to save those eyes of thine from weeping,
Being to write a Story of us two,
In stead of Ink, dip'd my sad Pen in blood.
When of thee I took leave, I went abroad
Onely for Pillage, as a Freebooter,                        100
What Gold soere I got, to make it thine.
To please a Father, I have Heaven displeas'd.
Striving to cast two wedding Rings in one,
Through my bad workmanship I now have none.
I have lost her and thee.
*Win.*                    I know she's dead:
But you have me still.

*Frank.* Nay, her this hand murdered;
And so I lose thee too.
*Win.* Oh me!
*Frank.* Be quiet,
For thou my evidence art, Jurie and Judge:
Sit quiet, and I'll tell all.

*As they whisper, enter at one end o'th'Stage Old Carter and
Katharine, Dog at th'other, pawing softly at Frank.*

*Kat.* I have run madding up and down to find you,     110
Being laden with the heaviest News that ever
Poor Daughter carried.
*O. Cart.* Why? is the Boy dead?
*Kat.* Dead, Sir! O Father, we are cozen'd: you are told
The Murtherer sings in Prison, and he laughs here.
This Villaine kil'd my Sister: see else, see,
A bloody Knife in's Pocket.
*O. Cart.* Bless me, patience!
*Frank.* The Knife, the Knife, the Knife!
*Kat.* What Knife?       *Exit* Dog.
*Frank.* To cut my Chicken up, my Chicken;
Be you my Carver, Father.
*O. Cart.* That I will.
*Kat.* How the Devil steels our brows after doing ill!     120
*Frank.* My stomack and my sight are taken from me;
All is not well within me.
*O. Cart.* I believe thee, Boy: I that have seen so many Moons clap
their Horns on other mens Foreheads to strike them sick, yet mine
to scape, and be well! I that never cast away a Fee upon Urinals,
but am as sound as an honest mans Conscience when hee's dying,
I should cry out as thou dost, All is not well within me, felt I but
the Bag of thy imposthumes. Ah poor Villaine! Ah my wounded
Rascal! all my grief is, I have now small hope of thee.
*Frank.* Do the Surgeons say, My wounds are dangerous then?    130
*O. Cart.* Yes, yes, and there's no way with thee but one.
*Frank.* Would he were here to open them.

    112 *O. Cart.*] *throughout this scene* Q *speech-prefix is:* Cart.

*O. Cart.*   Ile go to fetch him: Ile make an holiday to see thee as I
wish.                                    *Exit to fetch Officers.*
*Frank.*   A wondrous kinde old man.
*Win.*   Your sin's the blacker, so to abuse his goodness.   [*Aside.*]
Master, how do you?
*Frank.*                Pretty well now, boy:
I have such odd qualms come cross my stomack!
Ile fall too: boy, cut me.
*Win.*                You have cut me, I'm sure,        [*Aside.*]
A Leg or Wing, Sir.
*Frank.*            No, no, no: a Wing?                              140
Would I had Wings but to soar up yon Tower:
But here's a Clog that hinders me. What's that?

[*Enter*] *Father with her* [*Susan's body*] *in a Coffin.*

*O. Cart.*   That? what? O now I see her; 'tis a young Wench, my
Daughter, Sirrah, sick to the death: and hearing thee to be an
excellent Rascal for letting blood, she looks out at a Casement, and
crys, Help, help, stay that man; him I must have, or none.
*Frank.*   For pities sake, remove her: see, she stares
With one broad open eye still in my face.
*O. Cart.*   Thou puttest both hers out, like a Villaine as thou art;
yet see, she is willing to lend thee one againe to finde out the 150
Murtherer, and that's thy self.
*Frank.*   Old man, thou liest.
*O. Cart.*   So shalt thou i'th' Goal. Run for Officers.
*Kat.*   O thou merciless Slave!
She was (though yet above ground) in her Grave
To me, but thou hast torn it up againe.
Mine eyes too much drown'd, now must feel more raine.
*O. Cart.*   Fetch Officers.                        *Exit* Katharine.
*Frank.*   For whom?
*O. Cart.*   For thee, sirrah, sirrah: some knives have foolish Posies 160
upon them, but thine has a villanous one; look, Oh! it is enammeld
with the Heart-blood of thy hated Wife, my beloved Daughter.
What saist thou to this evidence? is't not sharp? does't not strike

136 sin's] Weber; sins Q

549

home? thou canst not answer honestly, and without a trembling
heart, to this one point, this terrible bloody point.

*Win.*    I beseech you, Sir,
Strike him no more; you see he's dead already.

*O. Cart.*    O, Sir! you held his Horses, you are as arrant a Rogue as
he: up, go you too.

*Frank.*    As y'are a man, throw not upon that Woman          170
Your loads of tyrannie, for she's innocent.

*O. Cart.*    How, how? a woman? is't grown to a fashion for women
in all Countries to wear the Breeches?

*Win.*    I am not as my disguise speaks me, Sir, his Page;
But his first onely wife, his lawful wife.

*O. Cart.*    How? how? more fire i'th' Bed-straw?

*Win.*    The wrongs which singly fell upon your Daughter,
On me are multiplyed: she lost a life,
But I, an Husband and my self must lose,
If you call him to a Bar for what he has done.          180

*O. Cart.*    He has done it then?

*Win.*    Yes, 'tis confess'd to me.

*Frank.*                    Dost thou betray me?

*Win.*    O pardon me, dear heart! I am mad to lose thee,
And know not what I speak: but if thou didst,
I must arraigne this Father for two sins,
Adultery and Murther.

                    *Enter* Katherine.

*Kat.*                    Sir, they are come.

*O. Cart.*    Arraigne me for what thou wilt, all *Middlesex* knows me
better for an honest man, then the middle of a Market place knows
thee for an honest woman: rise, Sirrah, and don your Tacklings,
rig your self for the Gallows, or I'll carry thee thither on my back: 190
your Trull shall to th' Goal go with you; there be as fine New-gate
birds as she, that can draw him in. Pox on's wounds.

*Frank.*    I have serv'd thee, and my wages now are paid,
Yet my worst punishment shall, I hope, be staid.

                                        *Exeunt.*

177 upon] Weber] on Q

## ACT. V, Scæna i

*Enter Mother* Sawyer *alone.*

*Sawy.*    Still wrong'd by every Slave? and not a Dog
Bark in his Dames defence? I am call'd Witch,
Yet am my self bewitched from doing harm.
Have I given up my self to thy black lust
Thus to be scorn'd? not see me in three days?
I'm lost without my *Tomalin*: prithee come,
Revenge to me is sweeter far then life;
Thou art my Raven, on whose cole-black wings
Revenge comes flying to me: O my best love!
I am on fire, (even in the midst of Ice)                         10
Raking my blood up, till my shrunk knees feel
Thy curl'd head leaning on them. Come then, my Darling,
If in the Aire thou hover'st, fall upon me
In some dark Cloud; and as I oft have seen
Dragons and Serpents in the Elements,
Appear thou now so to me. Art thou i'th' Sea?
Muster up all the Monsters from the deep,
And be the ugliest of them: so that my bulch
Shew but his swarth cheek to me, let earth cleave,
And break from Hell, I care not: could I run             20
Like a swift Powder-Mine beneath the world,
Up would I blow it all, to finde out thee,
Though I lay ruin'd in it. Not yet come!
I must then fall to my old Prayer:
*Sanctibiceter nomen tuum.*
Not yet come! worrying of Wolves, biting of mad Dogs, the
    Manges and the —

*Enter* Dog [*white*].

*Dog.*    How now! whom art thou cursing?
*Sawy.*    Thee. Ha! No, 'tis my black Cur I am cursing,

22 it ₐ all,] Gifford; ~ , ~ ₐ Q

*For not attending on me.* 30

*Dog.* I am that Cur.

*Sawy.* Thou liest: hence, come not nigh me.

*Dog.* Baugh, waugh.

*Sawy.* Why dost thou thus appear to me in white,
As if thou wert the Ghost of my dear love?

*Dog.* I am dogged, list not to tell thee: yet to torment thee, my whiteness puts thee in minde of thy winding Sheet.

*Sawy.* Am I near death?

*Dog.* Yes, if the Dog of Hell be near thee. When the Devil comes to thee as a Lamb, have at thy Throat. 40

*Sawy.* Off, Cur.

*Dog.* He has the back of a Sheep, but the belly of an Otter: devours by Sea and Land. Why am I in white? didst thou not pray to me?

*Sawy.* Yes, thou dissembling Hell-hound:
Why now in white more then at other times?

*Dog.* Be blasted with the News; whiteness is days Foot-boy, a forerunner to light, which shews thy old rivel'd face: Villaines are strip't naked, the Witch must be beaten out of her Cock-pit.

*Sawy.* Must she? she shall not; thou art a lying Spirit:
Why to mine eyes art thou a Flag of truce? 50
I am at peace with none; 'tis the black colour
Or none, which I fight under: I do not like
Thy puritan-paleness: glowing Furnaces
Are far more hot then they which flame outright.
If thou my old Dog art, go and bite such
As I shall set thee on.

*Dog.* I will not.

*Sawy.* I'll sell my self to twenty thousand Fiends,
To have thee torn in pieces then.

*Dog.* Thou canst not: thou art so ripe to fall into Hell, that no 60 more of my Kennel will so much as bark at him that hangs thee.

*Sawy.* I shall run mad.

*Dog.* Do so, thy time is come, to curse, and rave and die. The Glass of thy sins is full, and it must run out at Gallows.

*Sawy.* It cannot, ugly Cur, I'll confess nothing;

37 Sheet] Weber; Sweet Q

And not confessing, who dare come and swear
I have bewitched them? I'll not confess one mouthful.

*Dog.*  Chuse, and be hang'd or burn'd.

*Sawy.*  Spight of the Devil and thee,
I'll muzzle up my Tongue from telling Tales.          70

*Dog.*  Spight of thee and the Devil, thou'lt be condemn'd.

*Sawy.*  Yes, when?

*Dog.*  And ere the Executioner catch thee full in's Claws, thou'lt
confess all.

*Sawy.*  Out Dog!

*Dog.*          Out Witch! Thy tryal is at hand:
Our prey being had, the Devil does laughing stand.

> *The* Dog *stands aloof. Enter Old* Banks,
> Ratcliff, *and Countrymen.*

*O. Bank.*  She's here; attach her: Witch, you must go with us.

*Sawy.*  Whither? to Hell?

*O. Bank.*  No, no, no, old Crone; your Mittimus shall be made
thither, but your own Jaylors shall receive you. Away with her. 80

*Sawy.*  My *Tommie*! my sweet *Tom*-boy! O thou Dog!
Dost thou now fly to thy Kennel and forsake me?
Plagues and Consumptions ——          *Exeunt.*

*Dog.*          Ha, ha, ha, ha!
Let not the World, Witches or Devils condemn,
They follow us, and then we follow them.

> [*Enter*] *Young* Banks *to the Dog.*

*Clow.*  I would fain meet with mine Ingle once more; he has had
a Claw amongst 'um: my Rival that lov'd my Wench, is like to be
hang'd like an innocent; a kinde Cur, where he takes; but where he
takes not, a dogged Rascal. I know the Villaine loves me: no.
([Dog] *Barks.*) Art thou there? that's *Toms* voice, but'tis not he; 90
this is a Dog of another hair: this? bark and not speak to me? not
*Tom* then: there's as much difference betwixt *Tom* and this, as
betwixt white and black.

*Dog.*  Hast thou forgot me?

*Clow.*  That's *Tom* again: prithee Ningle speak, is thy name *Tom*?

*Dog.* Whilst I serv'd my old Dame *Sawyer*, 'twas: I'm gone from her now.

*Clow.* Gone? away with the Witch then too: shee'll never thrive if thou leav'st her; she knows no more how to kill a Cow, or a Horse, or a Sow, without thee, then she does to kill a Goose. 100

*Dog.* No, she has done killing now, but must be kill'd for what she has done: she's shortly to be hang'd.

*Clow.* Is she? in my conscience if she be, 'tis thou hast brought her to the Gallows, *Tom.*

*Dog.* Right: I serv'd her to that purpose, 'twas part of my Wages.

*Clow.* This was no honest Servants part, by your leave *Tom*: this remember, I pray you, between you and I; I entertain'd you ever as a Dog, not as a Devil.

*Dog.* True; and so I us'd thee doggedly, not divellishly. I have deluded thee for sport to laugh at. The Wench thou seek'st after, 110 thou never spakest with, but a Spirit in her form, habit and likeness. Ha, ha!

*Clow.* I do not then wonder at the change of your garments, if you can enter into shapes of Women too.

*Dog.* Any shape, to blind such silly eyes as thine; but chiefly those course Creatures, Dog or Cat, Hare, Ferret, Frog, Toad.

*Clow.* Louse or Flea?

*Dog.* Any poor Vermine.

*Clow.* It seems you Devils have poor thin souls, that you can bestow your selves in such small bodies: but pray you *Tom*, one 120 question at parting, I think I shall never see you more; where do you borrow those Bodies that are none of your own? the garment-shape you may hire at Brokers.

*Dog.* Why wouldst thou know that? fool, it availes thee not.

*Clow.* Onely for my mindes sake, *Tom*, and to tell some of my Friends.

*Dog.* I'll thus much tell thee: Thou never art so distant
From an evil Spirit, but that thy Oaths,
Curses and Blasphemies pull him to thine Elbow:
Thou never telst a lie, but that a Devil                                    130
Is within hearing it; thy evil purposes

98 *Clow.*] Weber; *Dog.* Q

Are ever haunted; but when they come to act,
As thy Tongue slaundering, bearing false witness,
Thy hand stabbing, stealing, cozening, cheating,
He's then within thee: thou play'st, he bets upon thy part;
Although thou lose, yet he will gaine by thee.

*Clow.* I? then he comes in the shape of a Rook.

*Dog.* The old Cadaver of some selfe-strangled wretch
We sometimes borrow, and appear humane.
The Carcase of some disease-slain strumpet,                    140
We varnish fresh, and wear as her first Beauty.
Didst never hear? if not, it has been done.
An hot luxurious Leacher in his Twines,
When he has thought to clip his Dalliance,
There has provided been for his embrace
A fine hot flaming Devil in her place.

*Clow.* Yes, I am partly a witness to this, but I never could embrace
her: I thank thee for that, *Tom*; well, againe I thank thee, *Tom*, for
all this counsel, without a Fee too; there's few Lawyers of thy
minde now: certainly *Tom*, I begin to pity thee.                150

*Dog.* Pity me? for what?

*Clow.* Were it not possible for thee to become an honest Dog yet?
'tis a base life that you lead, *Tom*, to serve Witches, to kill innocent
Children, to kill harmless Cattle, to stroy Corn and Fruit, &c.
'twere better yet to be a Butcher, and kill for your self.

*Dog.* Why? these are all my delights, my pleasures, fool.

*Clow.* Or *Tom*, if you could give your minde to ducking, I know
you can swim, fetch and carry, some Shop-keeper in *London* would
take great delight in you, and be a tender master over you: or if
you have a mind to the Game, either at Bull or Bear, I think I could    160
prefer you to *Mal-Cutpurse*.

*Dog.* Ha, ha! I should kill all the Game, Bulls, Bears, Dogs, and
all, not a Cub to be left.

*Clow.* You could do, *Tom*, but you must play fair, you should be
stav'd off else: or if your stomach did better like to serve in some
Noble Mans, Knights or Gentlemans Kitchin, if you could brook
the wheel, and turn the spit, your labour could not be much; when
they have Rost-meat, that's but once or twice in the week at most,

here you might lick your own Toes very well: Or if you could
translate your self into a Ladies Arming-puppy, there you might 170
lick sweet lips, and do many pretty Offices; but to creep under an
old Witches Coats, and suck like a great Puppy, Fie upon't!
I have heard beastly things of you, *Tom.*
*Dog.*   Ha, ha! The worse thou heardst of me, the better 'tis.
Shall I serve thee, Fool, at the self-same rate?
*Clow.*   No, I'll see thee hang'd, thou shalt be damn'd first; I know
thy qualities too well, Ile give no suck to such Whelps; therefore
henceforth I defie thee; out and avaunt.
*Dog.*   Nor will I serve for such a silly Soul.
I am for greatness now, corrupted greatness;                    180
There I'll shug in, and get a noble countenance:
Serve some Briarean Footcloth-strider,
That has an hundred hands to catch at Bribes,
But not a Fingers nayl of Charity.
Such, like the Dragons Tayl, shall pull down hundreds
To drop and sink with him: I'll stretch my self,
And draw this Bulk small as a Silver-wire,
Enter at the least pore Tobacco fume
Can make a breach for: hence silly fool,
I scorn to prey on such an Atome soul.                          190
*Clow.*   Come out, come out, you Cur; I will beat thee out of the
bounds of *Edmonton*, and to morrow we go in Procession, and after
thou shalt never come in againe: if thou goest to *London*, I'll make
thee go about by Tiburn, stealing in by Theeving Lane: if thou
canst rub thy Shoulder against a Lawyers Gown, as thou passest
by *Westminster*-Hall, do; if not, to the Stayers amongst the
Bandogs, take water, and the Devil go with thee.
                              *Exeunt Young* Banks, Dog *barking.*

169 your] Gifford; you Q

556

## [ACT V, Scene ii]

*Enter* Justice, *Sir* Arthur, Warbeck, [Somerton,]
[*Old*] Carter, Kate.

*Just.*    Sir *Arthur*, though the Bench hath mildly censur'd your
Errours, yet you have indeed been the Instrument that wrought all
their mis-fortunes: I would wish you pay'd down your Fine
speedily and willingly.
*Sir Art.*    I'll need no urging to it.
*O. Cart.*    If you should, 'twere a shame to you; for if I should
speak my conscience, you are worthier to be hang'd of the two,
all things considered; and now make what you can of it: but I am
glad these Gentlemen are freed.
*Warb.*    We knew our innocence.                              10
*Som.*    And therefore fear'd it not.
*Kat.*    But I am glad that I have you safe.         *Noise within.*
*Just.*    How now! what noyse is that?
*O. Cart.*    Young *Frank* is going the wrong way: Alas, poor youth!
now I begin to pity him.                                  [*Exeunt.*]


## [ACT V, Scene iii]

*Enter Young* [Frank] *Thorney and Holberts* [*and Exeunt.*]
*Enter as to see the Execution,* Old *Carter,* Old *Thorney,*
Katharine, Winnifride *weeping.*

*O. Thor.*    Here let our sorrows wait him: to press neerer
The place of his sad death, some apprehensions
May tempt our grief too much, at height already.
Daughter, be comforted.
*Win.*                    Comfort and I
Are too far separated to be joyn'd
But in eternity.

6 *O. Cart.*] *throughout this scene* Q *speech-prefix is:* Cart.

557

I share too much of him that's going thither.

*O. Cart.*   Poor woman, 'twas not thy fault: I grieve to see thee
weep for him that hath my pity too.

*Win.*   My fault was lust, my punishment was shame;          10
Yet I am happy that my soul is free
Both from consent, fore-knowledge and intent
Of any Murther, but of mine own Honour,
Restor'd again by a fair satisfaction,
And since not to be wounded.

*O. Thor.*                    Daughter, grieve not
For what necessity forceth; rather resolve
To conquer it with patience.
Alas, she faints!

*Win.*                 My griefes are strong upon me:
My weakness scarce can bear them.

*Within.*   Away with her! hang her, Witch!          20

*Enter* Sawyer *to Execution, Officers with Holberts, country-people.*

*O. Cart.*   The Witch, that instrument of mischief! did not she
witch the Devil into my Son-in-law, when he kill'd my poor
Daughter? do you hear, Mother *Sawyer?*

*Sawy.*   What would you have? cannot a poor old woman
Have your leave to die without vexation?

*O. Cart.*   Did not you bewitch *Frank* to kill his wife? he could
never have don't without the Devil.

*Sawy.*   Who doubts it? but is every Devil mine?
Would I had one now whom I might command
To tear you all in pieces: *Tom* would have don't          30
Before he left me.

*O. Cart.*   Thou did'st bewitch *Anne Ratcliff* to kill her self.

*Sawy.*   Churl, thou ly'st; I never did her hurt:
Would you were all as neer your ends as I am,
That gave evidence against me for it.

*Countr.*   I'll be sworn, Mr. *Carter,* she bewitched Gammer *Wash-*
*bowls* Sow, to cast her Pigs a day before she would have farried;
yet they were sent up to *London,* and sold for as good *Westminster*

8 *O. Cart.*] *throughout this scene* Q *speech-prefix is:* Cart.

Dog-Pigs, at *Bartholomew* Fair, as ever great belly'd Ale-wife
longed for.                                                                    40
*Sawy.*  These Dogs will mad me: I was well resolv'd
To die in my repentance; though 'tis true,
I would live longer if I might: yet since
I cannot, pray torment me not; my conscience
Is setled as it shall be: all take heed
How they believe the Devil, at last hee'l cheat you.
*O. Cart.*  Th'adst best confess all truly.
*Sawy.*                                               Yet again?
Have I scarce breath enough to say my Prayers?
And would you force me to spend that in bawling?
Bear witness, I repent all former evil;                                        50
There is no damned Conjurer like the Devil.
*Omn.*  Away with her, away!
        [*Exeunt* Sawyer *with Officers, Country-people follow.*]

        *Enter* Frank *to Execution, Officers, Justice,*
            *Sir* Arthur, Warbeck, Somerton.

*O. Thor.*  Here's the sad Object which I yet must meet
With hope of comfort, if a repentant end
Make him more happy then mis-fortune would
Suffer him here to be.
*Frank.*                    Good Sirs, turn from me;
You will revive affliction almost kil'd
With my continual sorrow.
*O. Thor.*                        O *Frank, Frank!*
Would I had sunk in mine own wants, or died
But one bare minute ere thy fault was acted.                                   60
*Frank.*  To look upon your sorrows, executes me
Before my Execution.
*Win.*                        Let me pray you, Sir —
*Frank.*  Thou much wrong'd woman, I must sigh for thee,
As he that's onely loath to leave the World,
For that he leaves thee in it unprovided,
Unfriended; and for me to beg a pity
From any man to thee when I am gone,

Is more then I can hope; nor to say truth,
Have I deserv'd it: but there is a payment
Belongs to goodness from the great Exchequer                    70
Above; it will not fail thee, *Winnifride*;
Be that thy comfort.
*O. Thor.*                    Let it be thine too,
Untimely lost young man.
*Frank.*                    He is not lost,
Who bears his peace within him: had I spun
My Web of life out at full length, and dream'd
Away my many years in lusts, in surfeits,
Murthers of Reputations, gallant sins
Commended or approv'd; then though I had
Died easily, as great and rich men do,
Upon my own Bed, not compell'd by Justice,                    80
You might have mourn'd for me indeed; my miseries
Had been as everlasting, as remediless:
But now the Law hath not arraign'd, condemn'd
With greater rigour my unhappy Fact,
Then I my self have every little sin
My memory can reckon from my Child-hood:
A Court hath been kept here, where I am found
Guilty; the difference is, my impartial Judge
Is much more gracious then my Faults
Are monstrous to be nam'd; yet they are monstrous.                    90
*O. Thor.*   Here's comfort in this penitence.
*Win.*                    It speaks
How truly you are reconcil'd, and quickens
My dying comfort, that was neer expiring
With my last breath: now this Repentance makes thee
As white as innocence; and my first sin with thee,
Since which I knew none like it, by my sorrow,
Is clearly cancell'd: might our Souls together
Climb to the height of their eternity,
And there enjoy what earth denied us, Happiness:
But since I must survive, and be the monument                    100
Of thy lov'd memory, I will preserve it

With a Religious care, and pay thy ashes
A Widows duty, calling that end best,
Which though it stain the name, makes the soul blest.
*Frank.*    Give me thy hand, poor woman; do not weep:
Farewel. Thou dost forgive me?
*Win.*                                   'Tis my part
To use that Language.
*Frank.*                Oh that my Example
Might teach the World hereafter what a curse
Hangs on their heads, who rather chuse to marry
A goodly Portion, then a Dowr of Vertues!                    110
Are you there, Gentlemen? there is not one
Amongst you whom I have not wrong'd: you most;
I rob'd you of a Daughter; but she is
In Heaven; and I must suffer for it willingly.
*O. Cart.*    I, I, she's in Heaven, and I am glad to see thee so well
prepared to follow her: I forgive thee with all my heart; if thou
had'st not had ill counsel, thou would'st not have done as thou
didst: the more shame for them.
*Som.*    Spare your excuse to me, I do conceive
What you would speak: I would you could as easily            120
Make satisfaction to the Law, as to my wrongs.
I am sorry for you.
*Warb.*    And so am I, and heartily forgive you.
*Kate.*    I will pray for you, for her sake, who, I am sure,
Did love you dearly.
*Sir Art.*                Let us part friendly too:
I am asham'd of my part in thy wrongs.
*Frank.*    You are all merciful,
And send me to my Grave in peace. *Sir Arthur,*
Heavens send you a new heart. Lastly to you, Sir;
And though I have deserv'd not to be call'd                  130
Your Son, yet give me leave upon my knees,
To beg a blessing.
*O. Thor.*            Take it: let me wet

---

113 I] Weber; *dropped out in* Q

Thy Cheeks with the last Tears my griefs have left me.
O *Frank, Frank, Frank!*
*Frank.*        Let me beseech you, Gentlemen,
To comfort my old Father; keep him with yee;
Love this distressed Widow; and as often
As you remember what a graceless man
I was, remember likewise that these are
Both free, both worthy of a better Fate,
Then such a Son or Husband as I have been.                    140
All help me with your prayers. On, on, 'tis just
That Law should purge the guilt of blood and lust.
                              *Exit* [*with Officers, &c.*].
*O. Cart.*   Go thy ways: I did not think to have shed one tear for
thee, but thou hast made me water my plants spight of my heart.
Mr. *Thorney*, chear up, man; whilst I can stand by you, you shall
not want help to keep you from falling. We have lost our Children
both on's the wrong way, but we cannot help it: better or worse,
'tis now as 'tis.
*O. Thor.*   I thank you, Sir; you are more kinde then I
Have cause to hope or look for.                                   150
*O. Cart.*   Mr. *Somerton*, is *Kate* yours or no?
*Som.*   We are agreed.
*Kat.*                    And, but my Faith is pass'd,
I should fear to be married, Husbands are
So cruelly unkind: excuse me that
I am thus troubled.
*Som.*                    Thou shalt have no cause.
*Just.*   Take comfort Mistris *Winnifride*. Sir *Arthur*,
For his abuse to you, and to your Husband,
Is by the Bench enjoyn'd to pay you down
A thousand Marks.
*Sir Art.*                  Which I will soon discharge.
*Win.*   Sir, 'tis too great a sum to be imploy'd                  160
Upon my Funeral.
*O. Cart.*   Come, come, if luck had serv'd, Sir *Arthur*, and every
man had his due, somebody might have totter'd ere this, without

* 156 *Just.*] Weber; *Cart.* Q

paying Fines: like it as you list. Come to me *Winnifride*, shalt be welcome: make much of her, *Kate*, I charge you: I do not think but she's a good Wench, and hath had wrong as well as we. So let's every man home to *Edmonton* with heavy hearts, yet as merry as we can, though not as we would.

*Just.*    Joyn Friends in sorrow; make of all the best:
Harms past may be lamented, not redrest.                *Exeunt.* 170


## Epilogue.

Win.    *I am a Widow still, and must not sort*
       *A second choice, without a good report;*
       *Which though some Widows finde, and few deserve,*
       *Yet I dare not presume, but will not swerve*
       *From modest hopes. All noble tongues are free;*
       *The gentle may speak one kinde word for me.*
                                    PHEN.


FINIS.


166 had] Weber; has Q

# TEXTUAL NOTES

## I.i

**143 that]** Editors have followed Gifford's emendation *there*, but the error is not a natural one. Possibly the sense of the original is, 'But what is that which can be brought forward to acquit me of prior knowledge?' For *that* in the sense of 'that which', see III.ii.100.

**160 Then were my happiness]** Although the line may be corrupt (and an emendation *twere* desirable), this may be only a contorted way of saying, in effect, 'If this has been cleanly carried, it should be my happiness that I repent rather than any happiness that I have deceived Frank'.

## II.i

**259 make at Eaglet]** Gifford, followed by Coleridge and Dyce, emended to *a taglet*, the idea presumably being that Young Banks would cling like a taglet, or tendril, to her; but the idiom is suspect and the sense not greatly improved, perhaps. Other editors have supposed that some unidentified game is being referred to, and Mother Sawyer's encouragement *A ball well bandied: now the set's half won* might be taken as encouraging this interpretation except that *eaglet* does not seem to be a tennis term. Some deep-rooted corruption may exist. On the other hand, *to make* is a common contemporary term for winning or taking a trick, or series of tricks, at cards; and the O.E.D. lists 'eagle' as an early eighteenth-century term for a gamester. It may be, therefore, that the reference is to some now lost gambling game of cards.

## II.ii

**42 Som.]** The correctness of Gifford's assignment of this speech to Somerton rather than Q's to Old Carter is shown by the familiar address, *thou*. Old Carter and Warburton employ the formal 'you' to each other. The error may have been present in the manuscript since memorial contamination by the compositor is unlikely here.

**126** Gifford, followed by Dyce, indicates that the rest of the speech beginning *she has't* is an aside, whereas the latest editors, Baskervill, Heltzel, and Nethercot, assign the whole speech as aside. Neither solution is wholly satisfactory. True, *she has't before thee* is thereby interpreted as 'she has my marriage vows before thee'; but left unexplained is Susan's use of *presage* to apply to the palmist's prophecy, and Frank's confusion, at first, about what she means by *or say it should be true*. Gifford's allocation leaves unexplained, also, the reason why Frank should call Winifred, *The poor Girl* (in Nether-cot, etc., this applies to Susan, of course). The last editors' attempt to get around the difficulty leads them to an un-Elizabethan staging whereby Frank's aside is taken by Susan as an unspoken hesitation to answer her and she is therefore forced to repeat her question. The difficulties would appear to be solved if we interpret *she has't before thee* as said to Susan and meaning *she has already died*. The presage then revolves on the fact that a woman has died who waited on him before Susan and this is an ill omen for Susan. Susan refuses to take the *presage* seriously. That her immediately following *or say it should be true* refers to a different matter, and goes back to the palmist's prophecy about Frank's re-marriage, is shown by Frank's un-certainty as to its application.

## III.i

90 Oh help]   Weber, followed by all editors, moved to its necessary position in the text Q's stage-direction '*Exeunt Spirit and* Banks', which in the original is placed at the right after the end of the whole speech.

## V.iii

156 *Just.*]   The context is not decisive in this traditional emendation for Q's *Cart.*, but the verse tips the scales, for Old Carter is not a verse-speaking character.

# EMENDATIONS OF ACCIDENTALS

## I.i

5-7 You...satisfaction] Q *lines*:
 You...man; | I...satisfaction
55 how —] ~ .
70-71 Thus...house] *one line in* Q
76-77 *prose in* Q
80 duty, you] duty. You
103 pound] *l.*
111 Q *lines*: promise. | We
121-123 *prose in* Q

139 me;] *point slightly doubtful but
 seems to be a semi-colon rather
 than a comma*
150 policy:] ~ ‸
188 thoroughly] throughly
202 Sir] *Sir*
212-213 Yes...honesty.] *one line in*
 Q

## I.ii

S.D. ii] 2.
 5 *Hertfordshire*] *Hertforshire*
9-13 *prose in* Q
26-28 *prose in* Q
30 Yeoman's] Yoeman's
31 Kickshaws] Kick-|shaws
41-49 *prose in* Q
49 Gentility —] ~ .
52 thine —] ~ .

53-54 *prose in* Q
65-66 *one line in* Q
84 Mr.] M.
103 Q *lines*: indeed. | Your
108 Vertuous ‸ Mrs.] ~ . ~ ‸
118 fore-noon] fore-|noon
188 to] To
191-202 *prose in* Q

## II.i

35 invocations,] ~ ?
63 us —.] ~ .
83 cross'd —] ~ .
117-118 *prose in* Q
141 tear —] ~ .

142 Q *lines*: blood. | See
145-146 And...*Banks* —] *one line
 in* Q
166 thee; ...ill,] ~ , ... ~ ;
186 are —] ~ ‸

## II.ii

S.D. ii] 2.
 8 promise —] ~ .
36 seal'd —] ~ ,
46-49 *prose in* Q
61-94 *prose in* Q
99 In thy] — In thy Q
117-119 Two...me?] *prose in* Q

124-132 I hope...goodness.] *prose
 in* Q
126 poor] poot
132 Sir...fate] Q *lines*: Sir...you; |
 Yet...fate
137 Prithee, prithee] Pritheee, prithe
137-159 *prose in* Q

566

## III.i

84–88 *prose in* Q
100 barks] braks

126 *Tom,* ...that;] ~ ; ... ~ ,

## III.ii

7 about,] ~ .
37–38 Q *lines:* ...come. | Go...
    thee.
46–47 Q *lines:* Tush...necessary. |
    On, ...brief.
62 me;] ~ ,
63 do,] ~ ;

104–105 Q *lines:* Prithee...thee, |
    And...instantly.
107–109 Q *lines:* Pray...last |
    Service...sight.
109–110 Q *lines:* Why...other |
    Business,..part.
118 sweet,] ~ .
125 Request —] ~ .

## III.iii

4–5 What...ever] *one line in* Q
22–26 *prose in* Q
68 fail‚] ~ ,
69 scratches,] ~ ‚
76–82 *prose in* Q

87 To] to
95 His] his
99 that] rhat
104–105 *one line in* Q
114 full] sull

## III.iv

2–4 Q *lines:* The... kinde|To ...
    Morrice.
59–60 Q *lines:* You'll...power; |
    'Twill...fairer.

62 Morrice-men] Morrice-|men
64 foot-way] foot-|way

## IV.i

3 upon't is] upon 't is
12 Maid-|servants] Maid-|servants
37 Gun-powder] Gun-|powder
163 churning] churming
173 Wind-mill] Wind-|mill

193 Chamber:] *colon inks in very few*
    *copies*
198–199 My...mine,] *prose in* Q
255 sudden;] ~ ,

## IV.ii

S.D. ii] 2.
12–14 *each speech as one line in* Q
16–17 Why...asleep.] *one line in* Q
24–25 Why...calling?] *one line in*
    Q

25–27 Q *lines:* Yes...place | To
    ...this.
32 Happy] Hapyy
49–50 Q *lines:* Slaves!...Slaves! |
    Speak...them.

61–62 Q *lines*: How...ear. | Stay
...higher.
62–85 *prose in* Q
83 Horse-boy] Horse-|boy
93–94 *Winnifride...fast?*] *one line in* Q

105–114 *prose in* Q
118–122 *prose in* Q
136–186 *prose in* Q
158 S.D. Katharine] Katharaine

## V.i

29–30 *prose in* Q
34–35 *prose in* Q
36 thee: ...thee,] ~ , ... ~ :
44–45 *prose in* Q
55–56 *one line in* Q
58–59 *prose in* Q
63–64 Q *lines*: die. | The

69–70 *prose in* Q
81–83 *prose in* Q
109–112 Q *lines*: True...divel-
lishly. | I...at. | The...with, |
But...ha!
122 garment-|shape] garment-|shape
133 witness,] ~ .

## V.iii

6–7 *one line in* Q
8–9 Q *lines*: see | Thee
13 Honour,] ~ .
14–15 *one line in* Q
15–19 *prose in* Q
20 S.D. *Execution*] *Fxecution*
24–25 *prose in* Q
30–31 *one line in* Q
33–35 *prose in* Q
36 *Wash-|bowls*] *Wash-|bowls*
52 S.D. *Enter*] *Fnter*
61–62 *one line in* Q
62 Sir —] ~ .
98 eternity] erernity

115–118 Q *lines*: I...see | Thee...
her: | I...thou | Had'st...
have | Done...them.
124–132 *prose in* Q
132–134 Q *lines*: Take...last |
Tears...*Frank*!
134–135 Q *lines*: Gentlemen, to |
Comfort
145 Mr.] M.
149–150 *prose in* Q
152–155 *prose in* Q
153 be married] bemarried
160–161 *one line in* Q

# THE
# WONDER
## OF
## A Kingdome.

*Quod non Dant proceres, Dabit Hiſtrie.*

---

*Written by* THOMAS DEKKER.

---

---

*LONDON:*

Printed by *Robert Raworth,* for *Nicholas Vavasour*; and are
to bee ſold at his Shop in the Inner *Temple,* neere the
Church-doore. 1636.

# TEXTUAL INTRODUCTION

*The Wonder of a Kingdom* (Greg, *Bibliography*, no. 508), though not printed until 1636, was first entered in the Stationers' Register (licensed by Herbert) to J. Jackman on 16 May 1631, during Dekker's lifetime. Nicholas Vavasour re-entered the play on 24 February 1636. In both entries Dekker is named as the author, but the repetition means nothing in view of Greg's belief that it was the same manuscript that was re-entered in 1636.

Although small errors are numerous, and the verse is mislined with some frequency, the substantives of the text appear to be reasonably well transmitted. Dekker was dead by the date of the printing; hence the proof-reading must be unauthoritative, and indeed the press-variants give every indication of printing-house origin without reference to copy. Although some few substantive alterations are unquestionably correct, none certainly required consultation of the manuscript; and the positive errors introduced by the proof-reader, as at I.i.48, 64, provide encouragement for an editor to reject such apparent sophistications as *have* at I.i.34 and doubtless the addition of *Sir* at I.i.26. It should be observed, too, that a comma was placed after *Pimtillioes* at I.i.31 without recognition that the word was in error, nor were the errors *Pimtoes* in the same line and *Passees* in I.i.29 discerned.

No distinction in authority can be made between the first two stages of correction in inner forme A. It would seem that the proof-reader took considerable pains at the very start to check on the compositor's way with the text. Since the extensive correction of this forme was not subsequently repeated, so far as evidence has been recovered, it may be that as a result of the massive correction of inner A the reader gave specific instructions that were followed to his general satisfaction. But we cannot be sure that the press-variants observed in later sheets represent the original corrections: if the inner B variant is not a simple case of a pulled type, it very likely evidences a second reading, and possibly the uncorrected states of inner C and inner D have already undergone one stage of alteration. The order assigned the second and the third stages of correction for inner A is somewhat arbitrary, but the alteration of the hyphen at I.i.75 to the proper dash seems to be decisive. Moreover, the order *wihi*, *weihi*, *weihy*, *wihy* is more probable than *wihi*, *weihi*, *wihy*, *weihy*. Probably the proof-reader, much concerned with this forme, looked over the second round of correction very soon after printing resumed, and was dissatisfied with the correction. Just possibly, from the start what he had wanted was only a terminal -*y* for -*i*; if so, the third round was to delete the intrusive *e* that had, perhaps, been overlooked in the correction of the type for the second round.

One press printed the quarto, and one compositor—who may or may not have been relieved for short intervals—set the type. Two skeleton-formes were transferred from sheet to sheet with complete regularity from sheet B to the end.

Little evidence concerning the manuscript seems to be preserved. Numerous stage-directions are unquestionably authorial, but prompt-copies are accustomed to retain many such directions. Although a fair number of brief marginal directions specifying action exist, similar directions are found in texts almost certainly set from Dekker's own papers. Some confusion obtains whether Lord Vanni's name is *Nicoletto* or *Nicoletti* but the circumstances of this confusion are obscure.

There may be some question whether the manuscript shows the effects of cuts. The provision for 'Two Curtizans' among the *Persons*, although such characters never appear, may reflect the excision of some scene involving Torrenti, or part of a scene; on the other hand, they may perhaps have been among the entertainers described in the opening direction to IV.i, or attendant upon him in some other scene. No sign of a cut is present unless (rather unlikely) they were depicted as deserting Torrenti in an excised part of V.ii. This latter scene is unusual in Dekker for its abrupt change of place, without accompanying direction, from Jacomo Gentili's house to that of the Duke at V.ii.23. One might argue for stage abridgement here of a much longer scene in which Torrenti was humbled. Yet the comments in V.ii.7–23 on Torrenti, and the contrast drawn with Gentili, might preclude further detail or action. To tie up all the loose ends the Duke must visit Gentili; and Torrenti's downfall —already adumbrated in IV.i.25–61—must be exhibited. To extend the scene would be dramatically superfluous so near the end of the play; and though Dekker was not above illustrating moral sentiments somewhat remorselessly, we may perhaps give him credit here for a sense of dramaturgy. Although not elsewhere found in Dekker, and comparatively rare in the drama of this date, the transition from one place to another without exit posed no problems on the Elizabethan stage. The lack of a direction for the withdrawal of Gentili is odd, however, since there is no indication that he joins the Duke's party. Perhaps the most that can be said is this. If indeed there has been abridgement here (and it is far from certain), V.ii.5–22 represent substituted lines which must have been written by Dekker himself as part of a revision for staging.

Since there would seem to be no positive evidence to associate this text strictly with stage-copy, we may guess that the printer used a Dekker manuscript or a transcript of one. But it must be admitted that a private transcript of a prompt-book could produce a text resembling what we have.

The other point of interest lies in the relation of this play to John Day's *Parliament of Bees* (1641). Five of the twelve Characters in this *Parliament* have an obvious relationship to various scenes in the *Wonder*, a relationship that extends to very close paraphrase in speech and even to verbal identity. Character 2 in the *Parliament* (sigs. C2ᵛ–4) parallels I.iv.8–125; Character 3 (sigs. C4–D1ᵛ) parallels III.i.1–230; Character 7 (sigs. E4–F1), IV.i.1–61; Character 9 (sigs. F3–4), IV.ii.94–153; and Character 10 (sigs. F4ᵛ–G2), IV.ii.1–93. The conventional view has been that Day borrowed from Dekker. In 1951, however, William Peery challenged this opinion in relation to two of the remaining Characters that parallel lines in *The Noble Spanish Soldier*, and argued that the integrity of Day's rhyming indicated that Dekker in the *Soldier* had been the borrower and was putting couplets into blank verse rather than the opposite.[1]

The case for the *Soldier* must stand or fall with the evidence from

---

[1] '*The Noble Soldier* and *The Parliament of Bees*', *Studies in Philology*, XLVIII (1951), 219–233.

the *Wonder*, of course. The critical section of this edition must argue on different grounds the merits of the controversy as finally drawn. The only obvious pieces of evidence I have myself noticed are perhaps contradictory. In the *Wonder*, IV.i.46–48 (part of a parallel passage) conveniently employ the bee frame of reference of the *Parliament*. On the other hand, in Character 9 of the *Parliament* anyone arguing for Dekker as the plagiarizer must explain why Day on sig. F4 first has his Apothecary bribe the servant with fifty *crowns* (as in the *Wonder*, IV.ii.135, 143, 151); and then shift later in a rhyme word to the rather absurd figure of fifty *pounds*. When one recalls that the theme of the *Parliament's* parallel Characters is the familiar Dekkerian praise of scholars, soldiers, and sailors in the formal vein of *If This Be Not a Good Play*, and when one associates the similar use of *crowns* in the passage noticed (appropriate for the *Wonder's* foreign setting, quite inappropriate for the *Parliament*), it may be that the burden of proof should rest on those who would argue that the most characteristic Dekker passages in the play are stolen from Day.

Except for the Pearson reprint of 1873, *The Wonder of a Kingdom* has been edited only by C. W. Dilke in vol. 3 of *Old English Plays* (1814).

The present text is based on a collation of the following twenty-one copies: British Museum, copy 1 (C.12.f.4[5]), copy 2 (644.b.23) (wants B2, C1–2, D1–2, E2), copy 3 (Ashley 619); Bodleian Library, copy 1 (Mal. 186[2]), copy 2 (Mal. 235[11]); Dyce Collection (Victoria and Albert Museum), copy 1 and copy 2; Eton College; National Library of Scotland (Bute Collection); Worcester College, Oxford (wants F1–4); William A. Clark Library; Henry E. Huntington Library; Yale University; Folger Shakespeare Library (only one copy presently available); Library of Congress; University of Chicago; Boston Public Library; Harvard University; New York Public Library; The Pierpont Morgan Library; and the University of Texas.

# DRAMMATIS PERSONÆ

DUKE OF FLORENCE

PRINCE OF PISA

LORD [NICOLETTO] VANNI

TREBATIO his Sonne

MUTIO  
PHILIPPO  
TORNELLI  
[MONTINELLO]  
} Courtiers

PIERO the Dukes Sonne

IASPARO his Friend

TIBALDO NERI, Lover of  
Dariene *Lord* Vanni's wife

ANGELO LOTTI, Lover of  
Fiametta

BAPTISTA, his friend

IACOMO GENTILI, The Noble House-keeper

SIGNIOR TORRENTI, The Riotous Lord [nephew to Lord Vanni]

FIAMETTA, the Dukes Daughter

DARIENE, Old Lord Vannies Wife

ALISANDRA, her Daughter

ALPHONSINA, sister to Tibaldo Neri

CARGO, Lord Vanni's man

A Nurse

[ASINIUS BUZARDO, A foolish Gentleman

Brother, to Torrenti

Gallants, attendant on Torrenti

Apothecary

Broker

Goldsmith

Lame Soldier

Friar

Servants]

Iasparo] Gasparo Q      Cargo] *below this,* Q *reads:* Two Curtizans

## *The Prologue.*

*Thus from the* Poet, *I am bid to say;*
*Hee knows what Iudges sit to Doome each Play,*
*(The Over-curious Critick, or the Wise)*
*The one with squint; 'Tother with Sunn-like eyes,*
*Shootes through each scæne; The one cries all things down;*
*Tother, hides strangers Faults, close as his Owne:*
    *Las! Those that out of custome come to jeere,*
*(Sung the full quire of the Nine* Muses *heere)*
*So Carping, — not from Wit, but Apish spite,*
*And Fether'd Ignorance, — Thus! our* Poet *does slight.*      10
    *'Tis not a gay sute, or Distorted Face,*
*Can beate his Merit off, — Which has won Grace*
*In the full Theater; — Nor can now feare*
*The Teeth of any Snaky whisperer;*
*But to the white, and sweete unclowded Brow,*
*(The heaven where true worth moves) our Poet do's bow:*
    *Patrons of Arts, and Pilots to the Stage,*
*Who guide it (through all Tempests) from the Rage*
*Of envious Whirlewindes, — ô, doe you but steere*
*His Muse, This day; And bring her toth' wished shore,*      20
*You are those Delphick Powers whom shee'le adore.*

1 *I am*] Q(u); *am I* Q(c²)          10 *our*] Q(c²); *ô* Q(u).

## The Wonder of a Kingdome.

### ACTUS PRIMUS, Scæna prima

*Enter Duke of* Florence, *Prince of* Pisa, Nicoletto Vanni, Trebatio *his sonne,* Mutio, Philippo, Tornelli, *Gallants,* Tibaldo Neri, Alphonsina *his sister,* Dariene *Old* Vannies *wife,* Cargo *a serving-man.*

*Flo.*  Wee surfit heere on Pleasures: Seas nor Land
Cannot invite us to a Feast more glorious,
Then this day we have sat at: my Lord *Vanni,*
You have an excellent seate heere; Tis a building
May entertaine a *Cæsar:* but you and I
Should rather talke of Tombs, then Pallaces,
Let's leave all to our heires, for we are old.
*Nic.*  Old! hem? all heart of brasse, sound as a bell,
Old? why, Ile tell your Graces; I have gone
But halfe the bridge ore yet; there lies before me          10
As much as I have pass'd, and I'le goe it all.
*Flo.*  Mad *Vanni* still.
*Nic.*                      Old Oakes doe not easily fall:
*Decembers* cold hand combes my head and beard,
But *May* swimmes in my blood; and he that walkes
Without his wooden third legge, is never old.
*Pisa.*  What is your age my Lord?
*Nic.*                      Age, what call you age?
I have liv'd some halfe a day, some halfe an houre.
*Flo.*  A tree of threescore-yeares growth; nothing?
*Tib.*                      A meere slip,
You have kept good diet my lord.
*Nic.*                      Let whores
Keepe diet, *Tibaldo;* never did Rivers runn          20

---

1 *Flo.*] Dilke; *om.* Q
*20 *Tibaldo;* never] Let whores keepe diet, | *Tibaldo* ner'e; never Q

578

In wilder, madder streames, then I have done,
I'le drinke as hard yet as an Englishman.
*Flo.*   And they are now best Drinkers.
*Pisa.*                   They put downe
The Dutch-men cleane.
*Nic.*                  Ile yet upon a wager
Hit any fencers button.
*Cargo.*   Some of 'em ha' no buttons to their doublets.
*Nic.*   Then knave Ile hit his flesh, and hit your cockscombe
If you crosse mine once more.          [*Exit* Cargo.]
*Flo.*                  Nay be not angry.
*Nic.*   I have my Passes Sir: and my Passadoes,
My Longes, my Stockadoes, Imbrocadoes,          30
And all my Puntoes, and Puntillioes,
Here at my fingers ends.
*Flo.*                  By my faith 'tis well.
*Nic.*   Old; why I ne're tooke Phisicke, nor ever will,
I'le trust none that has Art and leave to kill:
Now for that chopping herbe of hell Tobacco;
The idle-mans-Devill, and the Drunkards-whore,
I never medled with her; my smoake goes,
Out at my kitchin chimney, not my nose.
*Flo.*   And some Lords have no chimnies but their noses.
*Nic.*   Tobacco-shopps shew like prisons in hell;          40
Hote, smoaky, stinking, and I hate the smell.
*Pisa.*   Who'd thinke that in a coale so Ashy white,
Such fire were glowing?
*Flo.*                  May not a snuffe give light?
*Tib.*   You see it doe's in him.
*Alph.*                  A withered-tree,
Doth oft beare branches.
*Nic.*                  What thinke you then of me
Sweete Lady.

26 doublets.] Q(u); doublets Sir. Q(c²)
29 Passes] Dilke; Passees Q          29 Sir] Q(c²); *om.* Q(u)
31 Puntoes] Dilke; Pimtoes Q          31 Puntillioes] Dilke; Pimtillioes Q
32 ends] Q(u); end Q(c)          34 has] Q(u); have Q(c²)
42 so] Q(c²); of Q(u)

*Alph.*   Troth my Lord as of a horse, vilely, if he can neither wihi,
nor wagg's-Taile.

*Flo.*   The Lady *Alphonsina Neri*, has given it you my Lord.

*Nic.*   The time may come I may give it her too.                    50

*Flo.*   I doubt Lord *Vanni* she will cracke no Nutts,
With such a tough-shell, as is yours and mine,
But leaving this, lets see you pray, at Court —

*Nic.*   I thanke your grace.

*Flo.*                       Your wife, and your faire daughter,
One of the stars of *Florence*, with your sonne,
Heire to your worth and Honours, *Trebatio Vanni*.

*Treb.*   I shall attend your grace.

*Flo.*                       The holy knot,
*Hymen* shall shortly tie, and in faire bands,
Vnite *Florence* and *Pisa* by the hands,
Of *Fyametta* and this *Pisan* Duke                                 60
(Our Noble-son in law) and at this daie,
Pray be not absent.

*Nic.*                 We shall your wilf obey.

*Flo.*   We heare there is a gallant that out-vies
Vs, and our court for bravery, and expence,
For royall feasts, triumphs, and revellings.

*Nic.*   He's my neere kinsman, mine owne brothers son,
Who desperately a prodigall race doth ronne,
And for this riotous humour, he has the by-name,
Signior *Torrenti*, a swift Head-long streame.

*Flo.*   But ther's another layes on more then he.                  70

*Nic.*   Old *Iacomo*? open handed charitie,
Sit's ever at his gates to welcome guests,
He makes no bone-fires, as my riotous kinsman,
And yet his chimneis cast out braver smoake,
The Bellows which he blowes with are good deeds,
The rich he smiles upon, the poore he feeds.

*Flo.*   These gallants we'le be feasted by, and Feast;

48 wagg's-Taile] Q(u); wagge-Taile Q(c²)
64 and expence] Q(u); of expence Q(c²)

Fames praises of 'em, shall make us their guest,
Meane time we'le hence.            *Exit* Florence, Pisa, *&c.*

*Enter* Cargo.

*Cargo.*  I have News to tell your Lordship, Signior *Angelo* (of the 80
*Lotti Famely*) is banished.
*Dari.*  How, banish't? alas poore *Angelo Lotti.*
*Treb.*  Why must he goe from *Florence?*
*Cargo.*  Because he can stay there no longer.
*Nic.*  To what end is he driven from the Citie?
*Cargo.*  To the end he should goe into some other my Lord.
*Nic.*  Hoida.
*Cargo.*  I hope this is newes Sir.
*Nic.*  What speake the people of him?
*Cargo.*  As bells ring; some out, some in, all jangle, they say he has 90
dealt with the *Genoway* against the state: but whether with the men,
or the women; tis to be stood upon.
*Nic.*  Away Sir knave and foole.
*Cargo.*  Sir knave, a new word: fooles, and knaves Sir?        *Exit.*
*Nic.*  This muttering long agoe flew to mine eare,
The *Genoway* is but a line throwne out,
But *Fiametta's* love, the net that choakes him.
*Treb.*  He's worthy of her equall.
*Nic.*                      Peace foolish boy,
At these state bone-fires (whose flames reach so high)
To stand aloofe, is safer then too nigh.                        100
                                        *Exeunt.*


[ACT I, Scene ii]

*Enter* Tibaldo Neri, *and* Alphonsina.

*Alph.*  Why brother, what's the matter?
*Tib.*  I'me ill, exceeding ill.
*Alph.*  That's not well.
*Tib.*  Sure I did surfet at Lord *Vannies.*

100 S.D. *Exeunt*] Dilke; *Exit* Q

581

*Alph.* Surfet? you eate some Meate against your stomack.

*Tib.* No, but I had a stomack to one dish,
And the not tasting it, makes me sick at heart.

*Alph.* Was it fish or flesh?

*Tib.* Flesh sure, if I hit the marke right.

*Alph.* I'st not the missing of a marke (which you long to hit) makes 10
you draw sighes in stead of arrowes?

*Tib.* Would I had beene a thousand leagues from thence,
When I sat downe at's table, or bin partner
With *Angelo Lotti* in his banishment;
Oh! sister *Alphonsina*, there I dranke
My bane, the strongest poison that e're man
Drew from a Ladies eye, now swelling in me.

*Alph.* By casting of thy water then, I guesse thou would'st have
a medcine for the greene-sicknes.

*Tib.* 'Tis a greene wound indeed.                                    20

*Alph.* Tent it, tent it, and keepe it from ranckling, you are over
head and eares in love.

*Tib.* I am, and with such mortall Arrowes pierc't
I shall fall downe ——

*Alph.* There's no hurt in that.

*Tib.* And dye unlesse her pitty
Send me a quicke and sweete recovery.

*Alph.* And faith what doctresse is she must call you patient?

*Tib.* Faire *Dariene*, the Lord *Vannies* wife ——

*Alph.* How! *Dariene?* can no feather fit you but the broach in an 30
old mans hatt? were there so many dainty dishes to fill your belly,
and must you needs long for that dish the master of the house setts
up for his owne tooth.

*Tib.* Could love be like a subject, tied to lawes,
Then might you speake this language.

*Alph.* Love? a disease as common with young-gallants as swaggering and drinking Tobacco, there's not one of 'um all but will
to day ly drawing on for a woman, as if they were puffing and
blowing at a streight boot, and to morrow be ready to knock at
deathes doore, but I wo'd faine see one of you enter and set in his 40
staffe.

*Tib.*   You shall see me then do so.

*Alph.*   I shall looke so old first, I shall be taken for thy grandame; come, come 'tis but a worme betweene the skinne and the flesh, and to be taken out with the point of a waiting-womans needle, as well as a great Countesses.

*Tib.*   If this be all the comfort you will lend me,
Would you might leave me ——

*Alph.*   Leave thee in sicknes? I had more need give thee a caudle; and thrust thy adle-head into a night-Capp, for looke you 50 brother ——

*Tib.*   Even what you will must out.

*Alph.*   If what you will might so too, then would you be in tune: I warrant, if the sucket stood here before thee, thy stomack would goe against it.

*Tib.*   Yes sure my stomack would goe against it:
'Tis onely that which breeds in me despaire.

*Alph.*   Despaire for a woman? they hang about mens neckes in some places thicker then hops upon poles.

*Tib.*   Her walls of chastitie cannot be beaten downe.                60

*Alph.*   Walls of chastitie? walls of wafer-cakes, I have knowne a woman carry a fether-bed, and a man in't in her minde, when in the streete she cast up the white of her eye like a Puritane.

*Tib.*   Sister you do but stretch me on the racke
And with a laughing cheeke increase my paine,
Be rather pitifull and ease my torments
By teaching me how in this dreadfull storme,
I may escape ship-wrack and attaine that shore
Where I may live, heere else I'm sure to die.

*Alph.*   Well brother, since you will needs saile by such a starre as 70
I shall point out, looke you heere it is; if she were your Fether-makers, Taylors or Barbers wife, baite a hooke with gold, and with it ——

*Tib.*   I doe conjure you by that noble blood
Which makes me call you sister, cease to powre
Poison into a wound, so neere my heart,
And if to cure Loves-paines there be an Art,
Woman me thinkes should know it cause she breeds it.

*Alph.* That cunning woman you take me to be, and because I see you dissemble not, heer's my medcine. 80

*Tib.* I shall for ever thanke you.

*Alph.* First send for your Barber.

*Tib.* For heavens sake.

*Alph.* Your barber shall not come to rob you of your beard, I'le deale in no concealements ——

*Tib.* Oh! fie, fie, fie ——

*Alph.* But let him by rubbing of you quicken your spirits.

*Tib.* So so.

*Alph.* Then whistle your gold-finches (your gallants) to your fist.

*Tib.* Y'ar mad, y'ar mad. 90

*Alph.* Into a Tauerne, Drinke stiffe, sweare stiffe, have your musicke, and your brace, dance, and whiffe Tobacco, till all smoake agen, and split Sir.

*Tib.* You split my very heart in pieces.

*Alph.* And doe thus, but till the Moone cutts off her hornes; laugh in the day, and sleepe in the night: and this wenching fier will be burnt out of you.

*Tib.* Away, away, cruell you are to kill,
When to give life, you have both power and skill. *Exit.*

*Alph.* Alas, poore brother now I pitty thee, and wo'd doe any 100 thing to helpe thee to thy longing, but that a gap must be broken, in another mans hedge to rob his orchard, within there *Luca*, *Angelo*, give him musick:
Musicke has helpt some mad-men, let it then
Charme him, Love makes fooles of the wisest men.

*Exit.*

## [ACT I, Scene iii]

*Enter at one doore,* Angelo Lotti, *and* Baptista,
*at the other,* Piero, *and* Iaspero.

*Pier.* Yonders that villaine, keepe off *Iaspero:*
This prey I'le cease. *All draw.*

2 cease] *i.e.* seize

*Iasp.*          Be more advised Sir.

*Bapt.*   At whose life shoote you?

*Pier.*                    At that slaves there.

*Ang.*                                            Slave?
I know you for the Dukes sonne, but I know
No cause of quarrell, or this base reproach.

*Pier.*   Thou art a villaine.

*Ang.*                    Wherein?

*Pier.*                              And by witch-craft,
Had stole my sister *Fiamettas* heart,
Forceing her leave a Prince his bed for thine.

*Ang.*   If for her love you come to kill me; heere
I'le point you to a doore where you may enter                10
And fetch out a loath'd life.

*Pier.*   *Iaspero.*

*Iasp.*   Oh my Lord.

*Ang.*   Let him come, I ow her all;
And that debt will I pay her gladly.

*Iasp.*   Deare Sir heare him —

*Ang.*   But if on any other fier of rage,
You thirst to drinke my blood, heere I defie
You, and your malice; and returne the villaine
Into your throate.                                              20

*Pier.*   So brave sir!                    *Change a thrust or two.*

*Enter* Nicolletto, *and* Cargo.

*Nic.*   I charge you in the Dukes name, keepe the peace; beate
downe their weapons, knock em downe *Cargo.*

*Cargo.*   I have a Iustices warrant to apprehend your weapons;
therefore I charge you deliver.

*Nic.*   Oh my Lord: make a fray in an open streete? 'tis to make a
bon-fire to draw children and fooles together; Signior *Angelo,* pray
be wise, and be gon.

*Ang.*   I doe but guard my life (my Lord) from danger.

*Bapt.*   Sir, you doe exercise your violence          [*To* Piero.] 30
Vpon a man, stab'd to the heart with wounds;
You see him sinking, and you set your foote

Vpon his head, to kill him with two deathes;
Trample not thus on a poore banish'd man.
*Nic.*   If hee be banish'd, why dwells hee ith' house, whose tiles are
pull'd downe over his head? You must hunt no more in this Parke
of *Florence*; why then doe you lie sneaking heere, to steale venison?
*Ang.*   My Lords, I take my last leave of you all;
Of love, and fortunes ——
*Bapt.*                    Lower thou canst not fall.

                              *Exit* [Angelo *with* Baptista].

*Iasp.*   Trust mee, my Lord, This *Lotti* is a man,                    40
(Setting aside his rivall-ship in love,
For which you hate him) so abundant rich
In all the Vertues of a Gentle-man,
That had you read their file, as I haue done,
You would not onely fall in love with him,
And hold him worthy of a Princesse bed,
But grieve, that for a woman, such a man
Should so much suffer; in being so put downe,
Never to rise againe.
*Nic.*   A terrible case, i'de not be in't for all *Florence*.          50
*Pier.*   Troth deare friend,
The praises which have crown'd him with thy Iudgement,
Make mee to cast on him an open eye,
Which was before shut, and I pittie him.
*Iasp.*   I never heard 'mongst all your Romane spirits,
That any held so bravely up his head,
In such a sea of troubles (that come rowling
One on anothers necke) as *Lotti* doth,
Hee puts the spite of Fortune to disgrace,
And makes her, when shee frownes worst, turne her face.          60
*Pier.*   No more: I love him, and for all the Dukedome,
Would not have cut so Noble a spreading Vine,
To draw from it one drop of blood; Lord *Vanni*,
I thanke you that you cur'd our wounded peace,
So fare you well.                                          *Exit.*
*Nic.*   A good health to you both.

                    55 *Iasp.*] Dilke; Q *prefixes to line* 56

*Iasp.*   You play the Constable wisely.          [*Exit* Iasparo.]
*Cargo.*  And I his Beadle, I hope as wisely.
*Nic.*    The Constable wisely; *Cargo* he calls me foole by craft, but
let 'em passe.                                                      70
*Cargo.*  As Gentle-men doe by Creditors (muffled).
*Nic.*    I haue another case to handle: thou know'st the Donna
*Alphonsina*, of the *Neri* Familie.
*Cargo.*  The little Paraquinto that was heere when the Duke was
feasted, shee had quick-silver in her mouth, for her tongue, like
a Bride the first night, never lay still.
*Nic.*    The same Aspen-leafe, the same; is't not a Galley for the
Great Turke to be row'd in?
*Cargo.*  I thinke my Lord, in calme weather, shee may set upon a
Gally-ass bigge as your Lordship.                                  80
*Nic.*    Commend me to this *Angelica*.
*Cargo.*  *Angelica*-water is good for a cold stomach.
*Nic.*    I am all fire.
*Cargo.*  Shee's a cooler.
*Nic.*    Would 'twere come to that.
*Cargo.*  A small thing does it my Lord; in the time a Flemming
drinkes a Flap-dragon.
*Nic.*    Give her this paper, and this; in the one she may know my
minde, in the other, feele me: this a Letter, this a Iewell: Tell her,
I kisse the little white naile of her little white finger, of her more  90
little white hand, of her most little white bodie.
*Cargo.*  Her tell-tale, for all this will I bee.
*Nic.*    Thou hast beene my weavers shuttle to runne betwixt me and
my stuffes of *Procreandi causa*.
*Cargo.*  A suite of Stand-farther-off, had bin better sometimes.
*Nic.*    No *Cargo*, I have still the *Lapis mirabilis*; be thou close ——
*Cargo.*  As my Ladies Chamber-maide.
*Nic.*    Away then, nay quicke knave, thou rack'st mee.          *Exit.*
*Cargo.*  I goe to stretch you to your full length.

                                                              *Exit.*

## [ACT I, Scene iv]

*Enter* Iacomo Gentili, *in a suite of gray,* Velvet-gowne, Cap,
*Chaine,* Steward, *and Serving-men,* Mutio, Philippo,
Tornelli, Montinello.

*Gent.*   Happy be your arivall, Noble friends;
  You are the first, that like to Doves repaire
  To my new building; you are my first-borne guests,
  My eldest sonnes of hospitalitie;
  Here's to my hearty wellcomes.
*Mut.*                          Worthy Lord,
  In one word, and the word of one, for all,
  Our thankes are as your welcomes, Infinite.
*Phil.*   *Rome* in her Auncient pride, never rais'd up
  A worke of greater wonder, then this building.
*Gent.*   Tis finish'd, and the cost stands on no score,          10
  None can for want of payment, at my doore,
  Curse my foundation, praying the roofe may fall
  On the proud builders head, seeing the smoake goe
  Out of those Chimneys, for whose bricks I owe.
*Torn.*   To erect a frame so glorious, large, and hie,
  Would draw a very sea of silver drie.
*Mont.*   My Lord *Iacomo Gentili*, pray tell us,
  How much money have you buried under
  This kingly building?
*Gent.*                       Pray call it not so:
  The humble shrub, no Cedar heere shall grow;          20
  You see Three hundred Dorick pillars stand
  About one square, Three hundred Noble friends
  Lay'd (in their loves) at raising of those Columnes,
  A piece of gold under each Pedestall,
  With his name grav'd upon the bottome stone,
  Except that cost, all other was mine owne;
  See heere, each dayes expences are so great,
  They make a volume, for in this appeares,

It was no taske of weekes, or moneths, but yeares:
I trust my steward onely with the key,                              30
Which keepes that secret; heere's Arithmetick
For churles to cast up, there's the roote of all;
If you have skill in numbers, number that.
*Mont.*   Good Master Steward read it.
*Stew.*                              All the charge
In the grosse summe, amounteth to ——
*Gent.*                              To what?
Thou vaine vaine-glorious foole, goe burne that Booke,
No Herald needs to blazon Charities Armes;
Goe burne it presently.
*Stew.*                 Burne it?                    *Exit.*
*Gent.*                 Away,
I lanch not forth a ship, with drums and gunnes,
And Trumpets, to proclaime my gallantry;                            40
He that will reade the wasting of my gold,
Shall find it writ in ashes, which the winde
Will scatter ere he spends it; Another day,
The wheele may turne, and I that built thus high,
May by the stormes of want, be driven to dwell
In a thatch't Cottage; Rancor shall not then
Spit poyson at me, pinning on my backe
This card; Hee that spent thus much, now does lack.
*Mont.*   Why to your house adde you so many gates?
*Gent.*   My gates fill up the number of seuen dayes,              50
At which, of guests, seven severall sorts Ile welcome:
On Munday, Knights whose fortunes are sunke low;
On Tuesday, those that all their life-long read
The huge voluminous wonders of the deepe,
Sea-men (I meane) and so on other dayes,
Others shall take their turnes.
*Phil.*                 Why have you then
Built twelue such vaste roomes.
*Gent.*                 For the yeares twelue moones;
In each of which, twelue Tables shall be spread;
At them, such whom the world scornes, shall be fed,

The windowes of my building, which each morne,                    60
Are Porters, to let in mans comfort (light)
Are numbred just three hundred sixtie five,
And in so many daies the sunne does drive
His chariot stuck with beames of Burnish't gold,
My Almes shall such diurnall progresse make
As doe's the sunne in his bright-*Zodiack*.
*Torn.*  You differ from the guise of other lands,
Where Lords lay all their livings on the racke,
Not spending it in bread, but on the backe.
*Gent.*  Such Lords eate men, but men shall eate up me,                    70
My uncle the Lord *Abbot* had a soule
Subtile and quick, and searching as the fier,
By Magicke-stayers he went as deepe as hell,
And if in devills possession gold be kept,
He brought some sure from thence, 'tis hid in caves
Knowne (save to me) to none, and like a spring
The more 'tis drawne, the more it still doth rise,
The more my heape wastes, more it multiplies.
Now whither (as most rich-men doe) he pawn'd
His soule for that deare purchase none can tell,                    80
But by his bed-side when he saw death stand,
Fetching a deepe groane, me he catch't by'th hand,
Cal'd me his heire, and charg'd me well to spend
What he had got ill, deale (quoth he) a doale
Which round (with good mens prayers) may guard my soule
Now at her setting forth: let none feele want
That knock but at thy gates: do wrong to none,
And what request to thee so ear is made,
If honest, see it never be denay'd.
*Mont.*  And yow'le performe all this?
*Gent.*                                        Faire and upright,                    90
As are the strict vowes of an Anchorite:
A benefit given by a Niggards hand
Is stale and gravily bread, the hunger-sterv'd
Takes it, but cannot eate it; Ile give none such.

81 stand,] Dilke; ~ ₐ Q

Who with free heart shakes out but crums, gives much.
*Mont.* In such a ship of worldly cares my Lord
As you must saile now in, yow'le need more Pilots
Then your owne selfe to sit and steare the Helme.
You might doe therefore well to take a wife.
*Gent.* A wife? when I shall have one hand in heaven,                    100
To write my happinesse in leaves of starres;
A wife wo'd plucke me by the other downe:
This Barke hath thus long sail'd about the world,
My soule the Pilot, and yet never listen'd
To such a Mare-maids song: a wife, oh fetters,
To mans blest liberty! All this world's a prison,
Heaven the high wall about it, sin the jalour,
But the iron-shackles waying downe our heeles,
Are onely women, those light Angells turne us,
To fleshly devills, I that Sex admire,                                   110
But never will sit neere their wanton fier.
*Mut.* Who then shall reape the golden corne you sowe?
*Phil.* 'Tis halfe a curse to them, that build, and spare,
And hoard up wealth, yet cannot name an heire.
*Gent.* My heires shall be poore children fed on almes,
Souldiers that want limbes, schollers poore and scorn'd.
And these will be a sure inheritance;
Not to decay: Mannors and Townes will fall,
Lord-ships and Parkes, Pastures and woods be sold;
But this Land still continues to the Lord:                              120
No subtile trickes of law, can me beguile of this.
But of the beggers-dishe, I shall drinke healthes
To last for ever; whil'st I live, my roofe
Shall cover naked wretches; when I die,
'Tis dedicated to Saint Charitie.
*Mut.* The Duke inform'd, what trees of goodnesse grow,
Here of your planting; in true loue to your virtues,
Sent us to give you thankes, for crowning *Florence*,
With fame of such a subject, and entreats you
(Vntill he come himselfe) to accept this token,                        130
Of his faire wishes towards you.              [*Iewell.*]

*Gent.* Pray returne
My duty to the Duke, tell him I value
His love beyond all jewells in the world.
*Phil.* H'as vow'd ere long to be your visitant.
*Gent.* He shall be welcome when he comes, that's all;
Not to a Pallace, but my hospitall.
*Omn.* Wee'le leave your Lordship. [*Exeunt.*]
*Gent.* My best thoughts goe with you:
My Steward?

*Enter Steward, and a foolish Gentle-man* [Asinius Buzardo].

*Stew.* Heere my Lord.
*Gent.* Is the Booke fired?
*Stew.* As you commanded Sir, I saw it burn'd.
*Gent.* Keep safe that Iewell, and leave me; letters! from whome? 140
*Buʒ.* Signior *Ieronimo Guydanes.*
*Gent.* Oh sir,
I know the businesse: yes, yes, 'tis the same;
*Guidanes* lives amongst my bosome friends:
He writes to have me entertaine you sir.
*Buʒ.* That's the bough, my bolt flies at, my Lord.
*Gent.* What Qualities are you furnish't with?
*Buʒ.* My Education has bin like a Gentle-man.
*Gent.* Have you any skill in song, or Instrument?
*Buʒ.* As a Gentleman shoo'd have, I know all, but play on none:
I am no Barber. 150
*Gent.* Barber! no sir, I thinke it; Are you a Linguist?
*Buʒ.* As a Gentleman ought to be, one tongue serues one head;
I am no Pedler, to travell Countries.
*Gent.* What skill ha' you in horseman-ship?
*Buʒ.* As other Gentlemen have, I ha' rid some beasts in my time.
*Gent.* Can you write and reade then?
*Buʒ.* As most of your Gentle-men doe, my band has bin taken
with my marke at it.
*Gent.* I see you are a dealer, give me thy hand,
Ile entertaine thee howsoeuer, because 160

In thee I keepe halfe a score Gentlemen;
Thy name.

*Buʒ.*  *Asinius Buʒardo* ——
*Gent.*  I entertaine thee, good *Buʒardo.*
*Buʒ.*  Thankes sir.                                         [*Exit.*]
*Gent.*  This fellow's a starke foole, or too wise,
The triall will be with what wing he flies.

                                                                    *Exit.*


## ACTUS SECUNDUS, Sᴄᴀɴᴀ ᴘʀɪᴍᴀ

*Enter* Tibaldo *sicke in his chaire,* Alphonsina,
Mutio, Philippo, Tornelli, Montinello.

*Mut.*  In Lawes of courtesie, wee are bound sweete Lady,
(Being thus nigh) to see you and your brother,
Our noble friend, tho' the Duke had not sent.
*Alph.*  Thankes worthy sir.
*Phil.*  Signior *Tibaldo* hath desire to sleepe.
*Torn.*  Then leave him, Companie offends the sicke.
*Alph.*  Our humblest dutie to my Lord the Duke;
If in my Brothers name, and mine, you tender
For this his noble love, wee both shall rest
Highly indebted to you all.
*Mut.*                         Sweete Madam,                    10
You shall command our lives to worke your good.
*Alph.*  Signior, your love.
*Omn.*                         All at your service Madam.
*Mut.*  A quick, and good health to your noble Brother.
*Alph.*  And all faire fortunes doubled on your selfe.      *Exeunt.*
So: me-thinkes a Lady had more need have a new paire of lips,
then a new paire of gloves, for tho' they were both of one skinne,
yet one would weare out sooner then the other; I thinke these
Courtiers have al offices in the Spicerie, And taking my lips for

S.D. Montinello] Montivello Q          14 *Exeunt*] Dilke; *Exit* Q

sweet-meates, are as sawcie with 'em, as if they were Fees; I wonder
*Tibaldo* thou can'st sit still, and not come in for a share; If old 20
*Vanni*'s wife had beene heere, all the parts about you had mov'd.

*Tib.*  Thou think'st I lie in, heere's such a gossiping, as if 'twere a
Child-bed Chamber.

*Alph.*  So 'tis, for Ile sweare, all this stirre is about having a woman
brought to bed; marry I doubt it must be a mans lying in.

*Tib.*  I would thy tongue were a man then, to lie.

*Alph.*  I had rather it were a woman, to tell trueth.

*Tib.*  Good sister *Alphonsina*, you still play
The bad Phisicion, I am all on fire,
And you to quench mee, powre on scoopes of oyle;                  30
I feele ten thousand plummets at my heart,
Yet you cry, Lay on more, and are more cruell
Then all my tortures.

*Alph.*                  Sadnesse, I pittie thee,
And will to doe thee service, venture life,
Mine honour being kept spotlesse.

*Tib.*                  Gentle sister,
The easiest thing ith' world to begge, I crave,
And the poorest Almes to give.

*Alph.*                  But aske and have.

*Tib.*  A friendly counsell, loe that's all.

*Alph.*                  'Tis yours.
Be rul'd by me then; in an ashie sheete,
Cover these glowing embers of desire.                             40

*Tib.*  Embers? I wo'd you felt em, 'tis a fire ——

*Alph.*  Come, and set hand to paper, Ile indite.

*Tib.*  And shee'le condemne me; no, I will not write.

*Alph.*  Then prethee take this Phisick; be not the sea,
To drinke strange Rivers up, yet still be drie;
Be like a noble streame, covet to runne
Betwixt faire bankes, which thou may'st call thine owne,
And let those bankes be some faire Ladies armes,
Fit for thy youth, and birth.

*Tib.*                  Against your charmes,
Witch, thus I stop mine eares.                                   50

*Alph.*　Ile hollow then: this Deere runnes in my Lords Parke, and
if you steale it, looke to have Blood-hounds scent you.

*Tib.*　Are you mad?

*Alph.*　Yes, you shall finde venison-sawce deerer then other flesh.

*Tib.*　No, no, none else must, none shall, none can,
My hunger feede but this; downe will I dive,
And fetch this Pearle, or nere come up alive ——

*Alph.*　Are all my warme cawdles come to this? now I see th'art
too farre gone, this Lady hath overspent thee, therefore settle thine
estate, plucke up a good heart, and Ile pen thy will.　　　　　60

*Tib.*　Oh fie, fie.

*Alph.*　Bequeath thy kisses to some Taylor, that hunts out weddings
every sunday; *Item*, Thy sighes to a noyse of fidlers ill paid, thy
palenesse to a Fencer fighting at sharpe, thy want of stomack to one
of the Dukes guard.

*Tib.*　I begge it at thy hands, that being a woman,
Thou'lt make a wonder.

*Enter* Cargo.

*Alph.*　　　　　　　　What's that?

*Tib.*　　　　　　　　Hold thy tongue.

*Alph.*　It's an Instrument ever plaid on, cause well strung,
Who's that come into the Chamber there? Oh, Master *Cargo*.

*Cargo.*　My Lord hath sent you a Iewell, lock't up in this paper, 70
and the moisture of a goose quill, that's to say, words in that ——

*Alph.*　Oh sir, I thanke your Lord, and this your paines; have him
into the Buttery [*Exit* Cargo] — let me see, *Lady, that I love you,
I dare sweare like a Lord* (I shall have oathes enough then) *I send
you all that is mine, in hope all shall bee mine that is yours; for it
stands to reason, that mine being yours, yours should bee mine, and
yours being mine, mine should be yours. Love me, or I die, If I die,
you kill me, If you kill me, I will say nothing, but take the blow
patiently.* I hold my life this Lord has bin bastinado'd, out upon
him rammish foxe, he stinks hither; Prethee good Brother reade. 80

*Tib.*　I will.　　　　　　　　　　　　　　*Reades.*

*Alph.*　Is't Gander moneth with him? How the devill is my

maydenhead blasted? that among such shoales of Gallants, that
swim up and downe the Court, no fish bites at the baite of my poore
beautie, but this tough Cods-head?

*Tib.* Oh sister, peace for heavens sake; heere lies health
Even in this bitter pill (for me) so you
Would play but my Phisician, and say, take it;
You are offered heere, to soiourne at his house:
Companion with his Lady.                                            90

*Alph.* Sir, I have you. And I goeing vpon so weightie a businesse,
as getting of children, you would ha' me pin you to my sleeve.

*Tib.* Most true.

*Alph.* You care not so I turne whore to pleasure you.

*Tib.* Oh Sister, your high worth is knowne full well,
Gainst base assault, a Fort Impregnable;
And therefore, as you love my life, ith' sprindge,
Catch this old Wood-cocke.

*Alph.*                     In the flame I'le sindge
My wings, unlesse I put the candle out,
That you i'th' darke may bring your hopes about.                    100
You have wonne me.

*Tib.* You revive me.

*Alph.* Have a care you cast not your selfe downe too soone now.

*Tib.* I warrant you.

*Alph.* As for my old Huck-sters artillery, I have walls of chastity
strong enough, shoote he never so hard, to keepe him from making
any breach.

*Tib.* 'Twill be a noble-battaile on each side;
Yet now my spirits are rouzed, a stratageme
Lies hatching heere, pray helpe me noble sister,                    110
To give it forme and life.

*Alph.*              My best.

*Tib.*                          What thinke you?
(The marke of man not yet set in my face)
If as your sister, or your kins-woman,
I goe in womans habit, for thereby,
Speech, free accesse, faire opportunity,
Are had without suspition.

*Alph.*                    Mine be your will;
Oh me! what paines we take to bring forth ill!
Such a disguise is safe too, since you never
But once were seene there.
*Tib.*                    My wise sister ever.
*Alph.*   Send in the fellow there that brought the letter;            120

*Enter* Cargo.

Why how now? doe his leggs faile him already?
A staffe for his declining age.
*Cargo.*   I have a pike-staffe of mine owne already, but I could not
keep out your scurvy desperate hoggs-head from coming in upon
me, I'me cut i'th' cockscombe.
*Alph.*   Nothing I see is so like an old-man, as a young-man drunke.
*Cargo.*   Or when he comes from a wench.
*Alph.*   Before he beare your answer let him sleep.
*Tib.*   Whil'st you laugh at what I could almost weepe.

*Exeunt.*

[ACT II, Scene ii]

*Enter* Angelo, *like a Doctour*, Baptista *his man.*

*Ang.*   Deare friend, I should both wrong my faith and fortunes,
To make 'em thus dance Antickes; I shall never
Play the dissembler.
*Bapt.*                    Then never play the Lover;
Death! for a woman, I'de be fleade alive,
Could I but finde one constant: i'st such a matter
For you then to put on a Doctours-gowne,
And his flat velvet-Cap, and speake the gibbering
Of an Apothecary.
*Ang.*                    If thus disguis'd
I'me taken, all the phisicke in the world
Cannot prolong my life.
*Bapt.*                    And dying for her,            10

129 *Exeunt*] Dilke; *Exit* Q      S.D. Baptista‿] ~ , Q; [i.e. *like his man*]

You venture bravely, all women o're your grave
Will pray that they so kinde a man may have,
As to die for 'em; say your banishment
Had borne you hence, what hells of discontent,
Had rack'd your soule for her, as hers for you?
Should you but faint, well might you seeme untrue,
Where this attempt your loyalty shall approve,
Who ventures farthest winns a Ladies-love.
*Ang.*   How are my beard and haire?
*Bapt.*                          Friend I protest,
So rarely counterfeit, as if a painter                              20
Should draw a Doctour: were I sicke my selfe,
And met you with an urinall in my hand,
I'de cast it at your head, unlesse you cast
The water for me, come, all's passing well;
Love which makes pale the cheeks, gives you complexion,
Fit for a sallow French-man,
*Ang.*                          I will on then,
In *France* I long have liv'd, And know the Garbe
Of the French-Mounte-bankes, whose apish gesture,
Although in them I hold ridiculous,
My selfe shall practise.
*Bapt.*                          For a Doctours-man,                 30
You see I'me fitted, foote by foote I'le walke,
And meete all dangers sent against your breast.
*Ang.*   I thanke thee noble friend; let's then to court.
The pangs a lover suffers are but short.

                                                    *Exeunt.*


## [ACT II, SCENE iii]

*Enter* Florence, Pisa, Nicolletto, Philippo, Tornelli,
Piero, *met by an old Nurse.*

*Flo.*   How now *Nurse*, how does my *Fiametta*?
*Nurs.*   Oh my sweete Lord, shees at it agen, at it agen!

    11 your] Dilke; you Q        34 S.D. *Exeunt*] Dilke; *Exit* Q

*Flo.*  Who are with her? call for more helpe.

*Nurs.*  More helpe! alas there's my Lady *Vanni* with her, and Ladies upon Ladies, and Doctours upon Doctours, but all cannot doe.

*Pisa.*  How does it take her *Nurse*?

*Nurs.*  Oh sweete Princesse, it takes her all over with a pricking; first about her stomack, and then she heaves and heaves, that no one man with all his weight, can keepe her downe.                    10

*Pier.*  At this I wonder, that her sicknesse makes Her Doctours fooles.

*Nurs.*  He that she findes most ease in, is Doctour *Iordan*.

*Flo.*  I will give halfe my Duke-dome for her health.

*Nurs.*  Well, well, If death do take her, he shall have the sweetest bed-fellow that ever lay by leane mans-side.

*Flo.*  I entreate thee *Nurse* be tender over her.

*Nurs.*  Tender quoth a? I'me sure my heeles are growne as hard as hoofes, with trotting for her, I'le put you in one comfort.

*Flo.*  What's that Nurse?                                            20

*Nurs.*  In her greatest conflict sh'as had a worthy feeling of her selfe.

*Exit.*

*Flo.*  So, so, I'me glad of it. My Lord of *Pisa*, Vnder this common blow, which might have strooke The strongest heart here, pray doe not you shrinke.

*Pisa.*  Sicknes is lifes retainer, Sir, and I (What is not to be shun'd) beare patiently; But had she health as sound as hath the spring, She wo'd to me prove sickly Autumne still.

*Flo.*  Oh say not so.

*Pisa.*                          I finde it, for being loyall, As the touch-needle to one starre still turning,                      30 I loose that starre, my faith is paid with scorning. Who then with eagles wings of faith and truth, W'ud in her sun-beames plaie away his youth, And kisse those flames, which burne but out mine eyes, With scalding rivers of her cruelties?

*13, 15 *Nurs.*] *Nic.* Q          22 it. My] Dilke; it my Q

*Flo.*  'Tis but her way-ward sicknes casts this eye
Of slightnes on you.
*Pisa.*                    'Tis my Lord her hate;
For when death sits even almost on her browes,
She spreads her armes abroad, to welcome him,
When in my bridall-bed I finde a grave.                    40

*Enter* Mutio.

*Flo.*  Now *Mutio?*
*Mut.*                    There's a French-man come to court,
A profest Doctour, that has seen the Princesse,
And will on her recovery pawne his life.
*Flo.*  Comfort from heaven, I hope, let's see this Doctour.

*Enter* Angelo *like a Doctour,* Baptista *his man.*

*Flo.*  Welcome good Doctour: have you seen my daughter?
Restore her health, and nothing in my Duke-dome,
Shall be too deare for thee, how doe you Iudge her?
*Ang.*  Be me trat me Lord, I finde her a very bad lady, and no well.
*Flo.*  *Piero* take the Duke of *Pisa* pray
And be your sisters visitants ——
*Pier.*                    Sir we shall,                    50
If the Duke please ——
*Pisa.*                    The poysoned may drinke gall.    *Exeunt.*
*Flo.*  Attend the Duke.                    [*Exeunt attendants.*]

*Enter* Cargo, *with a letter.*

*Cargo.*  The party Sir.
*Nic.*                    Thou shalt have *Cæsars* pay ——
My Coach.
*Cargo.*        Old Ianuary goes to lie with May.
                    *Exeunt.* [*Manent* Florence *and* Angelo.]
*Flo.*  Doctor I thus have singled you, to sound
The depth of my girles sicknes, that if no skill
Of man can save her, I against heavens will,
May arme my breast with patience, therefore be free.

51, 54 *Exeunt*] Dilke; *Exit* Q

600

*Ang.*  By my tra' and fa' my Lor', me no point can play the hound, and fawne upon *de* most *puissant Roy in de* world; a French-man 60 beare the brave minde for dat.

*Flo.*  So, so, I like him better.

*Ang.*  Me gra tanke you, now for de maladie of de Princesse, me one two, tre time, feele her pulse, and ron up and downe all de oder parts of her body, and finde noting but dat she be trobla with le gran desire of de man.

*Flo.*  A great desire of a man?

*Ang.*  A my trat 'tis verament, she longa to do some ting in love upon le gentle home.

*Flo.*  Doctor thou hit'st her heart, 'tis there shee's wounded,    70
By a poyson'd Arrow, shot from a villaines hand,
One *Angelo* of the *Lotti* Familie;
And till that head be pluckt out, shee will pine,
Vnlesse controul'd by some deepe Art of thine.

*Ang.*  All tings possibela me sall undergoe, mee ha read *Gallen*, *Hipocratus*, *Avicen*, but no point can peeke out le remedie for de Madam in de bryars of love.

*Flo.*  No medicine you say in any of them for Love.

*Ang.*  A my trat, not worth a lowse, onely in my perigrination about le grand gloabe of de world, me find out a fine trick for 80 makea de man, and Voman doe, dat is tickla in love.

*Flo.*  The man and the woman doe? how doe, how doe?

*Ang.*  To be cura, and all whole, Admirable vell.

*Flo.*  As how pray?

*Ang.*  Me have had under my fingera, many brave vench, and most Noble gentle Dames, dat have bee much troubla, upon de wilde vorme in de taile for de man.

*Flo.*  Very good.

*Ang.*  And bee my tra my Lord, by experement me finde dat de heart of de man; you understanda me.    90

*Flo.*  Yes, yes, the heart of the man.

*Ang.*  Wee wee, de heart of de man being all dry as peppera —

*Flo.*  So so.

79 A my ₐ trat] A y me, trat ₐ Q (*see line 68 and also* III.ii.75)

*Ang.* And rub upon de ting (vat you call it) sall make it moulder
all to crumble and dust.

*Flo.* Oh, oh, a Grater.

*Ang.* Wee by my tra you say vell, rub a de mans dry Art upon de
Grater, and drinke de powder in de pot le Vine, by de Gentle-
voman, and by gars-blor, she presentamently kick up de heele at
de man she lova.                                                          100

*Flo.* Excellent.

*Ang.* No point more remembra, but cry out le French poo upon
le varlet.

*Flo.* So, shee will hate her lover.

*Ang.* Be-gar, as my selfe hate le puz-cat, cry mew at my shin; and
vill have de rombling a de gut, for de other gentle home.

*Flo.* Thou com'st up close to me now, my brave Doctor.

*Ang.* Be-gar me hope so, and derfore my Lord apply le desperate
Medicine, to le perilous maladie, and have dis *Angelo* be cut in de
troate, and be man-slaughtered.                                          110

*Flo.* You then advise me to have *Angelo* slaine.

*Ang.* Wee.

*Flo.* And then to have my daughter drincke his heart.

*Ang.* Wee, wee.

*Flo.* Grated and dried, and so ——

*Ang.* Wee, wee, wee.

*Flo.* I wo'd I grip'd it fast now in this hand,
And eat it panting hot, to teach a peasant
To climbe above his being, Doctor, hee dies.

*Ang.* Knocka de pate downe be-gar.                                      120

*Flo.* But stay, stay, hee's fled *Florence*; It will bee
A worke to find him first out, and being found,
A taske to kill him; for our Gallants speake
Much of his worth; The varlet is valiant.

*Ang.* No matera for dat; for two tree foure crowne, dar be rascalls
sall run him in on de backe-shide.

*Flo.* He shall be sought for, and being found, he dies.

*Ang.* Pray my lor' suffera le Princesse and me for be in private, le
Doctor uses for toucha doe Ooman ——

*Flo.*  Doe so, whil'st I for *Angeloes* death use speede,                    130
For till I have his heart, mine owne must bleede.            *Exit.*

*Enter* Baptista.

*Ang.*  Oh my *Baptista.*
*Bapt.*                    I have heard the thunder
Aym'd at your life.
*Ang.*                    And it will strike me dead,
With a most soddaine and Invisible blowe.
*Bapt.*  Now that you see his vengeance apt to fall,
Flie from it.
*Ang.*          How?
*Bapt.*                    By fayre, and free accesse,
Open your dangers to your Mistris eyes,
Were shee starke mad, so she be mad for love,
You'le bring her to her witts, if wisely now
You put her intoth' way; Gold bar'd with locks,            140
Is best being stolne; steale her then.
*Ang.*          'Tis but a wracke at most,
Oh on what boisterous Seas is True love tost!
                                             *Exeunt.*

## ACTUS TERTIUS, Scæna prima

*Trumpets sounding. Enter an Vsher bare, perfuming a roome,*
*Signior* Torrenti *gorgeously attyred, a company of Gallants.*

*Tor.*  This Roome smells.
1. *Gal.*                    It has bin new perfum'd.
*Tor.*  Then 'tis your breeches; stand off — and shines there (say
you)
A Sun in our horizon full as glorious,
As we our selfe?
2. *Gal.*          So cry the common people.
*Tor.*  The common people are Rascalls, lying devills,
Dung-hills, whose savor poisons brave mens fames,

108 Were] Dilke; Where Q

That Ape of greatnesse (imitating mee)
I meane that slavish Lord *Iacomo*
Shall die a beggar, If at the yeares end,
His totall of expence dares equall mine;                    10
How is his house built?
  1. *Gal.*                    Admirable faire.
*Tor.*    Faire? Ile guild mine (like *Pompey*'s Theater)
All ore to out-shine his; the richest hangings
Persian, or Turke, or Indian slaves can weave,
Shall from my purse be bought at any rates;
Ile pave my great hall with a floare of Clowdes,
Wherein shall move an artificiall Sunne,
Reflecting round about me, golden beames,
Whose flames shall make the roome seeme all on fire,
And when 'tis night, just as that Sun goes downe,                    20
A silver Moone shall rise, drawne up by starres,
And as that moves, I standing in her Orbe,
Will move with her, and be that man ith' moone,
So mock't in old wives tales; then over head,
A roofe of Woods, and Forests full of Deere,
Trees growing downwards, full of singing quiers,
And this i'le doe that men with prayse, may crowne
My fame, for turning the world upside downe:
And what brave gallants are *Gentilies* guestes?
  1. *Gal.*    The Lord *Iacomo Gentili* feeds                    30
All Beggars at his Table.
*Tor.*                    Hang *Iacomo*,
My boarde shalbe no manger for poore jades
To lick up provinder in.
  2. *Gal.*                    He welcomes souldiers.
*Tor.*    Let souldiors beg and starue, or steale and hange.
Wo'd I had heere ten-thousand Souldiors heads,
Their sculs set all in silver, to drinck healthes
To his confusion, first invented warre,
And the health drunck to drowne the bowles i'th Sea,
That very name of Souldior, makes me shrugg,
And thinck I crawle with vermin; give me Lutes,                    40

604

Mischiefe on drumms; for souldiors, fetch me whores,
These are mens blisse, those every Kingdomes soares;
Wee gave in charge to search through all the world
For the best Cookes, rarest musitians,
And fairest girles, that will sell sinne for gold.
1. *Gal.*   Some of all sorts you have.
*Tor.*                           Let me have more
Then the grand Signior, And my change as rare,
Tall, low, and middle size, the browne, and faire;
Ide give a Princes ransome now to kisse
Blacke *Cleopatra*'s cheeke; Onely to drinke                    50
A richer perle, then that of *Anthonyes*,
That Fame (where his name stands) might put downe mine.
Oh that my Mother had bin *Paris* Whore,
And I had liv'd to see a *Troy* on fire,
So that by that brave light, I might have danc'd
But one Lavalto with my Curtezan.

*Enter fourth Gallant.*

4. *Gal.*   Patterne of all perfection breath'd in man,
There's one without, before your Excellence
Desires accesse.
*Tor.*               What creature?
4. *Gal.*                           Your owne brother,
At least hee termes himselfe so.
*Tor.*                           Is he brave?                    60
4. *Gal.*   Hee's new come from Sea.
*Tor.*                           'Tis true, that *Iason*
Rig'd out a Fleete to fetch the Golden-Fleece;
'Tis a brave boy, all Elementall fire,
His shipps are great with Child of Turkish Treasure,
And heere shall be delivered; marshall him in
Like the seas proud commander, give our charge ——
*Omn.*   Sound drums, and trumpets for my Lord, away.

41 drumms; ...souldiors,] Dilke; ~ , ... ~ ; Q
42 blisse, ...soares;] Dilke; ~ ; ... ~ , Q
66 commander,] Dilke [;]; ~ ˄ Q

*Vsher him in Bare and ragged. At which* Torrenti
*starts, his hat falls off, offer it him.*

*Tor.*   Thou whoreson pesant, know me, burne that wind-fall,
It comes not to my head that drops so low,
— Another.                                                             70
1. *Gal.*   Hatts for my Lord.          *Hatt's brought in three or four.*
*Tor.*   It smells of earth, stood it againe so high,
My head would on a dung-hill seeme to lie.
How now? what scar-crow's this?
*Broth.*                                        Scar-crow? thy brother,
His bloud cleare as thine owne, but that it smoakes not,
With perfum'd fiers as thine doth.
*Tor.*                                        Has the poore snake,
A sting; can he hisse? What beggs the rogue for?
*Broth.*                                        Vengeance
From the just thunderer to throw *Lucifer* downe;
How high so ever thou rearest thy Babell-browes,
To thy confusion I this language speake:                             80
I am thy fathers sonne.
*Tor.*                         Ha, ha, the Skipper raves.
*Broth.*   The aw'd Venetian on Saint *Markes* proud-day,
Never went forth to marry the rich-sea
With casting in her lapp a ring of gold;
In greater bravery then my selfe did freight,
A fleete of gallant youthfull Florentines,
All vow'd to rescew *Rhodes,* from Turkish-slavery:
We went and waded up in our owne bloods,
Till most of us were drown'd.
*Tor.*                         Faire riddance on you.
*Broth.*   Where such a Peacock durst not spread his plumes,         90
We fought; and those that fell left Monuments
Of unmatch't valour to the whole race of man,
They that were ta'ne, (mongst whom my selfe was chiefe)
Were three yeeres chain'd up to the tugging o're,
See here the relicts of that misery,                    *Chaines.*
If thou wu'd'st know more, reade it on my backe,

Printed with the Bulls-peezele.

*Tor.*                    Hang the dogge.
What tellest thou me of Peezeles?
*Broth.*                    'Tis thy brother
Tells thee so, note me.
*Tor.*                    I know thee not;
Set mastives on him, worry him from my gates.          100
*Broth.*    The first unhappy breath I drew, mov'd heere,
And here I'le spend my last, e're brav'd from hence,
Heere I'le have meate and cloaths.
*Tor.*                    Kick the curre out.
*Broth.*    Who dares?
Take from that sumpter-horses backe of thine,
Some of those gaudie trappings to cloathe mine,
And keepe it from the keene aire, fetch me food,
You fawning spaniells.
*1. Gal.*            Some spirit of the buttery.
*2. Gal.*    It should be by his hunger.
*Broth.*                    I am starv'd,
Thirsty, and pinde to th' bare bones; heere, I'le eate          110
At thine owne scorneful board, on thine owne meate,
Or teare it from thy throate as 'tis chewing downe.
*Tor.*    I'le try that; if my dinner be prepared,
Serue me in my great state along'st this way,
And as you passe, two there with pistolls stand
To kill that ravenous Vulture; if he dare thrust
His tallents forth to make one dish his prey.          *Exeunt all.*
*Broth.*    Now view my face, and tho' perhaps you sham'd
To owne so poore a brother, let not my heart-strings,
In sunder cracke, if we now being lone,          120
You still disdaine me.
*Tor.*                    Wretch I know thee not,
And loath thy sight.
*Broth.*                    Slave, thou shalt know me then;
I'le beate thy braines out with my Gally-chaine.
*Tor.*    Wilt murther thine owne brother?
*Broth.*                    Pride doth it selfe confound,

What with both hands the Devill strove to have bound,
Heaven with one little finger hath untyed,
This proves that thou maiest fall, because one blast
Shakes thee already, feare not, I'le not take
The whip out of your hand and tho' thou break'st
Lawes of humanitie, and brother-hood,                          130
I'le not doe so; but as a begger should
(Not as a brother) knock I at the gate
Of thy hard heart for pitty to come forth,
And looke upon my wretchednes. A shot          *Kneeles.*
Toore to the keele that gally where I row'd;
Sunke her, the men slaine, I by dyving scaped,
And sat three leagues upon a broken-mast,
Wash't with the salt teares of the Sea, which wept,
In pitty, to behold my misery.
*Tor.*  Pox on your tarry misery.                               140
*Broth.*  And when heavens blest-hand hal'de me to a shoore,
To dry my wet-limbes, was I forc'd to fire,
A dead-mans straw-bed throwne into the streete.
*Tor.*  Foh, th'art infectious.
*Broth.*                    Oh remember this!
He that does good deeds, here waits at a Table,
Where Angells are his fellow servitours.
*Tor.*  I am no Robbin-red-breast to bring strawes
To cover such a coarse
*Broth.*                    Thou art turn'd devill.          *Rizes.*

*Trumpets sound. Enter an arm'd sewer, after him a company*
*with covered dishes: Coronets on their heads.*
*Two with pistolls to guard it.*

*Tor.*  Where's thy great stomack, eat, stand, let him choose
What dish he likes.
                    [Brother] *snatches a pistoll: all flye off.*
*Broth.*                    This then which I'le carve up        150
On thy base bosome, see thou Tryviall foole,
Thou art a Tyrant (o're me) of short reigne,
This cock out crow's thee, and thy petty kings,

Th'art a proud-bird, but fliest with rotten wings;
To shew how little for thy scorne I care,
See my revenge turn's all to idle-aire,                    *Shootes up.*
It upward flies and will from thence I feare
Shoote darts of lightning to confound thee heere.
Farewell thou huge *Leviathan*, when th'ast drunk dry,
That Sea thou rowl'st in, on some base shore dye.          [*Exit.*] 160

*Enter Gallants all drawne.*

*Omn.*   Where is the Traitor?
*Tor.*                        Now the house is fiered,
You come to cast on waters; barre up my doores,
But one such tattered ensigne here being spread,
Drawes numbers hither, here must no rogues be fed;
Command my carpenters invent od engines,
To manacle base beggers, hands and feete,
And by my name call 'em my whipping posts;
If you spye any man that has a looke,
Stigmatically drawne, like to a furies,
(Able to fright) to such I'le give large pay,                  170
To watch and ward for poore snakes night and day,
And whip 'em soundly if they approch my gates;
The poore are but the earths-dung fit to lie
Cover'd on muck-heapes not to offend the eye.

*Enter* 1. *Gallant.*

1. *Gal.*   Two Gentlemen sent from the *Florence* Duke,
Require speech with your Lord-ship ——
*Tor.*                              Give'm entrance.

*Enter* Mutio, Philippo.

What are you? and whence come you?
*Mut.*                            From the Duke.
*Tor.*   Your businesse?
*Mut.*                    This, fame sounding forth your worth
For hospitable princely house-keeping;

162 You] Dilke; *Torr.* You Q

Our Duke drawne by the wonder of report,                          180
Invites himselfe (by us) to be your guest.
*Tor.*   The honour of Embassadors be yours;
Say to the Duke that *Cæsar* never came,
More welcome to the Capitoll of *Rome*,
Then he to us — healthes to him — fill rich wines.
*Mut.*   You have this wonder wrought, now rare to men;
By you they have found the golden age agen.
*Tor.*   Which I'le uphold, so long as there's a sunne,
To play the *Alchymist.*
*Phil.*                         This proud fellow talkes          [*Aside.*]
As if he grasped the *Indies* in each hand.                       190
*Tor.*   Health to your Duke.
*Amb.*                         We pledge it on our knees.
*Tot.*   I'le stand to what I do, but kneele to none.

> *Musicke. Drinck, breake the glasse, they pledge it in plate,*
> *which offering, both servitours refuse to take.*

*Tor.*   Breake not our custome (pray ye): with one beame,
The god of mettailes makes both gold and wine.
To Imitate whose greatnesse; If on you
I can bestow Wine, I can give gold too.
Take them as free as *Bacchus* spends his blood;
And in them drinke our health.
*Mut.*                         Your bounty farre
Exceeds that of our *Cæsars.*
*Tor.*   Cæsar *ero, vel nihil ero:*                              200
What are Gold heapes? but a rich dust for Kings
To scatter with their breath, as chaffe by winde?
Let him then that hath gold, beare a Kings minde,
And give till his arme akes, who bravely powres
But into a wenches lap his golden showres,
May be *Ioves* equall, oh but hee that spends
A world of wealth, makes a whole world his debter,
And such a Noble spender is *Ioves* better;
That man Ile be. I'me *Alexanders* heire
To one part of his minde, I wish there were                       210

Ten Worlds, yet not to conquer, but to sell
For Alpine hills of silver, And that I
Might at one feast, spend all that treasure drie;
Who hoards up wealth, is base; who spends it, brave;
Earth breeds gold, so I tread but on my slave;
Beare backe our gratulations to your Duke. *Exit* [*with Gallants*].
*Amb.*  Wee shall great sir.
*Mut.*  *Torrenti* call you him; 'tis a prowd rough streame.
*Phil.*  Hee's of the *Romane* Family indeede.
*Mut.*  Lord *Vanni?* rather my Lord *Vanitie.*                    220
*Phil.*  And heapes of money sure have strucke him mad.
*Mut.*  Hee'le soone pick up his witts, let him but bleede
Thus many ownces at one time; All day
Could I drinke these deare healthes, yet nere be drunke.
*Phil.*  And carry it away most cleanely.
*Mut.*                                    Not a pin the worse;
What might his father leave him?
*Phil.*                                    A great estate,
Of some three hundred thousand Crownes a yeare.
*Mut.*  Strange hee's not begg'd, for fooles are now growne deare;
An admirable Cocks-combe!
*Phil.*                                    Let wonder passe,
Hee's both a brave Lord, and a golden Asse.                    230
                                    *Exeunt.*


[ACT III, Scene ii]

*A Bed discovered,* Fyametta *upon it. Enter two Dukes,* Piero,
*Gallants, Nurse, Ladies,* Angelo, Baptista, *ut antea* Fyametta.

*Ang.*  I pray you hush all, a little hush, le faire Lady by her owne
volunter disposition, has take a ting dat is of such a grand operation,
it shall makea de stone for slepe.
*Flo.*  What, Noble Doctor, is the name of it?
*Ang.*  'Tis not your scurvie English *Poppy,* nor *Mandragon,* nor

a ting so danger as *Oppium*, but tis de brave ting a de vorld, for
knocka de braine asleepe.

*Pisa.*   I am glad shee takes this rest.

*Ang.*   Peace, be gor it is snore and snore, two mile long; now if
your grace vill please for procure Musick, be restore as brave as de 10
first.

*Flo.*   Call for the Musicke.

*Ang.*   Makea no noise, but bring in de Fidlers, and play sweet ——

*Nurs.*   Oh out upon this Doctor; hang him, does he thinke to cure
dejected Ladies with Fidlers ——

*Ang.*   De grand French poo stopa de troate, pray void le Shambera.

*Flo.*   All, all part softly; peace Nurse, let her sleepe.

*Nurs.*   I, I, go out of her prospect, for shee's not to bee cur'd with
a song.                                                      *Exeunt.*

*Ang.*   *Baptista*, see the doore fast, watch that narrowly.          20

*Bapt.*   For one friend to keepe doore for another, is the office now
amongst gallants, common the Law; Ile bee your porter Sir.

*Ang.*   Shee does but slumber, *Fiametta*, Love.

*Fia.*   The *Pisan* Prince comes: daggers at my heart.

*Ang.*   Looke up, I am not hee, but *Angelo?*

*Fia.*   Ha! who names *Angelo?*

*Ang.*                          *Angelo* himselfe,
Who with one foote treads on the throat of death,
Whilst t'other stepps to embrace thee, thus ith' shape
Of a French Doctor.

*Fia.*                  Oh my life, my soule.

*Ang.*   Heare me.

*Fia.*                  Ime now not sicke, Ile have no Phisicke,          30
But what thy selfe shall give mee.

*Ang.*                          Let not Ioy
Confound our happinesse, I am but dead,
If it be knowne I am heere.

*Fia.*                      Thou shalt not hence.

*Ang.*   Be wise deare heart; see here the best of men,
Faithfull *Baptista* ——

*Fia.*             Oh, I love *Baptista*,
Cause he loves thee; But my *Angelo* I love bove kings.
*Bapt.*   Madam you'le spoile,
Vnlesse you joyne with us in the safe plot
Of our escape.
*Ang.*             Sweete *Fyametta* heare me,
For you shall hence with us.
*Fia.*                 Over ten worlds;                    40
But Ile not hence, my *Angelo* shall not hence,
True love, like gold, is best being tried in fire;
Ile defie Father, and a thousand deaths ——
For thee ——
*Ang.*         Vndone, vndone.                 *Knock within.*
*Bapt.*                 At the Court gate,
I see a Iebbit already, to hang's both;
Death! the Duke beates at the doore.
*Fia.*                           He shall come in;
                                        *Enter Omnes.*

One frowne at thee, my Tragedie shall begin;
See Father ——
*Flo.*             I told you that I heard —— her tongue ——
*Fia.*   See Father.
*Flo.*             What sweete girle?
*Fia.*                         That's *Angelo*,
And you shall pardon him.
*Flo.*                         With all my heart.               50
*Fia.*   Hee sayes hee pardons thee with all his heart.
*Ang.*   Mee Lor, be all mad, le braine crowe, and run whirabout like
de windmill saile, pardona moy, por quoy my sweete Madam,
pardon your povera Doctor.
*Fia.*   Because thou art my banish't *Angelo*.
*Flo.*   Starke mad.
*Pisa.*               This her recoverie?
*Fia.*                         Hee is no Doctor,
Nor that his man, but his deare friend *Baptista*;

45 already] *i.e.* all ready

H'as black't his beard like a Comœdian
To play the Mountibanke; away, Ile marry
None but that Doctor, and leave *Angelo*.                            60
*Ang.*    I doe pray Artely, Madam.
*Fia.*    Leave off thy gibberishe, and I prethee speake
Thy Native language.
*Ang.*    Par-ma-foy all French, be-gor shee be mad as the moone.
*Flo.*    Sweet girle, with gentle hands sir, take her hence.
*Fia.*    Stand from mee, I must follow *Angelo*.
*Pisa.*    Thine eyes drinke sleepe from the sweet god of rest.
*Fia.*    Oh, you shoote poyson'd arrowes thorow my breast.
                                                              [*Exeunt.*]
                    *Manent* Florence, Angelo, Baptista.

*Flo.*    What strange new furie now possesseth her?
*Ang.*    Begar her Imaginashon be out a de vitts, and so dazell de two  70
nyes, and come downe so into de bellie, and possibla for make her
tinke mee or you to be le shentle-man shee lovea, and so shee takea
my man for a Iack-a-nape, mee know not who.
*Bapt.*    For one *Baptista*.
*Ang.*    Povera garshon a my trat.
*Flo.*    I doe beleeve you both; but honest Doctor,
Straine all thy Art, and so thou leave her well,
I care not if you call up feinds from hell.
*Ang.*    Dar be too much devill in de body all ready be my trat my
Lor, mee no stay heere for ten hundred hundred Coronaes, she cry  80
upon mee 'tis Master *Angelo*, you tink so not one and two time, but
a tyrd time, you smella me out; And so cutta my troate; adue my
Lor.
*Flo.*    Still your opinion holds to kill that villaine,
And give her his heart dried.
*Ang.*    In de pot a vine, wee, very fine.
*Flo.*    This gold take for thy paines to make her sownde,
There needs a desperate cure to a desperate wounde.        *Exit.*
*Ang.*    How blowes it now?
*Bapt.*                              Faire, with a prosperous gale.
*Ang.*    Poore love, thou still art strucke with thine owne fate;    90

My life hangs at a thred, friend, I must flie.
*Bapt.*   How, to be safe?
*Ang.*                    I will take sanctuary,
I know a reverend Fryar, in whose cell
Ile lurke till stormes blow ore; If women knew
What men feele for them, None their scornes should rue.

[*Exeunt.*]

[ACT III, Scene iii]

*Enter* Tibaldo *in Womans attire,* Alphonsina.

*Alph.*   Is't come to this, have the walls of the Castle beene besieged
thus long, lien open for a breach; and dare you not give fier to one
piece? oh y'ar a proper soldyor, good sister, brother follow
your game more close, or i'le leave you.
*Tib.*   What wu'd you have me doe?
*Alph.*   Why I would ha' you (tho' you be in womans apparrell) to
be your selfe a man, and do what you come for.
*Tib.*   I have bin giving her a thousand on setts,
And still a blushing cheeke makes me retire;
I speake not three words, but my tongue is ready          10
To aske forgivenes of her.
*Alph.*   Must thou needs at thy first encounter tell her thou art a man,
why when you walke together, cannot you begin a tale to her, with
once upon a time, there was a loving couple that having tyred
themselves with walking, sat downe upon a banck, and kist, and
embraced, and plaid, and so by degrees bring the tale about to
your owne purpose. Can you not? fie, you are the worst at these
things Sir.
*Tib.*   I am sister indeed.
*Alph.*   And the more foole you indeed: you see how the old   20
stinking fox her husband is stil rubbing me as if I had the palsy, Ile
not have his wither'd hands (which are as moist as the side of a
stock-fish) lye pidling in my bosome, therefore determine some
thing, or farewell.

2 one] Dilke; once Q      *3 sister, brother] *stet* Q      22 a] *om.* Q

*Tib.*   I have deare sister, if you will but heare me.

*Alph.*   Come on, out with't then.

*Tib.*   Give you the old man promise of your love,
And the next night appoint him for your bed;
Rap'd with joy, he'le feigne businesse of state,
To leave his lady, and to lie alone.                                    30

*Alph.*   Very good.

*Tib.*   Then my request shall be, that for that night
She would accept me for her bed-fellow,
And there's no question sister of the grant,
Which being Injoy'd I doubt not but to manage
And carry all so even on levill ground,
That my offence shall in my love seeme drownde.

*Alph.*   The clocke for your businesse thus far goes true, but now
for me, what shall I do with the old cock in my Roost?

*Tib.*   Sister, you have some tricke (no doubt) to keepe              40
Him within compasse.

*Alph.*   No not I, beleeve me, I know not what to doe with him,
unlesse I should give him a little *Nux vomica*, to make him sleep
away the night, but brother, to pleasure you, Ile venter a joynte,
and yet it troubles me too, that I should prove a Traytor to my
sex, I doe betray an Innocent Lady, to what ill I know not.
But Love the author of it wil I hope
Turne it quite otherwise, and perhaps it may be
So welcome to her as a courtesie.

*Tib.*   I doubt not but it shall.

*Alph.*                        We nothing can,                          50
Vnlesse man woman helpe, and woman man.

                                                        *Exeunt.*

ACTUS QUARTUS, Scæna prima

*Trumpets sounding. Enter* Torrenti *very brave, betweene the two Dukes, attended by all the Courtiers, wondring at his costly habit. Enter a mask, women in strang habitts, Dance. Exit. He gives jewells, and ropes of pearle to the Duke; and a chaine of gold to every Courtier. Exeunt.* Nicholetto *and he stay.*

*Nic.*  Thou art my noble kinsman, and but thy mother
(Vpon my soule) was chast I should beleeve
Some Emperor begot thee.
*Tor.*                                        Why pray Vncle?
*Nic.*  Suppose all kingdomes on the earth were balls,
And that thou held'st a racket in thy hand,
To tosse 'em as thou wu'd'st, how wo'dst thou play?
*Tor.*  Why? as with balls, bandy 'em quite away.
*Nic.*  A tennes-court of kings could do no more;
But faith what doest thou thinke, that I now think,
Of thy this days expence?
*Tor.*                                     That it was brave.                    10
*Nic.*  I thinke thee a proud vaine-glorious bragging knaue.
That golden wombe thy father left so full,
Thou Vulture-like eat'st thorough: oh heeres trim stuffe;
A good-mans state, in Gartyres, strings and ruffe;
Hast not a saffron shirt on too? I feare
Th'art troubled with the greene-sicknes, thou look'st wan.
*Tor.*  With anger at thy snarling: must my hoase
Match your old greasy cod-piece?
*Nic.*  No, but I'de have thee live in compasse.
*Tor.*  Foole, I'le be                                                             20
As the sun in the Zodiack; I am he
That wood take *Phaetons* fall, tho' I set fire
On the whole world, to be heavens charioteire,
(As he was) but one day.

S.D. *Exeunt] Exit* Q          1 *Nic.*] Dilke; *Tor.* Q

*Nic.*                    Vaine riotous cockscombe,
  Tha'st fier'd to much already, Parkes, Forrests, chases,
  Have no part left of them, but names and places;
  'Tis voic'd abroad thy lands are all at pawne.
*Tor.*   They are, what then?
*Nic.*                    And that the mony went
  To entertaine the Popes great Nuntio,
  On whom you spent the ransome of a king.                    30
*Tor.*   You lye.
*Nic.*            I thanke you Sir.
*Tor.*                    Say all this true
  That I spent millions, what's that to you.
  Were there for every day i'th' yeare a Pope,
  For every houre i'th' yeare a Cardinall;
  I'd melt both *Indies*, but I'de feast 'em all.
*Nic.*   And leave your Curtezans bare, that leaving bare,
  Will one day leave thee naked, one nights waking,
  With a fresh-whore, cost thee four thousand duckets,
  Else the bawd lies.
*Tor.*            Wert thou not mine uncle
  I'de send thee with thy frozen-beard where furies                    40
  Should sindge it off with fire-brands, touching wenching,
  That art thy selfe an old rotten whore-master.
*Nic.*   I a whore-master?
  To shew how much I hate it, harke, when next
  Thy tomblers come to dance upon the ropes,
  Play this jigg to 'em.
*Tor.*            Goe, goe, idle droane,
  Thou enviest bees with stings, because thine is gone,
  Plate, jewells, revenues all shall flie.
*Nic.*                    They shall.
*Tor.*   And then Sir I'le turne pickled theefe, a Pirate,
  For as I to feed Rayot, a world did crave,                    50
  So nothing but the sea shall be my grave,
  Meane time that circle few began I've runne,
  Tho' the Devill stand i'th' Center.
*Nic.*                    What's that circle?

*Tor.*   The vanitie of all man-kinde be mine,
In me all prodigalls loosenes fresh shall flowe,
Wine, harlots, surfetts, rich embroidered cloaths,
Fashions, all sensuall sins, all new coin'd oathes,
Shall feed me, fill me; Ile feast every sence,
Nought shall become me ill, but innocence.          *Exit.*
*Nic.*   I hope a wallet hanging at thy backe,                    60
Who spends all young, ere age comes, all will lacke.
                                                     *Exit.*


## [ACT IV, Scene ii]

*Enter an Apothecary, give a serving-man gold, Iacomo [Gentili],
    Servants in blew-coats: Steward, Broker, Goldsmith,
        Torrenti's Brother, a Trumpet.*

*Gent.*   What sounds this trumpet for?
*Omn.*                          Dinner my Lord.
*Gent.*   To feast whome this day are my tables spread?
*Stew.*   For sea-men, wrack't, aged, or sicke, or lame,
And the late ransom'd captives from the Turke.
*Gent.*   Cheere them with harty welcomes in my name,
Attend them as great Lords, let no man dare,
To send 'em sad hence, bounty shall be plac'd
At the boards upper end; For Marriners
Are clocks of danger that do ne're stand still,
Their dialls-hand ere points to'th stroke of death,          10
And (albeit seldome windlesse) loose their breath;
I love 'em, for they eat the dearest bread,
That life can buy; when the elements make warrs,
Water and aire, they are sav'd by their good starrs.
And for the gally-slaves, make much of those,
Love that man
Who suffers onely for being christian;
What suiters waite?
*Stew.*   Come neere, one at once, keep back pray.
*Brok.*   A sorry man, a very sorry man.                    20

619

*Gent.*   What makes thee sorry?

*Brok.*   All I had is burnt, and that which touches me to the quick,
a boxe of my sweete evidence my Lord.

*Gent.*   Show me some proofe of this.

*Brok.*   Alas too good proofe, all burnt, nor stick, nor stone, left.

*Gent.*   What wo'dst have me doe?

*Brok.*   Bestow but a bare hundred pound on me, to set me up.

*Gent.*   Steward deliver him a hundred pound.

*Brok.*   Now all the ——

*Gent.*   Nay kneele not Sir, but heare me.                           30

*Brok.*   Oh my hony Lord!

*Gent.*   Faces are speaking pictures, thine's a booke,
Which if the leafe be truly printed shews
A page of close dissembling.

*Brok.*                         Oh my Lord!

*Gent.*   But say thou art such, yet the monie's thine,
Which I to Charitie give, not to her shrine;
If thou cheat'st me, thou art cheated? how? th'hast got
(Being licorish) rats-bane from a gally-pot,
Taking it for sugar; thou art now my debtor,
I am not hurt, nor thou I feare, much better;              40
Farewell.

*Enter lame legg'd Souldier.*

*Sould.*   Cannons defend me, Gun-powder of hell,
Whom doest thou blow up heere?

*Brok.*                         Some honest scullar,
Row this lame dog to hanging.

*Gent.*                         What noise is that?

*Stew.*   My Lord calls to you.

*Sould.*                         Was there ever call'd
A devill by name from hell? then this is one.

*Gent.*   My friend, what is hee?

*Sould.*                         A Citie pestilence,
A moath that eates up gownes, doublets and hose,
One that with Bills, leades smocks and shirts together
To linnen close adultery, and upon them                   50

620

Strowes lavender, so strongly, that the owners
Dare never smell them after; hee's a broaker.
*Gent.*   Suppose all this, what hurt hath hee done thee?
*Sould.*   More then my limbs losse; in one weeke he eate
My wife up, and three children, this christian Iew did;
Ha's a long lane of hellish Tenements,
Built all with pawnes.
*Gent.*                All that he had is burnt.
*Sould.*   He keepes a whore indeede, this is the Raven,
Cryed knocke before you call, he may be fir'd,
His lowsie wardropes are not; to this hell-hound          60
I pawn'd my weapons to buy browne bread
To feede my brats and me; (they forfited)
Twice so much as his money him I gave,
To have my Armes redeem'd, the griping slave
Swore (not to save my soule) vnlesse that I
Laid downe my stumpe heere, for the Interest,
And so hop home.
*Gent.*                Vnheard of villanie!
Broker, is this true?
*Brok.*                'Twere sinne my Lord, to lie.
*Gent.*   Souldier, what is't thou now crau'st at my hands?
*Sould.*   This my Pitition was, which now I teare,          70
My suite here was, When the next place did fall,
To be a Beades-man in your Hospitall:
But now I come most pitiously complaining
Against this three-pile rascall, widowes decayer,
The Orphans beggerer, and the poores betrayer;
Give him the Russian law for all these sinnes.
*Gent.*   How?
*Sould.*        But one hundred blowes on his bare shins.
*Brok.*   Come home and take thine Arms.
*Sould.*                        Ile have those leggs.
*Gent.*   Broaker, my soule foresaw goods thus ill got,
Would as ill thrive, you ask'd a hundred pound,          80
'Tis yours; but crafty Broaker, you plaid the knave

67 villanie] villaine Q

To begg, not needing. This man now must have
His request too, 'tis honest, faire, and just,
Take hence that varlet therefore, and on his shinnes,
In ready payment, give him an hundred blowes.

*Brok.*   My Lord, my pitifull Lord.

*Sould.*   I must bestirre my stumps too. Iustice; my Lord.

*Gent.*   I will not ravill out time; Broaker, I offer you
A hundred for a hundred.

*Sould.*                         That's his owne usury.

*Gent.*   A hundred pound, or else a hundred blowes,          90
Give him that money, he shall release you those.

*Brok.*   Take it, and may'st thou rot with't.          *Exit.*

*Sould.*                         Follow thee thy curse,
Wo'd blowes might make all Broakers still disburse.

*Gent.*   What next?

*Serv.*          The Party sir ——

*Gent.*                         What party sir?
If honest, speake, I love no whisperer.

*Serv.*   This Gentleman is a great shuter.

*Gent.*   In a Long-bow? how farre shootes hee?

*Serv.*   To your Lordship, to be your Apothecary.

*Gent.*   Vmph; what spie you in my face, that I sho'd buy
Your druggs and drenches? beares not my cheeke a colour          100
As fresh as any old mans? doe my bones
Ake with youth's ryotts? or my blood boile hot
With feavers? or is't num'd with dropsies cold,
Coughes, Rhumes, Catarrhes, Gowts, Apoplexie fits?
The common soares of age, on me never ran,
Nor Galenist, nor Paracelsian,
Shall ere reade Phisicall Lecture upon me.

*Apo.*   Two excellent fellowes my Lord.

*Gent.*   I honour their profession,
What the Creator does, they in part doe,          110
For a Phisician's a man-maker too,
— But honest friend,
My kitchin is my Doctor, and my Garden,
Trustie Apothecarie; when they give me pills,

So gently worke they, I'me not choak'd with bills,
Which are a stronger purge then the disease.

*Apo.*   Alas my Lord, and 'twere not for bills, our shops wo'd
downe.

*Gent.*   Sir, I beleeve you, bills nor pills Ile take;
I stand on sicknes shoare, and see men tost                      120
From one disease to another, at last lost;
But to such seas of surfetts, where they're drown'd,
I never ventering, am ever sound.

*Apo.*   Ever sound my Lord? if all our gallants sho'd bee so, Doctors,
Pothecaries, and Barber-surgeons, might feed upon Onyons and
Butter-milke; ever sound! a brave world then.

*Gent.*   'Tis their owne fault, if they feare springs or falls,
Wine-glasses fill'd too fast, make urynalls;
Man was at first borne sound, and hee growes ill
Seldome by course of nature, but by will ——                     130
Distempers are not ours, there should be then
(Were wee our selues) no Phisicke, men to men
Are both diseases cause, and the disease,
I'me free from (thankes good fate) either of these.

*Apo.*   My fifty Crownes.

*Serv.*   Not I.

*Apo.*   No, must I give you a Glister?

*Serv.*   Hist, hist.

*Apo.*   If your Lordship will not allow me minister to your selfe,
pray let me give your man a purgation.                           140

*Serv.*   Me a Purgation? my Lord, I'me passing well.

*Gent.*   Him a Purge, why?

*Apo.*   Or rather a vomit, that hee may cast up fifty Crownes ——
which he swallowed as a Bribe to preferre me.

*Gent.*   My health is bought and sold sir then by you,
A Doctor baits you next, whose mesh of potions
Striking me full of vlcers, a gibberish Surgion,
For fifty Crownes more, comes to drawe my will,
For mony, slaves their Soveraignes thus kill;
Nay, nay, so got, so keepe it; for his Fifty,                    150
Give him a hundred Crownes, because his will

Aym'd at my health I know, and not at ill:
Fare you well sir.
*Apo.* Who payes mee sir?
*Serv.* Follow me, I sir.                    *Exit Servant and Apothecary.*

*Enter* [*come forward*] *Gold-smith.*

*Gold.*  The fellow, my Lord, is fast.
*Gent.*                    What fellow sir?
*Gold.*  The thiefe that stole this Iewell from your honour,
Hee came unto my stall my Lord ——
*Gent.*                    So.
*Gold.*                    And ask'd mee
Not the fourth part in money it was worth,
And so smelling him out ——
*Gent.*          You did.
*Gold.*                    I did sir,                    160
Smell him out presently, and under hand
Sent for a Constable, examined him,
And finding that he is your Stewards man,
Committed him toth' Iale.
*Gent.*                    What money had hee
Upon this Iewell of you?
*Gold.*                    None my good Lord,
After I heard it yours.
*Gent.*                    Else you had bought it,
And beene the thiefes receiver, y'ar a varlet,
Go to, a sawcie knave; if I want money,
And send my servants servant (cause the world
Shall not take notice of it) to pawne, or sell                    170
Iewells, or Plate, tho' I loose halfe in halfe,
Must you sir, play the Marshall, and commit him,
As if he were a rogue; goe and release him,
Send him home presently, and pay his fees,
Doe you see sir.
*Gold.*  My Lord, I do see.
*Gent.*                    Least by the Innocent fellow,

I lay you fast byth' heeles, doe this y'are best;
You may be gone.
*Gold.*                Heere's a most excellent jeast.        *Exit.*

*Enter Steward.*

*Gent.*   Harke you, the Duke of *Florence* sent me once
A Iewell, have ye' it? For you laid it up.                180
*Stew.*   My Lord, I have it.
*Gent.*                Are you sure you have it?
Why change you colour? Know you this? doe you know
Your man, you sent to sell it? You belike
Thought in my memory it had beene dead,
And so your honesty too came buried,
'Tis well, out of mine eye; what wo'd you with mee?

*Enter [come forward]* Brother, *to* Torrenti.

*Broth.*   Your pitty on a wretch late wrackt at sea,
Beaten a shore by penury, three yeares
A Turkish Gally-slave.
*Gent.*                Your birth?
*Broth.*                Such Sir,
As I dare write my selfe a gentleman,                190
In *Florence* stood my cradle, my house great,
In mony, not in mercy; I am poore,
And dare not with the begger passe their doore.
*Gent.*   Name them, they shalbe forc't to thy reliefe.
*Broth.*   To steale compassion from them like a thiefe,
Good my Lord pardon me, under your noble wing,
I had rather sit, then on the highest tree sing,
That shadowes their gay buildings.
*Gent.*   Young man I doe commend thee, where's my steward?
Give me thy hand, I entertaine thee mine,                200
Make perfect your accounts, and see the books
Deliver'd to this Gentleman.
*Stew.*   This poore rogue Sir?
*Gent.*   Thou art a villaine, so to tearme the man,

195 *Broth.*] Dilke; *om.* Q

Whom I to liking take; Sir I discharge you;
I regard no mans out-side, 'tis the lineings
Which I take care for.
*Stew.*    Not if you knew how louzie they were.
*Gent.*    Cast not thy scorne upon him, prove thou but just,
Ile raise thee; Cedars spring out first from dust.        210

*Exeunt.*

[ACT IV, Scene iii]

*Enter* Nicolletto, Dariene, Alphonsina, Alisandra,
Tibaldo [*disguised*], Cargo.

*Nic.*    Madam this night I have received from court,
A booke of deepe import, which I must reade,
And for that purpose will I lie alone.
*Dar.*    Be Master of your owne content my Lord,
Ile change you for some femall bed-fellow.
*Nic.*    With all my heart.
*Tib.*                          Pray madam then take me.
*Nic.*    Doe prethee wife.
*Dar.*                          And Sir she is most welcome.
*Nic.*    Wo'ld I were at it, for it is a booke,
My fingers itch till I be turning o're;
Good rest; faire *Alphonsina* you'le not faile.        10
*Alph.*    No, feare me not.
*Nic.*                          All all to bed, to bed.  [*Exit with* Cargo.]
*Alph.*    Mine eyes are full of sleepe; Ile follow you.        *Exit.*
*Dar.*    I to my closet, and then bed-fellow
Expect your company.        [*Exit.*]
*Tib.*                          I will be for you Lady.
*Ales.*    Madam so please you forfeit to my mother,
And let your selfe and I be bed-fellowes.
*Tib.*    Deare heart I humbly thanke you, but I must not.
*Ales.*    Lady I rather wish your company,

210 thee; Cedars] the Cedars Q        210 S.D. *Exeunt*] *Exit* Q
14 you] Dilke; your Q

Because I know one maiden best conceales,
What's bosom'd in another: but Ile waite                           20
With patience a time fitting.
*Tib.*                    Worthy Lady,
This time is yours and mine.
*Ales.*                         Thus I begin then,
And if I cannot woe reliefe from you,
Let me at least win pitty, I have fixt
Mine eye upon your brother; whom I never
But once beheld here in this house, yet wish
That he beheld me now and heard me; You are
So like your brother, that me thinkes I speake to him,
And that provokes a blush to assaile my cheeke;
He smiles like you, his eyes like you; pray Lady         30
Where is the gentleman? 'twas for his sake
I would have lien with you, wo'd it were as lawfull
To fellow nights with him.
*Tib.*                    Troth I do wish it.
*Ales.*    And if in this you inrich me with your counsell,
Ile be a gratefull taker.
*Tib.*                    Sure my brother
Is blest in your affection, and shall have
Good time to understand so.
*Dar.*                  *Alesandra.*                  *Within.*
*Ales.*    Madam.
*Dar.*             A word, come quickly.        *Exit* [Alesandra].
*Tib.*                         O ye heavens!
How strangely one houre works upon an other.
I was but now heart-sick, and long'd for meat,          40
Which being set before me I abhorre.

                    *Enter* Alphonsina.
*Alph.*    Brother.
*Tib.*             What frights you thus from your chamber?
*Alph.*    Such a fury as thou.
*Tib.*                    How now? hast lost thy witts?

40 I] Dilke; It Q

*Alph.*   Ile sweare thou hast, for thou hast candied
Thy sweete but poysonous language to dishonour
Me thy most wretched sister, who no better
Then a vile instrument to thy desires,
Deserves to be stil'd Baud, worse then the bauds,
Who every day i'th' weeke shake hands with hell.
*Tib.*   Ha' patience dearest sister; I protest,                        50
By all the graces that become a man,
I have not wrong'd *Dariene* nor her Lord.
*Alph.*   Thou shalt not then by heaven.
*Tib.*                                        By all goodnes, not.
With a well blusht discourse faire *Alissandra*
Supposing me your sister hath discover'd
The true pangs of her fancy towards *Tibaldo*,
And in it crav'd my aide, which heard, Even then,
My Brutish purpose broke its neck, and I
Will proue the daughters husband, that came hither,
A traytour to the Mother.
*Alph.*                                  My noble brother,                        60
Our doings are alike, for by *Trebatio*
(Whome I with honour name) his fathers foulenes
Shall be cut off, and crost.
*Tib.*                                  Get to your chamber;
No longer will I play the womans part,
This night shall change my habit with my heart.

                                                        *Exeunt.*


## [ACT IV, Scene iv]

*Enter* Nicoletto *with a light.*

*Nic.*   In this chamber she lies, and that's her window, wo'd I were
in: the aire bites, but the bit that I shall bite anon sharpens my
stomack, the watch-word is a cornet, (*Cornet within*) it speakes, she
bids me come without a light, and reason, shes light enough her

65 S.D. *Exeunt*] *Exit*

selfe; wincke thou one-eyed baud, be thou an embleme of thy
Master and burne in secret.

*Enter* Alphonsina, *above.*

*Alph.*  My Lord.
*Nic.*  What sayes my most moist-handed sweete Lady.
*Alph.*  Who is there with you?
*Nic.*  No christian creature, I enter *solus.*                    10
*Alph.*  I feare I must entreate you to stay a little.
*Nic.*  As long as thou desir'st, but wilt come downe?
*Alph.*  I would be loth to loose all upon one rest ——
*Nic.*  Shall I mount then?
*Alph.*  For mine honour being once crack't ——
*Nic.*  Crack a pudding: Ile not meddle with thine honour.
*Alph.*  Say you should get me with childe.
*Nic.*  I hope I am not the first Lord has got a lady with childe.
*Alph.*  Is the night hush't?
*Nic.*  Ther's nothing stirring, the very mice are a sleepe, as I am  20
noble, Ile deale with thee like a gentleman.
*Alph.*  Ile doe that then, which some Citizens will not doe, to some
Lords.
*Nic.*  What's that?
*Alph.*  Take your word, I come.
*Nic.*  Vd's my life!                          *Musicke within.*
*Alph.*  What's the matter sir?
*Nic.*  I heare a lute, and sure it comes this way.
*Alph.*  My most lov'd Lord, step you aside, I would not have you
seene for the saving of my right hand, preserve mine honour, as  30
I preserve your love.

*Enter* Trebatio *with Musicke.*

*Nic.*  Pox on your Catts guts.
*Alph.*  To an unworthy window, who is thus kind?
*Treb.*  Looke out of it, and 'tis the richest casement
That ever let in Ayre.

13 upon one rest] Dilke; upon rest Q
23 Lords] Lord Q          26 *Musicke within.*] Q *places in line* 27

*Alph.*                    *Trebatio.*
*Treb.*                                I,
  My most faire Mistris.
*Alph.*                    Neither of both good sir;
  Pray play upon some other, you abuse mee,
  And that which seemes worse, in your fathers house.
*Nic.*    Brave girle.
*Alph.*    But you are young enough to be forgiven,                    40
  If you will mend hereafter, the night has in it
  Vnwholsome foggs, and blasts; to bed my Lord,
  Least they attach your beautie: nothing more,
  Ile pay you for your song.                    *Exit.*
*Treb.*                    Are you gone so?
  Well, you hard-hearted one, you shall not ever
  Be Lady of your selfe — away.        *Exit* [*with Musicke*].

                    *Enter* Cargo *running.*

*Cargo.*    Oh my Lord, I have stood Centinell as you bad me, but
  I am frighted.
*Nic.*    With what?
*Cargo.*    The Night-mare rides you, my Lady is conjured up.        50
*Nic.*    Now the devill lay her down, prevented in the very Act.
*Cargo.*    She workes by magick, and knowes all.

                    *Enter* Dariene.

*Dar.*    Doe you shrinke backe my Lord? you may with shame;
  Have I tane you napping my Lord?
*Nic.*    But not with the manner my Lady.
*Dar.*    Have you no bird to flie at, but what sits
  On your owne sonnes fiste?
*Nic.*                    How! my sonnes fiste?
*Dar.*                                Yes,
  The Lady whom you wrought to have bin your Harlot
  Your sonne has long since wonne to be his bride,
  Both they and I have this night exercis'd                    60
  Our witts to mocke your dotage.
*Nic.*                    Am I then gull'd?

*Cargo.*  Yes my Lord, and bull'd too, yonders *Tibaldo Neri* come this morning.

*Dar.*  So early, Is his sister with him?

*Cargo.*  Not that I saw, but I saw him kisse my yong Mistris, three or foure times, I thinke 'twere good to aske the banes of Matrimony.

*Nic.*  Wo't twere no worse, let's in, and give 'em the mornings Salutation.

*Dar.*  Ile tell him all.

*Nic.*  Sweete Lady, seal my pardon with a kisse,                    70
He ne're was borne, that never did amisse.

*Exeunt.*


## ACTUS QUINTUS, Scæna prima

*Enter* Florence, Piero, Pisa, Mutio, Tornelli, Philippo.

*Pier.*  Sir, I have found *Angelo*
With long and busie search.

*Flo.*                    And will he come?

*Pier.*  Your honour (as you charg'd me) I impawn'd
For his safe passage.

*Flo.*                    By my life hee shall;
When will hee come?

*Pier.*                    My friend brings him along.

*Flo.*  *Philippo*, *Mutio*, goe and perswade our daughter
To walke, and take the ayre.

*Pisa.*                    Ile play that Orator.            *Exit.*

*Flo.*  Attend the Duke of *Pisa*; prethee *Piero*  [*Exeunt courtiers.*]
Discover where this *Angelo* lay lurking.

*Pier.*  The world he has shut up, and now the booke        10
He reades, is onely heere, see where he comes.

*Enter* [*Fryar,*] Angelo *as a Fryar,* [*at another door*] Fyametta.

*Flo.*  Way for my daughter; looke you, there's *Angelo*.

*Fia.*  Ha? yes, 'tis the starre I saile by; hold me not,

62 Cargo.] Dilke; Dare. Q

Why doe you sticke like rocks, to barre my way,
And utterly to wracke mee?
*Flo.*                    Art thou mad?
*Fia.*  Yes, I am mad, oh my best life, my soule!    *Runs to him.*
*Ang.*  Whom seeke you Lady?
*Fia.*                    Doe you not know me sir?
*Ang.*  Yes.
*Fia.*      Doest thou not love mee?
*Ang.*                    Yes.
*Fia.*                        At very heart?
*Ang.*  Yes, at the very soule.
*Fia.*                    Burnes not your love,
With that most holy fire, the god of marriage                      20
Kindles in man and woman?
*Ang.*            Noe.
*Fia.*                Ha, no?
*Flo.*  Hee sayes no.
*Fia.*                Then so, *quod dedi perdidi.*
*Ang.*  How can I love you Lady?
I have clim'd too many of such fruitlesse trees.
*Fia.*  Have you indeede?
*Ang.*                    Yes, and have pull'd the apples —
*Fia.*  Now I beshrew your fingers.
*Ang.*  And when I touch'd 'em, found 'em turn'd to dust.
Why should you love me? I have chang'd my pleasure
In beautious dames, more then I have my dreames,
Foure in one night.
*Flo.*                Hee'le prove a lustie Larrence;                      30
This is the starre you sayle by tho.
*Ang.*  Why should you love me? I am but a Tombe,
Gay out-side, but within, rotten and foule.
*Fia.*  Ile sweare th'art most diseas'd, even in thy soule;
Oh thou, thou most perfidious man alive,
So prosper, as my poore sicke heart doth thrive;
Give me thy hand, I hate thee, fare-thee-well.
Come, I make thee my heaven, wer't once my Hell.    *To* Pisa.
*Pisa.*  I'me rap't above the spheares, Ioy strikes me dumbe.

*Flo.*  Th'ast lent unto mine age a score of yeares,                    40
More then ere nature promis'd, by thy loving
This Noble Prince; th'art his then?
*Fia.*                    His — to prove it;
Hence thou from mee; ne're more behold mine eyes.
*Ang.*  Now finde I, that a Lovers heart last dies.          *Exit.*
*Flo.*  I, I, so, so; If it die, it shall be buried.
*Fia.*  Good reverend Sir, stay you, and as you witnesse
This my divorce, so shall you seale my contract.
*Fryar.*  I will, your pleasure.
*Flo.*  *Fyametta,*
Make choice thy selfe of thine owne wedding day.                    50
*Fia.*  To morrow be it, Loves poyson is delay.
*Flo.*  Gallants, pray stirre betimes, and rowse your Mistresses;
Let some invite Lord *Vanni* and his Lady;
Wee dine to day with Lord *Iacomo,*
Thither let's hasten.
*Fia.*                    Sir, this holy man,
Shall be this night my confessor; about mid-night,
Expect my sending for you.
*Fryar.*                    Your devotion
Commands my service.
*Flo.*                    'Ware least i'th fryers stead,
The Prince be your confessor; girle prepare
To play the bride to morrow, and then being laid,                    60
One night past o're, thinke nere to rise a maide.
                              *Exeunt.*

52 *Flo.*] Dilke; *om.* Q          55 *Fia.* Dilke; *om.* Q
58 *Flo.*] Dilke; *om.* Q          61 S.D. *Exeunt*] Dilke; *Exit* Q

## [ACT V, SCENE ii]

*Trumpets sounding, services carried coverd over the stage, Poore*
*attending, Torrenti one, then enter Iacomo bare betwixt the*
*two Dukes, Piero, Philippo, Tornelli, Mutio.*

*Flo.*  No more of complement, my Lord *Gentili*;
Such noble welcomes have we had this day,
We must take blushing leaves, cause we can pay
Nothing but thanks.
*Gent.*              That's more then the whole debt comes to.
*Flo.*  Ne're saw I tables crown'd with braver store;
I know no man that spends, nay nor gives more,
And yet a full sea still: why yonder fellow,
The brave mock-prodigall has spent all indeed,
He that made beggers proud, begs now himselfe for need.
*Gent.*  But who releeves him now? none, for I know      10
He that in riotous feasting, wastes his store,
Is like a faire tree which in sommer bore
Boughes laden till they crackt, with leaves and fruite,
Whose plenty lasting, all men came unto't;
And pluckt and filld their lapps and carry away;
But when the boughes grow bare, and leaves decay,
And the great tree stands saplesse, wither'd dry,
Then each one casts on it a scornfull eye,
And grieves to see it stand, nay do not greeve,
Albeit the Axe downe to the roote it cleave;      20
The fall of such a tree, will I beware,
I know both when to spend, and when to spare.
*Flo.*  'Tis nobly spoke.
                          [*Exeunt* Gentili *and his household.*]
*Pisa.*              Nay good my Lord make hast.
*Pier.*  Here's a childe lost i'th staying.
*Flo.*                          Get two at night for't.
What is the bride yet drest?

5 *Flo.*] Dilke; *om.* Q

*Pier.*                     She's rigging Sir.
*Flo.*   'Tis well. Musicke? from whence? What chambers that?
*Mut.*   It Ioynes close to the lodgings of the bride.
*Flo.*   Inquire if she be ready, *Mutio*,
Say her bride-groome attends on her below.
*Mut.*   I shall my Lord.                                    30

Fiametta *above*.

*Pier.*   Tarry, she looks her selfe out.
*Flo.*                     Come, come loiterer.
*Fia.*   Faire welcome to your grace, and to that Prince,
That should have bin my bridegroome.
*Flo.*                     Should ha beene?
*Pier.*   Is the Moone chang'd already?
*Fia.*                     In her changes
The Moone is constant, man is onely varying,
And never in one Circle long is tarying,
But one man in the moone at once appeares,
Such praise (being true to one) a woman beares.
*Flo.*   Take thou that praise, and to this Prince be true,
Come downe and marry him.
*Fia.*                     What would the world say,    40
If I should marry two men in one day?
*Flo.*   That villaine has bewitch't her.
*Pier.*                     Sir what villaine?
*Flo.*   That slave, the banish't runnagate.
*Pier.*                     Cast not on him
Such foule aspersions, till you know his guilt;
Even now you said he was a worthy spirit,
Crown'd him with praise, and do you now condemne
An absent man unheard?
*Flo.*                     Ile hang thee traitor.
*Pisa.*   Locke all the gates of *Florence*, least he scape.
*Flo.*   Our pardon, whosoever takes and kill him.
*Pier.*   Oh! who would trust in Princes, the vaine breath,    50
Who in a minute gives one man life and death?

28 Inquire if] Dilke; Inquire. | If Q

*Fia.*   Come forth thou threatned man, here kill him all,
Lower then what you stand on, none can fall.

Angelo above.

*Ang.*   I now must stand your arrowes, but you shoote
Against a breast as innocent ——
*Flo.*                                     As a traytors.
*Ang.*   Your patience Sir.
*Pisa.*                      Talk'st thou of patience?
That by thy most perfidious ——
*Ang.*                          Heare me, pray.
Or if not me, heare then this reverend man.

Enter frier above.

*Pisa.*   What makes that Fryer there?
*Pier.*                         Father speake your minde.
*Fryar.*   I was enjoyned to be her confessor,                     60
And came, but then she wonn me to a vow,
By oath of all my orders, face to face,
To heare her speake unto *Angelo*, 'twas done,
He came, when falling downe on both her knees,
Her eyes drown'd all in teares, she opes a booke,
Chardging him read his oaths and promises,
The contract of their hands, hearts, yea and soules,
And askd if *Angelo* would marry her.
*Flo.*                                Very good.
*Fryar.*   He looking pale as death, said faintly no.
*Pisa.*   Faintly, he then was willing?
*Pier.*                           Pray heare him out.          70
*Fryar.*   Thrice tried: he thrice cried no; At which this Ladie
Desperately snatching from her side two knives,
Had stab'd her selfe to'th' heart, but that we knit
Our force against it, what should I doe in this?
Not marry her, or rob her of heavens blisse?
Which glory had bin greater, to have tane
A husband from her, or to have seene her slaine?
*Flo.*   Then you have married her?

636

*Fryar.*                    I have.
*Pier.*                              Brave girle.
*Pisa.*   Ile cut that knot asunder with my sword.
*Fryar.*   The hands which heaven hath joyn'd, no man can part.   80
*Fia.*   The hands they may, but never shall the heart.
*Flo.*   Why didst thou make to him thy promise then?
*Fia.*   Women are borne, but to make fooles of men.
She that's made sure to him, she loves not well,
Her banes are ask'd here, but she wedds in hell;
Parents that match their children gainst their will,
Teach them not how to live, but how to kill.
*Flo.*   Parrot, Parrot,
Ile stop your prating; breake into her chamber,
And lay the villaine bleeding at her feete.                *Draw.* 90
*Fia.*   Villaine? it is my husband.
*Flo.*                        Enter and kill him.
*Pier.*   Enter, but kill him he that dares, I blush
To see two Princes so degenerate.
*Fia.*   Oh noble brother!
*Pier.*                What would you have him doe?
He well deserves to have her to his wife,
Who gives to you a daughter, her a life;
In sight of angels she to him was given,
So that in striking him, you fight with heaven.
*Flo.*   You see there is no remedie.
*Pisa.*                        Troth none,
I threw at all and (gamesters lucke) all's gone;       100
Farewell brave spirited girle, he that gainst winde,
Fier and the sea, law and a womans minde,
Strives, is a foole, that's I, Ile now be wise,
And neuer more put trust in womans eyes.
*Fia.*   I love thee for that word with-all my heart.
*Flo.*   Will you come downe pray?
*Fia.*                        Sweare as you are a Duke.
*Flo.*   Yet more a doe.
*Pisa.*                Will you not trust your father?
*Fia.*   Why should I? you see there is no trust i'th' daughter;

Sweare by your hopes of good you will not touch
His naile to hurt him.
*Flo.*                     By my hopes I sweare.                    110
*Fia.*   And you too?
*Pisa.*                     Yes, what's falling none can reare.
*Fia.*   Wee come then: noble friend, flagg not thy wings,
In this warr I defie a campe of Kings.          *Exeunt ⌐above⌐.*

> *Enter* Nicolletto, Tibaldo, Alphonsina, Dariene,
> Alissandra, Trebatio.

*Flo.*   See, see, more shoales of friends, most beauteous Ladies,
Faire welcomes to you all.
*Nic.*                     My Lord those tides,
Are turn'd, these Ladies are transform'd to brides.
*Flo.*   We heard the happy newes, and therefore sent,
To marry joyes with joyes, yours, with our owne,
Yours (I see) prosper, ours are overthrowne.
*Nic.*   How meane you overthrowne?                    120

> *Enter* Angelo, Fiametta.

*Flo.*   Your owne eyes shall be witnesse how: nay, nay, pray rise,
I know your heart is up, tho your knees downe.
*Ang.*   All that we stand in feare of is your frowne.
*Fia.*   And all deare father which I begge of you,
Is that you love this man but as I doe.
*Flo.*   What begg you of this Prince?
*Fia.*                     That he would take
One favour from me, which my selfe shall make.
*Pisa.*   Pray let it be of willow.
*Fia.*                     Well then it shall.
*Alph.*   Why willow? is the noble Prince forsaken?
*Pier.*   All womens faults, one for another taken.          130
*Alph.*   Now in good sooth my Lord, shee has but vs'd you
As watermen use their fares, for shee look'd one way,
And row'd another, you but wore her glove,
The hand was *Angeloes*, and she dealt wisely.
Let woman ne're love man, or if she doe,

Let him nere know it, make him write, waite, woe,
Court, cogge, and curse, and sweare, and lie, and pine,
Till Love bring him to death's doore, else hee's not mine;
That flesh eates sweetest that's pick'd close toth' bone,
Water drinkes best, that's hew'd euen from the stone;            140
Men must be put to't home.
*Nic.*                          He that loves ducking,
Let him come learne of thee.
*Flo.*                          Shee has good skill;
At table will wee heare a full discourse
Of all these changes, and these Marriages,
Both how they shuffled, cut, and dealt about,
What cards are best, after the trumpes were out,
Who plaid false play, who true, who sought to save
An Ace ith' bottome, and turn'd up a knave;
For Love is but a Card-play, and all's lost,
Vnlesse you cogg, hee that pack's best, wins most.               150
*Alph.*   Since such good gamsters are together met,
As you like this, wee'le play another sett.

                                        *Exeunt.*


                    *FINIS.*

# TEXTUAL NOTES

## I.i

20 *Tibaldo*; never] Q '*Tibaldo* ner'e; never' could be the result of following a manuscript error and correction, but need not be, for the compositor correcting himself but failing to remove the metrically wrong form could as well be the explanation.

## II.i

51 hollow then] *hollow* is not 'to scoop out' but a form of *holla*, or *halloo*. We must assume minim error and compositorial misunderstanding to account for Q's *them*.

## II.iii

13 *Nurs.*] Assignment of these speeches at lines 13 and 15 to the Nurse, emending Q speech-prefix *Nic.*, is required by their content and style. The similar error at III.ii.14, when Nicoletto is in Rome and could not have been present in the scene is sufficient to confirm.

## III.iii

3 sister, brother] Despite the temptation to hyphenate Q *sister, brother* for maximum humour, it would seem preferable to follow Q and take it that *brother* begins a new independent clause coinciding with the shift in the metaphor.

# PRESS VARIANTS

[Copies collated: BM¹ (British Museum C.12.f.4[5]), BM² (644.b.23), wants B2, C1–2, D1–2, E2, BM³ (Ashley 619); Bodl¹ (Bodleian Mal. 186[2]), Bodl² (Mal. 235[11]); Dyce¹ (Victoria and Albert Museum), Dyce²; Eton (Eton College); NLS (National Library Scotland); Worc (Worcester College, Oxford), wants F1–4; CLUC (W. A. Clark Library); CSmH (Henry E. Huntington Library); CtY (Yale University); DFo (Folger Shakespeare Library); DLC (Library of Congress); ICU (University of Chicago); MB (Boston Public Library); MH (Harvard University); NN (New York Public Library); NNP (Pierpont Morgan Library); TxU (University of Texas).]

## Sheet A (*inner forme*)

*1st stage corrected:* Bodl².
*Uncorrected:* BM¹.

Sig. A2.
*Prologue*
9 *Carping, Not*] *Carping,* — *not*
10 *Ignorance,*] *Ignorance,* —
10 *our*] *δ*
12 *off,*] *off,* —
13 *Theater;*] *Theater;* —
19 *Whirlewindes,*] *Whirlewindes,* —

Sig. A3ᵛ.
I.i.22 Englifhman.] Englifhman,
24 cleane.] cleane,
27 knave,] knave
27 cockfcombe,] cockfcombe
31 Pimtillioes,] Pimtillioes
33 Old; why] Old why;
34 Art,] Art
37 her;] her,
47 weihi] wihi

Sig. A4.
*r-t Kingdome*] *king dome*
I.i.53 pray'] pray,
55 fonne,] fonne
64 bravery] brauery
67 runne] ronne
75 with,] with
76 rich he] richhe

77 Feaſt;] Feaſt
79 hence.] hence
81 *Famely*)] *Famely*
*d–l:* [*unsigned*]] A 4

*2nd stage corrected:* NLS.

Sig. A 2.

*Prologue*
1 *am I*] *I am*
6 *Owne.*] *Owne:*
21 *cw Drama-*] *Dramma-*

Sig. A 3ᵛ.

I.i.18 growth,] growth;
18 nothing?] nothing.
20 keepe] kepe
25 button.] button,
26 doublets Sir.] doublets.
29 Paſſees Sir:] Paſſees:
32 end] ends
33 Old?] Old;
34 have] has
42 ſo] of
45 me-] me
45 Lady?] Lady.
47 weihy] weihi
48 wagge-Taile] wagg's-Taile

Sig. A 4.

I.i.51 *Vanni,*] *Vanni*
52 mine.] mine,
55 *Florence,*] *Florence*
64 of] and
71 open-handed] open handed
72 gueſts.] gueſts,
74 ſmoake.] ſmoake,
79 *Exit*] *Exit.*
79 *Florence*] *Florence*
81 *Lotti Family*] *Locti Famely*
81 *cw Dari.*] *Pari.*

*3rd stage corrected:* BM²⁻³, Bodl¹, Dyce¹⁻², Eton, Worc, CLUC, CSmH,
CtY, DFo, DLC, ICU, MB, MH, NN, NNP, TxU.

Sig. A 3ᵛ.

I.i.45 me—] me-
47 wihy] weihy

642

## SHEET B (*inner forme*)

*Correct:* BM², Dyce², CtY, MH.
*Error:* BM¹⁻³, Bodl¹⁻², Dyce¹, Eton, NLS, Worc, CLUC, CSmH, DFo, DLC, ICU, MB, NN, NNP, TxU.

Sig. B4.
  I.iv.32 the] nhe

## SHEET C (*inner forme*)

*Corrected:* BM²⁻³, Bodl¹⁻², Dyce¹⁻², Eton, NLS, Worc, CLUC, CSmH, CtY, DFo, DLC, ICU, MB, MH, NN, NNP, TxU.

*Uncorrected:* BM¹.

Sig. C1ᵛ.
  I.iv.152 Gentleman] Gentielman
Sig. C3ᵛ.
  II.ii.S.D. Doctor] *Doctour*
Sig. C4.
  II.ii.2 Antickes;] Antickes
   22 met] meet

## SHEET D (*inner forme*)

*Corrected:* BM³, Bodl¹⁻², Dyce², NLS, Worc, CSmH, CtY, DFo, ICU, MB, MH, NNP, TxU.
*Uncorrected:* BM¹⁻², Dyce¹, Eton, CLUC, DLC, NN.

Sig. D3ᵛ.
  III.i.67 S.D. *Bare*] *Pare*
   67 S.D. | *offer*] | *Offer*
   71 *Hatt's brought in* 3. *or* 4.] Hatt's brought in 3. or 4.
   95 *Chainas.*] Chaines,
Sig. D4.
  III.i.107 keene] .keene
   108 ſpaniells.] ſpaniells
   115 paſſe,] paſſe
   118 ſham'd] ſhamd

41-2

# EMENDATIONS OF ACCIDENTALS

## Persons

DRAMMATIS] Q(u) *cw*: *Dramma-*; Q *text*: DRAMATIS

## Prologue

5 *down;*] ~ ₐ
6 *Owne:*] Q(u); ~ . Q(c²)
9 *Carping, —not*] Q(u); *Carping, Not* Q(c¹)

10 *Ignorance, —*] Q(u); ~ , ₐ Q(c¹)
12 *off, —*] Q(u); ~ , ₐ Q(c¹)
13 *Theater; —*] Q(u); ~ ; ₐ Q(c¹)
19 *Whirlewindes, —*] Q(u); ~ , ₐ Q(c¹)

## I.i

S.D. *serving-|man*] *serving-man*
14 blood;] *point doubtful in most copies*
16 *Nic.*] *Nie.*
18 growth;] Q(u); ~ , Q(c²)
18–19 A meere...lord.] *one line in* Q
23–24 They...cleane.] *one line in* Q
24–25 Ile...button.] *one line in* Q
27 knaveₐ] Q(u); ~ , Q(c¹)
27 cockscombeₐ] Q(u); ~ , Q(c¹)
33 Old; why ₐ] Q(c¹); ~ ₐ ~ ; Q(u); ~ ? ~ ₐ Q(c²)
34 Artₐ] Q(u); ~ , Q(c¹)
44–45 A...branches.] *one line in* Q

45 meₐ] Q(u); ~ — Q(c³)
46 Lady.] Q(u); ~ ? Q(c²)
47–48 Q *lines*: can | Neither
47 wihi] Q(u); weihi Q(c¹); weihy Q(c²), wihy Q(c³)
51 *Vanni* ₐ] Q(u); ~ , Q(c²)
52 mine,] Q(u); ~ . Q(c²)
53 pray,] Q(u); ~ ' Q(c¹)
53 Court —] ~ ,
67 ronne] Q(u); runne Q(c¹)
69, 80 Signior] *Signior*
71 open handed] Q(u); open-handed Q(c²)
72 guests,] Q(u); ~ . Q(c²)
74 smoake,] Q(u); ~ . Q(c²)
75 withₐ] Q(u); ~ , Q(c¹)
81 *Famely*] Q(u); *Family* Q(c²)
82 How,] ~ ₐ
90 has] | Has

## I.ii

6–7 No...heart.] *prose in* Q
10 makes] | Makes
18 have] | Have
21 over] | Over

30–33 Q *lines*: How! ...an | Old ...dishes | To...dish | The... tooth.
36–41 Q *lines*: Love? ...as |

Swaggering...one | Of...a |
Woman...boot, | And...
doore, | But...in | His staffe.
43 grandame] gran-|dame
44–46 Q *lines*: ...skinne | And...
a | Waiting- ...great | Coun-
tesses.
49–51 Q *lines*: Leave...a | Caudle
... -Capp, | for...
53–55 Q *lines*: If...in | Tune...
before. | Thee...it.
58–59 Q *lines*: mens | Neckes
61–63 Q *lines*: Walls...have |
Knowne...in't | In...of | Her
...Puritane.

70–73 Q *lines*: Well... a|Starre...
were | Your...wife, | Baite...
it—
70 needs] need s
71 Fether-|makers] Fether-makers
77–78 Art, ...it.] ~ .... ~ ,
87 Q *lines*: quicken | Your
92–93 Q *lines*: Tobacco, | Till
93 agen] Agen
96 laugh] | Laugh
100–103 Q *lines*: Alas...doe | Any
...a | Gap...rob | His...him |
Musick: |
102 *Luca*,] ~ ∧

## I.iii

3–4 Slave? ...know] *one line in Q*
5 No cause] noc ause
9 If for] Iffor
10–11 *prose in Q*
17 rage,] ~ ;
22–23 Q *lines*: peace; | Beate
25 therefore] | Therefore
26–28 Q *lines*: Oh...to | Make...
fooles | Together...gon.
35–37 Q *lines*: If...whose | Tiles
...hunt | No...then | Doe...
venison?
55 never] Never

55 Romane] *Romane*
55 spirits,] ~ .
69–70 Q *lines*: craft, | But
72 Donna] *Donna*
74–76 Q *lines*: The...Duke | Was
for | Her...still.
77–78 Q *lines*: for | The
78 Turke] *Turke*
79–80 Q *lines*: upon | A
86–87 Q *lines*: a | Flemming
89–91 Q *lines*: ...Iewell: | Tell...
white | Finger...most | Little
...bodie.

## I.iv

S.D. Iacomo] Iocomo
S.D. Tornelli,] *comma faintly inks in
very few copies*
17 *Iacomo*] *Iocomo*
18–19 How...building?] *one line
in* Q
20,30 *line indented in* Q
34 Master] Mr.
56–57 Why...roomes.] *one line in*
Q
82 hand,] ~ ∧
85 Which] which

90 Faire] Fairc
114 And] and
127 planting; ...virtues,] ~ , ...
~ ;
132 My] my
132–133 Q *lines*: value his love |
beyond...
141–142 Oh...same;] *one line in Q*
155 time] | Time
157–158 Q *lines*: bin | Taken
159–162 *prose in Q*

## II.i

44–49 *prose in* Q
51 and] | And
66–67 I...wonder.] *prose in* Q
95 well,] ~ ∧
105 chastity] Q *lines:* of | Chastity
106 enough,] ~ ∧
106 from] | From
111 To] to

115 opportunity,] ~ ;
118–119 Q *lines:* Such...once |
    Were...there.
124 keep] | Keep
124 out] our
124 in] Q *lines:* coming | In
126 Q *lines:* young-|man

## II.ii

S.D. *Doctour*] Q(u); *Doctor* Q(c)
3 Play] | play

12 Will] will
32 And] and

## II.iii

S.D. Tornelli,] Tonell,
12 Her] her
22 *Pisa,*] ~ .
23–24 Q *lines:* Vnder...the |
    strongest...shrinke.
24 heart here,] ~ , ~ ∧
28 wo'd to] wo'dto
31 faith is] faithis
37 Of] of
49–51 *prose in* Q
53–54 *prose in* Q
59–61 Q *lines:* By...play | The...
    world; | A...dat.
63–66 Q *lines:* Me...Princesse, |

Me...all | De...dat | She...
    man.
68 love] | Love
71–72 hand, ...Familie;] ~ ; ...
    ~ ,
73 And till] Andtill
81 makea] make a
92 peppera —] ~ .
98 Gentle-|voman] Gentle-voman
104 So,] ~ ∧
116 Wee] Wce
125 rascalls] Q lines: be | Rascalls
128 le] | Le
130 Doe∧] ~ ,
132–133 I...life.] *one line in* Q

## III.i

S.D. *Signior*] Signi-|nior
2–4 *prose in* Q
14 Persian...Turke...Indian]
    *Persian...Turke...Indian*
64 Turkish] *Turkish*
67 trumpets ∧ ...Lord,] ~ , ...
    ~ ∧
69–70 *one line in* Q

76–77 Q *lines:* Has...hisse? |
    What...for?
83 sea ∧] *a mark after this seems to be
    the inked lower part of a space, not
    a broken comma*
86 Florentines] *Florentines*
90–91 plumes, ... fought;] ~ ;...
    ~ , (*final comma clear in very
    few copies*)

646

95 *Chaines*] Q(u); *Chainas* Q(c)
98–99 Tis...me.] *one line in* Q
110–112 Q *lines*: Thirsty...thine |
Owne...from | Thy...downe.
110 bones; heere,] ~ , ~ ;
116–117 Q *lines*; To...tallents |
Forth...prey.
130–131 brother-hood, ...so;] ~ ;
...~ ,
134 wretchednes.] ~ ,
140 your_A] ~ ,
141 shoore,] ~ _A

148 *Rizes*] *Kizes*
148 S.D. *Two with*] *Two* | *With*
165 engines,] ~ .
176 entrance.] ~ _A
177 are] re (a *dropped out*)
192 S.D. *Drinck*] *drinck*
192 S.D. *which*] | *Which*
193 ye):] ~ ) _A
194 wine.] ~ _A
196 too.] ~ ,
209 be.] ~ ,
214 brave;] ~ ,

## III.ii

3 makea] make a
7 knocka] knock a
31–32 Let...dead,] *one line in* Q
40–41 worlds; ...Ile not hence,]
~ , ... ~ ;
43–44 Ile...thee —] *one line in* Q
49–50 That's... him.] *one line in* Q

58 H'as] Has
64 French,] ~ _A
76 both;] *semi-colon certain chiefly
in* CLUC
91 friend,] ~ _A
95 feele for] feelefor

## III.iii

2–4 Q *lines*: ...not | Give...
good | Sister...you.
11 aske forgivenes] askeforgivenes
18 things Sir] things      Sir

24 or farewell] orfarewell
25 will but] willbut
38 Q *lines*: true, | but

## IV.i

S.D. Nicholetto] Nicholettti
11 knaue.] ~ ,
12–13 Q *lines*: That...thou |
Vulture- ...stuffe;
15–16 Q *lines*: Hast...th'art |
Troubled...wan.
17 snarling:] ~ _A
23 world,] ~ _A
28–29 Q *lines*: And...to | Enter-
taine...Nuntio,

31 Sir] Sr
41–42 Q *lines*: Should...touching|
Wenching, ...-master.
44–45 Q *lines*: To...tomblers |
Come...ropes,
52–53 Q *lines*: Meane...the
Devill...Center.
55 In] *text*; in *cw*

## IV.ii

S.D. *Apothecary,*] ~ _A
13 buy; ...warrs,] ~ , ... ~ ;

15–18 Q *lines*: And...man | Who
...waite?

27, 28 pound] l.
37 thou cheat'st] thoucheat'st
40–41 *one line in* Q
43–44 Some. . .hanging.] *one line in*
  Q
76 Russian] *Russian*
86 *Brok.*] *Rroak.*
94 sir —] ~ :
103 dropsies ‸ cold,] ~ , ~ ‸
111–112 *one line in* Q
116 are a] area
144 which] | Which
158 Lord —] ~ .

160 out —] ~ .
164–166 What. . .yours.] *each speech
  one line in* Q
174–175 *one line in* Q
188–189 Q *lines:* Beaten. . .Turkish|
  Gally-slave
190 gentleman] gentlema
193 passe their doore] *type loose in
  some copies*
198 buildings.] ~ ..
201–202 Q *lines:* Make. . .deliver'd |
  To. . .Gentleman.

## IV.iii

S.D. Dariene,] ~ .
4 Master] Mr.
7 Sir] Sr.
10 rest;] ~ ‸
26 house,] *comma very faint al.
  copies*
27–28 Q *lines:* That. . .me; | You
  . . .him.
29 assaile] a ssaile
31 'twas] 't was
32–33 *prose in* Q
34–35 Q *lines:* And. . .Ile | Be. . .
  taker.

34 your] yonr
38–40 *prose in* Q
46–48 Q *lines:* Me. . .vile | Instru-
  ment. . .stil'd, | Baud. . .bauds.
48 stil'd‸] ~ ,
48 bauds,] ~ .
53 not.] ~ ‸
54 blusht] blush
62–63 Q *lines:* (Whome. . .be |
  Cut. . .crost.
63 off,] *comma clear in* DFo *but a
  speck else*

## IV.iv

S.D. Nicoletto] Nicoletti
4 a light] a lighr
6 Master] Mr.
12 but wilt] but-wilt
13 rest —] ~ ,
15 crack't —] ~ .

35–36 I, | My. . .Mistris.] *one line in*
  Q
37 abuse] a buse
56–57 *prose in* Q
57–58 Yes. . .Harlot] *one line in* Q

## V.i

1–2 Sir. . .search.] *one line in* Q
4–5 By. . .come?] *one line in* Q
6 *Philippo,*] ~ ‸
25 apples —] ~ .

42–43 Q *lines:* His. . .hence | Thou
  . . .eyes.
51 delay.] ~ ,
58 'Ware] W'are
58 stead,] ~ .

## V.ii

S.D. *sounding,* ...*attending,*] ∼ ∧
... ∼ ∧
16 decay,] ∼ :
26 Musicke] musicke
26 Q *lines*: whence? | What
27 Q *lines*: the | Lodgings
28–29 Q *lines*: Inquire | If...
-groome | Attends...below.
29 attends] Q *text* (| Attends);
Attend Q *cw*
31 Tarry,] *punctuation uncertain*;
*might be semi-colon*
34–35 Q *lines*: In...the | Moone
...varying,
53 on,] ∼ .

56–57 Talk'st...perfidious —] *one*
*line in* Q
57 me,] ∼ ∧
84 made sure] madesure
89 prating;] *punctuation mark un-*
*certain; might be comma*
95–96 wife, ...life;] ∼ ; ... ∼ ,
99–100 none, ...gone;] ∼ ; ...
∼ ,
100 and (gamesters] (∼ ∧ ∼
106 Sweare as] Sweare        as
112 then:] ∼ ∧
113 S.D. Dariene] Daariene
113 S.D. Alissandra,] Alissand,
141–142 He...thee.] *one line in* Q
143 wee heare] weeheare